TAKING SIDES

Clashing Views on Controversial

Issues in American History, Volume II, Reconstruction to the Present

NINTH EDITION

Selected, Edited, and with Introductions by

Larry Madaras
Howard Community College

and

James M. SoRelle
Baylor University

McGraw-Hill/Dushkin
A Division of The McGraw-Hill Companies

To Maggie and Cindy

Photo Acknowledgment
Cover image: © 2001 by PhotoDisc, Inc.

Cover Art Acknowledgment
Charles Vitelli

Manufactured in the United States of America

Ninth Edition

123456789BAHBAH4321

Library of Congress Cataloging-in-Publication Data
Main entry under title:
Taking sides: clashing views on controversial issues in American history, volume ii, reconstruction to the present/selected, edited, and with introductions by Larry Madaras and James M. SoRelle.—9th ed.
Includes bibliographical references and index.
1. United States—History—1865–. I. Madaras, Larry, comp. II. SoRelle, James M., comp.
973
0-07-243080-X
ISSN: 1091-8833

Printed on Recycled Paper

Preface

T he success of the past eight editions of *Taking Sides: Clashing Views on Controversial Issues in American History* has encouraged us to remain faithful to its original objectives, methods, and format. Our aim has been to create an effective instrument to enhance classroom learning and to foster critical thinking. Historical facts presented in a vacuum are of little value to the educational process. For students, whose search for historical truth often concentrates on *when* something happened rather than on *why*, and on specific events rather than on the *significance* of those events, *Taking Sides* is designed to offer an interesting and valuable departure. The understanding that the reader arrives at based on the evidence that emerges from the clash of views encourages the reader to view history as an *interpretive* discipline, not one of rote memorization.

As in previous editions, the issues are arranged in chronological order and can be easily incorporated into any American history survey course. Each issue has an issue *introduction,* which sets the stage for the debate that follows in the pro and con selections and provides historical and methodological background to the problem that the issue examines. Each issue concludes with a *postscript,* which ties the readings together, briefly mentions alternative interpretations, and supplies detailed *suggestions for further reading* for the student who wishes to pursue the topics raised in the issue. Also, Internet site addresses (URLs), which should prove useful as starting points for further research, have been provided on the *On the Internet* page that accompanies each part opener. At the back of the book is a listing of all the *contributors to this volume* with a brief biographical sketch of each of the prominent figures whose views are debated here.

Changes to this edition In this edition we have continued our efforts to maintain a balance between the traditional political, diplomatic, and cultural issues and the new social history, which depicts a society that benefited from the presence of African Americans, women, and workers of various racial and ethnic backgrounds. With this in mind, we present eight entirely new issues: *Did the Industrial Revolution Disrupt the American Family?* (Issue 3); *Was City Government in Late-Nineteenth-Century America a "Conspicuous Failure"?* (Issue 5); *Did Racial Segregation Improve the Status of African Americans?* (Issue 7); *Did the Women's Movement Die in the 1920s?* (Issue 9); *Did President Roosevelt Deliberately Withhold Information About the Attack on Pearl Harbor From the American Commanders?* (Issue 11); *Should America Remain a Nation of Immigrants?* (Issue 15); *Did President Reagan Win the Cold War?* (Issue 16); and *Will History Consider William Jefferson Clinton a Reasonably Good Chief Executive?* (Issue 17). Also, for Issue 6 on the cause of the Spanish-American War, the NO side has been replaced to bring a fresh perspective to the debate. In all there are 17 new selections.

A word to the instructor   An *Instructor's Manual With Test Questions* (multiple-choice and essay) is available through the publisher for the instructor using *Taking Sides* in the classroom. A general guidebook, *Using Taking Sides in the Classroom,* which discusses methods and techniques for integrating the pro-con approach into any classroom setting, is also available. An online version of *Using Taking Sides in the Classroom* and a correspondence service for *Taking Sides* adopters can be found at http://www.dushkin.com/usingts/.

Taking Sides: Clashing Views on Controversial Issues in American History is only one title in the Taking Sides series. If you are interested in seeing the table of contents for any of the other titles, please visit the Taking Sides Web site at http://www.dushkin.com/takingsides/.

Acknowledgments   Many individuals have contributed to the successful completion of this edition. We appreciate the evaluations submitted to McGraw-Hill/Dushkin by those who have used *Taking Sides* in the classroom. Special thanks to those who responded with specific suggestions for the ninth edition:

Gary Best
University of Hawaii–Hilo

James D. Bolton
Coastline Community College

Mary Borg
University of Northern Colorado

John Whitney Evans
College of St. Scholastica

Maryann Irwin
Diablo Valley College

Mark Hickerson
Chaffey College

Gordon Lam
Sierra College

Jon Nielson
Columbia College

Andrew O'Shaugnessy
University of Wisconsin-Oshkosh

Manian Padma
DeAnza College

Robert M. Paterson
Armstrong State College

Charles Piehl
Mankato State University

Ethan S. Rafuse
University of Missouri–Kansas City

John Reid
Ohio State University–Lima

Murray Rubinstein
CUNY Baruch College

Neil Sapper
Amarillo College

Preston Shea
Plymouth State College

Jack Traylor
William Jennings Bryan College

We are particularly indebted to Maggie Cullen, Cindy SoRelle, Barry A. Crouch, Virginia Kirk, Joseph and Helen Mitchell, and Jean Soto, who shared their ideas for changes, pointed us toward potentially useful historical works, and provided significant editorial assistance. Megan Arnold performed indispensable typing duties connected with this project. Susan E. Myers and Elu Ciborowski in the library at Howard Community College provided essential help in acquiring books and articles on interlibrary loan. Finally, we are sincerely grateful for the commitment, encouragement, and patience provided over the years by David Dean, former list manager for the Taking Sides series; David Brackley, senior developmental editor; and the entire staff of McGraw-Hill/ Dushkin. Indispensible to this project is Ted Knight, the current list manager.

Larry Madaras
Howard Community College

James M. SoRelle
Baylor University

Contents In Brief

Contents

Preface   i

Introduction: The Study of History   xii

Historian Matthew Josephson depicts John D. Rockefeller as an unconscionable manipulator who employed deception, bribery, and outright conspiracy to eliminate his competitors for control of the oil industry in the United States. Business historians Ralph W. Hidy and Muriel E. Hidy argue that Rockefeller and his associates were innovative representatives of corporate capitalism who brought stability to the often chaotic petroleum industry.

Professor of history Christine Stansell contends that women on the Great Plains were separated from friends and relatives and consequently endured lonely lives and loveless marriages. Professor of history Glenda Riley argues that women on the Great Plains created rich and varied social lives through the development of strong support networks.

Elaine Tyler May, a professor of American studies and history, argues that the Industrial Revolution in the United States, with its improved technology, increasing income, and emerging consumerism, led to higher rates of divorce because family wage earners failed to meet rising expectations for material accumulation. History professors Jacquelyn Dowd Hall, Robert Korstad, and James Leloudis contend that the cotton mill villages of the New South, rather than destroying family work patterns, fostered a labor system that permitted parents and children to work together as a traditional family unit.

Professor of history Carl N. Degler maintains that the American labor movement accepted capitalism and reacted conservatively to the radical organizational changes brought about in the economic system by big business. Professor of history Herbert G. Gutman argues that from 1843 to 1893, American factory workers attempted to humanize the system through the maintenance of their traditional, artisan, preindustrial work habits.

Professor of political science and political economy Ernest S. Griffith (1896–1981) argues that the city governments that were controlled by the political bosses represented a betrayal of the public trust. Professor of history Jon C. Teaford argues that municipal governments in the late nineteenth century achieved remarkable success in dealing with the challenges presented by rapid urbanization.

Journalist W. A. Swanberg argues that newspaper mogul William Randolph Hearst used the sensational and exploitative stories in his widely circulated *New York Journal* to stir up public opinion and to force President William McKinley to wage a war against Spain to free Cuba. Historian David Nasaw maintains that even if Hearst had not gone into publishing, the United States would have entered the war for political, economic, and security reasons.

Issue 7.   Did Racial Segregation Improve the Status of African Americans?   146

Professor of history Howard N. Rabinowitz suggests that racial segregation represented an improvement in the lives of African Americans in that it provided access to a variety of public services and accommodations from which they otherwise would have been excluded in the late-nineteenth-century South. Professor of American history Leon F. Litwack argues that "the age of Jim Crow," wherein efforts by whites to deny African Americans equal protection of the laws or the privileges and immunities guaranteed other citizens seemingly knew no bounds, created a highly repressive environment for blacks.

Issue 8.   Did the Progressives Fail?   170

Professor of history Richard M. Abrams maintains that progressivism was a failure because it never seriously confronted the inequalities that still exist in American society. Professors of history Arthur S. Link and Richard L. McCormick argue that the Progressives were a diverse group of reformers who confronted and ameliorated the worst abuses that emerged in urban industrial America during the early 1900s.

Issue 9.   Did the Women's Movement Die in the 1920s?   194

Professor of history William L. O'Neill contends that the women's movement died following the success of the suffrage campaign because women were not united in support of many of the other issues that affected them and because the increasingly militant feminism of the Woman's Party alienated many supporters of women's rights. Anne Firor Scott, a professor emeritus of history, maintains that the suffrage victory produced a heightened interest in further social and political reform, which inspired southern women to pursue their goals throughout the 1920s.

Professor of history Roger Biles contends that, in spite of its minimal reforms, the New Deal created a limited welfare state that implemented economic stabilizers to avert another depression. Professor of history Gary Dean Best argues that Roosevelt's regulatory programs retarded the nation's economic recovery from the Great Depression until World War II.

Retired rear admiral Robert A. Theobald argues that President Franklin D. Roosevelt deliberately withheld information from the commanders at Pearl Harbor in order to encourage the Japanese to make a surprise attack on the weak U.S. Pacific Fleet. Historian Roberta Wohlstetter contends that even though naval intelligence broke the Japanese code, conflicting signals and the lack of a central agency coordinating U.S. intelligence information made it impossible to predict the Pearl Harbor attack.

Professor of history Thomas G. Paterson argues that the Truman administration exaggerated the Soviet threat after World War II because the United

Professor of history John Lewis Gaddis argues that President Reagan combined a policy of militancy and operational pragmatism to bring about the most significant improvement in Soviet-American relations since the end of World War II. Professors of political science Daniel Deudney and G. John Ikenberry contend that the cold war ended only when Soviet president Gorbachev accepted Western liberal values and the need for global cooperation.

Journalist Lars-Erik Nelson argues that President Bill Clinton is a sadly flawed human being but a reasonably good president whose administration was a time of peace and plenty for Americans. Political scientists James MacGregor Burns and Georgia J. Sorenson et al. argue that Clinton will not rank among the near-great presidents because he is a transactional broker who lacks the ideological commitment to tackle the big issues facing American society.

Introduction

The Study of History

Larry Madaras

James M. SoRelle

In a pluralistic society such as ours, the study of history is bound to be a complex process. How an event is interpreted depends not only on the existing evidence but also on the perspective of the interpreter. Consequently, understanding history presupposes the evaluation of information, a task that often leads to conflicting conclusions. An understanding of history, then, requires the acceptance of the idea of historical relativism. Relativism means the redefinition of our past is always possible and desirable. History shifts, changes, and grows with new and different evidence and interpretations. As is the case with the law and even with medicine, beliefs that were unquestioned 100 or 200 years ago have been discredited or discarded since.

Relativism, then, encourages revisionism. There is a maxim that says, "The past must remain useful to the present." Historian Carl Becker argued that every generation should examine history for itself, thus ensuring constant scrutiny of our collective experience through new perspectives. History, consequently, does not remain static, in part because historians cannot avoid being influenced by the times in which they live. Almost all historians commit themselves to revising the views of other historians, by either disagreeing with earlier interpretations or creating new frameworks that pose different questions.

Schools of Thought

Three predominant schools of thought have emerged in American history since the first graduate seminars in history were given at the Johns Hopkins University in Baltimore, Maryland, in the 1870s. The *progressive* school dominated the professional field in the first half of the twentieth century. Influenced by the reform currents of Populism, progressivism, and the New Deal, these historians explored the social and economic forces that energized America. The progressive scholars tended to view the past in terms of conflicts between groups, and they sympathized with the underdog.

The post–World War II period witnessed the emergence of a new group of historians who viewed the conflict thesis as overly simplistic. Writing against the backdrop of the cold war, these *neoconservative* and *consensus* historians argued that Americans possess a shared set of values and that the areas of agreement within the nation's basic democratic and capitalistic framework are more important than the areas of disagreement.

In the 1960s, however, the civil rights movement, women's liberation, and the student rebellion (with its condemnation of the war in Vietnam) fragmented the consensus of values upon which historians of the 1950s centered their interpretations. This turmoil set the stage for the emergence of another group of scholars. *New Left* historians began to reinterpret the past once again. They emphasized the significance of conflict in American history, and they resurrected interest in those groups ignored by the consensus school. In addition, New Left historians critiqued the expansionist policies of the United States and emphasized the difficulties confronted by Native Americans, African Americans, women, and urban workers in gaining full citizenship status.

Progressive, consensus, and New Left history is still being written. The most recent generation of scholars, however, focuses upon social history. Their primary concern is to discover what the lives of "ordinary Americans" were really like. These new social historians employ previously overlooked court and church documents, house deeds and tax records, letters and diaries, photographs, and census data to reconstruct the everyday lives of average Americans. Some employ new methodologies, such as quantification (enhanced by advancing computer technology) and oral history, while others borrow from the disciplines of political science, economics, sociology, anthropology, and psychology for their historical investigations.

The proliferation of historical approaches, which are reflected in the issues debated in this book, has had mixed results. On the one hand, historians have become so specialized in their respective time periods and methodological styles that it is difficult to synthesize the recent scholarship into a comprehensive text for the general reader. On the other hand, historians now know more about new questions or ones that previously were considered to be germane only to scholars in other social sciences. Although there is little agreement about the answers to these questions, the methods employed and the issues explored make the "new history" a very exciting field to study.

The topics that follow represent a variety of perspectives and approaches. Each of these controversial issues can be studied for its individual importance to American history. Taken as a group, they interact with one another to illustrate larger historical themes. When grouped thematically, the issues reveal continuing motifs in the development of American history.

Economic Questions

Issue 1 explores the dynamics of the modern American economy through investigations of the nineteenth-century entrepreneurs. Were these industrial leaders robber barons, as portrayed by contemporary critics and many history texts? Or were they industrial statesmen and organizational geniuses? Matthew Josephson argues that John D. Rockefeller is a key example of a monopoly capitalist who utilized ruthless and violent methods in organizing the oil industry. More favorable and representative of the business historian approach is the interpretation of Ralph W. Hidy and Muriel E. Hidy. They conclude that Rockefeller was among the earliest organizational innovators and that he standardized production and procedures and created a large integrated Industrial Corporation.

The Outsiders: Laborers, Blacks, Women, Family, and Immigrants

In the wake of industrialization during the late 1800s, the rapid pace of change created new working conditions for the laboring class. How did laborers react to these changes? Did they lose their autonomy in the large corporations? Did they accept or reject the wage system? Were they pawns of the economic cycles of boom and bust, to be hired and fired at will? Did they look for an alternative to capitalism by engaging in strikes, establishing labor unions, or creating a socialist movement? In Issue 4, Carl N. Degler maintains that American workers accepted capitalism and the changes that it brought forth. Herbert G. Gutman, however, argues that in the years 1843–1893, American factory workers attempted to humanize the system by maintaining their traditional artisan values. By the beginning of the twentieth century, however, the organizational innovations of Rockefeller and the assembly-line techniques pioneered by Henry Ford had revolutionized American capitalism.

In recent years, historians have shifted their focus to social issues. New questions have been asked and new frameworks have been developed. Issue 3 ponders whether the industrial revolution disrupted the American family. In her study of changing patterns of divorce between 1880 and 1920, Elaine Tyler May finds that higher consumer expectations, which resulted from the Industrial Revolution, disproportionately strained marital relations among the lower-middle and working classes because the husbands were unable to fulfill the economic demands of their wives. But in their study of cotton mill people in the Piedmont region of North and South Carolina, Jacquelyn Dowd Hall, Robert Korstad, and James Leloudis argue that rural families were able to use the mills to make a living and to keep their families and farms intact.

The Piedmont mills were composed of white workers only. By the 1890s rigid segregation laws and customs separated the white and black races in the South. Did segregation hurt or harm the black community? In Issue 7, Howard N. Rabinowitz advances a unique position. He argues that it was better for blacks to attend segregated schools, to ride segregated streetcars and trains, and to use segregated parks and restrooms rather than to be totally excluded from schools and other public facilities. Segregation, says Rabinowitz, was a halfway measure between total exclusion and full integration. But Leon F. Litwack disagrees with this interpretation. To the white Southerners, he argues, Negroes were segregated because they were considered inferior.

The situation for African Americans has vastly improved since the civil rights revolution of the 1960s. But did it improve race relations in the United States? In Issue 13, Robert Weisbrot details the many opportunities and social improvements that he believes are products of the civil rights movement. But Tom Wicker argues that, in the long run, the civil rights movement failed to bring either racial equality or racial harmony to the United States.

One of the less well known areas of American history is the impact of the frontier on the women who migrated west. In Issue 2, Christine Stansell maintains that women who migrated west in the late nineteenth century lost their networks of family and friends back east and that they were isolated and lonely on the Great Plains. Glenda Riley agrees that women faced many hardships on the frontier. However, she argues that women rebuilt friendships through church gatherings and quilting bee sessions.

Issue 15 asks, Should America remain a nation of immigrants? In the first selection, Reed Ueda maintains that the sheer magnitude and diversity of U.S. immigrants has continually reshaped the American character and made America a "permanently unfinished country." In the second selection, Richard D. Lamm argues that immigration should be severely curtailed because the most recent immigrants are members of the underclass who are culturally unassimilable and who take jobs away from the poorest citizens of an already overpopulated America.

The United States and the World

As the United States developed a preeminent position in world affairs, the nation's politicians were forced to consider the proper relationship between their country and the rest of the world. To what extent, many asked, should the United States seek to expand its political, economic, and moral influence around the world?

This was a particularly intriguing question for a number of political, military, and intellectual leaders at the close of the nineteenth century, who pondered whether or not it was necessary to acquire an overseas empire to be considered one of the world's great powers. Many historians consider the Spanish-American war a turning point in American history. In Issue 6, W. A. Swanberg argues that newspaper mogul William Randolph Hearst used the sensational and exploitative stories in his widely circulated and nationally influential *New York Journal* to stir up public opinion and to push President William McKinley into a questionable war. Taking a broader view, David Nasaw asserts that even if Hearst had not gone into publishing newspapers, the United States would have entered the war for political, economic, and security reasons.

One of the most controversial historical issues concerns the events leading to America's entrance into World War II. In Issue 11, Robert A. Theobald contends that President Franklin D. Roosevelt deliberately withheld information from the Hawaiian army and naval commanders at Pearl Harbor in order to encourage the Japanese to make a surprise attack on the weak U.S. Pacific Fleet. Roberta Wohlstetter, however, maintains that even though naval intelligence broke the Japanese code, conflicting signals and the lack of a central agency coordinating U.S. intelligence information made it impossible to predict the Pearl Harbor attack.

The United States had barely emerged victorious against Germany and Japan in 1945 when a cold war developed against its former ally, the Soviet Union. Issue 12 tackles the question of responsibility. Thomas G. Paterson blames the United States for exaggerating the Soviet threat to world peace.

John Lewis Gaddis, taking a different position, argues that the power vacuum that existed in Europe at the end of World War II exaggerated the countries' differences and made a clash between the democratic, capitalist United States and the totalitarian, communist USSR almost inevitable.

No discussion of American foreign policy is complete without some consideration of the Vietnam War. Was America's escalation of the war inevitable in 1965? In Issue 14, Brian VanDeMark argues that President Lyndon Johnson was afraid to pull out of Vietnam because he feared that his opponents would accuse him of being soft on communism and that they would also destroy his Great Society reforms. On the other side, H. R. McMaster blames Johnson and his advisers for failing to develop a coherent policy in Vietnam.

Now that the cold war is over, historians must assess why it ended so suddenly and unexpectedly. Did President Ronald Reagan's military buildup in the 1980s force the Soviet Union into economic bankruptcy? In Issue 16, John Lewis Gaddis gives Reagan high marks for ending the cold war. By combining a policy of militancy and operational pragmatism, he argues, Reagan brought about the most significant improvement in Soviet-American relations since the end of World War II. According to Daniel Deudney and G. John Ikenberry, however, the cold war ended only when the Soviets saw the need for international cooperation to end the arms race, prevent a nuclear holocaust, and liberalize their economy.

Political and Social Successes and Failures, 1880–1920

Issue 5 looks at the way urban government operated in the late nineteenth century. Ernest S. Griffith surveys the nature of municipal government in the last three decades of the nineteenth century and concludes that city politics was consumed by a "cancer of corruption" that predominated from 1880 to 1893. Jon C. Teaford, on the other hand, maintains that scholars like Griffith are too eager to condemn the activities of late-nineteenth-century municipal governments without recognizing their accomplishments. While admitting numerous shortcomings, Teaford argues that American city dwellers enjoyed a higher standard of public services than any other urban residents in the world.

The Progressive movement is examined in Issue 8. Richard M. Abrams attributes the failure of the movement to its limited scope. He maintains that it imposed a uniform set of values on a diverse people and did not address the inequalities that prevail in American society. Arthur S. Link and Richard L. McCormick, however, emphasize the reforms introduced by the Progressives to check the abuses of industrialization and urbanization during the early 1900s.

With the passage of the Nineteenth Amendment in 1919, women gained the right to vote. How did this impact the political system? And how did it affect the women's movement in the 1920s with regard to other gender issues? In Issue 9, William L. O'Neill argues that in the 1920s the women's movement splintered and lost its force as women pursued more individualistic and personal goals and broke through Victorian constraints on social and sexual mores. But Anne Firor Scott concentrates on southern women and concludes that the 1920s witnessed significant efforts by women to seek reforms in areas of interest to members of their sex and to society as a whole.

The Great Depression of the 1930s remains one of the most traumatic events in U.S. history. The characteristics of that decade are deeply etched in American folk memory, but the remedies that were applied to these social and economic ills—known collectively as the New Deal—are not easy to evaluate. In Issue 10, Roger Biles contends that the economic stabilizers created by New Deal programs prevented the recurrence of the Great Depression. Gary Dean Best, on the other hand, criticizes the New Deal from a 1990s conservative perspective. In his view, because New Deal agencies were antibusiness, they overregulated the economy and did not allow the free enterprise system to work out of the depression.

The last president of the twentieth century, William Jefferson Clinton, was the first president to be impeached since Andrew Johnson (1865–1869). Both presidents, however, were not convicted of their impeachment charges. Most historians consider Johnson a below-average president. Will history rank Clinton as a near-great, average, or below-average president? In the first selection of Issue 17, Lars-Erik Nelson argues that President Clinton is "a sadly flawed human being but a reasonably good President whose administration was, for Americans, a time of peace and plenty." In the second selection, James Mac-Gregor Burns and Georgia J. Sorenson et al. argue that Clinton will not rank among the near-great presidents, because he is a transactional broker who lacks the ideological commitment to tackle the big issues facing American society.

Conclusion

The process of historical study should rely more on thinking than on memorizing data. Once the basics of who, what, when, and where are determined, historical thinking shifts to a higher gear. Analysis, comparison and contrast, evaluation, and explanation take command. These skills not only increase our knowledge of the past but they also provide general tools for the comprehension of all the topics about which human beings think.

The diversity of a pluralistic society, however, creates some obstacles to comprehending the past. The spectrum of differing opinions on any particular subject eliminates the possibility of quick and easy answers. In the final analysis, conclusions are often built through a synthesis of several different interpretations, but even then they may be partial and tentative.

The study of history in a pluralistic society allows each citizen the opportunity to reach independent conclusions about the past. Since most, if not all, historical issues affect the present and future, understanding the past becomes necessary if society is to progress. Many of today's problems have a direct connection with the past. Additionally, other contemporary issues may lack obvious direct antecedents, but historical investigation can provide illuminating analogies. At first, it may appear confusing to read and to think about opposing historical views, but the survival of our democratic society depends on such critical thinking by acute and discerning minds.

On the Internet . . .

DUSHKIN ONLINE

John D. Rockefeller and the Standard Oil Company

This site, created by Swiss entrepreneur Francois Micheloud, provides a highly detailed history of the American oil industry, with John D. Rockefeller as a main focus. It includes the discovery of oil, the main players in the oil industry, the rise of the Standard Oil Company, the passing of the Sherman Antitrust Act, and the dismantling of Standard Oil, as well as both short and detailed chronologies of the company.

http://www.micheloud.com/FXM/SO/rock.htm

National Women's History Project

The National Women's History Project is a nonprofit organization dedicated to recognizing and celebrating the diverse and historic accomplishments of women by providing information and educational material and programs.

http://www.nwhp.org

Industrial Revolution

This site provides an extensive list of links to pages on the Industrial Revolution grouped into categories, including Child Labor, Disparity of Wealth, Unions, and Urban Planning.

http://members.aol.com/TeacherNet/Industrial.html

Gilded Age and Progressive Era Resources

This page of the Department of History at Tennessee Technological University offers over 100 links to sites on the Gilded Age and the Progressive era. Links include general resources, political leaders, transformation of the West, the rise of big business and American workers, and literary and cultural resources.

http://www.tntech.edu/www/acad/hist/gilprog.html

The Industrial Revolution: How It Changed Farms, Families, Cities, and the Workplace

*E*conomic expansion and the seemingly unlimited resources available in postbellum America offered great opportunity and created new political, social, and economic challenges. Political freedom and economic opportunity provided incentives for immigration to America. The need for cheap labor to run the machinery of the Industrial Revolution created an atmosphere for potential exploitation that was intensified by the concentration of wealth in the hands of a few capitalists. The labor movement took root, with some elements calling for an overthrow of the capitalist system, while others sought to establish political power within the existing system. Strains began to develop between immigrant and native-born workers as well as between workers and owners, husbands and wives, and parents and their children.

With the growth of industry, urban problems became more acute. Improvements in water and sewerage, street cleaning, housing, mass transit, and fire and crime prevention developed slowly because incredible population growth strained municipal services. Urban governments had limited powers, which often fell under the control of political bosses. Historians disagree as to whether or not attempts to remedy these problems through a brokered political system were successful.

- Was John D. Rockefeller a "Robber Baron"?

- Did Nineteenth-Century Women of the West Fail to Overcome the Hardships of Living on the Great Plains?

- Did the Industrial Revolution Disrupt the American Family?

- Were American Workers in the Gilded Age Conservative Capitalists?

- Was City Government in Late-Nineteenth-Century America a "Conspicuous Failure"?

ISSUE 1

Was John D. Rockefeller a "Robber Baron"?

YES: Matthew Josephson, from *The Robber Barons: The Great American Capitalists, 1861–1901* (Harcourt, Brace & World, 1962)

NO: Ralph W. Hidy and Muriel E. Hidy, from *History of Standard Oil Company (New Jersey)*, vol. 1: *Pioneering in Big Business, 1882–1911* (Harper & Brothers, 1955)

ISSUE SUMMARY

YES: Historian Matthew Josephson depicts John D. Rockefeller as an unconscionable manipulator who employed deception, bribery, and outright conspiracy to restrain free trade in order to eliminate his competitors for control of the oil industry in the United States.

NO: Business historians Ralph W. Hidy and Muriel E. Hidy argue that although Rockefeller and his associates at Standard Oil occasionally used their power ruthlessly, they were innovative representatives of corporate capitalism who brought stability to the often chaotic petroleum industry and made a significant contribution to the rapid development of the national economy as a whole.

Between 1860 and 1914 the United States was transformed from a country of farms, small towns, and modest manufacturing concerns to a modern nation dominated by large cities and factories. During those years the population tripled, and the nation experienced astounding urban growth. A new proletariat emerged to provide the necessary labor for the country's developing factory system. Between the Civil War and World War I, the value of manufactured goods in the United States increased 12-fold, and the capital invested in industrial pursuits multiplied 22 times. In addition, the application of new machinery and scientific methods to agriculture produced abundant yields of wheat, corn, and other foodstuffs, despite the decline in the number of farmers.

Why did this industrial revolution occur in the United States during the last quarter of the nineteenth century? What factors contributed to the rapid pace of American industrialization? In answering these questions, historians often point to the first half of the 1800s and the significance of the "transportation revolution," which produced better roads, canals, and railroads to move people and goods more efficiently and cheaply from one point to another. Technological improvements such as the Bessemer process, refrigeration, electricity, and the telephone also made their mark in the nation's "machine age." Government cooperation with business, large-scale immigration from Europe and Asia, and the availability of foreign capital for industrial investments provided still other underpinnings for this industrial growth. Finally, American industrialization depended upon a number of individuals in the United States who were willing to organize and finance the nation's industrial base for the sake of anticipated profits. These, of course, were the entrepreneurs.

American public attitudes have reflected a schizophrenic quality with regard to the activities of the industrial leaders of the late nineteenth century. Were these entrepreneurs "robber barons" who employed any means necessary to enrich themselves at the expense of their competitors? Or were they "captains of industry" whose shrewd and innovative leadership brought order out of industrial chaos and generated great fortunes that enriched the public welfare through the workings of the various philanthropic agencies that these leaders established? Although the "robber baron" stereotype emerged as early as the 1870s, it probably gained its widest acceptance in the 1930s, when, in the midst of the Great Depression, many critics were proclaiming the apparent failure of American capitalism. Since the depression, however, some historians, including Allan Nevins, Alfred D. Chandler, Jr., and Maury Klein, have sought to revise the negative assessments offered by earlier generations of scholars. In the hands of these business historians, the late-nineteenth-century businessmen have become "industrial statesmen" who skillfully oversaw the process of raising the United States to a preeminent position among the nations of the world. The following selections reveal the divergence of scholarly opinion as it applies to one of the most notable of these American entrepreneurs—John D. Rockefeller, founder of the Standard Oil Company, who came to epitomize both the success and excess of corporate capitalism in the United States.

Matthew Josephson, whose 1934 attack on monopolistic capitalism became the model for the "robber baron" thesis for post-depression-era historians, characterizes Rockefeller as a parsimonious, deceptive, and conspiratorial businessman. Rockefeller's fortune, Josephson argues, was built upon a series of secret agreements that wrung concessions from America's leading railroad magnates and allowed Rockefeller to decimate his competitors through the establishment of the South Improvement Company and, subsequently, Standard Oil.

Ralph W. Hidy and Muriel E. Hidy, on the other hand, accentuate Rockefeller's positive accomplishments in their study of Standard Oil of New Jersey. Rockefeller could be ruthless in his business dealings, they admit, but he operated within the law and introduced innovations that stabilized the petroleum industry, produced a mass-marketing system, and spearheaded the nation's economic growth in the late nineteenth and early twentieth centuries.

The Robber Barons

J ohn Rockefeller who grew up in Western New York and later near Cleveland, as one of a struggling family of five children, recalls with satisfaction the excellent practical training he had received and how quickly he put it to use. His childhood seemed to have been darkened by the misdeeds of his father, a wandering vendor of quack medicine who rarely supported his family, and was sometimes a fugitive from the law; yet the son invariably spoke of his parent's instructions with gratitude. He said:

> ... He himself trained me in practical ways. He was engaged in different enterprises; he used to tell me about these things ... and he taught me the principles and methods of business.... I knew what a cord of good solid beech and maple wood was. My father told me to select only solid wood ... and not to put any limbs in it or any punky wood. That was a good training for me.

But the elder Rockefeller went further than this in his sage instructions, according to John T. Flynn, who attributes to him the statement:

> I cheat my boys every chance I get, I want to make 'em sharp. I trade with the boys and skin 'em and I just beat 'em every time I can. I want to make 'em sharp.

If at times the young Rockefeller absorbed a certain shiftiness and trading sharpness from his restless father, it was also true that his father was absent so often and so long as to cast shame and poverty upon his home. Thus he must have been subject far more often to the stern supervision of his mother, whom he has recalled in several stories. His mother would punish him, as he related, with a birch switch to "uphold the standard of the family when it showed a tendency to deteriorate." Once when she found out that she was punishing him for a misdeed at school of which he was innocent, she said, "Never mind, we have started in on this whipping and it will do for the next time." The normal outcome of such disciplinary cruelty would be deception and stealthiness in the boy, as a defense.

But his mother, who reared her children with the rigid piety of an Evangelist, also started him in his first business enterprise. When he was seven years old she encouraged him to raise turkeys, and gave him for this purpose the family's surplus milk curds. There are legends of Rockefeller as a boy stalking a turkey with the most patient stealth in order to seize her eggs.

This harshly disciplined boy, quiet, shy, reserved, serious, received but a few years' poor schooling, and worked for neighboring farmers in all his spare time. His whole youth suggests only abstinence, prudence and the growth of parsimony in his soul. The pennies he earned he would save steadily in a blue bowl that stood on a chest in his room, and accumulated until there was a small heap of gold coins. He would work, by his own account, hoeing potatoes for a neighboring farmer from morning to night for 37 cents a day. At a time when he was still very young he had fifty dollars saved, which upon invitation he one day loaned to the farmer who employed him.

"And as I was saving those little sums," he relates, "I soon learned that I could get as much interest for $50 loaned at seven per cent—then the legal rate of interest—as I could earn by digging potatoes for ten days." Thereafter, he tells us, he resolved that it was better "to let the money be my slave than to be the slave of money."

In Cleveland whither the family removed in 1854, Rockefeller went to the Central High School and studied bookkeeping for a year. This delighted him. Most of the conquering types in the coming order were to be men trained early in life in the calculations of the bookkeeper, Cooke, Huntington, Gould, Henry Frick and especially Rockefeller of whom it was said afterward: "He had the soul of a bookkeeper."

In his first position as bookkeeper to a produce merchant at the Cleveland docks, when he was sixteen, he distinguished himself by his composed orderly habits. Very carefully he examined each item on each bill before he approved it for payment. Out of a salary which began at $15 a month and advanced ultimately to $50 a month, he saved $800 in three years, the lion's share of his total earnings! This was fantastic parsimony.

He spent little money for clothing, though he was always neat; he never went to the theater, had no amusements, and few friends. But he attended his Baptist Church in Cleveland as devoutly as he attended to his accounts. And to the cause of the church alone, to its parish fund and mission funds, he demonstrated his only generosity by gifts that were large for him then—first of ten cents, then later of twenty-five cents at a time.

In the young Rockefeller the traits which his mother had bred in him, of piety and the economic virtue—worship of the "lean goddess of Abstinence" —were of one cloth. The pale, bony, small-eyed young Baptist served the Lord and pursued his own business unremittingly. His composed manner, which had a certain languor, hid a feverish calculation, a sleepy strength, cruel, intense, terribly alert.

As a schoolboy John Rockefeller had once announced to a companion, as they walked by a rich man's ample house along their way: "When I grow up I want to be worth $100,000. And I'm going to be too." In almost the same words, Rockefeller in Cleveland, Cooke in Philadelphia, Carnegie in Pittsburgh, or a James Hill in the Northwestern frontier could be found voicing the same hope. And Rockefeller, the bookkeeper, "not slothful in business... serving the Lord," as John T. Flynn describes him, watched his chances closely, learned every detail of the produce business which engaged him, until finally in 1858 he made bold to open a business of his own in partnership with a young Englishman named Clark (who was destined to be left far behind). Rockefeller's grimly accumulated savings of $800, in addition to a loan from his father at the usurious rate of 10 per cent, yielded the capital which launched him, and he was soon "gathering gear" quietly. He knew the art of using loan credit to expand his operations. His first bank loan against warehouse receipts gave him a thrill of pleasure. He now bought grain and produce of all kinds in carload lots rather than in small consignments. Prosperous, he said nothing, but began to dress his part, wearing a high silk hat, frock coat and striped trousers like other merchants of the time. His head was handsome, his eyes small, birdlike; on his pale bony cheeks were the proverbial side-whiskers, reddish in color.

At night, in his room, he read the Bible, and retiring had the queer habit of talking to his pillow about his business adventures. In his autobiography he says that "these intimate conversations with myself had a great influence upon my life." He told himself "not to get puffed up with any foolish notions" and never to be deceived about actual conditions. "Look out or you will lose your head—go steady."

He was given to secrecy; he loathed all display. When he married, a few years afterward, he lost not a day from his business. His wife, Laura Spelman, proved an excellent mate. She encouraged his furtiveness, he relates, advising him always to be silent, to say as little as possible. His composure, his self-possession was excessive. Those Clevelanders to whom Miss Ida Tarbell addressed herself in her investigations of Rockefeller, told her that he was a hard man to best in a trade, that he rarely smiled, and almost never laughed, save when he struck a good bargain. Then he might clap his hands with delight, or he might even, if the occasion warranted, throw up his hat, kick his heels and hug his informer. One time he was so overjoyed at a favorable piece of news that he burst out: "I'm bound to be rich! *Bound to be rich!*" ...

The discovery of oil in the northwestern corner of Pennsylvania by [Edwin L.] Drake in 1859 was no isolated event, but part of the long overdue movement to exploit the subsoil of the country. When thousands rushed to scoop the silver and gold of Nevada, Colorado and Montana, the copper of Michigan, the iron ore of Pennsylvania and New York, technical knowledge at last interpreted the meaning of the greasy mineral substance which lay above ground near Titusville, Pennsylvania, and which had been used as a patent medicine ("Kier's Medicine") for twenty years. The rush and boom, out of which numerous speculators such as Andrew Carnegie had drawn quick profits and sold out—while so many others lost all they possessed—did not escape the attention of Rockefeller. The merchants of Cleveland, interested either in handling the new illuminating oil or investing in the industry itself, had sent the young Rockefeller to spy out the ground.

He had come probably in the spring of 1860 to the strange, blackened valleys of the Oil Regions where a forest of crude derricks, flimsy shacks and storehouses had been raised overnight. Here he had looked at the anarchy of the pioneer drillers or diggers of oil, the first frenzy of exploitation, with a deep disfavor that all conservative merchants of the time shared. There were continual fires, disasters and miracles; an oil well brought a fortune in a week, with the market price at twenty dollars a barrel; then as more wells came in the price fell to three and even two dollars a barrel before the next season! No one could tell at what price it was safe to buy oil, or oil acreage, and none knew how long the supply would last.

Returning to Cleveland, Rockefeller had counseled his merchant friends against investments in oil. At best the refining trade might be barely profitable if one could survive the mad dance of the market and if the supply of oil held out. Repugnance was strong in the infinitely cautious young merchant against the pioneering of the Oil Creek rabble. Two years were to pass before he approached the field again, while his accumulations increased with the fruitful wartime trade in provisions.

In 1862, when small refineries were rising everywhere, when more and more oil fields were being opened, the prospects of the new trade were immensely more favorable. A Clevelander named Samuel Andrews, owner of a small still, now came to the firm of Rockefeller & Clark with a proposal that they back him in setting up a sizable oil-refinery. The man Andrews was something of a technologist: he knew how to extract a high percentage of kerosene oil from the crude; he was one of the first to use the by-products developed in the refining process. Rockefeller and his partner, who appreciated the man's worth, invested $5,000 at the start with him. The affair flourished quickly, as demand widened for the new illuminant. Soon Rockefeller missed not a day from the refinery, where Andrews manufactured a kerosene better, purer than his competitors', and Rockefeller kept the books, conducted the purchasing of crude oil in his sharp fashion, and saved old iron, waste oils, made his own barrels, watched, spared, squirmed, for the smallest bargains.

In 1865, with uncanny judgment, Rockefeller chose between his produce business and the oil-refining trade. He sold his share in the house of Rockefeller & Clark, and purchased Clark's share in the oil-refinery, now called Rockefeller & Andrews. At this moment the values of all provisions were falling, while the oil trade was widening, spreading over all the world. Several great new wells had come in; supply was certain—10,000 barrels a day. Concentrating all his effort upon the new trade, he labored unremittingly to entrench himself in it, to be ready for all the hazards, which were great. He inaugurated ruthless economies; giving all his attention "to little details," he acquired a numerous clientele in the Western and Southern states; and opened an export selling agency in New York, headed by his brother William Rockefeller. "Low-voiced, soft-footed, humble, knowing every point in every man's business," Miss Tarbell relates, "he never tired until he got his wares at the lowest possible figures." "John always got the best of the bargain," the old men of Cleveland recall: "'savy fellow he was!" For all his fierce passion for money, he was utterly impassive in his bearing, save when some surprisingly good purchase of oil had been made at the creek. Then he could no longer restrain his shouts of joy. In the oil trade, John Rockefeller grew up in a hard school of struggle; he endured the merciless and unprincipled competition of rivals; and his own unpitying logic and coldly resolute methods were doubtless the consequence of the brutal free-for-all from which he emerged with certain crushing advantages.

While the producers of crude oil contended with each other in lawless fashion to drill the largest quantities, the refiners at different industrial centers who processed and reshipped the crude oil were also engaged in unresting trade conflicts, in which all measures were fair. And behind the rivalry of the producers and the refiners in different cities lay the secret struggles of the large railroad interests moving obscurely in the background. Drew's Erie, Vanderbilt's New York Central, Thomson and Scott's Pennsylvania, extending their lines to the Oil Regions, all hunted their fortune in the huge new traffic, pressing the interests of favored shipping and refining centers such as Cleveland or Pittsburgh or Buffalo to suit themselves. It would have been simplest possibly to have oil-refineries at the source of the crude material itself; but the purpose of the railroads forbade this; and there was no way of determining the outcome in this matter, as in any other phase of the organization of the country's new resources, whose manner of exploitation was determined only through pitched battles between the various gladiators, wherein the will of Providence was seen.

Rockefeller, who had no friends and no diversions, who was "all business," as John T. Flynn describes him, now gave himself to incessant planning, planning that would defeat chance itself. His company was but one of thirty oil-refiners located in Cleveland; in the Oil Regions, at Oil City and Titusville, there were numerous others, including the largest refineries of all, more favorably placed for shipping. But in 1867 Rockefeller invited into his firm as a partner, a business acquaintance of his, Henry M. Flagler, son-in-law of the rich whiskey distiller and salt-maker S. V. Harkness. Flagler, a bold and dashing fellow, was deeply attracted by the possibilities of the oil business. Thanks to Harkness, he brought $70,000 into the business, which at once opened a second refinery in Cleveland. Within a year or two the firm of Rockefeller, Flagler & Andrews was the biggest refinery in Cleveland, producing 1,500 barrels a day, having its own warehouses, its export agency in New York, its own wooden tank cars, its own staff of chemists or experts who labored to improve or economize the manufacturing processes. The company moved steadily to the front of the field, surpassing its rivals in quality, and outselling them by a small, though not certain or decisive, margin. How was this done?

In the struggle for business, Rockefeller's instinct for conspiracy is already marked. The partnership with Flagler brought an access of fresh capital and even more credit. Then in a further step of collusion, this of profound importance, Rockefeller and Flagler approached the railroad which carried so many carloads of their oil toward the seaboard, and whose tariff figured heavily in the ultimate cost. They demanded from it concessions in freight rates that would enable them to meet the advantages of other refining centers such as Pittsburgh, Philadelphia and New York. Their company was now large enough to force the hand of the railroad, in this case, a branch of Vanderbilt's New York Central system; and they were granted their demands: a secret reduction or "rebate" on all their shipments of oil. "Such was the railroad's method," Rockefeller himself afterward admitted. He relates:

> A public rate was made and collected by the railroad companies, but so far as my knowledge extends, was seldom retained in full; a portion of it was repaid to the shipper as a rebate. By this method the real rate of freight which

any shipper paid was not known by his competitors, nor by other railroads, the amount being a matter of bargain with the carrying companies.

Once having gained an advantage Rockefeller pressed forward relentlessly. The volume of his business increased rapidly. Thanks to the collaboration of the railroad, he had placed his rivals in other cities and in Cleveland itself under a handicap, whose weight he endeavored to increase.

The railroads, as we see, possessed the strategic power, almost of life and death, to encourage one industrial group or cause another to languish. Their policy was based on the relative costs of handling small or large volume shipments. Thus as the Rockefeller company became the largest shipper of oil, its production rising in 1870 to 3,000 barrels a day, and offered to guarantee regular daily shipments of as much as sixty carloads, the railroads were impelled to accept further proposals for rebates. It was to their interest to do so in view of savings of several hundred thousand dollars a month in handling. On crude oil brought from the Oil Regions, Rockefeller paid perhaps 15 cents a barrel less than the open rate of 40 cents; on refined oil moving from Cleveland toward New York, he paid approximately 90 cents against the open rate of $1.30. These momentous agreements were maintained in utter secrecy, perhaps because of the persisting memory of their illegality, according to the common law ever since Queen Elizabeth's time, as a form of "conspiracy" in trade.

In January, 1870, Rockefeller, Flagler & Andrews were incorporated as a joint-stock company, a form increasingly popular, under the name of the Standard Oil Company of Ohio. At this time their worth was estimated at one million dollars; they employed over a thousand workers and were the largest refiners in the world. Despite deeply disturbed conditions in their trade during 1870, profits came to them in a mounting flood, while in the same year, it is noteworthy, four of their twenty-nine competitors in Cleveland gave up the ghost. The pious young man of thirty who feared only God, and thought of nothing but his business, gave not a sign of his greatly augmented wealth, which made him one of the leading personages of his city. His income was actually a fabulous one for the time. The Standard Oil Company from the beginning earned something like 100 per cent on its capital; and Rockefeller and his brother owned a full half-interest in it in 1870. But with an evangelistic fervor John Rockefeller was bent only upon further conquests, upon greater extensions of the power over industry which had come into the hands of the group he headed.

In the life of every conquering soul there is a "turning point," a moment when a deep understanding of the self coincides with an equally deep sense of one's immediate mission in the tangible world. For Rockefeller, brooding, secretive, uneasily scenting his fortune, this moment came but a few years after his entrance into the oil trade, and at the age of thirty. He had looked upon the disorganized conditions of the Pennsylvania oil fields, the only source then known, and found them not good: the guerilla fighting of drillers, or refining firms, of rival railroad lines, the mercurial changes in supply and market value —very alarming in 1870—offended his orderly and methodical spirit. But one could see that petroleum was to be the light of the world. From the source, from the chaotic oil fields where thousands of drillers toiled, the grimy stream of the precious commodity, petroleum, flowed along many diverse channels to narrow into the hands of several hundred refineries, then to issue once more in a continuous stream to consumers throughout the world. Owner with Flagler and Harkness of the largest refining company in the country, Rockefeller had a strongly entrenched position at the narrows of this stream. Now what if the Standard Oil Company should by further steps of organization possess itself wholly of the narrows? In this period of anarchic individual competition, the idea of such a movement of rationalization must have come to Rockefeller forcibly, as it had recently come to others.

Even as early as 1868 the first plan of industrial combination in the shape of the pool had been originated in the Michigan Salt Association. Desiring to correct chaotic market conditions, declaring that "in union there is strength," the salt-producers of Saginaw Bay had banded together to control the output and sale of nearly all the salt in their region, a large part of the vital national supply. Secret agreements had been executed for each year, allotting the sales and fixing the price at almost twice what it had been immediately prior to the appearance of the pool. And though the inevitable greed and self-seeking of the individual salt-producers had tended to weaken the pool, the new economic invention was launched in its infantile form. Rockefeller's partners, Flagler and Harkness, had themselves participated in the historic Michigan Salt Association.

This grand idea of industrial rationalization owed its swift, ruthless, methodical execution no doubt to the firmness of character we sense in Rockefeller, who had the temper of a great, unconscionable military captain, combining audacity with thoroughness and shrewd judgment. His plan seemed to take account of no one's feelings in the matter. Indeed there was something revolutionary in it; it seemed to fly in the fact of human liberties and deep-rooted custom and common law. The notorious "South Improvement Company," with its strange charter, ingeniously instrumenting the scheme of combination, was to be unraveled amid profound secrecy. By conspiring with the railroads (which also hungered for economic order), it would be terribly armed with the power of the freight rebate which garrotted all opposition systematically. This plan of combination, this unifying conception Rockefeller took as his ruling idea; he breathed life into it, clung to it grimly in the face of the most menacing attacks of legislatures, courts, rival captains, and, at moments, even of rebellious mobs. His view of men and events justified him, and despite many official and innocent denials, he is believed to have said once in confidence, as Flynn relates:

> I had our plan clearly in mind. It was right. I knew it as a matter of conscience. It was right between me and my God. If I had to do it tomorrow I would do it again in the same way—do it a hundred times.

The broad purpose was to control and direct the flow of crude petroleum into the hands of a narrowed group of refiners. The refiners would be supported by the combined railroad trunk lines which shipped the oil; while the producers' phase of the stream would be left unorganized—*but with power over their outlet to market* henceforth to be concentrated into the few hands of the refiners.

Saying nothing to others, bending over their maps of the industry, Rockefeller and Flagler first drew up a short list of the principal refining companies who were to be asked to combine with them. Then having banded together a sufficient number, they would persuade the railroads to give them special freight rates—on the ground of "evening" the traffic—guaranteeing equitable distribution of freight business; and this in turn would be a club to force other elements needed into union with them. They could control output, drive out competitors, and force all foreign countries throughout the world to buy their product from them at their own terms. They could finally dictate market prices on crude oil, stabilize the margin of profit at their own process, and do away at last with the dangerously speculative character of their business.

Their plans moved forward rapidly all through 1871. For a small sum of money the "conspirators" obtained the Pennsylvania charter of a defunct corporation, which had been authorized to engage in almost any kind of business under the sun. Those who were approached by the promoters, those whom they determined to use in their grand scheme, were compelled in a manner typical of all Rockefeller's projects to sign a written pledge of secrecy:

> I, —— ——, do solemnly promise upon my honor and faith as a gentleman that I will keep secret all transactions which I may have with the corporation known as the South Improvement Company; that should I fail to complete any bargains with the said company, all the preliminary conversations shall ̶b̶e̶ ̶k̶e̶p̶t̶ ̶s̶t̶r̶ictly private; and finally that I will not disclose the price for which ̶o̶f any products or any other facts which may in any way bring to ̶i̶nternal workings or organization of the company. All this I do ̶p̶romise.

̶t̶h̶e̶ time, in confidential pourparlers with the officials of the Erie, ̶P̶e̶n̶n̶s̶y̶l̶v̶a̶n̶ia and the New York Central Railroads, the men of the Standard ̶r̶e̶p̶r̶e̶s̶e̶n̶t̶e̶d̶ themselves as possessing secret control of the bulk of the refin-̶i̶n̶g̶,̶ ̶t̶h̶us they obtained conditions more advantageous than anything ̶s̶e̶e̶n̶ before; and this weapon in turn of course ensured the triumph ̶o̶f̶ ̶t̶h̶e̶i̶r̶ ̶p̶o̶o̶l̶.

The refiners to be combined under the aegis of the South Improvement Company were to have a rebate of from 40 to 50 per cent on the crude oil they ordered shipped to them and from 25 to 50 per cent on the refined oil they shipped out. The refiners in the Oil Regions were to pay *twice as much* by the new code (though nearer to New York) as the Standard Oil Company at Cleveland. But besides the rebate the members of the pool were to be given also a "drawback" consisting of part of the increased tariff rate which "outsiders" were forced to pay. Half of the freight payments of a rival refiner would in many cases be paid over to the Rockefeller group. Their competitors were simply to be decimated; and to make certain of this the railroads agreed—all being set down in writing, in minutest detail—"to make manifests or way-bills of all petroleum or its product transported over any portion of its lines... which manifests shall state the name of the consignee, the place of shipment and the place of destination," this information to be furnished faithfully to the officers of the South Improvement Company.

The railroad systems, supposedly public-spirited and impartial, were to open all their knowledge of rival private business to the pool, thus helping to concentrate all the oil trade into the few hands chosen. In return for so much assistance, they were to have their freight "evened," and were enabled at last to enter into a momentous peace pact with each other by which the oil traffic (over which they had quarreled bitterly) was to be fairly allotted among themselves.

By January, 1872, after the first decade of the oil business, John Rockefeller, with the aid of the railroad captains, was busily carrying out a most "elaborate national plan" of his own for the control of his industry—such planned control as the spokesman of the business system asserted ever afterward was impossible. The first pooling of 1872, beautiful as was its economic architecture and laudable its motive, had defects which were soon plainly noticeable. All the political institutions, the whole spirit of American law still favored the amiable, wasteful individualism of business, which in Rockefeller's mind had already become obsolete and must be supplanted by a centralized, one might say almost *collectivist*—certainly coöperative rather than competitive—form of operation. Moreover, these "revolutionists" took little account of the social dislocations their juggernaut would bring. Like the railroad baron, Vanderbilt, working better than they knew, their eyes fixed solely upon the immediate task rather than upon some millennium of the future, they desired simply, as they often said, to be "the biggest refiners in the world. . . ."

To the principal oil firms in Cleveland Rockefeller went one by one, explaining the plan of the South Improvement Company patiently, pointing out how important it was to oppose the creek refiners and save the Cleveland oil trade. He would say:

"You see, this scheme is bound to work. There is no chance for anyone outside. But we are going to give everybody a chance to come in. You are to turn over your refinery to my appraisers, and I will give you Standard Oil Company stock or cash, as you prefer, for the value we put upon it. I advise you to take the stock. It will be for your good."

Then if the men demurred, according to much of the testimony at the Senate Investigation of 1876, he would point out suavely that it was useless to resist; opposition would certainly be crushed. The offers of purchase usually made were for from a third to a half the actual cost of the property.

Now a sort of terror swept silently over the oil trade. In a vague panic, competitors saw the Standard Oil officers come to them and say (as Rockefeller's own brother and rival, Frank, testified in 1876): "If you don't sell your property to us it will be valueless, because we have got the advantage with the railroads."

The railroad rates indeed were suddenly doubled to the outsiders, and those refiners who resisted the pool came and expostulated; then they became frightened and disposed of their property. One of the largest competitors in Cleveland, the firm of Alexander, Scofield & Co., held out for a time, protesting before the railroad officials at the monstrous unfairness of the deal. But these officials when consulted said mysteriously: *"Better sell—better get clear—*better sell out—no help for it." Another powerful refiner, Robert Hanna, uncle of the famous Mark Alonzo, found that the railroads would give him no relief, and also was glad to sell out at 40 or 50 cents on the dollar for his property value. To one of these refiners, Isaac L. Hewitt, who had been his employer in boyhood, Rockefeller himself spoke with intense emotion. He urged Hewitt to take stock. Hewitt related: "He told me that it would be sufficient to take care of my family for all time... and asking for reasons, he made this expression, I remember: *'I have ways of making money that you know nothing of.'* "

All this transpired in secret. For "silence is golden," the rising king of oil believed. Though many were embittered by their loss, others joined gladly. The strongest capitalists in Cleveland, such as the wealthy Colonel Oliver H. Payne, were amazed at the swift progress Rockefeller had made, at the enormous profits he showed them in confidence to invite their coöperation. Payne, among others, as a man of wealth and influence, was taken into the board of directors and made treasurer of the Standard Oil Company. (The officers of the South Improvement Company itself were "dummies.") Within three months by an economic *coup d'état* the youthful Rockefeller had captured all of Cleveland's oil-refining trade, all twenty-five competitors surrendered to him and yielded him command of one-fifth of America's output of refined oil.

Tomorrow all the population of the Oil Regions, its dismayed refiners, drillers, and workers of oil, might rise against the South Improvement Company ring in a grotesque uproar. The secret, outwardly peaceful campaigns would assume here as elsewhere the character of violence and lawlessness which accompanied the whole program of the industrial revolution. But Rockefeller and his comrades had stolen a long march on their opponents; their tactics shaped themselves already as those of the giant industrialists of the future conquering the pigmies. Entrenched at the "narrows" of the mighty river of petroleum they could no more be dislodged than those other barons who had formerly planted their strong castles along the banks of the Rhine could be dislodged by unarmed peasants and burghers.

Ralph W. Hidy and Muriel E. Hidy  **NO**

Pioneering in Big Business, 1882–1911

From Chaos to Combination

During the years from 1882 to 1911 the leaders of the Standard Oil group of companies, including the Standard Oil Company (New Jersey), carried out an extraordinary experiment in the management of a business. John D. Rockefeller and his associates successfully created and applied a system for operating a large, integrated industrial enterprise which was one of the earliest representatives of Big Business, to use the phrase popular in the United States. As executives of the large combination those men contributed greatly to the rapid development of the American petroleum industry and through it to the growth of the economy as a whole. Being innovators, however, they also made numerous mistakes and learned only slowly that large size and concentrated economic power in a democratic society required conduct conforming to new rules set by popular demand.

The early life of the Standard Oil Company (New Jersey), generally referred to as Jersey Standard, was marked by rapid growth from infancy to early parenthood. Organized as one of the units of the Standard Oil Trust in August, 1882, for its first ten years the corporation existed primarily as the owner of a refinery and other manufacturing establishments at Bayonne; late in the decade the company acquired a few wholesaling facilities in the same northern New Jersey area. As a consequence of a court decision in Ohio in 1892, Standard Oil executives reorganized their enterprise under twenty corporations of which Jersey Standard was one of the three largest; top managers vested this company with direct ownership of extensive additional manufacturing and marketing properties and also made it one of the holding companies within the group of sister corporations. The Jersey Company continued to perform operating functions after it had become the parent of the entire combination in 1899.

As the apex of a pyramid of companies dominating the American petroleum industry, Jersey Standard naturally became the symbol of the much-distrusted Standard Oil "monopoly" in the public mind. In 1911 the Supreme Court of the United States, affirming that general conviction, broke up the

From Ralph W. Hidy and Muriel E. Hidy, *History of Standard Oil Company (New Jersey), vol. 1: Pioneering in Big Business, 1882–1911* (Harper & Brothers, 1955). Copyright © 1955, 1983 by Business History Foundation, Inc. Reprinted by permission of HarperCollins Publishers, Inc. Notes omitted.

combination by divesting the Standard Oil Company (New Jersey) of thirty-three affiliates, thus bringing to a close one eventful and significant phase of the corporation's history. . . .

The Standard Oil Team and Its Early Policies

As an early corporate product of the Standard Oil combination, Jersey Standard fell heir to the policies and practices of the men who created the alliance. In the course of working together before 1882, this group of executives had set precedents for the management of the Standard Oil family of firms which were to influence vitally the life of the new company.

The Men Who Made Standard Oil

The Standard Oil alliance in 1881 was the creation of a team of men. As one man paraphrased John D. Rockefeller's own statement, the "secret of the success of the Standard Oil Company was that there had come together a body of men who from beginning to end worked in single-minded co-operation, who all believed in each other and had perfect confidence in the integrity of each other, who reached all their decisions after fair consideration with magnanimity toward each other" in order to assure "absolute harmony."

As an instrument for carrying out the ideas of those men, the combination necessarily took its character from those who made it and managed it. When they chose to create a new corporation, such as Jersey Standard, it became part of the mechanism for pursuing their policies. Extremely significant, therefore, for understanding the history of the company is acquaintance with the individuals who created and directed both the Standard Oil family of companies and the Jersey Company itself. Scores of men made material contributions to the early development of the combination but only a relatively few ranked as outstanding.

John D. Rockefeller (1839–1937) was captain of the team. By all odds the largest holder of shares, he probably would have been chosen the head for that reason alone. Although not the only person to have the conviction in the 1870's that the petroleum industry should be stabilized, he first formulated the idea that the only satisfactory means was to organize a commonly owned unit on a national scale. Allan Nevins has characterized Rockefeller as careful, patient, cautious, methodical, quick to observe and to learn, grave, pious, aloof, secretive, reticent, inscrutable, and taciturn. Rockefeller considered work a duty, loved simplicity, believed in discipline, and possessed little social warmth except with his family and intimate friends. He had a mind of extraordinary force, great power of concentration, and almost infinite capacity for detail. Although he was willing to make decisions and to act forcefully, he possessed not only remarkable foresight, broad vision, and cool judgment, but also willingness to consider the ideas of others.

In the early 1870's Rockefeller began to delegate most details of management to subordinates and thereafter devoted himself primarily to formulation of broad policy. His greatest contribution, beyond the concept of the Standard

Oil combination itself, was the persuasion of strong men to join the alliance and to work together effectively in its management. The remarkable fact was that Rockefeller, while still in his thirties, impressed a group of men, almost all older than himself, with his qualities of leadership. His most arduous task later was to preside over meetings of strongly individualistic, positive executives, while they discussed and determined, usually unanimously, strategy and tactics for the combination as a whole.

During the 1860's and 1870's the closest and strongest associate of John D. Rockefeller was Henry M. Flagler (1830–1913). Of average height, slight build, erect figure, unobtrusive and dignified manner, Flagler was an ambitious, patient, and shrewd man of business. It is difficult to determine where the ideas of Rockefeller stop and those of Flagler begin. They were warm personal friends; they talked over their business before, during, and after office hours. Flagler liked to build new things and possessed a faculty for reducing complex problems to their simplest components. His constructive imagination was as broad and as vivid as Rockefeller's. It was caught by a desire to develop Florida, and into its hotels, railroads, and other enterprises he put some $50,000,000, and more of his energy than into Standard Oil, during the 1880's and later. Yet he left his mark on the combination. Having an aptitude for legal affairs, he was a master in drawing up clear, concise contracts. The incorporation of Ohio Standard appears to have been his brain child, and he helped in the later organization of the Trust. Flagler also participated in many negotiations leading to entry of other firms into the Standard Oil family. His special function was the handling of all affairs concerning transportation of both raw materials and finished products, and he drove hard bargains with railroad managers. Gifted with a keen sense of humor and a feeling of personal responsibilities to employees, he won the warm respect and loyal support of most subordinates. Not the least important of Flagler's executive positions was the presidency of Jersey Standard during eight of its first seventeen years. . . .

Although never an executive, one other man colored the history of Standard Oil as much as many of the men who created and managed the combination. Samuel C. T. Dodd (1836–1907), the general solicitor of the organization from 1881 to 1905, began his practice at Franklin, Pennsylvania, in 1859. Short and rotund, affable and learned, he soon became expert in the legal technicalities of the petroleum business. A Democrat in politics, he actively participated in the Pennsylvania constitutional convention of 1872. Though Dodd thought the material prosperity of the United States was attributable "in a great measure" to large combinations of capital, he was equally convinced that they should be regulated by clearly framed laws. Outspokenly opposed to "unjust" railroad rate discriminations, he accepted the invitation to become counsel for Standard Oil in the Oil Regions in 1879 only on the condition that his employers fully recognize his determination to fight the practice of rebating. When Dodd, a Presbyterian elder, abandoned private practice to become general solicitor for Standard Oil in New York, he humorously explained his decision to become the "least victim of the monopoly" by remarking: "Well, as the ministers say when they get a call to a higher salary, it seems to be the Lord's will." Thereafter Dodd quietly and honestly told top managers what they could and could not do under existing law as he interpreted it and occasionally, as extant correspondence shows, advocated a course of action on moral rather than legal grounds. He had a most difficult assignment in charting a course for a large business in a period when a new public policy toward trusts and combinations was emerging.

The executives advised by Dodd were men of varied abilities and complementary qualities. While several of them had specialized at one time or another in separate functions of the petroleum industry, a number of them had broad experience over a number of years. Some were inventors. Others brought special aptitudes in organization and marketing. Almost all had begun their careers in mercantile enterprises. Before joining the Standard Oil alliance, all had engaged in either regional or national co-operative efforts. By 1882 they had worked together for a number of years; while differing in backgrounds and philosophies, they had evolved policies which were, with some modifications, to guide the Standard Oil combination throughout its early history and to affect the petroleum industry for a longer span of years.

Policies, Practices, and Precedents

Policies and practices pursued by Standard Oil executives during the years prior to 1882 emerged in a variety of ways. Some policies were evidenced by votes of directors of components of the alliance and gradually won more general acceptance among its members. In other instances precedents and practices developed into policies over time; no formalized statement ever indicated the direction in which the leaders were traveling, but in a succession of separate steps they evolved a significant behavior pattern.

Many of the concepts and procedures adopted by executives of the alliance stemmed from their early experience as small businessmen. Probably at no other time during the nineteenth century was economic activity more freely competitive than in the period from 1840 to 1865. The customs and mores of the small individual enterpriser became the accepted pattern for almost all men. Naturally enough, therefore, Rockefeller and his associates learned in their youth to believe in freedom of entry into any occupation, in the sanctity of private property, in the obligation of the owner to manage his own operations, and in the right to keep his business affairs secret, a concept dating from time immemorial. As a corollary of that idea, in courts or legislative investigative chambers a businessman testified to the legal truth, and no more, a practice still honored by general observance in spite of critical charges of evasiveness and ambiguity. Since most markets were local, every businessman could observe his competitors with relative ease, and did. His habit was to use any competitive device not clearly prohibited by law. Bargaining in the market place was almost universal, whether for products or for such services as the transportation of freight. Posted prices were a point of departure for haggling, and price reductions were the most widely utilized of competitive techniques.

In response to the chaotic and depressed years of the 1870's, however, Standard Oil men drastically modified some of their socially inherited concepts about competition. They apparently desired at first to bring all gatherers of crude oil and refiners of light petroleum fractions into one commonly owned unit—to create a monopoly. Late in the decade they added lubricating oil specialists and trunk pipelines to their list of components to be unified. By means of common ownership in an association of specializing firms, Rockefeller and his associates created a great horizontal and vertical combination, which, on the eve of the birth of Jersey Standard, maintained overwhelming dominance in gathering, storing, and processing petroleum and its derivatives.

Either by design or through pressure of circumstances, the Standard Oil group of executives had not achieved monopoly in any function by 1881. Strong minority interests in many domestic marketing companies within the alliance, and limited coverage of the market by them, set definite limits to the influence of top managers in that field of operations. In almost all sales for export foreign merchants bought oil from companies in the Standard Oil family and carried on marketing in foreign lands. The combination owned few producing properties. United Pipe Lines men failed to keep pace with expansion in Bradford production, and competing gathering and storing facilities kept appearing. Tide-Water Pipe had thrown the first trunk pipeline over the mountains toward the sea and remained a belligerent competitor. Under the agreement with the producers in 1880 the price of crude oil was set on the oil exchanges, not by Standard Oil. In manufacturing, the area of initial intent for monopoly, the top managers of the alliance had stopped short of their goal. They had refused to pay the prices asked by owners of some plants. Others had sprung up in response to inducements offered by the Pennsylvania Railroad, and in 1882 the editor of *Mineral Resources* noted that the combination had "for some reason" not renewed leases on a number of refineries, several of which were doing "a good trade" and "assuming considerable importance." Thus, by that year some of the firms classified by H. H. Rogers in 1879 as being "in harmony" with Standard Oil had gone their independent ways.

Standard Oil executives employed a variety of tactics in carrying out the expansionist program during the 1870's. After the consolidation in Cleveland and the disastrous South Improvement episode, Rockefeller and his associates first won the confidence of competitors through comprehensive voluntary association. They then brought into the alliance the strongest men and firms in specific areas or functions, a policy pursued, with some exceptions, until 1911. Exchange of stock in the different companies by individuals and guarantee of equality in management provided the final assurance needed to convince such strong individualists as [Charles] Lockhart, [William G.] Warden, [Charles] Pratt, and [Henry H.] Rogers that combination was to their advantage. All then co-operated eagerly in trying to unify the remaining firms in refining by bringing them into The Central Association, by buying plants whenever feasible, and by leasing other works. If a seller personally chose not to enter the combination, he usually signed an agreement not to engage in the petroleum business for a period of years. In any case, evidence in extant records substantiates the point that Standard Oil men completely and carefully inventoried all properties and paid "good," though not high, prices for them, including compensation for patents, trade-marks, brands, good-will, and volume of business. In many instances prices for properties reflected the desire of Standard Oil officials to enlist the inventive capacities or administrative abilities of the owners in the service of the alliance. The preponderance of the evidence indicates that Rockefeller and his fellow executives preferred to buy out rather than fight out competitors.

At the same time, when Standard Oil men felt it necessary to apply pressure as a means of persuading a rival to lease or sell his plant, they showed no hesitancy in utilizing the usual sharp competitive practices prevailing in the oil industry during the 1870's. On one occasion or another they pre-empted all available staves and barrels, restricted as completely as possible the available tank cars to their own business, and indulged in local price cutting. They meticulously watched and checked on competitive shipments and sales, sometimes in co-operation with railroad men, and diligently negotiated advantageous freight rates on railways, even to the point of receiving rebates or drawbacks on rivals' shipments. All acts were kept secret as long as possible. The size and resources of the alliance gave it overwhelming power, which was sometimes used ruthlessly, though it is worthy of note that numerous oilmen successfully resisted the pressure.

Within the alliance itself executives also retained many of their competitive habits. Although price competition almost completely disappeared within the combination, men and firms raced with each other in reducing costs, devising new techniques, developing products, improving their quality, and showing profits. Top managers believed in competition but not in the undisciplined variety.

In building the alliance the leaders of Standard Oil adopted a long-range view with emphasis on planning, even before they had achieved an organization to carry such an approach into successful operation. They showed a profound faith in the permanence of the industry, a belief not generally held in years when the petroleum business was characterized by instability, rapid exhaustion of producing fields, and doubts about the appearance of new ones. They wanted to plan and to have reasonable assurance that they were taking no more than calculated risks in pushing toward their objectives. A necessary requirement of planning was centralized policy formulation.

That responsibility devolved not upon one man but on a group of executives. The evolution of Standard Oil's committee system, the hallmark of its administrative methods, started early in the seventies. The original bylaws of Ohio Standard provided for an Executive Committee. Its first membership of two, John D. Rockefeller and Flagler, was increased to three during the consecutive terms of Samuel Andrews and O. H. Payne. [John D.] Archbold replaced the latter in 1879. William Rockefeller, Pratt, Warden, and [Jabez] Bostwick had joined the three Cleveland members the previous year. At that time the Executive Committee absorbed the "Advisory Committee," which had been established as early as 1873 to act in the New York area. William Rockefeller and Bostwick, its first members, had been joined by Pratt and Warden soon after they entered the alliance. The enlarged Executive Committee of 1878 held many of its almost daily meetings at 140 Pearl Street, New York, and two years later made four a quorum because of the geographic split in membership between Cleveland and New York. Members of other committees started consultations before 1882. If the making of decisions as a synthesis of opinion of a group after discussion is a characteristic of modern business, as a recent commentator has implied, then Standard Oil was modern in the 1870's.

In order to have easily available the best data and advice for making decisions, the Rockefellers and their associates built up staffs in Cleveland, New York, and other points. For the use of executives they collected, evaluated, and digested information on crude oil supplies, costs of manufacture, and markets all over the world. The practice of watching and reporting on marketing by competitors everywhere in the United States, not merely locally, was already inaugurated, though not yet systematized. S. C. T. Dodd was engaged as legal navigator; Standard Oil officials desired to operate within the law. A beginning was made in standardizing accounting procedures.

As the emergence of the Executive Committee and the formation of staffs indicated, the creation of the combination permitted a division of labor or specialization within the organization. As Archbold expressed the development in 1888, the grouping of talents within the alliance permitted "various individuals to take up the different features of the business as a specialty and accomplish greater efficiency than can possibly be accomplished by an individual who attempts to cover all in a business."

In the matter of finance, as in other aspects of operations, Ohio Standard set precedents on reporting and central review. In 1877 the directors of that company resolved that all persons responsible for different aspects of the business should make quarterly reports in writing to the board. Two years later, its members unanimously agreed that annual financial statements should be presented. In 1875 the directors had voted that expenditures for new construction in manufacturing exceeding $2,500 should be undertaken only with written consent of seven members of the board, but that resolution was repealed five years later and the company's Executive Committee was given full charge of all matters relating to repairs and new construction.

Since the goal of the members of the alliance was to maximize profits in the long run, they adopted practices to that end. Emphasis was placed on reducing costs, improving and standardizing the quality of products, and striving for new methods of refining, including the engaging of specialists. Stories about John D. Rockefeller's penchant for eliminating waste and effecting economies have been told and retold. As president of the Acme Oil Company in the Oil Regions, Archbold achieved substantial savings through buying supplies in quantity and by making annual contracts regarding the repairing of boilers and barrels for all plants under his jurisdiction. When he purchased a lubricating oil patent in 1879, Archbold guaranteed the owner, Eli E. Hendrick, a salary of $10,000 per year for ten years in return for the devotion of his inventive talents to Acme. Duplicating pipelines were removed, inefficient plants dismantled, strategically located refineries enlarged, and auxiliary manufacturing units developed, all in the name of economy and reduction of costs. By consistently stressing that practice in every function Standard Oil men moved gradually but inevitably toward mass manufacturing and, more slowly, toward mass marketing.

Gathering information, consultation, planning, and experimentation did not always lead to quick action, but the leaders of Standard Oil early indicated flexibility in adopting new methods and thoroughness in carrying them out. Critics voiced the opinion in the late 1870's that Standard Oil, having invested so much in refineries in the Oil Regions, could not take advantage of the pipeline revolution to establish large manufacturing units at the coast. Almost as soon as others had demonstrated the feasibility of building long trunk pipelines the Standard Oil group took action in 1879. It already possessed a system of gathering lines through the United Pipe Lines. After its organization in 1881, the National Transit Company pushed trunk pipeline building vigorously. By the next year it owned 1,062 miles of trunk lines, only 48 of which had been bought from firms outside the alliance. Its policies... illustrate the fact that Standard Oil was not always the earliest to initiate an innovation, but, once launched on a policy, the combination pushed it with a vigor and fervor made possible by efficient organization and ample financial resources.

Standard Oil's financial policy itself was an important element in the successful life of the combination and its components. Not only were the risks spread by the breadth of the alliance's activities, but profits made in one company or phase of the business flowed into development of another when desired. Early in the history of Standard Oil units short-term loans were often obtained from commercial banks, and temporary aid had to be obtained when the properties of The Empire Transportation Company were purchased. A conservative ratio of dividends to net income, however, was soon to permit the accumulation of funds for self-financing.

Ohio Standard furnished an example for the companies in the alliance on the matter of insurance against fire. On the assumption that loss by fire was a normal expense of the petroleum industry and could be carried by a large unit, the directors of the Ohio Company agreed in January, 1877, to insure property in any one place only on the excess of its valuation above $100,000.

As directors of The Standard Oil Company (Ohio), executives of the alliance also set a precedent regarding the ownership of producing properties. In April, 1878, apparently as a result of a suit by H. L. Taylor & Company against John D. Rockefeller and others for breach of contract in a joint producing operation, the directors unanimously voted not to invest any more money in the purchase of crude oil lands. Six months later they resolved to discontinue all activity in producing petroleum and instructed the Executive Committee to dispose of its properties. This point of view had an influence upon the Standard Oil alliance for a decade.

Quite the contrary was the action adopted in regard to pipelines. By 1881 the Standard Oil group was definitely launched on a program for large-scale expansion of its pipeline facilities and soon exercised a greater measure of control over the function. The combination poured an increasing quantity of capital into building lines; the profits from them provided a cushion for all operations of the alliance. The speculatively minded can ask whether the development of the oil industry would have been more rapid or socially beneficial had parallel pipelines competed with each other during the formative years of the industry, and whether the development would have been as efficient, or more so, had the railroad systems controlled competing lines, as had seemed possible in the 1870's. The point remains that the top managers of Standard Oil determined to keep this function in their own hands to the extent possible. . . .

The roots of Standard Oil's policies went deep into the personalities and early experiences of Rockefeller and his associates. Though few of their practices had been satisfactorily systematized by 1881, precedents had been established for many later policies of Jersey Standard and other members of the combination.

By the end of 1881 the general public was hard put to make an accurate estimate of Standard Oil's behavior. Legislative investigations and several legal cases had already elicited an enormous amount of conflicting testimony as to the relations of the combination with both railroads and competitors. Rockefeller and his associates had heightened uncertainty and speculation about their activities by their secrecy in building the alliance and by their evasive, often ambiguous, consistently legally accurate testimony on the witness stand. The very newness, size, dominance, and efficiency of the combination, not to mention its absorption of small competitors in adversity and its avid search for the lowest possible railroad rates, all tended to arouse antagonism. In 1882 S. H. Stowell closed his comments on Standard Oil in *Mineral Resources* with an unbiased observer's puzzlement: "There seems to be little doubt that the company has done a great work, and that through its instrumentality oil refining has been reduced to a business, and transportation has been greatly simplified; but as to how much evil has been mixed with this good, it is not practicable to make a definite statement." It was certain that through combination managers of Standard Oil had brought a measure of order to a formerly confused industry, though they thought that the administration of the alliance itself needed further systematization.

POSTSCRIPT

Was John D. Rockefeller a "Robber Baron"?

Regardless of how American entrepreneurs are perceived, there is no doubt that they constituted a powerful elite and were responsible for defining the character of society in the Gilded Age. For many Americans, these businessmen represented the logical culmination of the country's attachment to laissez-faire economics and rugged individualism. In fact, it was not unusual at all for the nation's leading industrialists to be depicted as the real-life models for the "rags-to-riches" theme epitomized in the self-help novels of Horatio Alger. Closer examination of the lives of most of these entrepreneurs, however, reveals the mythical dimensions of this American ideal. Simply put, the typical business executive of the late nineteenth century did not rise up from humble circumstances, a product of the American rural tradition or the immigrant experience, as is frequently claimed. Rather, most of these big businessmen were of Anglo-Saxon origin and reared in a city by middle-class parents. According to one survey, over half the leaders had attended college at a time when even the pursuit of a high school education was considered unusual. In other words, instead of having to pull themselves up by their own bootstraps from the bottom of the social heap, these individuals usually started their climb to success at the middle of the ladder or higher.

Earl Latham and Peter d'A. Jones have assembled excellent collections of the major viewpoints on the "robber baron" thesis in their respective edited anthologies *John D. Rockefeller: Robber Baron or Industrial Statesman?* (D. C. Heath, 1949) and *The Robber Barons Revisited* (D. C. Heath, 1968). For a critique of Josephson's work, see Maury Klein, "A Robber Historian," *Forbes* (October 26, 1987). Studies focusing specifically upon Rockefeller include David Freeman Hawke, *John D.: The Founding Father of the Rockefellers* (Harper & Row, 1980) and Ron Chernow, *Titan: The Life of John D. Rockefeller, Sr.* (Random House, 1998). Biographical studies of other late-nineteenth-century businessmen include Harold Livesay, *Andrew Carnegie and the Rise of Big Business* (Little, Brown, 1975) and Maury Klein, *The Life and Legend of Jay Gould* (Johns Hopkins University Press, 1986).

The works of Alfred D. Chandler, Jr., are vital to the understanding of American industrialization. See *The Visible Hand: The Managerial Revolution in American Business* (Harvard University Press, 1977) and *Scale and Scope: The Dynamics of Industrial Capitalism* (Harvard University Press, 1990). Chandler's most important essays are collected in Thomas K. McCraw, ed., *The Essential Alfred Chandler: Essays Toward a Historical Theory of Big Business* (Harvard Business School Press, 1988).

ISSUE 2

Did Nineteenth-Century Women of the West Fail to Overcome the Hardships of Living on the Great Plains?

YES: Christine Stansell, from "Women on the Great Plains 1865–1890," *Women's Studies* (vol. 4, 1976)

NO: Glenda Riley, from *A Place to Grow: Women in the American West* (Harlan Davidson, 1992)

ISSUE SUMMARY

YES: Professor of history Christine Stansell contends that women on the Great Plains were torn from their eastern roots, isolated in their home environment, and separated from friends and relatives. She concludes that they consequently endured lonely lives and loveless marriages.

NO: Professor of history Glenda Riley argues that in spite of enduring harsh environmental, political, and personal conditions on the Great Plains, women created rich and varied social lives through the development of strong support networks.

In 1893 young historian Frederick Jackson Turner (1861–1932) delivered an address before the American Historical Association entitled "The Significance of the Frontier in American History." Turner's essay not only sent him from Wisconsin to Harvard University, it became one of the most important essays ever written in American history. According to Turner's thesis, American civilization was different from European civilization because the continent contained an abundance of land that was settled in four waves of migration from 1607 through 1890. During this process the European heritage was shed and the American characteristics of individualism, mobility, nationalism, and democracy developed.

This frontier theory of American history did not go unchallenged. Some historians argued that Turner's definition of the frontier was too vague and imprecise; he underestimated the cultural forces that came to the West from

Europe and the eastern states; he neglected the forces of urbanization and industrialization in opening the West; he placed an undue emphasis on sectional developments and neglected class struggles for power; and, finally, his provincial view of American history prolonged the isolationist views of a nation that had become involved in world affairs in the twentieth century. By the time Turner died, his thesis had been widely discredited. Historians continued to write about the West, but new fields and new theories were competing for attention.

Younger historians have begun to question the traditional interpretation of western expansion. For example, the older historians believed that growth was good and automatically brought forth progress. New historians William Cronin, Patricia Limerick, and others, however, have questioned this assumption in examining the disastrous ecological effects of American expansionism, such as the elimination of the American buffalo and the depletion of forests.

Until recently, most historians did not consider women part of western history. One scholar who searched 2,000 pages of Turner's work could find only one paragraph devoted to women. Men built the railroads, drove the cattle, led the military expeditions, and governed the territories. "Women," said one writer, "were invisible, few in number, and not important to the taming of the West."

When scholars did acknowledge the presence of women on the frontier, perceptions were usually based on stereotypes that were created by male observers and had become prevalent in American literature. According to professor of history Sandra L. Myres (1933–1991), there were three main images. The first image was that of a frightened, tearful woman who lived in a hostile environment and who was overworked and overbirthed, depressed and lonely, and resigned to a hard life and an early death. The second image, in contrast, was of a helpmate and a civilizer of the frontier who could fight Indians as well as take care of the cooking, cleaning, and rearing of the children. A third image of the westering woman was that of the "bad woman," who was more masculine than feminine in her behavior and who was "hefty, grotesque and mean with a pistol."

The proliferation of primary source materials since the early 1970s—letters, diaries, and memoirs written by frontierswomen—led to a reassessment of the role of westering women. They are no longer what professor of history Joan Hoff-Wilson once referred to as the "orphans of women's history." There are disagreements in interpretation, but they are based upon sound scholarship. One area where scholars disagree is how women were changed by their participation in the westward movements of the nineteenth century.

In the following selection, Christine Stansell, arguing from a feminist perspective, asserts that women on the Great Plains were torn from their eastern roots, isolated in their home environments, and forced to endure lonely lives and loveless marriages because they could not create networks of female friendships. In the second selection, Glenda Riley argues that in spite of harsh environmental, political, and personal conditions on the Great Plains, women were able to create rich and varied social lives through the development of strong support networks.

 **YES**

Women on the Great Plains 1865–1890

In 1841, Catharine Beecher proudly attested to the power of her sex by quoting some of Tocqueville's observations on the position of American women. On his tour of 1831, Tocqueville had found Americans to be remarkably egalitarian in dividing social power between the sexes. In his opinion, their ability to institute democratic equality stemmed from a clearcut division of work and responsibilities: "in no country has such constant care been taken... to trace two clearly distinct lines of action for the two sexes, and to make them keep pace with the other, but in two pathways which are always different." In theory, men and women controlled separate "spheres" of life: women held sway in the home, while men attended to economic and political matters. Women were not unaware of the inequities in a trade-off between ascendancy in the domestic sphere and participation in society as a whole. Attached to the metaphorical bargain struck between the sexes was a clause ensuring that women, through "home influence," could also affect the course of nation-building. For Miss Beecher, domesticity was also imperial power "to American women, more than to any others on earth, is committed the exalted privilege of extending over the world those blessed influences, which are to renovate degraded man, and 'clothe all climes with beauty.'"

Yet despite Beecher's assertions to the contrary, by 1841 one masculine "line of action" was diverging dangerously from female influences. Increasing numbers of men were following a pathway which led them across the Mississippi to a land devoid of American women and American homes. In the twenty-odd years since the Santa Fe trade opened the Far West to American businessmen, only men, seeking profits in furs or trading, had gone beyond the western farmlands of the Mississippi Valley; no women participated in the first stages of American expansion. Consequently, by 1841 the West was in one sense a geographical incarnation of the masculine sphere, altogether untouched by "home influence." Although in theory American development preserved a heterosexually balanced democracy, in actuality, the West, new arena of political and economic growth, had become a man's world.

In 1841, the first Americans intending to settle in the trans-Mississippi region rather than only trap or trade began to migrate over the great overland road to the coast. For the first time, women were present in the caravans, and

From Christine Stansell, "Women on the Great Plains 1865–1890," *Women's Studies*, vol. 4 (1976). Adapted from Christine Stansell, *City of Women: Sex and Class in New York, 1789–1860* (Alfred A. Knopf, 1986). Copyright © 1982, 1986 by Christine Stansell. Reprinted by permission of Alfred A. Knopf, a division of Random House, Inc. Notes omitted.

in the next decades, thousands of women in families followed. Their wagon trains generally carried about one-half men, one-half women and children: a population with the capacity to reinstate a heterosexual culture. Only during the Gold Rush years, 1849–1852, were most of the emigrants once again male. Many of the forty-niners, however, chose to return East rather than to settle. In the aftermath of the Rush, the numerical balance of men and women was restored. By 1860, the sex ratio in frontier counties, including those settled on the Great Plains, was no different from the average sex ratio in the East.

Despite the heterosexual demography, however, the West in the years after 1840 still appeared to be masculine terrain. Everywhere, emigrants and travellers saw "such lots of men, but very few ladies and children." In mining camps, "representatives of the gentler sex were so conspicuous by their absence that in one camp a lady's bonnet and boots were exhibited for one dollar a look." Similarly, "the Great Plains in the early period was strictly a man's country." Even later, historians agree that "the Far West had a great preponderance of men over women," and that the absence of "mothers and wives to provide moral anchorage to the large male population" was a primary cause of its social ills. What accounts for the disparity between these observations and the bare facts of demography? In many frontier regions, women failed to reinstitute their own sphere. Without a cultural base of their own, they disappeared behind the masculine preoccupations and social structure which dominated the West. Despite their numbers, women were often invisible, not only in the first two decades of family settlement but in successive phases as well.

In this [selection], I try to sketch out some ways of understanding how the fact of this masculine imperium affected women's experiences in the great trans-Mississippi migrations. The following pages are in no way a monograph but rather a collection of suggestions which I have developed through reading and teaching about the West, and which I hope will encourage others to begin investigating this neglected area. Western migration constituted a critical rite of passage in nineteenth century culture; its impact still reverberates a century later in our own "Western" novels, movies, and television serials. Women's relationship to this key area of the "American experience" has remained submerged and unquestioned. There are only a few secondary books on women in the West, and the two best-known works are simplistic and sentimental. Few writers or scholars have attempted to look at frontier women in the light of the newer interpretations of women's history which have evolved over the last four years. There are a wealth of questions to investigate and a wealth of sources to use. To demonstrate how new analyses can illuminate conventional teaching and lecture material, I have chosen one clearly defined area of "pioneer experience," settlers on the Great Plains from 1865–1890....

Until after the Civil War, emigrants usually travelled over the Great Plains without a thought of stopping. Explorers, farmers, and travellers agreed that the dry grasslands of the "Great American Desert"—the Dakotas, western Kansas, and western Nebraska—were not suitable for lucrative cultivation. In the late 60's, however, western land-grant railroads attempting to boost profits from passenger fares and land sales by promoting settlement in the region launched an advertising campaign in America and Europe which portrayed the Plains as a new Eden of verdant grasslands, rich soil, and plenteous streams. The railroad propaganda influenced a shift in public opinion, but technological advances in wheat-growing and steadily expanding urban markets for crops were far more significant in attracting settlers from Europe and the Mississippi Valley to the region. Emigrants came to take advantage of opportunities for more land, more crops, and more profits.

Who decided to move to the new lands? In the prevailing American notions of family relations, decisions about breadwinning and family finances were more or less in the hands of the male. Of course, removal to the Plains was a significant matter, and it is doubtful that many husbands and fathers made a unilateral decision to pull up stakes. Unfortunately, no large body of evidence about the choice to migrate to the Plains has been found or, at least, utilized in scholarly studies. I have sampled, however, some of the more than seven hundred diaries of men and women travelling to California and Oregon twenty years earlier. These indicate that the man usually initiated a plan to emigrate, made the final decision, and to a greater or lesser degree imposed it on his family. Men's involvement with self-advancement in the working world provided them with a logical and obvious rationale for going West.

The everyday concerns of "woman's sphere," however, did not provide women with many reasons to move. In the system that Tocqueville praised and Beecher vaunted, women's work, social responsibilities, and very identities were based almost entirely in the home. Domesticity involved professionalized housekeeping, solicitous child-rearing, and an assiduous maintenance of a proper moral and religious character in the family. Clearly, women could keep house better, literally and metaphorically, in "civilized" parts, where churches, kinfolk, and women friends supported them. The West held no promise of a happier family life or a more salutary moral atmosphere. On the contrary, it was notoriously destructive to those institutions and values which women held dear.

The Plains region was an especially arid prospect for the transplantation of womanly values. Lonely and crude frontier conditions prevailed into the 90's; in some areas, the sparse population actually declined with time: "following the great boom of the 80's, when the tide of migration began to recede, central Dakota and western Nebraska and Kansas presented anything but a land of occupied farms." The loneliness which women endured "must have been such as to crush the soul," according to one historian of the region. Another asserts that "without a doubt" the burden of the adverse conditions of Plains life—the aridity, treelessness, heat, perpetual wind, and deadening cold —fell upon the women. Almost without exception, others concur: "although the life of the frontier farmer was difficult special sympathy should go to his wife" ... "it is certain that many stayed until the prairie broke them in spirit or body while others fled from the monotonous terror of it." An observer who visited the Plains in the 50's found life there to be "peculiarly severe upon women and oxen." The duration as well as the severity of cultural disruption which Plains women experienced was perhaps without parallel in the history of nineteenth-century frontiers.

First of all, emigrant women did not move into homes like the ones they had left behind, but into sod huts, tarpaper shacks, and dugouts. Seldom as temporary as they planned to be, these crude structures still existed as late as the nineties. Most settlers lived in one room "soddies" for six or seven years: if luck left a little cash, they might move into a wooden shack. Thus a farmer's wife often spent years trying to keep clean a house made of dirt. The effort became especially disheartening in rainstorms, when leaking walls splattered mud over bedclothes and dishes: "in those trying times the mud floors were too swampy to walk upon and wives could cook only with an umbrella held over the stove; after they were over every stitch of clothing must be hung out to dry." Dry weather gave no respite from dirt, since dust and straw incessantly sifted down from the walls. Housekeeping as a profession in the sense that Catharine Beecher promulgated it was impossible under such circumstances. Soddies were so badly insulated that during the winter, water froze away from the stove. In summer, the paucity of light and air could be stifling.

Often there was simply no money available to build a decent house. Drought, grasshoppers, or unseasonable rains destroyed many of the harvests of the 80's and 90's. Even good crops did not necessarily change a family's living conditions, since debts and mortgages which had accrued during hard times could swallow up any profits. But in any case, home improvements were a low priority, and families often remained in soddies or shacks even when there was cash or credit to finance a frame house. The farmer usually earmarked his profits for reinvestment into the money-making outlay of better seeds, new stock, machinery, and tools. Farm machinery came first, labor-saving devices for women last: "there was a tendency for the new homesteader to buy new machinery to till broad acres and build new barns to house more stock and grain, while his wife went about the drudgery of household life in the old way in a little drab dwelling overshadowed by the splendour of machine farming." Washers and sewing machines graced some farms in the 80's, but "for the most part ... the machine age did not greatly help woman. She continued to operate the churn, carry water, and run the washing machine—if she were fortunate enough to have one—and do her other work without the aid of horse power which her more fortunate husband began to apply in his harvesting, threshing, and planting."

Against such odds, women were unable to recreate the kinds of houses they had left. Nor could they reinstate the home as a venerated institution. A sod house was only a makeshift shelter; no effort of the will or imagination could fashion it into what one of its greatest defenders eulogized as "the fairest garden in the wide field of endeavour and achievement." There were other losses as well. Many feminine social activities in more settled farm communities revolved around the church, but with the exception of the European immigrant enclaves, churches were scarce on the Plains. At best, religious observance was makeshift; at worst, it was non-existent. Although "it is not to be supposed that only the ungodly came west," one historian noted, "there seemed to exist in some parts of the new settlements a spirit of apathy if not actual hostility toward religion." Circuit-riders and evangelical freelancers drew crowds during droughts and depressions, but during normal times, everyday piety was rare. Few families read the Bible, sang hymns, or prayed together: "when people heard that a family was religious, it was thought that the head of the household must be a minister."

Women were also unable to reconstitute the network of female friendships which had been an accustomed and sustaining part of daily life "back home." Long prairie winters kept everyone housebound for much of the year. During summers and warmer weather, however, men travelled to town to buy supplies and negotiate loans, and rode to nearby claims to deliver mail, borrow tools, or share news. "As soon as the storms let up, the men could get away from the isolation," wrote Mari Sandoz, Nebraska writer and daughter of a homesteader: "But not their women. They had only the wind and the cold and the problems of clothing, shelter, food, and fuel." On ordinary days men could escape, at least temporarily, "into the fields, the woods, or perhaps to the nearest saloon where there was warmth and companionship, but women had almost no excuses to leave. Neighbors lived too far apart to make casual visiting practicable; besides, a farmer could seldom spare a wagon team from field work to take a woman calling. Hamlin Garland, who moved to the Plains as a young boy, remembered that women visited less than in Wisconsin, his former home, since "the work on the new farms was never-ending": "I doubt if the women—any of them—got out into the fields or meadows long enough to enjoy the birds and the breezes."

In most respects, the patterns of life rarely accommodated women's needs. Plains society paid little mind to women, yet women were essential, not incidental, to its functioning. Without female labor, cash-crop agriculture could never have developed. A man could not farm alone, and hired help was almost impossible to come by. Ordinarily, a farmer could count only on his wife and children as extra hands. On the homestead, women's responsibilities as a farm-hand, not as a home-maker or a mother, were of first priority. Women still cooked, sewed, and washed, but they also herded livestock and toted water for irrigation.

The ambitious farmer's need for the labor power of women and children often lent a utilitarian quality to relations between men and women. For the single settler, marriage was, at least in part, a matter of efficiency. Courtships were typically brief and frank. Molly Dorsey Sanford, a young unmarried homesteader in Nebraska territory, recorded in her diary over half a dozen proposals in a few years. Most of her suitors were strangers. One transient liked her cooking, another heard about a "hull lot of girls" at the Dorsey farm and came to try his luck, and an old man on the steamboat going to Nebraska proposed after an hour's acquaintance. Jules Sandoz, father of Mari Sandoz, married four times. Three wives fled before he found a woman who resigned herself to the emotionless regimen of his farm. Stolid and resilient, the fourth, Mari's mother, lived to a taciturn old age, but her daughter could not forget others of her mother's generation who had not survived their hasty marriages: "after her arrival the wife found that her husband seldom mentioned her in his letters or manuscripts save in connection with calamity. She sickened and left her work undone . . . so the pioneer could not plow or build or hunt. If his luck was exceedingly bad, she died and left him his home without a housekeeper until she could be replaced."

With characteristic ambivalence, Sandoz added, "at first this seems a calloused, even a brutal attitude, but it was not so intended."

Instrumentality could also characterize other family relations. Jules Sandoz "never spoke well of anyone who might make his words an excuse for less prompt jumping when he commanded. This included his wife and children." Garland described himself and his fellows as "a Spartan lot. We did not believe in letting our wives and children know they were an important part of our contentment." Jules' wife "considered praise of her children as suspect as self praise would be." Preoccupied by her chores, she maintained only minimal relationships with her family and assigned the care of the younger children to Mari, the oldest daughter.

In the domestic ideology of the family, careful and attentive child-rearing was especially important. Unlike the stoic Mrs. Sandoz, the American women who emigrated were often openly disturbed and troubled by a situation in which mothering was only peripheral to a day's work, and keenly felt the absence of cultural support for correct child-rearing. Mrs. Dorsey, the mother of diarist Molly Sanford, continually worried that her children, exiled from civilization, would turn into barbarians. In towns like Indianapolis, the family's home, schools, churches, and mothers worked in concert. In Nebraska, a mother could count on few aids. The day the Dorseys reached their claim, Molly wrote, "Mother hardly enters into ecstasies ... she no doubt realizes what it is to bring a young rising family away from the world ... if the country would only fill up, if there were only schools or churches or even some society. We do not see women at all. All men, single, or bachelors, and one gets tired of them." Molly occasionally responded to her mother's anxiety by searching herself and her siblings for signs of mental degeneration, but Mrs. Dorsey's fears were never warranted. The children grew up healthy and dutiful: in Molly's words, "the wild outdoor life strengthens our physical faculties, and the privations, our powers of endurance." To her confident appraisal, however, she appended a cautionary note in her mother's mode: "so that we do not degenerate mentally, it is all right; Heaven help us." Mrs. Dorsey, however, could seldom be reassured. When a snake bit one of the children, "Poor Mother was perfectly prostrated ... she sometimes feels wicked to think she is so far away from all help with her family." On her mother's fortieth birthday, Molly wrote, "I fear she is a little blue today. I do try so hard to keep cheerful. I don't know as it is hard work to keep myself so, but it is hard with her. She knows now that the children ought to be in school. We will have to do the teaching ourselves." ...

As Mrs. Dorsey saw her ideas of child-rearing atrophy, she also witnessed a general attenuation of the womanliness which had been central to her own identity and sense of importance in the world. Her daughters particularly taxed her investment in an outmoded conception of womanhood. Molly, for instance, was pleased with her facility in learning traditionally male skills. "So it seems I can put my hand to almost anything," she wrote with pride after helping her father roof the house. Mrs. Dorsey regarded her daughter's expanding capacities in a different light. When Molly disguised herself as a man to do some chores, "it was very funny to all but Mother, who fears I am losing all the dignity

I ever possessed." Molly was repentant but defensive: "I know I am getting demoralized, but I should be more so, to mope around and have no fun."

Mrs. Dorsey's partial failure to transmit her own values of womanhood to her daughter is emblematic of many difficulties of the first generation of woman settlers. Women could not keep their daughters out of men's clothes, their children in shoes, their family Bibles in use, or their houses clean; at every step, they failed to make manifest their traditions, values, and collective sensibility. It was perhaps the resistance of the Plains to the slightest feminine modification rather than the land itself which contributed to the legend of woman's fear of the empty prairies: "literature is filled with women's fear and distrust of the Plains... if one may judge by fiction, one must conclude that the Plains exerted a peculiarly appalling effect on women." The heroine of [O. E.] Rolvaag's *Giants in the Earth* echoed the experience of real women in her question to herself: "how will human beings be able to endure this place?... Why, there isn't even a thing that one can *hide behind!*" The desolation even affected women who passed through on their way to the coast. Sarah Royce remembered shrinking from the "chilling prospect" of her first night on the Plains on the Overland Trail: "surely there would be a few trees or a sheltering hillside.... No, only the level prairie.... Nothing indicated a place for us—a cozy nook, in which for the night we might be guarded."

Fright was not a rarity on the Plains. Both men and women knew the fear of droughts, blizzards, and accidental death. Yet the reported frequency of madness and suicide among women is one indication that [Everett] Dick may have been right in his contention that "the real burden... fell upon the wife and mother." Men's responsibilities required them to act upon their fears. If a blizzard hung in the air, they brought the cattle in; if crops failed, they renegotiated the mortgages and planned for the next season. In contrast, women could often do nothing in the face of calamity. "If hardships came," Sandoz wrote, "the women faced it at home. The results were tersely told by the items in the newspapers of the day. Only sheriff sales seem to have been more numerous than the items telling of trips to the insane asylum."

Men made themselves known in the acres of furrows they ploughed up from the grassland. Women, lacking the opportunities of a home, had few ways to make either the land or their neighbors aware of their presence. The inability of women to leave a mark on their surroundings is a persistent theme in Sandoz's memoirs. When Mari was a child, a woman killed herself and her three children with gopher poison and a filed down case knife. The neighbors agreed that "she had been plodding and silent for a long time," and a woman friend added sorrowfully, "If she could 'a had even a geranium, but in that cold shell of a shack...." In Sandoz's memory, the women of her mother's generation are shadows, "silent... always there, in the dark corner near the stove."

I have emphasized only one side of woman's experience on the Plains. For many, the years brought better times, better houses, and even neighbors. A second generation came to maturity: some were daughters like the strong farm women of Willa Cather's novels who managed to reclaim the land that had crushed their mothers. Yet the dark side of the lives of the first women on the Plains cannot be denied. Workers in an enterprise often not of their own making, their labor was essential to the farm, their womanhood irrelevant. Hamlin Garland's *Main Travelled Roads*, written in part as a condemnation of "the futility of woman's life on a farm," elicited this response from his mother: "you might have said more but I'm glad you didn't. Farmer's wives have enough to bear as it is."

Glenda Riley   ← **NO**

Women, Adaptation, and Change

Gender norms and expectations affected all types of western women
—African American, Native American, Asian American, Anglo, and
Spanish-speaking—in some way. Yet many women pushed at customary boundaries and tested limits. Sometimes they had feminist
intentions, but other times they sought to fulfill their own needs,
talents, and desires. As a result, women turned up everywhere, and
often in unexpected places: holding jobs, fighting for the right of
suffrage, forming labor organizations, and divorcing their spouses at
a higher rate than women in any other region of the country.

Other women, who are less obvious in the historical record,
fought against other forms of injustice—prejudicial attitudes and
discriminatory practices. Although historical accounts often present
women of color only as victims of oppression and exploitation, in
reality they frequently resisted and developed their own ways to live
in an often hostile world. A wide variety of resources gave women
of diverse races and ethnic backgrounds the strength to live in a
West composed of groups of people who persistently belittled and
shunned other groups who differed from them.

Women's Responses to the Challenges of Plains Living

The Great Plains region is an especially revealing case study of women's adaptation and survival in the West. Here, women, as in other western regions, carried
the primary responsibility for home and family. Not only wives and mothers,
but all women, young or old, single or married, white or black, Asian or Hispanic, whether employed outside the home or not, were expected to attend
to, or assist with, domestic duties. In addition, women helped with the family
enterprise and often held paid employment outside the home. They were also
socially, and sometimes even politically, active. In all these realms, women had
to deal on a daily basis with the particular limitations imposed upon them by
the harsh and demanding Plains environment. This essay examines how the
Plains affected women's duties and concerns, and how the majority of women
triumphed over these exigencies.

From Glenda Riley, *A Place to Grow: Women in the American West* (Harlan Davidson, 1992). Copyright
© 1992 by Harlan Davidson, Inc. Reprinted by permission of Harlan Davidson, Inc.

Between the early 1860s and the early 1910s the Great Plains attracted much controversy. It had vehement boosters and equally determined detractors. Land promoters and other supporters were quick to claim that a salubrious climate, rich farming and grazing lands, and unlimited business opportunities awaited newcomers. This "boomer" literature presented an attractive image that did not always seem completely truthful to those men and women who actually tried to profit from the area's purported resources.

Particularly during the early years of settlement, many migrants widely bemoaned the lack of water and relatively arid soil as well as their own inability to grapple effectively with these natural features of the Plains. At times their hardships were so severe that special relief committees and such groups as the Red Cross and the United States Army had to supply food, clothing, and other goods to help them survive.[1] Consequently, twentieth-century historical accounts have often focused on the ongoing struggles of existence. Until recently, only a few of these studies documented or analyzed the special problems that the Plains posed to women. Fortunately, a growing sensitivity to women's roles in history has led to an examination of women's own writings. This analysis of diaries, letters, and memoirs has clearly and touchingly revealed the details of their lives.[2]

The challenges that confronted women on the Plains can be grouped into three categories: the natural environment; political upheavals over such crucial issues as slavery, racism, and economic policy; and personal conflict with other people, including spouses. Obviously, all these factors also affected men, but they had a particular impact upon women.

The Natural Environment

The physical environment of the Plains created numerous difficulties for women. They showed, for instance, tremendous creativity and energy in obtaining the water that constantly was in such short supply. They carried water in pails attached to neck yokes or in barrels on "water sleds." They melted snow to obtain cooking and wash water. They used sal soda to 'break' the alkali content of water. Women also helped build windmills and dig wells. And in their desperation they even resorted to hiring a 'water-witch' or diviner to help them locate a vein of water.[3]

The aridity of the Plains created another problem for women—horribly destructive prairie fires. Men feared these fires because they endangered the animals, crops, and buildings that were largely their responsibilities, but women thought first of their children and homes as well as their cows, pigs, and chickens. In 1889 a fire in North Dakota destroyed one man's horses and barn and also claimed his wife's precious cows and chickens. Four years later, another fire in Fargo, North Dakota, burned to the ground both the shops where primarily men labored and the homes where primarily women worked. Recalling her childhood, a Kansas woman explained that because most buildings were made of wood, the "greatest danger" they faced was fire. She added that her father immediately turned all stock loose in the face of an oncoming fire because the animals instinctively headed for the safety of the river valley, while her mother placed her in the middle of the garden on the presumption that fire would not "pass into the ploughed land." Other women described the deafening noise and blinding smoke of the fires that threatened their families and homes.[4]

In addition, many women claimed that the Plains climate plagued them and interfered with their work. Destructive storms and blizzards were a constant threat, while summer heat and winter cold were regular annoyances. A Norwegian woman confronted her cold kitchen each winter morning dressed in overshoes, heavy clothing, and a warm head-scarf. Another woman simply wrote in her journal, "the snow falls upon my book while I write by the stove."[5]

Ever-present insects and animals also challenged women at every turn. Grasshoppers not only demolished crops, but could destroy homes and household goods as well. The "hoppers" gnawed their way through clothing, bedding, woodwork, furniture, mosquito netting, and stocks of food. Bliss Isely of Kansas claimed that she could remember the grasshopper "catastrophe" of 1874 in vivid detail for many years after its occurrence. As she raced down the road trying to outrun the "glistening white cloud" of grasshoppers thundering down from the sky, she worried about the baby in her arms. When the grasshoppers struck, they ate her garden to the ground, devoured fly netting, and chewed a hole in her black silk shawl. "We set ourselves to live through a hungry winter," she remembered. In the months that followed, she "learned to cook wheat and potatoes in every way possible." She made coffee from roasted wheat and boiled wheat kernels like rice for her children. Another Kansas woman who survived the grasshopper attack bitterly declared that Kansas had been "the state of cyclones, the state of cranks, the state of mortgages—and now grasshopper fame had come!"[6]

Political Upheaval

As if the physical environment wasn't enough to discourage even the hardiest and most determined women, another problem, political conflict, beset them as well. The ongoing argument over slavery especially affected the Kansas Territory when in 1856 an outbreak of violence between free-staters and proslavery factions erupted. "Border ruffians" added to the chaos by crossing frequently into "Bleeding Kansas" from Missouri in an attempt to impose slavery on the territory by force. Sara Robinson of Lawrence felt terrorized by frequent "street broils" and saw her husband imprisoned during what she termed the "reign of terror" in Kansas. Another Kansas woman lamented that there was no respite between this convulsive episode and the Civil War, which plucked men out of homes for military service. Women not only lost the labor and income of their men, but they feared the theft of food and children and the threat of rape for themselves and their daughters at the hands of raiders, thieves, and other outlaws made bold by the absence of men. In addition, the departure of men caused the burden of families, farms, and businesses to fall on the shoulders of already beleaguered women.[7]

The disputes that followed in the wake of the Civil War continued to disrupt women's lives. The period of Reconstruction between 1865 and 1877 included, for example, the chaotic entry of Exodusters (former slaves) into Kansas and other Plains states. In turn, prejudice against Exodusters created difficulties for African American women who had hoped they were migrating to a more hospitable region than the American South. Also during this period, economic unrest and dissatisfaction with federal and state government policies resulted in Populist agitation through the Plains during the 1880s and 1890s. By 1900, it seemed to many women that their lives had been entangled in a long series of political upheavals.

Personal Conflict

Women experienced personal conflict as well. Prejudice against Catholics, Jews, and people of other faiths led to intolerance at best and violence at worst. Ethnic and racial groups also received their share of distressing treatment. African American, Asian, and Mexican women were expected to work in the most menial, low-paid jobs, were barred from shops and other businesses, and were personally treated with disdain by many other migrants. This situation was especially difficult for women because they were frequently told that they were to be the arbitrators of society, yet they felt helpless to right this situation. Women also wanted desperately to shield their children from such treatment.

Some women also faced trouble within their own homes. Anecdotal evidence demonstrates that some husbands were domineering, demanding, and physically or verbally abusive. A young Jewish woman whose father had insisted that his family migrate to North Dakota remembered continual strife between her mother and father. "How can one bring the close, intimate life of the Russian *shtetl* to the vast open wilderness of the prairie?" she asked. But her mother tried. According to her daughter, "she rose early and cooked and baked and washed and scrubbed and sewed. She prayed and observed the fast days and holidays by making special dishes." Yet she also regretted and complained. Unable to understand her sorrow or offer her some much-needed sympathy, her husband argued and remonstrated. One day, much to his daughter's relief, he ran from the house storming and raging. Jumping into a buggy and seizing the reins, he shouted, "Goodbye, goodbye—I am leaving. This is more than human flesh can bear.... This is the end. I can take no more. It is beyond enduring. Goodbye, goodbye." When he soon returned, her joy dissipated: "My father had not kept his promise to go away and leave us in peace. He had returned. We were all trapped."[8]

On the Plains, and throughout the West, thousands of women deserted such husbands or sought relief in divorce courts. Census figures indicate that western women sought and received a higher proportion of divorces than women in other regions of the country. Whether economic opportunities encouraged this proclivity to divorce or whether western women had a spirit that sought independence is as yet unclear.[9]

Given the many difficulties that beset women, a reasonable person might ask why they stayed on the Plains. In fact, many did not stay. They and their families returned to former homes or moved onward to try life in another western region or town. After spending two years in Kansas, Helen Carpenter was delighted to become a new bride about to migrate to California. In 1857, Carpenter began her trail journal by going "back in fancy" over the two years she had spent in Kansas. She recalled the initial "weary journey of three weeks on a river boat" when all the children fell ill. Then, she wrote, it was "the struggle to get a roof over our heads . . . then followed days of longing for youthful companions . . . and before the summer waned, the entire community was stricken with fever and ague." Just as she finally made some friends and established something of a social life, "such pleasures were cut short by border troubles and an army of 'Border Ruffians' . . . who invaded the neighborhood, with no regard for life or property." She admitted that Kansas was "beautiful country" with its tall grass and lush wildflowers, but added that "the violent thunderstorms are enough to wreck the nerves of Hercules and the rattlesnakes are as thick as the leaves on the trees, and lastly 'but not leastly,' the fever and ague are corded up ever ready for use." Given the nature of her memories, it is not surprising that Carpenter concluded, "in consideration of what we have undergone physically and mentally, I can bid Kansas Good Bye without a regret." Another Kansas woman whose family left the region said that her father had taken sick and that her "Auntie wanted to get away from a place always hideous in her eyes."[10]

Fortunately, not all women felt so strongly about the drawbacks of their environment. Many women had already experienced a demanding life and, as Laura Ingalls Wilder put it, they saw the rigors of the Plains as "a natural part of life." They hung on because they had hope for the future, or according to one migrant, because they didn't expect the hard times to last. Often, their optimism was rewarded, and conditions did improve. Innovative technology gradually conquered the arid Plains, and economic booms occasionally appeared. A Nebraska woman of the early 1900s summed up her triumph in a pithy way when she wrote, "we built our frame house and was thru with our old leaky sod house. . . . We now had churches, schools, Telephones, Rural Mail."[11]

Still we must ask: did the women who remained on the Plains suffer disillusionment and despair, growing old and ill before their time? Did they blame their menfolk who had seen economic opportunity in the Plains for their misfortunes? The answer is "yes": many women who stayed on the Plains did so with resentment and hostility. Their writings tell of crushing work loads, frequent births, illnesses and deaths, recurring depression, loneliness, homesickness, and fear. A common complaint was the absence of other women; Plains women also longed for family members who had stayed at home. A Wyoming woman even claimed that the wind literally drove her crazy and that she could no longer bear to spend long winters on a remote ranch with no other women.[12]

Some women's lamentations were unrelenting, but others gradually included more pleasant observations. They noted that other people, including women, soon moved in and that often members of their own families joined them. Gradually, the depression of many hostile women ebbed and was replaced by a sense of affection for their new homes. Even the Wyoming woman who feared for her own mental stability later maintained that "those years on the Plains were hard years but I grew to like the West and now I would not like to live any other place."[13]

Numerous women did blame men for their circumstances. But it is often difficult to determine which women had fair cause to lay blame. Because women were hesitant to record personal troubles in journals or letters sent back home, it is not always clear how responsible men were for women's difficulties. Certainly, sad stories do exist of men who verbally or physically abused women or who were alcoholic, lazy, financially inept, or generally irresponsible. In the patriarchal family structure of the time, men were often slow to recognize the importance of women's labor, allow women a voice in family decisions, and extend understanding for women's concerns. As early as 1862, the U.S. Commissioner of Agriculture's annual report suggested that the supposedly prevalent insanity of plainswomen resulted more from the harsh treatment doled out by their own men than from the Plains climate, family finances, or infant mortality. In following years, newspaper reports of wife-beating or journal accounts of alcoholic husbands gave credence to his assertion.[14]

Here again, the negative testimony is balanced by other accounts. Countless women wrote about the energy, responsibility, support, community participation, and kindness of fathers, brothers, husbands, and sons. Women spoke of men's "cheerful spirits," patience, thoughtfulness, sympathy, and companionship. Army wives Ada Vogdes and Elizabeth Custer both felt that the hardships of their lives as women in western forts were greatly offset by the courtesy and consideration of their husbands, other officers, and enlisted men. More important, a considerable number of plucky women faced challenges with creativity, energy, optimism, and motivation. They battled the circumstances of their environment by confronting the necessities of each day while maintaining hope for a better future. They met political upheaval and violence with religious faith and a commitment to help establish order. And they endured conflict with family members, neighbors, and members of other cultural groups by persevering and seeking the companionship of others, especially other women.

A Kansan of the 1880s, Flora Moorman Heston, is one example of a woman who confronted poverty, hard work, loneliness, and other problems with buoyant spirits. In a letter home, she maintained that "we have the best prospect of prosperity we ever had and believe it was right for us to come here." She added that "I have a great deal more leasure [sic] time than I used to have it dont take near the work to keep one room that it does a big house."[15] Like women in the Midwest, Southwest, and Far West, plainswomen relied on their inner strength and kept a positive outlook. Although these qualities are often forgotten in conventional descriptions of the darker side of Plains living, they did indeed exist.

How Women Adapted

Most women who ventured to the Plains states were highly motivated. They sought wealth, health, a more promising future for their children, lower taxes, and end to slavery, less prejudice or more freedom from governmental control. During the hard times and disasters, their hopes sustained them. When their fathers, brothers, or husbands talked of moving elsewhere, they often reminded the men of the particular dream that had brought them to the Plains in the first place. Others relied upon religious faith, or clung to their belief that they were civilizing a raw region, or some other commitment to keep them strong in the face of adversity.

Many women migrants created rich and varied social lives out of limited opportunities. They relieved their own isolation by writing in cherished journals or penning letters to friends and family. A young Nebraska woman who lamented the lack of women in the neighborhood wrote daily in her journal. "What should I do without my journal!" she exclaimed on one of its pages. Yet, as time passed, her entries became less frequent while her apologies to her neglected journal increased.[16]

Women also turned to the books and newspapers they had brought with them, borrowed from others, or had purchased with hoarded butter-and-egg money. Bliss Isely explained that even when she and her husband could "not afford a shotgun and ammunition to kill rabbits" they subscribed to newspapers and bought books. She made it a personal rule that "no matter how late at night it was or how tired [she] was, never to go to bed without reading a few minutes from the Bible and some other book." Other women wrote of their longing for more books, of feeling settled when their books were unpacked, and of borrowing books from others. Faye Cashatt Lewis poignantly wrote: "Finishing the last book we borrowed from the Smiths, and having it too stormy for several days to walk the mile and a half to return it and get more, was a frequent and painful experience. Seeing the end of my book approaching was like eating the last bite of food on my plate, still hungry, and no more food in sight."[17]

Music also provided solace and sociability. Frequently women insisted upon bringing guitars, pianos, and miniature parlor organs to the Plains. Despite the fact that Ada Vogdes and her husband were transported from fort to fort in army ambulances with limited space, she clung to her guitar. In her journal, she frequently mentioned the pleasure that playing guitar and singing along brought to her and others.[18] Vogdes, like many others, also depended upon mail to keep her amused and sane. When a snowstorm stopped the mail for two long weeks, Vogdes proclaimed that she could not wait much longer. To many women, the arrival of the mail provided a lifeline to home and family and brought news of the larger world through magazines, journals, ethnic and other newspapers, and books.[19]

The coming of the railroad had great social implications. Not only did railroad companies bring additional people, but they sponsored fairs and celebrations and provided ties with other regions of the country. An Indian agent's wife in Montana wrote that "the coming of the Northern Pacific Railroad in 1883 brought us in closer touch with civilization, with kin and friends, with medical and military aid, but put an end to the old idyllic days." In 1907, a Wyoming woman was delighted to see the railroad come into her area and claimed that its very existence alleviated her depression. She explained that with "no trees and few buildings" to hamper her view of passing trains, she felt that she kept "in touch with the outside pretty well."[20]

Women also became effective instigators and organizers of a huge variety of social events including taffy pulls, oyster suppers, quilting bees, dinners, picnics, box suppers, church "socials," weddings and chivarees, spelling bees, dances, theatricals, song fests, puppet shows, and readings. Perhaps most important were the celebration of such special holidays as Thanksgiving, Hanukkah, Christmas, and the Fourth of July. The menus concocted by women on special occasions often confounded other women. After a particularly splendid dinner, one woman wrote, "however she got up such a variety puzzled me, as she cooks by the fireplace and does her baking in a small covered skillet."[21]

A third way in which women adapted was in their belief that they were family and cultural conservators. Women often derived great satisfaction and a sense of significance by establishing "real" homes for their families, preserving traditional values, folkways, and mores, passing on family and ethnic traditions, contributing to local schools and churches, and establishing women's organizations. Many would have probably agreed with the poetic woman who said of them, "Without their gentle touch, the land/Would still be wilderness." Certainly, women spent a good deal of time and energy recording and relating their cultural activities.[22]

In this role, women placed a great deal of emphasis on material goods. They preserved, but also used, family treasures. Some insisted on fabric rather than oilcloth table coverings, served holiday eggnog to cowhands in silver goblets, and used their best silver and chinaware whenever the occasion arose. Years after coming to the Plains, Faye Lewis still proudly displayed her mother's Haviland china. She explained that "Father had urged strongly that this china be sold, but the thought was so heartbreaking to mother that he relented and helped her pack it." Lewis perceptively saw that her mother's china was "more than a set of dishes to her, more than usefulness, or even beauty. They were a tangible link, a reminder, that there are refinements of living difficult to perpetuate . . . perhaps in danger of being forgotten." Certainly Mary Ronan felt this way. On an isolated Indian reservation in Montana, she still regularly set her dinner table with tablecloths and ivory napkin rings. She explained that "heavy, satiny damask" cloths gave her "exquisite satisfaction" although her children did not like them. She added that she had "one beautiful set of dishes" but used them only on "gala occasions."[23]

Rituals such as the celebration of Christmas were also important. In the early years, the Christmas trees in many Plains homes were scraggly, ornaments few and homemade, and Christmas dinner far from lavish. But as their situations improved financially, women provided more festive trees, elaborate presents, and special foods. They placed trees decorated with nuts, candy, popcorn balls, strings of cranberries, wax candles, and homemade decorations in schools and churches. They then surrounded the trees with gifts for family and friends as well as presents for poor children who might otherwise be deprived of a Christmas celebration. Often music, singing, speeches, and prayers preceded the arrival of a local man dressed as Santa Claus.[24]

It is important to note that women contributed to a diversity of cultural patterns because of their own mixed ethnic and racial stock. European, Native American, African American, Mexican, and Asian women who desired to preserve their own rich heritages subscribed to a variety of newspapers and magazines in their own languages, continued to wear traditional clothing, practiced their customary holiday rituals, and added their own words, foods, and perspectives to the evolving society. A Norwegian woman in Nebraska continued to speak Norwegian in her home, sent her children to parochial school, and cooked Norwegian food. African American women were another group who added their folkways to the cultural blend, especially after the Civil War when significant numbers of them migrated to Plains states as Exodusters.[25]

Jewish women were yet another group who brought their own culture to the Plains. Although many Jewish settlers first came to the Plains as members of agricultural communities, particularly under the auspices of the Jewish Colonization Association and the Hebrew Emigrant Aid Society, they soon relocated in such cities as Omaha, Nebraska, and Grand Forks, North Dakota. Here they established businesses and communities that could support rabbis and supply other religious needs. This relocation was important to many Jewish women who despaired of their inability to provide their children with religious education and keep a kosher home when separated from a sizable Jewish community.[26]

A fourth, and crucial, factor that aided many women in their adaptation to life on the Plains was their ability to bond with other women and to create what we would today call supportive networks. On the Plains, as elsewhere, women turned to each other for company, encouragement, information, and help in times of need. Women's longing for female companionship is clearly revealed by their laments about the lack of other women. One of only three known women migrants in a remote region of North Dakota stated simply, "Naturally I was very lonely for women friends."

Consequently, women frequently overcame barriers of age, ethnicity, social class, and race in forming friendships. Arriving in Oklahoma Territory in the early 1900s, Leola Lehman formed an extremely close friendship with a Native American woman whom she described as "one of the best women" she had known in her lifetime. A Kansas woman similarly characterized an African American woman who was first a domestic, then a confidante and friend, as "devoted, kind-hearted, hard-working." Still other women told how they found a way around language barriers in order to gain companionship from women of other races and cultures.[27]

Typically, women began a friendship with a call or chat. Lehman was hanging out her wash when the Indian woman who became her friend quietly appeared and softly explained, "I came to see you.... I thought you might be lonesome." The company of other women was especially important in male-dominated military forts, where a woman began receiving calls upon arrival. Ada Vogdes recorded her gratitude for being whisked off by another officer's wife the moment she first arrived at Fort Laramie. Her journal overflowed with mention of calls, rides, and other outings with women friends. When her closest friends left the fort, Vogdes described herself as feeling "forsaken and forlorn" and overwhelmed by an aching heart. Some years later, Fanny McGillycuddy at Fort Robinson in South Dakota also logged calls and visits with other women and noted their great importance to her.[28]

Women also established friendships, gave each other information and support and passed on technical information, often through quilting bees and sewing circles. Bliss Isely remembered that as a young woman she was always invited to the "sewings and quiltings" held by the married women in her neighborhood. On one occasion, she invited them in return and was pleased that "they remained throughout the day." Isely felt that these events gave her invaluable training in much-needed domestic skills and that the women had "a good time helping each other" with their work.[29]

Older women lavished new brides with maternal attention and were often very generous in sharing their time, energy, and skills with the novice. In 1869 the *Bozeman Chronicle* quoted a recent bride as saying, "In all there were just fourteen women in the town in 1869, but they all vied with each other to help us and make us welcome." This hospitality even included much-needed cooking lessons for the seventeen-year-old wife. A decade later, another bride arriving in Miles City, Montana, recalled that she met with a similar welcome: "Ladies called. . . . I wasn't at all lonely."[30]

Women were also quick to offer their services to other women in times of childbirth, illness, and death. Such aid in time of need created strong bonds between women that often stretched beyond racial, ethnic, and class lines. In 1871, the *Nebraska Farmer* quoted a settler who claimed that such women acted "without a thought of reward" and that their mutual aid transformed women into "unbreakable friends." During the early 1880s, a Jewish woman in North Dakota explained that when a woman was about to give birth she would send her children "to the neighbors to stay for the time" so that she "could have rest and quiet the first few days, the only rest many of these women ever knew." She added that "the rest of us would take home the washing, bake the bread, make the butter, etc." Other women said that in time of illness or death they would take turns watching the patient, prepare medicines, bring food, prepare a body with herbs, sew burial clothes, organize a funeral, and supply food.[31] The crucial nature of another woman's assistance in time of physical need was perhaps best expressed by Nannie Alderson, a Montana ranch wife during the 1880s. When she was ill, male family members and ranch hands strongly urged her to call a doctor from Miles City. Her reply: "I don't want a doctor. I want a woman!" When the men surrounding her failed to understand her need, they again pressed her to call a doctor. She sent for a neighbor woman instead. After her recovery, she justified her action by saying, "I simply kept quiet and let her wait on men, and I recovered without any complications whatever."[32]

As the number of women increased in an area, women began to join together in the public arena as well as in private. They formed a myriad of social, education, and reform associations. Women's literary clubs studied books and started libraries. Temperance societies—the most famous of which was the national Women's Christian Temperance Union—attempted to help control the evil of alcoholism that was so damaging to women and children who were economically dependent upon men. And woman suffrage groups fought for the right to vote. Nebraskan Clara Bewick Colby, suffragist and editor of *The Woman's Tribune*, noted again and again that the Plains states were particularly fertile ground for suffrage reform.[33]

Plainswomen split, however, on the issue of suffrage. Nebraskan Luna Kellie explained that she "had been taught that it was unwomanly to concern oneself with politics and that only the worst class of women would ever vote if they had a chance." But when a tax reform proposed to cut the length of the school term, Kellie, a mother of several small children, "saw for the first time that a woman might be interested in politics and want a vote." With her father's and husband's help, she promoted a campaign that resulted in woman suffrage in local school elections. Kellie's husband urged her to continue her efforts to obtain women's right to vote in general elections.[34] In 1888, one Kansas women placed a cap bearing presidential candidate Belva Lockwood's name on her daughter's head. Still, many women opposed the suffrage cause, maintaining that the vote should belong to men only. These women believed that women should focus on their homes and families rather than on making political decisions. Some of these women even organized anti-suffrage associations.[35]

But advocates of woman suffrage were not so easily deterred. After the National Woman Suffrage Association was organized in 1869 (the same year that Wyoming Territory granted women the right to vote), Elizabeth Cady Stanton and Susan B. Anthony traveled through the West promoting suffrage. Stanton thought that Wyoming was a "blessed land... where woman is the political equal of man." Although Esther Morris is usually given credit for bringing woman suffrage to Wyoming Territory and was later called the Mother of Woman Suffrage, some people dispute the centrality of her role. Evidently, many women worked to convince the Democratic legislature to adopt a Women's Rights Bill in December 1869 and persuaded Republican governor John A. Campbell to sign the bill on December 10, 1869.[36]

In addition to suffrage organizations, thousands of other women's clubs and associations existed, including hospital auxiliaries, housekeepers' societies, current events clubs, musical groups, tourist clubs, world peace groups, Red Cross units, and Women's Relief Corps chapters. By the 1880s, so many organizations existed that one Wyoming woman termed the era "the golden age of women's clubs." One leading Oklahoma clubwoman established or led over forty associations during her life.[37]

Unfortunately, much of the sharing that had existed during the early days of a region now began to dissipate. Many women's clubs were segregated; women of color formed their own groups and fought for suffrage or reforms in their own way. For instance, African American women worked energetically within their own communities to provide medical care, playgrounds, and better educational facilities.

Some men's organizations also invited women (usually only white women, however) to join their membership and support their causes. A few even expanded their platforms to include women's issues. As a result, women joined the Patrons of Husbandry (the Grange), the Farmers' Alliance, and the Populist party. Annie La Porte Diggs of Kansas, for example, was an active Populist speaker and writer known for her religious liberalism. Of course, the most famous Populist woman orator was Mary Elizabeth Lease, a woman who was admitted to the Kansas bar in 1885 and who gave in 1890 over 160 speeches in support of the Populist cause. She became famous for her admonition to farmers to "raise less corn and more hell" and was dubbed by the media "Mary Yellin'." So many other women spoke from wagons and platforms, carried banners, and marched in parades that political humorist Joseph Billings wrote, "Wimmin is everywhere."[38]

Women also began to run for office on the Populist ticket. They had long held elected positions on local, county, and state school boards so the idea was not totally unacceptable to many women and men. In 1892, Ella Knowles, a Montana lawyer who in 1889 successfully lobbied for a statute allowing women to practice law in the state, ran unsuccessfully for attorney general. She was, however, appointed to a four-year term as assistant attorney general, and during the mid 1890s was a delegate to Populist conventions and a member of the Populist National Committee. During this period, Olive Pickering Rankin served as the only woman on the school board in Missoula, Montana. She was also the mother of Jeanette Rankin, the first woman to serve in the U.S. Congress and the person who introduced the "Anthony Amendment" for woman suffrage into the U.S. House of Representatives.[39]

Many men also supported women in other areas of life. Cases of supportive, helpful, sympathetic men who offered a helping hand and a listening ear when needed abounded in all communities. Faye Cashatt Lewis, whose mother so plaintively complained that the great trouble with North Dakota was that "there is nothing to make a shadow," claimed that her father was her mother's "saving support" throughout her various travails. Lewis said that her mother "could never have felt lost while he was by her side."[40] Children too offered assistance, company, and comfort to the older women of a family. While the men were gone in the fields, working in a shop, practicing a profession, or making trips, children were often women's solace, friends, and helpers. According to Lewis, she and her siblings were not only her mother's assistants, but her friends and confidantes as well.[41]

The ability of many women to concentrate on their hopes and dreams, create and enjoy socializing, serve as cultural conservators, and form strong bonds with others—both female and male—helped them triumph over the innumerable demands of the West. Although the Plains was an especially difficult environment for women, they were not generally disoriented, depressed, or in disarray. Rather, the majority of them managed to maintain homes and families, carry out domestic functions, and perpetuate the many values associated with the home. While depression, insanity, or bitterness characterized some women's lives, many more were able to respond to the challenges and hardships involved in Plains living in ways that insured survival and often brought contentment and satisfaction as well.

Notes

1. Gilbert C. Fite, "The United States Army and Relief to Pioneer Settlers, 1874–1875," *Journal of the West* 6 (January 1967), 99–107.

2. Louise Pound, *Pioneer Days in the Middle West: Settlement and Racial Stocks* (Lincoln: Nebraska State Historical Society, n.d.); Mary W. M. Hargreaves, "Homesteading and Homemaking on the Plains: A Review," *Agricultural History* 47 (April 1973), 156–63; Lillian Schlissel, "Women's Diaries on the Western Frontier," *American Studies* 18 (Spring 1977), 87–100, and Lillian Schlissel, "Mothers and Daughters on the Western Frontier," *Frontiers* 3 (1979), 29–33; Christine Stansell, "Women on

the Great Plains, 1865–1900," *Women's Studies* 4 (1976), 87–98; John Mack Faragher and Christine Stansell, "Women and Their Families on the Overland Trail to California and Oregon, 1842–1867," *Feminist Studies* 2 (1975), 150–66; Glenda Riley, *The Female Frontier: A Comparative View of Women on the Prairie and the Plains* (Lawrence: University Press of Kansas, 1988).

3. See Myra Waterman Bickel, Lydia Burrows Foote, Eleanor Schubert, and Anna Warren Peart, Pioneer Daughters Collection, SDHRC; Abbie Bright, Diary, 1870–1871, KHS; Barbara Levorsen, "Early Years in Dakota," *Norwegian-American Studies* 21 (1961), 167–69; Kathrine Newman Webster, "Memories of a Pioneer," in *Old Times Tales*, Vol. 1, Part 1 (Lincoln: Nebraska State Historical Society, 1971); Bertha Scott Hawley Johns, "Pioneer Memories 1975," WSAMHD; Emma Crinklaw (interview by Mary A. Thon), "One Brave Homesteader of '89," 1989, WSAMHD. Regarding 'witching' for water in Kansas see Bliss Isely, *Sunbonnet Days* (Caldwell, Idaho: Caxton Printers, 1935), 176–79.

4. Ellen Stebbins Emery, letter to "Dear Sister Lizzie," December 31, 1889, from Emerado, SHSND (used by permission); "Prairie Pioneer: Some North Dakota Homesteaders," *North Dakota History* 43 (Spring 1976), 22; Adela E. Orpen, *Memories of the Old Emigrant Days in Kansas, 1862–1865* (New York: Harper & Brothers, 1928), 65–69; Florence Marshall Stote, "Of Such is the Middle West," n.d., KHS; Meri Reha, Pioneer Daughters Collection, SDHRC.

5. Amanda Sayle Walradth, Pioneer Daughters Collection, SDHRC, and Ada Vogdes, Journal, 1868–1872, HL.

6. Isely, *Sunbonnet Days*, 196–201, and Anne E. Bingham, "Sixteen Years on a Kansas Farm,] 1870–1886," Kansas State Historical Society *Collections* 15 (1919/20), 516.

7. Sara Tappan Doolittle Robinson, *Kansas, Its Interior and Exterior Life* (Freeport, New York: Books for Libraries Press, 1856), 85, 249–69, 347; Georgiana Packard, "Leaves from the Life of a Kansas Pioneer," 1914, KHS; Marian Lawton Clayton, "Reminiscences—The Little Family," 1961, KHS.

8. From Sophie Trupin, *Dakota Diaspora: Memoirs of a Jewish Homesteader* (Lincoln: University of Nebraska Press, 1984), 35, 39, 41–42.

9. For a fuller discussion of western divorce see Glenda Riley, *Divorce: An American Tradition* (New York: Oxford University Press, 1991), ch. 4.

10. Helen M. Carpenter, "A Trip Across the Plains in an Ox Wagon," 1857, HL, and Orpen, *Memories of the Old Immigrant Days*, 8.

11. Laura Ingalls Wilder, *The First Four Years* (New York: Harper & Row, 1971); Mollie Dorsey Sanford, *Mollie: The Journal of Mollie Dorsey Sanford in Nebraska and Colorado Territories, 1857–1886* (Lincoln: University of Nebraska Press, 1976), 54; Eva Klepper, "Memories of Pioneer Days," n.d., in May Avery Papers, NHS.

12. Sarah Ettie Armstrong, "Pioneer Days," n.d., WSAMHD.

13. Ibid.

14. U.S. Commissioner of Agriculture, *Annual Report,* 1862, 462–70; *Laramie Sentinel,* October 10, 1885; Martha Farnsworth, Diary, 1882–1922, KHS. See also John Mack Faragher, "History from the Inside-Out: Writing the History of Women in Rural America," *American Quarterly* 33 (Winter 1981), 537–57, and Melody Graulich, "Violence Against Women in Literature of the Western Family," *Frontiers* 7 (1984), 14–20.

15. Flora Moorman Heston, " 'I think I will Like Kansas': The Letters of Flora Moorman Heston, 1885–1886," *Kansas History* 6 (Summer 1983), 92.

16. Sanford, *Mollie,* 38.

17. Isely, *Sunbonnet Days,* 180, and Lewis, *Nothing to Make a Shadow,* 76.

18. Vogdes, Journal.

19. Ibid.

20. Margaret Ronan, *Frontier Woman: The Story of Mary Ronan* (Helena: University of Montana, 1973), 123, and Mrs. Charles Robinson, "Pioneer Memories," 1975, WSAMHD.

21. Sanford, *Mollie,* 63. Descriptions of social events can be found in Nannie T. Alderson and Helen H. Smith, *A Bride Goes West* (Lincoln: University of Nebraska Press, 1969), 169; Mary and George Baillie, "Recollections in the Form of a Duet," 1939, WSAMHD; Enid Bennets, "Rural Pioneer Life," 1939, WSAMHD; Minnie Doehring, "Kansas One-Room Public School," 1981, KHS; W. H. Elznic, Pioneer Daughters Collection, SDSHRC; Lottie Holmberg (recorder), Laura Ingraham Bragg, Recollections, n.d., WSAMHD; Lena Carlile Hurdsman, "Mrs. Lena Hurdsman of Mountain View," 1939, WSAMHD; Levorson, "Early Years in Dakota," 161; Alice Richards McCreery, "Various Happenings in the Life of Alice Richards McCreery," n.d., WSAMHD; Minnie Dubbs Millbrook, ed., "Rebecca Visits Kansas and the Custers: The Diary of Rebecca Richmond," *Kansas Historical Quarterly* 42 (Winter 1976), 366–402; Graphia Mewhirter Wilson, "Pioneer Life," 1939, WAHC.

22. Catherine E. Berry, "Pioneer Memories," 1975, WSAMHD. For discussions of women reconstructing their known lifestyle patterns on the Plains see James I. Fenton, "Critters, Sourdough, and Dugouts: Women and Imitation Theory on the Staked Plains, 1875–1910," in John R. Wunder, ed., *At Home on the Range: Essays on the History of Western Social and Domestic Life* (Westport, Conn.: Greenwood Press, 1985), 19–38; Jacqueline S. Reinier, "Concepts of Domesticity on the Southern Plains Agricultural Frontier," in Wunder, ed., *At Home on the Range,* 55–70.

23. Mrs. G. W. Wales, Reminiscences, 1866–1877, SHSND; Florence McKean Knight, "Anecdotes of Early Days in Box Butte County," *Nebraska History* 14 (April–June 1933), 142; Alderson and Smith, *A Bride Goes West,* 89; Lewis, *Nothing to Make a Shadow,* 71–72; Ronan, *Frontier Woman,* 115.

24. Lorshbough, "Prairie Pioneers," 78–79; Walter F. Peterson, "Christmas on the Plains," *American West* 1 (Fall 1964), 53–57; Anna Warren Peart, Pioneer Daughters Collection, SDHRC; Mabel Cheney Moudy, "Through My Life," n.d., WAHC.

25. Hannah, Birkley, "Mrs. Iver O. Birkley," 1957, NHS. For descriptions of Exodusters see Roy Garvin, "Benjamin, or 'Pap' Singleton and His Followers," *Journal of Negro History* 33 (January 1948), 7–8; Glen Schwendemann, "Wyandotte and the First 'Exodusters' of 1879," *Kansas Historical Quarterly* 26 (Autumn 1960), 233–49, and "The 'Exodusters' on the Missouri," *Kansas Historical Quarterly* 29 (Spring 1963), 25–40; Arvarh E. Strickland, "Toward the Promised Land: The Exodus to Kansas and Afterward," *Missouri Historical Review* 69 (July 1975), 405–12; Nell Irvin Painter, *Exodusters: Black Migration to Kansas after Reconstruction* (New York: Alfred A. Knopf, 1977; reprint, Lawrence: University Press of Kansas, 1986), 108–17; George H. Wayne, "Negro Migration and Colonization in Colorado, 1870–1930," *Journal of the West* 15 (January 1976), 102–20; "Washwomen, Maumas, Exodusters, Jubileers," in *We Are Your Sisters: Black Women in the Nineteenth Century,* ed. Dorothy Sterling (New York: Norton, 1984), 355–94.

26. For descriptions of Jewish women and men on the Plains see Lipman Goldman Feld, "New Light on the Lost Jewish Colony of Beersheba, Kansas, 1881–1886," *American Jewish Historical Quarterly* 60 (December 1970), 159, 165–67; Susan Leaphart, ed., "Frieda and Belle Fligelman: A Frontier-City Girlhood in the 1890s," *Montana: The Magazine of Western History* 32 (Summer 1982), 85–92; James A. Rudin, "Beersheba, Kansas: 'God's Pure Air on Government Lands,'" *Kansas Historical Quarterly* 34 (Autumn 1968), 282–98; Elbert L. Sapinsley, "Jewish Agricultural Colonies in the West: The Kansas Example," *Western States Jewish Historical Quarterly* 3 (April 1971), 157–69; Lois Fields Schwartz, "Early Jewish Agricultural Colonies in North Dakota," *North Dakota History* 32 (October 1965), 217, 222–32;

William C. Sherman, *Prairie Mosaic: An Ethnic Atlas of Rural North Dakota* (Fargo: North Dakota Institute for Regional Studies, 1983), 19–20, 53–54, 70, 112.

27. Mrs. W. M. Lindsay, "My Pioneer Years in North Dakota," 1933, SHSND; Leola Lehman, "Life in the Territories," *Chronicles of Oklahoma* 41 (Fall 1963), 373; Orpen, *Memories of the Old Emigrant Days,* 219; Lucy Horton Tabor, "An Old Lady's Memories of the Wyoming Territory," n.d., WSAMHD; Emma Vignal Borglum, "The Experience at Crow Creek: A Sioux Indian Reservation at South Dakota," 1899, SDHRC.

28. Lehman, "Life in the Territories," 373; Vogdes, Journal; Fanny McGillycuddy, Diary, 1877–78, SDHRC.

29. Isely, *Sunbonnet Days,* 78–79. For other descriptions of the importance of quilting see Mrs. Henry (Anna) Crouse, Reminiscence, January 12, 1939, MSU; Ellen Calder DeLong, "Memories of Pioneer Days in Cavalier County," n.d., SHSND; Agnes Henberg, Interview, September 6, 1979, WAHC; Olivia Holmes, Diary, 1872, KHS; Sarah Bessey Tracy, Diary, 1869, MSU.

30. *Bozeman Chronicle,* August 10, 1954; unidentified newspaper clipping, "Journey from Missouri to Montana in 1880 Great Adventure According to Mrs. Mary Myer," n.d., MSU.

31. *Nebraska Farmer,* December 8, 1934; Martha Thal, "Early Days: The Story of Sarah Thal, Wife of a Pioneer Farmer of Nelson County, N.D.," *American Jewish Archives* 23 (April 1971), 59; Mary Raymond, "My Experiences as a Pioneer," 1929, 1933, NHS; Allen, Diary; Lindsay, "My Pioneer Years"; Eleanor Schubert and Mary Louise Thomson, Pioneer Daughters Collection, SDHRC.

32. Alderson and Smith, *A Bride Goes West,* 205–06.

33. Clara Bewick Colby, Scrapbook of Clippings from *The Woman's Tribune,* 1883–1891, Clara Colby Collection, HL. See in particular pp. 24, 25, 257.

34. Luna Kellie, "Memoirs," n.d., NHS.

35. Catherine Wiggins Porter, "Sunday School Houses and Normal Institutes: Pupil and Teacher in Northern Kansas, 1886–1895," KHS, and Bingham, "Sixteen Years on a Kansas Farm," 502.

36. Stanton is quoted in Beverly Beeton and G. Thomas Edwards, "Susan B. Anthony's Woman Suffrage Crusade in the American West," *Journal of the West* 21 (April 1982), 5. See also Virginia Scharff, "The Case for Domestic Feminism: Woman Suffrage in Wyoming," *Annals of Wyoming* 56 (Fall 1984), 29–37; Dr. Grace Raymond Hebard, "How Woman Suffrage Came to Wyoming," n.d., WSAMHD; Katharine A. Morton, "How Woman Suffrage Came to Wyoming," n.d., Woman Suffrage Collection, WSAMHD; Staff of the Library of the University of Wyoming, "Esther Hobart Morris and Suffrage," n.d., Woman Suffrage File, WAHC; and Mary Lee Stark, "One of the First Wyoming Women Voters Tells How Franchise Was Granted," n.d., WAHC.

37. Mathilda C. Engstad, "The White Kid Glove Era," n.d., SHSND, and Marilyn Hoder-Salmon, "Myrtyle Archer McDougal: Leader of Oklahoma's 'Timid Sisters,'" *Chronicles of Oklahoma* 60 (Fall 1982), 332–43.

38. Marilyn Dell Brady, "Populism and Feminism in a Newspaper by and for Women of the Kansas Farmers' Alliance, 1891–1894," *Kansas History* 7 (Winter 1984/85), 280–90; O. Gene Clanton, "Intolerant Populist? The Disaffection of Mary Elizabeth Lease," *Kansas Historical Quarterly* 34 (Summer 1968), 189–200; Katherine B. Clinton, "What Did You Say, Mrs. Lease?" *Kansas Quarterly* 1 (Fall 1969), 52–59; and Richard Stiller, *Queen of the Populists: The Story of Mary Elizabeth Lease* (New York: Crowell, 1970). See also Elizabeth Cochran, "Hatchets and Hoopskirts: Women in Kansas History," *Midwest Quarterly* 2 (April 1961), 229–49.

39. Richard B. Knowles, "Cross the Gender Line: Ella L. Knowles, Montana's First Woman Lawyer," *Montana: The Magazine of Western History* 32 (Summer 1982), 64–75, and Olive Pickering Rankin, Montana American Mothers Bicentennial Project, MHSA.

40. Stote, "Of Such is the Middle West," KHS; Bingham, "Sixteen Years on a Kansas Farm," 517; Alderson and Smith, *A Bride Goes West,* 206, 233–34, Elizabeth B. Custer, *"Boots and Saddles" Or Life in Dakota With General Custer* (New York: Harper & Brothers, 1885), 126, 145; Vogdes, Journal; Faye Cashatt Lewis, *Nothing to Make a Shadow* (Ames: Iowa State University Press, 1971), 33–34.

41. Lewis, *Nothing to Make a Shadow,* 33–34.

POSTSCRIPT

Did Nineteenth-Century Women of the West Fail to Overcome the Hardships of Living on the Great Plains?

In her study of 700 letters, journals, and diaries, Stansell concludes that nineteenth-century women were forced by their husbands to move to a primitive, isolated environment and to live in sod houses far removed from their families and friends in the more civilized states east of the Mississippi River. In Stansell's view, women regressed from the traditional cult of motherhood adhered to by middle-class eastern women who attended to the moral and physical needs of their homes and their children. Out on the frontier, says Stansell, women were isolated from their support systems of other women, and their marriages were often dominated by males who showed their wives neither love and affection nor respect. In short, Stansell paints a very grim picture of frontier life for women.

Riley grants that women on the Great Plains faced physical hardships, political disputes, and personal family tragedies. But she also shows how women adapted to the new environment and developed close friendships through church services, holiday parties, and quilting bees. In addition, it was in the West that women began to move out of the home through the Prohibition and Populist reform movements and eventually achieved voting rights.

Riley's research indicates the new directions in which western women's history has been moving. First, she has established the multicultural links that women felt toward one another on the frontier, exemplified by the friendships that developed between white and Indian women. Second, Riley has studied the West as a continuum that transcends several generations down to the present time. See *Building and Breaking Families in the American West* (University of New Mexico Press, 1996).

Two major anthologies that sample new western history are William Cronon, George Miles, and Jay Gitlin, eds., *Under an Open Sky: Rethinking America's Western Past* (W. W. Norton, 1992) and Patricia N. Limerick, Charles Rankin, and Clyde A. Milner, Jr., eds., *Trails: Toward a New Western History* (University of Kansas Press, 1991). These readers deal with the environment, industrialization, painting, film, minorities, and women—areas of the West neglected by Frederick Jackson Turner and his followers.

The two best overviews of the new western history are Patricia N. Limerick's *The Legacy of Conquest: The Unbroken Past of the American West* (W. W. Norton, 1988) and Richard White's *"It's Your Misfortune and None of My Own": A New History of the American West* (University of Oklahoma Press, 1992).

ISSUE 3

Did the Industrial Revolution Disrupt the American Family?

YES: Elaine Tyler May, from "The Pressure to Provide: Class, Consumerism, and Divorce in Urban America, 1880–1920," *Journal of Social History* (Winter 1978)

NO: Jacquelyn Dowd Hall, Robert Korstad, and James Leloudis, from "Cotton Mill People: Work, Community, and Protest in the Textile South, 1880–1940," *The American Historical Review* (April 1986)

ISSUE SUMMARY

YES: Elaine Tyler May, a professor of American studies and history, argues that the Industrial Revolution in the United States, with its improved technology, increasing income, and emerging consumerism, led to higher rates of divorce because family wage earners failed to meet rising expectations for material accumulation.

NO: History professors Jacquelyn Dowd Hall, Robert Korstad, and James Leloudis contend that the cotton mill villages of the New South, rather than destroying family work patterns, fostered a labor system that permitted parents and children to work together as a traditional family unit.

The Industrial Revolution fueled the rise of the United States to a preeminent position among the nations of the world by 1914. It affected virtually every institution—political, economic, and social—in the country. Politically, municipal, state, and federal governments recognized the benefits of cooperating in a variety of ways with corporate America, so much so that the doctrine of laissez-faire existed more in theory than in actual practice. Economically, industrialization laid the foundation for monopolization; fueled occupational opportunities for residents, both native and foreign-born; placed in jeopardy the value of skilled artisans; and transformed the workplace for millions of Americans. Socially, the economic forces dominating the United States in the last quarter of the nineteenth century played a significant role in encouraging geographical mobility, subordinating rural values to those associated with large industrial cities, and generating tensions and conflicts along racial, ethnic, class, and gender lines.

As the factory came to replace the farm as the workplace for more and more Americans, the United States developed an identifiable proletariat—a mass of unskilled, often propertyless workers whose labor was controlled by someone other than themselves. Moreover, despite the optimistic promises of "rags-to-riches" advancement associated with the American Dream, these workers could anticipate that they would remain unskilled and propertyless for their entire lives. Within the factories, mills, and mines of industrial America, corporate management dictated company policy regarding wages, hours, and other conditions of employment and tended to view itself, not the laborers, as the producers. Wages may have been relatively higher but so, too, were prices, and a dollar a day was not enough for a man to feed, clothe, and house his family, to say nothing of providing medical attention. Consequently, many working-class, married women entered the labor force to help make ends meet, not because they found the prospect of wage earning to be liberating. In doing so, they were accused of stepping outside their proper sphere of domesticity and of violating the Victorian "cult of true womanhood." Their children also moved into the industrial workforce since little physical strength was required to carry out many of the tasks of the factory. Also, the owners could justify paying youngsters lower wages, which reduced production costs.

This scenario suggests that the processes of industrialization had the potential to alter the traditional structure of the American family wherein the husband and father was expected to provide the necessities of life. What happened to the family during the Industrial Revolution? How similar or different was it from the preindustrial family? Did industrialization have a sustaining or transformative impact on family life in the United States? These questions are addressed from different perspectives by the selections that follow.

Elaine Tyler May compares divorce records in California and New Jersey for the 1880s and 1920 and finds that the increased prosperity of the industrial era created money problems that affected marriages among the wealthy and the poor alike. In particular, assumptions of vastly improved material circumstances did not always match the realities of household income. As a result, arguments over money created a "pressure to provide" that led to the breakup of many families.

In contrast, Jacquelyn Dowd Hall, Robert Korstad, and James Leloudis emphasize factors that maintained family stability during the Industrial Revolution. Their study of the culture of cotton mill villages in the South after Reconstruction presents a portrait of a much smoother transition from farm to factory than is often associated with the Industrial Revolution. Specifically, they describe a work environment in the cotton mills that preserved rather than destroyed the traditional family labor system.

Elaine Tyler May

 **YES**

The Pressure to Provide

In an era of massive production of consumer goods, what determines the normative standard of living, and what constitutes the necessities of life? These questions became increasingly difficult to answer during the decades surrounding the turn of the century, when profound economic changes ushered in corporate America. Scholars have documented a number of crucial developments, including standardized industrial technology, a mushrooming national bureaucracy, a shorter work week, and increased wages. Some observers hail these changes for providing security and material abundance to enhance the home and enrich private life. Others lament the loss of the craft tradition, and the intrinsic satisfactions that went with it. Still others claim that consumerism was a ploy to buy off workers and women, making them complacent while discouraging effective unionization and political action. But, as yet, no study has used empirical data to probe the impact of these developments on American families, or determined how they affected individuals on different levels of the class order. This article examines and compares the effects of heightened material aspirations upon wealthy, white-collar, and blue-collar Americans. While the rising standard of living may well have enhanced family life for some among the comfortable classes, it often wreaked havoc in the homes of those who could not afford the fruits of abundance. It is no accident that the emergence of the affluent society paralleled the skyrocketing of the American divorce rate.

One way to explore the way in which prosperity took its toll is to examine the casualties themselves. I have used hundreds of divorce cases filed during these years to uncover some of the economic problems that plagued American marriages. The samples include 500 litigations from Los Angeles in the 1880s, and another 500 from 1920. A comparative sample includes 250 divorces filed throughout New Jersey in 1920. The proceedings cover a developing west-coast city with little manufacturing, and an eastern industrial state with a large rural population. Within the samples are individuals from virtually every ethnic group and occupational category. By comparing the accusations mentioned in the 1880s and in 1920, we can determine the effects of economic change over time, during these crucial transitional years. The testimonies of the litigants in these cases reveal the limits of abundance, and suggest that no class or locale was immune to the ill effects of rising material aspirations.

From Elaine Tyler May, "The Pressure to Provide: Class, Consumerism, and Divorce in Urban America, 1880–1920," *Journal of Social History*, vol. 12, no. 2 (Winter 1978). Copyright © 1978 by *Journal of Social History*. Notes omitted.

Obviously, financial problems did not erupt in American homes with the onset of the corporate economy. In fact, money conflicts appeared in divorce cases well before the 20th century. Yet the turn-of-the-century decades did witness a profound change. In the first place, the number of divorces increased dramatically. Secondly, issues surrounding money—who should make it, how much is adequate, and how it should be spent—became increasingly prevalent. The divorce samples from Los Angeles and New Jersey reflect this trend. Although the percentage of cases filed on the grounds of "neglect to provide" did not rise significantly between the two samples taken, these problems did become more complicated in the later decades. The Lynds found a similar development in Muncie, Indiana. In spite of the fairly constant rate of neglect complaints in divorce litigations from 1890 to the 1920s, "economic considerations figure possibly more drastically than formerly as factors in divorce."

At first glance, this appears rather perplexing. The nation was more prosperous in the later period than the earlier, and the standard of living was rising steadily for all classes. Moreover, women found greater opportunities to work, and both males and females experienced increasing wages and more free time off the job. During the same years, an unprecedented abundance of consumer goods became available on a mass level. Presumably, these developments would contribute to easing tensions between husbands and wives rather than creating them, while fostering a more pleasant, epressive, and comfortable existence. However, with the standard of living rising, and affluence filtering down to a greater proportion of the population, the "provider" was often expected to fulfill the increased demands sparked by widespread prosperity.

The evidence in the divorce proceedings suggests that this was not a major problem in the 1880s. Although financial conflicts appeared often, there was no controversy over what constituted the necessities of life. Either a husband supported his family, or he did not. Virtually all of the cases in the early sample that dealt with issues of neglect were clear-cut. If a man did not provide enough food, clothing, and shelter for his wife to live comfortably, she was entitled to a divorce. No husband questioned that; and no quarrels ensued over what his obligation entailed.

... Women who placed heavy demands upon their husbands were not merely selfish or lazy. Although these were the years of women's presumed "emancipation," females still faced limited options outside the home. Middle-class wives in particular may have felt restless as well as powerless. While their numbers in the work force increased, it was still considered undesirable for a married woman to work. If a wife did seek employment, she did not have access to the most lucrative, prestigious, and rewarding occupations. Most jobs available to women were routine and monotonous, with low pay and few chances for advancement.

What was left, then, to give these married females personal satisfaction? Even at home they may have felt a sense of uselessness. Childbearing and household responsibilities utilized less of a woman's creative energies as the birth rate declined and labor-saving devices proliferated. New avenues for self-expression had to be explored. The economy offered little in the way of jobs; yet it provided seemingly unlimited possibilities for consumerism. Indeed, female emancipation found its most immediate expression not in the work force, but in the realms of styles and leisure pursuits. These were purchasable, provided one had the means. If wives began spending to adorn their homes and themselves, it may have reflected their constraints elsewhere. It is no wonder that, for some women, this gave rise to an obsession with material goods and private indulgence. Thus, they turned the full force of their pent-up energies to these endeavors.

With limited financial resources of their own, women often looked to men to provide the means for their consumption desires. This pressure was one of many new challenges facing 20th-century males. While public notice focused on new female activities, parallel shifts that affected men went virtually unnoticed. Males continued to work, their clothing styles remained practically unaltered, and their public behavior did not change dramatically. Yet they were experiencing a subtle transformation in sex-role expectations that, while not as obvious as the new status of women, was no less profound.

For white-collar men, the most far-reaching changes came with the maturation of the corporate system. The engulfing bureaucracies stabilized many uncertainties of the earlier era, and offered at least a modicum of security. The 20th-century businessman was less likely to enter business on his own, with the full burden of success or failure resting on his shoulders. If one followed the rules, he would advance up the hierarchy in a steady, predictable manner, and reach a moderate level of success and prosperity. There may have been [a] few examples of men making a fortune overnight within the modern system; but, in fact, the Carnegies of the previous era served as little more than encouragement to fantasies. The top of the ladder was virtually closed then as well as later. However, successful men had been models of 19th-century striving. In spite of new rewards, the corporations took away some of the unique triumphs of individual enterprise.

With the mechanization of industry, increasing production, the declining work week, and a rising standard of living, the benefits were obvious. In terms of purely material considerations, the corporate economy offered abundance and leisure. The tragedy, however, was that the aspiration for affluence was more widespread than the luxurious life itself. Even if an individual entered the white-collar ranks, he still faced enormous pressures to advance and succeed. Supplying increased demands necessitated continual striving. This was difficult enough for relatively successful businessmen, but infinitely more so for employees with modest salaries, or for petty proprietors without the cushion of corporate security.

We know from national statistics that the white-collar level of society shifted away from self-employed businessmen to corporate bureaucrats and clerical workers. Our Los Angeles samples reflect a similar trend. These white-collar groups, possibly more than any other level in society, were striving for upward mobility, afraid of slipping down the socioeconomic ladder, and concerned with deriving the fruits of their labor in tangible material goods. Arno Mayer has suggested that, historically, the petite bourgeoisie was possibly the most insecure and status-conscious level in western nations. This group had its own unique aspirations and cultural forms geared toward emulating the more affluent groups above them. If this premise holds for 20th-century America, and I believe it does, then petty proprietors facing competition from large corporations, as well as rank and file white-collar workers, would be feeling these pressures most intensely.

Looking at the divorce samples from Los Angeles, we find that, by 1920, the low-white-collar level is overrepresented, compared to its proportion of the general population. In the later sample, the proportion of divorces granted to the wealthy classes declined dramatically as the more bureaucratic clerical and sales categories mushroomed. At the same time, the percentage of petty proprietors in the work force shrank; but these small businessmen remained heavily overrepresented in the divorce samples. Those who remained among the entrepreneurial ranks may well have felt new pressures. As large chains and department stores began drawing local patrons and customers away from independent enterprises, owners of small shops and businesses may have faced increasing insecurity. To add to these burdens, many of them had to purchase goods from larger firms, making them dependent upon a national marketing system. Undersold by large competitors who often controlled production and supply as well as distribution, and bound by wholesale merchandise prices, they may have tried to cut costs by turning to family labor. This was not always a satisfactory solution, especially if proprietors of small concerns had to cope with diminishing returns as well as increasing consumer demands. It is perhaps no wonder that this group had more than its share of divorce.

Unfortunately, relatively few of the divorce litigants articulated how financial and status considerations affected their marriages and their lives. As with virtually every complex issue that eroded these relationships, we must glean insights from a handful of cases where evidence is rich and detailed. In terms of material considerations, we are able to discern a pattern of discontent for each of the major socioeconomic levels represented.... [A]ffluence did not preclude the possibility of money squabbles. The leisured wife of a man with means might make a quasi-career out of purchasing goods and adorning herself and her abode. Even wealthy husbands may have reacted against frivolous or wasteful expenditures. But if a man's income was consistently a measure below his wife's aspirations for comfortable living, the tension could become chronic and destroy a marriage that otherwise might have survived.

In the divorce proceedings, conflicts over status and mobility stand out in bold relief, particularly among white-collar families on the west coast. It is here that we can best perceive the intensified pressures placed upon men to supply heightened material desires. Norman Shinner, for example, admitted that he deserted his wife after five years of marriage because of his "inability to support her in the manner she desired on my salary, and on this account we could not live together in an amiable manner." Rather than struggling to meet up to his wife's aspirations, Norman Shinner simply left.

Oscar Lishnog faced similar difficulties. He married Martha in Chicago in 1908, and had four children prior to their Los Angeles divorce. While the Lishnogs appeared to be a fairly comfortable suburban family, financial strain ultimately caused their union to collapse. Oscar was in the insurance and real estate business, working as an employee or salesman rather than executive or proprietor. His income was steady but modest. He spent some time living apart from his family while working in San Pedro; nevertheless, Oscar and Martha exchanged frequent loving, chatty, but slightly distant letters to each other. He sent her money, she tried to save, and they expressed affection for one another. Now and then Martha would tell Oscar to "mind the store and not waste time or money." Revealing her material aspirations, she wrote that many of her neighbors owned automobiles, for there was no street car line nearby. This suggests that their Los Angeles home was in a fairly new suburban development, removed from the downtown district and transportation network. Martha also reminded her husband that she was paying mortgage on the house, and the "kids want a hammock." She usually closed with affection, saying she was "waiting for him."

But in 1920, Martha filed for divorce on the grounds of willful neglect, saying that Oscar spent his $35 per week salary in "riotous living away from his family," squandering his money while depriving his wife and children. Claiming that she was not skilled in any vocation, Martha said she had to rely on the charity of friends. She asked for custody of the children. Oscar denied the charges, insisting that he earned only $21 per week and gave it all to his wife except a small amount for living expenses. He asked that the divorce be denied, and, assuming that they would remain living apart, requested joint custody of the children. Nevertheless, the court granted Martha the divorce, plus custody, $9 per week for the children, and $3 per month for her "personal recreation." This final item, though minimal in amount, suggests that courts were willing to designate some money for amusements and consumption within the category of necessities—which men were required to provide. Whatever other problems may be hidden from our view that contributed to this couple's woes, it is clear that money was a sore spot for a long time. Oscar's salary was hardly abundant, and he was finally unable to supply the demands of his wife and children to maintain their suburban lifestyle.

Perhaps one of the most telling of these cases was the Los Angeles divorce of Margaret and Donald Wilton. She was a devout midwestern Protestant whose marriage to her clerk husband lasted two years. At one point, she wrote to her estranged spouse, hoping to be reconciled. She recommended that he read some bible passages relating to the duties of husbands and wives, and promised to be a "good Christian wife." In a revealing passage at the end, she wrote, "I heard something about you that made my heart sing with joy; you have climbed another rung on the ladder of success. I am proud to know it, dear...." In spite of Donald's improved status, their marriage was beyond repair. After a rather bitter case, Margaret Wilton was granted a divorce.

Families such as the ones mentioned above may not have suffered severe deprivation. But, like other 20th-century couples, they faced a greater potential for disappointment when a modicum of luxury became the anticipated norm. As the standard of living continued to climb, the golden age of affluence seemed imminent, and it was anticipated with almost religious fervor. For much of the American population, increasing prosperity appeared as a signal from the Divine that the culmination of progress was at hand. One observer perceived, "To most people a millennium implies spiritual overtones. So does the standard of living." For a male provider, then, inability to keep up with this sanctified progress meant failure and damnation.

Although these pressures were particularly acute for the lower middle class, they were also severe for workers. Financial difficulties among working-class couples, however, were qualitatively different from those facing white-collar families. Laborers faced a double-edged problem. They may not have felt the same status anxieties as petty proprietors or rank and file bureaucrats, but it was often difficult for them to make ends meet. Blue-collar families lived with the uncertainties of a fluid labor market and usually lacked the cushion of corporate security. Weak or non-existent labor unions left them virtually un-protected. This is not to deny the fact that some of the abundance filtered down among the working classes. By 1900, their improved circumstances prompted Samuel Gompers, when asked if he thought the conditions of workers were worsening, to reply, "Oh, that is perfectly absurd." In our samples, we find that financial conflicts among blue-collar families actually decreased somewhat between 1880 and 1920. However, their percentage of the total number of lit-igants increased markedly. This may reflect a number of factors. It is possible that in the 1880s, the very price of a divorce precluded legal action for many blue-collar couples. When they did come to court, nearly one-third of them included money conflicts among their complaints. By 1920, more workers may have been able to afford a divorce, and the wives might have been less likely to complain of financial desperation. Yet status and spending concerns might well have helped erode these unions as well. To add to the problem of meeting basic needs, working-class families also shared new consumer desires with their more affluent peers. But for those with meager incomes, luxuries were out of the question, and the affluence they saw everywhere around them only served to heighten frustrations.

Working-class couples, then, faced compounded difficulties. Often the breadwinner's earnings were inadequate and his job insecure. Moreover, he was subject to the same sorts of demands for mass-produced goods as his white-collar contemporaries. One of the crucial features of the consumer-oriented economy was the way it transcended class boundaries. On one level, this con-tributed to a certain superficial "classless" quality. But, on another level, it served to homogenize tastes in a society where wealth remained unequally dis-tributed. Once self-esteem and validation came to rest upon supplying material goods, those on the bottom rungs would be considered less worthy....

Alberta Raschke was a blue-collar wife in Los Angeles with a five-year-old daughter. She filed for a divorce on the grounds of desertion and neglect, claiming that her husband forced her to rely on her parents' charity. The couple married in Indiana in 1913, and separated four years later. At some point, Alberta came to California and William remained in Chicago. In a letter, she accused him of refusing to support her, and claimed that she was in a "weakened condi-tion." "You have had ample time to *make a man of yourself* in all these six years, if you cared for your wife and baby, instead of driving a wagon for $12 a week. You would not take work offered you at $21 a week, so it is not because you could not find better. I stood for all the terrible abuse you gave me, and went without the very necessities of life to see if you would not come to your senses, but now I am tired of waiting and have decided to file suit for divorce... I am as ever Alberta."

Although Alberta Raschke probably had a valid complaint, the pressure put upon William to "make a man" of himself may have been unfair. It is not clear why he did not take the job allegedly offered to him for more pay, but perhaps he simply enjoyed what he was doing. The conflict between working at a job one liked and working for money may have ultimately led to this divorce. Although William Raschke apparently found the lower paying job more satisfying, as far as his wife was concerned the primary purpose of his work was to make money. Undoubtedly, it was not easy for this woman to live on $12 a week with a five-year-old child. However, the equation of manhood with the ability to provide placed a particularly heavy burden on a working-class husband.

In general, working-class wives were less obsessed with status considerations and more concerned with bread and butter issues. Most blue-collar divorces that included money difficulties revolved around basic needs, similar to the conflicts that surfaced in the 1880s proceedings. These problems erupted frequently in New Jersey, where the majority of divorces were among blue-collar couples. It is important to keep in mind that New Jersey only permitted divorces on the grounds of adultery and desertion—not financial neglect. Nevertheless, money was at the heart of many New Jersey litigations. In fact, a number of these couples struggled, quite literally, just to keep a roof over their heads.

A severe housing shortage in urban areas placed serious strains on several marriages. Providers with meager earnings often found themselves unable to provide a home. Numerous couples lived with parents or other relatives, or moved from one form of lodging to another. For these couples, the inability to acquire adequate housing was the fundamental issue that destroyed their marriages. The Shafers were one such family. "I want one thing," pleaded Anna Shafer to her husband. "Won't you please come back and make a home for me, I don't care if it is only two rooms, if you can afford to pay for two rooms." They had been married since 1910, when they ran away together to Hoboken, New Jersey. Anna claimed that William deserted her three years later. She said that her husband was "a drinking man who never made a home or provided for her and their child," although he worked for an insurance company. Anna was granted a divorce and restored to her maiden name. The same problems ended the marriage of Harris and Catherine Martin, two blue-collar workers in Newark. "I told him I would go anyplace with him as long as he could furnish me with a home," explained Catherine. "I didn't care where it was, even if it was only one room and I was alone." But after three months they separated, and Catherine was granted a divorce plus the return of her maiden name.

Lack of housing and insecure work also disrupted the marriage of a Jewish couple in New Jersey, Sarah and Morris Dubin, who married in 1910, and had one child that died. Morris was a tailor by trade, but was unable to practice his craft. Instead, he worked for the railroad, and as a cook in a sanitarium. It appears that this duo had a rather stormy marriage, with Morris deserting now and then and Sarah continually begging him to make a home for her. Whenever she asked, "Why won't you make me a home and support me?" he replied, "I won't and can't live in Newark with you." Newark was particularly plagued by the housing shortage at this time, which aggravated the situation for Morris, who was unable to find work that utilized his tailoring skills. But the court had little mercy. The interviewer concluded that Morris was "apparently one of those people who find it difficult to settle down and perform his obligations for any length of time." Sarah won her suit and the return of her maiden name.

Although a chronic shortage of basic needs eroded most of these blue-collar marriages, a number of working-class couples quarreled over consumer spending and status concerns as well. A few cases illustrate how squabbles might ensue over how money should be spent. Emma Totsworth was 19 when she married David Totsworth, a 22-year-old machinist, in Jersey City. Five years later she deserted. When asked about their difficulties, David said they argued "over different things, like going out and clothes, no clean clothes and all around jealousy. Simple meanness. She spent money on clothes that should have gone for eating." It appears that David Totsworth preferred to see his hard-earned income used for less frivolous items.

Charles and Ada Davis were plagued by similar problems. They were married in New Jersey in 1902 and had one child. After nine years, Ada deserted and went to New York. Apparently Charles, a railroad brakeman, never managed to provide for her in the style that she wanted. According to the interviewer, Ada became "dissatisfied with her surroundings and complained of the style of life her husband afforded her. She wouldn't speak or recognize her husband sometimes for days at a time. Finally she left, saying she wanted to live where she wanted to, and also wanted him to support her." Charles' brother stood up for the aggrieved husband, saying that he "always worked steadily and was a good provider for his home and did everything he could for his wife and family that a man could do under his circumstances." But apparently it was not enough. Charles testified that Ada "insisted upon telling me how much more the neighbors had than she had, and what the neighbor's husband did, and what they didn't do. I told her that if she would stop listening to outsiders and live for me and our little girl as she had done up to that time, everything could be very nice and we could get along." But Ada's dissatisfaction increased until she finally left, and Charles was granted a New Jersey divorce on the grounds of desertion.

These blue-collar couples were plagued by status anxieties. Both Emma Totsworth and Ada Davis had aspirations for material goods beyond the reach of their husbands' pay checks. Some wives not only held their spouses' incomes in disdain, they also looked down upon the work itself. Olivia Garside was a New Jersey housekeeper bent on feverish social climbing. After 26 years of marriage and three children, she finally left her husband Frederick, a machinist, who could not supply the lifestyle she craved. According to Frederick,

> My wife never considered me her equal. She told me this shortly after her marriage, and she was never satisfied with anything I might undertake to do and that I was not as neat appearing as a professional man. She would say my conversation wasn't as it should be and she felt I was socially beneath her. I have always turned over every cent I made to my wife outside of my travelling expenses. I have never been intoxicated in my life. I would very

often work overtime and on Sundays around the neighborhood to earn a few
dollars more. My wife always complained I wasn't making enough money.

This husband took pride in his hard work, his efforts to support his wife, his
sobriety and discipline. But to his wife, he lacked polish and grace—and the ample income to go with it. The court granted Frederick a divorce on the grounds
of desertion.

The evidence in these cases suggests that mass consumption was not
necessarily a positive outgrowth of the society's industrial development, even
though it held the potential for increased financial security and a more comfortable lifestyle. Rather, these marital conflicts represent a failure or inability
to come to terms with the changing economic order. For affluent couples,
tensions emerged over how the family's resources should be spent. For those
among the lower-white-collar ranks, status considerations clashed with limited incomes, creating enormous pressures upon the family breadwinner. For
many working-class couples, mass consumption remained virtually out of
reach, contributing to a greater sense of economic insecurity and heightened
frustrations.

The testimonies of divorce litigants reflect the discrepancy between material desires and reality, for it was difficult to meet the soaring demands put
before every consumer's eyes. Perhaps many Americans did indeed benefit from
new opportunities created by the mature industrial system. But among those
whose marriages fell apart during these years, and undoubtedly among thousands more whose thoughts and feelings are beyond the reach of scholars, there
was a great deal of disappointment, disillusion, and despair that the good life
they had hoped for could not be grasped.

Jacquelyn Dowd Hall, Robert Korstad, and James Leloudis

Cotton Mill People

Textile mills built the New South. Beginning in the 1880s, business and professional men tied their hopes for prosperity to the whirring of spindles and the beating of looms. Small-town boosterism supplied the rhetoric of the mill-building campaign, but the impoverishment of farmers was industrialization's driving force. The post–Civil War rise of sharecropping, tenantry, and the crop lien ensnared freedmen, then eroded yeoman society. Farmers of both races fought for survival by clinging to subsistence strategies and habits of sharing even as they planted cash crops and succumbed to tenantry. Meanwhile, merchants who had accumulated capital through the crop lien invested in cotton mills. As the industry took off in an era of intensifying segregation, blacks were relegated to the land, and white farmers turned to yet another strategy for coping with economic change. They had sold their cotton to the merchant; now they supplied him with the human commodity needed to run his mills. This homegrown industry was soon attracting outside capital and underselling northern competitors. By the end of the Great Depression, the Southeast replaced New England as the world's leading producer of cotton cloth, and the industrializing Piedmont replaced the rural Coastal Plain as pacesetter for the region.

Despite the lasting imprint of textile manufacturing on regional development and labor relations, we have no modern survey of the industry's evolution. Nor has the outpouring of research on working-class history been much concerned with factory workers in the New South. To be sure, recent studies have uncovered sporadic, and sometimes violent, contention over the shape of the industrial South. But those findings have done little to shake the prevailing wisdom: The South's mill villages supposedly bred a "social type" compounded of irrationality, individualism, and fatalism. Unable to unite in their own interests, textile workers remained "silent, incoherent, with no agency to express their needs."

We have reached different conclusions. Our research began with a collaborative oral history project aimed at discovering how working people made sense of their own experience. We did not view memory as a direct window on the past. But we did presume the moral and intellectual value of listening to those who lacked access to power and, thus, the means of affecting historical debate.

Adapted from Jacquelyn Dowd Hall, Robert Korstad, and James Leloudis, "Cotton Mill People: Work, Community, and Protest in the Textile South, 1880–1940," *The American Historical Review*, vol. 91, no. 2 (April 1986). Copyright © 1986 by Jacquelyn Dowd Hall, Robert Korstad, and James Leloudis. Reprinted by permission of the authors. Notes omitted.

Our effort was repaid in two major ways. Oral autobiographies dissolved static images, replacing them with portrayals of mill village culture drawn by the men and women who helped create it. Workers' narratives also steered us away from psychological interpretations and toward patterns of resistance, cultural creativity, and structural evolution. Later we turned to the trade press, particularly the *Southern Textile Bulletin*. Published by David Clark in Charlotte, North Carolina, the *Bulletin* spoke for factory owners at the cutting edge of industrial innovation. Finally, from the eloquent letters textile workers wrote to Franklin D. Roosevelt and the National Recovery Administration, we gained a view of the New Deal from below. Together, retrospective and contemporary evidence revealed the social logic that underlay daily practices and suggested an analysis that distinguished one epoch from another in a broad process of technological, managerial, and cultural change.

❦

Nothing better symbolized the new industrial order than the mill villages that dotted the Piedmont landscape. Individual families and small groups of local investors built and owned most of the early mills. Run by water wheels, factories flanked the streams that fell rapidly from the mountains toward the Coastal Plain. Of necessity, owners provided housing where none had been before. But the setting, scale, and structure of the mill village reflected rural expectations as well as practical considerations. Typically, a three-story brick mill, a company store, and a superintendent's house were clustered at one end of the village. Three- and four-room frame houses, owned by the company but built in a vernacular style familiar in the countryside, stood on lots that offered individual garden space, often supplemented by communal pastures and hog pens. A church, a company store, and a modest schoolhouse completed the scene. By 1910 steam power and electricity had freed the mills from their dependence on water power, and factories sprang up on the outskirts of towns along the route of the Southern Railway. Nevertheless, the urban mill village retained its original rural design. Company-owned villages survived in part because they fostered management control. Unincorporated "mill hills" that surrounded towns such as Charlotte and Burlington, North Carolina, and Greenville, South Carolina, enabled owners to avoid taxes and excluded workers from municipal government. But the mill village also reflected the workers' heritage and served their needs.

Like the design of the mill village, the family labor system helped smooth the path from field to factory. On farms women and children had always provided essential labor, and mill owners took advantage of these traditional roles. They promoted factory work as a refuge for impoverished women and children from the countryside, hired family units rather than individuals, and required the labor of at least one worker per room as a condition for residence in a mill-owned house. But this labor system also dovetailed with family strategies. The first to arrive in the mills were those least essential to farming and most vulnerable to the hazards of commercial agriculture: widows, female heads of households, single women, and itinerant laborers. By the turn of the century, families headed by men also lost their hold on the land. Turning to the mills, they sought not a "family wage" that would enable a man to support his dependents but an arena in which parents and children could work together as they had always done.

The deployment of family labor also helped maintain permeable boundaries between farm and mill. The people we interviewed moved with remarkable ease from farming to mill work and back again or split their family's time between the two. James Pharis's father raised tobacco in the Leaksville-Spray area of North Carolina until most of his six children were old enough to obtain mill jobs. The family moved to a mill village in the 1890s because the elder Pharis "felt that all we had to do when we come to town was to reach up and pull the money off of the trees." From the farm Pharis saved his most valuable possession: his team of horses. While the children worked in the mill, he raised vegetables on a plot of rented ground and used his team to do "hauling around for people." Betty Davidson's landowning parents came up with the novel solution of sharing a pair of looms. "My father would run the looms in the wintertime," Davidson remembered, "and go to and from work by horseback. And in the summertime, when he was farming, my mother run the looms, and she stayed in town because she couldn't ride the horse. Then, on the weekends, she would come home."

This ability to move from farming to factory work—or combine the two—postponed a sharp break with rural life. It also gave mill workers a firm sense of alternative identity and leverage against a boss's demands. Lee Workman recalled his father's steadfast independence. In 1918 the superintendent of a nearby cotton mill came to the Workmans' farm in search of workers to help him meet the demand for cloth during World War I. The elder Workman sold his mules and cow but, contrary to the superintendent's advice, held on to his land. Each spring he returned to shoe his neighbors' horses, repair their wagons and plows, and fashion the cradles they used to harvest grain. "He'd tell the superintendent, 'You can just get somebody else, because I'm going back to make cradles for my friends.' Then he'd come back in the wintertime and work in the mill." This type of freedom did not sit well with the mill superintendent, but the elder Workman had the upper hand. " 'Well,' he told them, 'if you don't want to do that, I'll move back to the country and take the family.' "

Although Lee Workman's father periodically retreated to the farm, his sons and daughters, along with thousands of others, eventually came to the mills to stay. There they confronted an authority more intrusive than anything country folk had experienced before. In Bynum, North Carolina, the mill owner supervised the Sunday School and kept tabs on residents' private lives. "If you stubbed your toe they'd fire you. They'd fire them here for not putting out the lights late at night. Old Mr. Bynum used to go around over the hill at nine o'clock and see who was up. And, if you were up, he'd knock on the door and tell you to cut the lights out and get into bed." Along with surveillance came entanglement with the company story. Mill hands all too familiar with the crop lien once again found themselves in endless debt. Don Faucette's father often talked about it. "Said if you worked at the mill they'd just take your wages and put it in the company store and you didn't get nothing. For years and years they didn't get no money, just working for the house they lived in and what they got at the company store. They just kept them in the hole all the time."

The mill village undeniably served management's interests, but it also nurtured a unique workers' culture. When Piedmont farmers left the land and took a cotton mill job, they did not abandon old habits and customs. Instead, they fashioned familiar ways of thinking and acting into a distinctively new way of life. This adaptation occurred at no single moment in time; rather, it evolved, shaped and reshaped by successive waves of migration off the farm as well as the movement of workers from mill to mill. Village life was based on family ties. Kinship networks facilitated migration to the mill and continued to play a powerful integrative role. Children of the first generation off the land married newcomers of the second and third, linking households into broad networks of obligation, responsibility, and concern. For many couples, marriage evolved out of friendships formed while growing up in the village. One married worker recalled, "We knowed each other from childhood. Just raised up together, you might say. All lived here on the hill, you see, that's how we met." As single workers arrived, they, too, were incorporated into the community. Mary Thompson explained that the boarding houses run by widowed women and older couples "were kind of family like. There ain't no place like home, but I guess that's the nearest place like home there is, a boarding house." Mill folk commonly used a family metaphor to describe village life. Hoyle McCorkle remembered the Highland Park mill village in Charlotte as a single household knit together by real and fictive kin: "It was kind of one big family; it was a 200-house family."

Mill hands also brought subsistence strategies from the countryside, modifying them to meet mill village conditions. Just as farmers had tried to bypass the furnishing merchant, mill workers struggled to avoid "living out of a tin can." Edna Hargett's father planted a large garden every spring but could not afford a mule to help till the land. He made do by putting a harness around himself and having his children "stand behind and guide the plow." Louise Jones's family also gardened and raised "homemade meat." Her parents "had a big garden and a corn patch and a few chickens around the yard. We'd have maybe six or eight hens, and we'd let the hens set on the eggs and hatch chickens and have frying-size chickens, raise our own fryers." Self-sufficiency, however, was difficult to achieve, especially when every family member was working a ten- to twelve-hour day for combined wages that barely made ends meet. Even with their gardens, few families could sustain a varied diet through the winter months. As a result, pellagra was a scourge in the mill villages. Life was lived close to the bone.

Under these conditions, necessity and habit fostered rural traditions of mutual aid. Although each family claimed a small plot of land, villagers shared what they grew and "live[d] in common." In late summer and early fall, they gathered for the familiar rituals of harvest and hog killing. Paul and Don Faucette remembered how it was done in Glencoe, North Carolina. "We'd kill our hogs this time, and a month later we'd kill yours. Well, you can give us some, and we can give you some. They'd have women get together down in the church basement. They'd have a quilting bee, and they'd go down and they'd all quilt. They'd have a good crop of cabbage, [and] they'd get together and all make kraut." Villagers helped one another, not with an expectation of immediate return but with the assurance of community support in meeting their individual needs. "They'd just visit around and work voluntarily. They all done it, and nobody owed nobody nothing."

Cooperation provided a buffer against misery and want at a time when state welfare services were limited and industrialists often refused to assume responsibility for job-related sickness and injury. It bound people together and reduced their dependence on the mill owners' charity. When someone fell ill, neighbors were quick to give the stricken family a "pounding." "They'd all get together and help. They'd cook food and carry it to them—all kinds of food— fruits, vegetables, canned goods." Villagers also aided sick neighbors by taking up a "love offering" in the mill. Edna Hargett organized such collections in the weave room at the Chadwick-Hoskins Mill in Charlotte. "When the neighbors got paid they'd come and pay us, and we'd take their money and give it to [the family of the weaver who was ill], and they'd be so proud of it, because they didn't have any wage coming in." To the people we interviewed, the village was "just one big community and one big family" whose members "all kind of hung together and survived."

Community solidarity did not come without a price. Neighborliness could shade into policing; it could repress as well as sustain. Divorced women and children born out of wedlock might be ostracized, and kinship ties could give mill supervisors an intelligence network that reached into every corner of the village. Alice Evitt of Charlotte remarked that "people then couldn't do like they do now. They was talked about. My daddy would never allow us to be with people that was talked about. This was the nicest mill hill I ever lived on. If anybody done anything wrong and you reported them, they had to move." A Bynum proverb summed up the double-edged quality of village life. "If you went along, they'd tend to their business and yours, too, if you let them, your neighbors would. Tend to your business and theirs, too. And the old saying here, you know, 'Bynum's red mud. If you stick to Bynum, it'll stick to you when it rains.' "

Given such tensions, we were struck by how little ambivalence surfaced in descriptions of mill village life. Recollections of factory work were something else again, but the village—red mud and all—was remembered with affection. The reasons are not hard to find. A commitment to family and friends represented a realistic appraisal of working people's prospects in the late nineteenth- and early twentieth-century South. Only after World War II, with the expansion of service industries, did the Piedmont offer alternatives to low-wage factory work to more than a lucky few. Until then, casting one's lot with others offered more promise and certainly more security than the slim hope of individual gain. To be sure, mill people understood the power of money; they struggled against dependency and claimed an economic competence as their due. Nevertheless, they had "their own ideas . . . about what constitute[d] the 'good life.'" Communal values, embodied in everyday behavior, distance mill folk from the acquisitiveness that characterized middle-class life in New South towns. . . .

◈

The physical and social geography of the mill village . . . was less a product of owners' designs than a compromise between capitalist organization and workers' needs. For a more clear-cut embodiment of the manufacturers' will, we must look to the factory. The ornate facades of nineteenth-century textile mills reflected their builders' ambitions and the orderly world they hoped to create. The mill that still stands at Glencoe is an excellent example. Situated only a few hundred yards from the clapboard houses that make up the village, the mill is a three-story structure complete with "stair tower, corbelled cornice, quoined stucco corners, and heavily stuccoed window labels." In contrast to the vernacular form of the village, the architecture of the factory, modeled on that of New England's urban mills, was highly self-conscious, formal, and refined.

At Glencoe, and in mills throughout the Piedmont, manufacturers endeavored to shape the southern yeomanry into a tractable industrial workforce. Workers' attitudes toward factory labor, like those toward village life, owed much to the cycles and traditions of the countryside. Owners, on the other hand, sought to substitute for cooperation and task orientation a labor system controlled from the top down and paced by the regular rhythms of the machine. Barring adverse market conditions, work in the mills varied little from day to day and season to season. Workers rose early in the morning, still tired from the day before, and readied themselves for more of the same. For ten, eleven, and twelve hours they walked, stretched, leaned, and pulled at their machines. Noise, heat, and humidity engulfed them. The lint that settled on their hair and skin marked them as mill workers to the outside world. The cotton dust that silently entered their lungs could also kill them.

Owners enforced this new pattern of labor with the assistance of a small coterie of supervisors. As a rule, manufacturers delegated responsibility for organizing work and disciplining the help to a superintendent and his overseers and second hands. A second hand in a pre–World War I mill recalled, "You had the cotton, the machinery, and the people, and you were supposed to get out the production. How you did it was pretty much up to you; it was production management was interested in and not how you got it." Under these circumstances, supervision was a highly personal affair; there were as many different approaches to its problems as there were second hands and overseers. As one observer explained, "There was nothing that could be identified as a general pattern of supervisory practice."

At times, discipline could be harsh, erratic, and arbitrary. This was particularly true before 1905, when most workers in southern mills were women and children. Even supervisors writing in the *Southern Textile Bulletin* admitted that "some overseers, second hands, and section men have a disposition to abuse the help. Whoop, holler, curse, and jerk the children around." James Pharis remembered that "you used to work for the supervisor because you were scared. I seen a time when I'd walk across the road to keep from meeting my supervisor. They was the hat-stomping kind. If you done anything, they'd throw their hat on the floor and stomp it and raise hell."

In the absence of either state regulation or trade unions, management's power seemed limitless, but there were, in fact, social and structural constraints. Although manufacturers relinquished day-to-day authority to underlings, they were ever-present figures, touring the mill, making decisions on wages and production quotas, and checking up on the help. These visits were, in part, attempts to maintain the appearance of paternalism and inspire hard work and company loyalty. At the same time, they divided power in the mill. Workers had direct access to the owner and sometimes saw him as a buffer between themselves and supervisors, a "force that could bring an arbitrary and unreasonable [overseer] back into line." Mack Duncan recalled that in the early years "most all the mill owners seemed like they had a little milk of human kindness about them, but some of the people they hired didn't. Some of the managers didn't have that. They were bad to exploit people." Under these circumstances, the commands of an overseer were always subject to review. Workers felt free to complain about unjust treatment, and owners, eager to keep up production, sometimes reversed their lieutenants' orders. Federal labor investigators reported in 1910 that "when an employee is dissatisfied about mill conditions he may obtain a hearing from the chief officer of the mill . . . and present his side of the case. Not infrequently when complaints are thus made, the overseer is overruled and the operative upheld." . . .

⁂

[The] tradeoff between a relatively relaxed work pace on the one hand and long hours and low wages on the other was tenuous at best. Despite manufacturers' efforts to create a secure world in the mill and village, there were recurrent symptoms of unrest. During the 1880s and 1890s, southern mill hands turned first to the Knights of Labor and then to the National Union of Textile Workers (NUTW) to defend their "freedom and liberty." In 1900 an intense conflict led by the NUTW flared in Alamance County, center of textile manufacturing in North Carolina, when an overseer at the Haw River Mill fired a female weaver for leaving her loom unattended. The next day, September 28, union members "threw up" their machines, defending the woman's right to "go when she pleased and where she pleased." By mid-October, workers at other mills throughout the county had joined in a sympathy strike.

The mill owners, conveniently overstocked with surplus goods, posted armed guards around their factories, declared they would employ only nonunion labor, and threatened to evict union members from company-owned houses. Undeterred, the workers resolved to stand together as "free men and free women"; five thousand strong, they brought production in Alamance mills virtually to a halt. But by the end of November evictions had overwhelmed the NUTW's relief fund, and the Alamance mill hands were forced to accept a settlement on management's terms.

The Haw River strike capped more than two decades of unrest. During those years, Populists and factory laborers challenged the power of planters, merchants, and industrialists. Between 1895 and 1902, southern Democrats turned to race baiting, fraud, and intimidation to destroy this interracial movement. The passage of state constitutional amendments disfranchising blacks and many poor whites, accompanied by a flurry of Jim Crow laws, restructured the political system, narrowing the terms of public discourse, discouraging lower-class political participation, and making it impossible for opposition movements to survive.

As prospects for collective protest diminished, Piedmont mill hands opted for a personal strategy as old as the industry itself—relocation. In Alamance County alone, more than three hundred workers left to find new jobs in south Carolina and Georgia. "Among them," reported the *Alamance Gleaner,* "are a great many excellent people who prefer to go elsewhere rather than surrender rights and privileges which they as citizens deem they should own and enjoy." In choosing to leave in search of better conditions, the Haw River workers set a pattern for decades to come. Until the end of World War I, quitting was textile workers' most effective alternative to public protest or acquiescence. One student of the southern textile industry declared that a mill hand's "ability to move at a moment's notice was his Magna Carta, Declaration of Independence, and Communist Manifesto."

This movement from job to job could be touched off by any number of factors—curtailed production, a promise of higher wages, or a simple desire to move on—but it could also be a response to a perceived abuse of authority. Josephine Glenn of Burlington explained. "A lot of people in textile mills come and go. They're more or less on a cycle. They're not like that as a whole, but a lot of them are. They're dissatisfied, you might say, restless. They just go somewhere and work awhile, and, if everything don't go just like they think it should, why, they walk out. Sometimes they'd be mad, and sometimes they'd just get on a bender and just not come back. Maybe something personal, or maybe something about the work, or just whatever they got mad about. They'd just [say], 'I've had it,' and that was it." Workers expected to be treated with respect; when it was lacking, they left. George Dyer of Charlotte offered this advice: "Sometimes some boss don't like you, gets it in for you. It's best then just to quit. Don't work under conditions like that. I didn't want to work under a man that don't respect me."

The decision to move was usually made by men, and it could be hard on women and children. Family ties could fray under the wear and tear of factory life. Although Edna Hargett also worked in the mills, she was evicted from her house every time her husband quit his job. "He was bad about getting mad and quitting. He was just hot-tempered and didn't like it when they wanted to take him off his job and put him on another job. When you work in the card room, you have to know how to run about every piece of machinery in there. He liked to be a slubber, and they wanted to put him on drawing or something else. Well, he didn't like to do that." Edna understood her husband's motives but finally left to settle down and rear their children on her own.

Divorce, however, was uncommon. Most families stayed together, and their moves from mill to mill were facilitated by kinship and cushioned by community. A study completed in the late 1920s revealed that 41 percent of mill families had moved less than three times in ten years. Most settled families were headed by middle-aged men and women who had "just kept the road hot" before and immediately after marriage and had then stayed in a village they liked. This relatively stable core of residents made movement possible by providing the contacts through which other workers learned of job opportunities. Established residents also mitigated the ill effects of transiency and preserved ways of life that made it easy for newcomers to feel at home. Women played central roles in this process, keeping up with the events in the village, coordinating informal acts of relief, and keeping the web of social relations intact.

In these ways, the Piedmont became what journalist Arthur W. Page described in 1907 as "one long mill village." Individual communities were woven together—through kinship, shared occupational experiences, and popular culture—into an elaborate regional fabric. According to Lacy Wright, who worked at Greensboro's White Oak Mill, "We had a pretty fair picture, generally speaking, of what you might say was a 200-mile radius of Greensboro. News traveled by word of mouth faster than any other way in those days, because that's the only way we had. In other words, if something would happen at White Oak this week, you could go over to Danville, Virginia, by the weekend and they'd done heard about it. It looked like it always worked out that there would be somebody or another that would carry that information all around." Rooted in a regional mill village culture, workers like Wright took the entire Piedmont as their frame of reference.

POSTSCRIPT

Did the Industrial Revolution Disrupt the American Family?

In his study of family life in Plymouth Colony, John Demos identifies six important functions performed by the family in preindustrial America. As the central social unit, says Demos, the family served as business, school, vocational institute, church, house of correction, and welfare institution. This pattern prevailed for the most part until the Industrial Revolution when these traditional functions began to be delegated to institutions outside the household. For example, children received their formal education in public schools and private academies established for that purpose, rather than from their parents. Similarly, religious instruction occurred more often than not in a church building on Sunday morning, not in a home where family members gathered around a table for Bible readings. The explanation for this change is that work opportunities existed outside the home, and various family members were spending less and less time in the physical presence of one another because of the exigencies of the industrial workplace. See John Demos, *A Little Commonwealth: Family Life in Plymouth Colony* (Oxford University Press, 1970) and *Past, Present, and Personal: The Family and the Life Course in American History* (Oxford University Press, 1986).

May's work offers a variation of Demos's interpretation by focusing upon the destructive influence of industrialization on the family, but May is less concerned with the altered functions of the family than with the powerful influence of heightened expectations of the acquisition of material wealth. Hall, Korstad, and Leloudis, on the other hand, suggest that the changes produced in American families were not as drastic as some scholars believe. Their portrait of cotton mill workers reveals significant levels of continuity with the rural past and the family labor patterns that were not all that different from those described by Demos for seventeenth-century Plymouth.

The study of the history of families is an outgrowth of the "new social history" that began to emerge in the 1960s. Since that time, scholars have devoted considerable attention to such topics as changing household structure and the influence of economic forces on family units and individual family members. For a general summary of the scholarly attention given to the American family, see Estelle B. Freedman's essay "The History of the Family and the History of Sexuality," in Eric Foner, ed., *The New American History*, rev. and exp. ed. (Temple University Press, 1997). Carl Degler, *At Odds: Women and the Family in America* (Oxford University Press, 1980); Steven Mintz and Susan Kellogg, *Domestic Revolutions: A Social History of American Family Life* (Free Press,

1988); and Stephanie Coontz, *The Social Origins of Private Life: A History of American Families, 1600–1900* (Verso, 1988) present introductory surveys of American family history. May expands the coverage of some of the issues explored in her essay in *Great Expectations: Marriage and Divorce in Post-Victorian America* (University of Chicago Press, 1980). Additional works addressing southern families in the industrial era include Carol Bleser, ed., *In Joy and in Sorrow: Women, Family, and Marriage in the Victorian South* (Oxford University Press, 1991) and Peter Bardaglio, *Reconstructing the Household: Families, Sex and the Law in the Nineteenth-Century South* (University of North Carolina Press, 1995). Tamara Hareven, *Family Time and Industrial Time: The Relationship Between the Family and Work in a New England Industrial Community* (Cambridge University Press, 1982) and Michael Grossberg, *Governing the Hearth: Law and the Family in Nineteenth-Century America* (University of North Carolina Press, 1985) are important monographs of the industrial era. For studies of family life among African Americans and immigrants, see E. Franklin Frazier, *The Negro Family in the United States* (University of Chicago Press, 1939); Herbert G. Gutman, *The Black Family in Slavery and Freedom, 1750–1925* (Pantheon, 1976); Virginia Yans McLaughlin, *Family and Community: Italian Immigrants in Buffalo, 1880–1930* (Cornell University Press, 1977); and Judith Smith, *Family Connections: A History of Italian and Jewish Immigrant Lives in Providence, Rhode Island, 1900–1940* (State University of New York Press, 1985). Finally, for the past quarter century, cutting-edge scholarship on the American family has appeared in the issues of the *Journal of Family History*.

ISSUE 4

Were American Workers in the Gilded Age Conservative Capitalists?

YES: Carl N. Degler, from *Out of Our Past: The Forces That Shaped Modern America*, 3rd ed. (Harper & Row, 1984)

NO: Herbert G. Gutman, from *Work, Culture, and Society in Industrializing America: Essays in American Working-Class and Social History* (Alfred A. Knopf, 1976)

ISSUE SUMMARY

YES: Professor of history Carl N. Degler maintains that the American labor movement accepted capitalism and reacted conservatively to the radical organizational changes brought about in the economic system by big business.

NO: Professor of history Herbert G. Gutman argues that from 1843 to 1893, American factory workers attempted to humanize the system through the maintenance of their traditional, artisan, preindustrial work habits.

The two major labor unions that developed in the late nineteenth century were the Knights of Labor and the American Federation of Labor. Because of hostility toward labor unions, the Knights of Labor functioned for 12 years as a secret organization. Between 1879 and 1886 the Knights of Labor grew from 10,000 to 700,000 members. Idealistic in many of its aims, the union supported social reforms such as equal pay for men and women, the prohibition of alcohol, and the abolition of convict and child labor. Economic reforms included the development of workers' cooperatives, public ownership of utilities, and a more moderate, eight-hour workday. The Knights declined after 1886 for several reasons. Although it was opposed to strikes, the union received a black eye (as did the whole labor movement) when it was blamed for the bombs that were thrown at the police during the 1886 Haymarket Square riot in Chicago. According to most historians, other reasons that are usually associated with the decline of the Knights include the failure of some cooperative businesses, conflict between skilled and unskilled workers, and, most important, competition from the American Federation of Labor. By 1890 the Knight's membership had dropped to 100,000. It died in 1917.

A number of skilled unions got together in 1896 and formed the American Federation of Labor (AFL). Samuel Gompers was elected its first president, and his philosophy permeated the AFL during his 37 years in office. He pushed for practical reforms—better hours, wages, and working conditions. Unlike the Knights, the AFL avoided associations with political parties, workers' cooperatives, unskilled workers, immigrants, and women. Decision-making power was in the hands of locals rather than the central board. Gompers was heavily criticized by his contemporaries, and later by historians, for his narrow craft unionism. But despite the depression of the 1890s, membership increased from 190,000 to 500,000 by 1900, to 1,500,000 by 1904, and to 2,000,000 by the eve of World War I.

Gompers's cautiousness is best understood in the context of his times. The national and local governments were in the hands of men who were sympathetic to the rise of big business and hostile to the attempts of labor to organize. Whether it was the railroad strike of 1877, the Homestead steel strike of 1892, or the Pullman car strike of 1894, the pattern of repression was always the same. Companies would cut wages, workers would go out on strike, scab workers would be brought in, fights would break out, companies would receive court injunctions, and the police and state and federal militia would beat up the unionized workers. After a strike was broken, workers would lose their jobs or would accept pay cuts and longer workdays.

On the national level, Theodore Roosevelt became the first president to show any sympathy for the workers. As a police commissioner in New York City and later as governor of New York, Roosevelt observed firsthand the deplorable occupational and living conditions of the workers. Although he avoided recognition of the collective bargaining rights of labor unions, Roosevelt forced the anthracite coal owners in Pennsylvania to mediate before an arbitration board for an equitable settlement of a strike with the mine workers.

In 1905 a coalition of socialists and industrial unionists formed America's most radical labor union: the Industrial Workers of the World (IWW). There were frequent splits within this union and much talk of violence. But in practice, the IWW was more interested in organizing workers into industrial unions than in fighting, as were the earlier Knights of Labor and the later Congress of Industrial Organizations. Strikes were encouraged to improve the daily conditions of the workers through long-range goals, which included reducing the power of the capitalists by increasing the power of the workers.

Were the American workers of the Gilded Age conservative supporters of American capitalism? In the following selection, Carl N. Degler argues in the affirmative. He concludes that, led by the bread-and-butter leader of the American Federation of Labor, Samuel Gompers, the American worker sought a larger slice of the profits in the form of better hours, wages, and benefits. In the second selection, however, Herbert G. Gutman argues that in the Gilded Age, the American worker tried to humanize the factory system through the maintenance of traditional, cultural, artisan, preindustrial work habits.

Carl N. Degler

 **YES**

Out of Our Past

The Workers' Response

To say that the labor movement was affected by the industrialization of the postwar years is an understatement; the fact is, industrial capitalism created the labor movement. Not deliberately, to be sure, but in the same way that a blister is the consequence of a rubbing shoe. Unions were labor's protection against the forces of industrialization as the blister is the body's against the irritation of the shoe. The factory and all it implied confronted the workingman with a challenge to his existence as a man, and the worker's response was the labor union.

There were labor unions in America before 1865, but, as industry was only emerging in those years, so the organizations of workers were correspondingly weak. In the course of years after Appomattox, however, when industry began to hit a new and giant stride, the tempo of unionization also stepped up. It was in these decades, after many years of false starts and utopian ambitions, that the American labor movement assumed its modern shape.

Perhaps the outstanding and enduring characteristic of organized labor in the United States has been its elemental conservatism, the fantasies of some employers to the contrary notwithstanding. Indeed, it might be said that all labor unions, at bottom, are conservative by virtue of their being essentially reactions against a developing capitalism. Though an established capitalist society views itself as anything but subversive, in the days of its becoming and seen against the perspective of the previous age, capitalism as an ideology is radically subversive, undermining and destroying many of the cherished institutions of the functioning society. This dissolving process of capitalism is seen more clearly in Europe than in America because there the time span is greater. But, as will appear later, organized labor in the United States was as much a conservative response to the challenge of capitalism as was the European trade union movement.

Viewed very broadly, the history of modern capitalism might be summarized as the freeing of the three factors of production—land, labor, and capital —from the web of tradition in which medieval society held them. If capitalism was to function, it was necessary that this liberating process take place.

Only when these basic factors are free to be bought and sold according to the dictates of the profit motive can the immense production which capitalism promises be realized. An employer, for example, had to be free to dismiss labor when the balance sheet required it, without being compelled to retain workers because society or custom demanded it. Serfdom, with its requirement that the peasant could not be taken from the land, was an anachronistic institution if capitalism was to become the economic ideology of society. Conversely, an employer needed to be unrestricted in his freedom to hire labor or else production could not expand in accordance with the market. Guild restrictions which limited apprenticeships were therefore obstacles to the achievement of a free capitalism.

The alienability of the three factors of production was achieved slowly and unevenly after the close of the Middle Ages. By the nineteenth century in most nations of the West, land had become absolutely alienable—it could be bought and sold at will. With the growth of banking, the development of trustworthy monetary standards, and finally the gold standard in the nineteenth century, money or capital also became freely exchangeable. Gradually, over the span of some two centuries, the innovating demands of capitalism stripped from labor the social controls in which medieval and mercantilistic government had clothed it. Serfdom as an obstacle to the free movement of labor was gradually done away with; statutes of laborers and apprenticeships which fixed wages, hours, and terms of employment also fell into disuse or suffered outright repeal. To avoid government interference in the setting of wage rates, the English Poor Law of 1834 made it clear that the dole to the unemployed was always to be lower than the going rate for unskilled labor. Thus supply and demand would be the determinant of wage levels. Both the common law and the Combination Acts in the early nineteenth century in England sought to ensure the operation of a free market in labor by declaring trade unions to be restraints on trade.

Like land and capital, then, labor was being reduced to a commodity, freely accessible, freely alienable, free to flow where demand was high. The classical economists of the nineteenth century analyzed this long historical process, neatly put it together, and called it the natural laws of economics.

To a large extent, this historical development constituted an improvement in the worker's status, since medieval and mercantilist controls over labor had been more onerous than protective. Nevertheless, something was lost by the dissolution of the ancient social ties which fitted the worker into a larger social matrix. Under the old relationship, the worker belonged in society; he enjoyed a definite if not a high status; he had a place. Now he was an individual, alone; his status was up to him to establish; his urge for community with society at large had no definite avenue of expression. Society and labor alike had been atomized in pursuit of an individualist economy. Herein lay the radical character of the capitalist ideology.

That the workingman sensed the radical change and objected to it is evident from what some American labor leaders said about their unions. Without rejecting the new freedom which labor enjoyed, John Mitchell, of the Mine Workers, pointed out that the union "stands for fraternity, complete and absolute." Samuel Gompers' eulogy of the social microcosm which was the trade union has the same ring. "A hundred times we have said it," he wrote, "and we say it again, that trade unionism contains within itself the potentialities of working class regeneration." The union is a training ground for democracy and provides "daily object lessons in ideal justice; it breathes into the working classes the spirit of unity"; but above all, it affords that needed sense of community. The labor union "provides a field for noble comradeship, for deeds of loyalty, for self-sacrifice beneficial to one's fellow-workers." In the trade union, in short, the workers could obtain another variety of that sense of community, of comradeship, as Gompers put it, which the acid of individualistic capitalism had dissolved.

And there was another objection to the transformation of labor into an exchangeable commodity. The theoretical justification for the conversion of the factors of production into commodities is that the maximum amount of goods can be produced under such a regime. The increased production is deemed desirable because it would insure greater amounts of goods for human consumption and therefore a better life for all. Unfortunately for the theory, however, labor cannot be separated from the men who provide it. To make labor a commodity is to make the men who provide labor commodities also. Thus one is left with the absurdity of turning men into commodities in order to give men a better life! ...

Seen in this light, the trade union movement stands out as a truly conservative force. Almost instinctively, the workers joined labor unions in order to preserve their humanity and social character against the excessively individualistic doctrines of industrial capitalism. Eventually, the workers' organizations succeeded in halting the drive to the atomized society which capitalism demanded, and in doing so, far from destroying the system, compelled it to be humane as well as productive.

The essential conservatism of the labor movement is to be seen in particular as well as in general. The organizations of American labor that triumphed or at least survived in the course of industrialization were conspicuous for their acceptance of the private property, profit-oriented society. They evinced little of the radical, anticapitalist ideology and rhetoric so common among European trade unions. Part of the reason for this was the simple fact that all Americans —including workers—were incipient capitalists waiting for "the break." But at bottom it would seem that the conservatism of American labor in this sense is the result of the same forces which inhibited the growth of socialism and other radical anticapitalist ideologies. ...

"The overshadowing problem of the American labor movement," an eminent labor historian has written, "has always been the problem of staying organized. No other labor movement has ever had to contend with the fragility so characteristic of American labor organizations." So true has this been that even today the United States ranks below Italy and Austria in percentage of workers organized (about 25 per cent as compared, for instance, with Sweden's 90 per cent). In such an atmosphere, the history of organized labor in America has been both painful and conservative. Of the two major national organizations of workers which developed in the latter half of the nineteenth century, only the cautious, restrictive, pragmatic American Federation of Labor [A.F. of

L.] lived into the twentieth century. The other, the Knights of Labor, once the more powerful and promising, as well as the less accommodating in goals and aspirations, succumbed to Selig Perlman's disease of fragility.

Founded in 1869, the Noble Order of the Knights of Labor recorded its greatest successes in the 1880's, when its membership rolls carried 700,000 names. As the A.F. of L. was later to define the term for Americans, the Knights did not seem to constitute a legitimate trade union at all. Anyone who worked, except liquor dealers, bankers, lawyers, and physicians, could join, and some thousands of women workers and Negroes were members in good standing of this brotherhood of toilers. But the crucial deviation of the Knights from the more orthodox approach to labor organization was its belief in worker-owned producers' co-operatives, which were intended to make each worker his own employer. In this way, the order felt, the degrading dependence of the worker upon the employer would be eliminated. "There is no good reason," Terence V. Powderly, Grand Master Workman of the order, told his followers, "why labor cannot, through co-operation, own and operate mines, factories and railroads."

In this respect the order repudiated the direction in which the America of its time was moving. It expressed the small-shopkeeper mentality which dominated the thinking of many American workers, despite the obvious trend in the economy toward the big and the impersonal. As the General Assembly of 1884 put it, "our Order contemplates a radical change, while Trades' Unions... accept the industrial system as it is, and endeavor to adapt themselves to it. The attitude of our Order to the existing industrial system is necessarily one of war." Though the order called this attitude "radical," a more accurate term, in view of the times, would have been "conservative" or "reactionary."

In practice, however, the Knights presented no more of a threat to capitalism than any other trade union. Indeed, their avowed opposition to the strike meant that labor's most potent weapon was only reluctantly drawn from the scabbard. The Constitution of 1884 said, "Strikes at best afford only temporary relief"; members should learn to depend on education, co-operation, and political action to attain "the abolition of the wage system."

Though the order officially joined in political activity and Grand Master Workman Powderly was at one time mayor of Scranton, its forays into politics accomplished little. The experience was not lost on shrewd Samuel Gompers, whose American Federation of Labor studiously eschewed any alignments with political parties, practicing instead the more neutral course of "rewarding friends and punishing enemies."

In a farewell letter in 1893, Powderly realistically diagnosed the ills of his moribund order, but offered no cure: "Teacher of important and much-needed reforms, she has been obliged to practice differently from her teachings. Advocating arbitration and conciliation as first steps in labor disputes she has been forced to take upon her shoulders the responsibilities of the aggressor first and, when hope of arbitrating and conciliation failed, to beg of the opposing side to do what we should have applied for in the first instance. Advising against strikes we have been in the midst of them. While not a political party we have been forced into the attitude of taking political action."

For all its fumblings, ineptitude, and excessive idealism, the Knights did organize more workers on a national scale than had ever been done before. At once premature and reactionary, it nonetheless planted the seeds of industrial unionism which, while temporarily overshadowed by the successful craft organization of the A.F. of L., ultimately bore fruit in the C.I.O. [Committee for Industrial Organization]. Moreover, its idealism, symbolized in its admission of Negroes and women, and more in tune with the mid-twentieth century than the late nineteenth, signified its commitment to the ideals of the democratic tradition. For these reasons the Knights were a transitional type of unionism, somewhere between the utopianism of the 1830's and the pragmatism of the A.F. of L. It seemed to take time for labor institutions to fit the American temper.

In the course of his long leadership of the American Federation of Labor, Samuel Gompers welcomed many opportunities to define the purposes of his beloved organization....

"The trade unions are the business organizations of the wage-earners," Gompers explained in 1906, "to attend to the business of the wage-earners." Later he expressed it more tersely: "The trade union is not a Sunday school. It is an organization of wage-earners, dealing with economic, social, political and moral questions." As Gompers' crossing of swords with Hillquit demonstrated, there was no need or place for theories. "I saw," the labor leader wrote years later, in looking back on his early life in the labor movement, "the danger of entangling alliances with intellectuals who did not understand that to experiment with the labor movement was to experiment with human life.... I saw that the betterment of workingmen must come primarily through workingmen."

In an age of big business, Samuel Gompers made trade unionism a business, and his reward was the survival of his Federation. In a country with a heterogeneous population of unskilled immigrants, reviled and feared Negroes, and native workers, he cautiously confined his fragile organization to the more skilled workers and the more acceptable elements in the population. The result was a narrow but lasting structure.

Though never ceasing to ask for "more," the A.F. of L. presented no threat to capitalism. "Labor Unions are *for* the workingman, but against no one," John Mitchell of the United Mine Workers pointed out. "They are not hostile to employers, not inimical to the interests of the general public.... There is no necessary hostility between labor and capital," he concluded. Remorselessly pressed by Morris Hillquit as Gompers was, he still refused to admit that the labor movement was, as Hillquit put it, "conducted against the interests of the employing people." Rather, Gompers insisted, "It is conducted for the interests of the employing people." And the rapid expansion of the American economy bore witness to the fact that the Federation was a friend and not an enemy of industrial capitalism. Its very adaptability to the American scene—its conservative ideology, if it was an ideology at all—as Selig Perlman has observed, contained the key to its success. "The unionism of the American Federation of Labor 'fitted'... because it recognized the virtually inalterable conservatism of the American community as regards private property and private initiative in economic life."

This narrow conception of the proper character of trade unionism—job consciousness, craft unionism, lack of interest in organizing the unskilled, the eschewing of political activity—which Gompers and his Federation worked out for the American worker continued to dominate organized labor until the earthquake of the depression cracked the mold and the Committee for Industrial Organization issued forth.

Nobody Here But Us Capitalists

"By any simple interpretation of the Marxist formula," commented Socialist Norman Thomas in 1950, "the United States, by all odds the greatest industrial nation and that in which capitalism is most advanced, should have had long ere this is a very strong socialist movement if not a socialist revolution. Actually," he correctly observed, "in no advanced western nation is organized socialism so weak." Nor was this the first time Socialists had wondered about this. Over eighty years ago, in the high noon of European socialism, Marxist theoretician Werner Sombart impatiently put a similar question: *"Warum gibt es in den Vereinigten Staaten keinen Sozialismus?"*

The failure of the American working class to become seriously interested in socialism in this period or later is one of the prominent signs of the political and economic conservatism of American labor and, by extension, of the American people as a whole. This failure is especially noteworthy when one recalls that in industrialized countries the world over—Japan, Italy, Germany, Belgium, to mention only a few—a Socialist movement has been a "normal" concomitant of industrialization. Even newly opened countries like Australia and New Zealand have Labour parties. Rather than ask, as Americans are wont to do, why these countries have nurtured such frank repudiators of traditional capitalism, it is the American deviation from the general pattern which demands explanation.

In large part, the explanation lies in the relative weakness of class consciousness among Americans. Historically, socialism is the gospel of the *class-conscious* working class, of the workingmen who feel themselves bound to their status for life and their children after them. It is not accidental, therefore, that the major successes of modern socialism are in Europe, where class lines have been clearly and tightly drawn since time immemorial, and where the possibility of upward social movement has been severely restricted in practice if not in law. Americans may from time to time have exhibited class consciousness and even class hatred, but such attitudes have not persisted, nor have they been typical. As Matthew Arnold observed in 1888, "it is indubitable that rich men are regarded" in America "with less envy and hatred than rich men in Europe." A labor leader like Terence Powderly was convinced that America was without classes. "No matter how much we may say about classes and class distinction, there are no classes in the United States.... I have always refused to admit that we have classes in our country just as I have refused to admit that the labor of a man's hand or brain is a commodity." And there was a long line of commentators on American society, running back at least to Crèvecoeur, to illustrate the prevalence of Powderly's belief.

The weakness of American class consciousness is doubtless to be attributed, at least in part, to the fluidity of the social structure. Matthew Arnold, for example, accounted for the relative absence of class hatred on such grounds, as did such very different foreign observers as Werner Sombart and Lord Bryce. The British union officials of the Mosely Commission, it will be recalled, were convinced of the superior opportunities for success enjoyed by American workers. Stephan Thernstrom in his study of Newburyport gave some measure of the opportunities for economic improvement among the working class when he reported that all but 5 per cent of those unskilled workers who persisted from 1850 to 1900 ended the period with either property or an improvement in occupational status.

Men who are hoping to move upward on the social scale, and for whom there is some chance that they can do so, do not identify themselves with their present class. "In worn-out, king-ridden Europe, men stay where they are born," immigrant Charles O'Conor, who became an ornament of the New York bar, contended in 1869. "But in America a man is accounted a failure, and certainly ought to be, who has not risen about his father's station in life." So long as Horatio Alger means anything to Americans, Karl Marx will be just another German philosopher.

The political history of the United States also contributed to the failure of socialism. In Europe, because the franchise came slowly and late to the worker, he often found himself first an industrial worker and only later a voter. It was perfectly natural, in such a context, for him to vote according to his economic interests and to join a political party avowedly dedicated to those class interests. The situation was quite different in America, however, for political democracy came to America prior to the Industrial Revolution. By the time the industrial transformation was getting under way after 1865, all adult males could vote and, for the most part, they had already chosen their political affiliations without reference to their economic class; they were Republicans or Democrats first and workers only second—a separation between politics and economics which has become traditional in America. "In the main," wrote Lord Bryce about the United States of the 1880's, "political questions proper have held the first place in a voter's mind and questions affecting his class second." Thus, when it came to voting, workers registered their convictions as citizens, not as workingmen. (In our own day, there have been several notable failures of labor leaders to swing their labor vote, such as John L. Lewis' attempt in 1940 and the C.I.O.'s in 1950 against Senator Taft and the inability of union leaders to be sure they could hold their members to support Hubert Humphrey in the Presidential election of 1968.) To most workers, the Socialist party appeared as merely a third party in a country where such parties are political last resorts.

Nor did socialism in America gain much support from the great influx of immigration. It is true that many Germans came to this country as convinced Socialists and thus swelled the party's numbers, but they also served to pin the stigma of "alien" upon the movement. Even more important was the fact that the very heterogeneity of the labor force, as a result of immigration, often made animosities between ethnic groups more important to the worker than class antagonism. It must have seemed to many workers that socialism, with its central concern for class and its denial of ethnic antagonism, was not dealing with the realities of economic life.

In the final reckoning, however, the failure of socialism in America is to be attributed to the success of capitalism. The expanding economy provided opportunities for all, no matter how meager they might appear or actually be at times. Though the rich certainly seemed to get richer at a prodigious rate, the poor, at least, did not get poorer—and often got richer. Studies of real wages between 1865 and 1900 bear this out. Though prices rose, wages generally rose faster, so that there was a net gain in average income for workers during the last decades of the century. The increase in real wages in the first fifteen years of the twentieth century was negligible—but, significantly, there was no decline. The high wages and relatively good standard of living of the American worker were patent as far as the twenty-three British labor leaders of the Mosely Commission were concerned. The American is a "better educated, better housed, better clothed and more energetic man than his British brother," concluded the sponsor, Alfred Mosely, a businessman himself.

But America challenged socialism on other grounds than mere material things. Some years ago an obscure Socialist, Leon Samson, undertook to account for the failure of socialism to win the allegiance of the American working class; his psychological explanation merits attention because it illuminates the influence exercised by the American Dream. Americanism, Samson observes, is not so much a tradition as it is a doctrine; it is "what socialism is to a socialist." Americanism to the American is a body of ideas like "democracy, liberty, opportunity, to all of which the American adheres rationalistically much as a socialist adheres to his socialism—because it does him good, because it gives him work, because, so he thinks, it guarantees him happiness. America has thus served as a substitute for socialism."

Socialism has been unable to make headway with Americans, Samson goes on, because "every concept in socialism has its substitutive counterconcept in Americanism." As Marxism holds out the prospect of a classless society, so does Americanism. The opportunities for talent and the better material life which socialism promised for the future were already available in America and constituted the image in which America was beheld throughout the world. The freedom and equality which the oppressed proletariat of Europe craved were a reality in America—or at least sufficiently so to blunt the cutting edge of the Socialist appeal. Even the sense of mission, of being in step with the processes of history, which unquestionably was one of the appeals of socialism, was also a part of the American Dream. Have not all Americans cherished their country as a model for the world? Was not this the "last, best hope of earth"? Was not God on the side of America, as history, according to Marx, was on the side of socialism and the proletariat?

Over a century ago, Alexis de Tocqueville predicted a mighty struggle for the minds of men between two giants of Russia and the United States. In the ideologies of socialism and the American Dream, his forecast has been unexpectedly fulfilled.

Herbert G. Gutman

 **NO**

Work, Culture, and Society in Industrializing America

The traditional imperial boundaries (a function, perhaps, of the professional subdivision of labor) that have fixed the territory open to American labor historians for exploration have closed off to them the study of such important subjects as changing work habits and the culture of work. Neither the questions American labor historians usually ask nor the methods they use encourage such inquiry. With a few significant exceptions, for more than half a century American labor history has continued to reflect both the strengths and the weaknesses of the conceptual scheme sketched by its founding fathers, John R. Commons and others of the so-called Wisconsin school of labor history. Even their most severe critics, including the orthodox "Marxist" labor historians of the 1930s, 1940s, and 1950s and the few New Left historians who have devoted attention to American labor history, rarely questioned that conceptual framework. Commons and his colleagues asked large questions, gathered important source materials, and put forth impressive ideas. Together with able disciples, they studied the development of the trade union as an institution and explained its place in a changing labor market. But they gave attention primarily to those few workers who belonged to trade unions and neglected much else of importance about the American working population. Two flaws especially marred this older labor history. Because so few workers belonged to permanent trade unions before 1940, its overall conceptualization excluded most working people from detailed and serious study. More than this, its methods encouraged labor historians to spin a cocoon around American workers, isolating them from their own particular subcultures and from the larger national culture. An increasingly narrow "economic" analysis caused the study of American working-class history to grow more constricted and become more detached from larger developments in American social and cultural history and from the writing of American social and cultural history itself. After 1945 American working-class history remained imprisoned by self-imposed limitations and therefore fell far behind the more imaginative and innovative British and Continental European work in the field....

[T]he focus in these pages is on free white labor in quite different time periods: 1815–1843, 1843–1893, 1893–1919. The precise years serve only as guide-posts to mark the fact that American society differed greatly in each period. Between 1815 and 1843, the United States remained a predominantly prein-dustrial society and most workers drawn to its few factories were the products of rural and village preindustrial culture. Preindustrial American society was not premodern in the same way that European peasant societies were, but it was, nevertheless, premodern. In the half-century after 1843 industrial devel-opment radically transformed the earlier American social structure, and during this Middle Period (an era not framed around the coming and the aftermath of the Civil War) a profound tension existed between the older American prein-dustrial social structure and the modernizing institutions that accompanied the development of industrial capitalism. After 1893 the United States ranked as a mature industrial society. In each of these distinctive stages of change in Ameri-can society, a recurrent tension also existed between native and immigrant men and women fresh to the factory and the demands imposed upon them by the regularities and disciplines of factory labor. That state of tension was regularly revitalized by the migration of diverse premodern native and foreign peoples into an industrializing or a fully industrialized society. The British economic historian Sidney Pollard has described well this process whereby "a society of peasants, craftsmen, and versatile labourers became a society of modern indus-trial workers." "There was more to overcome," Pollard writes of industrializing England,

> than the change of employment or the new rhythm of work: there was a whole new culture to be absorbed and an old one to be traduced and spurned, there were new surroundings, often in a different part of the coun-try, new relations with employers, and new uncertainties of livelihood, new friends and neighbors, new marriage patterns and behavior patterns of chil-dren within the family and without.

That same process occurred in the United States. Just as in all moderniz-ing countries, the United States faced the difficult task of industrializing whole cultures, but in this country the process was regularly repeated, each stage of American economic growth and development involving different first-generation factory workers. The social transformation Pollard described occurred in England between 1770 and 1850, and in those decades premodern British cultures and the modernizing institutions associated primarily with fac-tory and machine labor collided and interacted. A painful transition occurred, dominated the ethos of an entire era, and then faded in relative importance. After 1850 and until quite recently, the British working class reproduced itself and retained a relative national homogeneity. New tensions emerged but not those of a society continually busy (and worried about) industrializing persons born out of that society and often alien in birth and color and in work habits, customary values, and behavior. "Traditional social habits and customs," J. F. C. Harrison reminds us, "seldom fitted into the patterns of industrial life, and they had ... to be discredited as hindrances to progress." That happened regularly in the United States after 1815 as the nation absorbed and worked to transform new groups of preindustrial peoples, native whites among them. The result, however, was neither a static tension nor the mere recurrence of similar cycles, because American society itself changed as did the composition of its laboring population. But the source of the tension remained the same, and conflict often resulted. It was neither the conflict emphasized by the older Progressive historians (agrarianism versus capitalism, or sectional disagreement) nor that emphasized by recent critics of that early twentieth-century synthesis (conflict between competing elites). It resulted instead from the fact that the American working class was continually altered in its composition by infusions, from within and without the nation, of peasants, farmers, skilled artisans, and casual day laborers who brought into industrial society ways of work and other habits and values not associated with industrial necessities and the industrial ethos. Some shed these older ways to conform to new imperatives. Others fell victim or fled, moving from place to place. Some sought to extend and adapt older patterns of work and life to a new society. Others challenged the social system through varieties of collective associations. But for all—at different historical moments—the transition to industrial society, as E. P. Thompson has written, "entailed a severe restructuring of working habits—new disciplines, new incentives, and a new human nature upon which these incentives could bite effectively."

Much in the following pages depends upon a particular definition of culture and an analytic distinction between culture and society. Both deserve brief comment. "Culture" as used here has little to do with Oscar Lewis's inadequate "culture of poverty" construct and has even less to do with the currently fashionable but nevertheless quite crude behavioral social history that defines class by mere occupation and culture as some kind of a magical mix between ethnic and religious affiliations. Instead this [selection] has profited from the analytic distinctions between culture and society made by the anthropologists Eric Wolf and Sidney W. Mintz and the exiled Polish sociologist Zygmunt Bauman. Mintz finds in culture "a kind of resource" and in society "a kind of arena," the distinction being "between sets of historically available alternatives or forms on the one hand, and the societal circumstances or settings within which these forms may be employed on the other." "Culture," he writes, "is *used;* and any analysis of its use immediately brings into view the arrangements of persons in societal groups for whom cultural forms confirm, reinforce, maintain, change, or deny particular arrangements of status, power, and identity." ...

Despite the profound economic changes that followed the American Civil War, Gilded Age artisans did not easily shed stubborn and time-honored work habits. Such work habits and the life-styles and subcultures related to them retained a vitality long into these industrializing decades. Not all artisans worked in factories, but some that did retained traditional craft skills. Mechanization came in different ways and at different times to diverse industries. Samuel Gompers recollected that New York City cigarmakers paid a fellow craftsman to read a newspaper to them while they worked, and Milwaukee cigarmakers struck in 1882 to retain such privileges as keeping (and then selling) damaged cigars and leaving the shop without a foreman's permission. "The difficulty with many cigarmakers," complained a New York City manufacturer in 1877, "is this. They come down to the shop in the morning; roll a few cigars and then go to a beer saloon and play pinnocio or some other game, ... working probably only two or three hours a day." Coopers felt new machinery "hard and insensate," not a blessing but an evil that "took a great deal of joy out of life" because machine-made barrels undercut a subculture of work and leisure. Skilled coopers "lounged about" on Saturday (the regular payday), a "lost day" to their employers. A historian of American cooperage explained:

> Early on Saturday morning, the big brewery wagon would drive up to the shop. Several of the coopers would club together, each paying his proper share, and one of them would call out the window to the driver, "Bring me a Goose Egg," meaning a half-barrel of beer. Then others would buy "Goose Eggs," and there would be a merry time all around. . . . Little groups of jolly fellows would often sit around upturned barrels playing poker, using rivets for chips, until they had received their pay and the "Goose Egg" was dry.
>
> Saturday night was a big night for the old-time cooper. It meant going out, strolling around the town, meeting friends, usually at a favorite saloon, and having a good time generally, after a week of hard work. Usually the good time continued over into Sunday, so that on the following day he usually was not in the best of condition to settle down to the regular day's work.
>
> Many coopers used to spend this day [Monday] sharpening up their tools, carrying in stock, discussing current events, and in getting things in shape for the big day of work on the morrow. Thus, "Blue Monday" was something of a tradition with the coopers, and the day was also more or less lost as far as production was concerned.
>
> "Can't do much today, but I'll give her hell tomorrow," seemed to be the Monday slogan. But bright and early Tuesday morning, "Give her hell" they would, banging away lustily for the rest of the week until Saturday which was pay day again, and its thoughts of the "Goose Eggs."

Such traditions of work and leisure—in this case, a four-day work week and a three-day weekend—angered manufacturers anxious to ship goods as much as it worried Sabbatarians and temperance reformers. Conflicts over life- and work-styles occurred frequently and often involved control over the work process and over time. The immigrant Staffordshire potters in Trenton, New Jersey, worked in "bursts of great activity" and then quit for "several days at a time." "Monday," said a manufacturer, "was given up to debauchery." After the potters lost a bitter lockout in 1877 that included torchlight parades and effigy burnings, the *Crockery and Glass Journal* mockingly advised:

> Run your factories to please the crowd. . . . Don't expect work to begin before 9 a.m. or to continue after 3 p.m. Every employee should be served hot coffee and a bouquet at 7 a.m. and allowed the two hours to take a free perfumed bath. . . . During the summer, ice cream and fruit should be served at 12 p.m. to the accompaniment of witching music.

Hand coopers (and potters and cigarmakers, among others) worked hard but in distinctly preindustrial styles. Machine-made barrels pitted modernizing technology and modern habits against traditional ways. To the owners of competitive firms struggling to improve efficiency and cut labor costs, the Goose Egg and Blue Monday proved the laziness and obstinacy of craftsmen as well as the tyranny of craft unions that upheld venerable traditions. To the skilled cooper, the long weekend symbolized a way of work and life filled with almost ritualistic meanings. Between 1843 and 1893, compromise between such conflicting interests was hardly possible.

Settled premodern work habits existed among others than those employed in nonfactory crafts. Owners of already partially mechanized industries complained of them, too. "Saturday night debauches and Sunday carousels though they be few and far between," lamented the *Age of Steel* in 1882, "are destructive of modest hoardings, and he who indulges in them will in time become a striker for higher wages." In 1880 a British steelworker boasted that native Americans never would match immigrants in their skills: "adn't the 'ops, you know." Manufacturers, when able, did not hesitate to act decisively to end such troubles. In Fall River new technology allowed a print cloth manufacturer to settle a long-standing grievance against his stubborn mule spinners. "On Saturday afternoon after they had gone home," a boastful mill superintendent later recollected, "we started right in and smashed a room full of mules with sledge hammers.... On Monday morning, they were astonished to find that there was not work for them. That room is now full of ring frames run by girls." Woolen manufacturers also displaced handjack spinners with improved machinery and did so because of "the disorderly habits of English workmen. Often on a Monday morning, half of them would be absent from the mill in consequence of the Sunday's dissipation." Blue Monday, however, did not entirely disappear. Paterson artisans and factory hands held a May festival on a Monday each year ("Labor Monday") and that popular holiday soon became state law, the American Labor Day. It had its roots in earlier premodern work habits.

The persistence of such traditional artisan work habits well into the nineteenth century deserves notice from others besides labor historians, because those work habits did not exist in a cultural or social vacuum. If modernizing technology threatened and even displaced such work patterns, diverse nineteenth-century subcultures sustained and nourished them. "The old nations of the earth creep on at a snail's pace," boasted Andrew Carnegie in *Triumphant Democracy* (1886), "the Republic thunders past with the rush of an express." The articulate steelmaster, however, had missed the point. The very rapidity of the economic changes occurring in Carnegie's lifetime meant that many, unlike him, lacked the time, historically, culturally, and psychologically, to be separated or alienated from settled ways of work and life and from relatively fixed beliefs. Continuity not consensus counted for much in explaining working-class and especially artisan behavior in those decades that witnessed the coming of the factory and the radical transformation of American society. Persistent work habits were one example of that significant continuity. But these elements of continuity were often revealed among nineteenth-century American workers cut off by birth from direct contact with the preindustrial American past, a fact that has been ignored or blurred by the artificial separation between labor history and immigration history. In Gilded Age America (and afterward in the Progressive Era despite the radical change in patterns of immigration), working-class and immigration history regularly intersected, and that intermingling made for powerful continuities. In 1880, for example, 63 of every 100 Londoners were native to that city, 94 coming from England and Wales, and 98 from Great Britain and Ireland. Foreign countries together contributed only 1.6 percent to London's massive population. At that same moment, more than 70 of every 100 persons in San Francisco (78), St. Louis (78), Cleveland (80), New York (80), Detroit (84), Milwaukee (84), and Chicago (87) were immigrants or the children of immigrants, and the percentage was just as high in many smaller American industrial towns and cities. "Not every foreigner is a workingman," noticed the clergyman Samuel Lane Loomis in 1887, "but in the cities, at least, it may almost be said that every workingman is a foreigner." And until the 1890s most immigrants came from Northern and Western Europe, French- and English-speaking Canada, and China. In 1890, only 3 percent of the nation's foreign-born residents—290,000 of 9,200,000 immigrants —had been born in Eastern or Southern Europe. (It is a little recognized fact that most North and West European immigrants migrated to the United States after, not before, the American Civil War.) When so much else changed in the industrializing decades, tenacious traditions flourished among immigrants in ethnic subcultures that varied greatly among particular groups and according to the size, age, and location of different cities and industries. ("The Irish," Henry George insisted, "burn like chips, the English like logs.") Class and occupational distinctions within a particular ethnic group also made for different patterns of cultural adaptation, but powerful subcultures thrived among them all.

Suffering and plain poverty cut deeply into these ethnic working-class worlds. In reconstructing their everyday texture there is no reason to neglect or idealize such suffering, but it is time to discard the notion that the large-scale uprooting and exploitative processes that accompanied industrialization caused little more than cultural breakdown and social anomie. Family, class, and ethnic ties did not dissolve easily. "Almost as a matter of definition," the sociologist Neil Smelzer has written, "we associate the factory system with the decline of the family and the onset of anonymity." Smelzer criticized such a view of early industrializing England, and it has just as little validity for nineteenth-century industrializing America. Family roles changed in important ways, and strain was widespread, but the immigrant working-class family held together. Examination of household composition in sixteen census enumeration districts in Paterson in 1880 makes that clear for this predominantly working-class immigrant city, and while research on other ethnic working-class communities will reveal significant variations, the overall patterns should not differ greatly. The Paterson immigrant (and native white) communities were predominantly working class, and most families among them were intact in their composition. For this population, at least (and without accounting for age and sex ratio differences between the ethnic groups), a greater percentage of immigrant than native white households included two parents. Ethnic and predominantly working-class communities in industrial towns like Paterson and in larger cities, too, built on these strained but hardly broken familial and kin ties. Migration to another country, life in the city, and labor in cost-conscious and ill-equipped factories and workshops tested but did not shatter what the anthropologist Clifford Geertz has described as primordial (as contrasted to civic) attachments, "the 'assumed' givens ... of social existence: immediate contiguity and kin connections mainly, but beyond them, the givenness that stems from being born into a particular religious community, speaking a particular language, and following particular social patterns." Tough familial and kin ties made possible that transmission and adaptation of European working-class cultural patterns and beliefs to industrializing America. As late as 1888, residents in some Rhode Island mill villages figured their wages in British currency. Common rituals and festivals bound together such communities. Paterson silk weavers had their Macclesfield wakes, and Fall River cotton mill workers their Ashton wakes. British immigrants "banded together to uphold the popular culture of the homeland" and celebrated saints' days: St. George's Day, St. Andrew's Day, and St. David's Day. Even funerals retained an archaic flavor. Samuel Sigley, a Chartist house painter, had fled Ashton-under-Lyne in 1848, and built American trade unions. When his wife died in the late 1890s a significant ritual occurred during the funeral: some friends placed a chaff of wheat on her grave. Mythic beliefs also cemented ethnic and class solidarities. The Irish-American press, for example, gave Martin O'Brennan much space to argue that Celtic had been spoken in the Garden of Eden, and in Paterson Irish-born silk, cotton, and iron workers believed in the magical powers of that town's "Dublin Spring." An old resident remembered:

> There is a legend that an Irish fairy brought over the water in her apron from the Lakes of Killarney and planted it in the humble part of that town.... There were dozens of legends connected with the Dublin Spring and if a man drank from its precious depository ... he could never leave Paterson [but] only under the fairy influence, and the wand of the nymph would be sure to bring him back again some time or other.

When a "fairy" appeared in Paterson in human form, some believed she walked the streets "as a tottering old woman begging with a cane." Here was a way to assure concern for the elderly and the disabled.

Much remains to be studied about these cross-class but predominantly working-class ethnic subcultures common to industrializing America. Relations within them between skilled and unskilled workers, for example, remain unclear. But the larger shape of these diverse immigrant communities can be sketched. More than mythic beliefs and common work habits sustained them. Such worlds had in them what Thompson has called "working-class intellectual traditions, working-class community patterns, and a working-class structure of feeling," and men with artisan skills powerfully affected the everyday texture of such communities. A model subculture included friendly and benevolent societies as well as friendly local politicians, community-wide holiday celebrations, an occasional library (the Baltimore Journeymen Bricklayer's Union taxed members one dollar a year in the 1880s to sustain a library that included the collected works of William Shakespeare and Sir Walter Scott's Waverley novels), participant sports, churches sometimes headed by a sympathetic clergy, saloons, beer gardens, and concert halls or music halls and, depending upon circumstances, trade unionists, labor reformers, and radicals. The Massachusetts cleric Jonathan Baxter Harrison published in 1880 an unusually detailed description of one such ethnic, working-class institution, a Fall River music hall and saloon. About fifty persons were there when he visited it, nearly one-fourth of them young women. "Most of those present," he noticed, were "persons whom I had met before, in the mills and on the streets. They were nearly all operatives, or had at some time belonged to that class." An Englishman sang first, and then a black whose songs "were of many kinds, comic, sentimental, pathetic, and silly.... When he sang 'I got a mammy in the promised land,' with a strange, wailing refrain, the English waiter-girl, who was sitting at my table, wiped her eyes with her apron, and everybody was very quiet." Harrison said of such places in Fall River:

> All the attendants... had worked in the mills. The young man who plays the piano is usually paid four or five dollars per week, besides his board. The young men who sing receive one dollar per night, but most of them board themselves.... The most usual course for a man who for any reason falls out of the ranks of mill workers (if he loses his place by sickness or is discharged) is the opening of a liquor saloon or drinking place.

Ethnic ties with particular class dimensions sometimes stretched far beyond local boundaries and even revealed themselves in the behavior of the most successful practitioners of Gilded Age popular culture. In 1884, for example, the pugilist John L. Sullivan and the music-hall entertainers Harrigan and Hart promised support to striking Irish coal miners in the Ohio Hocking Valley. Local ties, however, counted for much more and had their roots inside and outside of the factory and workshop. Soon after Cyrus H. McCormick, then twenty-one, took over the management of his father's great Chicago iron machinery factory (which in the early 1880s employed twelve hundred men and boys), a petition signed by "Many Employees" reached his hands:

> It only pains us to relate to you... that a good many of our old hands is not here this season and if Mr. Evarts is kept another season a good many more will leave.... We pray for you... to remove this man.... We are treated as though we were dogs.... He has cut wages down so low they are living on nothing but bread.... We can't talk to him about wages if we do he will tell us to go out side the gate.... He discharged old John the other day he has been here seventeen years.... There is Mr. Church who left us last Saturday he went about and shook hands with every old hand in the shop... this brought tears to many men's eyes. He has been here nineteen years and has got along well with them all until he came to Mr. Evarts the present superintendent.

Artisans, themselves among those later displaced by new technology, signed this petition, and self-educated artisans (or professionals and petty enterprisers who had themselves usually risen from the artisan class) often emerged as civic and community leaders. "Intellectually," Jennie Collins noticed in Boston in the early 1870s, "the journeymen tailors... are ever discussing among themselves questions of local and national politics, points of law, philosophy, physics, and religion."

Such life-styles and subcultures adapted and changed over time. In the Gilded Age piece-rates in nearly all manufacturing industries helped reshape traditional work habits. "Two generations ago," said the Connecticut Bureau of Labor Statistics in 1885, "time-work was the universal rule." "Piece-work" had all but replaced it, and the Connecticut Bureau called it "a moral force which corresponds to machinery as a physical force." Additional pressures came in traditional industries such as shoe, cigar, furniture, barrel, and clothing manufacture, which significantly mechanized in these years. Strain also resulted where factories employed large numbers of children and young women (in the 1880 manuscript census 49.3 percent of all Paterson boys and 52.1 percent of all girls aged eleven to fourteen had occupations listed by their names) and was especially common among the as yet little-studied pools of casual male laborers found everywhere. More than this, mobility patterns significantly affected the structure and the behavior of these predominantly working-class communities. A good deal of geographic mobility, property mobility (home ownership), and occupational mobility (skilled status in new industries or in the expanding building trades, petty retail enterprise, the professions, and public employment counted as the most important ways to advance occupationally) reshaped these ethnic communities as Stephan Thernstrom and others have shown. But so little is yet known about the society in which such men and women lived and about the cultures which had produced them that it is entirely premature to infer "consciousness" (beliefs and values) only from mobility rates. Such patterns and rates of mobility, for example, did not entirely shatter working-class capacities for self-protection. The fifty-year period between 1843 and 1893 was not conducive to permanent, stable trade unions, but these decades were a time of frequent strikes and lockouts and other forms of sustained conflict.

Not all strikes and lockouts resulted in the defeat of poorly organized workers. For the years 1881 to 1887, for example, the New Jersey Bureau of Labor Statistics collected information on 890 New Jersey industrial disputes involving mostly workers in the textile, glass, metal, transportation, and building trades: 6 percent ended in compromise settlements; employers gained the advantage in 40 percent; strikers won the rest (54 percent). In four of five disputes concerning higher wages and shorter hours, New Jersey workers, not their employers, were victorious. Large numbers of such workers there and elsewhere were foreign-born or the children of immigrants. More than this, immigrant workers in the mid-1880s joined trade unions in numbers far out of proportion to their place in the labor force. Statistical inquiries by the Bureau of Labor Statistics in Illinois in 1886 and in New Jersey in 1887 make this clear. Even these data may not have fully reflected the proclivity of immigrants to seek self-protection. (Such a distortion would occur if, for example, the children of immigrants apparently counted by the bureaus as native-born had remained a part of the ethnic subcultures into which they had been born and joined trade unions as regularly as the foreign-born). Such information from Illinois and New Jersey suggests the need to treat the meaning of social mobility with some care. So does the sketchy outline of Hugh O'Donnell's career. By 1892, when he was twenty-nine years old, he had already improved his social status a great deal. Before the dispute with Andrew Carnegie and Henry Clay Frick culminated in the bitter Homestead lockout that year, O'Donnell had voted Republican, owned a home, and had in it a Brussels carpet and even a piano. Nevertheless this Irish-American skilled worker led the Homestead workers and was even indicted under a Civil War treason statute never before used. The material improvements O'Donnell had experienced mattered greatly to him and suggested significant mobility, but culture and tradition together with the way in which men like O'Donnell interpreted the transformation of Old America defined the value of those material improvements and their meaning to him.

Other continuities between 1843 and 1893 besides those rooted in artisan work habits and diverse ethnic working-class subcultures deserve brief attention as important considerations in understanding the behavior of artisans and other workers in these decades. I have suggested in other writings that significant patterns of opposition to the ways in which industrial capitalism developed will remain baffling until historians re-examine the relationship between the premodern American political system and the coming of the factory along with the strains in premodern popular American ideology shared by workers and large numbers of successful self-made Americans (policemen, clergymen, politicians, small businessmen, and even some "traditional" manufacturers) that rejected the legitimacy of the modern factory system and its owners. One strain of thought common to the rhetoric of nineteenth-century immigrant and native-born artisans is considered here. It helps explain their recurrent enthusiasm for land and currency reform, cooperatives, and trade unions. It was the fear of dependence, "proletarianization," and centralization, and the worry that industrial capitalism threatened to transform "the Great Republic of the West" into a "European" country. In 1869, the same year that saw the completion of the transcontinental railroad, the chartering of the Standard Oil Company, the founding of the Knights of Labor, and the dedication of a New York City statue to Cornelius Vanderbilt, some London workers from Westbourne Park and Notting Hill petitioned the American ambassador for help to emigrate. "Dependence," they said of Great Britain, "not independence, is inculcated. Hon. Sir, this state of things we wish to fly from ... to become citizens of that great Republican country, which has no parallels in the world's history." Such men had a vision of Old America, but it was not a new vision. Industrial transformation between 1840 and 1890 tested and redefined that vision. Seven years after their visit, the New York *Labor Standard,* then edited by an Irish socialist, bemoaned what had come over the country: "There was a time when the United States was the workingman's country, ... the land of promise for the workingman.... We are now in an *old country."* This theme recurred frequently as disaffected workers, usually self-educated artisans, described the transformation of premodern America. "America," said the Detroit *Labor Leaf,* "used to be the land of promise to the poor.... The Golden Age is indeed over—the Age of Iron has taken its place. The iron law of necessity has taken the place of the golden rule." We need not join in mythicizing preindustrial American society in order to suggest that this tension between the old and the new helps give a coherence to the decades between 1843 and 1893 that even the trauma of the Civil War does not disturb.

POSTSCRIPT

Were American Workers in the Gilded Age Conservative Capitalists?

D egler agrees with the traditional labor historians that the American worker accepted capitalism and wanted a bigger piece of the pie. But he reverses the radical-conservative dichotomy as applied to the conflict between the worker and the businessman. In his view, the real radicals were the industrialists who created a more mature system of capitalism. Labor merely fashioned a conservative response to the radical changes brought about by big business. The system led to its demise. Its place was taken by the American Federation of Labor, whose long-time leader Samuel Gompers was famous for his acceptance of the wage system and American capitalism. The American Federation of Labor adopted practical goals; it strove to improve the lot of the worker by negotiating for better hours, wages, and working conditions. "In an age of big business," says Degler, "Samuel Gompers made trade unionism a business, and his reward was the survival of his Federation."

In explaining the failure of socialism in America, Degler argues that Americans lacked a working-class consciousness because they believed in real mobility. Also, a labor party failed to emerge because Americans developed their commitment to the two-party system before the issues of the industrial revolution came to the forefront. The influx of immigrants from a variety of countries created the heterogeneous labor force, and animosities between rival ethnic groups appeared more real than class antagonisms. "In the final reckoning," says Degler, "the failure of socialism in America is to be attributed to the success of capitalism."

For the past 25 years historians have been studying the social and cultural environment of the American working class. The approach is modeled after Edward P. Thompson's highly influential and sophisticated Marxist analysis *The Making of the English Working Class* (Vintage Books, 1966), which is the capstone of an earlier generation of British and French social historians. The father of the "new labor history" in the United States is Gutman, who was the first to discuss American workers as a group separate from the organized union movement. Gutman's distinction between preindustrial and industrial values laid the groundwork for a whole generation of scholars who have performed case studies of both union and nonunion workers in both urban and rural areas of America. Such works have proliferated in recent years but should be sampled first in the following collections of articles: Daniel J. Leab and Richard B. Morris, eds., *The Labor History Reader* (University of Illinois Press, 1985); Charles Stephenson and Robert Asher, eds., *Life and Labor: Dimensions of American Working-Class History* (State University of New York Press, 1986); and Milton

Cantor, ed., *American Working Class Culture: Explorations in American Labor and Social History* (Greenwood, 1979).

Gutman's essay differs from Degler's more traditional approach in several ways. Gutman abandons the division of American history at the Civil War/Reconstruction fault line. He proposes a threefold division for free, white workers: (1) the premodern early industrial period from 1815 to 1843; (2) the transition to capitalism, which encompasses the years 1843–1893; and (3) the development of a full-blown industrial system, which took place from the late 1890s through World War I. Gutman's unique periodization enables us to view the evolution of the free, white nonunion worker, whose traditional values withstood the onslaughts of an increasingly large-scale dehumanized factory system that emphasized productivity and efficiency until the depression of 1893.

Gutman also challenges the view that workers were helpless pawns of the owners and that they were forced to cave in every time a strike took place. He shows that on a local level in the 1880s, immigrants workers not only joined unions but also usually won their strikes. This is because small shopkeepers and workers in other industries often supported those who were out on strike. Gutman also argues from census data of the 1880s that immigrant families were more stable and less prone to divorce and desertion than native-born families. Gutman applied many of these insights to slaves in his prizewinning book *The Black Family in Slavery and Freedom* (Pantheon, 1976).

To learn more about the rise and fall of the Knights of Labor, see the case studies in Leon Fink's *Workingmen's Democracy: The Knights of Labor and American Politics* (University of Illinois Press, 1983). See also Fink's collection of articles *In Search of the Working Class* (University of Illinois Press, 1994). Two other noteworthy books on the Knights of Labor are Robert E. Weir, *Beyond Labor's Veil: The Culture of the Knights of Labor* (Penn State University Press, 1996) and Kim Voss, *The Making of American Exceptionalism: The Knights of Labor and Class Formation in the Nineteenth Century* (Cornell University Press, 1993).

Two journals have devoted entire issues to the American labor movement: the fall 1989 issue of *The Public Historian* and the February 1982 issue of *Social Education*. Students who wish to sample the diverse scholarships on the American worker should consult "A Round Table: Labor, Historical Pessimism, and Hegemony," *Journal of American History* (June 1988).

The question of why the United States never developed a major socialist movement or labor party has been the subject of much speculation. A good starting point is John H. Laslett and Seymour Martin Lipset, eds., *Failure of a Dream? Essays in the History of American Socialism* (University of California Press, 1984). Political scientist Theodore J. Lowi argues that the U.S. political system of federalism prevented a socialist movement in "Why Is There No Socialism in the United States?" *Society* (January/February 1985). Finally, see Rick Halpern and Jonathan Morris, eds., *American Exceptionalism? U.S. Working-Class Formation in an International Context* (St. Martin's Press, 1997).

ISSUE 5

Was City Government in Late-Nineteenth-Century America a "Conspicuous Failure"?

YES: Ernest S. Griffith, from *A History of American City Government: The Conspicuous Failure, 1870–1900* (National Civic League Press, 1974)

NO: Jon C. Teaford, from *The Unheralded Triumph: City Government in America, 1860–1900* (Johns Hopkins University Press, 1984)

ISSUE SUMMARY

YES: Professor of political science and political economy Ernest S. Griffith (1896–1981) focuses upon illegal and unethical operations of the political machine and concludes that the governments controlled by the bosses represented a betrayal of the public trust.

NO: Professor of history Jon C. Teaford argues that scholars traditionally have overlooked the remarkable success that municipal governments in the late nineteenth century achieved in dealing with the challenges presented by rapid urbanization.

During the late nineteenth century, American farmers based their grievances on revolutionary changes that had occurred in the post–Civil War United States. Specifically, they saw themselves as victims of an industrial wave that had swept over the nation and submerged their rural, agricultural world in the undertow. Indeed, the values, attitudes, and interests of all Americans were affected dramatically by the rapid urbanization that accompanied industrial growth. The result was the creation of the modern city, with its coordinated network of economic development, which emphasized mass production and mass consumption.

In the years from 1860 to 1920, the number of urban residents in the United States increased much more rapidly than the national population as a whole. For example, the Census Bureau reported in 1920 that the United States housed 105,711,000 people, three times the number living in the country on the eve of the Civil War. Urban dwellers, however, increased ninefold during the same period. The number of "urban" places (incorporated towns with 2,500 or more residents, or unincorporated areas with at least 2,500 people per square mile) increased from 392 in 1860 to 2,722 in 1920. Cities with populations in excess of 100,000 increased from 9 in 1860 to 68 in 1920.

Reflecting many of the characteristics of "modern" America, these industrial cities produced a number of problems for the people who lived in them—problems associated with fire and police protection, sanitation, utilities, and a wide range of social services. These coincided with increased concerns over employment opportunities and demands for transportation and housing improvements. Typically, municipal government became the clearinghouse for such demands. What was the nature of city government in the late-nineteenth-century United States? How effectively were American cities governed? To what extent did municipal leaders listen to and redress the grievances of urban dwellers? In light of James Lord Bryce's blunt statement in 1888 that city government in the United States was a "conspicuous failure," it is worthwhile to explore scholarly assessments of Bryce's conclusion.

In the following selection, Ernest S. Griffith surveys the nature of municipal government in the last three decades of the nineteenth century and concludes that city politics was consumed by a "cancer of corruption" that predominated in the years from 1880 to 1893. He identifies numerous factors that contributed to this unethical environment, as well as the disreputable and illegal lengths gone to that perpetuated the power of the bosses but prevented city government from operating in the true interest of the people.

In the second selection, Jon C. Teaford contends that scholars like Griffith are too eager to condemn the activities of late-nineteenth-century municipal governments without recognizing their accomplishments. Teaford argues that, although there were numerous shortcomings, American city dwellers enjoyed a higher standard of public services than any other urban residents in the world. Also, in contrast to the portrait of boss dominance presented by Griffith and others, Teaford maintains that authority was widely distributed among various groups that peacefully coexisted with one another. For Teaford, nineteenth-century cities failed to develop a political image but succeeded to a remarkable degree in meeting the needs of those who were dependent upon them.

Ernest S. Griffith

 **YES**

The Cancer of Corruption

Introduction

Corruption may be defined as personal profit at the expense of the public—stealing and use of office for private gain, including the giving and taking of bribes outside of the law. More broadly defined, it is any antisocial conduct that uses government as an instrument. Its twilight zone is never the same from age to age, from community to community, or even from person to person. . . .

Historically, the motivations of the electorate, the uses to which tax money and campaign contributions were put, the pressures of reward and punishment to which candidates and officeholders were subjected, were never very far from the gray zone in which the line between the corrupt and the ethical —or even the legal—had somehow to be drawn. Votes were "coin of the realm" in a democracy; office holding or power-wielding was secured by votes. They might be freely and intelligently given; they might be the result of propaganda, friendship, or pressure; they might be purchased by money or otherwise; they might be manufactured out of election frauds. Those who were members of the government, visible or invisible, were ultimately dependent on the voters for their opportunity to serve, for their livelihood, for the chance to steal or betray. These conditions existed in the late nineteenth century; with differing emphases they still exist today.

What, then, determined whether a late-nineteenth-century city government was corrupt or ethical, or something in between? Ethically speaking, the nadir of American city government was probably reached in the years between 1880 and 1893. Why and how? There was obviously no one answer. The time has long since passed when municipal reformers, not to mention historians, believed there was a single answer. There was present a highly complex situation—a *Gestalt*, or pattern—never identical in any two places, but bearing a family resemblance in most respects. The path to better municipal governance was long and difficult because of this very complexity. The story of the 1890's and of the Progressive Era of the first twelve or fifteen years of the twentieth century was the story of a thousand battles on a thousand fronts—the unraveling of a refractory network of unsuitable charters and procedures, of a human nature that at times led to despair, of an economic order that put a premium

From Ernest S. Griffith, *A History of American City Government: The Conspicuous Failure, 1870–1900* (National Civic League Press, 1974). Copyright © 1974 by The National Municipal League. Reprinted by permission of University Press of America.

on greed, of a social order of class and ethnic divisions reflected often in incompatible value systems—all infinitely complicated by rapidity of growth and population mobility....

Patronage

... [H]ow are we to account for the corrupt machine in the first place, and for what came to be its endemic character in American cities for two or three decades? This is part of a broader analysis, and will be undertaken presently. As always, in the end the legacy of a corrupt and corrupting regime was a malaise of suspicion, discouragement, and blunted ideals in society as a whole.

In examining the fact of corruption, it was obvious that the city—any city, good or bad—provided livelihood for scores, hundreds, even thousands of people directly employed. They would fight if their livelihood were threatened. There were also large numbers dependent upon the city for contracts, privileges, and immunities. Not as sharply defined, and often overlapping one or both of these categories, were persons who served as organizers, brokers, or instruments of these other two groups, and whose livelihoods therefore also depended upon the city. They, too, would fight to attain, keep, or augment this livelihood, and probably the sense of power (and occasionally the constructive achievements) that their positions carried with them. They were the "machine," the "ring," the "boss," the professional politician, the political lawyer. This is to say, for many people (as regards the city) employment, power, and access to those with power were matters of economic life or death for themselves and their families—and, if these same people were wholly self-seeking, to them the end justified the means.

First, consider the municipal employees. "To the victors belong the spoils" —the party faction and machine rewarded their own and punished the others. In 1889 the mayor of Los Angeles appointed all of his six sons to the police force, but this helped to defeat him in the next election. In the smaller cities, and in the larger ones before skills seemed essential, a change of administration or party was the signal for wholesale dismissals and wholesale patronage. This fact created the strongest incentive for those currently employed to work for the retention in power of those influential in their employment; that they had so worked constituted a logical basis for their dismissal; given the success of the opposing candidates. That the city might suffer in both processes was unimportant to those whose livelihood was at stake in the outcome of the struggle. Those involved, in many instances, would not even respect the position of school teacher, and could usually find ways and means to subvert the civil service laws when they emerged, in intent if not in formal ritual. In Brooklyn, for example, during the Daniel Whitney administration of 1885, only favored candidates were informed of the dates of the examinations in time to apply. Examinations were then leniently graded, to put it mildly. One illiterate received a grade of 97.5 per cent on a written test. About 1890, each member of the Boston city council received a certain number of tickets corresponding to his quota of men employed by the city. No one was eligible without such a ticket, and existing employees were discharged to make room if necessary.

Sale of Privileges and Immunities

As regards the sale for cash of privileges and immunities, many politicians and officials did not stop with the twilight zone of liquor violations, gambling, and prostitution, but went on to exploit what would be regarded as crime in any language or society. Denver (incidentally, at least until the 1960's) was one of the worst. From the late 1880's until 1922, Lou Blonger, king of the city's underworld, held the police department in his grasp. For many of these years he had a direct line to the chief of police, and his orders were "law." Criminals were never molested if they operated outside the city limits, and often not within the limits, either. He contributed liberally to the campaign funds of both parties, those of the district attorneys being especially favored. Blonger was sent to jail in 1922 by Philip Van Cise, a district attorney who had refused his conditional campaign contribution of $25,000.

Yet, it was the insatiable appetite of men for liquor, sex, and the excitement and eternal hope of gambling that proved by all the odds the most refractory and the most corrupting day-to-day element. . . .

The police of most cities, and the politicians and officials, took graft or campaign contributions from the liquor interests so that they would overlook violations of the law. Judging from extant material of the period, corruption by the liquor trade occurred more frequently than any other. Over and over again the question of enforcement of whatever laws existed was an issue at the polls. The fact was that, at this time, the trade did not want *any* regulation and resented all but the most nominal license fee, unless the license in effect granted a neighborhood semimonopoly, and increased profitability accordingly. It was prepared to fight and pay for its privileges. Council membership was literally jammed with saloon keepers, and Buffalo (1880) was not too exceptional in having a brewer as mayor. Apparently in one instance (in Nebraska), the liquor interests resorted to assassination of the clerk of the U.S. Federal Circuit Court in revenge for his part in the fight against them.

More clearly illegal, because here it was not a question of hours of sale but of its right to exist, was commercial gambling. State laws and even municipal ordinances were fairly usual in prohibiting it, but these laws were sustained neither by enforcement nor by public opinion. If the public opinion calling for enforcement was present, the requisite ethical standard was not there that would preclude the offering and accepting of the bribes that made the continuance of gambling possible—except for an occasional spasm of raids and reform.

Oklahoma City will serve as a case study. At one point gambling houses regularly paid one fine a month. Four-fifths of the businessmen refused to answer whether they would favor closing such joints; going on record either way would hurt their business. Citing District Attorney William T. Jerome's views of attempts to secure enforcement of this type of law, one writer commented: "The corrupt politician welcomes the puritan as an ally. He sees in laws that cannot and will not be permanently enforced a yearly revenue in money and in power."

The situation regarding commercialized vice was similar. Laws and ordinances forbidding brothels were on the statute books. Brothels existed in every large city and most of the smaller ones. Especially in the Western cities where men greatly outnumbered women, they appeared in large numbers, and the same might be said of the commercial centers and the seaport towns. A boss like Boies Penrose of Philadelphia patronized them. So, in fact, did a number of presumably otherwise respectable citizens. Many of this last group also drew rent from the brothels.

What this meant to the city government of a place like Seattle may be illustrated by an episode in 1892:

> The police department thought it had a vested property right in the collections from prostitutes and gamblers. The new mayor, Ronald, was waited on almost immediately by a group of high ranking police officers who asked him how much of a cut he wanted out of the monthly "pay off" for gambling and prostitution. "Not a cent! Moreover, there isn't going to be any collection or places that pay protection money," he said as he pounded the table. The committee patiently explained that it was "unofficial licensing," a very effective way to control crime. The mayor exploded again and one of the captains took out a revolver and dropped it on the table. "Somebody is going to get hurt—maybe." The mayor tried as hard as ever anyone could to clean up, but found it impossible. He was powerless because he had no real support. He resigned in less than a year.

For the depths of degradation into which the combination of lust and greed can sink a city government, one can only cite the example of Kansas City, where girls at the municipal farm were sold by the politicians (who of course pocketed the money) and sent to brothels in New Orleans....

Each city, as the pressures of urban living forced regulation, found itself under conflicting demands. The people as a whole probably wanted "nuisances" cleared up—unsanitary dwellings, cattle in the streets, sign encroachments, garbage left around, and a hundred other annoying matters—the counterpart in today's world of illegal parking. But to the particular person involved, there was an interest in leaving things as they were—an interest for which he was prepared to pay by a tip or a vote. Compulsory education laws ran up against parents who regarded them as a violation of their God-given right to employ their children as they wished. Political revenge might well await the enforcer —the truant officer, health officer, inspector of meat, dairies, or housing, or policeman. Political and often pecuniary rewards awaited those who would overlook matters of this type. There were other favors, tips on the location of a proposed public improvement or on the location of a road or a park relevant to real estate value. These were advantageous to the official and his friends to know and to control for their own personal profit. Real estate profit through advance notice or an actual share in the decision on a municipal improvement or purchase was one of the most lucrative perquisites of councilors or the "ring" members. A special instance of this was the desire of many members of Congress for seats on the low-status District of Columbia Committee so as to secure advance information as to what would be profitable real estate purchases in the District. In general, these examples came under the heading of "honest graft" in those days, as not necessarily costing the city treasury an undue amount. The term was invented by George W. Plunkett of Tammany as a rationalization.

Graft From Contracts and Franchises

Quite otherwise were the profits, direct and indirect, from lucrative city contracts. Probably in the majority of cities there was a tacit understanding that a favored contractor would "kick back" a substantial amount (10 per cent or more being quite usual) either to party campaign funds for which accounting was rare, as fees to a "political lawyer," with the ultimate distribution uncertain, or as out-and-out bribes to those with the power to make the decisions. There were always any number of devices to evade the intent of the law, even in situations where the law called for competitive bidding. Pittsburgh for years found that William Flinn, one of its two bosses, was always the lowest "responsible" bidder for contracts. In other instances, specifications were such that only the favored one could meet them. In New Orleans, around 1890, in spite of the protests of the property owners, almost all paving was with rosetta gravel (in which one man had a monopoly). In other cases, the lowest bid was accepted, but there would be advance assurance (private and arranged) that the inspectors would not insist that the contractor meet the specifications. Contractors in Portland (Oregon) in 1893 whose men voted "right" were laxly supervised. In still other instances, the bidders themselves formed rings, bid high, and arranged for distribution of the contracts among themselves. This practice seems to have been a particular bent among paving contractors. William Gabriel of Cleveland, high in Republican circles, will serve as an example. This was not incompatible with generous bribes to municipal officials or rings as well. Graft in contracts extended to the schools—to their construction and to the textbooks purchased. Things were probably not so flagrant in Cleveland, where campaign contributions and not bribes were the favored means of business.

Franchises and privileges for the railroads and the various utilities came to be special sources of demoralization, particularly for the councils that usually had the responsibility for granting them. Initially, a community welcomed the railroad and even subsidized its coming. With growing urbanization, it looked forward to waterworks, lighting (gas or electricity), street cars (horse or cable), and eventually electricity and the telephone. The earliest of the franchises were likely to be most liberal with respect to rate allowed, duration, and service rendered. The cities wanted the utilities and often urged their coming. Later, as the latter proved enormously profitable, the stakes grew high, and betrayal of the public interest probably took place in the majority of cases. Power to grant franchises greatly increased the desirability of membership on the council. Hazen Pingree, mayor of Detroit in the early 1890's wrote:

> My experiences in fighting monopolistic corporations as mayor of Detroit, and in endeavoring to save to the people some of their right as against their greed, have further convinced me that they, the corporations, are responsible for nearly all the thieving and boodling with which cities are made to suffer from their servants. They seek almost uniformly to secure what

they want by means of bribes, and in this way they corrupt our councils and commissions.

Providence, in the 1890's allowed only property owners to vote. They elected businessmen to the city council. This council then awarded Nelson Aldrich, the state boss, a perpetual franchise, which he sold out at an enormous profit. He went to the Senate through wholesale bribery of rural voters, with money contributed by the sugar magnates for whom as congressman he had arranged a protective tariff. The city of Pawtucket, which sought to block a franchise, was overridden by the rurally dominated state legislature.

It was Lincoln Steffens who later dramatized beyond any forgetting the unholy link between the protected underworld, the city governments, and the portion of the business community in search of contracts and franchises—a link found in city after city. The story of his exposures belongs to the Progressive Era. At the time, these betrayals of the public interest were either not known or, if known, were enjoyed and shared, shrugged off and rationalized, or endured in futile fury.

Two or three further examples of documented franchise bribery might be cited. In 1884, in New York City, the Broadway Surface Railroad paid $25,000 to each of eighteen alderman and received the franchise. The rival company had offered the *city* $1 million. Another corporation set aside $100,000 to buy the council. The street-car companies of Indianapolis contributed to both political parties. So it went in city after city.

Some other examples of business corruption might be cited. Governor John P. Altgeld of Illinois sent a message (1895) to the state legislature, calling attention to the fantastically low rents paid by newspapers for school lands. In a most complex arrangement involving shipping companies, boarding-house keepers, "crimps" (recruiters of seamen), and the city authorities, the San Francisco waterfront instituted a reign of near-peonage, in which seamen were grossly overcharged for their lodging and shore "amenities," prevented from organized resistance, and virtually terrorized and blackmailed into signing on the ships again. In the early 1870's, local speculators of Dubuque, including two former mayors, bought up city bonds for a small amount and held out for redemption at par. Favored banks (that is, those contributing through appropriate channels to the city treasurer, the party, or the boss) received city deposits without having to pay interest thereon, or, as in Pittsburgh, paying the interest to the politicians. Finally, the employer power structure threw its weight and its funds in support of almost any administration that would protect strikebreakers, break up "radical" gatherings, and otherwise preserve the "American system" against alien ideas—this, without reference to the extent of the known corruption of the administration.

Theft, Assessment Favoritism, "Kickbacks," "Rake-Offs"

As might be expected, there were a number of examples of actual theft, most frequently by a city treasurer. Judges would occasionally keep fines. A certain amount of this was to be expected in an age of ruthless money-making when business ethics condoned all kinds of sharp practices in the private sector. What was more discouraging was that many of these thieves remained unpunished, as the machine with its frequent control over the courts protected its own. City officials of Spokane even stole funds contributed for relief after its great fire (1889).

How widespread was political favoritism in tax assessment would be extraordinarily difficult to determine. The practice of underassessment across the board to avoid litigation was almost universal, and in some communities it had a statutory base. Certainly many corporations were favored, in part because they were deemed an asset to the community's economic life. What was more probable was the widespread fear that, if a person were to criticize the city administration, he would find his underassessment raised. This particular form of blackmail took place in blatant fashion at one time in Jersey City. It also occurred under Park Board administration in the Bronx in 1874. From time to time, there would be exposures in the local press of assessment anomalies, but the press was itself vulnerable to punitive retaliation of this type because of its frequent underassessment.

The practice of compensating certain employees by fees instead of fixed salaries lingered on, in spite of or often because of the large amounts of money involved. Such employees were usually expected, by virtue of their election or appointment, to "kick back" a substantial portion to the party organization. Such "kickbacks" from the receiver of taxes amounted in Philadelphia to $200,000 in one of the years after 1873—divided among the small number who constituted the gas-house ring. Other compensations by the fee system were abandoned in 1873, and the employees were put on salaries. Some nominations and appointments were sold, with the receipts going, it was hoped, to the party campaign funds, concerning the use of which there was rarely in these days any effective accounting. Political assessments of city employees probably ruled in the majority of the cities.

How much graft in fact found its way into the pockets of the city employees for their betrayal of trust or, for that matter, for services they should have rendered in any event, how much "rake-off" the ring or the boss took, will never be known. What was graft and what was "rake-off" shaded into a gray zone after a while. The amount must have been colossal in the cities—certainly enough, had it been dedicated to municipal administration, to have enhanced efficiency and service enormously, or to have cut the tax rate drastically. Utility rates would have tumbled and service improved. . . .

Extortion and Blackmail

Extortion and blackmail, if not standard practice, were frequent enough to call for comment. Once in a while, as in Fort Worth (1877), they were used in an intriguing and perhaps constructive fashion. It was proposed that the sale of intoxicants be forbidden at the theaters. The ordinance was tabled, with the notation that it would be passed unless one of the theater owners paid his taxes.

In Brooklyn during the Whitney administration, the head of the fire department blocked an electric franchise until he was given one-fifth of the company's stock and several other politicians had taken a cut.

The newspapers were particularly vulnerable to blackmail. A threat of loss of the city's advertising was a marvelous silencer. In Tacoma (1889), enough businessmen believed a particular gambling house was a community asset that the newspaper that had denounced its protected status as a result lost heavily in both advertising and circulation.

The gangs of Detroit seemed to be immune in the 1880's and able to bring about the promotion or dismissal of a policeman. Sailors, tugmen, longshoremen made up the bulk of their personnel. In the early 1880's in Indianapolis, citizens were arrested on trumped-up charges and fined by judges who at that time were paid by the fines.

Police and the Courts

... [D]ifficulties stemmed from the key role played by the police in the electoral process, the graft from the under-world, and the desire on the part of the allegedly more respectable for immunities. In Tacoma, the mayor reprimanded the chief of police for raiding a brothel in which a number of the city's influential men were found. All these factors meant that in city after city the police force was really regarded as an adjunct of the political party or machine. In some of the smaller cities, the patronage aspect was expressed in extreme form. For example, until 1891 each new mayor of Wilmington (Delaware) appointed a new set of policemen, usually of his own party.

Nor were the courts immune as adjuncts to corruption. The district attorney and the judges, especially the local ones, were usually elected, and by the same processes as the mayors and councils. The same network of political and corrupt immunities that pervaded the police and stemmed from the rings and other politicians was present in the courts. Four hazards to justice were thus in a sense vulnerable to pressure and purchase—the stages of arrest, prosecution, the verdicts (and delays) of the judge, and the possibilities of a packed or bribed jury. William Howard Taft commented at a later date as follows:

> [The] administration of criminal law is a disgrace to our civilization, and the prevalence of crime and fraud, which here is greatly in excess of that in European countries, is due largely to the failure of the law to bring criminals to justice.

Quite apart from overt corruption, there were numerous ways in which courts could reward the party faithful, such as by appointment as favored bondsmen, stenographers, or auctioneers.

It was not surprising that an exasperated and otherwise respectable public occasionally fought back by violent means. In Cincinnati (1884), so flagrant had been the court delays and acquittals that a mass meeting, held to protest the situation, evolved into a mob bent on direct action. They burned the courthouse and attempted to storm the jail. For days the mob ruled. Police and militia failed, and only federal troops finally restored order. There were over fifty deaths. In Dallas, in the early 1880's, the "respectable" element, despairing of action by the city government in closing some of the worst resorts, took to burning them. Acquittal of the murderers of the chief of police of New Orleans by a probably corrupted jury was followed by lynchings. . . .

Summary Scenario

This in general was the scenario of most American cities about 1890: fitful reforms, usually not lasting; charters hopelessly tangled, with no agreement on remedies; civil service laws circumvented in the mad search for patronage opportunities; election frauds virtually normal; an underworld capitalizing on man's appetites and finding it easy to purchase allies in the police and the politician; countless opportunities for actual theft; business carrying over its disgraceful private ethics into subverting city government for its own ends, and city officials competing to obtain the opportunity to be lucratively subverted; citizens who might be expected to lead reforms generally indifferent, discouraged, frightened, and without the time necessary to give to the effort; a community with conflicting value systems into which the exploiter entered, albeit with an understanding and a sympathy denied to those from another class; ballots complicated; a nomination process seemingly built to invite control by the self-seeking; sinecures used to provide fulltime workers for the party machine; state governments ready to step in to aid in the corruption if local effort proved inadequate; confusion over the claims of party loyalty; a press often intimidated and frequently venal; countless opportunities to make decisions that would favor certain real estate over other locations; a burgeoning population rapidly urbanizing and dragging in its train innumerable problems of municipal services and aspirations.

For the unraveling of this tangled mess, the reformer and the career administrator had no acceptable philosophy.

NO ✔

Jon C. Teaford

Trumpeted Failures and
Unheralded Triumphs

In 1888 the British observer James Bryce proclaimed that "there is no denying that the government of cities is the one conspicuous failure of the United
States." With this pronouncement he summed up the feelings of a host of Americans. In New York City, residents along mansion-lined Fifth Avenue, parish-
ioners in the churches of then-sedate Brooklyn, even petty politicos at party
headquarters in Tammany Hall, all perceived serious flaws in the structure of
urban government. Some complained, for example, of the tyranny of upstate
Republican legislators, others attacked the domination of ward bosses, and still
others criticized the greed of public utility companies franchised by the municipality. Mugwump reformer Theodore Roosevelt decried government by Irish
political machine hacks, the moralist Reverend Charles Henry Parkhurst lam-
basted the reign of rum sellers, and that pariah of good-government advocates,
New York City ward boss George Washington Plunkitt, also found fault, attacking the evils of civil service. For each, the status quo in urban government was
defective. For each, the structure of municipal rule needed some revision. By
the close of the 1880s the litany of criticism was mounting, with one voice after
another adding a shrill comment on the misrule of the cities.

During the following two decades urban reformers repeated Bryce's words
with ritualistic regularity, and his observation proved one of the most-quoted
lines in the history of American government. Time and again latter-day Jeremi-
ahs damned American municipal rule of the late nineteenth century, denounc-
ing it as a national blight, a disgrace that by its example threatened the survival
of democracy throughout the world. In 1890 Andrew D. White, then-president
of Cornell University, wrote that "without the slightest exaggeration... the city
governments of the United States are the worst in Christendom—the most expensive, the most inefficient, and the most corrupt." Four years later the reform
journalist Edwin Godkin claimed that "the present condition of city governments in the United States is bringing democratic institutions into contempt
the world over, and imperiling some of the best things in our civilization." Such
preachers as the Reverend Washington Gladden denounced the American city
as the "smut of civilization," while his clerical colleague Reverend Parkhurst

From Jon C. Teaford, *The Unheralded Triumph: City Government in America, 1860–1900* (Johns Hopkins University Press, 1984). Copyright © 1984 by Johns Hopkins University Press. Reprinted by
permission.

said of the nation's municipalities: "Virtue is at the bottom and knavery on top. The rascals are out of jail and standing guard over men who aim to be honorable and law-abiding." And in 1904 journalist Lincoln Steffens stamped American urban rule with an indelible badge of opprobrium in the corruption-sated pages of his popular muckraking exposé *The Shame of the Cities*. Books, magazines, and newspapers all recited the catalog of municipal sins.

Likewise, many twentieth-century scholars passing judgment on the development of American city government have handed down a guilty verdict and sentenced American urban rule to a place of shame in the annals of the nation. In 1933 a leading student of municipal home rule claimed that "the conduct of municipal business has almost universally been inept and inefficient" and "at its worst it has been unspeakable, almost incredible." That same year the distinguished historian Arthur Schlesinger, Sr., in his seminal study *The Rise of the City*, described the development of municipal services during the last decades of the nineteenth century and found the achievements "distinctly creditable to a generation... confronted with the phenomenon of a great population everywhere clotting into towns." Yet later in his study he returned to the more traditional position, recounting tales of corruption and describing municipal rule during the last two decades of the century as "the worst city government the country had ever known." Writing in the 1950s, Bessie Louise Pierce, author of the finest biography to date of an American city, a multivolume history of Chicago, described that city's long list of municipal achievements but closed with a ritual admission of urban shortcomings, citing her approval of Bryce's condemnation. Similarly, that lifelong student of American municipal history, Ernest Griffith, subtitled his volume on late-nineteenth-century urban rule "the conspicuous failure," though he questioned whether municipal government was a greater failure than state government.

Historians such as Schlesinger and Griffith were born in the late nineteenth century, were raised during the Progressive era, and early imbibed the ideas of such critics as Bryce and White. Younger historians of the second half of the twentieth century were further removed from the scene of the supposed municipal debacle and could evaluate it more dispassionately. By the 1960s and 1970s, negative summations such as "unspeakable" and "incredible" were no longer common in accounts of nineteenth-century city government, and historians professing to the objectivity of the social sciences often refused to pronounce judgment on the quality of past rule. Yet recent general histories of urban America have continued both to describe the "deterioration" of city government during the Gilded Age and to focus on political bosses and good-government reformers who were forced to struggle with a decentralized, fragmented municipal structure supposedly unsuited to fast-growing metropolises of the 1880s and 1890s. Some chronicles of the American city have recognized the material advantages in public services during the late nineteenth century, but a number speak of the failure of the municipality to adapt to changing realities and of the shortcomings of an outmoded and ineffectual municipal framework. Sam Bass Warner, Jr., one of the leading new urban historians of the 1960s, has characterized the pattern of urban rule as one of "weak, corrupt, unimaginative municipal government." Almost one hundred years after

Bryce's original declaration, the story of American city government remains at best a tale of fragmentation and confusion and at worst one of weakness and corruption.

If modern scholars have not handed down such damning verdicts as the contemporary critics of the 1880s and 1890s, they have nevertheless issued evaluations critical of the American framework of urban rule. As yet, hindsight has not cast a golden glow over the municipal institutions of the late nineteenth century, and few historians or political scientists have written noble tributes to the achievements of American municipal government. Praise for the nation's municipal officials has been rare and grudging. Though many have recognized the elitist predilections of Bryce and his American informants, the influence of Bryce's words still persists, and the image of nineteenth-century city government remains tarnished. Historians have softened the harsh stereotype of the political boss, transforming him from a venal parasite into a necessary component of a makeshift, decentralized structure. Conversely, the boss's good-government foes have fallen somewhat from historical grace and are now typified as crusaders for the supremacy of an upper-middle-class business culture. But historians continue to aim their attention at these two elements of municipal rule, to the neglect of the formal, legal structure. They write more of the boss than of the mayor, more on the civic leagues than on the sober but significant city comptroller. Moreover they continue to stage the drama of bosses and reformers against a roughly sketched backdrop of municipal disarray. The white and black hats of the players may have shaded to gray, but the setting of the historian's pageant remains a ramshackle municipal structure.

Nevertheless, certain nagging realities stand in stark contrast to the traditional tableau of municipal rule. One need not look far to discover the monuments of nineteenth-century municipal achievement that still grace the nation's cities, surviving as concrete rebuttals to Bryce's words. In 1979 the architecture critic for the *New York Times* declared Central Park and the Brooklyn Bridge as "the two greatest works of architecture in New York... each... a magnificent object in its own right; each... the result of a brilliant synthesis of art and engineering after which the world was never quite the same." Each was also a product of municipal enterprise, the creation of a city government said to be the worst in Christendom. Moreover, can one visit San Francisco's Golden Gate Park or enter McKim, Mead, and White's palatial Boston Public Library and pronounce these landmarks evidence of weakness or failure? Indeed, can those city fathers be deemed "unimaginative" who hired the great landscape architect Frederick Law Olmsted to design the first public park systems in human history? And were the vast nineteenth-century water and drainage schemes that still serve the cities the handiwork of bumbling incompetents unable to cope with the demands of expanding industrial metropolises? The aqueducts of Rome were among the glories of ancient civilization; the grander water systems of nineteenth-century New York City are often overlooked by those preoccupied with the more lurid aspects of city rule.

A bright side of municipal endeavor did, then, exist. American city governments could claim grand achievements, and as Arthur Schlesinger, Sr., was willing to admit in 1933, urban leaders won some creditable victories in the struggle for improved services. Certainly there were manifold shortcomings: Crime and poverty persisted; fires raged and pavements buckled; garbage and street rubbish sometimes seemed insurmountable problems. Yet no government has ever claimed total success in coping with the problems of society; to some degree all have failed to service their populations adequately. If government ever actually succeeded, political scientists would have to retool and apply themselves to more intractable problems, and political philosophers would have to turn to less contemplative pursuits. Those with a negative propensity can always find ample evidence of "bad government," and late-nineteenth-century critics such as Bryce, White, and Godkin displayed that propensity. In their writings the good side of the municipal structure was as visible as the dark side of the moon.

Thus, observers of the late-nineteenth-century American municipality have usually focused microscopic attention on its failures while overlooking its achievements. Scoundrels have won much greater coverage than conscientious officials. Volumes have appeared, for example, on that champion among municipal thieves, New York City's political boss William M. Tweed, but not one book exists on the life and work of a perhaps more significant figure in nineteenth-century city government, Ellis Chesbrough the engineer who served both Boston and Chicago and who transformed the public works of the latter city. Only recently has an admirable group of studies begun to explore the work of such municipal technicians who were vital to the formulation and implementation of public policy. But prior to the 1970s accounts of dualistic conflicts between political bosses and good-government reformers predominated, obscuring the complexities of municipal rule and the diversity of elements actually vying for power and participating in city government. And such traditional accounts accepted as axiomatic the inadequacy of the formal municipal structure. Critics have trumpeted its failures, while its triumphs have gone unheralded.

If one recognizes some of the challenges that municipal leaders faced during the period 1870 to 1900, the magnitude of their achievements becomes clear. The leaders of the late nineteenth century inherited an urban scene of great tumult and stress and an urban population of increasing diversity and diversion.... The melting pot was coming to a boil, and yet throughout the 1870s, 1880s, and 1890s, waves of newcomers continued to enter the country, including more and more representatives of the alien cultures of southern and eastern Europe. To many in 1870, social and ethnic diversity seemed to endanger the very foundation of order and security in the nation, and municipal leaders faced the need to maintain a truce between Protestants and Catholics, old stock and new, the native business elite and immigrant workers.

The rush of migrants from both Europe and rural America combined with a high birth rate to produce another source of municipal problems, a soaring urban population.... During the last thirty years of the century, the nation's chief cities absorbed thousands of acres of new territory to accommodate this booming population, and once-compact cities sprawled outward from the urban core. This expansion sprawl produced demands for the extension of services and the construction of municipal facilities. The newly annexed peripheral wards needed sewer lines and water mains; they required fire and police protection; and residents of outlying districts expected the city to provide paved streets and lighting. Municipal governments could not simply maintain their services at existing levels; instead, they had to guarantee the extension of those services to thousands of new urban dwellers.

Improved and expanded municipal services, however, required funding, and revenue therefore posed another challenge for city rulers.... Inflation in the 1860s and economic depression in the 1870s exacerbated the financial problems of the city, leading to heightened cries for retrenchment. And throughout the 1880s and 1890s city governments faced the difficult problem of meeting rising expectations for services while at the same time satisfying demands for moderate taxes and fiscal conservatism. This was perhaps the toughest task confronting the late-nineteenth-century municipality.

During the last three decades of the century, American city government did, however, meet these challenges of diversity, growth, and financing with remarkable success. By century's close, American city dwellers enjoyed, on the average, as high a standard of public services as any urban residents in the world. Problems persisted, and there were ample grounds for complaint. But in America's cities, the supply of water was the most abundant, the street lights were the most brilliant, the parks the grandest, the libraries the largest, and the public transportation the fastest of any place in the world. American city fathers rapidly adapted to advances in technology, and New York City, Chicago, and Boston were usually in the forefront of efforts to apply new inventions and engineering breakthroughs to municipal problems. Moreover, America's cities achieved this level of modern service while remaining solvent and financially sound. No major American municipality defaulted on its debts payments during the 1890s, and by the end of the century all of the leading municipalities were able to sell their bonds at premium and pay record-low interest. Any wise financier would have testified that the bonds of those purported strongholds of inefficiency and speculation, the municipal corporations, were far safer investments than were the bonds of those quintessential products of American business ingenuity: the railroad corporations.

Not only did the city governments serve their residents without suffering financial collapse, but municipal leaders also achieved an uneasy balance of the conflicting forces within the city, accommodating each through a distribution of authority. Though commentators often claimed that the "better elements" of the urban populace had surrendered municipal administration to the hands of "low-bred" Irish saloonkeepers, such observations were misleading. Similarly incorrect is the claim that the business and professional elite abandoned city government during the late nineteenth century to decentralized lower-class ward leaders. The patrician, the plutocrat, the plebeian, and the professional bureaucrat all had their place in late-nineteenth-century municipal government; each staked an informal but definite claim to a particular domain within the municipal structure.

Upper-middle-class business figures presided over the executive branch and the independent park, library, and sinking-fund commissions. Throughout the last decades of the nineteenth century the mayor's office was generally in the hands of solid businessmen or professionals who were native-born Protestants. The leading executive officers were persons of citywide reputation and prestige, and during the period 1870 to 1900 their formal authority was increasing. Meanwhile, the legislative branch—the board of aldermen or city council —became the stronghold of small neighborhood retailers, often of immigrant background, who won their aldermanic seats because of their neighborhood reputation as good fellows willing to gain favors for their constituents. In some cities men of metropolitan standing virtually abandoned the city council, and in every major city this body was the chief forum for lower-middle-class and working-class ward politicians.

At the same time, an emerging body of trained experts was also securing a barony of power within city government. Even before the effective application of formal civil service laws, mayors and commissioners deferred to the judgment and expertise of professional engineers, landscape architects, educators, physicians, and fire chiefs, and a number of such figures served decade after decade in municipal posts, despite political upheavals in the executive and legislative branches. By the close of the century these professional civil servants were securing a place of permanent authority in city government. Their loyalty was not to downtown business interests nor to ward or ethnic particularism, but to their profession and their department. And they were gradually transforming those departments into strongholds of expertise.

The municipal professional, the downtown business leader, and the neighborhood shopkeeper and small-time politico each had differing concepts of city government and differing policy priorities. They thus represented potentially conflicting interests that could serve to divide the municipal polity and render it impotent. Yet, during the period 1870 to 1900, these elements remained in a state of peaceful, if contemptuous, coexistence. Hostilities broke out, especially if any element felt the boundaries of its domain were violated. But city governments could operate effectively if the truce between these elements was respected; in other words, if ward business remained the primary concern of ward alderman, citywide policy was in the hands of the business elite, and technical questions were decided by experts relatively undisturbed by party politics. This was the informal détente that was gradually developing amid the conflict and complaints.

Such extralegal participants as political parties and civic leagues also exerted their influence over municipal government, attempting to tip the uneasy balance of forces in their direction. The political party organization with its ward-based neighborhood bosses was one lever that the immigrants and less affluent could pull to affect the course of government. Civic organizations and reform leagues, in contrast, bolstered the so-called better element in government, the respected businessmen who usually dominated the leading executive offices and the independent commissions. Emerging professional groups such as engineering clubs and medical societies often lent their support to the rising ambitions and growing authority of the expert bureaucracy and permanent civil servants. And special-interest lobbyists like the fire insurance underwriters also urged professionalism in such municipal services as the fire department. Municipal government was no simple dualistic struggle between a citywide party boss with a diamond shirt stud and malodorous cigar and a good-government reformer with a Harvard degree and kid gloves. Various forces were pushing and pulling the municipal corporations, demanding a response to petitions and seeking a larger voice in the chambers of city government.

State legislatures provided the structural flexibility to respond to these demands. The state legislatures enjoyed the sovereign authority to bestow municipal powers and to determine the municipal structure, but when considering local measures, state lawmakers generally deferred to the judgment of the legislative delegation from the affected locality. If the local delegation favored a bill solely affecting its constituents, the legislature usually ratified the bill without opposition or debate. This rule of deference to the locality no longer applied, however, if the bill became a partisan issue, as it occasionally did. But in most cases authorization for new powers or for structural reforms depended on the city's representatives in the state legislature, and each session the state assemblies and senates rubber-stamped hundreds of local bills. Thus, indulgent legislators provided the vital elasticity that allowed urban governments to expand readily to meet new challenges and assume new responsibilities....

Even so, this process of perpetual adjustment resulted in a mechanism that succeeded in performing the job of city government. Municipal leaders adapted to the need for experts trained in the new technologies and hired such technicians. Moreover, downtown businessmen and ward politicos, the native-born and the immigrants, Protestants and Catholics, loosened the lid on the melting pot and reduced the boiling hostility of the midcentury to a simmer. The cities provided services; they backed off from the brink of bankruptcy; and the municipal structure guaranteed a voice to the various elements of society in both immigrant wards and elite downtown clubs.

Why, then, all the complaints? Why did so many critics of the 1880s and 1890s indulge in a rhetoric of failure, focusing on municipal shortcomings to the neglect of municipal successes? Why was municipal government so much abused? The answer lies in a fundamental irony: The late-nineteenth-century municipal structure accommodated everyone but satisfied no one. It was a system of compromise among parties discontented with compromise. It was a marriage of convenience, with the spouses providing a reasonably comfortable home for America's urban inhabitants. But it was not a happy home. The parties to the nuptials tolerated one another because they had to. Nevertheless, the businessman-mayors and plutocrat park commissioners disliked their dependence on ward politicians, whom they frequently regarded as petty grafters, and they frowned upon the power of the immigrant voters. Likewise, the emerging corps of civil servants was irked by interference from laypersons of both high and law status. And the plebeian party boss opposed efforts to extend the realm of the civil servants who had performed no partisan duties and thus merited no power. None liked their interdependence with persons they felt to be unworthy, incompetent, or hostile.

Enhancing this dissatisfaction was the cultural absolutism of the Victorian era. The late nineteenth century was an age when the business elite could refer to itself as the "best element" of society and take for granted its "God-given" superiority. It was an age when professional engineers, landscape architects, public health experts, librarians, educators, and fire fighters were first becoming aware of themselves as professionals, and with the zeal of converts they defended their newly exalted state of grace. It was also an age when most Protestants viewed Catholics as papal pawns and devotees of Italian idolatry, while most Catholics believed Protestants were little better than heathens and doomed to a quick trip to hell with no stops in purgatory. The late nineteenth century was not an age of cultural relativism but one of cultural absolutes, an age when people still definitely knew right from wrong, the correct from the erroneous. The American municipality, however, was a heterogeneous polyarchy, a network of accommodation and compromise in an era when accommodation and compromise smacked of unmanly dishonor and unprincipled pragmatism. Municipal government of the 1870s, 1880s, and 1890s rested on a system of broker politics, of bargaining and dealing....

Late-nineteenth-century urban government was a failure not of structure but of image. The system proved reasonably successful in providing services, but there was no prevailing ideology to validate its operation. In fact, the beliefs of the various participants were at odds with the structure of rule that governed them. The respectable elements believed in sobriety and government by persons of character. But the system of accommodation permitted whiskey taps to flow on the Sabbath for the Irish and for Germans, just as it allowed men in shiny suits with questionable reputations to occupy seats on the city council and in the municipal party conventions. The ward-based party devotees accepted the notions of Jacksonian democracy and believed quite literally in the maxim To the victor belong the spoils. But by the 1890s they faced a growing corps of civil servants more devoted to their profession than to any party. Although new professional bureaucrats preached a gospel of expertise, they still had to compromise with party-worshiping hacks and the supposedly diabolical forces of politics. Likewise, special-interest lobbyists such as the fire insurance underwriters were forced to cajole or coerce political leaders whom they deemed ignorant and unworthy of public office. Each of these groups worked together, but only from necessity and not because they believed in such a compromise of honor. There was no ideology of heterogeneous polyarchy, no system of beliefs to bolster the existing government structure. Thus late-nineteenth-century city government survived without moral support, and to many urban dwellers it seemed a bargain with the devil.

Twentieth-century historians also had reasons for focusing on urban failure rather than urban success. Some chroniclers in the early decades accepted rhetoric as reality and simply repeated the condemnations of critics such as Bryce, White, and Godkin. By the midcentury greater skepticism prevailed, but so did serious ills. In fact, the urban crisis of the 1960s provided the impetus for a great upsurge of interest in the history of the city, inspiring a search for the historical roots of urban breakdown and collapse. Urban problems were the scholars' preoccupation. Not until the much-ballyhooed "back-to-the-city" movement of the 1970s did the city become less an object of pity or contempt and more a treasured relic. By the late 1970s a new rhetoric was developing, in which sidewalks and streets assumed a nostalgic significance formerly reserved to babbling brooks and bucolic pastures.

The 1980s, then, seem an appropriate time to reevaluate the much-maligned municipality of the late nineteenth century. Back-to-the-city euphoria, however, should not distort one's judgment of the past. Instead, it is time to understand the system of city government from 1870 to 1900 complete with blemishes and beauty marks. One should not quickly dismiss the formal mechanisms of municipal rule as inadequate and outdated, requiring the unifying grasp of party bosses. Nor should one mindlessly laud municipal rule as a triumph of urban democracy. A serious appreciation of the municipal structure is necessary.

POSTSCRIPT

Was City Government in Late-Nineteenth-Century America a "Conspicuous Failure"?

The opposing viewpoints expressed by Griffith and Teaford represent a long-standing scholarly debate about the consequences of boss politics in the United States. James Bryce, *The American Commonwealth*, 2 vols. (Macmillan, 1888); Moisei Ostrogorski, *Democracy and the Organization of Political Parties* (1902; Anchor Books, 1964); and Lincoln Steffens, *The Shame of the Cities* (McClure, Phillips, 1904), present a litany of misdeeds associated with those who controlled municipal government. Political bosses, these authors charge, were guilty of malfeasance in office and all forms of graft and corruption.

Efforts to rehabilitate the sullied reputations of the machine politicians can be dated to the comments of one of Boss Tweed's henchmen, George Washington Plunkitt, a New York City ward heeler whose turn-of-the-century observations included a subtle distinction between "honest" and "dishonest" graft. A more scholarly effort was presented by Robert K. Merton, a political scientist who identified numerous "latent functions" of the political machine. According to Merton, city bosses created effective political organizations that humanized the dispensation of assistance, offered valuable political privileges for businessmen, and created alternative routes of social mobility for citizens, many of them immigrants, who typically were excluded from conventional means of personal advancement.

There are several excellent urban history texts that devote space to the development of municipal government in the late nineteenth century. Among these are David R. Goldfield and Blaine A. Brownell, *Urban America: From Downtown to No Town* (Houghton Mifflin, 1979); Howard P. Chudacoff and Judith E. Smith, *The Evolution of American Urban Society*, 3rd ed. (Prentice Hall, 1981); and Charles N. Glaab and A. Theodore Brown, *A History of Urban America*, 3rd ed. (Macmillan, 1983). Various developments in the industrial period are discussed in Blake McKelvey, *The Urbanization of America, 1860–1915* (Rutgers University Press, 1963) and Raymond A. Mohl, *The New City: Urban America in the Industrial Age, 1860-1920* (Harlan Davidson, 1985). Boss politics is analyzed in William L. Riordon, *Plunkitt of Tammany Hall* (E. P. Dutton, 1963); Robert K. Merton, *Social Theory and Social Structure* (Free Press, 1957); and John M. Allswang, *Bosses, Machines, and Urban Voters: An American Symbiosis* (Kennikat Press, 1977). The most famous urban boss is analyzed in Alexander B. Callow, Jr., *The Tweed Ring* (Oxford University Press, 1966) and Leo Hershkowitz, *Tweed's New York: Another Look* (Anchor Press, 1977). Scott Greer, ed., *Ethnics, Machines, and the American Future* (Harvard University Press, 1981) and Bruce M. Stave and Sondra Astor Stave, eds., *Urban Bosses, Machines, and Progressive Reformers,* 2d ed. (D. C. Heath, 1984) are excellent collections of essays on urban political machinery. Significant contributions to urban historiography are Sam Bass Warner, Jr., *Streetcar Suburbs: The Process of Growth in Boston, 1870–1900* (Harvard University Press, 1962); Stephan Thernstrom, *Poverty and Progress: Social Mobility in the Nineteenth-Century City* (Harvard University Press, 1964); Gunther Barth, *City People: The Rise of Modern City Culture in Nineteenth-Century America* (Oxford University Press, 1980); and Martin V. Melosi, *Garbage in the Cities: Refuse, Reform, and the Environment, 1880–1980* (Texas A & M University Press, 1982).

The Spanish-American War

This site from the Hispanic Division of the Library of Congress details events leading up to and occurring during the Spanish-American War. Included are links to pages on many of the key players, with a particular emphasis on Cuban patriots.

http://lcweb.loc.gov/rr/hispanic/1898/trask.html

Sallie Bingham Center for Women's History and Culture

The Sallie Bingham Center for Women's History and Culture is an integral part of Duke University's Special Collections Library, which houses a broad range of rare and unique primary source material. This page offers links to online collections, archives, and bibliographies on women's history.

http://odyssey.lib.duke.edu/women/

New Deal Network

Launched by the Franklin and Eleanor Roosevelt Institute (FERI) in October 1996, the New Deal Network (NDN) is a research and teaching resource on the World Wide Web devoted to the public works and arts projects of the New Deal. At the core of the NDN is a database of photographs, political cartoons, and texts (speeches, letters, and other historic documents from the New Deal period). Currently, there are over 20,000 items in this database.

http://newdeal.feri.org/index.htm

World War II Resources

This site links to primary source materials on the Web related to World War II, including original documents regarding all aspects of the war. From here you can see documents on Nazi-Soviet relations from the archives of the German Foreign Office, speeches of Franklin D. Roosevelt on foreign policy, and much more.

http://metalab.unc.edu/pha/

PART 2

The Response to Industrialism: War, Depressions, and Reforms, 1898–1945

*T**he maturing of the industrial system, a major economic depression, agrarian unrest, and labor violence all came to a head in 1898 with the Spanish-American war. The victory gave overseas territorial posses-sions to the United States and served notice to the world that the United States was a "great power." At the end of the nineteenth century, the African American population began fighting for civil rights, political power, and integration into society. Spokespeople for the blacks began to emerge, but their often unclear agendas frequently touched off con-troversy among both black people and white people. At the turn of the century, reformers known as the Progressives attempted to ameliorate the worst abuses brought about in the factories and slums of America's cities. However, it is argued that the most serious problems of inequality were never addressed by the Progressives.*

In the 1920s tensions arose between the values of the nation's rural past and the new social and moral values of modern America. There is controversy over whether the women's movement over those years lost momentum once the vote was achieved. The onset of a more activist federal government accelerated with the Great Depression. With more than one-quarter of the workforce unemployed, Franklin D. Roosevelt was elected on a promise to give Americans a "New Deal." World War II short-circuited these plans and led to the development of a cold war between the United States and the Soviet Union.

- Did Yellow Journalism Cause the Spanish-American War?

- Did Racial Segregation Improve the Status of African Americans?

- Did the Progressives Fail?

- Did the Women's Movement Die in the 1920s?

- Was the New Deal an Effective Answer to the Great Depression?

- Did President Roosevelt Deliberately Withhold Information About the Attack on Pearl Harbor From the American Commanders?

ISSUE 6

Did Yellow Journalism Cause the Spanish-American War?

YES: W. A. Swanberg, from *Citizen Hearst: A Biography of William Randolph Hearst* (Charles Scribner's Sons, 1961)

NO: David Nasaw, from *The Chief: The Life of William Randolph Hearst* (Houghton Mifflin, 2000)

ISSUE SUMMARY

YES: Journalist W. A. Swanberg argues that newspaper mogul William Randolph Hearst used the sensational and exploitative stories in his widely circulated *New York Journal* to stir up public opinion and to force President William McKinley to wage a war against Spain to free Cuba.

NO: Historian David Nasaw maintains that even if Hearst had not gone into publishing, the United States would have entered the war for political, economic, and security reasons.

Although Spanish rule over Cuba dated from 1511, most American presidents from the 1840s through the 1890s assumed that Cuba's strategic location, 90 miles from Florida, made it inevitable that the island would eventually come under some form of American control. American politicians were convinced that Spain was a declining power with limited influence in the Americas. However, repeated attempts to buy the island from Spain failed. Meanwhile, Cuban insurgents unsuccessfully rebelled against the Spanish government from 1868 until 1878. In 1894, in the midst of a depression, the U.S. Congress imposed a tariff on Cuban sugar, which had been entering the United States duty-free. An economic depression also hit the island and encouraged another rebellion against Spanish rule. The Spanish government retaliated by imposing a policy of "reconcentration." Approximately 300,000 Cubans were rounded up into fortified towns and camps to separate the insurgents from their supporters. As the atrocities were played up by sensationalist American newspapers, a new Spanish government came to power in Madrid that modified "reconcentration" and promised Cuba some autonomy.

Three events in the first few months of 1898 sabotaged a peaceful resolution of the Cuban crisis. On February 9 the *New York Journal* published a stolen private letter from Enrique Dupuy de Lome, the Spanish minister in Washington, which cast doubt on the sincerity with which the Spanish government was pursuing a policy of autonomy for Cuba. Even worse, de Lome stated, "McKinley is weak and a bidder for the admiration of the crowd, besides being a would be politician who tries to leave a door open behind himself while keeping on good terms with the jingos of his party."

The second event stirred up public opinion even more than the de Lome letter. Early in January antireform, pro-Spanish loyalists rioted in Havana. In response, President William McKinley ordered the battleship U.S.S. *Maine* to Havana's harbor to protect the lives of American citizens. On February 15 the *Maine* blew up, killing 260 American service personnel. Two separate investigations were made. The Spanish government said that the explosion was caused by internal failures, while the U.S. panel reported that a mine destroyed the *Maine*.

The third factor that pushed McKinley in the direction of a confrontation with Spain were the reports—official and unofficial—that the president received from public officials. In June 1897 William J. Calhoun, a political friend of the president, reported that the principal cause of the war "can be found in the economic conditions that have prevailed there for many years past." Calhoun's picture of the countryside outside of the military posts was particularly gloomy. Events moved rapidly in spring 1898. There were failed attempts at negotiating an end to "reconcentration," establishing an armistice in the Spanish-Cuban war, and setting up a truly autonomous government with a Cuban relationship to Spain similar to that of Canada's to Great Britain.

Why did President McKinley intervene in Cuba? In his address to Congress on April 11, 1898, the president listed four reasons: (1) "To put an end to the barbarities, bloodshed, starvation, and miseries now existing there"; (2) "to afford our citizens in Cuba protection and indemnity for life and property"; (3) to avoid "very serious injury to the commerce, trade, and business of our people, and by the wanton destruction of property and devastation of the island"; and (4) "the present condition of affairs in Cuba is a constant menace to our peace . . . where our traditional vessels are liable to seizure and are seized at our very door by war ships of a foreign nation, the expenditures of filibustering and the irritating questions and entanglements thus arising."

Implied in the president's message was the goal of independence for Cuba. Congress supported McKinley's request for intervention with a joint resolution that contained one exception: Senator Henry M. Teller of Colorado added an amendment that forbade the United States from annexing Cuba.

Historians continue to debate the reasons for the war. In the following selection, W. A. Swanberg argues that the war was started by propaganda created by the new yellow journalism of newspaper mogul William Randolph Hearst. In the second selection, David Nasaw contends that even if Hearst had not gone into publishing, political, economic and security reasons would have brought the United States into a war against Spain.

Citizen Hearst

The Cuban Joan of Arc

The Power of the Press

The two loudest warmongers in the United States, [William Randolph] Hearst and [Joseph] Pulitzer, were both six feet two inches tall, both millionaires who spent money royally while they espoused the causes of the masses. Both were singularly shy. The similarity ended there. Hearst was in a perfect health, placid and courteous. Pulitzer was blind, a nervous wreck who could fly into profane rages. Hearst was at his office daily, exercising personal control. Pulitzer was rarely at his proud, gold-domed skyscraper. He was only occasionally at his New York home on East Fifty-fifth Street, which was equipped with soundproof rooms to shield his quaking nerves. The rest of the time he was either at one of his four other mansions in Maine, New Jersey, Georgia and France, or aboard his palatial ocean-going yacht *Liberty*, keeping in touch with his editors by telegram or cable. Hearst believed in fighting Spain almost from the start of the Cuban trouble. Pulitzer, at first opposed to United States involvement, came around reluctantly for war, as he later candidly admitted, because it meant circulation.

It is safe to say that had not Pulitzer been locked in a bitter circulation struggle with Hearst, and had he not witnessed the added circulation Hearst's frenetic treatment of the Cuban news brought him, Pulitzer and his mighty *World* would have remained on the side of peace. Thus Hearst, in addition to his own potent newspapers, was responsible for dragging the morning and evening *World*, with the largest circulation in the nation, into the pro-war camp.

These two men addressed literally millions of Americans. In 1897, the circulation of Pulitzer's two papers was more than 800,000 daily. Hearst's morning and evening *Journal* were hardly 100,000 behind, and his San Francisco *Examiner* had 80,000. They had on their pro-war side the influential New York *Sun*, with about 150,000. Through the Associated Press and other news-service affiliations, the *Journal*, *World* and *Sun* dispatches were reprinted in many other important papers across the nation.

Against them they had the strongly anti-war *Herald* (100,000), the *Evening Post* (25,000), the conservative *Tribune* (75,000) and the high-priced *Times* (three cents, under 25,000 circulation). The remaining several New York papers were even smaller, had no funds for coverage of the Cuban rebellion, and exercised small weight.

The total circulation of New York's pro-war newspapers was about 1,560,000, against the anti-war total of 225,000.

However, all of these papers were of much more than local moment. The prestige of the large New York dailies on either side was a strong and determining influence on hundreds of fresh-water editors throughout the country who knew little of foreign affairs and traditionally had looked to the New York journals for guidance since the days of [Horace] Greeley, [James Gordon] Bennett and [Henry Jarvis] Raymond. Since the newspapers were the greatest mass medium then existing, their influence in shaping public opinion would be decisive. And since the New York newspapers in one way or another swayed most of the rest, it could be said that—given a situation where war or peace hung in almost equal balance—the clacking Underwoods and Remingtons in the grubby warrens around Printing House Square would decide whether it would be the olive branch or the sword.

No one could discount the national influence of the anti-war *Herald, Post, Tribune* and *Times.* Yet the plain fact was that their relatively quiet, sensible columns were dull newswise. They were like reasonable men speaking in normal tones. Naturally they were outshouted by the screams of the *Journal* and *World.* The majority of the public found it more exciting to read about the murder of Cuban babies and the rape of Cuban women by the Spaniards than to read conscientious accounts of complicated political problems and injustices on both sides. The hero-villain concept of the war was simple, easy to grasp and satisfying. In addition to having the loudest voices and the most money, Hearst and Pulitzer had the best writers and illustrators and had many more dispatch boats, jeweled swords and correspondents in Key West and Cuba than all the other papers combined. Hearst alone sent a total of at least thirty-five writers and artists to "cover the war" at various times. . . .

The Fate of the *Maine*

Hail Thee City Born Today!

. . . Like Caesar and Napoleon, Hearst enjoyed power. He derived pleasure from controlling masses of people, manipulating them to bring about events of national or international importance. Unlike Caesar and Napoleon, the bashful Hearst did his manipulating from behind the scenes with the aid of cylinder presses and tons of newsprint. By now, most other newspaper proprietors in New York regarded him with aversion as a man who would do anything for sensation, devoid of honesty or principle, a Polyphemus of propaganda who ate his enemies and kept his Cyclops eye on circulation. They misjudged the man by his methods. An incurable romantic, swayed by gusts of sentiment, Hearst was sincerely devoted to the Cuban cause and at the same time felt that American interests demanded the expulsion of Spain from the hemisphere. But he had no scruples against linking these defensible aims with a ruthless and vulgar drive for circulation, so that in the view of people of taste he had no unselfish impulses at all.

Considerations of taste in journalism did not disturb him. He had long since decided that the great majority of people, the masses, had no time or training for such a luxury as taste and could be reached and molded most effectively by the noise, sensation and repetition which he liked himself. Since these are the ingredients of modern mass advertising, Hearst deserves some dubious recognition as a pioneer.

His megalomania had grown. In San Francisco, his campaigns had been largely local, even his feud with the S.P. being inspired by local grievances. In New York he had started with local sensations—murders, public utility franchises, soup kitchens, bicycle carnivals. Now he was expanding his zone of operations into the nation and the world. His enemies were McKinley, Hanna, Weyler, Spain, France. The liberation of Miss Cisneros had been so successful that Hearst now had Karl Decker mapping an expedition to Devil's Island to free the wronged Captain Dreyfus and humiliate France as Spain had been humiliated.

In Spain, the American newspaper outcry, the continuation of the Cuban rebellion and the uprising in the Philippines caused the fall of the government and the formation of a new cabinet. Spain, with only some 18,000,000 people, grievously in debt, naturally feared the rich United States with its 75,000,000. In its anxiety to retain Cuba, its most treasured possession, it pocketed American insults and took steps to mollify the Yankees as well as the Cuban rebels. The new government under Práxedes Mateo Sagasta almost entirely accepted the United States position on Cuba. It promised the Cubans self-government under Spain. It dismissed General Weyler, who left Havana to the accompaniment of a valedictory in Hearst's *Journal* calling him "the monster of the century" who should be hanged for his "innumerable murders." It replaced him with General Ramón Blanco y Erenas, a kindly man not yet known as a murderer. It would be General Blanco's job to install the autonomous Cuban government and restore order.

But Hearst demanded independence for Cuba, not mere autonomy. He wrote a letter dated December 1, 1897, addressed to the unrecognized president of an unrecognized republic.

His Excellency Bartolomé Masso,

President of the Republic of Cuba:

Sir:—Will you kindly state through the New York *Journal*, acting for the people of the United States, the position of the Cuban Government on the offer of autonomy for the island by the Government of Spain?....

—Yours truly, W. R. Hearst.

Although some would dispute Hearst's right to act for "the people of the United States," Señor Masso did not. Apparently the letter was smuggled through to Masso, who eventually replied from Camaguey in part:

> ... We hold ourselves an independent nation, unrecognized though we may be by the civilized world. Autonomy is not for one moment considered by us. We absolutely reject it.
> We have no faith left in Spain or her promises....

Along with Hearst, the insurgents with one voice rejected autonomy. Estrada Palma branded the conciliatory measures as ruses to defeat the rebellion by typical Spanish treachery. Rebel army leaders warned that all Cubans who cooperated with the new Spanish schemes would be considered "traitors to the republic," meaning that they would be shot on sight. The militarily feeble rebels could not have taken this intransigent stand had they not seen how American public opinion had already forced the Spaniards to back down. Counting on further American support to drive the Spaniards out entirely, they continued their pillaging of plantations and villages.

The *Journal* agreed that the Cubans "would be fools if they trust Spanish promises," and boasted that "Spain fears the *Journal* and Karl Decker." Not surprisingly, attempts were made to dynamite the *Journal*'s Havana office. But President McKinley, impressed by the conciliatory efforts of the Sagasta government, was disposed to give it every opportunity for success. When Spain agreed to permit American contributions of food and clothing to be distributed to destitute Cubans by the Red Cross, and the relief work got under way, the outlook for peace on the troubled island seemed improved at last....

In Cuba, Consul General Lee kept hearing rumors of an "anti-American plot" in Matanzas. Although this never materialized, he urged protection for American nationals and property in Cuba. It was on Lee's recommendation that the twenty-four-gun battleship *Maine* was moved first to Key West, then to Havana, as a "friendly act of courtesy" to Spain. Spain, not deceived by the polite words, readied its armored cruiser *Vizcaya* to pay a "friendly visit" to New York.

The *Maine*, commanded by solemn, bespectacled Captain Charles D. Sigsbee, passed under the guns of Morro Castle and anchored in Havana harbor on January 25, 1898. The Spanish commander sent a case of fine sherry to Sigsbee and his officers, who later went ashore to dine with General Lee and enjoy a bullfight.

Hearst had hardly been aware of the *Maine* when she was launched in San Francisco in 1890, but now she loomed large. "OUR FLAG IN HAVANA AT LAST," headlined the *Journal*, urging that American vessels occupy all Cuban ports and demand the withdrawal of the Spanish troops, i.e., to make war. Although Captain Sigsbee and his men were enjoying a quiet sojourn in Havana, the *Journal* saw so many war clouds there that it momentarily forgot its *bête noire*, the Spanish minister in Washington, Dupuy de Lome. De Lome, who for three years had conducted himself with dignity in the capital despite painful provocation, chose this moment to commit an error. He wrote a letter critical of President McKinley to a friend in Havana, José Canalejas. A rebel sympathizer, Gustavo Escoto, who worked in Canalejas' office, read the letter, saw its propaganda possibilities, and stole it, boarding the next boat for New York.

The letter brought joy to Estrada Palma and the Peanut Club. Palma was so grateful to the *Journal* for its efforts for Cuba that he translated the letter and took it in person to the *Journal* office, handing it in triumph to Sam Chamberlain. In commenting on McKinley's pacific message to Congress, De Lome wrote:

> The message has undeceived the insurgents, who expected something else, and has paralyzed the action of Congress, but I consider it bad.... Besides the natural and inevitable coarseness with which he [McKinley] repeats all that the press and public opinion of Spain have said of Weyler, it shows once more what McKinley is: weak and catering to the rabble and, besides, a low politician who desires to leave the door open to himself and to stand well with the jingoes of his party....

Although this was a private letter, stolen, and although the *Journal* had leveled far worse insults of its own about McKinley multiplied by some 800,000 circulation, it flew into a front-page rage at De Lome that lasted for five days. The letter was too provocative for the Peanut Club to give it exclusively to the *Journal*. It gave it to all the newspapers, handing the *Journal* a beat, however, in giving it exclusive right to publish a facsimile. The *Journal* used *all of its front page* to publicize the letter, headlining it "THE WORST INSULT TO THE UNITED STATES IN ITS HISTORY" and demanding the minister's instant dismissal. It dredged up a book which De Lome had published twenty-two years earlier, stressing critical remarks he had made about American women. It perpetrated an enormity in doggerel:

> Dupuy de Lome, Dupuy de Lome, what's this I hear of you?
> Have you been throwing mud again, is what they're saying true?
> Get out, I say, get out before I start to fight.
> Just pack your few possessions and take a boat for home.
> I would not like my boot to use but—oh—get out, De Lome.

It ran a huge Davenport cartoon showing an angry Uncle Sam thumbing away a quaking De Lome, with a one-word caption, "Git." "Now let us have action immediate and decisive," it said. "The flag of Cuba Libre ought to float over Morro Castle within a week." All this went out over the Associated Press.

In Washington, De Lome instantly cabled his resignation to Madrid. This took the sting out of the State Department's demand for his dismissal, for he was already packing. The Spanish government promptly disavowed his letter and apologized for it. In a few days, United States officials realized that what the *Journal* and a few other New York newspapers chose to construe as a gross affront was nothing more than a comic diplomatic blunder. In Cuba, the new autonomous government was beginning to function. The outlook was promising. The De Lome incident would have been forgotten had it not been followed almost immediately by an event of violence and tragedy that still poses one of history's impenetrable mysteries.

The *Maine* had now been in Havana for three weeks. Its usefulness there was questionable, since there were no anti-American demonstrations. Navy Secretary John D. Long had contemplated recalling it early in February, only to desist because of Consul General Lee's advice that it stay. On the sultry night of February 15, as the clear bugle notes of "Taps" pealed across the quiet harbor, Captain Sigsbee was in his cabin writing a letter in some embarrassment to his wife. He explained that in a uniform pocket he had discovered a letter to her from an old friend which he had forgotten for ten months. He had just sealed the envelope at 9:40 when the *Maine* blew up all around him.

Though shaken, Sigsbee was unhurt. The vessel's lights blacked out. Screams came from wounded and dying men. Fire broke out forward, causing small-caliber ammunition to start popping like firecrackers. Survivors jumped into the water as the ship began settling slowly into the mud. Dazed bluejackets put out a boat to pick up the swimmers. Other boats came from the Spanish cruiser *Alfonso XII* and an American vessel nearby. Spaniards and Americans joined gallantly in the dangerous rescue work as ammunition continued to explode. At his palace, Spain's General Blanco burst into tears at the news and sent officers to express regret and organize assistance. Of the *Maine's* 350 officers and men, 260 died in the catastrophe. Sigsbee dispatched a telegram to "Secnav" in Washington, describing it and adding:

> Public opinion should be suspended until further report.... Many Spanish officers including representatives of General Blanco now with me to express sympathy.

Hearst had left the *Journal* earlier than usual that evening, probably to go to the theater. He returned to his apartment in the Worth House quite late without stopping at his office. He found his man Thompson waiting for him.

"There's a telephone from the office," Thompson said. "They say it's important news."

Hearst telephoned the *Journal*. "Hello," he said. "What is the important news?"

"The battleship *Maine* has been blown up in Havana Harbor," the editor replied.

"Good heavens, what have you done with the story?"

"We have put it on the first page, of course."

"Have you put anything else on the front page?"

"Only the other big news," said the editor.

"There is not any other big news," Hearst said. "Please spread the story all over the page. This means war."

There Is No Other News

Hearst's coverage of the *Maine* disaster still stands as the orgasmic acme of ruthless, truthless newspaper jingoism. As always, when he wanted anything he wanted it with passionate intensity. The *Maine* represented the fulfillment not of one want but two—war with Spain and more circulation to beat Pulitzer.

He fought for these ends with such abandonment of honesty and incitement of hatred that the stigma of it never quite left him even though he still had fifty-three years to live.

Intelligent Americans realized the preposterousness of the idea that Spain had blown up the *Maine*. Proud Spain had swallowed insult to avoid a war she knew she would lose. Her forbearance had borne fruit until the explosion in Havana caused journalistic insanity in New York. The disaster was the worst blow Spain could have suffered. The *Maine* might have been wrecked by an accidental explosion of her own magazines. If she was sunk by plotters, it was most reasonable to suspect those who stood to gain from the crime—the Cuban rebels, whose cause was flagging and would be lost unless the United States could be dragged into the struggle. There was one other possibility: that a group of Spaniards or Cuban loyalists, working off their hatred unknown to the Spanish government, were responsible.

Even the *Journal* admitted disbelief that Spain had officially ordered the explosion. But this was tucked away in small type and later disavowed. The big type, the headlines, the diagrams, the cartoons, the editorials, laid the blame inferentially or flatly on Spain. For a week afterward, the *Journal* devoted a daily average of eight and one-half pages to the *Maine* and war. In the face of Sigsbee's wise suggestion that "public opinion be suspended," the *Journal* lashed public opinion day after day.

Some idea of the *Journal's* enormities, though an inadequate one, is given by a day-by-day recapitulation of its headlines and stories.

February 16: "CRUISER MAINE BLOWN UP IN HAVANA HARBOR." This was simple truth, written before the propaganda machine got into motion. It was the last truthful front-page headline for almost two weeks.

February 17: "THE WARSHIP MAINE WAS SPLIT IN TWO BY AN ENEMY'S SECRET INFERNAL MACHINE." The cause, of course, was unknown. This issue had a seven-column drawing of the ship anchored over mines, and a diagram showing wires leading from the mines to a Spanish fortress on shore—a flight of fancy which many readers doubtless took as fact. The hatred of Spaniards for Americans was mentioned. The caption read, "If this [plot] can be proven, the brutal nature of the Spaniards will be shown in that they waited to spring the mine until after all men had retired for the night." The *Journal* said, "Captain Sigsbee Practically Declares that His Ship was Blown Up by a Mine or Torpedo." Sigsbee said no such thing. He later wrote, "A Spanish officer of high rank... showed me a New York paper of February 17 in which was pictured the *Maine* anchored over a mine. On another page was a plan showing wires leading from the *Maine* to shore. The officer asked me what I thought of that. It was explained that we had no censorship in the United States.... Apparently the Spanish officer could not grasp the idea."

February 18: "THE WHOLE COUNTRY THRILLS WITH THE WAR FEVER." This came at a time when Spanish and Cuban military, civil and ecclesiastical leaders were giving the victims a solemn state funeral in Havana, with every mark of respect, dedicating the plots used at Colon Cemetery to the United States in perpetuity. On this day, for the first time, the combined circulation of the morning and evening *Journal* passed a million.

February 20 (over a drawing:) "HOW THE MAINE ACTUALLY LOOKS AS IT LIES, WRECKED BY SPANISH TREACHERY, IN HAVANA BAY."

February 21: "HAVANA POPULACE INSULTS THE MEMORY OF THE MAINE VICTIMS." This was over a story alleging that Spanish officers had been overheard to boast that any other American ship visiting Havana would "follow the *Maine*."

February 23: "THE MAINE WAS DESTROYED BY TREACHERY."

Although the *Journal* knew all along who sank the ship, it offered $50,000 reward for the solution of the mystery. It also began a drive for a memorial to be erected to those lost in the explosion, Hearst donating the first $1000. It began as usual by soliciting famous men whose participation could be exploited, among them ex-President Cleveland. Cleveland won some measure of immortality by replying, "I decline to allow my sorrow for those who died on the *Maine* to be perverted to an advertising scheme for the New York *Journal*." Other "big names" were less percipient, General Nelson Miles, Levi Morton, Chauncey Depew and O. H. P. Belmont being among the many who lent their prestige to the drive.

On February 18, at this most inopportune of times, the Spanish cruiser *Vizcaya* arrived in New York harbor from Cartagena on her "courtesy call." Her commander, Captain Antonio Eulate, shocked when informed of the *Maine* tragedy, ordered his colors half-masted and said he would take no part in any festivities planned in his honor. In view of the public hysteria, the police and naval authorities took strenuous measures to protect the *Vizcaya*, surrounding her with a cordon of patrol boats. The *World*, almost as frenetic in its Hispanophobia as the *Journal*, warned that the *Vizcaya* might have treacherous intentions, saying, "While lying off the Battery, her shells will explode on the Harlem River and in the suburbs of Brooklyn." However, the *Vizcaya* did not fire a shot.

The Spanish authorities, incensed by the *Journal*'s warmongering, retaliated. *Journal* men were forbidden to board the *Vizcaya*. More important, the *Journal* was denied further use of the cables from Havana. It took cognizance of this with an announcement headed, "SPANISH COURTESIES TO AN AMERICAN NEWSPAPER," and boxed on the front page with a flowing American flag. It read:

> The *Journal* takes great pride in announcing that on account of its too decided Americanism and its work for the patriots of Cuba this newspaper and its reporters have been forbidden entrance on board the Spanish warship *Vizcaya;* its dispatches are refused transmission over the Government cables from Havana.
>
> These Spanish acts, of course, do not prevent the *Journal* from getting all the news.... The *Journal* is flattered by these delicate attentions from Spain.... It expects to merit still more attention when the United States decides to end Spanish misrule and horrors in America.

The *Journal* also presented its readers with a newly-devised "Game of War With Spain," to be played by four persons with cards. Two contestants would portray the crew of the United States battleship *Texas*, doing their best to "sink" the other two, who manned the *Vizcaya*.

Hearst had rounded up a carefully-selected group of jingoistic legislators who were not averse to a free trip to Cuba. Senators Hernando Money of Mississippi, John W. Thurston of Nebraska and J. H. Gallinger of New Hampshire, and Representatives William Alden Smith of Michigan and Amos Cummings of New York, embarked from Fort Monroe on the Hearst yacht *Anita* as *"Journal* Commissioners"* to make a survey of conditions on the island and to write reports for the *Journal*, their expenses being paid by Hearst. Representatives Smith and Cummings were members of the House Foreign Affairs and Naval Affairs committees respectively. The *Journal* meanwhile appealed to its readers to write their Congressmen, and said it had so far relayed 15,000 such letters demanding war.

The *Journal* raged at Senator Mark Hanna for deprecating the war talk. It referred to him frequently as "President Hanna," to indicate how completely McKinley was his puppet. The cowardly peace policy of the administration was dictated by a base desire for profits in Wall Street, which could be depressed by war. "President Hanna... announced that there will be no war," said the *Journal*. "... This attitude is fairly representative of the eminently respectable porcine citizens who—for dollars in the money-grubbing sty, support 'conservative' newspapers and consider the starvation of... inoffensive men, women and children, and the murder of 250 [sic] American sailors... of less importance than the fall of two points in a price of stock."

Anyone advocating peace was a traitor or a Wall Street profiteer, probably both. When Navy Secretary Long dared to say that "Spanish official responsibility for the *Maine* explosion might be considered eliminated," Long joined the *Journal*'s list of officials who had sold out the nation's honor to Wall Street. This was all part of a money-making coup engineered by Hanna, said the *Journal*, with Long as his pawn, for Hanna had advised his friends before the announcement to buy stocks which rose several points as a result of Long's words and netted them $20,000,000.

The treasonous President McKinley had already publicly stated his opinion that the *Maine* was wrecked by an accidental explosion of her own magazines. The perfidious Secretary of the Navy had defended Spain. In Havana at the time was sitting a United States naval board of inquiry, sending down divers to examine the *Maine*'s hull and taking testimony from survivors in an effort to determine the cause of the disaster. Spain had asked, and been promised, that no American newspaper correspondents would take part in the investigation. The *Journal*, with the *World* and *Sun* close behind, was whipping public fury to a point where all these official efforts were rendered useless, a trivial shadow play unheard behind the din of the headlines.

The Nearest Approach to Hell

In Cuba, Hearst's junketing group of Senators and Congressmen were finding plenty of destitution, which indeed was so bad that it could scarcely be exaggerated. The *Journal* praised them as "brave congressmen [who] faced death to get at the truth in Cuba." Each of the five legislators wrote articles for the *Journal* describing the suffering they saw. Mrs. Thurston, wife of the Senator from Nebraska, who had accompanied her husband, wrote an especially stirring appeal to *Journal* mothers:

> Oh! Mothers of the Northland, who tenderly clasp your little ones to your loving hearts! Think of the black despair that filled each [Cuban] mother's heart as she felt her life-blood ebb away, and knew that she had left her little ones to perish from the pain of starvation and disease.

While in the harbor of Matanzas, Mrs. Thurston suffered a heart attack and died aboard the Hearst yacht—a misfortune the *Journal* blamed on the destitution she had seen. The five "*Journal* Commissioners" returned to make speeches in Congress praising the *Journal*'s patriotic motives and declaring that newspaper reports of conditions in Cuba were not exaggerated. For weeks, while the naval court continued its investigation in Havana, American citizens were conducted into a theater world of Cuban horror, Spanish treachery and United States dishonor staged with primitive efficiency by Producer-Director Hearst and aped by the rabble-rousing Pulitzer (now sadly reduced to the role of imitator) and the respected *Sun*. Edwin Godkin vainly tried to stem the tide in his *Evening Post*, with its puny 25,000 circulation.

"... when one of [the yellow journals] offers a yacht voyage," Godkin wrote, "with free wine, rum and cigars, and a good bed, under the guise of philanthropy, or gets up a committee for Holy purposes, and promises to puff it, it can get almost any one it pleases to go on the yacht voyage and serve on the committee—senators, lawyers, divines, scholars, poets, presidents and what not.... Every one who knows anything about 'yellow journals' knows that everything they do and say is intended to promote sales.... No one—absolutely no one—supposes a yellow journal cares five cents about the Cubans, the *Maine* victims, or any one else. A yellow journal is probably the nearest approach to hell, existing in any Christian state."

Theodore Roosevelt, who had displeased the *Journal* as head of the New York police, was now Assistant Secretary of the Navy under Long and a jingo after Hearst's own heart. Roosevelt had decided instantly that the *Maine* was sunk by treacherous Spaniards. He privately referred with contempt to McKinley as having "no more backbone than a chocolate eclair." The *Journal*, always doubly glad when it could praise itself as it rapped its enemies, quoted Roosevelt in a front-page interview as saying: "It is cheering to find a newspaper of the great influence and circulation of the *Journal* tell [sic] the facts as they exist and ignore the suggestions of various kinds that emanate from sources that cannot be described as patriotic or loyal to the flag of this country."

Roosevelt immediately repudiated the statement, saying, "The alleged interview with me in today's New York *Journal* is an invention from beginning to end. It is difficult to understand the kind of infamy that resorts to such methods." Roosevelt later won a reputation for occasional denials of indiscreet things he had said, but perhaps in this instance it is safer to trust him than the *Journal*.

Long before the Navy report on the *Maine* was ready, the *Journal* anticipated it with sheer falsehood, saying, "the Court of Inquiry finds that Spanish government officials blew up the *Maine*," and that the warship "was purposely moved where a Spanish mine exploded by Spanish officers would destroy it." "The *Journal* can stake its reputation as a war prophet on this assertion: There will be a war with Spain as certain as the sun shines unless Spain abases herself in the dust and voluntarily consents to the freedom of Cuba." The Spaniards were universally painted as such cowardly, two-faced wretches that Madrid editors not surprisingly began railing at the "Yankee pigs," which in turn was faithfully reported by the *Journal* and its contemporaries.

Under these daily onslaughts, multiplied by many extra editions and news-service transmission from coast to coast, the nation was seething. The public was deceived, misled and tricked by its only source of information. McKinley, a kindly man of peace, could deal expertly with legislators but lacked the dynamism, the spark of leadership that grips and sways the public mind. The country was getting away from him. The Presidency of the United States was being preempted by batteries of cylinder presses.

On March 28, McKinley handed the report of the naval court to Congress. The court's opinion was that "the *Maine* was destroyed by the explosion of a submarine mine, which caused the partial explosion of two or more of the forward magazines." The court admitted its inability to fix the blame. A Spanish court of inquiry which had made a similar investigation, but which the Americans had denied an opportunity for close inspection, found for an accidental explosion within the ship. This report was ignored. The guilt for the disaster, if guilt there was, was a mystery then as it is today. No one ever collected the *Journal*'s $50,000 reward.

However, public sentiment was so inflamed that the United States court's opinion that the explosion came from outside and thus was not accidental was enough to lay the blame on Spain. The *Journal*, dissatisfied, declared that the truth was being hidden from the public, saying, "the suppressed testimony shows Spain is guilty of blowing up the *Maine*." Even the heavens demonstrated the inevitability of war. On the night of April 4, the moon was surrounded by two pale rings. "Many persons insisted," said the *Journal*, "that the contact of the two rings meant nothing short of war; the smaller ring standing for the pretension of Spain in the Island of Cuba and the larger circle for the United States and its immensely superior power."

This whimsy was lost in the prevailing theme of American dishonor. "Write to your Congressmen at once," the *Journal* urged its readers. "... Give Congress a chance to know what the people think." The same issue featured a cartoon depicting Hanna, with his puppet McKinley stuck in his back pocket, poking a white feather into the star-studded hat of Uncle Sam, and suggested satirically that the stars on the flag be changed to dollar signs and the stripes to rows of dollar bills. It ran a front-page headline in three-inch type: "HANNA VS. HONOR." When some Ohio politicians charged that Hanna was elected to the Senate by fraud, the *Journal*'s cartoon showed him in prison stripes with the caption, "Here is Our 'President-Maker!' How Do You Like Him?" It warned that "Spain's powerful flotilla" was believed to be "stealing toward our shore." Blasting McKinley and his Wall Street bosses for waiting for Spain to strike the first blow, it demanded, in an issue dotted with American flags, "In the name of 266 [sic] American seamen, butchered in cold blood by the Spaniards, what is a 'blow' in the McKinley concept of war?" It ran an imaginative drawing showing Spanish soldiers bayoneting helpless Cubans, with the caption, "The wires bring news of the butchery of two hundred more reconcentrados.... Two hundred murders more or fewer is of little importance in Spain's record, and McKinley can hardly be expected to get excited about this."

The *Journal* pointed out how ridiculously easy it would be to crush Spain. It talked of organizing a regiment of giant athletes including Heavyweights Bob Fitzsimmons and James J. Corbett, Ballplayer Cap Anson, Hammer Thrower Jim Mitchell and Indian Footballer Red Water, all of whom agreed to join. "Think of a regiment composed of magnificent men of this ilk!" glowed the *Journal*. "They would overawe any Spanish regiment by their mere appearance. They would scorn Krag-Jorgensen and Mauser bullets."

According to the *Journal,* volunteers were itching to avenge the *Maine.* Frank James, ex-bandit brother of the legendary Jesse, offered to lead a company of cowboys. Six hundred Sioux Indians were ready and willing to scalp Spaniards in Cuba. The *World* improved on this, reporting the statement of "Buffalo Bill" Cody that 30,000 Indian fighters could clear the Spaniards out of Cuba in sixty days. The *Journal* came back with a report of riots in Havana that had "2,000 AMERICANS IN PERIL," presenting a four-column drawing showing exactly how the Navy would bombard Morro Castle and land men around Havana. *Journal* reporters were sent to interview the mothers of sailors who died in the *Maine* living in the New York area. All made pathetic appeals for vengeance.

"How would President McKinley have felt, I wonder," said one of them, "if he had a son on the *Maine* murdered as was my little boy? Would he then forget the crime and let it go unpunished while the body of his child was lying as food for the sharks in the Spanish harbor of Havana?" Another mother was quoted as saying in part, "I ask that mine and other mothers' sons be avenged.... I ask it for justice [sic] sake and the honor of the flag."

In Madrid, United States Minister Stewart Woodford was working efficiently for peace, although he was ostracized by Spanish society as De Lome previously had been in Washington. Being out of range of the *Journal*, which attacked his peace efforts as "twaddle," he felt that peace could be preserved. It would have been had not his efforts been junked by the administration. He found the Spanish government ready to go the limit to avoid war. "They cannot go further in open concessions to us," Woodford earlier had informed McKinley, "without being overthrown by their own people here in Spain.... They want peace if they can keep peace and save the dynasty. They prefer the chances of war, with the certain loss of Cuba, to the overthrow of the dynasty." On April 9, Woodford cabled that the Queen's government had gone still farther and had surrendered to all the important United States demands, even to the extent of offering to grant an immediate armistice there. Woodford was confident that this last concession meant peace, saying:

> I hope that nothing will now be done to humiliate Spain as I am satisfied that the present government is going, and is loyally ready to go, as fast and as far as it can. With your power of action sufficiently free, you will win the fight on your own lines.

Here was the key to an amicable settlement, if the United States wanted it. But McKinley knew that the majority of the American people, misled by their newspapers, wanted war. He knew that many legislators, influenced by their angry constituents, wanted war. And he knew that his administration and the Republican party would suffer unpopularity and loss of confidence if it made a stand for peace.

Mr. McKinley bowed to Mr. Hearst. He went over to the war party. Without taking any stand, he submitted the whole problem to Congress in a message given on April 11. He dramatized his own abandonment of peace by burying the all-important Spanish concessions in the last two paragraphs of his speech. Everybody knew that this meant war, but the *Journal* was impatient at the delay in making it official, as one of its headlines showed:

SUICIDE

LAMENTED

THE MAINE

AGED MRS. MARY WAYT ENHALED [*sic*] GAS
THROUGH A TUBE.

GRIEVED OVER OUR DELAY

"The Government May Live in Dishonor," Said She,

"I Cannot."

Possibly the President was surprised at the peace sentiment still existing when the Senate on April 19 passed a war resolution by the narrow vote of 42 to 35. Only four more Senators on the peace side would have swung the balance, indicating that determined Presidential leadership might have foiled Hearst. But when the House concurred with the Senate in a 310–6 vote for war, it demonstrated that McKinley, had he won peace, would have won unpopularity along with it.

It was an unnecessary war. It was the newspapers' war. Above all, it was Hearst's war. It is safe to say that had not Hearst, with his magnificently tawdry flair for publicity and agitation, enlisted the women of America in a crusade they misunderstood, made a national heroine of the jail-breaking Miss Cisneros, made a national abomination of Dupuy de Lome, made the *Maine* a mistaken symbol of Spanish treachery, caused thousands of citizens to write their Congressmen, and dragged the powerful *World* along with him into journalistic ill-fame, the public would have kept its sanity, McKinley would have shown more spunk, at least four more Senators would have taken counsel with reason, and there would have been no war.

"The outbreak of the Spanish-American war found Mr. Hearst in a state of proud ecstasy," recalled James Creelman, who was working with Hearst daily. "He had won his campaign and the McKinley Administration had been forced into war." Willis Abbot wrote: "Hearst was accustomed to refer to the war, in company with his staff, as 'our war.' "

He rallied the United States with a headline in four-inch type:

"NOW TO AVENGE THE MAINE!"

David Nasaw ⬅ **NO**

"How Do You Like the *Journal*'s War?"

There are no accounts of Hearst's life nor are there histories of the Spanish-American War that do not include some discussion of the role of the Yellow Press in general and Hearst in particular in fomenting war in Cuba. Still, it is safe to say from the vantage point of one hundred years that even had William Randolph Hearst never gone into publishing, the United States would nonetheless have declared war on Spain in April of 1898. That Hearst has received so large a measure of credit or blame for that "glorious war" is a tribute to his genius as a self-promoter. It was Hearst who proclaimed the war in Cuba to be the *New York Journal*'s war and he who convinced the rest of the nation that without the Hearst press leading the way there would have been no war.

⟡

The first Cuban revolution against Spanish colonialism had begun in 1868, when Hearst was five years old, and was only subdued after ten years of fighting. In early 1895, the rebellion was reignited after the United States imposed a new American tariff on Cuban exports that led to massive unemployment on the sugar plantations and economic hardship throughout the island. By the fall, the Cuban revolutionaries had freed enough territory from Spanish rule to proclaim their own provisional government. "The reports indicate that Cuba is likely to gain her independence," the *San Francisco Examiner* editorialized in August of 1895, "but not before many battles have been fought, many lives have been lost, much property has been destroyed." Concluding that Spain was prepared to "fight a war to extermination" in Cuba, the *Examiner* called on the government in Washington to protect the innocent men, women, and children of Cuba from the fate that had recently befallen the Armenians at the hands of the Turks: "It may not be our duty to interfere in Turkey, but we certainly cannot permit the creation of another Armenia in this hemisphere... Cuba is our Armenia, and it is at our doors.... We are determined that no more butcheries and arsons shall be laid to our door. Cuba must not stand in the relation to us that Armenia does to England."

In early 1896, Spain responded to the growing insurrection in Cuba by sending 150,000 troops to the island commanded by General Valeriano Weyler

From David Nasaw, *The Chief: The Life of William Randolph Hearst* (Houghton Mifflin, 2000). Copyright © 2000 by David Nasaw. Reprinted by permission of Houghton Mifflin Company. All rights reserved. Notes omitted.

(soon to be known in the American press as "Butcher" Weyler). Weyler tried to quell the rebellion by herding Cuban peasants into concentration camps to prevent them from supporting the rebel armies with food and new recruits. Hundreds of thousands of Cubans were forced from their land to die of starvation and disease behind barbed wire. The suffering was unimaginable. Pulitzer's *World*, Dana's *Sun*, and the *Journal*, which were fed a steady diet of stories from the Junta, the rebels' unofficial diplomatic and publicity arm, covered the events in Cuba as if they were happening next door.

That Spain had no moral or political right to maintain a colonial empire in the New World was not, for Hearst, a matter of debate. But this was not the primary reason why the Cuban conflict was given a prominent place on his front pages. What made Cuba such a compelling story was the fact that events on the island lent themselves to Hearst's favorite plot line. Here was raw material for tales of corruption more horrific than any yet told. The villains were lecherous and bloodthirsty Spanish officials and army officers; the victims, innocent Cuban women and children; the heroes, crusading *Journal* reporters and their publisher.

"Credible witnesses have testified," read an editorial from December 1896, "that all prisoners captured by Weyler's forces are killed on the spot; that even helpless inmates of a hospital have not been spared, and that Weyler's intention seems to be to murder all the pacificos in the country.... The American people will not tolerate in the Western Hemisphere the methods of the Turkish savages in Armenia, no matter what the cost of putting an end to them might be. Twenty Spains would prove no efficacious obstacle in the way of a righteous crusade like that. Let us not act hastily, but let us act."

In early 1897, Hearst offered Richard Harding Davis $3,000 a month plus expenses to serve as the *Journal's* special correspondent in Cuba. Artist Frederic Remington was sent along to illustrate Davis's articles. The two were transported to Cuba—with a full crew of assistants—in Hearst's new steam-driven 112-foot yacht, the *Vamoose*, which he had purchased in the early 1890s and kept moored in New York. Unfortunately the *Vamoose*, though a magnificent-looking yacht and reportedly the fastest ship in New York Harbor, was entirely unsuited for the mission. After three attempts at landing, the captain had to turn back. Davis was so frustrated at being marooned offshore that, as he wrote his mother, he lay on the deck and cried. The *Vamoose* returned to Key West, where Hearst wired his reporters an additional $1,000 to buy or lease another boat. Davis and Remington decided instead to take the regularly scheduled passenger steamer to Havana.

Hearst made the most of his stars' heroic entry onto the battle-scarred island. In mid-January, the *Journal* reported triumphantly that its representatives had caught up with the insurgent Cuban army. Davis was outraged. As he had written his mother a few days earlier, not only had he not found any army in the field, he had in his entire time in Cuba not "heard a shot fired or seen an insurgent.... I am just 'not in it' and I am torn between coming home and making your dear heart stop worrying and getting one story to justify me being here and that damn silly page of the Journal's.... All Hearst wants is my name and

I will give him that only if it will be signed to a different sort of a story from those they have been printing."

While Davis never did find any fighting, he was able to find enough material to write a few magnificent front-page stories on the devastation the war had visited on Cuba and its peoples. Frederic Remington was not so fortunate. Disgusted by the lack of action and his inability to find scenes worth illustrating, he telegrammed Hearst from Havana that he wished to return to New York. "Everything is quiet. There is no trouble here. There will be no war." Hearst, according to James Creelman, who wrote about the incident in his autobiography, answered Remington by return cable, "Please remain. You furnish the pictures, and I'll furnish the war."

Though many pages have been written about these telegrams, there is no record of them outside of Creelman's 1901 autobiography. Hearst himself, in a letter to the *London Times* in 1907, referred to the intimation that he was chiefly responsible for the Spanish war as a kind of "clotted nonsense" which "could only be generally circulated and generally believed in England."

Despite his disclaimers, Hearst might well have written the telegram to Remington, but if he did, the war he was referring to was the one already being fought between the Cuban revolutionaries and the Spanish army, not the one the Americans would later fight. There is no mention of or reference to American intervention in the telegrams; the groundswell that would lead to intervention after the sinking of the *Maine* had not yet begun. The war in question, the war Hearst may have claimed he would furnish, was the one between Cubans and Spaniards being waged in January of 1897, not the one that would be declared in Washington fifteen months later.

The question that is much more interesting than whether or not Hearst wrote the telegram is why its contents have been so universally misinterpreted. The answer is simple: Hearst, with his genius for self-promotion, so deftly inserted himself and his newspapers into the narrative of the Spanish-American War that historians and the general public have accepted the presumption that he furnished it.

❧

Though Hearst tried his best to keep Cuba on his front pages, events conspired against him. By April of 1897, Cuba was no longer front-page news. Hearst focused his attention instead on the threatened war between Greece and Turkey, dispatching to the front a full complement of star reporters led by Stephen Crane, Julian Ralph, two "female correspondents," and a full "contingent of Greek couriers, translators, and orderlies."

By the summer of 1897, peace having settled over Greece, Hearst and his editors were left without a viable front-page story cycle. They found it in August in Cuba where, as they reported in huge bold headlines and artfully engraved line drawings, Evangelina Cosio y Cisneros, the young and innocent daughter of a jailed insurgent, had been cast into an airless dungeon for daring to protect her chastity against the brutal advances of a lust-crazed Spanish colonel. Evangelina was the perfect heroine for Hearst's melodrama: a beautiful eighteen-year-old "Cuban Joan of Arc, with long black hair." As Creelman recalled in his autobiography—no doubt with some embellishment—Hearst, on hearing of Evangelina's plight, took command of the newsroom and barked out orders to the assembled editors and reporters:

> "Telegraph to our correspondent in Havana to wire every detail of this case. Get up a petition to the Queen Regent of Spain for this girl's pardon. Enlist the women of America. Have them sign the petition. Wake up our correspondents all over the country. Have distinguished women sign first. Cable the petitions and the names to the Queen Regent. Notify our minister in Madrid. We can make a national issue of this case. . . . That girl must be saved if we have to take her out of prison by force or send a steamer to meet the vessel that carries her away—but that would be piracy, wouldn't it?"

"Within an hour," continues Creelman's account, "messages were flashing to Cuba, and to every part of the United States. The petition to the Queen Regent was telegraphed to more than two hundred correspondents in various American cities and towns. Each correspondent was instructed to hire a carriage and employ whatever assistance he needed, get the signatures of prominent women of the place, and telegraph them to New York as quickly as possible."

Hearst himself telegraphed the most prominent women in the nation, including Mrs. McKinley in the White House: "Will you not add your name to that of distinguished American women like Mrs. Julia Ward Howe . . . who are cabling petitions to Queen Regent of Spain for release of Evangelina Cisneros eighteen years old . . . who is threatened with twenty years imprisonment? She is almost a child, sick, defenseless, and in prison. A word may save her. Answer at our expense. William Hearst."

Hundreds of responses followed—from Clara Barton, Mrs. Jefferson Davis, President McKinley's mother, and many more—each one of them reproduced on the pages of the *Journal*. While the *World*, citing the American consul general in Havana, screamed that the Cisneros story was more hoax than fact, and *Town Topics*, the weekly guide to gossip and politics in New York, echoing the opinion of the city's respectable classes, complained that the *Journal*'s coverage was both "senseless and pernicious," Hearst continued to trumpet the story, with the focus shifted from what had been done to Evangelina Cisneros to what the *Journal* was doing for her.

As it became apparent that Spain was not about to release Evangelina, Hearst ordered the reporter and adventurer Karl Decker to sail for Cuba and help Evangelina escape. Miraculously, with the help of some well-placed bribes, Decker succeeded in springing Cisneros from her dungeon and transporting her to New York City: "An American Newspaper Accomplishes at a Single Stroke What the Red Tape of Diplomacy Failed to Bring About in Many Months." In New York, Hearst dressed Evangelina like a princess in a long white gown, installed her in a suite at the Waldorf, and paraded her through the streets to a huge rally at Madison Square Garden, followed by a dinner at Delmonico's, a ball in the Waldorf's Red Room, and a trip to Washington, D.C., for a reception with President McKinley at the White House.

Hearst's rescue of Cisneros was significant not because, as his supporters and critics would later argue, it embarrassed the Spanish and pushed the United States toward involvement in the Caribbean, but because it strengthened his sense of entitlement and bolstered his confidence that because he was acting on behalf of the American people, he could make his own rules—subverting, if need be, common sense and international law.

~◆~

The Evangelina Cisneros rescue was a sideshow. The real story was being played out in Cuba, where the insurgents continued their battle for independence, and in Spain, where the new Liberal party government found itself caught between the Cuban insurrectionists, who demanded complete independence, and the Conservative opposition, army officers, Spanish landholders in Cuba, and colonial officials, who threatened civil war should the Liberal government cede the island to the Cubans. With no compromise possible, the war continued. American businessmen watched hopelessly as the Cuban economy disintegrated, trade halted, and tens of millions of dollars in American investments were rendered virtually worthless.

On January 11, 1898, antigovernment riots broke out in Havana, incited this time not by the Cuban revolutionaries but by Spanish army officers who feared that the government in Madrid might give in to the revolutionaries. President McKinley ordered the battleship U.S.S. *Maine* to sail from Key West to protect American interests on the island.

Two weeks later, a representative of the Cuban Junta appeared at the *Journal* office with a stolen letter in which Dupuy de Lôme, the Spanish ambassador to the United States, referred to President McKinley as "weak, vacillating, and venal." The Cubans had offered the letter to the *Herald*, but when the *Herald* editors delayed publication pending authentication, the rebels withdrew it and marched to Hearst's office. The *Journal* published the letter next morning in an inflammatory English translation. The headline read, "Worst Insult to the United States in Its History."

Under ordinary circumstances, Hearst could have wrung headlines out of this story for weeks, but events were now moving so fast he did not have to. On the evening of February 15, 1898, the U.S.S. *Maine*, under circumstances which even today are not entirely clear, exploded in Havana Harbor, instantly killing more than 250 of the sailors, marines, and officers on board. This event, if we are to judge only from the size of the headlines, became at once the biggest newspaper story since the assassination of President Lincoln.

According to Hearst's account, he was awakened with news of the *Maine's* sinking by his butler, George Thompson:

> "There's a telephone call from the office. They say it's important news."
>
> The office was called up.
>
> "Hello, what is the important news?"

"The battleship Maine *has been blown up in Havana Harbor."*

"Good heavens, what have you done with the story?"

"We have put it on the first page of course."

"Have you put anything else on the front page?"

"Only the other big news."

"There is not any other big news. Please spread the story all over the page. This means war."

While President McKinley convened a naval court of inquiry to determine the cause of the *Maine* explosion and newspapers across the country cautioned readers to await the gathering of evidence before jumping to conclusions, Pulitzer's *World* and Hearst's *Journal* determined, after only forty-eight hours, that the explosion had been detonated by a Spanish mine. "Destruction of the Warship *Maine* Was the Work of An Enemy," read the *Journal's* front-page headline on February 17, 1897. In the middle of the page was a drawing of the *Maine* in Havana Harbor with a mine placed directly underneath it. The caption read: "The Spaniards, it is believed, arranged to have the *Maine* anchored over one of the Harbor mines. Wires connected the mine with a powder magazine and it is thought the explosion was caused by sending an electric current through the wire."

"*Maine* is great thing. Arouse everybody. Stir up Madrid," Hearst telegrammed James Creelman in London. Having determined that the Spanish were responsible for the explosion, Hearst positioned the *Journal* in the center of the story as the hero who would avenge the murder of the American sailors. He offered a $50,000 reward for the solution to the mystery of the *Maine* explosion, began a drive for a *Maine* memorial and contributed the first $1,000, devised a new "War with Spain" card game, enlisted a delegation of senators and congressmen to travel to Cuba on a Hearst yacht as "*Journal* commissioners," and implored his readers to write their congressmen. The combined circulation of the morning and evening *Journals* reached one million and continued to grow.

Pulitzer and his editors tried but failed to keep up with Hearst's newspapers on this, the biggest story since the Civil War. The *World* did not have the funds—or the Hearst-owned yachts—to send dozens of correspondents and artists to report firsthand on Cuba, nor did it have the staff to put out six to eight pages of articles, editorials, cartoons, interviews, and illustrated features on the Cuban crisis each day. The *Journal's* coverage was bigger, more spectacular, more varied, and more imaginative than that of any other paper in the city. There were dozens of stories on the *Maine* explosion, on the funeral procession for the *Maine* victims, on the mounting horrors in "Butcher" Weyler's death camps, on the findings of the "*Journal* commissioners" to Cuba. While McKinley awaited the report from his naval court of inquiry on the cause of the *Maine* explosion, the Hearst papers attacked the president together with Mark Hanna, the "conservative" newspapers that refused to join the crusade, and "the eminently respectable porcine citizens" who resisted the call to battle. To graphically demonstrate to the public how easy it would be to win this war, the *Journal* contacted America's most famous oversized athletes, including heavyweight champions James J. Corbett and Bob Fitzsimmons, baseball star Cap Anson, and champion hammer-throwers and wrestlers, to ask if they would consider joining a regiment of athletes. "Think of a regiment composed of magnificent men of this ilk!" the *Journal* gloated on March 29, 1898. "They would overawe any Spanish regiment by their mere appearance."

"Whatever else happens, the *World* must go," declared *Town Topics* in early April. "It has been beaten on its own dunghill by the *Journal*, which has bigger type, bigger pictures, bigger war scares, and a bigger bluff. If Mr. Pulitzer had his eyesight he would not be content to play second fiddle to the *Journal* and allow Mr. Hearst to set the tone."

When, less than two months after the *Maine* explosion, Congress passed a joint resolution demanding that Spain "relinquish its authority and government on the island of Cuba" and directing the president "to use the land and naval forces of the United States to carry these resolutions into effect," Hearst's *Journal* greeted the news, in headlines a full four inches high, "NOW TO AVENGE THE MAINE!" Five days later, on April 25, rockets were set off from the roof of the *Journal* building to celebrate the signing of the declaration of war and the *Journal* offered a prize of $1,000 to the reader who came up with the best ideas for conducting the war. A week later, Hearst, unable to contain his euphoria, asked on the very top of his front page, "How do you like the *Journal's* war?"

Though Hearst claimed that the war in Cuba was the *Journal's* war, it was not. President McKinley had not asked for a declaration of war, nor had Congress granted him one, to please William R. Hearst. The "yellows" had been clamoring for war for several years, with no discernible effect, their strident voices balanced by more conservative Republican voices like Whitelaw Reid's *Tribune* and E. L. Godkin's *Evening Post,* which urged restraint. Hearst was a cheerleader not a policy maker. McKinley had his own sources of information in Cuba; he did not need a Hearst or Pulitzer to tell him what was going on there nor did he place much trust in what they had to say. According to the historian Walter LaFeber, he did not even read the "yellows." As John Offner, the author of *An Unwanted War,* has concluded, sensational journalism had "only a marginal impact" on the decision to go to war with Spain: "Hearst played on American prejudices; he did not create them. Although he and other sensationalists supplied many false stories, they did not fabricate the major events that moved the United States.... Had there been no sensational press, only responsible editors, the American public nevertheless would have learned about the terrible conditions in Cuba [and] would have wanted Spain to leave."

What prompted McKinley, Congress, and most of the business community to support intervention in early 1898, after resisting for so many years, was the recognition that Spain had lost control of Cuba and would not be able to regain it. Politically, McKinley could not afford to allow the Democrats to blame him and his party for so much human suffering and bloodshed so close to home. Economically, he could not allow the millions of dollars invested on the island to lie fallow or, worse yet, be lost forever should the Cubans oust the Spanish.

POSTSCRIPT

Did Yellow Journalism Cause the Spanish-American War?

In his biography of the newspaper mogul, Swanberg argues that Hearst sent dozens of his first-rate reporters into Cuba to publicize the failure of the Spanish government to maintain control over the last vestiges of its empire in the Caribbean. The Spanish government contributed to the Hearst propaganda machine with its imprisonment of Evangelina Cosio y Cisneros, the letter of Spanish minister de Lome castigating President McKinley as "weak... catering to the rabble, and... [a] low politician," and, finally, what later proved to be the accidental blowing up of the battleship *Maine* in Havana harbor. There is little doubt that in major cities like San Francisco and New York the Hearst newspapers—with their sensational headlines, inflammatory stories, and artistic sketches—greatly impacted public opinion.

Marcus M. Wilkerson, *Public Opinion and the Spanish American War: A Study in War Propaganda* (Russell & Russell, 1932, 1967) and Joseph E. Wisan, *The Cuban Crisis as Reflected in the New York Press (1895–1898)* (Octagon Press, 1934, 1965) both support Swanberg's view that newspaper propaganda caused the Spanish-American War. Interestingly, the two books were written in the 1930s and reprinted in the 1960s, both periods of antiwar sentiments in the United States. Some journal articles discount the impact of pro-war newspapers on public opinion in midwestern states. See Mark M. Welter, "The 1895–98 Cuban Crisis in Minnesota Newspapers: Testing the 'Yellow Journalism' Theory," *Journalism Quarterly* (Winter 1970) and Harold J. Sylvester, "The Kansas Press and the Coming of the Spanish American War," *Historian* (vol. 31, 1969), pp. 251–267, which examines 18 newspapers and finds that only 2 are highly jingoistic.

The history of the American newspaper receives its fullest treatment in Frank Luther Mott, *American Journalism: A History, 1690–1960,* 3rd ed. (Macmillan, 1962). Though detailed, it contains an excellent chapter entitled "Yellow Journalism and the War With Spain." Briefer but useful is John Tebbel, *The Compact History of the American Newspaper* (Hawthorn Books, 1963). The correspondents' views of the war from the bottom up can be found in Joyce Milton, *The Yellow Kids: Foreign Correspondents in the Heyday of Yellow Journalism* (Harper & Row, 1989) and Charles H. Brown, *The Correspondent's War: Journalists in the Spanish-American War* (Charles Scribner's Sons, 1967).

Nasaw disagrees with Swanberg and others who argue that Hearst started the Spanish-American War. In a massive new biography, and based on an examination of Hearst papers that were previously unavailable to researchers, Nasaw makes several telling points. First, Hearst sent veteran reporter Richard Harding

Davis and artist Frederick Remington to Cuba to write about the war. Supposedly, when Remington cabled Hearst that "everything is quiet," Hearst replied, "Please remain. You furnish the pictures and I'll furnish the war." According to Nasaw, the evidence for this exchange is very slim. The actual telegrams have never been found. The story originates in veteran reporter James Creelman's autobiography, *On the Great Highway: The Wanderings and Adventures of a Special Correspondent* (Lothrop, 1901). If Hearst said this, Nasaw argues, he was probably referring to the war between the Cuban rebels and the Spaniards. In 1907 Hearst himself referred to the notion that he was responsible for the Spanish-American War as "clotted nonsense."

Nasaw, like Ian Mugridge in *The View From Xanadu: William Randolph Hearst and United States Foreign Policy* (McGill-Queens University Press, 1995), argues that Swanberg and others have failed to demonstrate a causal link between propaganda, public opinion, and emotionalism and the decision for war made by President McKinley, his cabinet, and Congress. Such an interpretation assumes that McKinley was a passive individual with the "backbone of a chocolate éclair" (to quote then-assistant secretary of the navy Theodore Roosevelt) who could be easily swayed by Cuban rebels, big business, or Hearst himself to go to war. Recent biographers of McKinley see him as a man in charge of situations, a decision maker who reluctantly went to war when Spain refused to allow him to mediate the dispute between the Cuban rebels and the Spanish government. Why the breakdown in relations occurred is clear in hindsight. Spain wanted an armistice and was willing to grant Cuba autonomy. The United States wanted Cuba to become independent, a goal the Spanish government was not willing to concede. See, for example, John L. Offner, *An Unwanted War: The Diplomacy of the United States and Spain Over Cuba, 1895–1898* (University of North Carolina Press, 1992); H. Wayne Morgan, *America's Road to Empire: The War With Spain and Overseas Expansion* (John Wiley, 1965); and Lewis L. Gould, *The Spanish-American War and President McKinley* (University of Kansas Press, 1982). Both Morgan and Gould have also written full-scale biographies of McKinley.

Why the *Maine* was sunk is as controversial today as it was in 1898. In 1976 the Naval History Division of the Department of the Navy published Admiral Hyman D. Rickover's *How the Battleship Maine Was Destroyed*. Disputing the official naval verdicts in 1898 and 1911, Rickover concluded that a fire in a coal bunker had detonated munitions in an adjacent magazine. The February 1998 *National Geographic* uses computer technology to present both sides of the controversy. Joseph R. L. Sterne, in "Battleship Blowup Still a Mystery," *The Baltimore Sun* (February 15, 1998), summarizes the most recent scholarship.

Three books that detail the military as well as the social and diplomatic aspects of the war are Frank Friedel's pictorial *The Splendid Little War* (Little, Brown, 1958) and two other full-scale studies: David F. Trask, *The War With Spain in 1898* (Macmillan, 1981) and Ivan Musicant, *Empire by Default: The Spanish-American War and the Dawn of the American Century* (Henry Holt, 1998).

ISSUE 7

Did Racial Segregation Improve the Status of African Americans?

YES: Howard N. Rabinowitz, from "From Exclusion to Segregation: Southern Race Relations, 1865–1890," *The Journal of American History* (September 1976)

NO: Leon F. Litwack, from *Trouble in Mind: Black Southerners in the Age of Jim Crow* (Alfred A. Knopf, 1998)

ISSUE SUMMARY

YES: Professor of history Howard N. Rabinowitz suggests that racial segregation represented an improvement in the lives of African Americans in that it provided access to a variety of public services and accommodations from which they otherwise would have been excluded in the late-nineteenth-century South.

NO: Professor of American history Leon F. Litwack argues that "the age of Jim Crow," wherein efforts by whites to deny African Americans equal protection of the laws or the privileges and immunities guaranteed other citizens seemingly knew no bounds, created a highly repressive environment for blacks.

In the late nineteenth and early twentieth centuries, most black Americans' lives were characterized by increased inequality and powerlessness. Although the Thirteenth Amendment had fueled a partial social revolution by emancipating approximately 4 million southern slaves, the efforts of the Fourteenth and Fifteenth Amendments to provide all African Americans with the protections and privileges of full citizenship had been undermined by the U.S. Supreme Court.

By 1910, 75 percent of all African Americans resided in rural areas. Ninety percent lived in the South, where they suffered from abuses associated with the sharecropping and crop-lien systems, political disfranchisement, and antagonistic race relations, which often boiled over into acts of violence, including race riots and lynchings. Black southerners who moved north in the decades preceding World War I to escape the ravages of racism instead discovered a society in which the color line was drawn more rigidly to limit black opportunities.

Residential segregation led to the emergence of racial ghettos. Jim Crow also affected northern education, and competition for jobs produced frequent clashes between black and white workers. By the early twentieth century, then, most African Americans endured a second-class citizenship reinforced by segregation laws (both customary and legal) in the "age of Jim Crow."

The response by black Americans to the developing patterns of racial segregation in the late nineteenth century was often reflected in the philosophies of those recognized as "leaders of the race." Prior to 1895 the foremost spokesman for the nation's African American population was former slave and abolitionist Frederick Douglass, whose crusade for blacks emphasized the importance of civil rights, political power, and immediate integration. Historian August Meier has called Douglass "the greatest living symbol of the protest tradition during the 1880's and 1890's." At the time of Douglass's death in 1895, however, this tradition was largely replaced by the emergence of Booker T. Washington. Born into slavery in Virginia in 1856, Washington became the most prominent black spokesman in the United States as a result of a speech delivered in the year of Douglass's death at the Cotton States Exposition in Atlanta, Georgia. Known as the "Atlanta Compromise," this address, with its conciliatory tone, found favor among whites and gave Washington a reputation as a "responsible" spokesman for black America.

One of the earliest and most outspoken critics of Washington's program was his contemporary, W. E. B. Du Bois. In a famous essay in *The Souls of Black Folk* (1903), Du Bois leveled an assault upon Washington's apparent acceptance of segregation and attachment to industrial education. By submitting to disfranchisement and segregation, Du Bois charged, Washington had become an apologist for racial injustice in the United States. He also argued that Washington's national prominence had been bought at the expense of black interests throughout the nation.

In more reflective moments, Du Bois undoubtedly understood the immense difficulty of eradicating Jim Crow laws in a South where whites embraced the doctrine of white supremacy with great fervor. As a witness to the Atlanta race riot of 1906, he also knew the dangers of challenging the "white man's laws" too forcefully. Moreover, both Du Bois and Washington recognized that segregation, no matter how firmly entrenched, was not slavery and that certain benefits presented themselves to African Americans within this otherwise discriminatory caste system.

In the first of the selections that follow, Howard N. Rabinowitz asserts that racial segregation improved the circumstances of black southerners who had only recently been removed from chattel slavery by providing them access to education and public facilities, such as restaurants, theaters, parks, and transportation—areas from which blacks had been excluded prior to the war.

Leon F. Litwack, in the second selection, emphasizes the harshest realities confronting African Americans in a Jim Crow world. Subjected to insults, humiliations, and physical violence on a routine basis, black southerners living in the late nineteenth and early twentieth centuries, according to Litwack, faced "the most repressive period in the history of race relations in the South."

Howard N. Rabinowitz

From Exclusion to Segregation:
Southern Race Relations, 1865–1890

Since the appearance in 1955 of C. Vann Woodward's *The Strange Career of Jim Crow*, extensive research has been devoted to uncovering the origins of racial segregation in the South. Woodward challenges the traditional view that the restrictive Jim Crow codes were the product of the immediate post-Reconstruction period. Emphasizing the legal side of segregation, he argues that the separation of the races grew out of forces operating in the last decade of the nineteenth and the first years of the twentieth century. He has modified his original position, but the existence of a law enforcing segregation remains the key variable in evaluating the nature of race relations. Because of the alleged absence of these statutes, Woodward contends that "forgotten alternatives" existed in the period between redemption and the full-scale arrival of Jim Crow.

Although George Tindall had in part anticipated Woodward's arguments, it is the "Woodward thesis" over which historians have chosen sides. Charles E. Wynes, Frenise A. Logan, and Henry C. Dethloff and Robert P. Jones explicitly declare their support for Woodward (even though much of their evidence seems to point in the opposite direction); and the same is true of the more recent implicit endorsements by John Blassingame and Dale Somers. In his study of South Carolina blacks, however, Joel Williamson, unlike Woodward, emphasizes customs rather than laws and sees segregation so entrenched in the state by the end of Reconstruction that he refers to the early appearance of a "duo-chromatic order." Vernon Lane Wharton's account of Mississippi blacks reaches a similar conclusion, and it has been used to support the arguments of Woodward's critics. Richard C. Wade's work on slavery in antebellum southern cities, Roger A. Fischer's studies of antebellum and postbellum New Orleans, and Ira Berlin's treatment of antebellum free Negroes also question Woodward's conclusions.

The debate has been fruitful, shedding light on race relations in the postbellum South. But the emphasis on the alternatives of segregation or integration has obscured the obvious "forgotten alternative"—exclusion. The issue is not merely when segregation first appeared, but what it replaced. Before the Civil War, blacks were excluded from militia companies and schools, as well as most hospitals, asylums, and public accommodations. The first postwar governments

From Howard N. Rabinowitz, "From Exclusion to Segregation: Southern Race Relations, 1865–1890," *The Journal of American History*, vol. 63, no. 2 (September 1976). Copyright © 1976 by The Organization of American Historians. Reprinted by permission. Notes omitted.

during presidential reconstruction generally sought to continue the antebellum policy of exclusion. Nevertheless, by 1890—before the resort to widespread de jure segregation—de facto segregation had replaced exclusion as the norm in southern race relations. In the process the integration stage had been largely bypassed. This shift occurred because of the efforts of white Republicans who initiated it, blacks who supported and at times requested it, and Redeemers who accepted and expanded the new policy once they came to power.

The first postwar governments, composed of Confederate veterans and elected by white male suffrage, saw little need to alter the prewar pattern of exclusion of blacks from most sectors of southern life.

During the period from 1865 to 1867 southern whites sought to limit admission to poorhouses, orphanages, insane asylums, and institutions for the blind, deaf, and dumb to whites. The states that established systems of public education, such as Georgia, Arkansas, and Texas, opened the schools to whites only. The North Carolina public school system, which dated from antebellum years, was initially closed because of fears that it would be forced to admit blacks. Savannah officials made the same decision about their city's parks. Meanwhile, hotels, restaurants, and many theaters continued to exclude blacks.

Nevertheless, the policy of segregation rather than exclusion was already being forced upon the South. In Richmond and Nashville, for example, the United States Army and the Freedmen's Bureau made the local conservative governments provide poorhouse facilities to indigent blacks. In both cases blacks were placed in quarters separate from whites. The Nashville Board of Education, fearing that it would be forced to integrate its newly opened school system, voluntarily set up separate schools for blacks in 1867. A year earlier the new Nashville Street Railway, which previously had excluded blacks, began running a separate car for them. On the state level, Alabama conservatives admitted blacks for the first time on a segregated basis to the state insane asylum.

Further undermining the policy of exclusion were the practices in those facilities that had experienced the shift from exclusion to segregation during earlier years. The use of separate streetcars for blacks in New Orleans, for example, superseded exclusion during the antebellum and war years. Steamboats and railroads had for many years segregated those few blacks who traveled as paying passengers. This practice continued, and Texas, Mississippi, and Florida strengthened it through the passage of laws. Whatever exclusion there had been on boats and trains had not been forced; it had resulted from the absence of a large black clientele. Cemeteries suffered no such shortage. While most private cemeteries excluded all blacks except faithful servants, public cemeteries had by law or custom assigned blacks to special sections. This procedure continued after the war. Some places of amusement continued to exclude blacks; others retained their earlier pattern of segregated seating; still others as in Nashville opened their doors to freedmen for the first time, although on a segregated basis. Traveling circuses, especially popular with blacks, went so far in Montgomery as to establish separate entrances for the races. The Georgia Infirmary in Savannah and the Charity Hospital in New Orleans similarly continued as they had before the war to provide blacks with segregated medical care at city expense.

Most white southerners remained committed to exclusion as the best racial policy. They were thwarted by the imposition of congressional reconstruction in March 1867 and thereafter were forced by military and civilian authorities to grant new privileges and services to blacks. Nonetheless, the net effect of the Radical measures on race relations in the southern states was to institutionalize the shift from exclusion to segregation....

The Republicans stood for more than segregation. They called for separate but equal treatment for blacks. During debates on congressional civil rights legislation, for example, Senator Joshua Hill of Georgia and Representative Alexander White of Alabama argued that separate provisions for blacks in public carriers, places of amusement, or hotels and restaurants was not a violation of civil rights if the accommodations were equal to those of whites. The Alabama Republican party in its 1874 platform declared that "the republican party does not desire mixed schools or accommodations for colored people, but they ask that in all these advantages they shall be equal. We want no social equality enforced by law." Tennessee's Republican governor signed a separate but equal accommodations measure in 1881, and a Georgia Republican legislature passed a similar bill in 1870. Alabama Republicans pushed for such a measure and congratulated those railroads that voluntarily provided separate but equal accommodations. The Republican legacy to the Redeemers therefore consisted of the seemingly mutually exclusive policies of segregation and equality....

White opinion was not unified, but most Redeemers also adopted the rhetoric of the Republicans' separate but equal commitment. Despite the failure to honor this commitment, in several instances the Redeemers actually moved beyond their predecessors to provide segregated, if unequal, facilities in areas previously characterized by exclusion. Some whites distinguished between segregation and discrimination. Thus Tennessee law prohibited "discrimination" in any place of public amusement that charged a fee but nevertheless maintained that this provision did not outlaw "separate accommodations and seats for colored and white persons."

Additional public institutions opened their doors to blacks for the first time under the Redeemers. Among those states making initial provision for Negro blind, deaf, and dumb were Texas, Georgia, Alabama, Tennessee, and South Carolina; and in 1887, the same year that Tennessee provided a Negro department for the previously all-white and privately run Tennessee Industrial School. North Carolina opened its Colored Orphan Asylum.

Segregation may have also replaced exclusion in other areas of southern life after Reconstruction rather than integration. As early as 1872, Atlanta's Union Passenger Depot had a "Freedmen's Saloon," and at least by 1885 Nashville's Union Depot had "a colored passenger room." In 1885 Austin, Texas, was among the Texas cities required by city ordinance to have separate waiting rooms for both races. It is not known what facilities existed for blacks before the appearance of these Negro waiting rooms. The experiences of Montgomery, Alabama, and Raleigh, North Carolina, however, are instructive. The new Union Depot in Montgomery was described in 1877 as having "a ladies waiting room" and a "gents' waiting room"; the original plans for the Raleigh Union Depot in 1890 included a "ladies waiting room" and a "gentlemen's waiting room." Although there was no reference to a Negro waiting room, the use of the words "gents," "gentlemen," and "ladies" rather than "men" and "women" suggests the exclusion of blacks. The mention of three waiting rooms at the Montgomery Depot in 1885—one each for "ladies," "gentlemen," and "colored people"—and the revised plans for the Raleigh Depot that contained a separate waiting room for blacks suggest further evidence of the shift from exclusion to segregation.

Segregation persisted or replaced exclusion in theaters. For the most part blacks were confined to separate galleries. In Richmond, however, because of the 1875 Civil Rights Act blacks won access to a segregated portion of the once exclusively white dress circle. Most restaurants and hotels continued to exclude blacks, as did the better barrooms. Some bars catering to whites charged blacks outrageous prices or provided poor service; less subtle was the sign over the bar of a Nashville saloon in 1884—"No drinks sold to colored persons." In 1888 the Atlanta *Constitution* reported that of Atlanta's sixty-eight saloons, five served only blacks and only two catered to both blacks and whites. On those instances when blacks were admitted to primarily white restaurants, bars, and hotels, the races were carefully segregated. A restaurant in the rear of a Nashville saloon served "responsible and well behaved colored people" in its kitchen; the Planters Hotel in Augusta, Georgia, seated blacks at separate tables in the dining room; the St. Charles, the only Richmond hotel to accept a black delegate to the 1886 Knights of Labor convention, gave him second-class quarters and seated him at a table in the dining room farthest from the door and behind a screen; and in answer to the Civil Rights Act, Montgomery's Ruby Saloon set up "a small counter" apart from the main bar for black customers. Such examples probably marked only a transitory stage on the way to total segregation.

With the exception of New Orleans, athletic events in the South were rigidly segregated. Most cities had at least two black baseball teams. Militia companies similarly engaged in racially separated competition. Segregated places in parades and observances, usually in the rear, were provided for blacks as well.

Prostitution also suffered the effects of segregation. Even in New Orleans, houses of prostitution offering white and black women to a mixed clientele had become a rarity by 1880. White and black prostitutes resided on separate blocks in Atlanta. When two well dressed mulattoes sought admission to a brothel on Collins Street that served only whites, they were driven off by gunfire. If taken to court, the prostitutes would likely have found the spectators racially separated, and perhaps, like the procedure in Savannah's mayor's court in 1876, they would have sworn on a Bible set aside for their particular race.

The situation in parks was more complex. There were few formal parks and pleasure grounds in antebellum cities, and blacks were excluded from those that existed. Indeed, it was not until the mid-1870s, in most cases after Republicans had relinquished control of local governments, that the park movement began to affect southern urban life. Most of these new parks were privately owned, often by streetcar companies that used them to encourage traffic on their lines, but municipally owned parks became common by the 1880s.

Increasingly blacks were barred from many parks. Sometimes this can be surmised only from the language of the local press. In other cases speculation is unnecessary. Blacks taking the street railway to Atlanta's Ponce de Leon Springs in 1887 were informed "politely but forcibly" by policemen that they would not be admitted. Three years later blacks were excluded from the city's Inman Park. Already Atlanta blacks had begun to gravitate to the grounds and woods around Clark University, leading the Atlanta *Constitution* to call for construction of a park for them in that area. Then, too, in most southern cities blacks and whites continued to frequent separate picnic groves while the large all-white cemeteries served as parks for whites.

Nevertheless, the existence of separate parks for whites and blacks as a general phenomenon seems to have been the product of the post-1890 period. As of 1882, Nashville's Watkins Park was visited by "persons of all shades and sizes." As late as 1890, blacks and whites were invited to watch a Negro militia company drill in Atlanta's Piedmont Park, and on Independence Day, blacks were among the mostly white crowd that enjoyed the facilities at the city's Grant Park. Montgomery's Highland and Raleigh's Pullem Park were apparently open to blacks and whites as well.

In the absence of separate parks, segregation within the grounds became the norm. Although blacks enjoyed access to Atlanta's Ponce de Leon Springs until the late 1880s, the two races entertained themselves at separate dance halls and refreshment stands. Blacks attending the two free concerts given at Nashville's Glendale Park were barred from the new pavillion while those visiting Raleigh's Brookside Park could not use the swimming pool. When a new zoo opened in Atlanta's Grant Park, it contained eight cages occupying the center of the building and stretching from end to end. An aisle was railed off on each side of the row of cages: one was for blacks, the other for whites. "There is no communication between them," the Atlanta *Constitution* observed, "and two large double doors at each end of the building serve as entrance and exit to the aisles...."

Segregation also seems to have been the rule at expositions and fairs. Nashville Negroes had fairgrounds purchased by a black organization. Blacks could attend certain functions at the white fairgrounds but specifically which functions and when is not always clear. Negroes were barred, for example, from the interstate drill competition held in 1883. But again admittance of both races went hand in hand with segregation. There was a special gate provided for blacks in the exposition building at a Nashville fair in 1875; there was a "colored people's saloon" in addition to the main grandstand saloon at the 1871 Georgia State Fair in Macon; and at the Southern Exposition held in Montgomery in 1890 the two races ate in separate restaurants....

The situation in public conveyances is less discernible and there seems to have been a greater divergence in practice. As under the Republicans, steamboats remained the most segregated form of travel. Although Virginia did not pass a law requiring the racial separation of passengers on steamboats until 1900, the *City of Richmond* in service to Norfolk since 1880 had from its inception "a neat and comfortable dining room for colored passengers in the lower cabin." George Washington Cable discovered in 1887 that Louisiana Negroes had to confine themselves to a separate quarter of the boats called the "Freedman's bureau." And to Frederick Douglass it seemed ironic that the Negro had more freedom on steamboats as a slave since "he could ride anywhere, side by side with his white master.... [A]s a freeman, he was not allowed a cabin abaft the wheel."

Although there was greater integration in train travel, blacks were generally confined to the smoking and second-class cars. Occasionally they were provided with separate first class accommodations equal to those given to white passengers. During her trip through the United States in 1883, Iza Duffus Hardy was especially struck by the variety of methods used on trains to keep Negroes "in their place." On the train leaving Charleston, Negroes were in a separate second class car although they did pay a lower fare than whites. At Savannah on the Florida Express, the Negroes rode in the forward part of the smoking car nearest the engine. Somewhat farther south Hardy found a car labeled "For Coloured Passengers," that she discovered "was in every respect exactly like the car reserved for us 'white folk,' the same velvet seats, ice water tank; every comfort the same—and of course, the same fare." As opposed to this rare instance of a first-class car, the car assigned to Negroes in Charleston was described by her traveling companion, Lady Duffus Hardy, as "seedy looking." The association of Negroes with smoking cars was pronounced. While traveling on the Central Railroad in Georgia, Alexander Stephens and two other noted Georgians were ejected from a first-class Negro car because they had seen blacks in it and had assumed it was a second-class car where they could smoke.

The first class cars for Negroes on the Central Railroad reflected an effort by certain railroads and sympathetic whites to provide separate but equal accommodations for blacks able to afford first-class rates. Noting the noncompliance with the 1881 statute providing for separate but equal accommodations for the races on Tennessee's railroads, Nashville's *American* observed in 1885:

> The blacks are forced into the smoking cars where they are subjected not only to all the annoyance of smoke and dirt, but often to the additional hardship of association with the roughest and most quarrelsome class of whites.... Now these things *should not be.* They are bad for the black race and they are equally bad for the white race. The law which provides for separate cars and equal accommodations is right. It is only law which can be just to both of these classes of citizens, and at the same time prevent race conflicts, which would disturb the peace of the community.

As early as 1870, the Orange Railroad passenger trains in Virginia had a special car exclusively for Negroes where smoking was prohibited. A regular smoking car was to be used by both blacks and whites. The Houston and Texas Central agreed in 1883 to provide "separate, exclusive, equal accommodations for colored patrons." Two years later a Louisville and Nashville train running between Montgomery and Mobile had a first-class coach "specially provided for colored people." In the opinion of the Atlanta *Constitution,* it "was as good in every sense as the [white] car.... There was no smoking or disorder permitted."

In a case involving alleged discrimination on an Alabama railroad in 1887, the Interstate Commerce Commission held that different cars for the races could indeed be used provided that the accommodations were equal and that Negroes paying first-class fare received first-class facilities.

In only one area of southern life was the shift to segregation relatively incomplete by 1890. Most southern streetcar systems initially excluded blacks; separate cars for the races followed. Once blacks gained entrance to the white cars, documenting the existence of segregation becomes difficult. August Meier and Elliott Rudwick argue that segregation "declared after being instituted in many places prior to and just after the Civil War." There is evidence to support the contention that streetcars were the most integrated southern facility. Referring to the color line, the Nashville *American* observed in 1880 that "in Tennessee there is such a line, as every man, white and black, well knows, but on our street cars the races ride together without thought of it, or offensive exhibition, or attempt to isolate the colored passenger." Ten years later, when there was a rumor that the president of one of Richmond's street railways had been asked to provide separate cars for black passengers, the Richmond *Planet*, a Negro newspaper, expressed surprise and counseled against the plan since "we do not know of a city in the south in which discrimination is made on the street cars." In 1908 Ray Stannard Baker sadly concluded that "a few years ago the Negro came and went in the street cars in most cities and sat where he pleased, but gradually Jim Crow laws or local regulations were passed forcing him into certain seats at the back of the car."

Segregation, however, may have been more prevalent than these accounts indicate. In Richmond and Savannah segregated streetcars persisted at least until the mid-1870s. But segregation on horsecars could be inconvenient and expensive to maintain. Because the horses could pull only one rather small car at a time, the segregation of passengers required either the use of an entirely separate car and horse for blacks or limited them to a portion of the already crowded cars open to whites. This problem was remedied by the appearance on southern streets at the end of the 1880s of the dummy streetcar and the later electrification of the lines. The steam driven dummy derived its name from the attempt to disguise the engine as a passenger car in order to cut down on noise and to avoid frightening horses. Since it had two cars or else a single car larger than that pulled by horses, segregation of the races was easier.

Montgomery initiated dummy service in 1886 with the forward cars reserved for whites and the rear cars for blacks. Two years later the dummy also made possible the first clear indication of segregation in Atlanta. The dummy service, begun by the Metropolitan Street Railway Company in September 1888, included two cars plus the engine—one painted yellow for whites, the other red for blacks. Likewise, the first documented case of segregation in a Nashville streetcar after 1867 was contained in an 1888 report about a Negro minister's sermon. It simply noted that "in a sermon Sunday night, [the minister] attacked the management of the dummy line for insisting that he should move to another car or get off." During the following two years, however, the newspapers reported additional instances of blacks being told to go to separate cars.

The period of seeming flexibility came to an end with the passage of statutes enforcing segregation. Both blacks and the streetcar companies often objected to Jim Crow measures. But what were they protesting? Was it segregation or legal segregation that blacks were against? Did the streetcar owners object to any form of racial separation or simply to one that made them supply additional cars, usually an unprofitable venture. The fact that many Nashville blacks would have settled for separate cars in 1905 as long as there were black fare collectors suggests that the boycotts were not simply against segregation. The twentieth-century practice of dividing streetcars into black and white sections lends credence to the view that white owners objected less to the initiation of segregation than to the law requiring more cars. As the Richmond *Planet* noted, southern managers realized that "separate cars would not pay and what was worse there would be more trouble on account of it." Thanks to the cooperation of local officials the managers could handle the "trouble"; financial aspects were another matter.

Then, too, why would streetcars be immune from segregation, given its prevalence in most other areas of southern life? One answer would seem to rest less with the absence of white hostility than in the circumstances in which streetcars operated. The resistance of white managers might be a reason, but as important was the greater leverage blacks exercised over streetcar policy as compared, for example, to railroad policy. Clearly boycotts presented a more serious threat to local streetcar lines than they did to a railroad that drew passengers from many communities. In addition, boycotts could be better organized because of the existence of alternative means of transportation. Whether by using hacks, private carriages, or by simply walking, Negroes could go about their business without the streetcars.

This essay has been primarily concerned with the pervasiveness of segregation in the postbellum South as it came to replace exclusion as the dominant characteristic of race relations. It has been argued that both white Republicans and Redeemers came to embrace this new policy, though often for different reasons. But what helped to assure this shift was the attitude of the blacks themselves.

Blacks on occasion did challenge segregation. During Richmond's celebration of the passage of the Fifteenth Amendment, a Negro minister was accused by the Richmond *Dispatch* of saying that "the negroes must claim the right to sit with the whites in theatres, churches, and other public buildings, to ride with them on the cars, and to stay at the same hotels with them." Similarly after Tennessee passed its Jim Crow law in 1881, a minister from Nashville argued that "no man of color [should] ride in a car simply because it is set apart and *labeled* 'exclusively for negroes,' but rather let every individual choose of the regular coaches the one in which to ride." And six years later when Charles Dudley Warner asked a group of leading Nashville black businessmen "What do you want here in the way of civil rights that you have not?" the answer was, "we want to be treated like men, like anybody else regardless of color.... We want public conveyances open to us according to the fare we pay; we want the privilege to go to hotels and to theatres, operas and places of amusement...

[We] cannot go to the places assigned us in concerts and theatres without loss of self respect."

Negroes opposed segregation by deeds as well as by words. By 1870, Charleston, New Orleans, Richmond, Mobile, and Nashville were among the cities to experience challenges to exclusion or segregation on their streetcars. Suits were brought also against offending railroad companies. Challenges to segregation were most pronounced after passage of the 1875 Civil Rights Act. For the most part, blacks failed to break down the racial barriers in theaters, hotels, restaurants, public conveyances, and bars. More isolated and equally unsuccessful attempts occurred with decreasing frequency in subsequent years.

Despite this opposition to segregation, the majority of blacks, including their leaders, focused their attention elsewhere. The failure of a sustained attack on segregation perhaps resulted from the lack of support from white allies and the courts. There were other reasons as well. Five prominent Nashville blacks, for example, argued that Negroes would not use passage of the Civil Rights Act "to make themselves obnoxious" since they "had too much self respect to go where they were not wanted." Besides, they said, such actions would lead only to disturbances and "colored people wanted peace and as little agitation as possible." Bishop Henry M. Turner echoed this view in 1889, telling a reporter that "I don't find much trouble in traveling at [sic] the south on account of my color, for the simple reason that I am not in the habit of pushing myself where I am not wanted." A similar attitude might have governed the response of "several really respectable colored persons" in Charleston to the attempt of a Negro to buy a ticket for the orchestra or dress circle of the Academy of Music in 1870. Calling the move a cheap political trick, they "avowed their willingness to sit in the places provided for their own race when they visited the Academy."

Economic pressures also led blacks to accept segregation. Negroes who relied on a white clientele were especially reluctant to serve members of both races. Shortly after the passage of the Civil Rights Act two Negro barbers in Edgefield, across the river from Nashville, refused to serve black customers. The previous year a Negro delegation had been ejected when it demanded shaves at the shop of a black barber in Chattanooga. Asked if their money were not as good as a white man's, the barber, fearful of the loss of his white customers, answered, "Yes just as good, but there is not enough of it." Both whites and blacks understood the focus of economic power. In 1875 the Nashville *Union and American* listed twelve blacks who had been testing compliance to the Civil Rights Act. The fact that "most of them got their reward by losing their situations" helps explain why there were not more protestors.

Other blacks sought to work out an equitable arrangement within the confines of a segregated order. They accepted segregation because it was seen as an improvement over exclusion and because they believed, or at least hoped, that separate facilities could be equal. A rider in 1866 on the Nashville streetcar set apart for blacks did not complain about the segregation, but threatened a boycott unless the company protected black passengers from abusive whites who forced their way into the car and used obscene language in front of black women. A Norfolk, Virginia, Negro observing that the city was building a new opera house suggested that "colored theatregoers . . . petition the managers to give them a respectable place to sit, apart from those of a lewd character." To one Atlanta citizen, writing during a period of racial tension in his city, it seemed that whites and blacks should "travel each in their own distinct paths, steering clear of debatable ground, never forgetting to render one to the other that which equity and good conscience demands." And when the Negro principal of the Alabama State Normal School brought suit against the Western and Atlantic Railroad on the ground that despite his possession of a first-class ticket he was ejected from the first-class car and removed to the Negro car, he admitted the right of the company to classify passengers by race, but maintained it was the duty of the railroad to furnish equal facilities and conveniences for both races. This belief in the need to guarantee separate but equal treatment was expressed in a resolution offered in the Virginia senate by a Negro legislator in 1870. It provided that whites would be forbidden from traveling in portions of boats, trains, and streetcars reserved for blacks. In a letter to the Richmond *Dispatch,* the legislator attributed his action to the fact that there was little possibility of blacks being allowed to ride wherever they wanted and this would protect them, especially the women, from the intrusion of undesirable whites.

In other areas, acceptance of segregation did not necessarily mean passivity on the part of blacks. Again, the targets of protest were exclusion and unequal treatment rather than segregation. For example, blacks placed more emphasis on securing better schools and welfare institutions than on achieving integrated institutions. Blacks went even further. They called for black control of separate facilities through the use of black staff or black directors of public institutions, such as penitentiaries and institutions for the blind, deaf, and dumb. The increase in the number of black colleges, like Tuskegee and Morris Brown, founded and run by blacks was another manifestation of this desire for control over separate institutions.

When the white community persisted in its policy of exclusion, blacks responded by opening their own hospitals, orphanages, hotels, ice cream parlors, and skating rinks. Part of this response was an accommodation to white prejudice; but it was also related to the development of a group identity among blacks. Though it cannot be equated with the racism of whites, by moving in this direction blacks themselves contributed to the emergence of the separate black and white worlds that characterized southern life by 1890.

Although the sanction of law underwrote much of the system of parallel facilities, the separation of the races was accomplished largely without the aid of statutes for as long as both races accepted its existence. As early as 1866, an English traveler, William Dixon, noted that the Negro in Richmond, Virginia, regardless of his legal rights, knew "how far he may go, and where he must stop." He knew also that "[h]abits are not changed by paper law." In 1880 two of the Negro witnesses testifying before a congressional committee pointed to this difference between the power of law and the power of custom. When asked if there were any laws in Alabama applied solely to one race, James T. Rapier answered: "Custom is law in our country now, and was before the war." Asked again if there were any discriminatory provisions in the constitution or state statutes, he replied: "None that I know of; but what we complain of is the administration of the law—the custom of the country." James O'Hara of

North Carolina made a similar statement. "These are matters [segregation in public accommodations] that are and must be regulated purely by prejudice and feeling, and that the law cannot regulate...."

Though prejudice persisted during the quarter century after 1865, a profound change occurred in southern race relations. The policy of exclusion was largely discarded. Instead, by 1890 segregation had been extended to every major area of southern life. Doubts remained as to the possibility of keeping Negroes fully "in their place" without resort to laws. During the last decade of the nineteenth and the first decade of the twentieth century, these doubts resulted in the legalization of practices in effect since the end of the war. As Gilbert Stephenson pointed out for train travel: "The 'Jim Crow' laws... coming later, did scarcely more than to legalize an existing and widespread custom." For whether under Radical Reconstruction, or Redemption, the best that blacks could hope for in southern racial policy was separate but equal access. In fact, they usually met with either exclusion or separate but unequal treatment. Integration was rarely permitted. When it did occur, it was only at the initiation of whites and was confined as a rule to the least desirable facilities—cheap bars, inferior restaurants, second-class and smoking cars on trains. Whites were there because they chose to be; blacks were there because they had no choice.

NO ⮐

Leon F. Litwack

White Folks: Acts

On boarding the streetcar, the woman took the most convenient seat available. "What do you mean?" the conductor shouted at her. "Niggers don't sit with white folks down here. You must have come from 'way up yonder." The woman replied that she was a visitor and had no knowledge of the new law. "Well, no back talk now," the conductor loudly admonished her, playing very much to his audience; "that's what I'm here [for]—to tell niggers their places when they don't know them." The whites in the car laughed over her discomfort. "Not one of them thought that I was embarrassed, wounded, and outraged by the loud, brutal talk of the conductor and the sneering, contemptuous expressions on their own faces." Rather than move to the Jim Crow section she left the car, prompting one of the passengers to remark, "These niggers get more impudent every day; she doesn't want to sit where she belongs."

After walking downtown, the woman attempted to use an elevator in a public building, only to be told to heed the sign posted at the entrance. "I guess you can't read," the elevator operator told her, "but niggers don't ride in this elevator; we're white folks here, we are. Go to the back and you'll find an elevator for freight and niggers." The whites who then occupied the elevator appeared to enjoy her dismay.

The day's events in this Alabama city had left their mark on the woman. As a native Southerner, the daughter of a former slave, it had not been her first experience with the ways of white folks, only a different manifestation of the same phenomenon. "I have been humiliated and insulted often," she declared, "but I never get used to it; it is new each time, and stings and hurts more and more." Her children, she knew, would be better educated than her generation, and she expected the accumulation of insults and humiliations to add to their dislike of whites. "I dread to see my children grow. I know not their fate.... It does not matter how good or wise my children may be, they are colored. When I have said that, all is said. Everything is forgiven in the South but color." ...

꒰꒷꒰

Racial segregation was hardly a new phenomenon. Before the Civil War, when slavery had fixed the status of most blacks, no need was felt for statutory

From Leon F. Litwack, *Trouble in Mind: Black Southerners in the Age of Jim Crow* (Alfred A. Knopf, 1998). Copyright © 1998 by Leon F. Litwack. Reprinted by permission of Alfred A. Knopf, a division of Random House, Inc. Notes omitted.

measures segregating the races. The restrictive Black Codes, along with the few segregation laws passed by the first postwar governments, did not survive Reconstruction. What replaced them, however, was not racial integration but an informal code of exclusion and discrimination. Even the Radical legislatures in which blacks played a prominent role made no concerted effort to force integration on unwilling and resisting whites, especially in the public schools; constitutional or legislative provisions mandating integration were almost impossible to enforce. The determination of blacks to improve their position during and after Reconstruction revolved largely around efforts to secure accommodations that equaled those afforded whites. Custom, habit, and etiquette, then, defined the social relations between the races and enforced separation in many areas of southern life. Whatever the Negro's legal rights, an English traveler noted in Richmond in 1866, he knows "how far he may go, and where he must stop" and that "habits are not changed by paper laws."

But in the 1890s whites perceived in the behavior of "uppity" (and invariably younger) blacks a growing threat or indifference to the prevailing customs, habits, and etiquette. Over the next two decades, white Southerners would construct in response an imposing and extensive system of legal mechanisms designed to institutionalize the already familiar and customary subordination of black men and women. Between 1890 and 1915, state after state wrote the prevailing racial customs and habits into the statute books. Jim Crow came to the South in an expanded and more rigid form, partly in response to fears of a new generation of blacks unschooled in racial etiquette and to growing doubts that this generation could be trusted to stay in its place without legal force. If the old Negro knew his "place," the New Negro evidently did not. "The white people began to begrudge these niggers their running around and doing just as they chose," recalled Sam Gadsden, a black South Carolinian born in 1882. "That's all there is to segregation, that caused the whole thing. The white people couldn't master these niggers any more so they took up the task of intimidating them."

What made the laws increasingly urgent was the refusal of blacks to keep to their place. In the late nineteenth century, economic and social changes swept through the South, introducing new sites and sources of potential racial contact and conflict; at the same time, white women in increasing numbers moved into the public arena and workplace. Both races availed themselves of the expanding means of rail transportation, with middle-class blacks in particular asserting their independence and social position. Refusing to be confined to the second-class or "smoking" car, they purchased tickets in the first-class or "ladies" car, much to the consternation of whites who resented these "impudent" assertions of social equality. In response to white complaints, conductors expelled blacks from the first-class seats they had purchased, resulting in disruptive incidents and litigation.

Segregation, even more than disfranchisement, came to be linked to white fears of social equality. The railroad and the streetcar became early arenas of confrontation, precisely because in no other area of public life (except the polling place) did blacks and whites come together on such an equal footing. "In their homes and in ordinary employment," as one observer noted, "they meet as master and servant; but in the street cars they touch as free citizens, each paying for the right to ride, the white not in a place of command, the Negro without an obligation of servitude. Street car relationships are, therefore, symbolic of the new conditions." In daily travel, the proximity of the races was likely to be much closer, more intimate, more productive of evil, as a New Orleans newspaper suggested: "A man that would be horrified at the idea of his wife or daughter seated by the side of a burly negro in the parlor of a hotel or at a restaurant cannot see her occupying a crowded seat in a car next to a negro without the same feeling of disgust." An English visitor heard the Jim Crow car defended not only as a necessary means to keep the peace but "on the ground of the special aversion which . . . the negro male excites in the white woman."

In South Carolina, where legislation segregating public transportation had been previously defeated, the question took on a new urgency in the late 1890s. Explaining that urgency and why it no longer opposed such legislation, a Columbia newspaper referred to the "many" and "constant" complaints over racial intermingling on the railway trains.

> The seeming humiliation put upon respectable colored people is to be regretted, but they suffer from the conduct of those of their race who have not appreciated the privileges which they were accorded on the railroads of this state. The obtrusiveness and hardly-veiled insolence of many negroes constantly offends ladies traveling and this settles it.

Legislators and editors voiced support of segregation while lamenting the passage of the "old Negro." The linkage seemed obvious. The new laws, explained a state senator, were not needed to protect whites from "good old farm hands and respectable negroes" but from "that insolent class who desired to force themselves into first class coaches."

To resolve this growing problem, state after state, beginning in the 1880s, responded by designating cars for whites and blacks, in many instances making the "smoking" or second-class car the only car available to black passengers. The same assertiveness by blacks on the urban streetcars and trolleys including the refusal to sit in separate sections or to give up seats to whites, prompted municipalities to take similar action. In Jacksonville, Florida, for example, the city council enacted a separate streetcar ordinance after reports of disturbances on the cars and growing complaints from whites about "the attitude" of black passengers.

Some municipalities prescribed separate cars; most settled on partitions that separated the races on the same car, with blacks relegated to the rear seats. On boarding a streetcar in Atlanta, for example, the passenger would see over each door a sign reading

> White People Will Seat From Front of Car Toward the Back and Colored People from Rear Toward Front

With some exceptions, that became the standard arrangement. In Birmingham, blacks sat in the front section, and attempts to reverse the order clashed with custom. "After all," one white resident noted, "it is not important which end of the car is given to the nigger. The main point is that he must sit where he is told."

Variations appeared in the way municipalities chose to define and enforce the restrictions. In the absence of clear demarcations within the car, it might be left to the discretion of the conductor. "Heh, you nigger, get back there," an Atlanta conductor shouted, and the black man, who had taken a seat too far forward, complied with the demand. But in most places, as in New Orleans, screens clearly defined where blacks could sit, and if whites filled their section, the screen could be moved farther to the rear. To listen to black passengers, the restrictions were often enforced arbitrarily, almost always to their discomfort and disadvantage. In responding to the complaint of a black woman, who objected to a white man smoking in a car assigned black passengers, the conductor placed the entire Jim Crow apparatus in its proper context: "The law was made to keep you in your place, not the white people."

The new railway stations in Birmingham, Atlanta, Charleston, and Jacksonville impressed visitors with their spaciousness and impressive architecture. Each station also had its separate entrances, waiting rooms, and ticket offices marked "For White Passengers" and "For Colored Passengers." The rod separating the white section from the black section, unlike the screens in streetcars, as one visitor noted, was neither provisional nor movable "but fixed as the foundations of the building." Throughout the South, segregation was extended to waiting rooms, most often confining blacks to smaller and cramped quarters. In one station, the waiting rooms were designated "White Men," "White Women," "Black Men," and "Black Women," but some of the local whites became alarmed at the limited scope of the term "Black" and authorities substituted "Colored."

Although blacks had previously experienced segregation in various forms, the thoroughness of Jim Crow made it strikingly different. What the white South did was to segregate the races by law and enforced custom in practically every conceivable situation in which whites and blacks might come into social contact: from public transportation to public parks, from the workplace to hospitals, asylums, and orphanages, from the homes for the aged, the blind, deaf, and dumb, to the prisons, from saloons to churches. Not only were the races to be kept apart in hospitals (including a special section for black infants requiring medical attention), but some denied admission to blacks altogether. Laws or custom also required that black and white nurses tend only the sick of their own race. By 1885, most states had already legally mandated separate schools. Where intermarriage and cohabitation had not been outlawed, states quickly moved to place such restrictions in law.

The signs "White Only" and "Colored" (or "Negroes") would henceforth punctuate the southern landscape, appearing over the entrances to parks, theaters, boardinghouses, waiting rooms, toilets, and water fountains. Movie houses were becoming increasingly popular, and Jim Crow demanded not only separate ticket windows and entrances but also separate seating, usually in the balcony—what came to be known as the "buzzard roost" or "nigger heaven." And blacks came to learn that in places where they were permitted to mix with whites—stores, post offices, and banks, for example—they would need to wait until all the whites had been served. Special rules also restricted blacks when shopping in white stores, forbidding women, for example, from trying on dresses, hats, and shoes before purchasing them.

The rapid industralization of the South introduced another set of problems, increasing racial tensions in places employing both races. Where whites and blacks worked in the same factories, the law would now mandate segregation wherever feasible. The code adopted in South Carolina, for example, prohibited textile factories from permitting black and white laborers to work together in the same room, or to use the same entrances, pay windows, exits, doorways, or stairways at the same time, or the same "lavatories, toilets, drinking water buckets, pails, cups, dippers or glasses" at any time. Under certain conditions, such as an emergency, the code permitted black firemen, floor scrubbers, and repairmen to associate with white laborers.

Separation of the races often meant the total exclusion of black men and women from certain facilities. The expansion of recreation in the late nineteenth century mandated exclusion of blacks from most amusement parks, roller skating rinks, bowling alleys, swimming pools, and tennis courts. It was not uncommon to find a sign at the entrance to a public park reading "Negroes and Dogs Not Allowed." Excluding blacks from parks deprived them not only of a recreational area but of free public entertainment. "Think of it," a black visitor to Atlanta informed a friend in New York, "Negroes not allowed in some of the parks here, to listen to [a] band which plays here on Sundays." Some communities admitted blacks to parks on certain days, designated a portion for their use, or made arrangements for separate parks.

With few exceptions, municipal libraries were reserved for the exclusive use of whites. Between 1900 and 1910, some public libraries extended limited service—that is, blacks were still denied access to the reading room or the privilege of browsing in the stacks, but they might in some instances borrow books for home use. Rather than make any such provisions in the main library, some cities chose to establish separate branches to serve black patrons. But for whites who feared educated blacks, barring them from libraries altogether made eminently good sense. "[T]he libraries in the Southern States are closed to the low down negro eyes... because he is not worthy of an education," a Florida white man wrote to a northern critic. "All the mean crimes, that are done are committed by some educated negro...." In one community, the librarian had a ready answer to a question about why blacks could not be permitted to check out books: "[T]he southern people do not believe in 'social equality.' "

Although most business establishments welcomed back customers, there were exceptions and restrictions. Many laundries, for example, posted signs reading "We Wash For White People Only"; in Nashville, a laundry declared on the sides of its delivery wagons and on advertisements in streetcars "No Negro Washing Taken." Where custom had largely governed which if any restaurants blacks could patronize, laws in some states mandated separate accommodations, often a small room with a separate entrance, and many restaurants barred blacks altogether.

In the early twentieth century, the growing availability of automobiles to both races precipitated a variety of measures. While some communities limited the access of black motorists to the public streets, others placed restrictions on where they might park. In much of the South, racial etiquette dictated that black drivers should make no effort to overtake buggies and wagons driven by whites on unpaved roads. Not only could such behavior be construed as "impudence," but also the white passengers might be enveloped by a cloud of dust. "As a rule," Benjamin Mays recalled, "Negroes did not pass white people on either a dusty or a muddy road.... I have been with my father when he apologized for passing a white driver by saying, 'Excuse me, Boss, I'm in a hurry.' Did this mean that my father mentally accepted or emotionally approved this cringing behavior? I doubt it.... It was a technique of survival."

If the use of roads could be legislated, so could a town's sidewalks, where custom had always dictated that blacks step aside to provide ample room for whites. In Danville, Virginia, after hearing complaints about black children occupying the entire sidewalk on their way to and from school, a new police rule limited their use of those sidewalks when white children were coming or going in the other direction. Of course, whether by law or custom, blacks of any age were expected to step aside when white adults approached.

In the towns and cities, segregated residential patterns were now legally sanctioned, making it difficult for blacks of any class to move into a white block and accelerating the appearance or growth of a distinct district designated as "darktown" or "niggertown." Whether by custom or ordinance, the newer and most rapidly growing cities tended to be the most segregated; by the mid-1890s, for example, racially exclusive sections characterized Atlanta, Richmond, and Montgomery. In some of the older antebellum communities, where house slaves and free blacks had lived near their white employers, black housing tended to be more widely scattered. Some whites thought laws or ordinances restricting where blacks could live were unnecessary, that public sentiment would expeditiously settle the issue. "[T]here is no use to make a law that says one set of men can do this or do that," a resident of Greensboro, North Carolina, argued. "In this white man's town when an African proposed to 'move into' a white section, he was given to understand that it wouldn't do. And if he had moved in he would have moved out a great deal quicker—and a pile of ashes would have marked the house. That is what the White Man will do, law or no law, and that is understood." In a small community south of Clinton, Mississippi, as in Forsyth County, Georgia, public sentiment and night riders imposed their own version of exclusivity by driving out all the black residents.

The legislation of Jim Crow affected all classes and ages, and it tended to be thorough, far-reaching, even imaginative: from separate public school textbooks for black and white children and Jim Crow Bibles on which to swear in black witnesses in court, to separate telephone booths, separate windows in the banks for black and white depositors, and Jim Crow elevators in office buildings, one for whites and one for blacks and freight. New Orleans went so far as to adopt an ordinance segregating black and white prostitutes; Atlanta confined them to separate blocks, while a Nashville brothel settled for a plan by which black prostitutes were placed in the basement and white prostitutes on the ground and upper floors. In Atlanta, the art school that had used black models needed no law to dispense with their employment.

Even as the laws decreed that black babies would enter the world in separate facilities, so blacks would occupy separate places at the end of their lives. The ways in which Jim Crow made its mark on the ritual of death could assume bizarre dimensions. Will Mathis, a convicted white felon, appealed to a judge that he be hanged at a different hour than Orlando Lester, a black man, and from a different set of gallows. The same plea was made by a white Tennessean convicted of the brothel murder of his wife. After he objected to going to the gallows with three black men, the authorities agreed to hang them first. Custom, if not ordinances, dictated that blacks and whites be buried in separate cemeteries. "If a colored person was to be buried among the whites," one observer noted sarcastically in Alabama, "the latter would all rise from their graves in indignation. How they tolerate the 'niggers' in heaven is a mystery, unless the mansions there are provided with kitchens and stables." On the edge of Little Rock, Arkansas, in still another unique expression of white supremacy, a section of the cemetery once reserved for blacks was converted into an exclusively white cemetery. "There are a lot of colored folks buried there and white folks on top of them," a black resident observed. "They didn't move the colored because there wasn't nobody to pay for moving. They just buried the whites on top of them."

Enforcement of the Jim Crow laws could be as harsh and vigorous as the spirit and rhetoric that had demanded them. Had these laws not been adopted, an English visitor thought, "the South would have been a nation of saints, not of men. It is in the methods of its enforcement that they sometimes show themselves not only human but inhuman." The often savage beatings and expulsions on railroads and streetcars attested not only to white determination to enforce the law but also to black resistance to its implementation. Calling the Jim Crow car an "unmixed blessing," a Richmond newspaper noted that those "ill-advised" blacks who had protested it "only accentuated its need and its usefulness." Law and custom interacted to keep blacks in their place, and it would be the responsibility of blacks to learn how to adapt to these conditions as way of life. That required a knowledge not only of local customs and laws but also of the way these might differ from place to place. "Every town had its own mores, its own unwritten restrictions," a black educator recalled. "The trick was to find out from local [black] people what the 'rules' were."

Perhaps the most revealing aspects of Jim Crow were the exceptions made for black domestic workers. If a black servant, for example, accompanied a white child into a railroad coach or into a park reserved for whites, that was perfectly acceptable, since the association did not imply an equal relationship. "Everything was all right," a Georgia house servant revealed, "so long as I was in the white man's part of the street car or in the white man's coach as a servant—a slave—but as soon as I did not present myself as a menial, and the relationship of master and servant was abolished by my not having the white children with me, I would be forthwith assigned to the 'nigger' seats or the 'colored people's coach.'" The same exception applied to black servants overseeing white children in public parks that barred blacks. Some of the parks bore signs reading "No Negroes Allowed on These Grounds Except as Servants." A black teacher ventured into a restricted park in Charleston in the company of a white friend and fellow teacher and precipitated no objections. "Of course," she noted, "every one thought I was her maid."

Whether in the exceptions made for black employees or in the quality of the facilities afforded blacks, the position of superior and inferior had to be absolutely clear. "The black nurse with a white baby in her arms, the black valet looking after the comfort of a white invalid," an Episcopal minister in Napoleonville, Louisiana, explained, "have the label of their inferiority conspicuously upon them; they understand themselves, and everybody understand them, to be servants, enjoying certain privileges for the sake of the person served. Almost anything the Negro may do in the South, and anywhere he may go, provided the manner of his doing and his going is that of an inferior. Such is the premium put upon his inferiority; such his inducement to maintain it." On this basis, the poorest illiterate white could claim a standing in society denied to the wealthiest and most intelligent and educated black. . . .

<hr/>

In Richland County, South Carolina, in the 1920s, a black story-teller reflected about the law and the courts and how they operated half a century after the abolition of slavery. "Dere ain' no use. De courts er dis land is not for niggers. . . . It seems to me when it come to trouble, de law an' a nigger is de white man's sport, an' justice is a stranger in them precincts, an' mercy is unknown." The Bible, he noted, asked people to pray for their enemy, and so he offered up this prayer: "Drap on you' knee, brothers, an' pray to God for all de crackers an' de judges an' de courts an' solicitors, sheriffs an' police in de land. . . ."

As the storyteller suggested, the perversion of justice had become a lasting legacy of the New South. The mechanisms of legal violence—that is, violence sanctioned by the day-to-day workings of the legal system—functioned after Reconstruction as a formidable instrument of social control. In the name of the law and justice, whites (including those sworn to uphold and enforce the law) made a mockery of law and justice. The legal system was only one mechanism in the arsenal of white power, but it proved to be a critical and formidable one. Unequal justice interacted with disfranchisement, segregation, economic exploitation, inferior schooling, and violence to remind blacks of all ages and classes of where power rested in this society. By 1907, a newspaper in Yazoo, Mississippi, could observe with satisfaction how the South had become to all intents and purposes a closed society. "With every official in Mississippi a white man, and every jury composed of whites; every judge upon the bench white, and all elections conducted by and only participated in by whites, there can be no possible danger of negro rule."

In communities across the South, blacks came to perceive the law and its enforcers as an outside and alien force, an intrusive and repressive agency against which appeals for fairness and impartiality, humane and just treatment, were all but useless. Even as the United States in the wake of World War I promoted the cause of international justice, blacks demanded some semblance of domestic justice. In the black press and at black meetings, the abuse of the law and the double standard of justice applied to the two races took increasing precedence over other issues. The remark made in a Georgia court that not half of the blacks sentenced would be convicted if properly represented resonated with blacks throughout the South. Addressing a biracial audience in Oklahoma City, a black editor confided to them how black people thought about the legal system:

> I think you ought to know how the black man talks and feels at times when he knows that you are nowhere about, and I want to tell you, if you were to creep up to-night to a place where there are 10,000 Negroes gathered, you would find no division on this one point. I know that they all would say, "WE HAVE NO CONFIDENCE IN WHITE POLICEMEN." Let there be one hundred or one hundred thousand, they would with one accord all say, "WE HAVE NO CONFIDENCE IN THE WHITE MAN'S COURT." I think you ought to know this, for it is with what men think that we have to deal. They would say in such a meeting that they know before they get into the court what the verdict will be. If their cause is the cause of a black man against a white man they will say that they know that a verdict would be rendered in favor of the white man.

This view of southern justice rested on an abundance of evidence, on tens of thousands of cases tried and not tried. The differences between the courtroom and the lynch mob were not always clear in the New South. Nor in the eyes of black men and women were there discernible differences between a speedy trial and mob justice, between lawless lynchers and lawless judges, sheriffs, constables, policemen, wardens, and prison guards. "The fact is," a black educator noted in 1915, "that lynching has gone on so long in many parts of our country that it is somewhat difficult to draw at this time a sharp line marking off distinctly the point where the lynching spirit stops and the spirit of legal procedure commences. You cannot tell what the most peaceable community will do at any moment under certain conditions."

The most repressive period in the history of race relations in the South also became the most violent. The race chauvinism, the often rabid Negrophobia, the intense feelings and emotions stirred up by the campaigns to disfranchise and segregate blacks expressed themselves simultaneously in an era of unprecedented racial violence. Rather than allay white fears, the campaigns to repress blacks heightened those fears. Rather than provide safe alternatives, the campaigns exacerbated race relations. Once dehumanized, black life was cheapened and made even more expendable. The effort to solidify the subordination of black men and women knew no limits.

POSTSCRIPT

Did Racial Segregation Improve the Status of African Americans?

There is little question that racial segregation created a separate and subordinate status for African Americans. Rabinowitz's selection is important in that it recognizes that patterns of Jim Crow represented a middle ground between total exclusion and full integration and that few blacks living in the United States at the turn of the century could have assumed that integration was a realistic possibility. Moreover, Rabinowitz, in this and other works (see especially *Race Relations in the Urban South, 1865–1890* [Oxford University Press, 1978]), challenges the interpretation of the origins of segregation developed by C. Vann Woodward in *The Strange Career of Jim Crow* (Oxford University Press, 1955). Writing in the wake of the explosive response by white segregationists to the U.S. Supreme Court's decision in *Brown v. Board of Education of Topeka* (1954), Woodward attempted to restore some sense of calm by declaring that segregation of the races was not an "immutable folkway" of the South. Looking back at the first 25 years following the Civil War, Woodward depicted a South in which no color line was rigidly drawn. In other words, Woodward, a native southerner, was challenging the notion that prevailed among most whites in the mid-twentieth-century South that segregation of the races had been in force ever since emancipation. While making a distinction between customary and *de jure* segregation, Woodward argued that the latter form did not appear in full until 1890.

Rabinowitz demonstrates that, in fact, numerous examples of legal segregation of the races could be found in the South during the Reconstruction period, especially in southern cities. Litwack, in *North of Slavery: The Negro in the Free States, 1790–1860* (University of Chicago Press, 1961), and Richard C. Wade, in *Slavery in the Cities: The South, 1820–1860* (Oxford University Press, 1964), also make a case for an earlier starting point for Jim Crow. Woodward answered some of his critics in "The Strange Career of a Historical Controversy," published in his *American Counterpoint: Slavery and Racism in the North-South Dialogue* (Little, Brown, 1971).

Discussions of race relations in the late-nineteenth- and early-twentieth-century United States invariably focus upon the ascendancy of Booker T. Washington, his apparent accommodation to existing patterns of racial segregation, and the conflicting traditions within black thought, which were epitomized by the clash between Washington and Du Bois. A thorough assessment of the protest and accommodationist views of black Americans is presented in August Meier, *Negro Thought in America, 1880–1915* (University of Michigan Press, 1963). For a study that coincides with the tone set in the selection by Litwack, see Rayford Logan, *The Betrayal of the Negro: From Rutherford*

B. Hayes to Woodrow Wilson (Macmillan, 1965). By far the best study of Booker T. Washington is Louis Harlan's 2-volume biography *Booker T. Washington: The Making of a Black Leader, 1856–1901* (Oxford University Press, 1972) and *Booker T. Washington: The Wizard of Tuskegee, 1901–1915* (Oxford University Press, 1983). In addition, Harlan has edited the 13-volume *Booker T. Washington Papers* (University of Illinois Press, 1972–1984). For assessments of two of Washington's harshest critics, see Stephen R. Fox, *The Guardian of Boston: William Monroe Trotter* (Atheneum, 1970) and David Levering Lewis, *W. E. B. Du Bois: Biography of a Race, 1868–1919* (Henry Holt, 1993) and *W. E. B. Du Bois: The Fight for Equality and the American Century, 1919–1963* (Henry Holt, 2000). John H. Bracey, Jr., August Meier, and Elliott Rudwick, in *Black Nationalism in America* (Bobbs-Merrill, 1970), provide an invaluable collection of documents pertaining to black nationalism. See also Edwin S. Redkey, *Black Exodus: Black Nationalist and Back-to-Africa Movements, 1890–1910* (Yale University Press, 1969) and Hollis R. Lynch, *Edward Wilmot Blyden: Pan-Negro Patriot, 1832–1912* (Oxford University Press, 1967). Diverse views of Marcus Garvey, who credited Booker T. Washington with inspiring him to seek a leadership role on behalf of African Americans, are found in Edmund David Cronon, *Black Moses: The Story of Marcus Garvey and the Universal Negro Improvement Association* (University of Wisconsin Press, 1955); Tony Martin, *Race First: The Ideological and Organizational Struggles of Marcus Garvey and the UNIA* (Greenwood Press, 1976); and Judith Stein, *The World of Marcus Garvey: Race and Class in Modern Society* (Louisiana State University Press, 1986). Some of Garvey's own writings are collected in Amy Jacques-Garvey, ed., *Philosophy and Opinions of Marcus Garvey* (1925; Atheneum, 1969).

ISSUE 8

Did the Progressives Fail?

YES: Richard M. Abrams, from "The Failure of Progressivism," in Richard Abrams and Lawrence Levine, eds., *The Shaping of the Twentieth Century*, 2d ed. (Little, Brown, 1971)

NO: Arthur S. Link and Richard L. McCormick, from *Progressivism* (Harlan Davidson, 1983)

ISSUE SUMMARY

YES: Professor of history Richard M. Abrams maintains that progressivism was a failure because it tried to impose a uniform set of values upon a culturally diverse people and never seriously confronted the inequalities that still exist in American society.

NO: Professors of history Arthur S. Link and Richard L. McCormick argue that the Progressives were a diverse group of reformers who confronted and ameliorated the worst abuses that emerged in urban industrial America during the early 1900s.

P*rogressivism* is a word used by historians to define the reform currents in the years between the end of the Spanish-American War and America's entrance into the Great War in Europe in 1917. The so-called Progressive movement had been in operation for over a decade before the label was first used in the 1919 electoral campaigns. Former president Theodore Roosevelt ran as a third-party candidate in the 1912 election on the Progressive party ticket, but in truth the party had no real organization outside of the imposing figure of Theodore Roosevelt. Therefore, as a label, "progressivism" was rarely used as a term of self-identification for its supporters. Even after 1912, it was more frequently used by journalists and historians to distinguish the reformers of the period from socialists and old-fashioned conservatives.

The 1890s was a crucial decade for many Americans. From 1893 until almost the turn of the century, the nation went through a terrible economic depression. With the forces of industrialization, urbanization, and immigration wreaking havoc upon the traditional political, social, and economic structures of American life, changes were demanded. The reformers responded in a variety of ways. The proponents of good government believed that democracy was threatened because the cities were ruled by corrupt political machines while the state legislatures were dominated by corporate interests. The cure was to purify democracy and place government directly in the hands of the people through such devices as the initiative, referendum, recall, and the direct election of local school board officials, judges, and U.S. senators.

Social justice proponents saw the problem from a different perspective. Settlement workers moved into cities and tried to change the urban environment. They pushed for sanitation improvements, tenement house reforms, factory inspection laws, regulation of the hours and wages of women, and the abolition of child labor.

A third group of reformers considered the major problem to be the trusts. They argued for controls over the power of big business and for the preservation of the free enterprise system. Progressives disagreed on whether the issue was size or conduct and on whether the remedy was trust-busting or the regulation of big business. But none could deny the basic question: How was the relationship between big business and the U.S. government to be defined?

How successful was the Progressive movement? What triggered the reform impulse? Who were its leaders? How much support did it attract? More important, did the laws that resulted from the various movements fulfill the intentions of its leaders and supporters?

In the following selections, Richard M. Abrams distinguishes the Progressives from other reformers of the era, such as the Populists, the Socialists, the mainstream labor unions, and the corporate reorganization movement. He then argues that the Progressive movement failed because it tried to impose a uniform set of middle-class Protestant moral values upon a nation that was growing more culturally diverse, and because the reformers supported movements that brought about no actual changes or only superficial ones at best. The real inequalities in American society, says Abrams, were never addressed.

In contrast, Arthur S. Link and Richard L. McCormick view progressivism from the point of view of the reformers and rank it as a qualified success. They survey the criticisms of the movement made by historians since the 1950s and generally find them unconvincing. They maintain that the Progressives made the first real attempts to change the destructive direction in which modern urban-industrial society was moving.

Richard M. Abrams  **YES**

The Failure of Progressivism

Our first task is definitional, because clearly it would be possible to beg the whole question of "failure" by means of semantical niceties. I have no intention of being caught in that kind of critics' trap. I hope to establish that there was a distinctive major reform movement that took place during most of the first two decades of this century, that it had a mostly coherent set of characteristics and long-term objectives, and that, measured by its own criteria—not criteria I should wish, through hindsight and preference, to impose on it—it fell drastically short of its chief goals.

One can, of course, define a reform movement so broadly that merely to acknowledge that we are where we are and that we enjoy some advantages over where we were would be to prove the "success" of the movement. In many respects, Arthur Link does this sort of thing, both in his and William B. Catton's popular textbook, *American Epoch,* and in his article, "What Happened to the Progressive Movement in the 1920's?" In the latter, Link defines "progressivism" as a movement that "began convulsively in the 1890's and waxed and waned afterward to our own time, to insure the survival of democracy in the United States by the enlargement of governmental power to control and offset the power of private economic groups over the nation's institutions and life." Such a definition may be useful to classify data gathered to show the liberal sources of the enlargement of governmental power since the 1890's; but such data would not be finely classified enough to tell us much about the *non*liberal sources of governmental power (which were numerous and important), about the distinctive styles of different generations of reformers concerned with a liberal society, or even about vital distinctions among divergent reform groups in the era that contemporaries and the conventional historical wisdom have designed as progressive....

Now, without going any further into the problem of historians' definitions which are too broad or too narrow—there is no space here for such an effort—I shall attempt a definition of my own, beginning with the problem that contemporaries set themselves to solve and that gave the era its cognomen, "progressive." That problem was *progress*—or more specifically, how American

From Richard M. Abrams, "The Failure of Progressivism," in Richard Abrams and Lawrence Levine, eds., *The Shaping of the Twentieth Century,* 2d ed. (Little, Brown, 1971). Copyright © 1971 by Richard M. Abrams. Reprinted by permission of the author.

society was to continue to enjoy the fruits of material progress without the accompanying assault upon human dignity and the erosion of the conventional values and moral assumptions on which the social order appeared to rest....

To put it briefly and yet more specifically, a very large body of men and women entered into reform activities at the end of the nineteenth century to translate "the national credo" (as Henry May calls it) into a general program for social action. Their actions, according to Richard Hofstadter, were "founded upon the indigenous Yankee-Protestant political tradition [that] assumed and demanded the constant disinterested activity of the citizen in public affairs, argued that political life ought to be run, to a greater degree than it was, in accordance with general principles and abstract laws apart from and superior to personal needs, and expressed a common feeling that government should be in good part an effort to moralize the lives of individuals while economic life should be intimately related to the stimulation and development of individual character."

The most consistently important reform impulse, among *many* reform impulses, during the progressive era grew directly from these considerations. It is this reform thrust that we should properly call "the progressive movement." We should distinguish it carefully from reform movements in the era committed primarily to other considerations.

The progressive movement drew its strength from the old mugwump reform impulse, civil service reform, female emancipationists, prohibitionists, the social gospel, the settlement-house movement, some national expansionists, some world peace advocates, conservation advocates, technical efficiency experts, and a wide variety of intellectuals who helped cut through the stifling, obstructionist smokescreen of systematized ignorance. It gained powerful allies from many disadvantaged business interests that appealed to politics to redress unfavorable trade positions; from some ascendant business interests seeking institutional protection; from publishers who discovered the promotional value of exposés; and from politicians-on-the-make who sought issues with which to dislodge long-lived incumbents from their place. Objectively it focused on or expressed (1) a concern for responsive, honest, and efficient government, on the local and state levels especially; (2) recognition of the obligations of society—particularly of an affluent society—to its underprivileged; (3) a desire for more rational use of the nation's resources and economic energies; (4) a rejection, on at least intellectual grounds, of certain social principles that had long obstructed social remedies for what had traditionally been regarded as irremediable evils, such as poverty; and, above all, (5) a concern for the maintenance or restoration of a consensus on what conventionally had been regarded as *fixed moral* principles. "The first and central faith in the national credo," writes Professor May, "was, as it always had been, the reality, certainty, and eternity of moral values.... A few thought and said that ultimate values and goals were unnecessary, but in most cases this meant that they believed so deeply in a consensus on these matters that they could not imagine a serious challenge." Progressives shared this faith with most of the rest of the country, but they also conceived of themselves, with a grand sense of stewardship, as its heralds, and its agents.

The progressive movement was (and is) distinguishable from other contemporary reform movements not only by its devotion to social conditions regarded, by those within it as well as by much of the generality, as *normative,* but also by its definition of what forces threatened that order. More specifically, progressivism directed its shafts at five principal enemies, each in its own way representing reform:

1. The *socialist reform movement*—because, despite socialism's usually praiseworthy concern for human dignity, it represented the subordination of the rights of private property and of individualistic options to objectives that often explicitly threatened common religious beliefs and conventional standards of justice and excellence.
2. The corporate reorganization of American business, which I should call *the corporate reform movement* (its consequence has, after all, been called "the corporate revolution")—because it challenged the traditional relationship of ownership and control of private property, because it represented a shift from production to profits in the entrepreneurial definition of efficiency, because it threatened the proprietary small-business character of the American social structure, because it had already demonstrated a capacity for highly concentrated and socially irresponsible power, and because it sanctioned practices that strained the limits of conventionality and even legality.
3. *The labor union movement*—because despite the virtues of unionized labor as a source of countervailing force against the corporations and as a basis for a more orderly labor force, unionism (like corporate capitalism and socialism) suggested a reduction of individualistic options (at least for wage-earners and especially for small employers), and a demand for a partnership with business management in the decision-making process by a class that convention excluded from such a role.
4. *Agrarian radicalism*, and populism in particular—because it, too, represented (at least in appearance) the insurgency of a class conventionally believed to be properly excluded from a policy-making role in the society, a class graphically represented by the "Pitchfork" Bens and "Sockless" Jerrys, the "Cyclone" Davises and "Alfalfa" Bills, the wool hat brigade and the rednecks.
5. *The ethnic movement*—the demand for specific political and social recognition of ethnic or ex-national affiliations—because accession to the demand meant acknowledgment of the fragmentation of American society as well as a retreat from official standards of integrity, honesty, and efficiency in government in favor of standards based on personal loyalty, partisanship, and sectarian provincialism.

Probably no two progressives opposed all of these forces with equal animus, and most had a noteworthy sympathy for one or more of them. . . .

So much for what progressivism was not. Let me sum it up by noting that what it rejected and sought to oppose necessarily says much about what it was —perhaps even more than can be ascertained by the more direct approach.

My thesis is that progressivism failed. It failed in what it—or what those who shaped it—conceived to be its principal objective. And that was, over and above everything else, to restore or maintain the conventional consensus on a particular view of the universe, a particular set of values, and a particular constellation of behavioral modes in the country's commerce, its industry, its social relations, and its politics. Such a view, such values, such modes were challenged by the influx of diverse religious and ethnic elements into the nation's social and intellectual stream, by the overwhelming economic success and power of the corporate form of business organization, by the subordination of the work-ethic bound up within the old proprietary and craft enterprise system, and by the increasing centrality of a growing proportion of low-income, unskilled, wage-earning classes in the nation's economy and social structure. Ironically, the *coup de grâce* would be struck by the emergence of a philosophical and scientific rationale for the existence of cultural diversity within a single social system, a rationale that largely grew out of the very intellectual ferment to which progressivism so substantially contributed.

Progressivism sought to save the old view, and the old values and modes, by educating the immigrants and the poor so as to facilitate their acceptance of and absorption into the Anglo-American mode of life, or by excluding the "unassimilable" altogether; by instituting antitrust legislation or, at the least, by imposing regulations upon corporate practices in order to preserve a minimal base for small proprietary business enterprise; by making legislative accommodations to the newly important wage-earning classes—accommodations that might provide some measure of wealth and income redistribution, on-the-job safety, occupational security, and the like—so as to forestall a forcible transfer of policy-making power away from the groups that had conventionally exercised that power; and by broadening the political selection process, through direct elections, direct nominations, and direct legislation, in order to reduce tensions caused unnecessarily by excessively narrow and provincial cliques of policy-makers. When the economic and political reforms failed to restore the consensus by giving the previously unprivileged an ostensible stake in it, progressive energies turned increasingly toward using the force of the state to proscribe or restrict specifically opprobrious modes of social behavior, such as gaming habits, drinking habits, sexual habits, and Sabbatarian habits. In the ultimate resort, with the proliferation of sedition and criminal syndicalist laws, it sought to constrict political discourse itself. And (except perhaps for the disintegration of the socialist movement) *that* failed, too.

One measure of progressivism's failure lies in the xenophobic racism that reappeared on a large scale even by 1910. In many parts of the country, for example, in the far west and the south, racism and nativism had been fully blended with reform movements even at the height of progressive activities there. The alleged threats of "coolie labor" to American living standards, and of "venal" immigrant and Negro voting to republican institutions generally, underlay the alliance of racism and reform in this period. By and large, however, for the early progressive era the alliance was conspicuous only in the south and on the west coast. By 1910, signs of heightening ethnic animosities, most notably anti-Catholicism, began appearing in other areas of the country as well.

As John Higham has written, "It is hard to explain the rebirth of anti-Catholic ferment [at this time] except as an outlet for expectations which progressivism raised and then failed to fulfill." The failure here was in part the inability of reform to deliver a meaningful share of the social surplus to the groups left out of the general national progress, and in part the inability of reform to achieve its objective of assimilation and consensus.

The growing ethnic animus, moreover, operated to compound the difficulty of achieving assimilation. By the second decade of the century, the objects of the antagonism were beginning to adopt a frankly assertive posture. The World War, and the ethnic cleavages it accentuated and aggravated, represented only the final blow to the assimilationist idea; "hyphenate" tendencies had already been growing during the years before 1914. It had only been in 1905 that the Louisville-born and secular-minded Louis Brandeis had branded as "disloyal" all who "keep alive" their differences of origin or religion. By 1912, by now a victim of anti-Semitism and aware of a rising hostility toward Jews in the country, Brandeis had become an active Zionist; before a Jewish audience in 1913, he remarked how "practical experience" had convinced him that "to be good Americans, we must be better Jews, and to be better Jews, we must become Zionists."

Similarly, American Negroes also began to adopt a more aggressive public stance after having been subdued for more than a decade by antiblack violence and the accommodationist tactics suggested in 1895 by Booker T. Washington. As early as 1905, many black leaders had broken with Washington in founding the Niagara Movement for a more vigorous assertion of Negro demands for equality. But most historians seem to agree that it was probably the Springfield race riot of 1908 that ended illusions that black people could gain an equitable share in the rewards of American culture by accommodationist or assimilationist methods. The organization of the NAACP in 1909 gave substantive force for the first time to the three-year-old Niagara Movement. The year 1915 symbolically concluded the demise of accommodationism. That year, the Negro-baiting movie, "The Birth of a Nation," played to massive, enthusiastic audiences that included notably the president of the United States and the chief justice of the Supreme Court; the KKK was revived; and Booker T. Washington died. The next year, black nationalist Marcus Garvey arrived in New York from Jamaica.

Meanwhile, scientific knowledge about race and culture was undergoing a crucial revision. At least in small part stimulated by a keen self-consciousness of his own "outsider" status in American culture, the German-Jewish immigrant Franz Boas was pioneering in the new anthropological concept of "cultures," based on the idea that human behavioral traits are conditioned by historical traditions. The new view of culture was in time to undermine completely the prevailing evolutionary view that ethnic differences must mean racial inequality. The significance of Boas's work after 1910, and that of his students A. L. Kroeber and Clyde Kluckhohn in particular, rests on the fact that the racist thought of the progressive era had founded its intellectual rationale on the monistic, evolutionary view of culture; and indeed much of the progressives' anxiety over the threatened demise of "the American culture" had been founded on that view.

Other intellectual developments as well had for a long time been whittling away at the notion that American society had to stand or fall on the unimpaired coherence of its cultural consensus. Yet the new work in anthropology, law, philosophy, physics, psychology, and literature only unwittingly undermined that assumption. Rather, it was only as the ethnic hostilities grew, and especially as the power of the state came increasingly to be invoked against dissenting groups whose ethnic "peculiarities" provided an excuse for repression, that the new intelligence came to be developed. "The world has thought that it must have its culture and its political unity coincide," wrote Randolph Bourne in 1916 while chauvinism, nativism, and antiradicalism were mounting; now it was seeing that cultural diversity might yet be the salvation of the liberal society—that it might even serve to provide the necessary countervailing force to the power of the state that private property had once served (in the schema of Locke, Harrington, and Smith) before the interests of private property became so highly concentrated and so well blended with the state itself.

The telltale sign of progressivism's failure was the violent crusade against dissent that took place in the closing years of the Wilson administration. It is too easy to ascribe the literal hysteria of the postwar years to the dislocations of the War alone. Incidents of violent repression of labor and radical activities had been growing remarkably, often in step with xenophobic outbreaks, for several years before America's intervention in the War. To quote Professor Higham once more. "The seemingly unpropitious circumstances under which antiradicalism and anti-Catholicism came to life [after 1910] make their renewal a subject of moment." It seems clear that they both arose out of the sources of the reform ferment itself. When reform failed to enlarge the consensus, or to make it more relevant to the needs of the still disadvantaged and disaffected, and when in fact reform seemed to be encouraging more radical challenges to the social order, the old anxieties of the 1890's returned.

The postwar hysteria represented a reaction to a confluence of anxiety-laden developments, including the high cost of living, the physical and social dislocations of war mobilization and the recruitment of women and Negroes into war production jobs in the big northern cities, the Bolshevik Revolution, a series of labor strikes, and a flood of radical literature that exaggerated the capabilities of radical action. "One Hundred Per Cent Americanism" seemed the only effective way of meeting all these challenges at once. As Stanley Coben has written, making use of recent psychological studies and anthropological work on cultural "revitalization movements": "Citizens who joined the crusade for one hundred per cent Americanism sought, primarily, a unifying force which would halt the apparent disintegration of their culture.... The slight evidence of danger from radical organizations aroused such wild fear only because Americans had already encountered other threats to cultural stability."

Now, certainly during the progressive era a lot of reform legislation was passed, much that contributed genuinely to a more liberal society, though more that contributed to the more absolutistic moral objectives of progressivism. Progressivism indeed had real, lasting effects for the blunting of the sharper edges of self-interest in American life, and for the reduction of the harsher cruelties suffered by the society's underprivileged. These achievements deserve emphasis, not least because they derived directly from the progressive habit of looking to standards of conventional morality and human decency for the solution of diverse social conflicts. But the deeper nature of the problem confronting American society required more than the invocation of conventional standards; the conventions themselves were at stake, especially as they bore upon the allocation of privileges and rewards. Because most of the progressives never confronted that problem, in a way their efforts were doomed to failure.

In sum, the overall effect of the period's legislation is not so impressive. For example, all the popular government measures put together have not conspicuously raised the quality of American political life. Direct nominations and elections have tended to make political campaigns so expensive as to reduce the number of eligible candidates for public office to (1) the independently wealthy; (2) the ideologues, especially on the right, who can raise the needed campaign money from independently wealthy ideologues like themselves, or from the organizations set up to promote a particular ideology; and (3) party hacks who pay off their debt to the party treasury by whistle-stopping and chicken dinner speeches. Direct legislation through the Initiative and Referendum device has made cities and states prey to the best-financed and -organized special-interest group pressures, as have so-called nonpartisan elections. Which is not to say that things are worse than before, but only that they are not conspicuously better. The popular government measures did have the effect of shaking up the established political organizations of the day, and that may well have been their only real purpose.

But as Arthur Link has said, in his text, *The American Epoch,* the popular government measures "were merely instruments to facilitate the capture of political machinery.... They must be judged for what they accomplished or failed to accomplish on the higher level of substantive reform." Without disparaging the long list of reform measures that passed during the progressive era, the question remains whether all the "substantive reforms" together accomplished what the progressives wanted them to accomplish.

Certain social and economic advantages were indeed shuffled about, but this must be regarded as a short-term achievement for special groups at best. Certain commercial interests, for example, achieved greater political leverage in railroad policy-making than they had had in 1900 through measures such as the Hepburn and Mann-Elkins Acts—though it was not until the 1940's that any real change occurred in the general rate structure, as some broad regional interests had been demanding at the beginning of the century. Warehouse, farm credits, and land-bank acts gave the diminishing numbers of farm owners enhanced opportunities to mortgage their property, and some business groups had persuaded the federal government to use national revenues to educate farmers on how to increase their productivity (Smith-Lever Act, 1914); but most farmers remained as dependent as ever upon forces beyond their control—the bankers, the middlemen, the international market. The FTC, and the Tariff Commission established in 1916, extended the principle of using government agencies to adjudicate intra-industrial conflicts ostensibly in the national interest, but these agencies would develop a lamentable tendency of deferring to and even confirming rather than moderating the power of each industry's dominant interests. The Federal Reserve Act made the currency more flexible, and that certainly made more sense than the old system, as even the bankers agreed. But depositers would be as prey to defaulting banks as they had been in the days of the Pharaoh—bank deposit insurance somehow was "socialism" to even the best of men in this generation. And despite Woodrow Wilson's brave promise to end the banker's stifling hold on innovative small business, one searches in vain for some provision in the FRA designed specifically to encourage small or new businesses. In fact, the only constraints on the bankers' power that emerged from the era came primarily from the ability of the larger corporations to finance their own expansion out of capital surpluses they had accumulated from extortionate profits during the War.

A major change almost occurred during the war years when organized labor and the principle of collective bargaining received official recognition and a handful of labor leaders was taken, temporarily, into policy-making councils (e.g., in the War Labor Board). But actually, as already indicated, such a development, if it had been made permanent, would have represented a defeat, not a triumph, for progressivism. The progressives may have fought for improved labor conditions, but they jealously fought against the enlargement of union power. It was no aberration that once the need for wartime productive efficiency evaporated, leading progressives such as A. Mitchell Palmer, Miles Poindexter, and Woodrow Wilson himself helped civic and employer organizations to bludgeon the labor movement into disunity and docility. (It is possible, I suppose, to argue that such progressives were simply inconsistent, but if we understand progressivism in the terms I have outlined above I think the consistency is more evident.) Nevertheless, a double irony is worth noting with respect to progressivism's objectives and the wartime labor developments. On the one hand, the progressives' hostility to labor unions defeated their own objectives of (1) counterbalancing the power of collectivized capital (i.e., corporations), and (2) enhancing workers' share of the nation's wealth. On the other hand, under wartime duress, the progressives did grant concessions to organized labor (e.g., the Adamson Eight-Hour Railway Labor Act, as well as the WLB) that would later serve as precedents for the very "collectivization" of the economic situation that they were dedicated to oppose.

Meanwhile, the distribution of advantages in the society did not change much at all. In some cases, from the progressive reformers' viewpoint at least, it may even have changed for the worse. According to the figures of the National Industrial Conference Board, even income was as badly distributed at the end of the era as before. In 1921, the highest 10 percent of income recipients received 38 percent of total personal income, and that figure was only 34 percent in 1910. (Since the share of the top 5 percent of income recipients probably declined in the 1910–20 period, the figures for the top 10 percent group suggest a certain improvement in income distribution at the top. But the fact that the share of the lowest 60 percent also declined in that period, from 35 percent to 30 percent, confirms the view that no meaningful improvement can be shown.) Maldistribution was to grow worse until after 1929.

American farmers on the whole and in particular seemed to suffer increasing disadvantages. Farm life was one of the institutional bulwarks of the mode of life the progressives ostensibly cherished. "The farmer who owns his land," averred Gifford Pinchot, "is still the backbone of the Nation; and one of the things we want most is more of him, ... [for] he is the first of home-makers." If only in the sense that there were relatively fewer farmers in the total population at the end of the progressive era, one would have to say farm life in the United States had suffered. But, moreover, fewer owned their own farms. The number of farm tenants increased by 21 percent from 1900 to 1920; 38.1 percent of all farm operators in 1921 were tenants; and the figures look even worse when one notices that tenancy *declined* in the most *impoverished* areas during this period, suggesting that the family farm was surviving mostly in the more marginal agricultural areas. Finally, although agriculture had enjoyed some of its most prosperous years in history in the 1910–20 period, the 21 percent of the nation's gainfully employed who were in agriculture in 1919 (a peak year) earned only 16 percent of the national income.

While progressivism failed to restore vitality to American farming, it failed also to stop the vigorous ascendancy of corporate capitalism, the most conspicuous challenge to conventional values and modes that the society faced at the beginning of the era. The corporation had drastically undermined the very basis of the traditional rationale that had supported the nation's freewheeling system of resource allocation and had underwritten the permissiveness of the laws governing economic activities in the nineteenth century. The new capitalism by-passed the privately-owned proprietary firm, it featured a separation of ownership and control, it subordinated the profit motive to varied and variable other objectives such as empire-building, and, in many of the techniques developed by financial brokers and investment bankers, it appeared to create a great gulf between the making of money and the producing of useful goods and services. Through a remarkable series of judicial sophistries, this nonconventional form of business enterprise had become, in law, a *person*, and had won privileges and liberties once entrusted only to men, who were presumed to be conditioned and restrained by the moral qualities that inhere in human nature. Although gaining legal dispensations from an obliging Supreme Court, the corporation could claim no theoretical legitimacy beyond the fact of its power and its apparent inextricable entanglement in the business order that had produced America's seemingly unbounded material success.

Although much has been written about the supposed continuing vitality of small proprietary business enterprise in the United States, there is no gainsaying the continued ascendancy of the big corporation nor the fact that it still lacks legitimation. The fact that in the last sixty years the number of small proprietary businesses has grown at a rate that slightly exceeds the rate of population growth says little about the character of small business enterprise today as compared with that of the era of the American industrial revolution; it does nothing to disparage the apprehensions expressed in the antitrust campaigns of the progressives. To focus on the vast numbers of automobile dealers and gasoline service station owners, for example, is to miss completely their truly humble dependence upon the very few giant automobile and oil companies, a foretold dependence that was the very point of progressives' anticorporation, antitrust sentiments. The progressive movement must indeed be credited with placing real restraints upon monopolistic tendencies in the United States, for most statistics indicate that at least until the 1950's business concentration showed no substantial increase from the turn of the century (though it may be pertinent to note that concentration ratios did increase significantly in the decade immediately following the progressive era). But the statistics of concentration remain impressive—just as they were when John Moody wrote *The Truth About the Trusts* in 1904 and Louis Brandeis followed it with *Other People's Money* in 1914. That two hundred corporations (many of them interrelated) held almost one-quarter of all business assets, and more than 40 percent of all corporate assets in the country in 1948; that the fifty largest manufacturing corporations held 35 percent of all industrial assets in 1948, and 38 percent by 1962; and that a mere twenty-eight corporations or one one-thousandth of a percentage of all nonfinancial firms in 1956 employed 10 percent of all those employed in the nonfinancial industries, should be sufficient statistical support for the apprehensions of the progressive era—*just as it is testimony to the failure of the progressive movement to achieve anything substantial to alter the situation.*

Perhaps the crowning failure of progressivism was the American role in World War I. It is true that many progressives opposed America's intervention, but it is also true that a great many more supported it. The failure in progressivism lies not in the decision to intervene but in the futility of intervention measured by progressive expectations.

**Arthur S. Link and
Richard L. McCormick**

 **NO**

Progressivism in History

Convulsive reform movements swept across the American landscape from the 1890s to 1917. Angry farmers demanded better prices for their products, regulation of the railroads, and the destruction of what they thought was the evil power of bankers, middlemen, and corrupt politicians. Urban residents crusaded for better city services and more efficient municipal government. Members of various professions, such as social workers and doctors, tried to improve the dangerous and unhealthy conditions in which many people lived and worked. Businessmen, too, lobbied incessantly for goals which they defined as reform. Never before had the people of the United States engaged in so many diverse movements for the improvement of their political system, economy, and communities. By around 1910, many of these crusading men and women were calling themselves progressives. Ever since, historians have used the term *progressivism* to describe the many reform movements of the early twentieth century.

Yet in the goals they sought and the remedies they tried, the reformers were a varied and contradictory lot. Some progressives wanted to increase the political influence and control of ordinary people, while other progressives wanted to concentrate authority in experts. Many reformers tried to curtail the growth of large corporations; others accepted bigness in industry on account of its supposed economic benefits. Some progressives were genuinely concerned about the welfare of the "new" immigrants from southern and eastern Europe; other progressives sought, sometimes frantically, to "Americanize" the newcomers or to keep them out altogether. In general, progressives sought to improve the conditions of life and labor and to create as much social stability as possible. But each group of progressives had its own definitions of improvement and stability. In the face of such diversity, one historian, Peter G. Filene, has even argued that what has been called the progressive movement never existed as a historical phenomenon ("An Obituary for 'The Progressive Movement,'" *American Quarterly*, 1970).

Certainly there was no *unified* movement, but, like most students of the period, we consider progressivism to have been a real, vital, and significant phenomenon, one which contemporaries recognized and talked and fought about.

From Arthur S. Link and Richard L. McCormick, *Progressivism* (Harlan Davidson, 1983), pp. 1–3, 8–10, 21–25, 113–118. Copyright © 1983 by Harlan Davidson, Inc. Reprinted by permission of Harlan Davidson, Inc.

Properly conceptualized, progressivism provides a useful framework for the history of the United States in the late nineteenth and early twentieth centuries.

One source of confusion and controversy about progressives and progressivism is the words themselves. They are often used judgmentally to describe people and changes which historians have deemed to be "good," "enlightened," and "farsighted." The progressives themselves naturally intended the words to convey such positive qualities, but we should not accept their usage uncritically. It might be better to avoid the terms progressive and progressivism altogether, but they are too deeply embedded in the language of contemporaries and historians to be ignored. Besides, we think that the terms have real meaning. In this [selection] the words will be used neutrally, without any implicit judgment about the value of reform.

In the broadest sense, progressivism was the way in which a whole generation of Americans defined themselves politically and responded to the nation's problems at the turn of the century. The progressives made the first comprehensive efforts to grapple with the ills of a modern urban-industrial society. Hence the record of their achievements and failures has considerable relevance for our own time.

Who Were the Progressives?

Ever since the early twentieth century, people have argued about who the progressives were and what they stood for. This may seem to be a strange topic of debate, but it really is not. Progressivism engaged many different groups of Americans, and each group of progressives naturally considered themselves to be the key reformers and thought that their own programs were the most important ones. Not surprisingly, historians ever since have had trouble agreeing on who really shaped progressivism and its goals. Scholars who have written about the period have variously identified farmers, the old middle classes, professionals, businessmen, and urban immigrants and ethnic groups as the core group of progressives. But these historians have succeeded in identifying *their* reformers only by defining progressivism narrowly, by excluding other reformers and reforms when they do not fall within some specific definition, and by resorting to such vague, catch-all adjectives as "middle class." . . .

The advocates of the middle-class view might reply that they intended to study the leaders of reform, not its supporters, to identify and describe the men and women who imparted the dominant character to progressivism, not its mass base. The study of leadership is surely a valid subject in its own right and is particularly useful for an understanding of progressivism. But too much focus on leadership conceals more than it discloses about early twentieth-century reform. The dynamics of progressivism were crucially generated by ordinary people—by the sometimes frenzied mass supporters of progressive leaders, by rank-and-file voters willing to trust a reform candidate. The chronology of progressivism can be traced by events which aroused large numbers of people—a sensational muckraking article, an outrageous political scandal, an eye-opening legislative investigation, or a tragic social calamity. Events such as these gave reform its rhythm and its power.

Progressivism cannot be understood without seeing how the masses of Americans perceived and responded to such events. Widely circulated magazines gave people everywhere the sordid facts of corruption and carried the clamor for reform into every city, village, and county. State and national election campaigns enabled progressive candidates to trumpet their programs. Almost no literate person in the United States in, say, 1906 could have been unaware that ten-year-old children worked through the night in dangerous factories, or that many United States senators served big business. Progressivism was the only reform movement ever experienced by the whole American nation. Its national appeal and mass base vastly exceeded that of Jacksonian reform. And progressivism's dependence on the people for its objectives and timing has no comparison in the executive-dominated New Deal of Franklin D. Roosevelt or the Great Society of Lyndon B. Johnson. Wars and depressions had previously engaged the whole nation, but never reform. And so we are back to the problem of how to explain and define the outpouring of progressive reform which excited and involved so many different kinds of people.

A little more than a decade ago, Buenker and Thelen recognized the immense diversity of progressivism and suggested ways in which to reorient the study of early twentieth-century reform. Buenker observed that divergent groups often came together on one issue and then changed alliances on the next ("The Progressive Era: A Search for a Synthesis," *Mid-America,* 1969). Indeed, different reformers sometimes favored the same measure for distinctive, even opposite, reasons. Progressivism could be understood only in the light of these shifting coalitions. Thelen, in his study of Wisconsin's legislature, also emphasized the importance of cooperation between different reform groups. "The basic riddle in Progressivism," he concluded, "is not what drove groups apart but what made them seek common cause."

There is a great deal of wisdom in these articles, particularly in their recognition of the diversity of progressivism and in the concept of shifting coalitions of reformers. A two-pronged approach is necessary to carry forward this way of looking at early twentieth-century reform. First, we should study, not an imaginary unified progressive movement, but individual reforms and give particular attention to the goals of their diverse supporters, the public rationales given for them, and the results which they achieved. Second, we should try to identify the features which were more or less common to different progressive reforms.

The first task—distinguishing the goals of a reform from its rhetoric and its results—is more difficult than it might appear to be. Older interpretations of progressivism implicitly assumed that the rhetoric explained the goals and that, if a proposed reform became law, the results fulfilled the intentions behind it. Neither assumption is a sound one: purposes, rationale, and results are three different things. Samuel P. Hays' influential article, "The Politics of Reform in Municipal Government in the Progressive Era" (*Pacific Northwest Quarterly,* 1964), exposed the fallacy of automatically equating the democratic rhetoric of the reformers with their true purposes. The two may have coincided, but the historian has to demonstrate that fact, not take it for granted. The unexamined identification of either intentions or rhetoric with results is also invalid, although it is still a common feature of the scholarship on progressivism. Only within the last decade have historians begun to examine the actual achievements of the reformers. To carry out this first task, in the following... we will distinguish between the goals and rhetoric of individual reforms and will discuss the results of reform whenever the current literature permits. To do so is to observe the ironies, complexities, and disappointments of progressivism.

The second task—that of identifying the common characteristics of progressivism—is even more difficult than the first but is an essential base on which to build an understanding of progressivism. The rest of this [selection] focuses on identifying such characteristics. The place to begin that effort is the origins of progressivism....

The Character and Spirit of Progressivism

Progressivism was characterized, in the first place, by a distinctive set of attitudes toward industrialism. By the turn of the century, the overwhelming majority of Americans had accepted the permanence of large-scale industrial, commercial, and financial enterprises and of the wage and factory systems. The progressives shared this attitude. Most were not socialists, and they undertook reform, not to dismantle modern economic institutions, but rather to ameliorate and improve the conditions of industrial life. Yet progressivism was infused with a deep outrage against the worst consequences of industrialism. Outpourings of anger at corporate wrongdoing and of hatred for industry's callous pursuit of profit frequently punctuated the course of reform in the early twentieth century. Indeed, antibusiness emotion was a prime mover of progressivism. That the acceptance of industrialism *and* the outrage against it were intrinsic to early twentieth-century reform does not mean that progressivism was mindless or that it has to be considered indefinable. But it does suggest that there was a powerful irony in progressivism: reforms which gained support from a people angry with the oppressive aspects of industrialism also assisted the same persons to accommodate to it, albeit to an industrialism which was to some degree socially responsible.

The progressives' ameliorative reforms also reflected their faith in progress—in mankind's ability, through purposeful action, to improve the environment and the conditions of life. The late nineteenth-century dissidents had not lacked this faith, but their espousal of panaceas bespoke a deep pessimism: "Unless this one great change is made, things will get worse." Progressive reforms were grounded on a broader assumption. In particular, reforms could protect the people hurt by industrialization, and make the environment more humane. For intellectuals of the era, the achievement of such goals meant that they had to meet Herbert Spencer head on and confute his absolute "truths." Progressive thinkers, led by Lester Frank Ward, Richard T. Ely, and, most important, John Dewey, demolished social Darwinism with what Goldman has called "reform Darwinism." They asserted that human adaptation to the environment did not interfere with the evolutionary process, but was, rather, part and parcel of the law of natural change. Progressive intellectuals and their popularizers produced a vast literature to condemn laissez faire and to promote the concept of the active state.

To improve the environment meant, above all, to intervene in economic and social affairs in order to control natural forces and impose a measure of order upon them. This belief in interventionism was a third component of progressivism. It was visible in almost every reform of the era, from the supervision of business to the prohibition of alcohol (John W. Chambers II, *The Tyranny of Change: America in the Progressive Era, 1900–1917*, 1980). Interventionism could be both private and public. Given their choice, most progressives preferred to work noncoercively through voluntary organizations for economic and social changes. However, as time passed, it became evident that most progressive reforms could be achieved only by legislation and public control. Such an extension of public authority made many progressives uneasy, and few of them went so far as Herbert Croly in glorifying the state in his *The Promise of American Life* (1909) and *Progressive Democracy* (1914). Even so, the intervention necessary for their reforms inevitably propelled progressives toward an advocacy of the use of governmental power. A familiar scenario during the period was one in which progressives called upon public authorities to assume responsibility for interventions which voluntary organizations had begun.

The foregoing describes the basic characteristics of progressivism but says little about its ideals. Progressivism was inspired by two bodies of belief and knowledge—evangelical Protestantism and the natural and social sciences. These sources of reform may appear at first glance antagonistic to one another. Actually, they were complementary, and each imparted distinctive qualities to progressivism.

Ever since the religious revivals from about 1820 to 1840, evangelical Protestantism had spurred reform in the United States. Basic to the reform mentality was an all-consuming urge to purge the world of sin, such as the sins of slavery and intemperance, against which nineteenth-century reformers had crusaded. Now the progressives carried the struggle into the modern citadels of sin —the teeming cities of the nation. No one can read their writings and speeches without being struck by the fact that many of them believed that it was their Christian duty to right the wrongs created by the processes of industrialization. Such belief was the motive force behind the Social Gospel, a movement which swept through the Protestant churches in the 1890s and 1900s. Its goal was to align churches, frankly and aggressively, on the side of the downtrodden, the poor, and working people—in other words, to make Christianity relevant to this world, not the next. It is difficult to measure the influence of the Social Gospel, but it seared the consciences of millions of Americans, particularly in urban areas. And it triumphed in the organization in 1908 of the Federal Council of Churches of Christ in America, with its platform which condemned exploitative capitalism and proclaimed the right of workers to organize and to enjoy a decent standard of living. Observers at the Progressive party's national convention of 1912 should not have been surprised to hear the delegates sing, spontaneously and emotionally, the Christian call to arms, "Onward, Christian Solders!"

The faith which inspired the singing of "Onward, Christian Soldiers!" had significant implications for progressive reforms. Progressives used moralistic appeals to make people feel the awful weight of wrong in the world and to exhort them to accept personal responsibility for its eradication. The resultant reforms could be generous in spirit, but they could also seem intolerant to the people who were "reformed." Progressivism sometimes seemed to envision life in a small town Protestant community or an urban drawing room—a vision sharply different from that of Catholic or Jewish immigrants. Not every progressive shared the evangelical ethos, much less its intolerance, but few of the era's reforms were untouched by the spirit and techniques of Protestant revivalism.

Science also had a pervasive impact on the methods and objectives of progressivism. Many leading reformers were specialists in the new disciplines of statistics, economics, sociology, and psychology. These new social scientists set out to gather data on human behavior as it actually was and to discover the laws which governed it. Since social scientists accepted environmentalist and interventionist assumptions implicitly, they believed that knowledge of natural laws would make it possible to devise and apply solutions to improve the human condition. This faith underpinned the optimism of most progressives and predetermined the methods used by almost all reformers of the time: investigation of the facts and application of social-science knowledge to their analysis; entrusting trained experts to decide what should be done; and, finally, mandating government to execute reform.

These methods may have been rational, but they were also compatible with progressive moralism. In its formative period, American social science was heavily infused with ethical concerns. An essential purpose of statistics, economics, sociology, and psychology was to improve and uplift. Leading practitioners of these disciplines, for example, Richard T. Ely, an economist at the University of Wisconsin, were often in the vanguard of the Social Gospel. Progressives blended science and religion into a view of human behavior which was unique to their generation, which had grown up in an age of revivals and come to maturity at the birth of social science.

All of progressivism's distinctive features found expression in muckraking—the literary spearhead of early twentieth-century reform. Through the medium of such new ten-cent magazines as *McClure's, Everybody's* and *Cosmopolitan,* the muckrakers exposed every dark aspect and corner of American life. Nothing escaped the probe of writers such as Ida M. Tarbell, Lincoln Steffens, Ray Stannard Baker, and Burton J. Hendrick—not big business, politics, prostitution, race relations, or even the churches. Behind the exposés of the muckrakers lay the progressive attitude toward industrialism: it was here to stay, but many of its aspects seemed to be deplorable. These could be improved, however, if only people became aware of conditions and determined to ameliorate them. To bring about such awareness, the muckrakers appealed to their readers' consciences. Steffens' famous series, published in book form as *The Shame of the Cities* in 1904, was frankly intended to make people feel guilty for the corruption which riddled their cities. The muckrakers also used the social scientists' method of careful and painstaking gathering of data—and with devastating effects. The investigative function—which was later largely taken over by governmental agencies—proved absolutely vital to educating and arousing Americans.

All progressive crusades shared the spirit and used the techniques discussed here, but they did so to different degrees and in different ways. Some voiced a greater willingness to accept industrialism and even to extol its potential benefits; others expressed more strongly the outrage against its darker aspects. Some intervened through voluntary organizations; others relied on government to achieve changes. Each reform reflected a distinctive balance between the claims of Protestant moralism and of scientific rationalism. Progressives fought among themselves over these questions even while they set to the common task of applying their new methods and ideas to the problems of a modern society....

In this analysis we have frequently pointed to the differences between the rhetoric, intentions, and results of progressive reform. The failure of reform always to fulfill the expectations of its advocates was not, of course, unique to the progressive era. Jacksonian reform, Reconstruction, and the New Deal all exhibited similar ironies and disappointments. In each case, the clash between reformers with divergent purposes, the inability to predict how given methods of reform would work in practice, and the ultimate waning of popular zeal for change all contributed to the disjuncture of rationale, purpose, and achievement. Yet the gap between these things seems more obvious in the progressive era because so many diverse movements for reform took place in a brief span of time and were accompanied by resounding rhetoric and by high expectations for the improvement of the American social and political environment. The effort to change so many things all at once, and the grandiose claims made for the moral and material betterment which would result, meant that disappointments were bound to occur.

Yet even the great number of reforms and the uncommonly high expectations for them cannot fully account for the consistent gaps which we have observed between the stated purposes, real intentions, and actual results of progressivism. Several additional factors, intrinsic to the nature of early twentieth-century reform, help to explain the ironies and contradictions.

One of these was the progressives' confident reliance on modern methods of reform. Heirs of recent advances in natural science and social science, they enthusiastically devised and applied new techniques to improve American government and society. Their methods often worked; on the other hand, progressive programs often simply did not prove capable of accomplishing what had been expected of them. This was not necessarily the reformers' fault. They hopefully used untried methods even while they lacked a science of society which was capable of solving all the great problems which they attacked. At the same time, the progressives' scientific methods made it possible to know just how far short of success their programs had sometimes fallen. The evidence of their failures thus was more visible than in any previous era of reform. To the progressives' credit, they usually published that evidence—for contemporaries and historians alike to see.

A second aspect of early twentieth-century reform which helps to account for the gaps between aims and achievements was the deep ambivalence of the progressives about industrialism and its consequences. Individual reformers were divided, and so was their movement as a whole. Compared to many

Americans of the late 1800s, the progressives fundamentally accepted an industrial society and sought mainly to control and ameliorate it. Even reformers who were intellectually committed to socialist ideas often acted the part of reformers, not radicals.

Yet progressivism was infused and vitalized, as we have seen, by people truly angry with their industrial society. Few of them wanted to tear down the modern institutions of business and commerce, but their anger was real, their moralism was genuine, and their passions were essential to the reforms of their time.

The reform movement never resolved this ambivalence about industrialism. Much of its rhetoric and popular passion pointed in one direction—toward some form of social democracy—while its leaders and their programs went in another. Often the result was confusion and bitterness. Reforms frequently did not measure up to popular, antibusiness expectations, indeed, never were expected to do so by those who designed and implemented them. Even conservative, ameliorative reformers like Theodore Roosevelt often used radical rhetoric. In doing so, they misled their followers and contributed to the ironies of progressivism.

Perhaps most significant, progressives failed to achieve all their goals because, despite their efforts, they never fully came to terms with the divisions and conflicts in American society. Again and again, they acknowledged the existence of social disharmony more fully and frankly than had nineteenth-century Americans. Nearly every social and economic reform of the era was predicated on the progressive recognition that diverse cultural and occupational groups had conflicting interests, and that the responsibility for mitigating and adjusting those differences lay with the whole society, usually the government. Such recognition was one of the progressives' most significant achievements. Indeed, it stands among the most important accomplishments of liberal reform in all of American history. For, by frankly acknowledging the existence of social disharmony, the progressives committed the twentieth-century United States to recognizing—and to lessening—the inevitable conflicts of a heterogeneous industrial society.

Yet the significance of the progressives' recognition of diversity was compromised by the methods and institutions which they adopted to diminish or eliminate social and economic conflict. Expert administrative government turned out to be less neutral than the progressives believed that it would be. No scientific reform could be any more impartial than the experts who gathered the data or than the bureaucrats who implemented the programs. In practice, as we have seen, administrative government often succumbed to the domination of special interests.

It would be pointless to blame the progressives for the failure of their new methods and programs to eradicate all the conflicts of an industrial society, but it is perhaps fair to ask why the progressives adopted measures which tended to disguise and obscure economic and social conflict almost as soon as they had uncovered it. For one thing, they honestly believed in the almost unlimited potentialities of science and administration. Our late twentieth-century skepticism of these wonders should not blind us to the faith with which the progressives embraced them and imbued them with what now seem magical properties. For another, the progressives were reformers, not radicals. It was one thing to recognize the existence of economic and social conflict, but quite another thing to admit that it was permanent. By and large, these men and women were personally and ideologically inclined to believe that the American society was, in the final analysis, harmonious, and that such conflicts as did exist could be resolved. Finally, the class and cultural backgrounds of the leading progressives often made them insensitive to lower-class immigrant Americans and their cultures. Attempts to reduce divisions sometimes came down to imposing middle-class Protestant ways on the urban masses. In consequence, the progressives never fulfilled their hope of eliminating social conflict. Reformers of the early twentieth century saw the problem more fully than had their predecessors, but they nonetheless tended to consider conflicts resolved when, in fact, they only had been papered over. Later twentieth-century Americans have also frequently deceived themselves in this way.

Thus progressivism inevitably fell short of its rhetoric and intentions. Lest this seem an unfairly critical evaluation, it is important to recall how terribly ambitious were the stated aims and true goals of the reformers. They missed some of their marks because they sought to do so much. And, despite all their shortcomings, they accomplished an enormous part of what they set out to achieve.

Progressivism brought major innovations to almost every facet of public and private life in the United States. The political and governmental systems particularly felt the effects of reform. Indeed, the nature of political participation and the uses to which it was put went through transitions as momentous as those of any era in American history. These developments were complex, as we have seen, and it is no easy matter to sort out who was helped and who was hurt by each of them or by the entire body of reforms. At the very least, the political changes of the progressive era significantly accommodated American public life to an urban-industrial society. On balance, the polity probably emerged neither more nor less democratic than before, but it did become better suited to address, or at least recognize, the questions and problems which arose from the cities and factories of the nation. After the progressive era, just as before, wealthier elements in American society had a disproportionate share of political power, but we can hardly conclude that this was the fault of the progressives.

The personal and social life of the American people was also deeply affected by progressivism. Like the era's political changes, the economic and social reforms of the early twentieth century were enormously complicated and are difficult to summarize without doing violence to their diversity. In the broadest sense, the progressives sought to mitigate the injustice and the disorder of a society now dominated by its industries and cities. Usually, as we have observed, the quests for social justice and social control were extricably bound together in the reformers' programs, with each group of progressives having different interpretations of these dual ends. Justice sometimes took second place to control. However, before one judges the reformers too harshly for that, it is well to remember how bad urban social conditions were in the late nineteenth century and the odds against which the reformers fought. It is also well to remember that they often succeeded in mitigating the harshness of urban-industrial life.

The problems with which the progressives struggled have, by and large, continued to challenge Americans ever since. And, although the assumptions and techniques of progressivism no longer command the confidence which early twentieth-century Americans had in them, no equally comprehensive body of reforms has ever been adopted in their place. Throughout this study, we have criticized the progressives for having too much faith in their untried methods. Yet if this was a failing, it was also a source of strength, one now missing from reform in America. For the essence of progressivism lay in the hopefulness and optimism which the reformers brought to the tasks of applying science and administration to the high moral purposes in which they believed. The historical record of their aims and achievements leaves no doubt that there were many men and women in the United States in the early 1900s who were not afraid to confront the problems of a modern industrial society with vigor, imagination, and hope. They of course failed to solve all those problems, but no other generation of Americans has done conspicuously better in addressing the political, economic, and social conditions which it faced.

POSTSCRIPT

Did the Progressives Fail?

In spite of their differences, both Abrams's and Link and McCormick's interpretations make concessions to their respective critics. Link and McCormick, for example, admit that the intended reforms did not necessarily produce the desired results. Furthermore, the authors concede that many reformers were insensitive to the cultural values of the lower classes and attempted to impose middle-class Protestant ways on the urban masses. Nevertheless, Link and McCormick argue that in spite of the failure to curb the growth of big business, the progressive reforms did ameliorate the worst abuses of the new urban industrial society. Although the Progressives failed to solve all the major problems of their times, they did set the agenda that still challenges the reformers of today.

Abrams also makes a concession to his critics when he admits that "progressivism had real lasting effects for the blunting of the sharper edges of self-interest in American life, and for the reduction of the harsher cruelties suffered by the society's underprivileged." Yet the thrust of his argument is that the progressive reformers accomplished little of value. While Abrams probably agrees with Link and McCormick that the Progressives were the first group to confront the problems of modern America, he considers their intended reforms inadequate by their very nature. Because the reformers never really challenged the inequalities brought about by the rise of the industrial state, maintains Abrams, the same problems have persisted to the present day.

Historians have generally been sympathetic to the aims and achievements of the progressive historians. Many, like Charles Beard and Frederick Jackson Turner, came from the Midwest and lived in model progressive states like Wisconsin. Their view of history was based on a conflict between groups competing for power, so it was easy for them to portray progressivism as a struggle between the people and entrenched interests.

It was not until after World War II that a more complex view of progressivism emerged. Richard Hofstadter's *Age of Reform* (Alfred A. Knopf, 1955) was exceptionally critical of the reformist view of history as well as of the reformers in general. Born of Jewish immigrant parents and raised in cities in New York, the Columbia University professor argued that progressivism was a moral crusade undertaken by WASP families in an effort to restore older Protestant and individualistic values and to regain political power and status. Both Hofstadter's "status revolution" theory of progressivism and his profile of the typical Progressive have been heavily criticized by historians. Nevertheless, he changed the dimensions of the debate and made progressivism appear to be a much more complex issue than had previously been thought.

Most of the writing on progressivism for the past 20 years has centered around the "organizational" model. Writers of this school have stressed the role of the "expert" and the ideals of scientific management as basic to an understanding of the Progressive Era. This fascination with how the city manager plan worked in Dayton or railroad regulation in Wisconsin or the public schools laws in New York City makes sense to a generation surrounded by bureaucracies on all sides. Two books that deserve careful reading are Robert Wiebe's *The Search for Order, 1877–1920* (Hill & Wang, 1967) and the wonderful collection of essays by Samuel P. Hayes, *American Political History as Social Analysis* (Knoxville, 1980), which brings together two decades' worth of articles from diverse journals that were seminal in exploring ethnocultural approaches to politics within the organizational model.

In a highly influential article written for the *American Quarterly* in spring 1970, Professor Peter G. Filene proclaimed "An Obituary for the 'Progressive Movement.' " After an extensive review of the literature, Filene concluded that since historians cannot agree on its programs, values, geographical location, members, and supporters, there was no such thing as a Progressive movement. Few historians were bold enough to write progressivism out of the pantheon of American reform movements. But Filene put the proponents of the early-twentieth-century reform movement on the defensive. Students who want to see how professional historians directly confronted Filene in their refusal to attend the funeral of the Progressive movement should read the essays by John D. Buenker, John C. Burnham, and Robert M. Crunden in *Progressivism* (Schenkman, 1977).

Three works provide an indispensable review of the literature of progressivism in the 1980s. Link and McCormick's *Progressivism* (Harlan Davidson, 1983) deserves to be read in its entirety for its comprehensive yet concise coverage. More scholarly but still readable are the essays on the new political history in McCormick's *The Party Period and Public Policy: American Politics From the Age of Jackson to the Progressive Era* (Oxford University Press, 1986). The more advanced student should consult Daniel T. Rodgers, "In Search of Progressivism," *Reviews in American History* (December 1982). While admitting that Progressives shared no common creed or values, Rodgers nevertheless feels that they were able "to articulate their discontents and their social visions" around three distinct clusters of ideas: "The first was the rhetoric of antimonopolism, the second was an emphasis on social bonds and the social nature of human beings, and the third was the language of social efficiency."

ISSUE 9

Did the Women's Movement Die in the 1920s?

YES: William L. O'Neill, from *Everyone Was Brave: A History of Feminism in America* (Quadrangle Books, 1971)

NO: Anne Firor Scott, from *The Southern Lady: From Pedestal to Politics, 1830–1930* (University of Chicago Press, 1970)

ISSUE SUMMARY

YES: Professor of history William L. O'Neill contends that the women's movement died following the success of the suffrage campaign because women were not united in support of many of the other issues that affected them and because the increasingly militant feminism of the Woman's Party alienated many supporters of women's rights.

NO: Anne Firor Scott, a professor emeritus of history, maintains that the suffrage victory produced a heightened interest in further social and political reform, which inspired southern women to pursue their goals throughout the 1920s.

On March 31, 1776, Abigail Adams wrote to her husband, John, "I long to hear that you have declared an independency—and by the way in the new Code of Laws which I suppose it will be necessary for you to make I desire you would Remember the Ladies, and be more generous and favourable to them than your ancestors." Apparently, John Adams, like so many husbands before and since, forgot his wife's supplication. Consequently, following the American Revolution, women benefited very little from the democratic forces that swept through the United States. Their failure to enjoy the same progress as men in terms of political democracy produced a status characterized by historian Gerda Lerner as "relative deprivation." This sense of deprivation helped to fuel the women's movement during the "age of reform" and culminated in the Women's Rights Convention of 1848 in Seneca Falls, New York.

The tone of the Seneca Falls meeting was set by Elizabeth Cady Stanton's presentation of the Declaration of Sentiments and Resolutions, which called for the elimination of the separate status of the two sexes by proclaiming that "all men and women are created equal." All of the resolutions passed unanimously except the one demanding women's suffrage. This proposal was finally adopted, but not without a floor fight. The right to vote, it appeared, was too radical.

Following the Civil War, suffragists hoped that the issue of women's political disfranchisment would be resolved satisfactorily in conjunction with efforts to extend voting rights to African Americans. The architects of the Fourteenth and Fifteenth Amendments, however, feared that proposals to enfranchise former slaves and women at the same time would jeopardize the primary goal of black political empowerment. Stanton argued that this decision made women relatively more powerless than before and renewed her call for women's suffrage. After 1890 the National American Woman Suffrage Association (NAWSA) began to view women's suffrage as a primary goal for the reform of American society. Benefiting from the organizational skills of Carrie Chapman Catt, who formulated her "Winning Plan" to gain the right to vote, American women won their campaign with the passage and ratification of the Nineteenth Amendment.

For many participants, the suffrage victory signaled the last step to full equality. For others, it marked another beginning. Was the struggle over? Had the final victory been won? Certainly there was no evidence that voting rights brought full equality for American women after 1920. On the other hand, there is some doubt about whether or not women in the 1920s developed the collective self-consciousness that had been displayed in the suffrage campaign and that would be required to achieve further gains in their status. What *did* happen to the women's movement in the 1920s? The selections that follow suggest the absence of a consensus on this question.

In the first selection, William L. O'Neill argues that, following the enactment of the Nineteenth Amendment, American women possessed no other reform initiatives to which they were committed so strongly as the right to vote. Without a unifying goal, the women's movement splintered along regional, racial, and class lines, and many women's organizations abandoned their interest in activism and operated primarily as social clubs. Furthermore, contends O'Neill, organizations like the League of Women Voters reflected much of the conservatism of the period, while the Woman's Party, under the leadership of Alice Paul, failed to temper its demands for an equal rights amendment with a willingness to engage in the art of political compromise.

In the second selection, Anne Firor Scott concentrates on southern women and concludes that the 1920s witnessed significant efforts by women to secure reforms in areas of interest to members of their sex and to society as a whole. By addressing issues such as child labor, minimum wage and maximum hour legislation, race relations, and political democracy, women contributed significantly to the success of progressivism in the South in the 1920s. Scott maintains that these efforts demonstrated the growing powers of the "new woman" of the postsuffrage era and revealed the desire of many women to increase their opportunities beyond the purely domestic sphere.

YES

The Post-Suffrage Era

The decline of social feminism after World War I was demoralizing to all concerned. Women reformers could, however, console themselves with the knowledge that their frustrations resulted from a nationwide swing to the right rather than any special defects peculiar to themselves. Ardent feminists were denied this comfort. The women's rights movement expired in the twenties from ailments that had gone untreated in its glory days. Chief among them was the feminists' inability to see that equal suffrage was almost the only issue holding the disparate elements of the woman movement together. Once it was resolved, voters who happened to be female were released from the politically meaningless category of "woman." This allowed their basic allegiances to come into play. As a popular journalist pointed out, "the woman 'bloc' does not tend to become more and more solidified, but tends to become more and more disintegrated. Women at the polling places in Vermont turn out to be different from women at the polling places in Iowa; and the differences of locality and of class turn out to overshadow the difference of sex." It quickly became evident that, except on matters like Prohibition and the sex lives of political figures, there was no women's vote. It also soon became clear that the anti-suffragists had more accurately foreseen the ballot's limitation than the suffragists. In 1920 it was still possible to argue, as Emily Greene Balch did, that if women voters were often ignorant and inexperienced, "they are also largely free from bad old political habits and traditions, and free to strike out a new political method, not dominated by party, in which social and moral values shall outweigh all others." At the first postwar convention of the International Woman Suffrage Alliance, Carrie Chapman Catt, while admitting that in many countries woman suffrage had come almost by accident as a consequence of the war, still believed "that had the vote been granted to women some twenty-five years ago when justice and logic and public opinion demanded... there would have been no World War."

The mood did not last long. By 1922 H. L. Mencken could say:

> Years ago I predicted that these suffragettes, tried out by victory, would turn out to be idiots. They are now hard at work proving it. Half of them devote themselves to advocating reforms, chiefly of a sexual character, so utterly preposterous that even male politicians and newspaper editors laugh

From William L. O'Neill, *Everyone Was Brave: A History of Feminism in America* (Quadrangle Books, 1971). Copyright © 1969, 1971 by William L. O'Neill. Notes omitted.

at them; the other half succumb absurdly to the blandishments of the old-time male politicians, and so enroll themselves in the great political parties. A woman who joins one of these parties simply becomes an imitation man, which is to say, a donkey. Thereafter she is nothing but an obscure cog in an ancient and creaking machine, the sole intelligible purpose of which is to maintain a horde of scoundrels in public office.

Unjust? Of course. Yet soon many suffragists admitted that fighting for the vote had been more rewarding than getting it. Mrs. Catt had expected this. Even before women voted in their first national election, she reminded them that they had no obligation to the major parties, for if either had "lived up to the high ideals of our Nation and courageously taken the stand for right and justice as against time-serving, vote-winning policies of delay, women would have been enfranchised long ago." It was partially for this reason that she founded the League of Women Voters [LWV], and the experience of 1920 confirmed her judgment. "Suffrage women last autumn numerously confessed that they found real politics 'pale and insipid' when it came time to use their first vote. It seemed sordid and commonplace to be striving merely to elect men whose platforms were so strangely confused they could not find a direct issue. They felt a vacancy where for years there had been purpose consecrated to an immortal principle." A few years later Mrs. Catt noted again that suffragists "are disappointed first of all because they miss the exaltation, the thrill of expectancy, the vision which stimulated them in the suffrage campaign. They find none of these appeals to their aspiration in the party of their choice."

It was one thing for the indomitable Mrs. Catt, whom no political party had anything of value to offer, to take this line; it was quite another for the typical suffragist who had been led to expect something more from the franchise than political tokens (such as the National Committee seats assigned women by both parties). Anne Martin, who several times ran for the Senate from Nevada, was annoyed in 1919 when the National Conference of Republican Women seemed more interested in the clichés of professional politicians than in her own efforts to organize a specifically feminine program. Having given up on the Republicans, she was even more discouraged when in 1924 the La Follette managers picked a Socialist candidate to run on the third-party ticket, even though she had outpolled him in a previous election. She saw the 1924 election as a debacle for women. Only one was elected to Congress, and she was not among the emancipated candidates supported by the Woman's party [WP]. Ignoring the women endorsed by the La Follette party, Miss Martin concluded that all the parties had shown themselves equally bigoted, and that by urging women to work within the established system "Mrs. Carrie Chapman Catt sounded the doom of feminism for many years to come." This was hardly fair to Mrs. Catt, who held no brief for the existing parties but saw no alternative to them, nor was it reasonable of Miss Martin to expect Mrs. Catt to organize another Woman's party when the drawbacks of that policy had, from a social feminist point of view, been so clearly demonstrated by the existing one.

Even so, women with more patience and less personal ambition than Anne Martin found the results of big-party politics disappointing. The first chairman of the Republican Women's Committee of Illinois observed that reform-minded women who joined the regular parties were simply swallowed up. Her experience demonstrated that while the parties were willing to give women symbolic appointments, they were carefully shut out of the decision-making process. This was not so much because they were women as because they were amateurs who did not share the regulars' passion for office. The professionals reasoned correctly that "once in the organization we could be controlled. Our nuisance value was gone. Not only that, our power for good was gone." It was a mistake, she concluded, to think women could reform the party from within.

Emily Newell Blair, who served as vice-chairman of the Democratic National Committee from 1921 to 1928, was less disillusioned but hardly more sanguine. She agreed that women had little influence on the parties, that they had been awarded few high offices, and that in general their services had not been adequately compensated. She thought there was a good reason for this. "Members of the party take responsibility and women have been backward about taking it. Their habit is to sit back and then complain because it is not offered them." Mrs. Blair understood the deeper problems enfranchisement had revealed. When women first gained the vote, she noted, male politicians had feared the consequences and treated women with respect and caution. But soon it became clear not only that women would not hang together, but that they would not even support for public office the best female candidates. Since there was no bloc vote, there was no reason for men to cater to it. All of which, she felt, resulted from the fundamental failure of suffragists to think deeply enough about what would happen when the vote was won. Anna Howard Shaw knew the suffragists had let their followers down in this respect. Once victory was assured, she told Mrs. Blair, "I am sorry for you young women who have to carry on the work in the next ten years, for suffrage was a symbol, and now you have lost your symbol. There is nothing for the women to rally round."

Before long it became evident that the League of Women Voters, though it did good work, was no substitute for the NAWSA [National American Women Suffrage Association]. It labored on too many fronts; the nature of its activities precluded either the exhilarating victories or heart-wrenching defeats that made life among the suffragists so exciting; and its determined neutrality denied it the passionate loyalties reserved for partisan organizations. Most of all, perhaps, the LWV lost a great many fights, and this did not commend it to younger women who came of age during the years when suffrage was a winning cause. Of course, politics as such diminished in interest during the 1920's, and many women who might otherwise have concerned themselves with public affairs were drawn off into the cultural, social, and recreational pursuits that made the New Era exciting. Marguerite Wells, while attempting to show that women profited from the vote, was forced to admit that "the net effect of suffrage on many clubs has been that they are less, rather than more, prone to 'take action' on political questions." And Rose Schneiderman, although she was careful to point out that she was no more disappointed in women's suffrage than she had been in men's suffrage, admitted that "the women's vote hasn't been of any sensible value in the measures which the Women's Trade Union League want. We started twelve years ago to fight for a forty-eight-hour week. We are still fighting for it, and I can't see that it is a bit easier now, that we make any more impression on the Legislature than we did before we could vote." So much for Florence Kelley's contention that politicians were unresponsive to the needs of working women because they could not vote. The rejoinder that woman suffrage was no worse in practice than man suffrage, although often used, was of course beside the point: a large part of the original justification for it had been that women would vote more sanely than men. If women were going to be no different as voters, there was little purpose to the long struggle except as a matter of simple justice, and mere justice was not why social feminists had invested so much in the cause. . . .

By 1936 it was possible for John Gordon Ross to sum up the results of woman suffrage in terms that require little modification today. In their sixteen years as voters women had overthrown no bosses, and few women in politics had established independent power bases. Women bureaucrats were no better than men—though less corruptible. The vote had not made women mannish, as had been feared, "rather their new responsibilities have brought out only the undesirable traits that women have always had," that is, fussiness, primness, bossiness, and the tendency to make unnecessary enemies. They did not trust each other as candidates. They had not come up with any useful new political ideas. As voters they tended to be excessively moralistic and intolerant. Only about half as many women as men registered to vote, and when they went to the polls they voted as their husbands did. "After a fair trial of sixteen years, it seems just to appraise women's suffrage as one of those reforms which, like the secret ballot, the corrupt-practices acts, the popular election of senators, and the direct primary, promised almost everything and accomplished almost nothing."

Except for a slightly mean-spirited satisfaction in the deflation of suffragist pretensions, this still seems a fair appraisal. The percentage of women who register to vote is much higher now than in 1936, but otherwise the situation is little changed. Ross did, however, admit to one area in which women excelled politically—lobbying. But, he pointed out, they had been successful lobbyists long before they got the vote, and their prowess in this area did not in any way weaken his argument. Quite so, yet it did raise again the possibility that antisuffragists had been right in thinking that the vote would diminish women's actual influence over politics. Emily Newell Blair later remarked that so long as the woman vote was an unknown quantity, professional politicians were obliged to respect it. Moreover, women in the pre-suffrage years spoke with virtually a single voice as they were never able to do again. Although some women of note opposed equal suffrage, almost none of them was publicly against the purposes of social feminism. In the Progressive era, before women were divided by partisan political affiliations, before the German scare and Russian scare unleashed an hysterical patriotism, before ex-suffragists fell out over their differing conceptions of equal rights, an apparent unanimity prevailed that lent great weight to the woman movement's expressions of opinion. Organized women did not understand the sources of their unity very well. They explained it by references to the bonds of motherhood and other more occult characteristics which supposedly bound them together, but it was no less real for being so misconstrued. As they did not understand the peculiar circumstances responsible for their unity, they could hardly preserve it in the postwar, postsuffrage, and post-Progressive world.

This is not to say, of course, that the woman movement could have been saved if only suffragists had adopted a sounder strategy in their voteless years, or if they had given up entirely on votes for women. The latter was not a real option. Too many years, too many tears had gone into the movement for anyone to arrest it on the eve of victory. Even if suffragists had appreciated that the vote would do organized women more harm than good, they would still have wanted it. Nor could they control the historical processes that were going to make class differences and ideological disagreements more important to women after 1917. But while recognizing that chance and circumstance sharply limited their field of maneuver, it is still clear that suffragists' neglect of certain alternatives was fatal to their larger purposes. They oversold the vote, which meant that both they and the generation that followed them were inevitably disillusioned with public affairs in general. They made too many compromises, from ignobly deserting their embattled sisters in the Woman's party to accepting American participation in a war they disliked. Practical politics made these choices essential, but expediency tarnished the moral quality that was the movement's most precious asset in the postsuffrage era. They failed to think seriously about what was to come after the federal amendment was passed. And, perhaps worst of all, in overconcentrating on politics they neglected other areas—economic, social, domestic—that more profoundly governed women's lives.

It might have been expected that the decline of feminism after 1920 would have been especially hard on the militant suffragists. They had wanted the vote more desperately than most women, and had risked more and suffered more to gain it. Militants lived a richly colored emotional life. Like children, zealots, and romantics, they were either way up or way down, but whether high or low they were always intense, doctrinaire, and assertive. Once their initial euphoria had passed, the members of the Woman's party, more so than other suffragists, found victory hardly less demoralizing than defeat. Previous setbacks had, after all, only been provisional; victory was final. Suffragists had sustained innumerable reverses with their morale intact. But the struggle had gone on for too long, had become, in fact, a way of life. Victory too long delayed loses its savor, and campaigns if endlessly prolonged become self-sustaining and self-justifying. Three generations of women had fought for the vote, and in doing so had become dependent on the cause to give their lives meaning. The vote was no compensation for the effort that had gone into winning it, no substitute for the emotions it displaced. The suffrage army was quickly demobilized. The thought patterns and modes of behavior it had required were not so easily converted to a peaceful, postsuffrage economy.

The NAWSA had anticipated some such denouement by founding in advance the League of Women Voters, a new bottle into which it hoped to pour the old feminist wine. But the prosaic LWV offered nothing to militants who, like discharged commandos, could see no way of using their special skills in the postwar world. Even before most women had a chance to cast their first vote, ultra-feminists were expressing their discontent and searching for ways to maintain the old faith. Mrs. Oliver Hazard Perry Belmont, an immensely rich and determined widow who had become the Woman's party's principal means of support, returned from Europe in July 1920 urging women to boycott the coming elections. "Husband your new power," she instructed them, adding that "suffragists did not fight for your emancipation for seventy years to have you now become servants to men's parties." Her vague admonitions became less opaque a few days later when she announced that the times demanded a new party to save women from the corruptions of big-party politics. Mrs. Belmont's lack of enthusiasm for the party system was widely shared. The League of Women Voters was, of course, scrupulously nonpartisan, in keeping with organized women's traditional aversion to regular politics, but many women were not. Charlotte Perkins Gilman endorsed Mrs. Belmont's position with some fervor:

> The power women will be able to exercise lies with their not joining in the party system of men. The party system of politics is a trick of men to conceal the real issues. Women should work for the measures they want outside of party politics. It is because the old political parties realize that women's influence will be negligible on the inside that they are so eager to get women to join with them.

On February 18, 1921, the old Woman's party was disbanded and a new one created in its stead. Florence Kelley was there and took its number in a slashing report for the *Survey.* She found the new Woman's party's position on the race issue singularly ignoble. The leadership declared that since Southern Negro women were discriminated against equally with Negro men, the principle of equal rights was not imperiled and the party not obliged to intervene. "An inglorious ideal of equality this! Acquiescence in the disfranchisement of millions of women, provided only that the men of their race also are deprived of their constitutional rights." The party's interpretation of equal rights in the industrial field was just as bad. It was inclined to regard protective legislation for working women as discriminatory, an attitude Mrs. Kelley believed to be both unjust and ill-informed. "How cruel, therefore, is the pretension of certain organizations of professional and business women to decide for the wage-earners, without consulting them, what statutory safeguards they are henceforth to do without." From the day of its birth, then, the battle lines between the new Woman's party and the social feminists for whom Mrs. Kelley spoke were clearly drawn. Although other social reformers were not so quick to react as Mrs. Kelley, she correctly gauged the dedication of the WP to equal rights thus construed, and prophetically warned Newton Baker that the struggle would go on "until an amendment of this general nature is adopted, or the leaders of the Woman's Party all die of old age." . . .

The Woman's party did earn much of the invective directed against it. Haughty and uncooperative under the best of circumstances, the party became truculent in the face of adversity. Mrs. Belmont and some other leaders were extraordinarily tactless. The party's manifesto began, "Women today, although enfranchised, are still in every way subordinate to men"—a statement which was not so much false as belittling of all that had been done for and by women in the recent past. The WP insisted that all grievances listed in the Seneca Falls declaration of 1848, save only votelessness, still obtained. This sweeping untruth irritated veteran suffragists who by the turn of the century had come to feel, as Susan B. Anthony put it, that "while women still suffer countless minor disadvantages, the fundamental rights have largely been secured except the suffrage." Equally offensive was the WP's claim to be the original suffragists' only heir. "Other women's organizations work for many things and for women incidentally; the Woman's Party works to acquire for women equal rights and opportunities, and this, in sum and substance, is the feminist movement."

The Woman's party sometimes appeared to have virtually a monopoly on the kind of woman condemned by the *American Mercury* as "a rabid feminist, one of the type that sees all history as a struggle between Woman, the beautiful builder, and Man, the eternal brute and wastrel." It continually obscured the merits of its program by flippancies which could only offend the serious. *Equal Rights* concluded one editorial on the probable judicial reaction to its amendment by observing that however "the courts may interpret the amendment, we can rest serene in our reliance on the righteousness of the principle of Equal Right for men and women and not worry as to the details of how it will work out. The establishing of a righteous principle will certainly bring only good results." But, of course, the "details of how it will work out" were precisely what the controversy over the amendment was all about.

Extreme feminists, while superb agitators, were hopelessly bad politicians with no feel for the bargaining and compromises that make the democratic machine go. Agitation had played its part in the suffrage struggle, but it was accompanied by a careful attention to the political arts. The Woman's party was, in this sense, completely unbalanced. Even when it did attempt to play politics, its approach was absurdly unrealistic. By 1924 it had given up its old strategy of attempting to hold the party in power responsible, but it was drifting toward a new and equally implausible theory—that a sufficient number of congresswomen would guarantee passage of the equal-rights amendment. For a time the party planned to support all women candidates, regardless of their position on the amendment, and urged women to vote exclusively for members of their own sex. Eventually the WP decided to support only those women candidates who endorsed the amendment. Five did so, all of them La Follette or minority candidates. All of them, despite the WP's help, were beaten. As usual, the party had gotten much, largely hostile, publicity, but the effort was so great and failure so complete that it never tried this tactic again.

. . . [T]he WP illustrates another familiar aspect of American social history: that radicals often more correctly analyze a given situation than their adversaries, but that the very traits responsible for their insight prevent them from exploiting it successfully. The militants were quick to understand that the vote had not materially improved the condition of women. They realized that many discriminatory laws and customs remained, and that to overcome them would require the same crusading energies that had gone into the suffrage campaign. In the end, this knowledge did them little good because the passions that led them to demand a feminist revival kept them from effecting it. Their theatrical demonstrations and doctrinaire rigor antagonized most other women, leaving the Woman's party in a position of solitary grandeur. Perhaps it didn't matter really. The feminist tide was ebbing so fast in the 1920's that it probably could not have been reversed under the best of circumstances. All the same, militancy insured the defeat of those hopes it meant to advance....

For all its symbolic triumphs, the WP had little to show at the decade's end for the nearly $800,000 it had spent since 1921. Wisconsin was still the only state with an equal-rights proviso in its constitution—the effects of which had been minimal. The party had been involved in preparing more than five hundred individual pieces of legislation across the country, but most of them were never made into law. It had alienated itself from the mainstream of organized womanhood and was soon to be confronted with an economic collapse that made its concentration on equal rights seem parochial if not downright cranky, and that was to dry up the supply of romantic youth which had given the organization its special force. From this point on the WP grew smaller, older, and poorer while the current of events moved ever more strongly against it.

Women With the Vote

W omen have been saying for years that the world, and they themselves, would be changed if they were granted the right to vote. When Tennessee ratified the Nineteenth Amendment, the old dream became reality. Would the predicted consequences follow?

For more than two decades increasing numbers of southern women had become deeply engaged in efforts to build a system of public schools, to clean up prisons and abolish the convict lease system, to restrict the use of child labor, to improve the working conditions and reduce the hours of work of women and of factory workers generally, and to diminish racial discrimination in the South. Progress in all these areas had been slow, and the World War diverted the energies of many reformers. Now the war was over, women had the ballot, and the time had come when it was possible to believe, as one young North Carolina woman put it, that "the advent of women into political life would mean the loosening of a great moral force which will modify and soften the relentlessly selfish economic forces of trade and industry.... the ideals of democracy and of social and human welfare will undoubtedly receive a great impetus."

Whatever the future was destined to reveal about the long-run consequences of adding women to the electorate, at the outset there was a burst of energy, a new drive for accomplishment. Among those who had long supported the idea of suffrage there was no lack of confidence that women would live up to their new opportunity. In Baton Rouge the daughter of a former governor edited a weekly paper entitled *Woman's Enterprise* with the goal of proving to the world that women "are as fully alive to the demands of the times as are the sterner sex." The newspaper encouraged women to register and vote, urged them to run for office, and issued constant reminders to officeholders that women now intended to be heard on all important issues. Women, the *Enterprise* thought, far from voting as their menfolk directed, were on the way to becoming the politically influential members of their families. "Place one energetic woman on a commission and a general house cleaning will result such as Baton Rouge has never enjoyed," the editors confidently asserted; "inefficiency in every department will disappear."

In addition to politics the *Enterprise* carried a steady stream of articles on working women's problems, education for women, and the "new concept of

From Anne Firor Scott, *The Southern Lady: From Pedestal to Politics, 1830–1930* (University of Chicago Press, 1970). Copyright © 1970 by Anne Firor Scott. Reprinted by permission of University of Chicago Press. Notes omitted.

marriage." It also directed a good deal of attention to the accomplishments of young women enrolled at the Louisiana State University.

For those who had taken it seriously the suffrage movement had been an excellent school in political methods. In the first flush of post-suffrage enthusiasm, the old hands undertook to try to teach the ways and means of political action to as many of the newly enfranchised as they could persuade to be interested. Even before the Nineteenth Amendment was ratified, state suffrage organizations transformed themselves into leagues of women voters, to educate women and work for "needed legislation." Charles Merriam, a well-known political scientist, was persuaded to offer an intensive training course for women leaders at the University of Chicago. "Citizenship schools" blossomed over the landscape, offering everything from the most serious reading in political theory to the simplest instruction in ballot marking. Meanwhile women established legislative councils in a concerted effort to attain the laws they felt were needed. The Alabama council, for example, was made up of sixteen organizations ranging from the Woman's Trade Union League to the Methodist Home Missionary Council. In Texas the Joint Legislative Council published a carefully compiled record of the work of congressmen, state legislators, and judges.

The central political concern had to do with the problems of children. In nearly every state women were active in the effort to secure better child labor laws. The case of Virginia is instructive. In 1921 women's groups urged the legislature to establish a Children's Code Commission, and when the legislature took their suggestion, they persuaded the governor to appoint five of their number to the commission. When the commission, in turn, brought in twenty-four recommendations for new laws, ranging from a statewide juvenile court system to compulsory education, the women went to work to secure legislative approval of the recommendations. Eighteen of the twenty-four were adopted.

Also in 1921 a combination of women's groups in Georgia secured the passage of a children's code, a child-placement bill, and a training school bill. In 1923 Georgia women tried, but failed, to persuade the state legislature to ratify the federal child labor amendment. In Arkansas, by contrast, a woman member of the legislature, working in conjunction with the members of the women's clubs, was given credit for that state's ratifying the amendment. The wife of the man who led the floor fight against ratification was reported to be unable to conceal her delight that he had failed. In other states when women failed to secure ratification of the child labor amendment they turned their attention to strengthening state labor laws, an effort in which they were more successful.

In 1921 southern women, along with women from over the nation, brought pressure upon the Congress to pass the Sheppard-Towner Act for maternal and infant health. Nineteen of 26 southern senators voted for the bill. In the House, 91 of the 279 votes in support of the bill came from the South and only 9 of 39 votes against it. This law, which pioneered federal-state cooperation in welfare, was the first concrete national achievement of newly enfranchised women. Since the law provided for federal-state cooperative financing, it was necessary for the women to follow up their congressional efforts with work to secure the matching appropriations from state legislatures. This campaign elicited a great deal of enthusiasm among women in every southern state. It was in those states particularly, where the machinery of public health was not well developed, that the favorable effects of the Act were most visible.

Next to children the subjects of most general interest to politically minded women had to do with the working conditions and wages of women workers. In Arkansas, for example, as early as 1919 the suffrage organization began to work for minimum wages and maximum hours in cotton mills. In Georgia women joined the Federation of Labor in an effort to secure a limit on hours of work for women. The hearing on this last measure brought out "every cotton mill man in Georgia," and while a woman's eloquent testimony persuaded the committee to report the bill, the millowners had enough influence to prevent its being brought to a vote. As a result of what they had learned about the conditions in which many factory women worked, clubwomen and the League of Women Voters developed a deepening concern for the problems of industrial labor generally. This concern often brought them into conflict with husbands and friends. The businessman's cherished "cheap labor" might be seen by his wife as an exploited human being, especially when the worker was a woman or a child. For years southern ladies had been praised for their superior sensitivity to human and personal problems, and now that their "sphere" was enlarging, such sensitivity took them in directions not always welcome to their husbands.

This particular drama of wives against husbands was played out, among other places, in North Carolina. Textile manufacturing was a major economic interest in that state, and working conditions in many mills were far from ideal. Wages were low, and it was common to find numbers of young children at work. Soon after the passage of the Nineteenth Amendment, North Carolina women began to develop an aggressive interest in these matters. It occurred to them to ask the state government to invite the Woman's Bureau of the United States Department of Labor to investigate working conditions in North Carolina mills. This suggestion aroused a strong opposition among millmen and their business colleagues. The governor was polite to the women but adamant: North Carolina had no need for the federal government to tell it how to run its affairs. Textile journals and newspapers accused the offending women of being unwomanly, of mixing in things about which they knew nothing, and of being the dupes of northern manufacturers bent on spoiling the competitive advantage which child labor and cheap female labor gave the South. The YWCA, one of the groups supporting the idea of a survey, was warned that it would soon find itself without funds. The state president of the League of Women Voters was summoned before a self-constituted panel of millmen and lectured severely. She was told that her husband's sales of mill machinery would diminish as long as she and the league continued their unseemly interest in working conditions in the mills.

The progressive movement came fully into being in the South in the 1920s, especially in relation to state government. Southern women contributed significantly to the political effort which led to the adoption of a wide range of social legislation in those years. In public, women continued to defer to men, but in their private correspondence they described their own efforts as more practical than those of men.

As time went by a small number of very respectable southern women became deeply involved in what could only be called, in the southern context, the radical aspect of the labor movement. Lucy Randolph Mason, whose name testified to her Virginia lineage, began by working with the YWCA in Richmond and became, as she said, more and more concerned about the lack of social control in the development of southern industry. In her YWCA work she became acutely aware of industrial problems, for the young women in the Y, during the twenties, were preoccupied with the study of the facts of industrial life. They worked out a legislative program which included the abatement of poverty, abolition of child labor, a living wage in every industry, the eight-hour day, and protection of workers from the hardships of continued unemployment. At Randolph-Macon members of the Y studied the problems of coal miners, and at Westhampton those of unemployment. College girls across the South formed a committee for student industrial cooperation, seeking, as they put it, to Christianize the social order.

In January 1923 the National Consumers League sponsored a conference on industrial legislation for the Mississippi Valley states. The session on hours of work for women was chaired by a New Orleans woman, and the one on minimum wages by a Kentucky woman. In the same year the chairman of the Women in Industry Committee of the Mississippi League of Women Voters urged members of local leagues to inform themselves about the working conditions of the 15,000 working women in Mississippi "in restaurants and shops, in bakeries and laundries and fisheries," about their inadequate wages, and their need for safety and sanitary protection. All this was to be in preparation for the next session of the Mississippi legislature.

Middle-class southern women set up two schools for factory girls. One, sponsored by the YWCA at Lake Junaluska in North Carolina, offered what its founders called a brief social-religious education. Although the organizers of this school realized that political action to improve their wages and working conditions could not be accomplished by the working women alone, they felt that these summer conferences might stimulate girls to begin to study and think about their own problems. The other experiment was the Southern Summer School for Women Workers in Industry, founded at Burnsville, North Carolina, in 1927. An outgrowth of the famous Bryn Mawr workers summer school, it offered training to factory girls many of whom, when the upsurge of unionization occurred in the 1930s, would become labor organizers.

By 1931 the Southern Council on Women and Children in Industry, made up of women, had been formed to work for shorter hours and to try to bring an end to night work in the textile industry. Lucy Mason worked for this group too, before she went on to her major effort in the 1930s as an organizer for the CIO [Congress of Industrial Organizations].

It is curious in view of the deep conservatism of the majority of southern women, many of whom never registered to vote, that those who did choose to live an active life were often found on the progressive side of the political spectrum. Part of the explanation is that the person who was bold enough to assume a role unusual for women was also likely to be radical on social questions generally. As the president of the Tennessee League of Women Voters remarked:

> Some good souls are pleased to call our ideas socialistic. They are indeed uncomfortable often for some folk. Some timid souls of both sexes are only half converted to the new order... [yet] every clear thinking, right feeling and high minded man and woman should consecrate his best talents to the gradual reorganization of society, national and international.

One evidence of the advanced thinking of many of the southern women who were most active in public life was the important part they played in what came to be called the interracial movement. Beginning in 1919, at a time when many Negroes were leaving the South and many others were coming home from the war with a new view of life, the interracial movement of the twenties was built on the foundation laid in the previous decades....

In 1920 at a meeting of southern churchwomen in Memphis four Negro women came on invitation to speak of the needs of southern Negroes. One of them, Charlotte Hawkins Brown, head of a school for Negroes in North Carolina, told the gathering that she had been forcibly removed from a Pullman car on her way to the meeting. In the emotional stir of the moment the ninety-odd white churchwomen constituted themselves the Woman's Department of Will Alexander's Commission [on Interracial Cooperation]. The first head of this group was Mrs. Luke Johnson of Griffin, Georgia, under whose leadership interracial committees were organized in every southern state. Mrs. Johnson thought race was "one of the livest issues of the day and... a real test of Christianity and of citizenship."

In Texas the women's interracial organization was put together by an energetic widow, businesswoman, and former suffrage worker, Jessie Daniel Ames. By 1924 women there were working to improve Negro housing, schools, libraries, to secure Negro farm agents to work with Negro farmers, for better health care, a school for delinquent girls, adequate railroad accommodations, and for textbooks dealing with the economic and racial development of the Negro people. They proposed an anti-lynching law which would have made every member of a mob liable to murder charges. The group also attempted to investigate particular problems of intimidation, and organized a speakers' bureau to take the discussion of race issues to the state. In North Carolina Mrs. Bertha Newell, superintendent of the Bureau of Christian Social Relations of the Women's Missionary Council of the Methodist Church, and Clara Cox, a Friend from High Point, carried on the same kind of effort. In 1926 Mrs. Newell began working to secure better job opportunities for educated Negro girls.

Women tried to deal with racial conflict and black problems in many ways. When the National League of Women Voters decided in 1924 to establish a committee on Negro problems with membership from every state that had more than 15 percent Negro population, women in eight southern states accepted appointment. Many of these same women served on local interracial committees, of which there were finally about eight hundred in the South. In Tennessee white women organized a special citizenship school for Negro women. Some individuals offered personal support to their Negro fellow citizens. Mary Cooke

Branch Munford of Richmond made a room of her house permanently available to Negroes for public meetings, and a busy doctor's wife in Alabama waged a one-woman campaign for better Negro education. When the Richmond city council considered a segregation statute in 1929, it was Lucy Randolph Mason who, almost single-handedly, persuaded the council to defeat it. In April 1924 the Mississippi Federation of Women's Clubs set up a committee on the condition of the colored people, and the president of the Colored Women's Federation was invited to tell the white convention about the problems of Negro domestic workers.

The most dramatic aspect of women's interracial work was the crusade against lynching, which began in the early twenties. A group of Georgia women sent a message to the *New York World:*

> We are convinced that if there is any one crime more dangerous than others, it is that crime which strikes at the roots of and undermines constituted authority, breaks all laws and restraints of civilization, substitutes mob violence and masked irresponsibility from established justice and deprives society of a sense of protection against barbarism.

By 1930 under the leadership of Jessie Daniel Ames, who by that time had left Texas for Atlanta, the Association of Southern Women for the Prevention of Lynching took shape. At its peak this organization enrolled 40,000 small-town and rural churchwomen in an effort to bring to an end this most spectacularly disgraceful form of race conflict.

In the meantime southern white women inaugurated an increasing number of interracial meetings, in which there was fairly open discussion of the problems Negroes faced. Though Negro women leaders, for the most part, took care to eschew any demand for social equality, they did hammer away on such things as discrimination in the administration of justice, housing, Jim Crow cars, inferior education, and the need for the ballot. It seems likely that these efforts, ineffectual as they seemed in the face of the magnitude of the problem, nevertheless represented the opening wedge which would ultimately bring an end to the monolithic position of southerners on the issue of white supremacy. From slavery through Reconstruction and into the twentieth century, relationships between white and black women were quite unlike those common between white and black men, sharing as they did many concerns about children and home life across the color line. The fact that women were very active in the interracial movement is not surprising.

In the twenties white women were speaking of their sympathy for Negro women who were, like themselves, mothers and homemakers. One point they made over and over was the need to protect the chastity of Negro women from the aggression of white men. Just as one antebellum woman had candidly remarked that she did not know whether her grandmother's sympathy for abolition stemmed from sympathy for slaves or for white women, so it might be wondered whether part of the concern for the chastity of Negro women was a reflection of the white women's distaste for the half-hidden miscegenation which existed in every southern community.

✦❧❀

The interest of women in humanitarian causes had deep roots in traditional feminine philanthropy. However, the twenties also witnessed the beginning of some newer interests. As they studied the mechanics of government in order to vote, women began to develop a concern for efficient organization. One of the tools for educating new voters to their responsibilities was the study of state and local government. As women went about looking at the way such governments actually operated they began to wonder whether they could be made more efficient. As early as 1922 women's groups in Virginia were working for improved election laws, and in the following year they undertook to learn about the executive budget. In 1924 the Virginia League of Women Voters concentrated upon tax administration, a subject which the controlling Democratic machine was not anxious to discuss. The same group successfully supported a bill to create a uniform fiscal year but failed in an effort to secure civil service, a conservation department, and reform of the county government and the state educational machinery.

Such interests were not confined to Virginia. Women in Georgia and Tennessee became convinced that outmoded constitutions were the source of much inefficiency; and in both states campaigns for constitutional revisions were launched and eventually succeeded. Kentucky women in 1927 began to work for home rule for cities, improvements in local charters, and the adoption of city manager government.

Women were interested not only in the structure of government; they wanted to make it more democratic. Their own long exclusion had made them sensitive to citizen participation. It was newly enfranchised women who invented the now commonplace idea of getting out the vote. In some places their efforts led to spectacular increases. In Alabama, for example, 54.4 percent of the qualified voters voted in 1924 following a get-out-the-vote effort, compared to less than 30 percent in 1920. One county, where women had been particularly active, turned out 84.1 percent of its qualified voters. Florida in the same year reported a 65.9 percent increase over 1920 in the number of voters going to the polls.

The poll tax was a subject of twofold concern. Women's groups opposed the tax on principle, but as long as it remained in force, they set out to collect it in order to increase the number of qualified voters. In 1925 Louisiana women collected $30,000 to this end. The work of North Carolina women for the Australian ballot, which finally succeeded in 1929, was another example of an effort to improve democratic procedures.

Close to home, yet a long way from women's traditional concerns, were two other political issues that developed strength in southern women's groups in the twenties: government ownership of Muscle Shoals and the regulation of utility rates. Interest in both these questions resulted from studies of the cost of living. The movement that would lead to the Tennessee Valley Authority gained the enthusiastic support of women in Alabama and Tennessee. On these as on other questions politically active women took a pragmatic view without reference to traditional free enterprise arguments.

. . . Many southern women showed an interest in running for elective office; and, though numerous obstacles lay between almost any woman and nomination, by 1930 only Louisiana had yet to have women in the state legislature. During the twenties women served as secretaries of state in Kentucky, Texas, and Louisiana, as clerks or deputy clerks of the Supreme Court in Georgia and Oklahoma, as commissioners of public welfare in North Carolina and Oklahoma, as commissioner of state lands in Arkansas, railroad commissioner in Florida, and superintendent of public instruction in Texas.

One woman who made her way to the center of power was Mrs. Nellie Nugent Somerville of Greenville, Mississippi, who had been an active politician long before the Nineteenth Amendment. At the first election after it was legal to do so, in 1923, she ran for the state legislature, in a campaign that was a model of thorough organization, and was elected. She had been observing party organization long enough to understand it rather well, and she hoped the newly enfranchised women would be similarly observant. She advised them to be certain they had a hand in choosing county committees and reminded them: "It now becomes the duty of women voters to take lively interests in the details of political machinery. When any meeting or election is ordered by your political party be sure you take part in it." . . .

Another politically minded woman who reached a position of genuine power in the party was Sue Shelton White of Tennessee, an independent court reporter, secretary to members of the Tennessee Supreme Court, and from 1920 to 1926 secretary to Senator Kenneth McKellar. In 1915 she drafted the first mother's pension law to be presented to the Tennessee legislature, which finally passed in 1920. She went from her job in Senator McKellar's office to practice law in Jackson, Tennessee, and was sufficiently effective in Democratic politics to be invited to work for the Democratic National Committee. With Nellie Davis (Tayloe) Ross she helped lay the groundwork for the extensive women's program of the party during the early Franklin D. Roosevelt years. . . .

An increasing number of southern women undertook simple party work of the doorbell-ringing and envelope-stuffing variety—a trend that still continues. And whether they helped make policy or not, women voters believed they were affecting the outcome of elections. Women claimed to have defeated James E. Ferguson and elected William P. Hobby governor of Texas in 1920. In Mississippi Henry L. Whitfield, former president of Mississippi State College for Women, was elected governor in 1923, largely through the efforts of alumnae of the college. South Carolina women thought they had a large hand in the defeat of Cole Blease. One South Carolina woman who worked through the whole campaign remarked innocently, "We made no partisan stand, we merely got out the vote." Tennessee Democrats, perhaps looking for a scapegoat, blamed women for the Republican victory in Tennessee in the 1920 election. The women themselves claimed credit for the return of Cordell Hull to Congress three years later.

In North Carolina in 1921 the federated women persuaded a reluctant governor to appoint their former president, Kate Burr Johnson, commissioner of charities and welfare. The legislature showed an equal reluctance to confirm the appointment, but, as Mrs. Johnson recalled it, "They were scared to death of what women with the vote might do, and one legislator was heard to remark, 'Well, we might as well put her in; she's pretty and won't give us any trouble.' " The forecast was inaccurate, since Mrs. Johnson, with the organized women behind her, became a prime mover in the struggle to secure a survey of working conditions in North Carolina mills, and by so doing soon stood high on the legislature's list of troublemakers....

Many of the women... who had been trained during the two or three decades before suffrage, and who had been acutely aware of the disadvantage of being barred from the polls, were eager to move into a more active and effective political role in 1920. Their general goals had been worked out in the preceding decades. Their underlying motivation was complex, but at least two main drives were clear: first, the drive to assert themselves as individual human beings with minds and capacities that could be used; and, second, the drive to improve the world in which they lived. The balance of these motives varied from person to person. Some, like Lucy Mason, were primarily interested in social reform:

> When I was fourteen, a missionary's sermon made me want to be a missionary myself. Later I recognized that religion can be put to work right in one's own community. It was this belief that took me into the Equal Suffrage League, and later the League of Women Voters, both of which were interested in labor and social legislation.

Others thoroughly enjoyed the game of politics and the feeling of power that occasionally accompanied it. Nearly all felt that significant reforms would be more easily achieved with women's help.

The Nineteenth Amendment changed a good many things, but it only partially modified southern culture. A number of difficulties remained in the way of women's full participation in public life. One major obstacle, in addition to the demands of home and family, was widespread male opposition, typified, perhaps, by the Texan who burned his wife's poll tax receipt to prevent her from voting. Equally important was the unwillingness of many women to assume and carry through large responsibilities. Often they had a vague desire to "do something" but needed leadership to find out what to do and how to do it, and there were never enough leaders to tap all the potential resources. A good example, no doubt an extreme one, was a Virginia town of which it was reported that when a certain Miss Terry was at home the town was alive with women's political activities but when she went to Europe all was quiet.

Around the handful of leaders there gathered a slowly growing number of supporters and workers, and when this support was effectively channeled, specific goals were achieved. In almost every instance—as in child labor reform, for example—groups of men were working to the same ends, and frequently there was cooperation. Women's efforts were crucial in the areas of race relations and factory regulation. Through it all, the outward aspect of the southern lady continued to be maintained as the necessary precondition for securing a hearing.

For some women, this was a perfectly compatible outward role, so long as their freedom of action was not seriously limited. Others impatiently called for an end to pedestals, but even they found it effective to operate within the ladylike tradition. The other side of the coin was that women were accused of not being proper southern ladies by those who objected to the substantive goals for which they were working, and who hoped thus to discredit the goals themselves....

When all this is said, however, the fact remains that the post-suffrage burst of political and social effort created a milieu in which the emerging new woman could try her powers. Along with expanding opportunities for work, education, and associated activity, the franchise added another dimension to women's lives, and another option for women who wanted more than purely domestic experience.

POSTSCRIPT

Did the Women's Movement Die in the 1920s?

Most students today associate the Equal Rights Amendment (ERA) with the women's liberation movement of the 1960s and 1970s, but the history of this amendment dates back to the 1920s. Proposed for the first time in 1923, the amendment stated, "Men and women shall have equal rights throughout the United States and every place subject to its jurisdiction." This notion of full equality met significant opposition when it was proposed—as it has in recent years—including challenges from women's organizations. Groups such as the League of Women Voters complained that the Equal Rights Amendment, if ratified, would roll back protective legislation in the areas of minimum wage and maximum hour laws and would jeopardize penalties for rape and sexual offenses against women. Hence, many of the fruits of the Progressive Era would be lost. For Alice Paul, leader of the National Women's Party that supported the amendment, the protective legislation enacted in the past represented a conspiracy to deny women full equality by singling them out for special treatment. These laws, Paul argued, set women apart as a separate and unequal class. The ideological struggle suggested by these divergent positions continued into the 1930s and reflected the serious divisions that surfaced in the women's movement following the suffrage victory.

The status of women in the decade after suffrage receives general treatment in William H. Chafe, *The American Woman: Her Changing Social, Economic, and Political Roles, 1920–1970* (Oxford University Press, 1972); June Sochen, *Herstory: A Woman's View of American History* (Alfred, 1974); Mary P. Ryan, *Womanhood in America: From Colonial Times to the Present* (New Viewpoints, 1975); Sheila M. Rothman, *Woman's Proper Place: A History of Changing Ideals and Practices, 1870 to the Present* (Basic Books, 1978); Lois Scharf and Joan Jensen, eds., *Decades of Discontent: The Women's Movement, 1910–1940* (Greenwood Press, 1983); and Nancy Woloch, *Women and the American Experience* (Alfred A. Knopf, 1984). Discussions of feminism in the 1920s are presented in J. Stanley Lemons, *The Woman Citizen: Social Feminism in the 1920s* (University of Illinois Press, 1973); Lois Banner, *Women in Modern America: A Brief History* (Harcourt Brace Jovanovich, 1974); Susan D. Baker, *The Origins of the Equal Rights Amendment: Feminism Between the Wars* (Greenwood Press, 1981); Dorothy Brown, *Setting a Course: American Women in the 1920s* (Twayne, 1987); and Robyn Muncy, *Creating a Female Dominion in American Reform, 1890–1935* (Oxford University Press, 1991). Felice D. Gordon, *After Winning: The Legacy of the New Jersey Suffragists, 1920–1947* (Rutgers University Press, 1986) and Kristi Anderson, *After Suffrage: Women in Partisan and Electoral Politics Before the New Deal* (University of Chicago Press, 1996) focus specifically on the continuing struggle for political empowerment following the ratification of the Nineteenth Amendment. Christine Lunardini, in *From Equal Suffrage to Equal Rights: Alice Paul and the National Woman's Party, 1910-1928* (New York University Press, 1986), examines one of the controversial advocates for an equal rights amendment in the 1920s. Nancy F. Cott, in *The Grounding of Feminism* (Yale University Press, 1987), argues that the diversity within the women's movement created important paradoxes. For example, although feminists in the 1920s desired equality with men, unity among themselves, and gender consciousness, they also focused upon their differences from men, the diversity of women, and the elimination of gender roles. David M. Kennedy, in *Birth Control in America: The Career of Margaret Sanger* (Yale University Press, 1970), examines an important issue that attracted the interest of many women's groups in the 1920s, while Jacqueline Dowd Hall, in *Revolt Against Chivalry: Jessie Daniel Ames and the Women's Campaign Against Lynching* (Columbia University Press, 1979), explores the role of women in the area of race relations. A valuable historiographical essay is Estelle B. Freedman, "The New Woman: Changing Views of Women in the 1920s," *Journal of American History* (September 1974).

ISSUE 10

Was the New Deal an Effective Answer to the Great Depression?

YES: Roger Biles, from *A New Deal for the American People* (Northern Illinois University Press, 1991)

NO: Gary Dean Best, from *Pride, Prejudice, and Politics: Roosevelt Versus Recovery, 1933–1938* (Praeger, 1990)

ISSUE SUMMARY

YES: Professor of history Roger Biles contends that, in spite of its minimal reforms and nonrevolutionary programs, the New Deal created a limited welfare state that implemented economic stabilizers to avert another depression.

NO: Professor of history Gary Dean Best argues that Roosevelt established an antibusiness environment with the creation of the New Deal regulatory programs, which retarded the nation's economic recovery from the Great Depression until World War II.

The catastrophe triggered by the 1929 Wall Street debacle crippled the American economy, deflated the optimistic future most Americans assumed to be their birthright, and ripped apart the values by which the country's businesses, farms, and governments were run. In the 1920s the whirlwind of a boom economy had sucked people into its vortex. During the next decade, the inertia of the Great Depression stifled their attempts to make ends meet.

The world depression of the 1930s began in the United States, which is where some of the most serious effects were felt. The United States had suffered periodic economic setbacks—in 1873, 1893, 1907, and 1920—but those slumps had been limited and temporary. The omnipotence of American productivity, the ebullient American spirit, and the self-deluding thought "it can't happen here" blocked out any consideration of an economic collapse that might devastate the capitalist economy and threaten U.S. democratic government.

All aspects of American society trembled from successive jolts; there were 4 million unemployed people in 1930 and 9 million more by 1932. Those who had not lost their jobs took pay cuts or worked for scrip. Charitable organizations attempted to provide for millions of homeless and hungry people, but their resources were not adequate. There was no security for those whose savings were lost forever when banks failed or stocks declined. Manufacturing halted, industry shut down, and farmers destroyed wheat, corn, and milk rather than sell them at a loss. Worse, there were millions of homeless Americans—refugees from the cities roaming the nation on freight trains, victims of the drought of the Dust Bowl seeking a new life farther west, and hobo children estranged from their parents. Physicians reported increased cases of malnutrition. Some people plundered grocery stores to avoid starvation.

Business and government leaders alike seemed immobilized by the economic giant that had fallen to its knees. "In other periods of depression there has always been hope, but as I look about, I now see nothing to give ground for hope—nothing of man," said former president Calvin Coolidge on New Year's Day 1933. Herbert Hoover, the incumbent president at the start of the Great Depression, attempted some relief programs. However, they were ineffective, considering the magnitude of the unemployment, hunger, and distress. Nor did Hoover's initiatives recognize the need for serious changes in the relationship between the federal government and society or for any modification of its relationship with individual Americans.

As governor of New York, Franklin D. Roosevelt (who was elected president in 1932) had introduced some relief measures, such as industrial welfare and a comprehensive system of unemployment remedies, to alleviate the social and economic problems facing the citizens of the state. Yet his campaign did little to reassure his critics that he was more than a "Little Lord Fauntleroy" rich boy who wanted to be president. In light of later developments, Roosevelt may have been the only presidential candidate to deliver more programs than he actually promised.

In the following selections, Roger Biles argues that in spite of its minimal reforms and nonrevolutionary programs, the New Deal created a limited welfare state that implemented economic stabilizers to avert another depression. Gary Dean Best is highly critical of Roosevelt's pragmatic approach to solving the depression. Roosevelt established an antibusiness environment, maintains Best, when he created a host of New Deal regulatory programs whose long-range effect was to retard the nation's economic recovery until World War II.

Roger Biles  **YES**

A New Deal for the American People

At the close of the Hundred Days, Franklin D. Roosevelt said, "All of the proposals and all of the legislation since the fourth day of March have not been just
a collection of haphazard schemes, but rather the orderly component parts of
a connected and logical whole." Yet the president later described his approach
quite differently. "Take a method and try it. If it fails admit it frankly and try
another. But above all, try something." The impetus for New Deal legislation
came from a variety of sources, and Roosevelt relied heavily at various times
on an ideologically diverse group of aides and allies. His initiatives reflected
the contributions of, among others, Robert Wagner, Rexford Tugwell, Raymond
Moley, George Norris, Robert LaFollette, Henry Morgenthau, Marriner Eccles,
Felix Frankfurter, Henry Wallace, Harry Hopkins, and Eleanor Roosevelt. An
initial emphasis on recovery for agriculture and industry gave way within two
years to a broader-based program for social reform; entente with the business
community yielded to populist rhetoric and a more ambiguous economic program. Roosevelt suffered the opprobrium of both the conservatives, who vilified
"that man" in the White House who was leading the country down the sordid
road to socialism, and the radicals, who saw the Hyde Park aristocrat as a confidence man peddling piecemeal reform to forestall capitalism's demise. Out of
so many contradictory and confusing circumstances, how does one make sense
of the five years of legislative reform known as the New Deal? And what has
been its impact on a half century of American life?[1]

A better understanding begins with the recognition that little of the New
Deal was new, including the use of federal power to effect change. Nor, for all of
Roosevelt's famed willingness to experiment, did New Deal programs usually
originate from vernal ideas. Governmental aid to increase farmers' income, pro-
pounded in the late nineteenth century by the Populists, surfaced in Woodrow
Wilson's farm credit acts. The prolonged debates over McNary-Haugenism in
the 1920s kept the issue alive, and Herbert Hoover's Agricultural Marketing Act
set the stage for further federal involvement. Centralized economic planning,
as embodied in the National Industrial Recovery Act, flowed directly from the
experiences of Wilson's War Industries Board; not surprisingly, Roosevelt chose
Hugh Johnson, a veteran of the board, to head the National Recovery Administration. Well established in England and Germany before the First World War,

From Roger Biles, *A New Deal for the American People* (Northern Illinois University Press, 1991).
Copyright © 1991 by Northern Illinois University Press. Reprinted by permission.

social insurance appeared in a handful of states—notably Wisconsin—before the federal government became involved. Similarly, New Deal labor reform took its cues from the path-breaking work of state legislatures. Virtually alone in its originality, compensatory fiscal policy seemed revolutionary in the 1930s. Significantly, however, Roosevelt embraced deficit spending quite late after other disappointing economic policies and never to the extent Keynesian economists advised. Congress and the public supported the New Deal, in part, because of its origins in successful initiatives attempted earlier under different conditions.

Innovative or not, the New Deal clearly failed to restore economic prosperity. As late as 1938 unemployment stood at 19.1 percent and two years later at 14.6 percent. Only the Second World War, which generated massive industrial production, put the majority of the American people back to work. To be sure, partial economic recovery occurred. From a high of 13 million unemployed in 1933, the number under Roosevelt's administration fell to 11.4 million in 1934, 10.6 million in 1935, and 9 million in 1936. Farm income and manufacturing wages also rose, and as limited as these achievements may seem in retrospect, they provided sustenance for millions of people and hope for many more. Yet Roosevelt's resistance to Keynesian formulas for pump priming placed immutable barriers in the way of recovery that only war could demolish. At a time calling for drastic inflationary methods, Roosevelt introduced programs effecting the opposite result. The NRA restricted production, elevated prices, and reduced purchasing power, all of which were deflationary in effect. The Social Security Act's payroll taxes took money from consumers and out of circulation. The federal government's $4.43 billion deficit in fiscal year 1936, impressive as it seemed, was not so much greater than Hoover's $2.6 billion shortfall during his last year in office. As economist Robert Lekachman noted, "The 'great spender' was in his heart a true descendant of thrifty Dutch Calvinist forebears." It is not certain that the application of Keynesian formulas would have sufficed by the mid-1930s to restore prosperity, but the president's cautious deflationary policies clearly retarded recovery.[2]

Although New Deal economic policies came up short in the 1930s, they implanted several "stabilizers" that have been more successful in averting another such depression. The Securities and Exchange Act of 1934 established government supervision of the stock market, and the Wheeler-Rayburn Act allowed the Securities and Exchange Commission to do the same with public utilities. Severely embroiled in controversy when adopted, these measures have become mainstays of the American financial system. The Glass-Steagall Banking Act forced the separation of commercial and investment banking and broadened the powers of the Federal Reserve Board to change interest rates and limit loans for speculation. The creation of the Federal Deposit Insurance Corporation (FDIC) increased government supervision of state banks and significantly lowered the number of bank failures. Such safeguards restored confidence in the discredited banking system and established a firm economic foundation that performed well for decades thereafter.

The New Deal was also responsible for numerous other notable changes in American life. Section 7(a) of the NIRA, the Wagner Act, and the Fair Labor Standards Act transformed the relationship between workers and business and breathed life into a troubled labor movement on the verge of total extinction. In the space of a decade government laws eliminated sweatshops, severely curtailed child labor, and established enforceable standards for hours, wages, and working conditions. Further, federal action eliminated the vast majority of company towns in such industries as coal mining. Although Robert Wagner and Frances Perkins dragged Roosevelt into labor's corner, the New Deal made the unions a dynamic force in American society. Moreover, as Nelson Lichtenstein has noted, "by giving so much of the working class an institutional voice, the union movement provided one of the main political bulwarks of the Roosevelt Democratic party and became part of the social bedrock in which the New Deal welfare state was anchored."[3]

Roosevelt's avowed goal of "cradle-to-grave" security for the American people proved elusive, but his administration achieved unprecedented advances in the field of social welfare. In 1938 the president told Congress: "Government has a final responsibility for the well-being of its citizenship. If private co-operative endeavor fails to provide work for willing hands and relief for the unfortunate, those suffering hardship from no fault of their own have a right to call upon the Government for aid; and a government worthy of its name must make fitting response." The New Deal's safety net included low-cost housing; old-age pensions; unemployment insurance; and aid for dependent mothers and children, the disabled, the blind, and public health services. Sometimes disappointing because of limiting eligibility requirements and low benefit levels, these social welfare programs nevertheless firmly established the principle that the government had an obligation to assist the needy. As one scholar wrote of the New Deal, "More progress was made in public welfare and relief than in the three hundred years after this country was first settled."[4]

More and more government programs, inevitably resulting in an enlarged administrative apparatus and requiring additional revenue, added up to a much greater role for the national government in American life. Coming at a time when the only Washington bureaucracy most of the people encountered with any frequency was the U.S. Postal Service, the change seemed all the more remarkable. Although many New Deal programs were temporary emergency measures, others lingered long after the return of prosperity. Suddenly, the national government was supporting farmers, monitoring the economy, operating a welfare system, subsidizing housing, adjudicating labor disputes, managing natural resources, and providing electricity to a growing number of consumers. "What Roosevelt did in a period of a little over 12 years was to change the form of government," argued journalist Richard L. Strout. "Washington had been largely run by big business, by Wall Street. He brought the government to Washington." Not surprisingly, popular attitudes toward government also changed. No longer willing to accept economic deprivation and social dislocation as the vagaries of an uncertain existence, Americans tolerated—indeed, came to expect —the national government's involvement in the problems of everyday life. No longer did "government" mean just "city hall."[5]

The operation of the national government changed as well. For one thing, Roosevelt's strong leadership expanded presidential power, contributing to what historian Arthur Schlesinger, Jr., called the "imperial presidency."

Whereas Americans had in previous years instinctively looked first to Capitol Hill, after Roosevelt the White House took center stage in Washington. At the same time, Congress and the president looked at the nation differently. Traditionally attentive only to one group (big business), policymakers in Washington began responding to other constituencies such as labor, farmers, the unemployed, the aged, and to a lesser extent, women, blacks, and other disadvantaged groups. This new "broker state" became more accessible and acted on a growing number of problems, but equity did not always result. The ablest, richest, and most experienced groups fared best during the New Deal. NRA codes favored big business, and AAA benefits aided large landholders; blacks received relief and government jobs but not to the extent their circumstances merited. The long-term result, according to historian John Braeman, has been "a balkanized political system in which private interests scramble, largely successfully, to harness governmental authority and/or draw upon the public treasury to advance their private agendas."[6]

Another legacy of the New Deal has been the Roosevelt revolution in politics. Urbanization and immigration changed the American electorate, and a new generation of voters who resided in the cities during the Great Depression opted for Franklin D. Roosevelt and his party. Before the 1930s the Democrats of the northern big-city machines and the solid South uneasily coexisted and surrendered primacy to the unified Republican party. The New Deal coalition that elected Roosevelt united behind common economic interests. Both urban northerners and rural southerners, as well as blacks, women, and ethnic immigrants, found common cause in government action to shield them from an economic system gone haywire. By the end of the decade the increasing importance of the urban North in the Democratic party had already become apparent. After the economy recovered from the disastrous depression, members of the Roosevelt coalition shared fewer compelling interests. Beginning in the 1960s, tensions mounted within the party as such issues as race, patriotism, and abortion loomed larger. Even so, the Roosevelt coalition retained enough commitment to New Deal principles to keep the Democrats the nation's majority party into the 1980s.[7]

Yet for all the alterations in politics, government, and the economy, the New Deal fell far short of a revolution. The two-party system survived intact, and neither fascism, which attracted so many followers in European states suffering from the same international depression, nor communism attracted much of a following in the United States. Vital government institutions functioned without interruption and if the balance of powers shifted, the national branches of government maintained an essential equilibrium. The economy remained capitalistic; free enterprise and private ownership, not socialism, emerged from the 1930s. A limited welfare state changed the meld of the public and private but left them separate. Roosevelt could be likened to the British conservative Edmund Burke, who advocated measured change to offset drastic alterations— "reform to preserve." The New Deal's great achievement was the application of just enough change to preserve the American political economy.

Indications of Roosevelt's restraint emerged from the very beginning of the New Deal. Rather than assume extraordinary executive powers as Abraham

Lincoln had done in the 1861 crisis, the president called Congress into special session. Whatever changes ensued would come through normal governmental activity. Roosevelt declined to assume direct control of the economy, leaving the nation's resources in the hands of private enterprise. Resisting the blandishments of radicals calling for the nationalization of the banks, he provided the means for their rehabilitation and ignored the call for national health insurance and federal contributions to Social Security retirement benefits. The creation of such regulatory agencies as the SEC confirmed his intention to revitalize rather than remake economic institutions. Repeatedly during his presidency, Roosevelt responded to congressional pressure to enact bolder reforms, as in the case of the National Labor Relations Act, the Wagner-Steagall Housing Act, and the FDIC. The administration forwarded the NIRA only after Senator Hugo Black's recovery bill mandating 30-hour workweeks seemed on the verge of passage.

As impressive as New Deal relief and social welfare programs were, they never went as far as conditions demanded or many liberals recommended. Fluctuating congressional appropriations, oscillating economic conditions, and Roosevelt's own hesitancy to do too much violence to the federal budget left Harry Hopkins, Harold Ickes, and others only partially equipped to meet the staggering need. The president justified the creation of the costly WPA in 1935 by "ending this business of relief." Unskilled workers, who constituted the greatest number of WPA employees, obtained but 60 to 80 percent of the minimal family income as determined by the government. Roosevelt and Hopkins continued to emphasize work at less than existing wage scales so that the WPA or PWA never competed with free labor, and they allowed local authorities to modify pay rates. They also continued to make the critical distinction between the "deserving" and "undeserving" poor, making sure that government aided only the former. The New Deal never challenged the values underlying this distinction, instead seeking to provide for the growing number of "deserving" poor created by the Great Depression. Government assumed an expanded role in caring for the disadvantaged, but not at variance with existing societal norms regarding social welfare.

The New Deal effected no substantial redistribution of income. The Wealth Tax Act of 1935 (the famous soak-the-rich tax) produced scant revenue and affected very few taxpayers. Tax alterations in 1936 and 1937 imposed no additional burdens on the rich; the 1938 and 1939 tax laws actually removed a few. By the end of the 1930s less than 5 percent of Americans paid income taxes, and the share of taxes taken from personal and corporate income levies fell below the amount raised in the 1920s. The great change in American taxation policy came during World War II, when the number of income tax payers grew to 74 percent of the population. In 1942 Treasury Secretary Henry Morgenthau noted that "for the first time in our history, the income tax is becoming a people's tax." This the New Deal declined to do.[8]

Finally, the increased importance of the national government exerted remarkably little influence on local institutions. The New Deal seldom dictated and almost always deferred to state and local governments—encouraging, cajoling, bargaining, and wheedling to bring parochial interests in line with national objectives. As Harry Hopkins discovered, governors and mayors angled to obtain as many federal dollars as possible for their constituents but with no strings attached. Community control and local autonomy, conditions thought to be central to American democracy, remained strong, and Roosevelt understood the need for firm ties with politicians at all levels. In his study of the New Deal's impact on federalism, James T. Patterson concludes: "For all the supposed power of the New Deal, it was unable to impose all its guidelines on the autonomous forty-eight states.... What could the Roosevelt administration have done to ensure a more profound and lasting impression on state policy and politics? Very little."[9]

Liberal New Dealers longed for more sweeping change and lamented their inability to goad the president into additional action. They envisioned a wholesale purge of the Democratic party and the creation of a new organization embodying fully the principles of liberalism. They could not abide Roosevelt's toleration of the political conservatives and unethical bosses who composed part of the New Deal coalition. They sought racial equality, constraints upon the southern landholding class, and federal intrusion to curb the power of urban real estate interests on behalf of the inveterate poor. Yet to do these things would be to attempt changes well beyond the desires of most Americans. People pursuing remunerative jobs and the economic security of the middle class approved of government aiding the victims of an unfortunate economic crisis but had no interest in an economic system that would limit opportunity. The fear that the New Deal would lead to such thoroughgoing change explains the seemingly irrational hatred of Roosevelt by the economic elite. But, as historian Barry Karl has noted, "it was characteristic of Roosevelt's presidency that he never went as far as his detractors feared or his followers hoped."[10]

The New Deal achieved much that was good and left much undone. Roosevelt's programs were defined by the confluence of forces that circumscribed his admittedly limited reform agenda—hostile judiciary; powerful congressional opponents, some of whom entered into alliances of convenience with New Dealers and some of whom awaited the opportunity to build on their opposition; the political impotence of much of the populace; the pugnacious independence of local and state authorities; the strength of people's attachment to traditional values and institutions; and the basic conservatism of American culture. Obeisance to local custom and the decision to avoid tampering with the fabric of American society allowed much injustice to survive while shortchanging blacks, women, small farmers, and the "unworthy" poor. Those who criticized Franklin Roosevelt for an unwillingness to challenge racial, economic, and gender inequality misunderstood either the nature of his electoral mandate or the difference between reform and revolution—or both.

If the New Deal preserved more than it changed, that is understandable in a society whose people have consistently chosen freedom over equality. Americans traditionally have eschewed expanded government, no matter how efficiently managed or honestly administered, that imposed restraints on personal success—even though such limitations redressed legitimate grievances or righted imbalances. Parity, most Americans believed, should not be purchased with the loss of liberty. But although the American dream has always entailed individual success with a minimum of state interference, the profound shock of capitalism's near demise in the 1930s undermined numerous previously unquestioned beliefs. The inability of capitalism's "invisible hand" to stabilize the market and the failure of the private sector to restore prosperity enhanced the consideration of stronger executive leadership and centralized planning. Yet with the collapse of democratic governments and their replacement by totalitarian regimes, Americans were keenly sensitive to any threats to liberty. New Deal programs, frequently path breaking in their delivery of federal resources outside normal channels, also retained a strong commitment to local government and community control while promising only temporary disruptions prior to the return of economic stability. Reconciling the necessary authority at the federal level to meet nationwide crises with the local autonomy desirable to safeguard freedom has always been one of the salient challenges to American democracy. Even after New Deal refinements, the search for the proper balance continues.

Notes

1. Otis L. Graham Jr., and Meghan Robinson Wander, eds., *Franklin D. Roosevelt, His Life and Times: An Encyclopedic View* (Boston: G. K. Hall, 1985), p. 285 (first quotation); Harvard Sitkoff, "Introduction," in Sitkoff, *Fifty Years Later*, p. 5 (second quotation).

2. Richard S. Kirkendall, "The New Deal as Watershed: The Recent Literature," *Journal of American History* 54 (March 1968), p. 847 (quotation).

3. Graham and Wander, *Franklin D. Roosevelt, His Life and Times*, p. 228 (quotation).

4. Leuchtenburg, "The Achievement of the New Deal," p. 220 (first quotation); Patterson, *America's Struggle against Poverty, 1900–1980*, p. 56 (second quotation).

5. Louchheim, *The Making of the New Deal: The Insiders Speak*, p. 15 (quotation).

6. John Braeman, "The New Deal: The Collapse of the Liberal Consensus," *Canadian Review of American Studies* 20 (Summer 1989), p. 77.

7. David Burner, *The Politics of Provincialism: The Democratic Party in Transition, 1918–1932* (New York: Alfred A. Knopf, 1968).

8. Mark Leff, *The Limits of Symbolic Reform*, p. 287 (quotation).

9. James T. Patterson, *The New Deal and the States: Federalism in Transition* (Princeton: Princeton University Press, 1969), p. 202.

10. Barry D. Karl, *The Uneasy State: The United States from 1915 to 1945* (Chicago: University of Chicago Press, 1983), p. 124

NO ↵

Gary Dean Best

Pride, Prejudice and Politics: Roosevelt Versus Recovery, 1933–1938

This book had its genesis in the fact that I have for a long time felt uncomfortable with the standard works written about Franklin Delano Roosevelt and the New Deal, and with the influence those works have exerted on others writing about and teaching U.S. history. Although I approach the subject from a very different perspective, Paul K. Conkin's preface to the second edition of *The New Deal* (1975) expressed many of my own misgivings about writings on the subject. Conkin wrote that "pervading even the most scholarly revelations was a monotonous, often almost reflexive, and in my estimation a very smug or superficial valuative perspective—approval, even glowing approval, of most enduring New Deal policies, or at least of the underlying goals that a sympathetic observer could always find behind policies and programs."

Studies of the New Deal such as Conkin described seemed to me to be examples of a genre relatively rare in U.S. historiography—that of "court histories." . . .

But, like most historians teaching courses dealing with the Roosevelt period, I was captive to the published works unless I was willing and able to devote the time to pursue extensive research in the period myself. After some years that became possible, and this book is the result.

My principal problem with Roosevelt and the New Deal was not over his specific reforms or his social programs, but with the failure of the United States to recover from the depression during the eight peacetime years that he and his policies governed the nation. I consider that failure tragic, not only for the 14.6 percent of the labor force that remained unemployed as late as 1940, and for the millions of others who subsisted on government welfare because of the prolonged depression, but also because of the image that the depression-plagued United States projected to the world at a crucial time in international affairs. In the late 1930s and early 1940s, when U.S. economic strength might have given pause to potential aggressors in the world, our economic weakness furnished encouragement to them instead.

From the standpoint, then, not only of our domestic history, but also of the tragic events and results of World War II, it has seemed to me that

From Gary Dean Best, *Pride, Prejudice, and Politics: Roosevelt Versus Recovery, 1933-1938* (Praeger, 1990), pp. ix-xv, xvii, 217-223. Copyright © 1990 by Gary Dean Best. Reprinted by permission of Greenwood Publishing Group, Inc., Westport, CT. Notes omitted.

Roosevelt's failure to generate economic recovery during this critical period deserved more attention than historians have given it.

Most historians of the New Deal period leave the impression that the failure of the United States to recover during those eight years resulted from Roosevelt's unwillingness to embrace Keynesian spending. According to this thesis, recovery came during World War II because the war at last forced Roosevelt to spend at the level required all along for recovery. This, however, seemed to me more an advocacy of Keynes' theories by the historians involved than an explanation for the U.S. failure to recover during those years. Great Britain, for example, managed to recover by the late 1930s without recourse to deficit spending. By that time the United States was, by contrast, near the bottom of the list of industrial nations as measured in progress toward recovery, with most others having reached the predepression levels and many having exceeded them. The recovered countries represented a variety of economic systems, from state ownership to private enterprise. The common denominator in their success was not a reliance on deficit spending, but rather the stimulus they furnished to industrial enterprise.

What went wrong in the United States? Simplistic answers such as the reference to Keynesianism seemed to me only a means of avoiding a real answer to the question. A wise president, entering the White House in the midst of a crippling depression, should do everything possible to stimulate enterprise. In a free economy, economic recovery means *business* recovery. It follows, therefore, that a wise chief executive should do everything possible to create the conditions and psychology most conducive to business recovery—to encourage business to expand production, and lenders and investors to furnish the financing and capital that are required. An administration seeking economic recovery will do as little as possible that might inhibit recovery, will weigh all its actions with the necessity for economic recovery in mind, and will consult with competent business and financial leaders, as well as economists, to determine the best policies to follow. Such a president will seek to promote cooperation between the federal government and business, rather than conflict, and will seek to introduce as much consistency and stability as possible into government economic policies so that businessmen and investors can plan ahead. While obviously the destitute must be cared for, ultimately the most humane contribution a liberal government can make to the victims of a depression is the restoration of prosperity and the reemployment of the idle in genuine jobs.

In measuring the Roosevelt policies and programs during the New Deal years against such standards, I was struck by the air of unreality that hung over Washington in general and the White House in particular during this period. Business and financial leaders who questioned the wisdom of New Deal policies were disregarded and deprecated because of their "greed" and "self-interest," while economists and business academicians who persisted in calling attention to the collision between New Deal policies and simple economic realities were dismissed for their "orthodoxy." As one "orthodox" economist pointed out early in the New Deal years,

> economic realism... insists that policies aiming to promote recovery will, in fact, retard recovery if and where they fail to take into account correctly of stubborn facts in the existing economic situation and of the arithmetic of business as it must be carried out in the economic situation we are trying to revive. The antithesis of this economic realism is the vaguely hopeful or optimistic idealism in the field of economic policy, as such, which feels that good intentions, enough cleverness, and the right appeal to the emotions of the people ought to insure good results in spite of inconvenient facts.

Those "inconvenient facts" dogged the New Deal throughout these years, only to be stubbornly resisted by a president whose pride, prejudices, and politics would rarely permit an accommodation with them.

Most studies of the New Deal years approach the period largely from the perspective of the New Dealers themselves. Critics and opponents of Roosevelt's policies and programs are given scant attention in such works except to point up the "reactionary" and "unenlightened" opposition with which Roosevelt was forced to contend in seeking to provide Americans with "a more abundant life." The few studies that have concentrated on critics and opponents of the New Deal in the business community have been by unsympathetic historians who have tended to distort the opposition to fit the caricature drawn by the New Dealers, so that they offer little to explain the impact of Roosevelt's policies in delaying recovery from the depression.

The issue of *why* businessmen and bankers were so critical of the New Deal has been for too long swept under the rug, together with the question of *how* Roosevelt and his advisers could possibly expect to produce an economic recovery while a state of war existed between his administration and the employers and investors who, alone, could produce such a recovery. Even a Keynesian response to economic depression is ultimately dependent on the positive reactions of businessmen and investors for its success, as Keynes well knew, and those reactions were not likely to be as widespread as necessary under such a state of warfare between government and business. Businessmen, bankers, and investors may have been "greedy" and "self-interested." They may have been guilty of wrong perceptions and unfounded fears. But they are also the ones, in a free economy, upon whose decisions and actions economic recovery must depend. To understand their opposition to the New Deal requires an immersion in the public and private comments of critics of Roosevelt's policies. The degree and nature of business, banking, and investor concern about the direction and consequences of New Deal policies can be gleaned from the hundreds of banking and business periodicals representative of every branch of U.S. business and finance in the 1930s, and from the letters and diaries of the New Deal's business and other critics during the decade.

Statistics are useful in understanding the history of any period, but particularly periods of economic growth or depression. Statistics for the Roosevelt years may easily be found in *Historical Statistics of the United States* published by the Bureau of the Census, U.S. Department of Commerce (1975). Some of the trauma of the depression years may be inferred from the fact that the population of the United States grew by over 17 million between 1920 and 1930, but by only about half of that (8.9 million) between 1930 and 1940.

Historical Statistics gives the figures... for unemployment, 1929–1940. These figures are, however, only estimates. The federal government did not monitor the number of unemployed during those years. Even so, these figures are shocking, indicating as they do that even after the war had begun in Europe, with the increased orders that it provided for U.S. mines, factories, and farms, unemployment remained at 14.6 percent.

One characteristic of the depression, to which attention was frequently called during the Roosevelt years, was the contrast between its effects on the durable goods and consumer goods industries. Between 1929 and 1933, expenditures on personal durable goods dropped by nearly 50 percent, and in 1938 they were still nearly 25 percent below the 1929 figures. Producers' durable goods suffered even more, failing by nearly two-thirds between 1929 and 1933, and remaining more than 50 percent below the 1929 figure in 1938. At the same time, expenditures on nondurable, or consumer, goods showed much less effect. Between 1929 and 1933 they fell only about 14.5 percent, and by 1938 they exceeded the 1929 level. These figures indicate that the worst effects of the depression, and resultant unemployment, were being felt in the durable goods industries. Roosevelt's policies, however, served mainly to stimulate the consumer goods industries where the depression and unemployment were far less seriously felt.

One consequence of Roosevelt's policies can be seen in the U.S. balance of trade during the New Deal years. By a variety of devices, Roosevelt drove up the prices of U.S. industrial and agricultural products, making it difficult for these goods to compete in the world market, and opening U.S. markets to cheaper foreign products.... With the exception of a $41 million deficit in 1888, these were the only deficits in U.S. trade for a century, from the 1870s to the 1970s.

... [W]hile suicides during the Roosevelt years remained about the same as during the Hoover years, the death rate by "accidental falls" increased significantly. In fact, according to *Historical Statistics,* the death rate by "accidental falls" was higher in the period 1934–1938 than at any other time between 1910 and 1970 (the years for which figures are given).

Interestingly, the number of persons arrested grew steadily during the depression years. In 1938 nearly twice as many (554,000) were arrested as in 1932 (278,000), and the number continued to increase until 1941. And, while the number of telephones declined after 1930 and did not regain the 1930 level until 1939, the number of households with radios increased steadily during the depression years. And Americans continued to travel. Even in the lowest year, 1933, 300,000 Americans visited foreign countries (down from 517,000 in

1929), while the number visiting national parks, monuments, and such, steadily increased during the depression—in 1938 nearly five times as many (16,331,000) did so as in 1929 (3,248,000).

Comparisons of the recovery of the United States with that of other nations may be found in the volumes of the League of Nations' *World Economic Survey* for the depression years. [A] table (from the volume of 1938/39) shows comparisons of unemployment rates. From this it can be seen that in 1929 the United States had the lowest unemployment rate of the countries listed; by 1932 the United States was midway on the list, with seven nations reporting higher unemployment rates and seven reporting lower unemployment. By mid-1938, however, after over five years of the New Deal, only three nations had higher unemployment rates, while twelve had lower unemployment. The United States, then, had lost ground in comparison with the other nations between 1932 and 1938.

The *World Economic Survey* for 1937/38 compared the levels of industrial production for 23 nations in 1937, expressed as a percentage of their industrial production in 1929.... It must be remembered that the figures for the United States reflect the level of industrial production reached just before the collapse of the economy later that year. Of the 22 other nations listed, 19 showed a higher rate of recovery in industrial production than the United States, while only 3 lagged behind. One of these, France, had followed policies similar to those of the New Deal in the United States. As the *World Economic Survey* put it, both the Roosevelt administration and the Blum government in France had "adopted far-reaching social and economic policies which combined recovery measures with measures of social reform." It added: "The consequent doubt regarding the prospects of profit and the uneasy relations between businessmen and the Government have in the opinion of many, been an important factor in delaying recovery," and the two countries had, "unlike the United Kingdom and Germany," failed to "regain the 1929 level of employment and production." The *World Economic Survey* the following year (1939) pointed out that industrial production in the United States had fallen from the 92.2 to 65 by June 1938, and hovered between 77 and 85 throughout 1939. Thus, by the end of 1938 the U.S. record was even sorrier than revealed by the [data].

◦◉◦

Every survey of American historians consistently finds Franklin Delano Roosevelt ranked as one of this nation's greatest presidents. Certainly, exposure to even a sampling of the literature on Roosevelt and the New Deal can lead one to no other conclusion. Conventional wisdom has it that Roosevelt was an opportune choice to lead the United States through the midst of the Great Depression, that his cheerful and buoyant disposition uplifted the American spirit in the midst of despair and perhaps even forestalled a radical change in the direction of American politics toward the right or the left. Roosevelt's landslide reelection victory in 1936, and the congressional successes in 1934, are cited as evidence of the popularity of both the president and the New Deal among the American people. Polls by both Gallup and the Democratic National Committee early in the 1936 campaign, however, give a very different picture, and suggest that the electoral victories can be as accurately accounted for in terms of the vast outpourings of federal money in 1934 and 1936, and the inability or unwillingness of Landon to offer a genuine alternative to the New Deal in the latter year. To this must be added the fact that after early 1936 two of the most unpopular New Deal programs—the NRA and the AAA—had been removed as issues by the Supreme Court.

Conventional wisdom, in fact, suffers many setbacks when the Roosevelt years are examined from any other perspective than through a pro-New Deal Prism—from the banking crisis of 1933 and the first inaugural address, through the reasons for the renewed downturn in 1937, to the end of the New Deal in 1937–1938. The American present has been ill-served by the inaccurate picture that has too often been presented of this chapter in the American past by biographers and historians. Roosevelt's achievements in alleviating the hardship of the depression are deservedly well known, his responsibility for prolonging the hardship is not. His role in providing long-overdue and sorely needed social and economic legislation is in every high school American history textbook, but the costs for the United States of his eight-year-long war against business recovery are mentioned in none.

Such textbooks (and those in college, too) frequently contain a chapter on the Great Depression, followed by one on the New Deal, the implication being that somewhere early in the second of the chapters the depression was ended by Roosevelt's policies. Only careful reading reveals that despite Roosevelt's immense labors to feed the unemployed, only modest recovery from the lowest depths of the depression was attained before the outbreak of World War II. Roosevelt, readers are told, was too old-fashioned, too conservative, to embrace the massive compensatory spending and unbalanced budgets that might have produced a Keynesian recovery sooner. But World War II, the books tell us, made such spending necessary and the recovery that might have occurred earlier was at last achieved.

Generations of Americans have been brought up on this version of the New Deal years. Other presidential administrations have been reevaluated over the years, and have risen or fallen in grace as a result, but not the Roosevelt administration. The conventional wisdom concerning the Roosevelt administration remains the product of the "court historians," assessments of the New Deal period that could not have been better written by the New Dealers themselves. The facts, however, are considerably at variance with this conventional wisdom concerning the course of the depression, the reasons for the delay of recovery, and the causes of the recovery when it came, finally, during World War II.

From the uncertainty among businessmen and investors about the new president-elect that aborted a promising upturn in the fall of 1932, to the panic over the prospect of inflationary policies that was a major factor in the banking crisis that virtually paralyzed the nation's economy by the date of his inauguration, Roosevelt's entry into the White House was not an auspicious beginning toward recovery. The prejudices that were to guide the policies and programs of the New Deal for the next six years were revealed in Roosevelt's inaugural address, although the message was largely overlooked until it had become more apparent in the actions of the administration later. It was an attitude of hostility toward business and finance, of contempt for the profit motive of capitalism, and of willingness to foment class antagonism for political benefit. This was not an attitude that was conducive to business recovery, and the programs and policies that would flow from those prejudices would prove, in fact, to be destructive of the possibility of recovery.

There followed the "hundred days," when Roosevelt rammed through Congress a variety of legislation that only depressed business confidence more. The new laws were served up on attractive platters, with tempting descriptions —truth in securities, aid for the farmer, industrial self-regulation—but when the covers were removed the contents were neither attractive nor did they match the labels. By broad grants of power to the executive branch of the government, the legislation passed regulation of the U.S. economy into the hands of New Dealers whose aim was not to promote recovery but to carry out their own agendas for radical change of the economic system even at the expense of delaying recovery. Thus, truth in securities turned to paralysis of the securities markets, aid for the farmer became a war against profits by processors of agricultural goods, and industrial self-regulation became government control and labor-management strife. International economic cooperation as a device for ending the depression was abandoned for an isolationist approach, and throughout 1933 the threat of inflation added further uncertainty for businessmen and investors.

The grant of such unprecedented peacetime authority to an American president aroused concern, but these after all were only "emergency" powers, to be given up once recovery was on its way. Or were they? Gradually the evidence accumulated that the Tugwells and the Brandeisians intended to institutionalize the "emergency" powers as permanent features of American economic life. By the end of 1933, opposition to the New Deal was already sizable. Business alternated between the paralysis of uncertainty and a modest "recovery" born of purchases and production inspired by fear of higher costs owing to inflation and the effects of the AAA and NRA. The implementation of the latter two agencies in the fall of 1933 brought a renewed downturn that improved only slightly during the winter and spring. A renewed legislative onslaught by the New Deal in the 1934 congress, combined with labor strife encouraged by the provisions of the NIRA, brought a new collapse of the economy in the fall of 1934, which lowered economic indices once again to near the lowest levels they had reached in the depression.

The pattern had been established. The war against business and finance was under way, and there would be neither retreat nor cessation. Roosevelt's pride and prejudices, and the perceived political advantages to be gained from the war, dictated that his administration must ever be on the offensive and never in retreat. But the administration suffered defeats, nevertheless, and embarrassment. The Supreme Court proved a formidable foe, striking down both the NRA and the AAA. Dire predictions from the administration about the implications for the economy of the loss of the NRA proved embarrassing when the economy began to show gradual improvement after its departure. But defeat did not mean retreat. Under the goading of Felix Frankfurter and his disciples, Roosevelt became even more extreme in his verbal and legislative assault against business. Their attempts to cooperate with the Roosevelt administration having been spurned, businessmen and bankers awakened to the existence of the war being waged upon them and moved into opposition. Roosevelt gloried in their opposition and escalated the war against them in the 1936 reelection campaign.

Reelected in 1936 on a tidal wave of government spending, and against a lackluster Republican campaigner who offered no alternative to the New Deal, Roosevelt appeared at the apogee of his power and prestige. His triumph was, however, to be short-lived, despite an enhanced Democratic majority in Congress. A combination of factors was about to bring the New Deal war against business to a stalemate and eventual retreat. One of these was his ill-advised attempt to pack the Supreme Court with subservient justices, which aroused so much opposition even in his own party that he lost control of the Democrat-controlled Congress. More important, perhaps, was the growing economic crisis that the Roosevelt administration faced in 1937, largely as a result of its own past policies. The massive spending of 1936, including the payment of the veterans' bonus, had generated a speculative recovery during that year from concern about inflationary consequences. Fears of a "boom" were increased as a result of the millions of dollars in dividends, bonuses, and pay raises dispensed by businesses late in 1936 as a result of the undistributed profits tax. The pay raises, especially, were passed on in the form of higher prices, as were the social security taxes that were imposed on businesses beginning with 1937. Labor disturbances, encouraged by the Wagner Labor Act and the Roosevelt alliance with John L. Lewis' Congress of Industrial Organizations in the 1936 campaign, added further to the wage-price spiral that threatened as 1937 unfolded. Massive liquidations of low-interest government bonds, and sagging prices of the bonds, fueled concern among bankers and economists, and within the Treasury, that a "boom" would imperil the credit of the federal government and the solvency of the nation's banks whose portfolios consisted mainly of low-interest government bonds.

In considering the two principal options for cooling the "boom"—raising interest rates or cutting federal spending—the Roosevelt administration chose to move toward a balanced budget. It was a cruel dilemma that the New Dealers faced. All knew that the economy had not yet recovered from the depression, yet they were faced with the necessity to apply brakes to an economy that was becoming overheated as a consequence of their policies. Moreover, the reduction in consumer purchasing power caused by the cuts in federal spending was occurring at the same time that purchasing power was already being eroded as a result of the higher prices that worried the administration. Private industry, it should have been obvious, could not "take up the slack," since the Roosevelt administration had done nothing to prepare for the transition from government to private spending that John Maynard Keynes and others had warned them was necessary. The New Dealers had been far too busy waging war against business to allow it the opportunity to prepare for any such transition.

In fact, far from confronting the emergency of 1937 by making long-overdue attempts to cooperate with business in generating recovery, Roosevelt was busy pressing a new legislative assault against them. Denied passage of his legislative package by Congress during its regular 1937 session, Roosevelt called a special session for November despite evidence that the economy had begun a new downturn. Even the collapse of the stock market, within days after his announcement of the special session, and the growing unemployment that soon followed, did not deter Roosevelt from his determination to drive the legislative assault through it. With the nation in the grips of a full-blown economic collapse, Roosevelt offered nothing to the special session but the package of antibusiness legislation it had turned down in the regular session. Once again he was rebuffed by Congress. The nation drifted, its economic indices falling, with its president unwilling to admit the severity of the situation or unable to come to grips with what it said about the bankruptcy of the New Deal policies and programs.

By early 1938, Roosevelt was faced with problems similar to those he had faced when he first entered the White House five years earlier, but without the political capital he had possessed earlier. In 1933 the Hoover administration could be blamed for the depression. In 1938 the American people blamed the Roosevelt administration for retarding recovery. Five years of failure could not be brushed aside. Five years of warfare against business and disregard of criticism and offers of cooperation had converted supporters of 1933 into cynics or opponents by 1938. Even now, however, pride, prejudice, and politics dominated Roosevelt, making it impossible for him to extend the needed olive branch to business. The best that he could offer in 1938 was a renewal of federal spending and more of the same New Deal that had brought the nation renewed misery. In the 1938 congressional session he continued to press for passage of the antibusiness legislation that had been rejected by both sessions of 1937.

But Congress was no longer the pliant body it had been in 1933, and in the 1938 congressional elections the people's reaction was registered when the Republicans gained 81 new seats in the House and 8 in the Senate—far more than even the most optimistic Republican had predicted. If the message was lost on Roosevelt, it was obvious to some in his administration, notably his new Secretary of Commerce Harry Hopkins and his Secretary of the Treasury Henry Morgenthau. Two of the earliest business-baiters in the circle of Roosevelt advisers, they now recognized the bankruptcy of that course and the necessity for the administration to at last strive for recovery by removing the obstacles to normal and profitable business operation that the New Deal had erected. This was not what Roosevelt wanted to hear, nor was it what his Frankfurter disciples wanted him to hear. These latter knew, as Hopkins and Morgenthau had learned earlier, just which Rooseveltian buttons could be pushed to trigger his antibusiness prejudices and spite. A battle raged within the New Deal between the Frankfurter radicals and the "new conservatives," Hopkins and Morgenthau, amid growing public suspicion that the former were not interested in economic recovery.

It was not a fair battle. Hopkins and Morgenthau knew how to play the game, including use of the press, and had too many allies. They did not hesitate to talk bluntly to Roosevelt, perhaps the bluntest talk he had heard since the death of Louis McHenry Howe. Moreover, Roosevelt could afford the loss of a Corcoran and/or a Cohen, against whom there was already a great deal of congressional opposition, but a break with both Hopkins and Morgenthau would have been devastating for an administration already on the defensive. Gradually the Frankfurter radicals moved into eclipse, along with their policies, to be replaced increasingly by recovery and preparedness advocates, including many from the business and financial world.

Conventional wisdom has it that the massive government spending of World War II finally brought a Keynesian recovery from the depression. Of more significance, in comparisons of the prewar and wartime economic policies of the Roosevelt administration, is the fact that the war against business that characterized the former was abandoned in the latter. Both the attitude and policies of the Roosevelt administration toward business during the New Deal years were reversed when the president found new, foreign enemies to engage his attention and energies. Antibusiness advisers were replaced by businessmen, pro-labor policies became pro-business policies, cooperation replaced confrontation in relations between the federal government and business, and even the increased spending of the war years "trickled down" rather than "bubbling up." Probably no American president since, perhaps, Thomas Jefferson ever so thoroughly repudiated the early policies of his administration as Roosevelt did between 1939 and 1942. This, and not the emphasis on spending alone, is the lesson that needs to be learned from Roosevelt's experience with the depression, and of the legacy of the New Deal economic policies.

The judgment of historians concerning Roosevelt's presidential stature is curiously at odds with that of contemporary observers. One wonders how scholars of the Roosevelt presidency are able so blithely to ignore the negative assessments of journalists, for example, of the stature of Raymond Clapper, Walter Lippmann, Dorothy Thompson, and Arthur Krock, to name only a few. Can their observations concerning Roosevelt's pettiness and spitefulness, their criticism of the obstacles to recovery created by his anticapitalist bias, and their genuine concern over his apparent grasp for dictatorial power be dismissed so cavalierly? Is there any other example in U.S. history of an incumbent president running for reelection against the open opposition of the two previous nominees of his own party? Will a public opinion poll ever again find 45 percent of its respondents foreseeing the likelihood of dictatorship arising from a president's policies? Will a future president ever act in such a fashion that the question will again even suggest itself to a pollster? One certainly hopes not.

Perhaps the positive assessment of Roosevelt by American historians rests upon a perceived liberalism of his administration. If so, one must wonder at their definition of liberalism. Surely a president who would pit class against class for political purposes, who was fundamentally hostile to the very basis of a free economy, who believed that his ends could justify very illiberal means, who was intolerant of criticism and critics, and who grasped for dictatorial power does not merit description as a liberal. Nor are the results of the Gallup poll mentioned above consistent with the actions of a liberal president. If the perception is based on Roosevelt's support for the less fortunate "one-third" of the nation, and his program of social legislation, then historians need to be reminded that such actions do not, in themselves, add up to liberalism, they having been used by an assortment of political realists and demagogues— of the left and the right—to gain and hold power.

There were certainly positive contributions under the New Deal, but they may not have outweighed the negative aspects of the period. The weight of the negative aspects would, moreover, have been much heavier except for the existence of a free and alert press, and for the actions of the Supreme Court and Congress in nullifying, modifying, and rejecting many of the New Deal measures. When one examines the full range of New Deal proposals and considers the implications of their passage in the original form, the outline emerges of a form of government alien to any definition of liberalism except that of the New Dealers themselves. Historians need to weigh more thoroughly and objectively the implications for the United States if Roosevelt's programs had been fully implemented. They need also to assess the costs in human misery of the delay in recovery, and of reduced U.S. influence abroad at a critical time in world affairs owing to its economic prostration. We can only speculate concerning the possible alteration of events from 1937 onward had the United States faced the world with the economic strength and military potential it might have displayed had wiser economic policies prevailed from 1933 to 1938. There is, in short, much about Roosevelt and the New Deal that historians need to reevaluate.

POSTSCRIPT

Was the New Deal an Effective Answer to the Great Depression?

Both Biles and Best agree that the New Deal concentrated a tremendous amount of power in the executive branch of the government. They also acknowledge that it was World War II—not the New Deal's reform programs—that pulled the United States out of the depression.

But the two historians disagree with each other in their assumptions and assessments of the New Deal. Biles argues that the New Deal was a nonrevolution compared to the economic and political changes that were taking place in communist Russia, fascist Italy, and Nazi Germany. The New Deal, in his view, was not so new. The Wilson administration had imposed strong governmental controls during World War I, and a number of the farm, business, and collective utility projects had been suggested and passed in different versions during the Harding, Coolidge, and Hoover presidencies.

Best's major failing is his inability to view the human side of the New Deal. By concentrating on the strengths and weaknesses of a business recovery, he seems to forget that the New Deal was much more than the sum total of a number of economic statistics. Since that time, people have come to expect the national government to manage the economy responsibly.

The most influential early books by historians on the New Deal were highly sympathetic and written from the perspective of Washington, D.C. A well-written, partisan, and never-to-be-completed history is Arthur M. Schlesinger, Jr.'s volumes in the Age of Roosevelt series, which consists of *The Crisis of the Old Order, 1919–1933* (1957), *The Coming of the New Deal* (1959), and *The Politics of Upheaval* (1960), all published by Houghton Mifflin. The best one-volume history of the New Deal from this perspective remains William E. Leuchtenburg's *Franklin D. Roosevelt and the New Deal* (Harper & Row, 1963). In a retrospective written 50 years later, "The Achievement of the New Deal," Leuchtenburg chides left-wing critics of the New Deal who blame Roosevelt for not ending racial segregation or hard-core poverty. Both Leuchtenburg and Biles remind us of what the New Deal accomplished, not what it failed to do. This essay, along with other important interpretative essays that the author wrote over many years, can be found in Leuchtenburg's *The FDR Years: On Roosevelt and His Legacy* (Columbia University Press, 1995).

John Braeman has written two bibliographical essays that critically analyze some of the major specialized works written in the 1970s and 1980s. See "The New Deal and the Broker State: A Review of the Recent Scholarly Literature," *Business History Review* (vol. 46, 1971) and "The New Deal: The Collapse of the Liberal Consensus," *Canadian Review of American Studies* (Summer 1989), which reviews a dozen or so books and concludes that, in the long term, the New Deal brought about "a balkanized political system in which private interests scramble, barely successfully, to harass governmental authority and/or draw upon the public treasury to advance their private agendas."

Comprehensive syntheses and bibliographies can be found in Robert S. McElvaine, *The Great Depression: America, 1929–1941* (Times Books, 1984) and Anthony J. Badger, *The New Deal: The Depression Years, 1933–1940* (Farrar, Straus & Giroux, 1989). For a convenient reproduction of approximately 150 of "the most important" articles on all aspects of the New Deal, see *The Great Depression and the New Deal* (Garland, 1990), edited by Melvyn Dubofsky and Stephen Burnwood.

Liberal criticisms of the New Deal can be found in the first volume of James MacGregor Burns's political biography *Roosevelt: The Lion and the Fox* (Harcourt Brace, 1956), a work so elegantly written that 40 years later the many other biographies pale in comparison. Burns argues that Roosevelt retarded the recovery and created a recession in 1937 when he attempted to balance the budget. Alan Brinkley, in *The End of Reform: New Deal Liberalism in Recession and War* (Alfred A. Knopf, 1995), a study of the much-neglected years 1937–1945, argues that Roosevelt and his advisers gave up on trying to redistribute income by centralized planning and concentrated instead on encouraging production in hopes that a rising tide would lift all boats. James Q. Wilson attacks Brinkley with conservative arguments similar to those of Best in "Liberal Ghosts," *The New Republic* (May 22, 1995).

Radical criticisms of the New Deal and its legacy became common in the 1960s. A good starting point is Howard Zinn, ed., *New Deal Thought* (Bobbs-Merrill, 1966). Two of the most sophisticated New Left criticisms are Barton J. Bernstein, *The New Deal: The Conservative Achievements of Liberal Reform* (Pantheon Books, 1967) and Paul K. Conklin, *The New Deal*, 2d ed. (Harlan Davidson, 1975). Steve Fraser and Gary Gerstle edited a series of social and economic essays, which they present in *The Rise and Fall of the New Deal Order, 1930–1980* (Princeton University Press, 1989). A standard work is Alan Brinkley's overview *Voices of Protest: Huey Long, Father Coughlin and the Great Depression* (Alfred A. Knopf, 1982).

The celebration of Roosevelt's 100th birthday in 1982 and the 50th anniversary of the New Deal in 1983 inspired a number of conferences and the subsequent publication of the resulting papers. Among the most important are Harvard Sitkoff, ed., *Fifty Years Later: The New Deal Evaluated* (Alfred A. Knopf, 1985); Wilbur J. Cohen, ed., *The Roosevelt New Deal: A Program Assessment Fifty Years After* (Lyndon B. Johnson School of Public Affairs, 1986); and Herbert D. Rosenbaum and Elizabeth Barteline, eds., *Franklin D. Roosevelt: The Man, the Myth, the Era, 1882–1945* (Greenwood Press, 1987).

ISSUE 11

Did President Roosevelt Deliberately Withhold Information About the Attack on Pearl Harbor From the American Commanders?

YES: Robert A. Theobald, from *The Final Secret of Pearl Harbor: The Washington Contribution to the Japanese Attack* (Devin-Adair, 1954)

NO: Roberta Wohlstetter, from *Pearl Harbor: Warning and Decision* (Stanford University Press, 1967)

ISSUE SUMMARY

YES: Retired rear admiral Robert A. Theobald argues that President Franklin D. Roosevelt deliberately withheld information from the commanders at Pearl Harbor in order to encourage the Japanese to make a surprise attack on the weak U.S. Pacific Fleet.

NO: Historian Roberta Wohlstetter contends that even though naval intelligence broke the Japanese code, conflicting signals and the lack of a central agency coordinating U.S. intelligence information made it impossible to predict the Pearl Harbor attack.

In 1899 and 1900 Secretary of State John Hay enunciated two notes, known as the Open Door policy. The first pronouncement attempted to provide equal access to commercial rights in China for all nations. The second note called on all countries to respect China's "territorial and administrative" integrity. For the next 40 years the open door was restated by every president from Theodore Roosevelt to Franklin Roosevelt for two reasons: (1) to prevent China from being taken over by Japan, and (2) to preserve the balance of power in the world. The Open Door policy appeared to work during World War I and the 1920s.

The Nine-Power Treaty of 1922 restated the Open Door principles, and its signatories agreed to assist China in forming a stable government. Japan supported the agreements because the world economy was reasonably stable.

But the worldwide depression had a major effect on the foreign policies of all nations. Japan decided that she wanted to extend her influence politically as well as economically in Asia. On the night of September 18, 1931, an explosion, probably staged by Japanese militarists, damaged the Japanese-controlled South Manchurian Railroad. Japanese troops not only overran Chinese troops stationed in South Manchuria but within five months established the puppet state of Manchukuo. When the League of Nations condemned Japan's actions, the Japanese gave their two-year's notice and withdrew from the league. A turn for the worse came for the Chinese on July 7, 1937, when a shooting incident at the Marco Polo Bridge between Chinese and Japanese troops led to a full-scale war on China's mainland. President Franklin Roosevelt took a strong verbal stand in a speech he delivered on October 5, 1937, demanding that nations stirring up "international anarchy" should be quarantined.

Roosevelt aided the Chinese with nonembargoed, nonmilitary goods when he found a loophole in the neutrality laws. Japan's goal to establish a "new order in East Asia" was furthered by the outbreak of World War II in Europe in the fall of 1939 and the ease with which the German army overran and defeated France the following spring. In September 1940 Japanese forces occupied northern French Indochina (later known as Vietnam). Although Franklin Roosevelt was unable to stop Japan's military expansionism, he did jar them with economic sanctions. When the Japanese occupied southern Indochina on July 25, 1941, Franklin Roosevelt again jolted the Japanese government by issuing an order freezing all Japanese assets in the United States, which created major problems. Japan had only 12 to 18 months of oil in reserves for military use. A military statement had developed in the war with China in part because the United States was funneling economic and military aid to her ally. Consequently, Japan sought an accommodation with the United States in the fall of 1941. Japan tried to negotiate two plans that would have resulted in a partial withdrawal from Indochina and the establishment of a coalition government in China proper that would be partially controlled by the Japanese and would take place once the war stopped. In return, America would resume trade with Japan prior to the July 26 freezing of Japanese assets.

Because American cryptologists had broken the Japanese diplomatic code for a second time in the summer of 1941, American policy makers knew that these were Japan's final proposals. Secretary of State Cordell Hull sent the Japanese a note on November 26 that restated America's Open Door policy and asked "the government of Japan [to] withdraw all military naval, air, and police forces from China and from Indochina." When Japan rejected the proposal both sides realized this meant war. Where or when was the question. Japan's surprise December 7 attack on Pearl Harbor provided the answer.

In the following selection, Robert A. Theobald argues that President Roosevelt deliberately withheld information from the Hawaiian army and naval commanders at Pearl Harbor in order to encourage the Japanese to make a surprise attack on the weak Pacific Fleet. In the second selection, Roberta Wohlstetter maintains that even though naval intelligence broke the Japanese code, conflicting signals made it impossible to predict the Pearl Harbor attack.

Robert A. Theobald  **YES**

The Final Secret of Pearl Harbor

Having been present at Pearl Harbor on December 7, 1941, and having appeared with Admiral Husband E. Kimmel when that officer testified before the Roberts Commission,[1] the author has ever since sought a full understanding of the background that made that day possible. For many years, he gathered and pieced together the available evidence which appeared to shed light upon the Washington happenings concerned with that attack. These studies produced very definite conclusions regarding the manner in which our country's strategy had been shaped to entice the Japanese to attack Pearl Harbor, and the efforts that have since been made to keep these facts from the knowledge of the American People.

For over three years, the thirty-nine-volume set which comprises the Record of Proceedings of all the Pearl Harbor Investigations has been available to the author. Serious study of these volumes has caused many revisions of errors in detail, but it has served to divest the writer's mind of all doubt regarding the soundness of his basic conclusions.

It is firmly believed that those in Washington who knew the facts, decided from the first that considerations of patriotism and loyalty to their wartime Commander-in-Chief required that a veil of secrecy should be drawn about the President's handling of the situation which culminated in the Pearl Harbor attack.

While there was great justification for this secrecy during the continuance of the war, the reasons for it no longer exist. The war is finished. President Roosevelt and his administration are now history. Dictates of patriotism requiring secrecy regarding a line of national conduct in order to preserve it for possible future repetition do not apply in this case because, in this atomic age, facilitating an enemy's surprise attack, as a method of initiating a war, is unthinkable. Our Pearl Harbor losses would preclude that course of action in the future without consideration of the increased destructiveness of present and future weapons. Finally, loyalty to their late President in the matter of Pearl Harbor would be better served today, if his friends would discard their policy of secrecy in favor of full publicity.

Another consideration which today strongly favors a complete understanding of the whole Pearl Harbor story, is the thought of justice to the

From Robert A. Theobald, *The Final Secret of Pearl Harbor: The Washington Contribution to the Japanese Attack* (Devin-Adair, 1954). Copyright © 1954 by Robert A. Theobald.

professional reputations of the Hawaiian Commanders, Admiral Kimmel and General Short—a justice which is long overdue.

Throughout the war, maintenance of the national morale at the highest possible level demanded complete public confidence in the President and his principal military advisers. During that time, the public could not be given cause to assign a tithe of blame for the Pearl Harbor attack to Washington. And so, dating from the report of the Roberts Commission, most of the responsibility for Pearl Harbor has been placed upon the two Hawaiian Commanders. This carefully executed plan which diverted all suspicion from Washington contributed its full measure to the successful conduct of the war.

The time has come when full publicity should be given to the Washington contribution to the Pearl Harbor attack, in order that the judgment of the American people may assign to Admiral Kimmel and General Short no more than their just and proper share of the responsibility for that tragic day.

Manifestly, many readers will be reluctant to agree with the main conclusions which have been reached in this study. In recognition of this fact, the normal sequence of deductive reasoning is discarded in favor of the order used in a legal presentation. The case is stated at the outset, and the evidence is then marshalled and discussed. The reader is thus enabled to weigh each fact, as it is presented, against the conclusions, which have been firmly implanted in the mind of the author by the summation of these facts.

The sole purpose of the subject matter contained herein is a searching for the truth, and it is hoped that the absence of any ulterior motive is apparent throughout. Comments of a critical character concerning the official actions of officers frequently intersperse the pages which follow. No criticism of the officer is intended. Those officers were obeying orders, under circumstances which were professionally most trying to them. Such comments are necessary to a full understanding of the discussion of the moment, however, but there is no intention to impugn the motives of any individual. Patriotism and loyalty were the wellsprings of those motives....

Main Deduction: President Roosevelt Circumvents American Pacifism

In the spring of 1940, Denmark, Norway, Holland, Belgium and France were conquered by Germany, and throughout the remainder of that year Great Britain's situation was so desperate that many expected her collapse early in the ensuing year. Fortunately, however, the Axis powers turned East in 1941 to conquer Greece and to attack Russia.

There is every reason to believe that when France was overcome President Roosevelt became convinced the United States must fight beside Great Britain, while the latter was still an active belligerent, or later sustain the fight alone, as the last democratic stronghold in a Nazi world. Never, however, had the country been less prepared for war, both psychologically and physically. Isolationism was a dominant philosophy throughout the land, and the armed forces were weak and consequently unready.

The United States not only had to become an active participant in democracy's fight as quickly as possible, but a people, completely united in support of the war effort, had to be brought into the arena. But, how could the country be made to fight? Only a cataclysmic happening could move Congress to enact a declaration of war; and that action would not guarantee that the nation's response would be the completely united support which victory has always demanded. This was the President's problem, and his solution was based upon the simple fact that, while it takes two to make a fight, either one may start it.

As the people of this country were so strongly opposed to war, one of the Axis powers must be forced to involve the United States, and in such a way as to arouse the American people to wholehearted belief in the necessity of fighting. This would require drastic action, and the decision was unquestionably a difficult one for the President to make.

In this connection, it should be remembered that Japan, Germany, and Italy signed the Tripartite Treaty on September 28, 1940, by which the three nations agreed to make common cause against any nation, not then a participant in the European war or the Sino-Japanese conflict, which attacked one of the signatories.

Thereafter, the fact that war with Japan meant war with Germany and Italy played an important part in President Roosevelt's diplomatic strategy. Throughout the approach to war and during the fighting, the primary U.S. objective was the defeat of Germany.

To implement the solution of his problem, the President: (1) instituted a successful campaign to correct the Nation's military unpreparedness; (2) offered Germany repeated provocations, by violations of neutrality and diplomatic usage; (3) applied ever-increasing diplomatic-economic pressure upon Japan, which reached its sustained climax on July 25, 1941, when the United States, Great Britain, and the Netherlands stopped their trade with Japan and subjected her to almost complete economic encirclement; (4) made mutual commitments with the British Prime Minister at Newfoundland in August, 1941, which promised mutual support in the event that the United States, Great Britain, or a third country not then at war were attacked by Japan in the Pacific; (5) terminated the Washington conference with the note of November 26, 1941, which gave Japan no choice but surrender or war; (6) retained a weak Pacific Fleet in Hawaiian waters, despite contrary naval advice, where it served only one diplomatic purpose, an invitation to a Japanese surprise attack; (7) furthered that surprise by causing the Hawaiian Commanders to be denied invaluable information from decoded Japanese dispatches [or "Magic"] concerning the rapid approach of the war and the strong probability that the attack would be directed at Pearl Harbor.

This denial of information was a vital feature of enticing a Japanese surprise attack upon Pearl Harbor. If Admiral Kimmel and General Short had been given the knowledge possessed by the Washington authorities, the Hawaiian Commands would have been alerted against an overseas attack. The Pacific Fleet would have kept the sea during the first days of December, 1941, until the issue of peace or war had been decided. With the highly effective Japanese espionage in Hawaii, this would have caused Tokyo to cancel the surprise attack.

The problem which faced Lincoln during March of 1861 was identical in principle—to unite the sentiment of the North behind the policy of compelling the seceded Southern states by force of arms to return to the Union. For a month after his inauguration, he made no move, and then South Carolina's insistent demands for the surrender of Fort Sumter gave him the answer to his problem. He refused to surrender the fort, and dispatched a fleet to reprovision it. South Carolina then fired the first shots of the Civil War. Pearl Harbor was President Roosevelt's Fort Sumter.

Diplomatically, President Roosevelt's strategy of forcing Japan to war by unremitting and ever-increasing diplomatic-economic pressure, and by simultaneously holding our Fleet in Hawaii as an invitation to a surprise attack, was a complete success. Militarily, our ship and personnel losses mark December 7, 1941 as the day of tragic defeat. One is forced to conclude that the anxiety to have Japan, beyond all possibility of dispute, commit the first act of war, caused the President and his civilian advisers to disregard the military advice which would somewhat have cushioned the blow. The President, before the event, probably envisaged a *Panay* incident[2] of somewhat larger proportions. Despite the fact that the attack laid the foundation for complete victory, a terrific price was paid, as the following account of the ship, plane, and personnel losses discloses.

The Pearl Harbor Losses: Facts and Figures

The Japanese clearly intended that their entire surprise attack should be delivered against military objectives. The first waves of the attack were delivered against the airfields on the Island of Oahu—Army, Navy, and Marine Corps—to reduce the air-borne opposition as much as possible. The main attacks began 15 minutes after these preliminary attacks, and were primarily directed against the capital ships in Pearl Harbor. Damage inflicted upon smaller vessels was clearly the incidental consequence of the main operation. Very few planes dropped their bombs upon the city of Honolulu. Three planes did so in the late phases of the attack, but their last-minute changes of course indicated that this was done because those particular pilots did not care to encounter the severe anti-aircraft fire that was then bursting over their main target area.

In December, 1941, the capital ships of the Pacific Fleet numbered twelve: 9 Battleships; 3 Carriers. Of these, eight Battleships but none of the Carriers were present in Pearl Harbor at the time of the Japanese attack: the Battleship *Colorado* was in the Bremerton Navy Yard; the Carrier *Enterprise* was in a Task Force returning from Wake; the *Lexington* was in a Task Force ferrying planes to Midway; the *Saratoga* was on the West Coast, having just completed a Navy Yard overhaul.

The results of the Japanese air attacks upon the U.S. Pacific Fleet in Pearl Harbor on December 7, 1941, were as follows:

Battleships:

Arizona: total loss, as her forward magazines blew up;

Oklahoma: total loss, capsized and sank in harbor—later raised solely
to clear harbor of the obstruction and resunk off Oahu;

California, West Virginia: sank in upright position at their berths with
quarterdecks awash—much later raised, repaired, and returned to
active war service;

Nevada: beached while standing out of the harbor, to prevent sinking
in deep water after extensive bomb damage—repaired and returned
to active war service;

Pennsylvania, Maryland, and Tennessee: all received damage but of a
less severe character.

Smaller Ships:

Cruisers: *Helena, Honolulu,* and *Raleigh* were all damaged, but were
repaired and returned to active war service;

Destroyers: Two damaged beyond repair; two others damaged but
repaired and returned to active war service;

Auxiliary Vessels: 1 Seaplane Tender, 1 Repair Ship, both severely
damaged but repaired and returned to active war service;

Target Ship: *Utah,* former battleship, sank at her berth.

The Japanese attacks upon the various Oahu airfields resulted in the following U.S. plane losses: Navy 80; Army 97.

U.S. military personnel casualties were: Navy, including Marine Corps,
3077 officers and enlisted men killed, 876 wounded; Army, including the Army
Air Corps, 226 officers and enlisted men killed, 396 wounded. Total: 4575.

The Japanese losses were 48 planes shot down and three midget sub-
marines destroyed. These vessels displaced 45 tons and were of little, if any,
military value.

The Final Summation

Review of the American Moves
Which Led to the Japanese Attack

Our Main Deduction is that President Roosevelt forced Japan to war by unrelenting diplomatic-economic pressure, and enticed that country to initiate
hostilities with a surprise attack by holding the Pacific Fleet in Hawaiian waters
as an invitation to that attack.

The evidence shows how surely the President moved toward war after June,
1940. His conversation with Admiral Richardson in October, 1940, indicated his
conviction that it would be impossible without a stunning incident to obtain a
declaration of war from Congress.

Despite the conditions of undeclared war which existed in the Atlantic
during the latter half of 1941, it had long been clear that Germany did not
intend to contribute to the creation of a state of formal war between her and

the United States. The Tripartite Treaty of September, 1940, however, supplied the President with the answer. Under that treaty, war with Japan meant war with Germany and Italy.

The highlights of the ever-increasing pressure upon Japan were:

1. the extension of financial and military aid to China in concert with Great Britain and the Netherlands, which began early in 1941;
2. the stoppage of Philippine exports to Japan by Executive Order on May 29, 1941;
3. the freezing of Japanese assets and the interdiction of all trade with Japan by the United States, Great Britain, and the Netherlands on July 25, 1941;
4. President Roosevelt's very frank statements of policy to Ambassador Nomura in their conference of August 17, 1941;
5. the termination of the Washington conference by the American note of November 26, 1941, which brought the war to the United States as the President so clearly intended it would.

That the Pearl Harbor attack was in accord with President Roosevelt's plans is attested by the following array of facts:

1. President Roosevelt and his military and naval advisers were well aware that Japan invariably started her wars with a surprise attack synchronized closely with her delivery of the Declaration of War;
2. In October, 1940, the President stated that, if war broke out in the Pacific, Japan would commit the overt act which would bring the United States into the war;
3. The Pacific Fleet, against contrary naval advice, was retained in Hawaii by order of the President for the alleged reason that the Fleet, so located, would exert a restrictive effect upon Japanese aggressions in the Far East;
4. The Fleet in Hawaii was neither powerful enough nor in the necessary strategic position to influence Japan's diplomatic decisions, which could only be accomplished by the stationing of an adequate naval force in Far Eastern waters;
5. Before that Fleet could operate at any distance from Pearl Harbor, its train (tankers, supply and repair vessels) would have had to be tremendously increased in strength—facts that would not escape the notice of the experienced Japanese spies in Hawaii;
6. President Roosevelt gave unmistakable evidence, in March, 1941, that he was not greatly concerned with the Pacific Fleet's effects upon Japanese diplomatic decisions, when he authorized the weakening of that Fleet, already inferior to that of Japan, by the detachment of 3 battleships, 1 aircraft carrier, 4 light cruisers, and 18 destroyers for duty in the Atlantic—a movement which would immediately be detected by Japanese espionage in Hawaii and Panama Canal Zone;

7. The successful crippling of the Pacific Fleet was the only surprise operation which promised the Japanese Navy sufficiently large results to justify the risk of heavy losses from land-based air attacks if the surprise failed;

8. Such an operation against the Fleet in Hawaii was attended with far greater chances of success, especially from the surprise standpoint, and far less risk of heavy losses than a similar attack against that Fleet based in U.S. West Coast ports;

9. The retention of the Fleet in Hawaii, especially after its reduction in strength in March, 1941, could serve only one possible purpose, an invitation to a surprise Japanese attack;

10. The denial to the Hawaiian Commanders of all knowledge of Magic was vital to the plan for enticing Japan to deliver a surprise attack upon the Fleet in Pearl Harbor, because, as late as Saturday, December 6, Admiral Kimmel could have caused that attack to be cancelled by taking his Fleet to sea and disappearing beyond land-based human ken.

Review of the Situation Known to Washington Before the Attack

From the beginning of the Washington conference in November, 1941, President Roosevelt and his advisers had repeated evidence that this was Japan's last and supreme effort to break the economic encirclement by peaceful means.

Throughout the negotiations, the Japanese secret dispatches stressed a "deadline date," after which "things were automatically going to happen."

Automatic events which were to follow the breakdown of such vital negotiations could only be acts of war, clear evidence that Japan intended to deliver a surprise attack to initiate the hostilities.

The fact that surprise was essential to the Japanese plans was repeatedly emphasized, on and after November 28, by the Tokyo dispatches and by telephone instructions to the two Ambassadors, cautioning them to keep alive the appearance of continuing negotiation.

Everyone familiar with Japanese military history knew that her first acts of war against China in 1894 and Russia in 1904 had been surprise attacks against the main fleets of those countries.

The only American Naval Force in the Pacific that was worth the risk of such an operation was the Fleet in Hawaiian waters.

The President and his military naval advisers well knew, on October 9, from the Tokyo dispatch to Honolulu of September 24, that Japan intended to plan a surprise air attack on the American Fleet in Pearl Harbor, and had daily evidence from the late decodes of certain Tokyo-Honolulu dispatches during the period, December 3–6 inclusive, that the planned attack was soon to occur.

On November 26, the recipients of Magic all had positive information from the Tokyo dispatch to Hong Kong of November 14 that Japan intended war with the United States and Great Britain if the Washington negotiations should fail.

The Tokyo dispatch to the Washington Embassy of November 28 definitely stated that the Japanese Government considered that the American note of the 26th had terminated all possibility of further negotiations.

The Tokyo-Berlin messages dated November 30 instructed the Japanese Ambassador to inform Hitler and von Ribbentrop that war between Japan and the Anglo-Saxon nations would come sooner than anyone expected.

The Japanese code-destruction messages of December 1 and 2 meant that war was extremely close at hand.

With the distribution of the Pilot Message at 3:00 P.M. on Saturday, December 6, the picture was complete for President Roosevelt and the other recipients of Magic, both in Washington and Manila. It said that the answer to the American note was about to arrive in the Embassy, that it was very lengthy, and that its delivery to the U.S. Government was to be especially timed. That timed delivery could only have meant that the answer was a Declaration of War, synchronized with a surprise attack. No other deduction was tenable.

The Saturday receipt of this definite information strongly supported the existing estimates in the War and Navy Departments, that the Japanese surprise attack would be delivered on a Sunday, and marked the morrow, Sunday, December 7, as the day. All this, beyond doubt, was known to President Roosevelt, General Marshall, and Admiral Stark at about 3:00 P.M. on that Saturday, Washington time, 21 hours before the next sunrise in Hawaii.

In obedience to the basic dictates of the Military Art, the information contained in the Pilot Message and the unmistakable implications thereof should have been transmitted to Admiral Kimmel and General Short at once. There was no military consideration that would warrant or tolerate an instant's delay in getting this word to those officers. There cannot be the slightest doubt that General Marshall and Admiral Stark would have had this done, if they had not been restrained from doing so by the orders of President Roosevelt. In the situation which then existed for them, no officer of even limited experience, if free to act, could possibly decide otherwise.

The fighting words in the selected passages of the 13-part message received on that same Saturday were merely additional evidence that this was a Declaration of War. The 14th part received early Sunday morning was further confirmation of that fact.

The 1:00 P.M. Washington delivery, ordered by the time-of-delivery dispatch, clearly indicated Pearl Harbor as the objective of the surprise attack, the final link in the long chain of evidence to that effect.

There Would Have Been No Pearl Harbor If Magic Had Not Been Denied to the Hawaiian Commanders

The recurrent fact of the true Pearl Harbor story has been the repeated withholding of information from Admiral Kimmel and General Short. If the War and Navy Departments had been free to follow the dictates of the Art of War, the following is the minimum of information and orders those officers would have received:

The Tokyo-Honolulu dispatches regarding the exact berthing of U.S. ships in Pearl Harbor and, in that connection, a reminder that Japan invariably started her wars with a surprise attack on the new enemy's Main Fleet; the dispatches concerning the Washington Conference and the deadline date after which things were automatically going to happen—evidence that this was Japan's last effort to solve U.S.-Japanese differences by peaceful means and the strong intimation of the surprise attack; the Tokyo-Hong Kong dispatch of November 14, which told of Japan's intentions to initiate war with the two Anglo-Saxon powers if the Washington negotiations failed; the Tokyo-Washington dispatch of November 28, which stated that the American note of November 26 had terminated those negotiations; the Pilot Message of December 6, which told that the Declaration of War was about to arrive in Washington, and that its delivery to the U.S. Government was to be especially timed, an essential feature for synchronizing the surprise attack with that delivery.

Not later than by November 28, the War and Navy Departments should have ordered the Hawaiian Commanders to place the Joint Army-Navy Coastal Frontier Defense Plans in effect, and to unify their Commands; the Navy Department should have ordered the mobilization of the Naval Establishment.

On November 28, the Chief of Naval Operations should have ordered Admiral Kimmel to recall the *Enterprise* from the Wake operation, and a few days later should have directed the cancellation of the contemplated sending of the *Lexington* to Midway.

... [N]ot one word of this information and none of the foregoing orders were sent to Hawaii.

General Marshall Looks Ahead, but Admiral Stark Lets the Cat Out of the Bag

Everything that happened in Washington on Saturday and Sunday, December 6 and 7, supports the belief that President Roosevelt had directed that no message be sent to the Hawaiian Commanders before noon on Sunday, Washington time.

General Marshall apparently appreciated that failure to act on the Declaration of War message and its timed delivery was going to be very difficult to explain on the witness stand when the future inevitable investigation into the incidents of those days took place. His avoidance of contact with the messages after the Pilot message until 11:25 on Sunday morning was unquestionably prompted by these thoughts. Otherwise, he would undoubtedly have been in his office by 8:00 A.M. on that fateful day.

Admiral Stark, on the other hand, did arrive in his office at 9:25 A.M. on Sunday, and at once accepted delivery of the full Declaration of War message. Against the advice of his assistants, he refused to inform Admiral Kimmel of its receipt. Forty minutes later, he knew that the 14-part message was to be delivered to the U.S. Government at 1:00 P.M., Washington time, which was 7:30 A.M., Hawaiian time, as was pointed out to him at once. Again, despite the urging of certain of his aides, he refused to send word to Admiral Kimmel.

Never before in recorded history had a field commander been denied information that his country would be at war in a matter of hours, and that everything pointed to a surprise attack upon his forces shortly after sunrise. No Naval Officer, on his own initiative, would ever make such a decision as Admiral Stark thus did.

That fact and Admiral Stark's decisions on that Sunday morning, even if they had not been supported by the wealth of earlier evidence, would reveal, beyond question, the basic truth of the Pearl Harbor story, namely that these Sunday messages and so many earlier ones, of vital import to Admiral Kimmel's exercise of his command, were not sent because Admiral Stark had orders from the President, which prohibited that action.

This deduction is fully supported by the Admiral's statement to the press in August, 1945, that all he did during the pre-Pearl Harbor days was done on order of higher authority, which can only mean President Roosevelt. The most arresting thing he did, during that time, was to withhold information from Admiral Kimmel.

President Roosevelt's Strategy Accomplishes Its Purpose

Thus, by holding a weak Pacific Fleet in Hawaii as an invitation to a surprise attack, and by denying the Commander of that Fleet the information which might cause him to render that attack impossible, President Roosevelt brought war to the United States on December 7, 1941. He took a fully aroused nation into the fight because none of its people suspected how the Japanese surprise attack fitted into their President's plans. Disastrous as it was from a naval standpoint, the Pearl Harbor attack proved to be the diplomatic prelude to the complete defeat of the Axis Powers.

As each reader will make up his own mind regarding the various questions raised by President Roosevelt's solution to his problem, nothing would be gained by an ethical analysis of that solution.

Notes

1. Admiral Kimmel had asked the author to act as his counsel before the Roberts Commission, but the Admiral was not allowed counsel. Nevertheless, although his status before the Commission was anomalous, the author did accompany the Admiral whenever the latter testified before that body, and late on the first day of that testimony was sworn as a witness. During the discussion connected with this swearing, the following exchange occurred:

   Justice Roberts: "So it is understood that you are not acting as counsel."
   Admiral Theobald: "No, sir."
   General McCoy: "The admiral is not on trial, of course."
   Justice Roberts: "No, this is not a trial of the admiral, in any sense."

   It has always been difficult to understand Justice Roberts' statement that Admiral Kimmel was not on trial. The Commission came into being to investigate the surprise attack upon the Fleet which he had commanded at the time, and it was generally recognized that the result of the inquiry would be the severe arraignments of Admiral Kimmel and General Short, which did constitute the principal findings of the Commission; findings which were given wide publicity at the earliest possible moment.

2. U.S.S. *Panay,* an American gunboat, sunk by Japanese bombing planes on the Yangtze River on December 12, 1937.

NO ↵

Roberta Wohlstetter

Surprise

If our intelligence system and all our other channels of information failed to produce an accurate image of Japanese intentions and capabilities, it was not for want of the relevant materials. Never before have we had so complete an intelligence picture of the enemy. And perhaps never again will we have such a magnificent collection of sources at our disposal.

Retrospect

To review these sources briefly, an American cryptanalyst, Col. William F. Friedman, had broken the top-priority Japanese diplomatic code, which enabled us to listen to a large proportion of the privileged communications between Tokyo and the major Japanese embassies throughout the world. Not only did we know in advance how the Japanese ambassadors in Washington were advised, and how much they were instructed to say, but we also were listening to top-secret messages on the Tokyo-Berlin and Tokyo-Rome circuits, which gave us information vital for conduct of the war in the Atlantic and Europe. In the Far East this source provided minute details on movements connected with the Japanese program of expansion into Southeast Asia.

Besides the strictly diplomatic codes, our cryptanalysts also had some success in reading codes used by Japanese agents in major American and foreign ports. Those who were on the distribution list for MAGIC had access to much of what these agents were reporting to Tokyo and what Tokyo was demanding of them in the Panama Canal Zone, in cities along the east and west coasts of the Americas from northern Canada as far south as Brazil, and in ports throughout the Far East, including the Philippines and the Hawaiian Islands. They could determine what installations, what troop and ship movements, and what alert and defense measures were of interest to Tokyo at these points on the globe, as well as approximately how much correct information her agents were sending her.

Our naval leaders also had at their disposal the results of radio traffic analysis. While before the war our naval radio experts could not read the content of any Japanese naval or military coded messages, they were able to deduce from a study of intercepted ship call signs the composition and location of the Japanese Fleet units. After a change in call signs, they might lose sight of some

From Roberta Wohlstetter, *Pearl Harbor: Warning and Decision* (Stanford University Press, 1967). Copyright © 1962 by The Board of Trustees of the Leland Stanford Junior University. Reprinted by permission of Stanford University Press.

251

units, and units that went into port in home waters were also lost because the ships in port used frequencies that our radios were unable to intercept. Most of the time, however, our traffic analysts had the various Japanese Fleet units accurately pinpointed on our naval maps.

Extremely competent on-the-spot economic and political analysis was furnished by Ambassador Grew and his staff in Tokyo. Ambassador Grew was himself a most sensitive and accurate observer, as evidenced by his dispatches to the State Department. His observations were supported and supplemented with military detail by frequent reports from American naval attachés and observers in key Far Eastern ports. Navy Intelligence had men with radio equipment located along the coast of China, for example, who reported the convoy movements toward Indochina. There were also naval observers stationed in various high-tension areas in Thailand and Indochina who could fill in the local outlines of Japanese political intrigue and military planning. In Tokyo and other Japanese cities, it is true, Japanese censorship grew more and more rigid during 1941, until Ambassador Grew felt it necessary to disclaim any responsibility for noting or reporting overt military evidence of an imminent outbreak of war. This careful Japanese censorship naturally cut down visual confirmation of the decoded information but very probably never achieved the opaqueness of Russia's Iron Curtain.

During this period the data and interpretations of British intelligence were also available to American officers in Washington and the Far East, though the British and Americans tended to distrust each other's privileged information.

In addition to secret sources, there were some excellent public ones. Foreign correspondents for *The New York Times, The Herald Tribune,* and *The Washington Post* were stationed in Tokyo and Shanghai and in Canberra, Australia. Their reporting as well as their predictions on the Japanese political scene were on a very high level. Frequently their access to news was more rapid and their judgment of its significance as reliable as that of our Intelligence officers. This was certainly the case for 1940 and most of 1941. For the last few weeks before the Pearl Harbor strike, however, the public newspaper accounts were not very useful. It was necessary to have secret information in order to know what was happening. Both Tokyo and Washington exercised very tight control over leaks during this crucial period, and the newsmen accordingly had to limit their accounts to speculation and notices of diplomatic meetings with no exact indication of the content of the diplomatic exchanges.

The Japanese press was another important public source. During 1941 it proclaimed with increasing shrillness the Japanese government's determination to pursue its program of expansion into Southeast Asia and the desire of the military to clear the Far East of British and American colonial exploitation. This particular source was rife with explicit signals of aggressive intent.

Finally, an essential part of the intelligence picture for 1941 was both public and privileged information on American policy and activities in the Far East. During the year the pattern of action and interaction between the Japanese and American governments grew more and more complex. At the last, it became especially important for anyone charged with the responsibility of ordering an alert to know what moves the American government was going to make with respect to Japan, as well as to try to guess what Japan's next move would be, since Japan's next move would respond in part to ours. Unfortunately our military leaders, and especially our Intelligence officers, were sometimes as surprised as the Japanese at the moves of the White House and the State Department. They usually had more orderly anticipations about Japanese policy and conduct than they had about America's. On the other hand, it was also true that State Department and White House officials were handicapped in judging Japanese intentions and estimates of risk by an inadequate picture of our own military vulnerability.

All of the public and private sources of information mentioned were available to America's political and military leaders in 1941. It is only fair to remark, however, that no single person or agency ever had at any given moment all the signals existing in this vast information network. The signals lay scattered in a number of different agencies; some were decoded, some were not; some traveled through rapid channels of communication, some were blocked by technical or procedural delays; some never reached a center of decision. But it is legitimate to review again the general sort of picture that emerged during the first week of December from the signals readily at hand. Anyone close to President Roosevelt was likely to have before him the following significant fragments.

There was first of all a picture of gathering troop and ship movements down the China coast and into Indochina. The large dimensions of this movement to the south were established publicly and visually as well as by analysis of ship call signs. Two changes in Japanese naval call signs—one on November 1 and another on December 1—had also been evaluated by Naval Intelligence as extremely unusual and as signs of major preparations for some sort of Japanese offensive. The two changes had interfered with the speed of American radio traffic analysis. Thousands of interceptions after December 1 were necessary before the new call signs could be read. Partly for this reason American radio analysts disagreed about the locations of the Japanese carriers. One group held that all the carriers were near Japan because they had not been able to identify a carrier call sign since the middle of November. Another group believed that they had located one carrier division in the Marshalls. The probability seemed to be that the carriers, wherever they were, had gone into radio silence; and past experience led the analysts to believe that they were therefore in waters near the Japanese homeland, where they could communicate with each other on wavelengths that we could not intercept. However, our inability to locate the carriers exactly, combined with the two changes in call signs, was itself a danger signal.

Our best secret source, MAGIC, was confirming the aggressive intentions of the new military cabinet in Tokyo, which had replaced the last moderate cabinet on October 17. In particular, MAGIC provided details of some of the preparations for the move into Southeast Asia. Running counter to this were increased troop shipments to the Manchurian border in October. (The intelligence picture is never clear-cut.) But withdrawals had begun toward the end of that month. MAGIC also carried explicit instructions to the Japanese ambassadors in Washington to pursue diplomatic negotiations with the United States with increasing energy, but at the same time it announced a deadline for the favorable conclusion of the negotiations, first for November 25, later postponed until November 29. In case of diplomatic failure by that date, the Japanese ambassadors were told, Japanese patience would be exhausted, Japan was determined to pursue her Greater East Asia policy, and on November 29 "things" would automatically begin to happen.

On November 26 Secretary Hull rejected Japan's latest bid for American approval of her policies in China and Indochina. MAGIC had repeatedly characterized this Japanese overture as the "last," and it now revealed the ambassadors' reaction of consternation and despair over the American refusal and also their country's characterization of the American Ten Point Note as an "ultimatum."

On the basis of this collection of signals, Army and Navy Intelligence experts in Washington tentatively placed D-day *for the Japanese Southeastern campaign* during the week end of November 30, and when this failed to materialize, during the week end of December 7. They also compiled an accurate list of probable British and Dutch targets and included the Philippines and Guam as possible American targets.

Also available in this mass of information, but long forgotten, was a rumor reported by Ambassador Grew in January, 1941. It came from what was regarded as a not-very-reliable source, the Peruvian embassy, and stated that the Japanese were preparing a surprise air attack on Pearl Harbor. Curiously the date of the report is coincident roughly with what we now know to have been the date of inception of Yamamoto's plan; but the coincidence is fairly pure. The rumor was traced to a Japanese cook in the Embassy who had been reading a novel that began with an attack on Pearl Harbor. Consequently everyone concerned, including Ambassador Grew, labeled the rumor as quite fantastic and the plan as absurdly impossible. American judgment was consistent with Japanese judgment at this time, since Yamamoto's plan was in direct contradiction to Japanese naval tactical doctrine.

Perspective

On the basis of this rapid recapitulation of the highlights in the signal picture, it is apparent that our decisionmakers had at hand an impressive amount of information on the enemy. They did not have the complete list of targets, since none of the last-minute estimates included Pearl Harbor. They did not know the exact hour and date for opening the attack. They did not have an accurate knowledge of Japanese capabilities or of Japanese ability to accept very high risks. The crucial question then, we repeat, is, If we could enumerate accurately the British and Dutch targets and give credence to a Japanese attack against them either on November 30 or December 7, why were we not expecting a specific danger to *ourselves?* And by the word "expecting," we mean expecting in the sense of taking specific alert actions to meet the contingencies of attack by land, sea, or air.

There are several answers to this question.... First of all, it is much easier *after* the event to sort the relevant from the irrelevant signals. After the event, of course, a signal is always crystal clear; we can now see what disaster it was signaling, since the disaster has occurred. But before the event it is obscure and pregnant with conflicting meanings. It comes to the observer embedded in an atmosphere of "noise," i.e., in the company of all sorts of information that is useless and irrelevant for predicting the particular disaster. For example, in Washington, Pearl Harbor signals were competing with a vast number of signals from the European theater. These European signals announced danger more frequently and more specifically than any coming from the Far East. The Far Eastern signals were also arriving at a center of decision where they had to compete with the prevailing belief that an unprotected offensive force acts as a deterrent rather than a target. In Honolulu they were competing *not* with signals from the European theater, but rather with a large number of signals announcing Japanese intentions and preparations to attack Soviet Russia rather than to move southward; here they were also competing with expectations of local sabotage prepared by previous alert situations.

In short, we failed to anticipate Pearl Harbor not for want of the relevant materials, but because of a plethora of irrelevant ones. Much of the appearance of wanton neglect that emerged in various investigations of the disaster resulted from the unconscious suppression of vast congeries of signs pointing in every direction except Pearl Harbor. It was difficult later to recall these signs since they had led nowhere. Signals that are characterized today as absolutely unequivocal warnings of surprise air attack on Pearl Harbor become, on analysis in the context of December, 1941, not merely ambiguous but occasionally inconsistent with such an attack. To recall one of the most controversial and publicized examples, the winds code, both General Short and Admiral Kimmel testified that if they had had this information, they would have been prepared on the morning of December 7 for an air attack from without. The messages establishing the winds code are often described in the Pearl Harbor literature as Tokyo's declaration of war against America. If they indeed amounted to such a declaration, obviously the failure to inform Honolulu of this vital news would have been criminal negligence. On examination, however, the messages proved to be instructions for code communication after normal commercial channels had been cut. In one message the recipient was instructed on receipt of an execute to destroy all remaining codes in his possession. In another version the recipient was warned that the execute would be sent out "when relations are becoming dangerous" between Japan and three other countries. There was a different code term for each country: England, America, and the Soviet Union.

There is no evidence that an authentic execute of either message was ever intercepted by the United States before December 7. The message ordering code destruction was in any case superseded by a much more explicit code-destruction order from Tokyo that was intercepted on December 2 and translated on December 3. After December 2, the receipt of a winds-code execute for code destruction would therefore have added nothing new to our information, and code destruction in itself cannot be taken as an unambiguous substitute for a formal declaration of war. During the first week of December the United States ordered all American consulates in the Far East to destroy all American codes, yet no one has attempted to prove that this order was equivalent to an American declaration of war against Japan. As for the other winds-code message, provided an execute had been received warning that relations were dangerous between Japan and the United States, there would still have been no way on the basis of this signal alone to determine whether Tokyo was signaling Japanese intent to attack the United States or Japanese fear of an American surprise attack (in reprisal for Japanese aggressive moves against American allies in the Far East). It was only after the event that "dangerous relations" could be interpreted as "surprise air attack on Pearl Harbor."

There is a difference, then, between having a signal available somewhere in the heap of irrelevancies, and perceiving it as a warning; and there is also a difference between perceiving it as a warning, and acting or getting action on it. These distinctions, simple as they are, illuminate the obscurity shrouding this moment in history.

Many instances of these distinctions have been examined in the course of this study. We shall recall a few of the most dramatic now. To illustrate the difference between having and perceiving a signal, let us [look at] Colonel Fielder.... Though he was an untrained and inexperienced Intelligence officer, he headed Army Intelligence at Pearl Harbor at the time of the attack. He had been on the job for only four months, and he regarded as quite satisfactory his sources of information and his contacts with the Navy locally and with Army Intelligence in Washington. Evidently he was unaware that Army Intelligence in Washington was not allowed to send him any "action" or policy information, and he was therefore not especially concerned about trying to read beyond the obvious meaning of any given communication that came under his eyes. Colonel Bratton, head of Army Far Eastern Intelligence in Washington, however, had a somewhat more realistic view of the extent of Colonial Fielder's knowledge. At the end of November, Colonel Bratton had learned about the winds-code setup and was also apprised that the naval traffic analysis unit under Commander Rochefort in Honolulu was monitoring 24 hours a day for an execute. He was understandably worried about the lack of communication between this unit and Colonel Fielder's office, and by December 5 he finally felt that the matter was urgent enough to warrant sending a message directly to Colonel Fielder about the winds code. Now any information on the winds code, since it belonged to the highest classification of secret information, and since it was therefore automatically evaluated as "action" information, could not be sent through normal G-2 channels. Colonel Bratton had to figure out another way to get the information to Colonel Fielder. He sent this message: "Contact Commander Rochefort immediately thru Commandant Fourteenth Naval District regarding broadcasts from Tokyo reference weather." Signal Corps records establish that Colonel Fielder received this message. How did he react to it? He filed it. According to his testimony in 1945, it made no impression on him and he did not attempt to see Rochefort. He could not sense any urgency behind the lines because he was not expecting immediate trouble, and his expectations determined what he read. A warning signal was available to him, but he did not perceive it.

Colonel Fielder's lack of experience may make this example seem to be an exception. So let us recall the performance of Captain Wilkinson, the naval officer who headed the Office of Naval Intelligence in Washington in the fall of 1941 and who is unanimously acclaimed for a distinguished and brilliant career. His treatment of a now-famous Pearl Harbor signal does not sound much different in the telling. After the event, the signal in question was labeled "the bomb-plot message." It originated in Tokyo on September 24 and was sent to an agent in Honolulu. It requested the agent to divide Pearl Harbor into five areas and to make his future reports on ships in harbor with reference to those areas. Tokyo was especially interested in the locations of battleships, destroyers, and carriers, and also in any information on the mooring of more than one ship at a single dock.

This message was decoded and translated on October 9 and shortly thereafter distributed to Army, Navy, and State Department recipients of MAGIC. Commander Kramer, a naval expert on MAGIC, had marked the message with an asterisk, signifying that he thought it to be of particular interest. But what was its interest? Both he and Wilkinson agreed that it illustrated the "nicety" of Japanese intelligence, the incredible zeal and efficiency with which they collected detail. The division into areas was interpreted as a device for shortening the reports. Admiral Stark was similarly impressed with Japanese efficiency, and no one felt it necessary to forward the message to Admiral Kimmel. No one read into it a specific danger to ships anchored in Pearl Harbor. At the time, this was a reasonable estimate, since somewhat similar requests for information were going to Japanese agents in Panama, Vancouver, Portland, San Diego, San Francisco, and other places. It should be observed, however, that the estimate was reasonable only on the basis of a very rough check on the quantity of espionage messages passing between Tokyo and these American ports. No one in Far Eastern Intelligence had subjected the messages to any more refined analysis. An observer assigned to such a job would have been able to record an increase in the frequency and specificity of Tokyo's requests concerning Manila and Pearl Harbor in the last weeks before the outbreak of war, and he would have noted that Tokyo was not displaying the same interest in other American ports. These observations, while not significant in isolation, might have been useful in the general signal picture.

There is no need, however, to confine our examples to Intelligence personnel. Indeed, the crucial areas where the signals failed to communicate a warning were in the operational branches of the armed services. Let us take Admiral Kimmel and his reaction to the information that the Japanese were destroying most of their codes in major Far Eastern consulates and also in London and Washington. Since the Pearl Harbor attack, this information has frequently been characterized by military experts who were not stationed in Honolulu as an "unmistakable tip-off." As Admiral Ingersoll explained at the congressional hearings, with the lucidity characteristic of statements after the event:

> If you rupture diplomatic negotiations you do not necessarily have to burn your codes. The diplomats go home and they can pack up their codes with their dolls and take them home. Also, when you rupture diplomatic negotiations, you do not rupture consular relations. The consuls stay on.
>
> Now, in this particular set of dispatches that did not mean a rupture of diplomatic negotiations, it meant war, and that information was sent out to the fleets as soon as we got it.... [1]

The phrase "it meant war" was, of course, pretty vague; war in Manila, Hong Kong, Singapore, and Batavia is not war 5000 miles away in Pearl Harbor. Before the event, for Admiral Kimmel, code burning in major Japanese consulates in the Far East may have "meant war," but it did not signal danger of an air attack on Pearl Harbor. In the first place, the information that he received was not the original MAGIC. He learned from Washington that Japanese consulates were burning "almost all" of their codes, not all of them, and Honolulu was not included on the list. He knew from a local source that the Japanese consulate in Honolulu was burning secret papers (not necessarily codes), and this back yard burning had happened three or four times during the year. In July, 1941, Kimmel had been informed that the Japanese consulates in lands neighboring Indochina had destroyed codes, and he interpreted the code burning in December as a similar attempt to protect codes in case the Americans or their British and Dutch allies tried to seize the consulates in reprisal for the southern advance. This also was a reasonable interpretation at the time, though not an especially keen one.

Indeed, at the time there was a good deal of evidence available to support all the wrong interpretations of last-minute signals, and the interpretations appeared wrong only *after* the event. There was, for example, a good deal of evidence to support the hypothesis that Japan would attack the Soviet Union from the east while the Russian Army was heavily engaged in the west. Admiral Turner, head of Navy War Plans in Washington, was an enthusiastic adherent of this view and argued the high probability of a Japanese attack on Russia up until the last week in November, when he had to concede that most of Japan's men and supplies were moving south. Richard Sorge, the expert Soviet spy who had direct access to the Japanese Cabinet, had correctly predicted the southern move as early as July, 1941, but even he was deeply alarmed during September and early October by the large number of troop movements to the Manchurian border. He feared that his July advice to the Soviet Union had been in error, and his alarm ultimately led to his capture on October 14. For at this time he increased his radio messages to Moscow to the point where it was possible for the Japanese police to pinpoint the source of the broadcasts.

It is important to emphasize here that most of the men that we have cited in our examples, such as Captain Wilkinson and Admirals Turner and Kimmel— these men and their colleagues who were involved in the Pearl Harbor disaster —were as efficient and loyal a group of men as one could find. Some of them were exceptionally able and dedicated. The fact of surprise at Pearl Harbor has never been persuasively explained by accusing the participants, individually or in groups, of conspiracy or negligence or stupidity. What these examples illustrate is rather the very human tendency to pay attention to the signals that support current expectations about enemy behavior. If no one is listening for signals of an attack against a highly improbable target, then it is very difficult for the signals to be heard.

For every signal that came into the information net in 1941 there were usually several plausible alternative explanations, and it is not surprising that our observers and analysts were inclined to select the explanations that fitted the popular hypotheses. They sometimes set down new contradictory evidence side by side with existing hypotheses, and they also sometimes held two contradictory beliefs at the same time. We have seen this happen in G-2 estimates for the fall of 1941. Apparently human beings have a stubborn attachment to old beliefs and an equally stubborn resistance to new material that will upset them.

Besides the tendency to select whatever was in accord with one's expectations, there were many other blocks to perception that prevented our analysts from making the correct interpretation. We have just mentioned the masses of conflicting evidence that supported alternative and equally reasonable hypotheses. This is the phenomenon of noise in which a signal is embedded. Even at its normal level, noise presents problems in distraction; but in addition to the natural clatter of useless information and competing signals, in 1941 a number of factors combined to raise the usual noise level. First of all, it had been raised, especially in Honolulu, by the background of previous alert situations and false alarms. Earlier alerts, as we have seen, had centered attention on local sabotage and on signals supporting the hypothesis of a probable Japanese attack on Russia. Second, in both Honolulu and Washington, individual reactions to danger had been numbed, or at least dulled, by the continuous international tension.

A third factor that served to increase the natural noise level was the positive effort made by the enemy to keep the relevant signals quiet. The Japanese security system was an important and successful block to perception. It was able to keep the strictest cloak of secrecy around the Pearl Harbor attack and to limit knowledge only to those closely associated with the details of military and naval planning. In the Japanese Cabinet only the Navy Minister and the Army Minister (who was also Prime Minister) knew of the plan before the task force left its final port of departure.

In addition to keeping certain signals quiet, the enemy tried to create noise, and sent false signals into our information system by carrying on elaborate "spoofs." False radio traffic made us believe that certain ships were maneuvering near the mainland of Japan. The Japanese also sent to individual commanders false war plans for Chinese targets, which were changed only at the last moment to bring them into line with the Southeastern movement.

A fifth barrier to accurate perception was the fact that the relevant signals were subject to change, often very sudden change. This was true even of the so-called static intelligence, which included data on capabilities and the composition of military forces. In the case of our 1941 estimates of the infeasibility of torpedo attacks in the shallow waters of Pearl Harbor, or the underestimation of the range and performance of the Japanese Zero, the changes happened too quickly to appear in an intelligence estimate.

Sixth, our own security system sometimes prevented the communication of signals. It confronted our officers with the problem of trying to keep information from the enemy without keeping it from each other, and, as in the case of MAGIC, they were not always successful. As we have seen, only a very few key individuals saw these secret messages, and they saw them only briefly. They had no opportunity or time to make a critical review of the material, and each one assumed that others who had seen it would arrive at identical interpretations. Exactly who those "others" were was not quite clear to any recipient. Admiral Stark, for example, thought Admiral Kimmel was reading all of MAGIC. Those who were not on the list of recipients, but who had learned somehow of the existence of the decodes, were sure that they contained military as well as diplomatic information and believed that the contents were much fuller and more precise than they actually were. The effect of carefully limiting the reading and discussion of MAGIC, which was certainly necessary to safeguard the secret of our knowledge of the code, was thus to reduce this group of signals to the point where they were scarcely heard.

To these barriers of noise and security we must add the fact that the necessarily precarious character of intelligence information and predictions was reflected in the wording of instructions to take action. The warning messages were somewhat vague and ambiguous. Enemy moves are often subject to reversal on short notice, and this was true for the Japanese. They had plans for canceling their attacks on American possessions in the Pacific up to 24 hours before the time set for attack. A full alert in the Hawaiian Islands, for example, was one condition that might have caused the Pearl Harbor task force to return to Japan on December 5 or 6. The fact that intelligence predictions must be based on moves that are almost always reversible makes understandable the reluctance of the intelligence analyst to make bold assertions. Even if he is willing to risk his reputation on a firm prediction of attack at a definite time and place, no commander will in turn lightly risk the penalties and costs of a full alert. In December, 1941, a full alert required shooting down any unidentified aircraft sighted over the Hawaiian Islands. Yet this might have been interpreted by Japan as the first overt act. At least that was one consideration that influenced General Short to order his lowest degree of alert. While the cautious phrasing in the messages to the theater is certainly understandable, it nevertheless constituted another block on the road to perception. The sentences in the final theater warnings—"A surprise aggressive move in any direction is a possibility" and "Japanese future action unpredictable but hostile action possible at any moment"—could scarcely have been expected to inform the theater commanders of any change in their strategic situation.

Last but not least we must also mention the blocks to perception and communication inherent in any large bureaucratic organization, and those that stemmed from intraservice and interservice rivalries. The most glaring example of rivalry in the Pearl Harbor case was that between Naval War Plans and Naval Intelligence. A general prejudice against intellectuals and specialists, not confined to the military but unfortunately widely held in America, also made it difficult for intelligence experts to be heard. McCollum, Bratton, Sadtler, and a few others who felt that the signal picture was ominous enough to warrant more urgent warnings had no power to influence decision. The Far Eastern code analysts, for example, were believed to be too immersed in the "Oriental point of view." Low budgets for American Intelligence departments reflected the low prestige of this activity, whereas in England, Germany, and Japan, 1941 budgets reached a height that was regarded by the American Congress as quite beyond reason.

In view of all these limitations to perception and communication, is the fact of surprise at Pearl Harbor, then, really so surprising? Even with these limitations explicitly recognized, there remains the step between perception and action. Let us assume that the first hurdle has been crossed: An available signal has been perceived as an indication of imminent danger. Then how do we resolve the next questions: What specific danger is the signal trying to communicate, and what specific action or preparation should follow?

On November 27, General MacArthur had received a war warning very similar to the one received by General Short in Honolulu. MacArthur's response had been promptly translated into orders designed to protect his bombers from possible air attack from Formosan land bases. But the orders were carried out very slowly. By December 8, Philippine time, only half of the bombers ordered to the south had left the Manila area, and reconnaissance over Formosa had not been undertaken. There was no sense of urgency in preparing for a Japanese air attack, partly because our intelligence estimates had calculated that the Japanese aircraft did not have sufficient range to bomb Manila from Formosa.

The information that Pearl Harbor had been attacked arrived at Manila early in the morning of December 8, giving the Philippine forces some 9 or 10 hours to prepare for an attack. But did an air attack on Pearl Harbor necessarily mean that the Japanese would strike from the air at the Philippines? Did they have enough equipment to mount both air attacks successfully? Would they come from Formosa or from carriers? Intelligence had indicated that they would have to come from carriers, yet the carriers were evidently off Hawaii. MacArthur's headquarters also pointed out that there had been no formal declaration of war against Japan by the United States. Therefore approval could not be granted for a counterattack on Formosan bases. Furthermore there were technical disagreements among airmen as to whether a counterattack should be mounted without advance photographic reconnaissance. While Brereton was arranging permission to undertake photographic reconnaissance, there was further disagreement about what to do with the aircraft in the meantime. Should they be sent aloft or should they be dispersed to avoid destruction in case the Japanese reached the airfields? When the Japanese bombers arrived shortly after noon, they found all the American aircraft wingtip to wingtip on the ground. Even the signal of an actual attack on Pearl Harbor was not an unambiguous signal of an attack on the Philippines, and it did not make clear what response was best.

Note

1. *Hearings,* Part 9, p. 4226.

POSTSCRIPT

Did President Roosevelt Deliberately Withhold Information About the Attack on Pearl Harbor From the American Commanders?

Theobald was an eyewitness to the Pearl Harbor attack. In his selection, Theobald defends his former boss, Admiral Husband E. Kimmel of the U.S. Pacific Fleet, from responsibility for the fleet's lack of preparation prior to Japan's surprise attack. He argues that President Roosevelt and his chief military aides deliberately withheld from Kimmel information that they had received from intelligence intercepts going to Japanese diplomats that the Japanese navy was going to attack Pearl Harbor on December 7. Why would Roosevelt do such a thing? Because, says Theobald, Roosevelt wanted to enter the war against Germany and Japan, and he could not mobilize a reluctant public for war unless the United States was attacked first. Disastrous as it was from a naval standpoint, says Theobald, "the Pearl Harbor attack proved to be the diplomatic prelude to the complete defeat of the Axis Powers."

Theobald wrote *The Final Secret of Pearl Harbor* at the height of the battle in the 1950s between the internationist historians, who defended Roosevelt's policies toward Germany and Japan, and the revisionists, who believed that Roosevelt unnecessarily and deliberately deceived the American public by enticing the Japanese to attack Pearl Harbor. Both groups held different assumptions about the nature of America's foreign policy before World War II. Internationalists believed that Germany and Japan constituted threats to world peace and the overall balance of power and that they had to be defeated with or without active U.S. participation in the war. Revisionist historians believed that Germany and Japan did not threaten America's security even if they controlled Europe and Asia. For the best defenses of President Roosevelt's foreign policies, see Robert Dallek, *Franklin Roosevelt and American Foreign Policy, 1932–1945* (Oxford University Press, 1979) and Waldo H. Heinrichs, *Threshold of War: Franklin D. Roosevelt and American Entry Into World War II* (Oxford University Press, 1988). Early revisionist studies of Roosevelt are summarized in Harry Elmer Barnes, ed., *Perpetual War for Perpetual Peace: A Critical Examination of the Foreign Policy of Franklin D. Roosevelt and Its Aftermath* (Caxton, 1953). Later criticisms include John T. Toland, *Infamy: Pearl Harbor and Its Aftermath* (Doubleday, 1982) and *Wind Over Sand: The Diplomacy of Franklin Roosevelt* (University of Georgia Press, 1988).

Theobald's account raises a number of questions. Did Roosevelt shift 3 battleships, 1 aircraft carrier, 4 light cruisers, and 18 destroyers for duty in the

Atlantic in March 1941 to bolster lend-lease shipments to aid Great Britain in her struggle against Germany (a possibility that Theobald does not mention)? Or was Roosevelt, who knew that their intelligence agents would be aware of the maneuvers, trying to entice the Japanese to attack Pearl Harbor? What about Theobald's charge that the commanders at Pearl Harbor were deliberately denied information about Japan's plans so that the Japanese Navy would be tempted to attack the fleet? If this is true, why wasn't Roosevelt tried as a war criminal (after his death)? Furthermore, if the president wanted to use the attack to get America into the war, why would he destroy most of his Pacific task force? Perhaps Gordon W. Prange is correct to reject revisionist historians in his massive, well-documented account *At Dawn We Slept: The Untold Story of Pearl Harbor* (McGraw-Hill, 1981). Prange faults the commanders at Pearl Harbor: Lieutenant General Walter C. Short, for example, was so obsessed with sabotage that ammunition was not available when the attack came. Short also failed to use radar and ignored Washington's orders to undertake reconnaissance.

Although most revisionists will disagree with her, Wohlstetter's analysis of the decision-making process provides an alternative to both the revisionist conspiratorial views of Roosevelt and his staunchest defenders. Wohlstetter makes several telling points. First, the intelligence community was organizationally divided between army and navy intelligence units in Washington, D.C., and Hawaii, so there was no systematic analysis of the decrypted diplomatic messages collectively known as MAGIC by the War Department's Signal Intelligence Service (SIS). Second, because of the abundance of information from public and private sources as well as from diplomatic intelligence intercepts, it was difficult to sort through the noise level and separate relevant materials from irrelevant materials. Third, the Japanese themselves provided misleading signals so that American observers would think the fleet was home—near the Marshall Islands. Fourth, even though President Roosevelt knew that war was coming with Japan, he thought the attack might be against Russia in Siberia, with its oil reserves, or in Southeast Asia against the British and Dutch possessions, especially Indonesia, with its important supply of rubber. Finally, Wohlstetter contends that even with an eight-hour warning, America's leaders in the Philippines were immobilized by bureaucratic indecisiveness and that Japanese planes destroyed most of the American aircraft at Clark Field because the planes were not moved to hidden areas.

The starting points for further study on Pearl Harbor are Hans Trefouse, *Pearl Harbor: The Continuing Controversy* (Krieger, 1982) and Akira Iriye, *Pearl Harbor and the Coming of the Pacific War: A Brief History With Documents and Essays* (St. Martin's Press, LLC, 1999). On Pearl Harbor itself see Gordon Prange, *Pearl Harbor: The Verdict of History* (McGraw-Hill, 1986). A trenchant analysis with a comprehensive bibliography of the whole period is Justus D. Doenecke and John E. Wiltz, *From Isolation to War: 1931–1941*, 2d ed. (Harlan Davidson, 1991). For a discussion of early interpretations, see Wayne S. Cole, "American Entry Into World War II: A Historiographical Appraisal," *Mississippi Valley Historical Review* (March 1957). For a more recent evaluation, see J. Gary Clifford, "Both Ends of the Telescope: New Perspectives on F.D.R. and American Entry Into World War II," *Diplomatic History* (Spring 1989).

On the Internet ...

Cold War Hot Links

This page contains links to Web pages on the cold war that a variety of people have created. They run the entire spectrum of political thought and provide some interesting views on the cold war and the state of national security.

http://www.stmartin.edu/~dprice/cold.war.html

Civil Rights: A Status Report

Kevin Hollaway is the author of this detailed history of black civil rights, from the discovery of the New World to the present. In his own words, "It is not my intent to complain about the present state of Black America, nor to provide excuses. My intent is [to] provide an unbiased picture of Black American history; something that is often missing from many classrooms in America."

http://www.ghgcorp.com/hollaway/civil.htm

The History Place Presents: The Vietnam War

This page of the History Place offers comprehensive timelines of U.S. involvement in the Vietnam conflict from 1945 to 1975, with quotes and analysis. You can also jump to specific events and topics, such as the Tet Offensive, the Geneva Conference, and the Pentagon Papers.

http://www.historyplace.com/unitedstates/vietnam/

American Immigration Resources on the Internet

This site contains many links to American immigration resources on the Internet. It includes a site on children's immigration issues, the Immigration and Naturalization Service home page, and a forum on immigration.

http://www.immigration-usa.com/resource.html

Bill Clinton

This site includes President Bill Clinton's Inaugural Address and all of his State of the Union Addresses, his Public Papers, an extensive list of links to pages and essays on the former president, and a selected bibliography.

http://www.interlink-cafe.com/uspresidents/42nd.htm

PART 3

The Cold War and Beyond

*T*he postwar years were a period of both affluence and anxiety. By 1947 a cold war between the Western powers and the Russians was in full swing. By 1950 a hot war of "containment" was being fought in Korea. By the mid-1950s the Korean War had subsided. But the containment policy in Asia never subsided. By 1968 President Lyndon Johnson had escalated America's participation in the Vietnam War to 550,000 troops and then tried to negotiate a peace.

From 1950 to 1974 most Americans were economically well-off. Presidents Harry S. Truman, Dwight D. Eisenhower, and John F. Kennedy managed an economy whose major problem was keeping inflation under control for a prosperous blue-collar labor force and an emerging baby boomer, white-collar class. The 1960s and early 1970s represented a turning point for African Americans and women, who rose up and demanded that they be granted their civil, political, and economic rights as first-class citizens.

The last quarter of the twentieth century has continued America's fluctuation between affluence and anxiety. Deindustrialization has hurt blue-collar factory workers, but unprecedented prosperity exists for the managers of the high-tech economy. Controversy surrounds whether President Ronald Reagan's policies were responsible for the demise of the Soviet Union's empire. The reputations of Presidents Reagan and Bill Clinton are heavily dependent upon the future course of America's prosperity and power in the twenty-first century.

- Was the United States Responsible for the Cold War?

- Did the Civil Rights Movement Improve Race Relations in the United States?

- Was America's Escalation of the War in Vietnam Inevitable?

- Should America Remain a Nation of Immigrants?

- Did President Reagan Win the Cold War?

- Will History Consider William Jefferson Clinton a Reasonably Good Chief Executive?

ISSUE 12

Was the United States Responsible
for the Cold War?

YES: Thomas G. Paterson, from *Meeting the Communist Threat: Truman to Reagan* (Oxford University Press, 1988)

NO: John Lewis Gaddis, from *Russia, the Soviet Union, and the United States: An Interpretive History*, 2d ed. (McGraw-Hill, 1990)

ISSUE SUMMARY

YES: Professor of history Thomas G. Paterson argues that the Truman administration exaggerated the Soviet threat after World War II because the United States had expansionist political and economic global needs.

NO: Professor of history John Lewis Gaddis argues that the power vacuum that existed in Europe at the end of World War II exaggerated and made almost inevitable a clash between the democratic, capitalist United States and the totalitarian, communist USSR.

Historians are unable to agree on exactly when the cold war began. This is because of the rocky relationship that existed between the United States and the Soviet Union since World War I. The Wilson administration became upset when the communist government declared its neutrality in the war and pulled Russia out of the allied coalition. The Russian leader V. I. Lenin resented the allied intervention in Siberia from 1918 to 1920 because he believed that the pretext for rescuing Czech troops was an excuse to undermine Russia's communist government. The relationship between the two countries improved in 1933 after President Franklin D. Roosevelt accorded diplomatic recognition to the communist government. In the late 1930s the relationship soured once again. Russia, unable to negotiate a security treaty with France, signed a nonaggression pact with Germany on August 23, 1939. This allowed Adolf Hitler to attack Poland in early September and Soviet leader Joseph Stalin to attack Finland and take over the Baltic states Latvia, Lithuania, and Estonia. In September 1939, as World War II was breaking out in Europe, the United States—like the USSR—was officially neutral. But the Roosevelt administration pushed modifications of the neutrality laws through Congress, which enabled significant amounts of economic and military assistance to be extended to England and France (until she surrendered to Germany in 1940). In one of history's great ironies, Stalin, who distrusted everyone, ignored British prime minister Winston Churchill's warnings and was caught completely off guard when Hitler occupied the Balkans and then launched his surprise attack against the Russians in June 1941. By November, lend-lease was extended to the Russians, who would receive a total of $11 billion by the end of the war.

The wartime coalition of the United States, Great Britain, and the USSR was an odd combination. Their common goal—defeat Hitler—temporarily submerged political differences. During the war the United States actually sided with Russia against Great Britain over the appropriate military strategy. Russia and the United States wanted a second front established in France.

As the military victory in Europe became clear, political differences began to crack open the alliance. A number of wartime conferences were held to coordinate military strategy; to establish political and economic international agencies, such as the United Nations and the World Bank; and to plan the reestablishment of governments in Eastern and Western Europe. Differences developed over the structure of the United Nations; the composition of the Polish and other Eastern European governments; and the boundaries, reparations, and occupational questions surrounding postwar Germany.

The military situation dominated the Yalta Conference in February 1945. Since the atomic bomb had not yet been tested, the United States thought that a landed invasion of the Japanese mainland would be necessary to win the war. At this time Russia and Japan were neutral toward each other. Stalin promised that three months after the war in Europe ended he would invade Japan. In return Roosevelt promised Stalin the territories and sphere of influence Russia held in Asia prior to 1905, which she had lost in a war with Japan.

Sole possession of the atomic bomb by the United States loomed in the background as the two powers failed to settle their differences after the war. Secretary of State James Byrnes hoped that the bomb would make the Russians more "manageable" in Europe, but atomic diplomacy was never really practiced. Nor were attempts at economic coercion successful.

By 1946 the cold war had begun. In February Stalin gave a speech declaring that communism and capitalism were incompatible and that future wars were inevitable. The next month, at a commencement address with President Truman at his side, Churchill declared that an "iron curtain" had descended over Eastern Europe. In May 1946 the allies refused to send any more industrial equipment to the Russian zone in Germany.

Who started the cold war? Was it inevitable, or should one side take more of the blame? In the following selection, Thomas G. Paterson argues that the Truman administration exaggerated the Soviet threat to world peace after World War II because the United States had its own expansionist, political, and economic global needs. In the second selection, John Lewis Gaddis asserts that the power vacuum that existed in Europe at the end of World War II exaggerated ideological, political, and economic differences and made a clash between the United States and the USSR almost inevitable.

Thomas G. Paterson

Harry S Truman, American Power, and the Soviet Threat

President Harry S Truman and his Secretary of State Dean Acheson, Henry A. Kissinger once remarked, "ushered in the most creative period in the history of American foreign policy." Presidents from Eisenhower to Reagan have exalted Truman for his decisiveness and success in launching the Truman Doctrine, the Marshall Plan, and NATO [North Atlantic Treaty Organization], and for staring the Soviets down in Berlin during those hair-trigger days of the blockade and airlift. John F. Kennedy and Lyndon B. Johnson invoked memories of Truman and the containment doctrine again and again to explain American intervention in Vietnam. Jimmy Carter has written in his memoirs that Truman had served as his model—that he studied Truman's career more than that of any other president and came to admire greatly his courage, honesty, and willingness "to be unpopular if he believed his actions were the best for the country." Some historians have gone so far as to claim that Truman saved humankind from World War III. On the other hand, he has drawn a diverse set of critics. The diplomat and analyst George F. Kennan, the journalist Walter Lippmann, the political scientist Hans Morgenthau, politicians of the left and right, like Henry A. Wallace and Robert A. Taft, and many historians have questioned Truman's penchant for his quick, simple answer, blunt, careless rhetoric, and facile analogies, his moralism that obscured the complexity of causation, his militarization of American foreign policy, his impatience with diplomacy itself, and his exaggeration of the Soviet threat. . . .

Because of America's unusual postwar power, the Truman Administration could expand the United States sphere of influence beyond the Western Hemisphere and also intervene to protect American interests. But this begs a key question: Why did President Truman think it necessary to project American power abroad, to pursue an activist, global foreign policy unprecedented in United States history? The answer has several parts. First, Americans drew lessons from their experience in the 1930s. While indulging in their so-called "isolationism," they had watched economic depression spawn political extremism, which in turn, produced aggression and war. Never again, they vowed. No more appeasement with totalitarians, no more Munichs. "Red Fascism" became a popular phrase to express this American idea. The message seemed evident: To

From Thomas G. Paterson, *Meeting the Communist Threat: Truman to Reagan* (Oxford University Press, 1988). Copyright © 1988 by Thomas G. Paterson. Reprinted by permission of Oxford University Press, Inc. Notes omitted.

prevent a reincarnation of the 1930s, the United States would have to use its vast power to fight economic instability abroad. Americans felt compelled to project their power, second, because they feared, in the peace-and-prosperity thinking of the time, economic doom stemming from an economic sickness abroad that might spread to the United States, and from American dependency on overseas supplies of raw materials. To aid Europeans and other people would not only help them, but also sustain a high American standard of living and gain political friends, as in the case of Italy, where American foreign aid and advice influenced national elections and brought defeat to the left. The American fear of postwar shortages of petroleum also encouraged the Truman Administration to penetrate Middle Eastern oil in a major way. In Saudi Arabia, for example, Americans built and operated the strategically important Dhahran Airport and dominated that nation's oil resources.

Another reason why Truman projected American power so boldly derived from new strategic thinking. Because of the advent of the air age, travel across the world was shortened in time. Strategists spoke of the shrinkage of the globe. Places once deemed beyond American curiosity or interest now loomed important. Airplanes could travel great distances to deliver bombs. Powerful as it was, then, the United States also appeared vulnerable, especially to air attack. As General Carl A. Spaatz emphasized: "As top dog, America becomes target No. 1." He went on to argue that fast aircraft left no warning time for the United States. "The Pearl Harbor of a future war might well be Chicago, or Detroit, or even Washington." To prevent such an occurrence, American leaders worked to acquire overseas bases in both the Pacific and Atlantic, thereby denying a potential enemy an attack route to the Western Hemisphere. Forward bases would also permit the United States to conduct offensive operations more effectively. The American strategic frontier had to be pushed outward. Thus the United States took the former Japanese-controlled Pacific islands of the Carolines, Marshalls, and Marianas, maintained garrisons in Germany and Japan, and sent military missions to Iran, Turkey, Greece, Saudi Arabia, China, and to fourteen Latin American states. The Joint Chiefs of Staff and Department of State lists of desired foreign bases, and of sites where air transit rights were sought, included such far-flung spots as Algeria, India, French Indochina, New Zealand, Iceland, and the Azores. When asked where the American Navy would float, Navy Secretary James Forrestal replied: "Wherever there is a sea." Today we may take the presumption of a global American presence for granted, but in Truman's day it was new, even radical thinking, especially after the "isolationist" 1930s.

These several explanations for American globalism suggest that the United States would have been an expansionist power whether or not the obstructionist Soviets were lurking about. That is, America's own needs—ideological, political, economic, strategic—encouraged such a projection of power. As the influential National Security Council Paper No. 68 (NSC-68) noted in April 1950, the "overall policy" of the United States was "designed to foster a world environment in which the American system can survive and flourish." This policy "we would probably pursue even if there were no Soviet threat."

Americans, of course, did perceive a Soviet threat. Thus we turn to yet another explanation for the United States' dramatic extension of power early in the Cold War: to contain the Soviets. The Soviets unsettled Americans in so many ways. Their harsh Communist dogma and propagandistic slogans were not only monotonous; they also seemed threatening because of their call for world revolution and for the demise of capitalism. In the United Nations the Soviets cast vetoes and even on occasion walked out of the organization. At international conferences their *"nyets"* stung American ears. When they negotiated, the Soviets annoyed their interlocuters by repeating the same point over and over again, delaying meetings, or abruptly shifting positions. Truman labeled them "pigheaded," and Dean Acheson thought them so coarse and insulting that he once allowed that they were not "housebroken."

The Soviet Union, moreover, had territorial ambitions, grabbing parts of Poland, Rumania, and Finland, and demanding parts of Turkey. In Eastern Europe, with their Red Army positioned to intimidate, the Soviets quickly manhandled the Poles and Rumanians. Communists in 1947 and 1948 seized power in Hungary and Czechoslovakia. Some Americans predicted that the Soviet military would roll across Western Europe. In general, Truman officials pictured the Soviet Union as an implaccable foe to an open world, an opportunistic nation that would probe for weak spots, exploit economic misery, snuff out individual freedom, and thwart self-determination. Americans thought the worst, some claiming that a Soviet-inspired international conspiracy insured perennial hostility and a creeping aggression aimed at American interests. To Truman and his advisers, the Soviets stood as the world's bully, and the very existence of this menacing bear necessitated an activist American foreign policy and an exertion of American power as a "counterforce."

But Truman officials exaggerated the Soviet threat, imagining an adversary that never measured up to the galloping monster so often depicted by alarmist Americans. Even if the Soviets intended to dominate the world, or just Western Europe, they lacked the capabilities to do so. The Soviets had no foreign aid to dispense; outside Russia Communist parties were minorities; the Soviet economy was seriously crippled by the war; and the Soviet military suffered significant weaknesses. The Soviets lacked a modern navy, a strategic air force, the atomic bomb, and air defenses. Their wrecked economy could not support or supply an army in the field for very long, and their technology was antiquated. Their ground forces lacked motorized transportation, adequate equipment, and troop morale. A Soviet *blitzkrieg* invasion of Western Europe had little chance of success and would have proven suicidal for the Soviets, for even if they managed to gain temporary control of Western Europe by a military thrust, they could not strike the United States. So they would have to assume defensive positions and await crushing American attacks, probably including atomic bombings of Soviet Russia itself—plans for which existed.

Other evidence also suggests that a Soviet military threat to Western Europe was more myth than reality. The Soviet Union demobilized its forces after the war, dropping to about 2.9 million personnel in 1948. Many of its 175 divisions were under-strength, and large numbers of them were engaged in occupation duties, resisting challenges to Soviet authority in Eastern Europe. American intelligence sources reported as well that the Soviets could not count on troops of the occupied countries, which were quite unreliable, if not rebellious. At most, the Soviets had 700,000 to 800,000 troops available for an attack against the West. To resist such an attack, the West had about 800,000 troops, or approximate parity. For these reasons, top American leaders did not expect a Soviet onslaught against Western Europe. They and their intelligence sources emphasized Soviet military and economic weaknesses, not strengths, Soviet hesitancy, not boldness.

Why then did Americans so fear the Soviets? Why did the Central Intelligence Agency, the Joint Chiefs of Staff, and the President exaggerate the Soviet threat? The first explanation is that their intelligence estimates were just that—estimates. The American intelligence community was still in a state of infancy, hardly the well-developed system it would become in the 1950s and 1960s. So Americans lacked complete assurance that their figures on Soviet force deployment or armaments were accurate or close to the mark. When leaders do not know, they tend to assume the worst of an adversary's intentions and capabilities, or to think that the Soviets might miscalculate, sparking a war they did not want. In a chaotic world, the conception of a single, inexorably aggressive adversary also brought a comforting sense of knowing and consistency.

Truman officials also exaggerated the Soviet threat in order "to extricate the United States from commitments and restraints that were no longer considered desirable." For example, they loudly chastised the Soviets for violating the Yalta agreements; yet Truman and his advisers knew the Yalta provisions were at best vague and open to differing interpretations. But, more, they purposefully misrepresented the Yalta agreement on the vital question of the composition of the Polish government. In so doing, they hoped to decrease the high degree of Communist participation that the Yalta conferees had insured when they stated that the new Polish regime would be formed by reorganizing the provisional Lublin (Communist) government. Through charges of Soviet malfeasance Washington sought to justify its own retreat from Yalta, such as its abandonment of the $20 billion reparations figure for Germany (half of which was supposed to go to the Soviet Union).

Another reason for the exaggeration: Truman liked things in black and white, as his aide Clark Clifford noted. Nuances, ambiguities, and counterevidence were often discounted to satisfy the President's preference for the simpler answer or his pre-conceived notions of Soviet aggressiveness. In mid-1946, for example, the Joint Chiefs of Staff deleted from a report to Truman a section that stressed Soviet weaknesses. American leaders also exaggerated the Soviet threat because it was useful in galvanizing and unifying American public opinion for an abandonment of recent and still lingering "isolationism" and support for an expansive foreign policy. Kennan quoted a colleague as saying that "if it [Soviet threat] had never existed, we would have had to invent it, to create a sense of urgency we need to bring us to the point of decisive action." The military particularly overplayed the Soviet threat in order to persuade Congress to endorse larger defense budgets. This happened in 1948–49 with the creation of the North Atlantic Treaty Organization. NATO was established not to halt a Soviet military attack, because none was anticipated, but to give Europeans a psychological boost—a "will to resist." American officials believed that the European Recovery Program would falter unless there was a "sense of security" to buttress it. They nurtured apprehension, too, that some European nations might lean toward neutralism unless they were brought together under a security umbrella. NATO also seemed essential to help members resist internal subversion. The exaggerated, popular view that NATO was formed to deter a Soviet invasion of Western Europe by conventional forces stems, in part, from Truman's faulty recollection in his published memoirs.

Still another explanation for why Americans exaggerated the Soviet threat is found in their attention since the Bolshevik Revolution of 1917 to the utopian Communist goal of world revolution, confusing goals with actual behavior. Thus Americans believed that the sinister Soviets and their Communist allies would exploit postwar economic, social, and political disorder, not through a direct military thrust, but rather through covert subversion. The recovery of Germany and Japan became necessary, then, to deny the Communists political opportunities to thwart American plans for the integration of these former enemies into an American system of trade and defense. And because economic instability troubled so much of Eurasia, Communist gains through subversion might deny the United States strategic raw materials.

Why dwell on this question of the American exaggeration of the Soviet threat? Because it over-simplified international realities by under-estimating local conditions that might thwart Soviet/Communist successes and by over-estimating the Soviet ability to act. Because it encouraged the Soviets to fear encirclement and to enlarge their military establishment, thereby contributing to a dangerous weapons race. Because it led to indiscriminate globalism. Because it put a damper on diplomacy; American officials were hesitant to negotiate with an opponent variously described as malevolent, deceitful, and inhuman. They especially did not warm to negotiations when some critics were ready to cry that diplomacy, which could produce compromises, was evidence in itself of softness toward Communism.

Exaggeration of the threat also led Americans to misinterpret events and in so doing to prompt the Soviets to make decisions contrary to American wishes. For example, the Soviet presence in Eastern Europe, once considered a simple question of the Soviets' building an iron curtain or bloc after the war, is now seen by historians in more complex terms. The Soviets did not seem to have a master plan for the region and followed different policies in different countries. Poland and Rumania were subjugated right away; Yugoslavia, on the other hand, was an independent Communist state led by Josip Tito, who broke dramatically with Stalin in 1948; Hungary conducted elections in the fall of 1945 (the Communists got only 17 percent of the vote) and did not suffer a Communist coup until 1947; in Czechoslovakia, free elections in May 1946 produced a non-Communist government that functioned until 1948; Finland, although under Soviet scrutiny, affirmed its independence. The Soviets did not have a firm grip on Eastern Europe before 1948—a prime reason why many American leaders believed the Soviets harbored weaknesses.

American policies were designed to roll the Soviets back. The United States reconstruction loan policy, encouragement of dissident groups, and appeal for free elections alarmed Moscow, contributing to a Soviet push to secure the area. The issue of free elections illustrates the point. Such a call was consistent with cherished American principle. But in the context of Eastern Europe and the Cold War, problems arose. First, Americans conspicuously followed a double standard which foreigners noted time and again; that is, if the principle of free elections really mattered, why not hold such elections in the United States' sphere of influence in Latin America, where an unsavory lot of dictators ruled? Second, free elections would have produced victories for anti-Soviet groups. Such results could only unsettle the Soviets and invite them to intervene to protect their interests in neighboring states—just as the United States had intervened in Cuba and Mexico in the twentieth century when hostile groups assumed power. In Hungary, for example, it was the non-Communist leader Ferenc Nagy who delayed elections in late 1946 because he knew the Communist Party would lose badly, thereby possibly triggering a repressive Soviet response. And, third, the United States had so little influence in Eastern Europe that it had no way of insuring free elections—no way of backing up its demands with power.

Walter Lippmann, among others, thought that the United States should tame its meddling in the region and make the best out of a bad arrangement of power. "I do believe," he said in 1947, "we shall have to recognize the principle of boundaries of spheres of influence which either side will not cross and have to proceed on the old principle that a good fence makes good neighbors." Kennan shared this view, as did one State Department official who argued that the United States was incapable of becoming a successful watchdog in Eastern Europe. American "barkings, growlings, snappings, and occasional bitings," Cloyce K. Huston prophesized, would only irritate the Soviets without reducing their power. Better still, argued some analysts, if the United States tempered its ventures into European affairs, then the Soviets, surely less alarmed, might tolerate more openness. But the United States did not stay out. Americans tried to project their power into a region where they had little chance of succeeding, but had substantial opportunity to irritate and alarm the always suspicious Soviets. In this way, it has been suggested, the United States itself helped pull down the iron curtain.

Another example of the exaggeration of the Soviet threat at work is found in the Truman Doctrine of 1947. Greece was beset by civil war, and the British could no longer fund a war against Communist-led insurgents who had a considerable non-Communist following. On March 12, Truman enunciated a universal doctrine: It "must be the policy of the United States to support free peoples who are resisting attempted subjugation by armed minorities or by outside pressures." Although he never mentioned the Soviet Union by name, his juxtaposition of words like "democratic" and "totalitarian" and his references to Eastern Europe made the menace to Greece appear to be the Soviets. But there was and is no evidence of Soviet involvement in the Greek civil war. In fact, the Soviets had urged both the Greek Communists and their allies the Yugoslavs to stop the fighting for fear that the conflict would draw the United States into the Mediterranean. And the Greek Communists were strong nationalists. The United States nonetheless intervened in a major way in Greek affairs, becoming responsible for right-wing repression and a military establishment that plagued Greek politics through much of its postwar history. As for Turkey, official Washington did not expect the Soviet Union to strike militarily against that bordering nation. The Soviets were too weak in 1947 to undertake such a major operation, and they were asking for joint control of the Dardanelles largely for defense, for security. Then why did the President, in the Truman Doctrine speech, suggest that Turkey was imminently threatened? American strategists worried that Russia's long-term objective was the subjugation of its neighbor. But they also wished to exploit an opportunity to enhance the American military position in the Mediterranean region and in a state bordering the Soviet Union. The Greek crisis and the Truman Doctrine speech provided an appropriate environment to build up an American military presence in the Eastern Mediterranean for use against the Soviets should the unwanted war ever come.

Truman's alarmist language further fixed the mistaken idea in the American mind that the Soviets were unrelenting aggressors intent upon undermining peace, and that the United States, almost alone, had to meet them everywhere. Truman's exaggerations and his commitment to the containment doctrine did not go unchallenged. Secretary Marshall himself was startled by the President's muscular anti-communist rhetoric, and he questioned the wisdom of overstating the case. The Soviet specialist Llewellyn Thompson urged "caution" in swinging too far toward "outright opposition to Russia...." Walter Lippmann, in reacting to both Truman's speech and George F. Kennan's now famous "Mr. 'X' " article in the July 1947 issue of the journal *Foreign Affairs,* labeled containment a "strategic monstrosity," because it made no distinctions between important or vital and not-so-important or peripheral areas. Because American power was not omnipresent, Lippmann further argued, the "policy can be implemented only by recruiting, subsidizing and supporting a heterogeneous array of satellites, clients, dependents and puppets." He also criticized the containment doctrine for placing more emphasis on confrontation than on diplomacy.

Truman himself came to see that there were dangers in stating imprecise, universal doctrines. He became boxed by his own rhetoric. When Mao Zedong's forces claimed victory in 1949 over Jiang's regime, conservative Republicans, angry Democrats, and various McCarthyites pilloried the President for letting China "fall." China lost itself, he retorted. But his critics pressed the point: if containment was to be applied everywhere, as the President had said in the Truman Doctrine, why not China? Truman appeared inconsistent, when, in fact, in the case of China, he was ultimately prudent in cutting American losses where the United States proved incapable of reaching its goals. Unable to disarm his detractors on this issue, Truman stood vulnerable in the early 1950s to political demagogues who fueled McCarthyism. The long-term consequences in this example have been grave. Democrats believed they could never lose "another China"—never permit Communists or Marxists, whether or not linked to Moscow, to assume power abroad. President John F. Kennedy later said, for example, that he could not withdraw from Vietnam because that might be perceived as "another China" and spark charges that he was soft on Communism. America, in fact, could not bring itself to open diplomatic relations with the People's Republic of China until 1979.

Jiang's collapse joined the Soviet explosion of an atomic bomb, the formation of the German Democratic Republic (East Germany), and the Sino-Soviet Friendship Treaty to arouse American feeling in late 1949 and early 1950 that the Soviet threat had dramatically escalated. Although Kennan told his State Department colleagues that such feeling was "largely of our own making" rather than an accurate accounting of Soviet actions, the composers of NSC-68 preferred to dwell on a more dangerous Soviet menace in extreme rhetoric not usually found in a secret report. But because the April 1950 document was aimed at President Truman, we can certainly understand why its language was hyperbolic. The fanatical and militant Soviets, concluded NSC-68, were seeking to impose "absolute authority over the rest of the world." America had to frustrate the global "design" of the "evil men" of the Kremlin, who were unrelentingly bent on "piecemeal aggression" against the "free world" through military force, infiltration, and intimidation. The report called for a huge American and allied military build-up and nuclear arms development.

NSC-68, most scholars agree, was a flawed, even amateurish document. It assumed a Communist monolith that did not exist, drew alarmist conclusions based upon vague and inaccurate information about Soviet capabilities, made grand, unsubstantiated claims about Soviet intentions, glossed over the presence of many non-democratic countries in the "free world," and recommended against negotiations with Moscow at the very time the Soviets were advancing toward a policy of "peaceful co-existence." One State Department expert on the Soviet Union, Charles E. Bohlen, although generally happy with the report's conclusions, faulted NSC-68 for assuming a Soviet plot for world conquest—for "oversimplifying the problem." No, he advised, the Soviets sought foremostly to maintain their regime and to extend it abroad "to the degree that is possible without serious risk to the internal regime." In short, there were limits to Soviet behavior. But few were listening to such cautionary voices. NSC-68 became American dogma, especially when the outbreak of the Korean War in June of 1950 sanctified it as a prophetic "we told you so."

The story of Truman's foreign policy is basically an accounting of how the United States, because of its own expansionism and exaggeration of the Soviet threat, became a global power. Truman projected American power after the Second World War to rehabilitate Western Europe, secure new allies, guarantee strategic and economic links, and block Communist or Soviet influence. He firmly implanted the image of the Soviets as relentless, worldwide transgressors with whom it is futile to negotiate. Through his exaggeration of the Soviet threat, Truman made it very likely that the United States would continue to practice global interventionism years after he left the White House.

John Lewis Gaddis   ◄ **NO**

The Origins of the Cold War: 1945–1953

It is, of course, a truism that coalitions tend not to survive their enemies' defeat. Certainly during World War II most observers of the international scene had expected differences eventually to arise among the victors. The hope had been, though, that a sufficiently strong framework of common interests—whether the United Nations or some mutually acceptable agreement on spheres of influence—would develop that could keep these differences within reasonable limits. This did not happen. Although both sides sought security, although neither side wanted a new war, disagreements over how to achieve those goals proved too great to overcome. With a rapidity that dismayed policymakers in both Washington and Moscow, allies shortly before united against the Axis found themselves in a confrontation with each other that would determine the shape of the postwar era. Russian-American relations, once a problem of rarely more than peripheral concern for the two countries involved, now became an object of rapt attention and anxiety for the entire world.

⋘◉⋙

It is no simple matter to explain how national leaders in the United States and the Soviet Union came to hold such dissimilar concepts of postwar security. There did exist, in the history of the two countries' encounters with one another, an ample basis for mutual distrust. But there were also strong motives for cooperation, not the least of which was that, had they been able to act in concert, Russians and Americans might have achieved something close to absolute security in an insecure world. Their failure to do so may be attributed, ultimately, to irreconcilable differences in four critical areas: perceptions of history, ideology, technology, and personality.

Clearly the divergent historical experiences of the two countries conditioned their respective views of how best to attain security. The Russians tended to think of security in terms of space—not a surprising attitude, considering the frequency with which their country had been invaded, or the way in which they had used distance to defeat their adversaries. That such a concept might be outmoded in an age of atomic weapons and long-range bombers appears not to

From John Lewis Gaddis, *Russia, the Soviet Union, and the United States: An Interpretive History,* 2d ed. (McGraw-Hill, 1990). Copyright © 1990 by The McGraw-Hill Companies. Reprinted by permission. Notes omitted.

have occurred to Stalin; Hitler's defeat brought no alteration in his determination to control as much territory along the periphery of the Soviet Union as possible. "He regarded as sure only whatever he held in his fist," the Yugoslav Communist Milovan Djilas has written. "Everything beyond the control of his police was a potential enemy."

Americans, on the other hand, tended to see security in institutional terms: conditioned by their own atypical historical experience, they assumed that if representative governments could be established as widely as possible, together with a collective security organization capable of resolving differences between them, peace would be assured. That such governments might not always harbor peaceful intentions toward their neighbors, that the United Nations, in the absence of great power agreement, might lack the means of settling disputes, occurred to only a few informed observers. The general public, upon whose support foreign policy ultimately depended, tended to accept Cordell Hull's vision of a postwar world in which "there will no longer be need for spheres of influence, for alliances, for balance of power, or any of the special arrangements through which, in the unhappy past, the nations sought to safeguard their security or to promote their interests."

There was, of course, room for compromising these conflicting viewpoints. Neither the United States nor its British ally had been prepared wholly to abandon spheres of influence as a means of achieving their own postwar security; both accepted the premise that the USSR was entitled to have friendly countries along its borders. The great difficulty was that, unlike the expansion of American and British influence into Western Europe and the Mediterranean, the Soviet Union's gains took place without the approval of most of the governments and most of the people in the areas involved. The Anglo-Americans simply did not find it necessary, in the same measure as did the Russians, to ensure their own security by depriving people within their sphere of influence of the right to self-determination. Given Western convictions that only the diffusion of democratic institutions could guarantee peace, given Hitler's all-too-vivid precedent, Moscow's imposition of influence in Eastern Europe seemed ominous, whatever its motives. Stalin found himself able to implement his vision of security only by appearing to violate that of the West. The result was to create for the Soviet Union new sources of hostility and, ultimately, insecurity in the world.

Ideological differences constituted a second source of antagonism. Stalin had deliberately downplayed the Soviet commitment to communism during the war, even to the point of abolishing the Comintern in 1943. Some Americans concluded that the Russians had abandoned that ideology altogether, if on no other grounds than that a nation that fought Germans so effectively could not be all bad. The European communist movement remained very much the instrument of Soviet policy, however, and the Russians used it to facilitate their projection of influence into Eastern Europe. This development raised fears in the West that Soviet collaboration against the Axis had been nothing but a marriage of convenience and that, victory having been achieved, the Kremlin was now embarking upon a renewed crusade for world revolution.

This was, it now appears, a mistaken view. Stalin had always placed the security of the Soviet state above the interests of international communism; it had been the former, not the latter, that had motivated his expansion into Eastern Europe. Far from encouraging communists outside the Soviet Union to seize power, Stalin initially advised restraint, especially in his dealings with such movements in France, Italy, Greece, and China. But the Soviet leader's caution was not all that clear in the West. Faced with the sudden intrusion of Russian power into Europe, faced with a revival of anticapitalist rhetoric among communists throughout the world, faced with painful evidence from the recent past of what happened when dictators' rhetoric was not taken seriously, observers in both Western Europe and the United States jumped to the conclusion that Stalin, like Hitler, had insatiable ambitions, and would not stop until contained.

Technological differences created a third source of tension. The United States alone emerged from World War II with an industrial plant superior to what it had possessed before that conflict started; the Soviet Union, in turn, had come out of the war with its land ravaged, much of its industry destroyed, and some twenty million of its citizens dead. The resulting disparity of power caused some Americans to exaggerate their ability to influence events in the rest of the world; it simultaneously produced in the Russians deep feelings of inferiority and vulnerability.

This problem manifested itself most obviously with regard to reconstruction. Stalin had hoped to repair war damage with the help of Lend-Lease and a postwar loan from the United States; his conviction that Americans would soon be facing a postwar depression led him to believe—drawing on clear Leninist principles—that Washington would have no choice but to provide such aid as a means of generating foreign markets for surplus products. His surprise was great when the United States passed up the economic benefits it would have derived from granting a loan in favor of the political concessions it hoped to obtain by withholding it. Nor would Washington allow the use of Lend-Lease for reconstruction; to compound the offense, the Truman administration also cut off, in 1946, the flow of reparations from the American zone in Germany. Whether more generous policies on these matters would have produced better relations with the Soviet Union is impossible to prove—certainly the Russians were never in such need of aid as to be willing to make major political concessions in order to get it. There is no doubt, though, that they bitterly resented their exclusion from these "fruits" of Western technology.

Another "fruit" of Western technology that impressed the Russians was, of course, the atomic bomb. Although Soviet leaders carefully avoided signs of concern about this new weapon, they did secretly accelerate their own bomb development project while simultaneously calling for the abolition of all such weapons of mass destruction. After much debate within the government, the United States, in the summer of 1946, proposed the Baruch Plan, which would have transferred control of all fissionable materials to the United Nations. In fact, however, neither the Russians nor the Americans had sufficient faith in the world organization to entrust their security completely to it. Washington at no point was willing to surrender its bombs until the control system had gone into effect, while Moscow was unwilling to accept the inspection provisions which would allow the plan to operate. Both sides had concluded by 1947 that they would find greater security in an arms race than in an unproven system of international control.

Finally, accidents of personality made it more difficult than it might otherwise have been to achieve a mutually agreeable settlement. The Russians perceived in the transition from Roosevelt to Truman an abrupt shift from an attitude of cooperation to one of confrontation. "The policy pursued by the US ruling circles after the death of Franklin D. Roosevelt," the official history of Soviet foreign policy asserts, "amounted to renunciation of dependable and mutually beneficial cooperation with the Soviet Union, a cooperation that was so effective... in the period of joint struggle against the nazi aggressors." In fact, though, Roosevelt's policy had been firmer than Stalin realized; Truman's was not as uncompromising as his rhetoric suggested. What was different was style: where Roosevelt had sought to woo the Soviet leader by meeting his demands wherever possible, the new chief executive, like a good poker player, tried to deal from positions of rhetorical, if not actual, strength. His tough talk was designed to facilitate, not impede, negotiations—any appearance of weakness, he thought, would only encourage the Russians to ask for more.

What Truman failed to take into account was the possibility that Stalin might also be bluffing. Given the history of Western intervention to crush Bolshevism, given the Soviet Union's ruined economy and weakened population, and given the atomic bomb's unexpected confirmation of American technological superiority, it seems likely that the aging Soviet dictator was as frightened of the West as the West was of him. Truman's tough rhetoric, together with Hiroshima's example, may well have reinforced Stalin's conviction that if *he* showed any signs of weakness, all would be lost. Both leaders had learned too well the lesson of the 1930s: that appeasement never pays. Prospects for an amicable resolution of differences suffered accordingly.

There was nothing in this set of circumstances that made the Cold War inevitable—few things ever are inevitable in history. But a situation such as existed in Europe in 1945, with two great powers separated only by a power vacuum, seemed almost predestined to produce hostility, whether either side willed it or not. As a result, the United States, the Soviet Union, and much of the rest of the world as well would have to suffer through that prolonged period of insecurity that observers at the time, and historians since, have called the "Cold War."

━━━◆◆◆━━━

The evolution of United States policy toward the Soviet Union between 1945 and 1947 can be seen as a three-stage process of relating national interests to national capabilities. From V-J Day through early 1946, there existed genuine confusion in Washington as to both Soviet intentions and appropriate methods for dealing with them. Coordination between power and policy was, as a result, minimal. By the spring of 1946, a consensus had developed favoring resistance to further Soviet expansion, but little had been done to determine what resources would be necessary to accomplish that goal or to differentiate between areas of primary and secondary concern. It was not until 1947 that there began to emerge an approach to the Soviet Union that bore some reasonable relationship to American capabilities for projecting influence in the world.

There appeared to be no lack of power available to the United States for the purpose of ordering the postwar environment as it saw fit, but the task of transforming technological superiority into political influence proved frustratingly difficult. Secretary of State James F. Byrnes had hoped to trade reconstruction assistance and a commitment to the international control of atomic energy for Soviet concessions on such outstanding issues as implementation of the Yalta Declaration on Liberated Europe, peace treaties with former German satellites, and, ultimately, a final resolution of the German question itself. But the Russians maintained a posture of ostentatious unconcern about the atomic bomb, nor would they yield on significant issues to obtain reconstruction assistance. Congressional skepticism about Moscow's intentions ensured that any loan would carry a political price far beyond what the Russians would willingly pay, while public opinion pushed Truman into a decision to seek United Nations control of atomic energy before Byrnes had made any attempt to extract Soviet concessions in return. Economic and technological superiority thus won the United States surprisingly few practical benefits in its early postwar dealings with the USSR.

In Washington, moreover, there still existed a substantial number of officials who viewed Soviet hostility as the product of misunderstandings and who expected that, with restraint on both sides, a mutually satisfactory resolution of differences might still occur. It is significant that as late as November, 1945, a State Department representative could rebuke the Joint Chiefs of Staff for confidentially suggesting that the wartime alliance might not survive victory. "We must always bear in mind," a Department memorandum noted the following month, "that because of the differences between the economic and political systems [of the United States and the Soviet Union], the conduct of our relations requires more patience and diligence than with other countries." Despite his tough rhetoric, President Truman shared this view. Disagreements with the Russians were to be expected once the common bond of military necessity had been removed, he told his advisers; in time, they would disappear because "Stalin was a fine man who wanted to do the right thing."

But events made this position increasingly difficult to sustain. The Russians remained adamant in their determination to exclude Western influence from Eastern Europe and the Balkans, while a continued Soviet presence in Iran and Manchuria raised fears that Moscow might try to impose control over those territories as well. Russian interest in the eastern Mediterranean seemed to be growing, with demands for trusteeships over former Italian colonies, boundary rectifications at Turkey's expense, and a revision of the Montreux Convention governing passage through the Dardanelles. And in February, 1946, news of Soviet atomic espionage became public for the first time with the revelation that the Canadian government had arrested a group of Russian agents for trying to steal information about the bomb. That same month, Stalin in his first major postwar foreign policy speech stressed the incompatibility between communism and capitalism, implying that future wars were inevitable until the world economic system was restructured along Soviet lines.

It was at this point that there arrived at the State Department a dispatch from George F. Kennan, now *chargé d'affaires* at the American embassy in Moscow, which did much to clarify official thinking regarding Soviet behavior. Russian hostility toward the West, Kennan argued, stemmed chiefly from the internal necessities of the Stalinist regime: the Soviet dictator required a hostile outside world in order to justify his own autocratic rule. Marxism provided Soviet leaders with

> justification for their instinctive fear of the outside world, for the dictatorship without which they did not know how to rule, for cruelties they did not dare not to inflict, for sacrifices they felt bound to demand.... Today they cannot dispense with it. It is the fig leaf of their moral and intellectual respectability.

It followed that Stalin was, by nature, incapable of being reassured. "Nothing short of complete disarmament, delivery of our air and naval forces to Russia and resigning of the powers of government to American Communists would even dent this problem," Kennan noted in a subsequent dispatch, "and even then Moscow would smell a trap and would continue to harbor the most baleful misgivings." The solution, Kennan suggested, was to strengthen Western institutions in order to render them invulnerable to the Soviet challenge while simultaneously awaiting the eventual mellowing of the Soviet regime.

There was little in Kennan's analysis that he and other career Soviet experts had not been saying for some time. What was new was Washington's receptivity to the message, a condition brought about both by frustration over Soviet behavior and by growing public and Congressional resistance to further concessions. In contrast to its earlier optimism about relations with Moscow, the State Department now endorsed Kennan's analysis as "the most probable explanation of present Soviet policies and attitudes." The United States, it concluded, should demonstrate to the Kremlin, "in the first instance by diplomatic means and in the last analysis by military force if necessary that the present course of its foreign policy can only lead to disaster for the Soviet Union."

The spring and summer of 1946 did see a noticeable toughening of United States policy toward the Soviet Union. In early March, Truman lent public sanction to Winston Churchill's strongly anti-Soviet "iron curtain" speech by appearing on the platform with him at Fulton, Missouri. That same month, Secretary of State Byrnes insisted on placing the issue of Iran before the United Nations, even after the Russians had agreed to withdraw their troops from that country. The termination of German reparations shipments came in May; three months later, Byrnes publicly committed the United States to support German rehabilitation, with or without the Russians. In July, Truman endorsed the continued presence of American troops in southern Korea on the grounds that that country constituted "an ideological battleground upon which our whole success in Asia may depend." Soviet pressure on Turkey for bases produced a decision in August to maintain an American naval force indefinitely in the eastern Mediterranean. In September, White House aide Clark Clifford submitted a report to the president, prepared after consultation with top military and diplomatic advisers, arguing that "this government should be prepared... to resist vigorously and successfully any efforts of the U.S.S.R. to expand into areas vital to American security."

But these policies were decided upon without precise assessments as to whether the means existed to carry them out. The atomic bomb was of little use for such purposes, given the strong inhibitions American officials felt about brandishing their new weapon in peacetime and given the limited number of bombs and properly equipped bombers available, if war came. Nor could the administration hold out the prospect of economic aid as a means of inducing more cooperative Soviet behavior, in the face of continued Congressional reluctance to appropriate funds for such purposes. Such conventional military power as the United States possessed was rapidly melting away under the pressures of demobilization, and although most Americans supported firmer policies toward the Soviet Union, the election of an economy-minded, Republican-controlled Congress in November suggested that few were prepared to assume the burdens, in the form of high taxes and military manpower levels, such policies would require.

Shortly thereafter a severe economic crisis, the product of remaining wartime dislocations and an unusually harsh winter, hit Western Europe. This development caused the British to announce their intention, in February, 1947, of terminating economic and military aid to Greece and Turkey, countries that had, up to that point, been regarded as within London's sphere of responsibility. It also raised the longer-range but even more frightening prospect that economic conditions in Western Europe generally might deteriorate to the point that communist parties there could seize power through coups or even free elections. Suddenly the whole European balance of power, which the United States had gone to war to restore, seemed once again in peril.

This situation, which appeared so to threaten European stability, was one the Russians had done little if anything to instigate; it was rather the product primarily of internal conditions within the countries involved. But there was little doubt of Moscow's ability to exploit the European economic crisis if nothing was done to alleviate it. And action was taken, with such energy and dispatch that the fifteen weeks between late February and early June, 1947, have come to be regarded as a great moment in the history of American diplomacy, a rare instance in which "the government of the United States operat[ed] at its very finest, efficiently and effectively."

Such plaudits may be too generous. Certainly the language Truman used to justify aid to Greece and Turkey ("at the present moment in world history nearly every nation must choose between alternative ways of life.... I believe that it must be the policy of the United States to support free peoples who are resisting attempted subjugation by armed minorities or by outside pressures") represented a projection of rhetoric far beyond either the administration's intentions or capabilities. Whatever its usefulness in prying funds out of a parsimonious Congress, the sweeping language of the "Truman Doctrine" would cause problems later on as the president and his foreign policy advisers sought to clarify distinctions between vital and peripheral interests in the world. That such distinctions were important became apparent with the announcement in June, 1947, of the Marshall Plan, an ambitious initiative that reflected, far more than did the Truman Doctrine, the careful calibration of ends to means characteristic of the administration's policy during this period.

The European Recovery Program, to use its official title, proposed spending some $17 billion for economic assistance to the non-communist nations of Europe over the next four years. (Aid was offered to the Soviet Union and its East European satellites as well, but with the expectation, which proved to be correct, that Moscow would turn it down.) It was a plan directed, not against Soviet military attack, a contingency United States officials considered remote, but against the economic malaise that had sapped self-confidence among European allies, rendering them vulnerable to internal communist takeovers. It involved no direct military commitments; rather, its architects assumed, much as had advocates of the "arsenal of democracy" concept before World War II, that the United States could most efficiently help restore the balance of power in Europe by contributing its technology and raw materials, but not its manpower. It represented a deliberate decision to focus American energies on the recovery of Europe at the expense of commitments elsewhere: it is significant that the spring of 1947 also saw the Truman administration move toward liquidating its remaining responsibilities in China and Korea. What took place in Washington during the famous "fifteen weeks," then, was not so much a proliferation of commitments as a reordering of priorities, executed with a sharp awareness of what the United States would have to accept in the world and what, given limited resources, it could realistically expect to change.

Unfortunately, rhetoric again obscured the point, this time by way of a mysterious article, entitled "The Sources of Soviet Conduct," which appeared in the July, 1947, issue of *Foreign Affairs*. Attributed only to a "Mr. X," it advanced the notion that

> the main element of any United States policy toward the Soviet Union must be that of a long-term, patient but firm and vigilant containment of Russian expansive tendencies.... Soviet pressure against the free institutions of the Western world is something that can be contained by the adroit and vigilant application of counter-force at a series of constantly shifting geographical and political points, corresponding to the shifts and maneuvers of Soviet policy.

Then, as now, nothing remained secret for very long, and word soon leaked out that "Mr. X" had been none other than Kennan, who had recently become head of the State Department's new Policy Planning Staff. This information gave the "X" article something of the character of an official document, and it quickly came to be seen as the definitive expression of administration policy toward the Soviet Union.

In fact, Kennan had not intended his article as a comprehensive prescription for future action; it was, rather, an elaboration of the analysis of Soviet behavior he had submitted in his February, 1946, telegram to the State Department. Such policy recommendations as Kennan did include reflected only in the most approximate and incomplete way the range of his thinking on Soviet-American relations. The article implied an automatic commitment to resist Russian expansionism wherever it occurred; there was in it little sense of the administration's preoccupation with limited means and of the consequent need to distinguish between primary and secondary interests. Nor did the piece make it clear that economic rather than military methods were to be employed as the chief instrument of containment. The safest generalization that can be made about the "X" article is that, like the Truman Doctrine, it was an outstanding demonstration of the obfuscatory potential of imprecise prose. It was not an accurate description of the policies the United States was, at that moment, in the process of implementing.

Kennan provided a much clearer explanation of what he meant by "containment" in a secret review of the world situation prepared for Secretary of State George C. Marshall in November, 1947. Soviet efforts to fill power vacuums left by German and Japanese defeats had largely been halted, Kennan argued, but this accomplishment had dangerously strained American resources: "The program of aid to Europe which we are now proposing to undertake will probably be the last major effort of this nature which our people could, or should, make.... It is clearly unwise for us to continue the attempt to carry alone, or largely singlehanded, the opposition to Soviet expansion." Further dispersal of resources could be avoided only by identifying clearly those parts of the world upon whose defense American security depended. Aside from the Western Hemisphere, Kennan's list included only non-communist Europe, the Middle East, and Japan. In China there was little the West could do, although there were as well "definite limitations on both the military and economic capabilities of the Russians in that area." Since Korea was "not of decisive strategic importance to us, our main task is to extricate ourselves without too great a loss of prestige." All in all, Kennan concluded, "our best answer is to strengthen in every way local forces of resistance, and persuade others to bear a greater part of the burden of opposing communism."

"Containment," then, involved no indiscriminate projection of commitments around the world: it was, instead, a policy precise in its identification of American interests, specific in its assessment of threats to those interests, frugal in its calculation of means required to ward off those threats, vague only in its public presentation. But this very vagueness would, in time, corrupt the concept, for where gaps between policy and rhetoric exist, it is often easier to bring the former into line with the latter than the other way around. The eventual consequence would be the promulgation of policies under the rubric of "containment" far removed from what that doctrine had been originally intended to mean.

⋅❀⋅

Despite its limited character, the vigor of the American response to Soviet post-war probes apparently caught Stalin by surprise. His response was to try to strengthen further the security of his own regime; first by increasing safeguards against Western influences inside the Soviet Union; second, by tightening control over Russia's East European satellites; and finally by working to ensure central direction of the international communist movement. By a perverse kind of logic, each of these moves backfired, as did a much earlier Soviet initiative whose existence only came to light at this point—the establishment, in the United States during the 1930s, of a major espionage network directed from Moscow. The result, in each of these cases, was to produce consequences that only made it more difficult for Stalin to obtain the kind of security he sought.

Soviet leaders had always faced a dilemma regarding contacts with the West. Such associations might carry substantial benefits—certainly this had been true of collaboration with Great Britain and the United States during World War II. But there were also costs, not the least of which was the possibility that prolonged exposure to Western ideas and institutions might erode the still vulnerable base of the Soviet regime. It is an indication of the seriousness with which Stalin viewed this problem that he shipped hundreds of thousands of returning prisoners-of-war off to labor camps in 1945, much to the horror of Americans who had forcibly repatriated many of them at the Russians' request. By 1947, Moscow's campaign against Western influence had extended to literature, music, history, economics, and even genetics. As a result, Soviet prestige suffered throughout the world; the effect of these policies on science, and, in turn, on the advancement of Russian military capabilities, can only be guessed at.

Even more striking in its impact on the West, though, was Stalin's harsh effort to consolidate his control over Eastern Europe. Subservience to Moscow, not ideological uniformity, had been the chief Soviet priority in that area until 1947, but in June of that year the Russians imposed a communist-dominated government in Hungary, a country in which relatively free elections had been held in the fall of 1945. "I think it's an outrage," President Truman told a press conference on June 5. "The Hungarian situation is a terrible one." In February, 1948, the Communist Party of Czechoslovakia overthrew the duly-constituted government of that country—an event that produced the death, by either murder or suicide, of the popular Czech foreign minister, Jan Masaryk. It would be difficult to exaggerate the impact of this development in the West, where guilty consciences still existed over what had been done to the Czechs at Munich ten years before. One immediate effect was to ensure Congressional passage of the Marshall Plan; another was to provoke Britain, France, and the Benelux countries into forming the Western Union, the first step toward a joint defensive alliance among the non-communist nations of Europe. There also followed the stimulation of something approaching a war scare in the United States, an administration request for Universal Military Training and the reinstitution of the draft, and a public condemnation by Truman of the Soviet Union as the "one nation [that] has not only refused to cooperate in the establishment of a just and honorable peace, but—even worse—has actively sought to prevent it."

Meanwhile, attempts to resolve the question of divided Germany had produced no results, despite protracted and tedious negotiations. In February, 1948, the three Western occupying powers, plus the Benelux countries, met in London and decided to move toward formation of an independent West German state. Stalin's response, after initial hesitation, was to impose a blockade on land access to Berlin, which the World War II settlement had left a hundred miles inside the Soviet zone. The Berlin crisis brought the United States and the Soviet Union as close to war as they would come during the early postwar years. Truman was determined that Western forces would stay in the beleaguered city, however untenable their military position there, and to reinforce this policy he ostentatiously transferred to British bases three squadrons of B-29 bombers. No atomic bombs accompanied these planes, nor were they even equipped to carry them. But this visible reminder of American nuclear superiority may well have deterred the Russians from interfering with air access to Berlin, and through this means the United States and its allies were able to keep their sectors of the city supplied for almost a year. Stalin finally agreed to lift the blockade in May, 1949, but not before repeating the dubious distinction he had achieved in the Russo-Finnish War a decade earlier: of appearing to be brutal and incompetent at the same time.

The Berlin blockade had two important consequences, both of which were detrimental from the Soviet point of view. It provided the impetus necessary to transform the Western Union into the North Atlantic Treaty Organization, a defensive alliance linking the United States, Canada, and ten Western European nations, established in April, 1949. Simultaneously, the blockade lessened prospects for a settlement of the German problem in collaboration with the Russians; the result was to accelerate implementation of the London program, a goal accomplished with the formation, in September, 1949, of the Federal Republic of Germany.

POSTSCRIPT

Was the United States Responsible for the Cold War?

Paterson's selection contains most of the arguments advanced by the revisionist critics of America's cold war policies: Truman's diplomatic style was blunt and impetuous, and he tended to oversimplify complex issues into black and white alternatives.

Paterson believes that the Truman administration exaggerated the Russian threat to the balance of power in Europe. It is not clear whether this was a deliberate miscalculation or whether the Truman administration misperceived the motive behind the "iron curtain" that Russia drew around Eastern Europe. The author maintains that Stalin was more concerned with Russia's security needs than with world conquest.

Gaddis is much less critical than Paterson of America's postwar policy. He believes that the United States and Russia would inevitably clash once the common enemy—Hitler—was defeated because the two countries had fundamentally different political and economic systems. Gaddis maintains that for nearly two years there was confusion and uncertainty in the United States' foreign policy in Europe. Truman, he says, did not reverse Roosevelt's policy. His manner was more blunt and, consequently, he showed less patience in dealing with Stalin.

Gaddis acknowledges revisionist criticisms that the Americans misperceived Stalin's attempts to control Eastern Europe. The Soviet premier used expansionist rhetoric when he was primarily concerned about protecting Russia from another invasion. By early 1946 both sides were pursuing policies that would lead to an impasse.

Students who wish to study the cold war in greater detail should consult *Containment: Documents on American Policy and Strategy, 1945–1950* edited by Thomas H. Etzold and John Lewis Gaddis (Columbia University Press, 1978), which remains the best collection of the major policy documents. Another sophisticated but comprehensive work is Melvyn P. Leffler, *A Preponderance of Power: National Security, the Truman Administration, and the Cold War* (Stanford University Press, 1992). The two best readers to excerpt the various viewpoints on the cold war are Thomas G. Paterson and Robert J. McMahon, eds., *The Origins of the Cold War*, 3rd ed. (D. C. Heath, 1991) and Melvyn P. Leffler and David S. Painter, eds., *Origins of the Cold War: An International History* (Routledge, 1994). Finally, David Reynolds has edited a series of essays in *The Origins of the Cold War: International Perspectives* (Yale University Press, 1994).

ISSUE 13

Did the Civil Rights Movement Improve Race Relations in the United States?

YES: Robert Weisbrot, from *Freedom Bound: A History of America's Civil Rights Movement* (Plume Books, 1990)

NO: Tom Wicker, from *Tragic Failure: Racial Integration in America* (William Morrow, 1996)

ISSUE SUMMARY

YES: Professor of history Robert Weisbrot describes the lasting achievements produced by the civil rights movement in the realm of school desegregation, access to public accommodations, the protection of voting rights for African Americans, and the deepening commitment to racial harmony.

NO: Political journalist Tom Wicker recognizes that legal segregation ended in the South in the 1960s but contends that in the 1970s and 1980s enthusiasm for racial integration waned as white animosity toward African American achievements drained momentum from the movement for true racial equality.

On a steamy August day in 1963, Martin Luther King, Jr., mounted a podium constructed in front of the Lincoln Memorial in Washington, D.C., and, in the studied cadence of a preacher, delivered his famous "I Have a Dream" speech. For many Americans, black and white, King's speech represented the symbolic climax of the civil rights movement. The Civil Rights Act of 1964 and the Voting Rights Act of 1965 were merely denouements.

There were other symbolic events at the March on Washington in addition to King's electrifying oration. The call for the march had been issued by A. Philip Randolph, a long-time civil rights activist, who had threatened in 1941 to stage a similar protest march to bring attention to the economic inequality suffered by African Americans. Randolph's presence at the head of the march reflected a realization of *his* dream. Moreover, several of the speakers that day paid homage to W. E. B. Du Bois, the godfather of the twentieth-century black protest movement in the United States, who had died the previous day (at the age of 95) in Ghana, West Africa, an embittered exile from the land of his birth.

For decades, African Americans had endured an enforced second-class citizenship. But in the 1940s and 1950s, following constitutional victories spearheaded by the National Association for the Advancement of Colored People (NAACP) in the areas of housing, voting, and education, black Americans awakened to the possibilities for change in their status. These victories coincided with the rise of independent nations in Africa, led by black leaders such as Kwame Nkrumah, and this fostered pride in the African homeland among many black Americans. Finally, the nonviolent direct action movement, pioneered by interracial organizations such as the Congress of Racial Equality (CORE) and individuals like Randolph, King, Ella Baker, James Farmer, and Fannie Lou Hamer, issued a clarion call to African Americans and their white supporters that full equality was around the corner.

Despite these idealistic predictions of the future, King's vision of a color-blind society, liberated from the harsh realities of prejudice and discrimination, faced serious barriers after the mid-1960s. King's desegregation campaigns had little impact on the economic plight of many African Americans, a point made consistently by Malcolm X prior to his assassination in 1965. The rise of black nationalism produced fissures within the leading civil rights organizations and alienated many whites who had committed their time and money to fostering interracial harmony. Following King's death in 1968, the federal government made efforts to enforce school integration and to legislate affirmative action programs. This fueled controversy that manifested itself in a conservative white backlash against much of the racial progress that had occurred during the previous generation. By the 1990s, in the midst of debates over hiring quotas and the racial implications of the sensationalist media attention devoted to the criminal and civil prosecutions of O. J. Simpson, serious questions could be raised concerning the long-term success of the civil rights movement.

In the first of the following selections, Robert Weisbrot acknowledges the illusory nature of many of the movement's hopes for racial progress and admits that the United States remains a race-conscious society. Nevertheless, he credits the nonviolent direct action campaigns of the 1950s and 1960s with sharply reducing the levels of ignorance, fear, and hate that are the products of the nation's racial heritage. Moreover, he recognizes a substantial record of achievement that includes the desegregation of schools and places of public accommodation, the protection of voting rights, and a severe weakening of the legal and social standing once accorded racism in America.

For Tom Wicker, the civil rights glass is half empty. In the second selection, he argues that, despite legal victories over segregation in the South during the 1960s, recent decades have witnessed a retrenchment campaign abetted by both major political parties and stimulated by white fears that black gains during the civil rights era were achieved at the expense of whites. Consequently, in the long run the civil rights movement failed to bring either racial equality or racial harmony to the United States.

Robert Weisbrot

 **YES**

The Shifting Politics of Race

Lagging progress toward equality led blacks in the 1970s to propose new, bolder answers to the riddle of "all deliberate speed." Instead of seeking merely to punish overt acts of discrimination, some civil rights spokesmen urged the government to guarantee fair representation of blacks in schools, jobs, and other areas of society. This strategy, pursued mainly through a sympathetic judiciary, broadened the concept of equal opportunity and the frontiers of federal regulation. Yet the idea of race-conscious and at times preferential treatment of blacks, even to remedy past injustice, strained the civil rights coalition and brought further backlash in an age of prolonged liberal eclipse....

The Receding Civil Rights Vision

It is now clear that the more expansive hopes for civil rights progress were markedly inflated. Residential segregation, seen in the persistence of inner-city black ghettos and lily-white suburbs, has easily survived federal fiats against housing discrimination. De facto segregation of churches, social centers, and private schools also remains routine, suggesting that in important respects the society's newfound emphasis on interracial harmony has been more rhetorical than real. Wealth, too, is largely segregated along racial lines; the median family income of blacks is barely half that of whites, and blacks are three times as likely to be poor. As for black political power, it is still embryonic with regard to national office holding and access to the circles that make foreign and domestic policy. In all, the roots of racial inequality have proved too deeply embedded in centuries of American history to be washed away by a decade's liberal reform.

Race relations have changed at a glacial pace in much of the rural South, where only the hardiest civil rights activists could weather the repressive social climate. Southern whites understandably regard black militancy as an urban malady, for only in the cities have blacks developed an independent business and professional class able to lead sustained protests. In many outlying towns, where whites monopolize credit and own the farms and textile mills that provide crucial jobs, the etiquette of racial deference persists.

Unwritten rules of segregation in small Southern communities still have the force of law. Harassment and occasional beatings discourage blacks from approaching the polls on election day, whatever the language of federal statutes. Blacks also know to avoid restaurants where they will draw stares instead of service, hotels that will always be "fully booked," and golf courses where management sand traps will foil their bids for access. Even white physicians who treat persons of both races commonly route their patients into separate waiting rooms with pre-1960 firmness. Here progress in race relations often comes in rudimentary concessions to black dignity, as in the recent removal of a chain-link fence dividing black and white plots in a Georgia county cemetery. Until that headline-making decision, black funeral processions had entered the cemetery through a back gate.

Challenges to old racial mores can bring spiraling retaliation. In Ludowici, Georgia, where students picked separate white and black homecoming queens until 1984, an argument in the high school lunchroom over interracial dating degenerated into an interracial brawl. Discipline was swift and selective: several students were expelled, all of them black. After local black leaders protested, hooded Klansmen visited the town, and within hours the home of a civil rights activist was burned to the ground. Fire marshals blamed faulty wiring, but Joseph Lowery of the Southern Christian Leadership Conference thought it absurd to deny the real problem: faulty white racial attitudes. The former SNCC [Student Nonviolent Coordinating Committee] worker Charles Sherrod observed, "Those people who shot at us, and blew up churches and all that 20 years ago, they haven't gone anywhere. The attitudes are still there. Their behavior has changed because we have got a little power. They won't do anything they can't get away with."

Few officials anywhere in the South still defy civil rights laws openly, for events in the 1960s showed the futility of shrill racist posturing. Softer sabotage, however, still limits the impact of federal guarantees. After passage of the Voting Rights Act in 1965, whites generally acquiesced in the registration of blacks but devised ways to undermine the new electorate. Testimony in 1982 before the Senate Judiciary Committee revealed that nearly half the counties of Alabama, Georgia, Louisiana, and South Carolina had disregarded the act's "preclearance" requirement by changing electoral laws—often for transparent racial reasons—without first obtaining federal approval. Cities with large black populations imported white voters by annexing adjacent suburbs, and cities with a few predominantly black areas discarded district elections for at-large voting. Legislators have also excluded black voters from communities through redistricting schemes of rare cartographic cunning. The understaffed Justice Department has trailed such infractions at a discouraging distance. An amendment to the North Carolina constitution, designed to gerrymander away the influence of new black voters, escaped challenge from federal attorneys until 1981, fourteen years after it was illegally implemented.

Outside the South racism treads more softly but still sequesters most blacks in ghettos. Blacks formed 6 percent of the suburban population in 1980 (up from 5 percent in 1970), and even this figure was inflated by spillover into older, industrial suburbs that white flight turned into segregated enclaves.

Federal studies show pervasive discrimination by white realtors and residents, resulting in hundreds of census tracts in New York, Cleveland, and other metropolitan areas that contain no nonwhites. Nor is housing bias entirely covert. Obscene phone calls, curses, threats, firebombings, and rocks and bricks crashing through windows are among the dozens of incidents that each year impart a rough frontier quality to black settlement in white neighborhoods. Such experiences confirm that the open-housing legislation of the 1960s has meant little beside the resolve of whites to maintain property values and "ethnic purity" in their communities.

Racial violence and harassment, a central target of civil rights protest, still occurs daily in every region of the country. The Justice Department conservatively recorded a rise in racist attacks from 99 in 1980 to 276 in 1986; the count by individual cities is more extensive. New York City's police department charted an increase in bias-related clashes from four a week to ten a week in early 1987. Chicago reported 240 episodes of racially motivated violence and harassment in 1986, an increase for the third consecutive year. The spark is often no more than the presence of a black person in a store, on the street, in a new home. For dejected white students at the University of Massachusetts at Amherst, the defeat of the Boston Red Sox in the 1986 World Series was enough reason to beat a black New York Mets fan unconscious and injure several others. Several months earlier, at Howard Beach, New York, three black "outsiders" fled an attack by eleven whites; one of the blacks, twenty-three-year-old Michael Griffith, was killed when he ran onto a parkway of speeding cars in his attempt to escape a beating. Kevin Nesmith, a black student at the Citadel Military School, in Charleston, South Carolina, resigned after whites in Klan robes burst into his room at two in the morning shouting racial slurs and hazing him. Something akin to a freedom ride befell black students returning from Newton North High School to their homes in Boston when whites smashed the bus windows with stones and a tire iron. These and other recent episodes do not approach the systematic, officially sanctioned terror against blacks that once scarred American history. They nonetheless point to the continued difficulty blacks face in securing basic civil rights.

Police each year kill dozens of blacks, including children. Defenders of police conduct stress the extreme danger facing officers in some ghetto neighborhoods, their need to use deadly force on occasion to survive, and their able protection of blacks, notably during civil rights marches that have drawn white hecklers. Still, cases abound of unprovoked, cold-blooded police shootings of ghetto residents that almost invariably go unpunished.

The criminal justice system is less blatantly harsh toward blacks than in the past, but patterns of punishment still appear skewed by racial prejudice. Blacks average longer prison terms than whites for the same offense and are the primary victims of capital punishment. Criminals of any race, moreover, are treated more severely for victimizing whites. In 1987 a case that challenged the death penalty as being tainted, in practice, by racial bias showed that in Georgia, even after accounting for 230 other factors, killers of white persons were four times more likely to be executed than killers of blacks. Despite corroborating evidence of prejudice in meting out capital punishment, the Supreme Court narrowly upheld the death penalty. The majority opinion asserted, in language shades removed from *Plessy v. Ferguson*, that the treatment of black and white prisoners was admittedly different but not discriminatory.

◦◉◦

Failure to include blacks fully in the nation's prosperity is the most glaring limitation of the movement for racial justice. In the South two-thirds of all black workers, compared with one-third of all whites, hold low-income jobs. The national economy today relegates more than half of all black workers to menial jobs, perpetuates a black underclass of deepening antisocial bent, and confines even educated blacks to the margins of wealth and opportunity. These problems can be traced to various causes—racial differences in family structure, education, and job experience among them—but they are also rooted in both past and persistent discrimination.

Title VII of the 1964 Civil Rights Act did not end bias in employment but drove it behind closed office doors. Managers commonly assigned blacks to dead-end jobs, minimized their executive role, scrutinized them more harshly than comparably trained whites, and excluded them from the after-hours fraternizing that can advance careers. In 1982 only one in thirty black men (compared with one in ten whites) filled management or administrative jobs, reflecting a ten-year increase so minute that it was probably a matter of statistical error. No black headed a corporation in *Fortune* magazine's top 1,000, and few had risen above the level of vice-president in any major firm. Tokenism thus became more intricate in the era of affirmative action, permitting a greater minority presence in the office but seldom in the conference suites where deals, promotions, and salaries are decided.

An aura of the closed medieval guild still surrounds craft unions, which have countered civil rights laws with subtler means of racial exclusion. One AFL-CIO union, representing New York City's electrical contractors, avoided punishment for racist practices by devising an "outreach training program" for minorities in 1971. Over a decade later state investigators charged that the program required black and Hispanic trainees to work eleven years before they could reach class A journeyman status, compared with five years for white apprentices. Nonwhite trainees were also taught a curriculum separate from that of whites, with obsolete textbooks and without the fifth year of classroom instruction needed to pass the union exam and obtain work at journeymen's wages. Many other AFL-CIO locals have also been exposed for turning affirmative action programs into a permanent racial obstacle course for minorities....

A Record of Change

Like other reform movements the crusade for racial justice inevitably fell short of the utopian goals that sustained it. Still, if America's civil rights movement is judged by the distance it traveled rather than by barriers yet to be crossed, a record of substantial achievement unfolds. In communities throughout the South, "whites only" signs that had stood for generations suddenly came down from hotels, rest rooms, theaters, and other facilities. Blacks and whites seldom mingle socially at home, but they are apt to lunch together at fast-food shops that once drew blacks only for sit-ins. Integration extends equally to Southern workers, whether at diner counters or in the high-rise office buildings that now afford every Southern city a skyline.

School desegregation also quickened its pace and by the mid-1970's had become fact as well as law in over 80 percent of all Southern public schools. Swelling private school enrollments have tarnished but not substantially reversed this achievement. A privileged 5 to 10 percent of all Southern white children may find shelter from the *Brown* [*v. Board of Education of Topeka, Kansas* (1954)] verdict at private academies; but the words "massive resistance" have virtually disappeared from the region's political vocabulary.

Hate groups once flourished without strong federal restraint, but the civil rights movement has curbed the Ku Klux Klan and other extremist threats. Beginning in 1964 the FBI infiltrated the Klan so thoroughly that by 1965 perhaps one in five members was an informant. During the 1980s, amid a rise in racial assaults, synagogue bombings, and armed robberies to bankroll fringe groups, the federal government mounted the largest campaign against organized subversion since World War II. In 1987, members of the Florida Realm of the United Klans of America were convicted of illegal paramilitary training exercises, and leaders of the Identity Movement, which preaches a theology of hatred toward Jews and blacks, were indicted for conspiring to overthrow the government. Federal action has encouraged private lawsuits, including one that bankrupted the United Klans of America. After a black teenager in Mobile, Alabama, was murdered by Klansmen and left hanging from a tree in 1981, the boy's family won a $7 million judgment. To pay damages the Klan had to cede its two-story national headquarters, near Tuscaloosa, Alabama, to the black litigants. Reeling from legal and financial adversity, Klan membership declined from 10,000 in 1981 to less than 5,500 in 1987, the lowest since the early seventies.

Protection of voting rights represents the movement's most unalloyed success, more than doubling black voter registration, to 64 percent, in the seven states covered by the 1965 act. Winning the vote literally changed the complexion of government service in the South. When Congress passed the Voting Rights Act, barely 100 blacks held elective office in the country; by 1989 there were more than 7,200, including 24 congressmen and some 300 mayors. Over 4,800 of these officials served in the South, and nearly every Black Belt county in Alabama had a black sheriff. Mississippi experienced the most radical change, registering 74 percent of its voting-age blacks and leading the nation in the number of elected black officials (646).

Black influence in electoral politics acquired a compelling symbol during the 1980s with the emergence of the Reverend Jesse Jackson of Chicago as a presidential contender. As a young aide to Dr. King from 1966 to 1968, Jackson had stood out for his eloquence, élan, and ambition. In the 1970s Jackson won national acclaim for spurring ghetto youths to excel in school, but his denunciations of American society as racist, capitalist, and imperialist kept him on the fringes of public life. Over the next decade, however, as blacks increasingly protested President Reagan's neglect of minorities and the poor, Jackson began to temper his revolutionary message in hopes of forging a revitalized reform coalition.

Jackson campaigned in the 1984 Democratic presidential primaries, drawing large crowds and intense media coverage with his mixture of evangelical fervor, nimble wit, and self-conscious identification with minority hopes. He spoke of a "Rainbow Coalition" that would transcend racial lines, though his campaign chiefly focused on mobilizing black voter registration and turnout with the aid of Negro churches. This strategy enabled Jackson to win nomination contests in South Carolina, Louisiana, and Washington, D.C., and to finish third in delegates at the Democratic National Convention. Partly offsetting this achievement was Jackson's failure to draw even 5 percent of the white voters, whether because of his race, radical image, or suspect character. (Jews in particular recoiled at Jackson's ties with the Black Muslim Louis Farrakhan, who had branded Judaism a "gutter religion.") Despite these weaknesses Jackson's campaign legitimized Black Power to the American people in a way that Stokely Carmichael and others in the 1960s had vainly tried to do from outside the political mainstream.

In 1988 Jackson hewed closer to the political center and reached well beyond his core supporters, in a second bid for the Democratic presidential nomination. The now seasoned candidate trimmed his radical rhetoric, conciliated many who had thought him opportunistic and divisive, and emphasized broadly appealing liberal themes of economic opportunity for all citizens. Jackson's approach, which this time afforded him second place among seven competitors, reflected and fostered a new openness toward blacks in the Democratic party and in the nation. An especially prominent landmark of political change was Jackson's Michigan primary victory, with 54 percent of the vote, just twenty years after that state's Democratic contest had gone to the Alabama segregationist George Wallace. The candidate's progress, as in 1984, remained in key respects exceedingly personal, for it did not appreciably change his party's stand on key issues nor dispel racism as a factor in national politics. Still, more than any black leader since Martin Luther King, Jr., Jackson had inspired Americans with the faith—crucial to every reform movement—that the decisive state of America's democratic odyssey lay just ahead.

⚜

Despite unsettling parallels with the aftermath of Reconstruction, the modern civil rights movement should prove better able to resist the undoing of black gains. A salient difference is the greater reluctance in recent times to risk convulsing society by spurning the ideal of equality. Blacks during Reconstruction had exerted relatively minor influence over the white leadership that instituted—and then abandoned—measures for racial justice. By contrast blacks a century later shook whole cities with mass demonstrations, demanded and secured sweeping changes in federal law, and reshaped the political agenda of two strong-minded chief executives. These protests brought a new respect for Afro-Americans, breaking forever the comfortable myth that blacks were content with a biracial society and proving that they had the rare courage needed to challenge it.

New currents in world affairs have reinforced the consensus to guarantee black civil rights. During the late nineteenth century Americans were largely indifferent to the nonwhite world except for the growing possibilities of colonizing or otherwise controlling it. The European nations that most influenced this country were themselves indulging in imperialism based on racial as well as national interests. Global pressures today are vastly different. Competition for the support of nonwhite nations and the near-universal ostracism of South Africa, which asserts a racist ideology, require American society to pay at least nominal homage to racial equality.

Pluralism is also more firmly rooted in American values than ever before. The black revolution stimulated others, including women, homosexuals, Hispanics, native Americans, and Asians, who frequently modeled their actions on the values and tactics popularized by Martin Luther King, Jr. Each emerging movement, while pursuing a discrete agenda, has bolstered the principle that government must guarantee equal rights and opportunities to all citizens.

Racism lost more than legal standing with the triumph of civil rights campaigns; it lost social standing. Even the Daughters of the American Revolution, an organization known for its racially exclusive character, apologized in 1982 for having spurned the singer Marian Anderson over four decades earlier. The DAR's president general, a native of Beulah, Mississippi, invited Anderson to perform at the organization's ninety-first convention in Constitution Hall. The eighty-year-old singer was by then too frail to attend, but the black soprano Leontyne Price, who treated the DAR to a concert ending with "The Battle Hymn of the Republic," assured her interracial audience that Anderson was "here in spirit."

The deepening interest in racial harmony has encouraged recognition of the black experience as central to American history. The 1977 television drama "Roots," which engaged audiences in the trauma of racial slavery and the struggle for freedom, became the most widely viewed special series in the history of the medium. Six years later Congress created a holiday to honor Martin Luther King, Jr., and by extension the civil rights movement he symbolized. Such a tribute had eluded Thomas Jefferson, Andrew Jackson, both Roosevelts, and other giants of American history. President Reagan, who had originally opposed enacting a holiday for King as an unwise "ethnic" precedent, signed the popular bill into law while standing alongside King's widow, Coretta.

⋖◉⋗

In the South, as in the rest of the nation, few whites seriously contemplate returning to the state of race relations before 1960. This outlook differs strikingly from Southern intransigence after Reconstruction and reflects the disparate ways in which the two eras of racial change occurred. Reconstruction came as a sudden, violently imposed upheaval in Southern race relations that virtually nothing in the region's history had prepared it to accept. The civil rights movement instead advanced nonviolently, secured small gains over decades, and fostered progress from within the region. The campaigns that ended legalized segregation in the sixties marked the culmination of this gradual change. Many white Southerners had by then reconciled themselves to reforms that seemed inevitable and even, perhaps, beneficial.

Freed from the albatross of defending Jim Crow at the expense of national respect and regional peace, Southerners could focus on tasks of economic and social modernization. Mississippi's leading journal, the *Jackson Clarion-Ledger*, offered a glimpse into this revolution in priorities. After the March on Washington in 1963, a front-page story reported that the capital was "clean again with Negro trash removed." Twenty years later the paper won a Pulitzer Prize in public serve for exposing the need for fuller desegregation and better funding of public schools.

Southern memories of black protests have mellowed to the point where both races treat them as parts of their history to be proud of. Montgomery motorists now drive down the Martin Luther King, Jr. Expressway, and the Dexter Baptist Church, where King was pastor, has become a national landmark. The prison cell King occupied in Birmingham is set aside as a library for inmates, his "Letter from a Birmingham Jail" framed on the wall. In Georgia's capitol a portrait of King hangs near a bust of Alexander Stephens, the Confederate vice-president. One elderly black tour guide, assigned to interpret these landmarks of the past, ignored the bust of Stephens, and beamed, "Here is Nobel prize winner Martin Luther King, Jr. He was born and bred right here in Atlanta on Auburn Avenue."

Political calculation has sealed this acceptance of racial change. Over a quiet bourbon and branch water in his Senate office, Mississippi's arch-segregationist James Eastland confided, "When [blacks] get the vote, I won't be talking this way anymore." Later Eastland was among the many officials who jettisoned their tested appeals to prejudice, learned to pronounce "Negro" in place of more casual epithets, and prefaced the names of newly valued black constituents with the once forbidden appellation "Mister."

Even the past master of race baiting, Alabama's George Wallace, was struck color-blind on the road to Montgomery in his 1982 gubernatorial campaign. Wallace, who like most politicians believed above all in winning elections today, tomorrow, and forever, spent much of his hard-fought contest kissing black babies and humbly supplicating their parents' support, assuring them of his reborn attitudes on race matters. (He won the campaign with the aid of a forgiving black electorate and welcomed several blacks to positions in his cabinet.) Whatever Wallace's deepest sentiments, his actions were a striking testament to the legacy of the civil rights protests that he once vowed to crush but that instead have left an indelible imprint on the nation's moral landscape.

⁕

The full impact of civil rights campaigns has yet to be felt. The movement could not wholly sweep away old Jim Crow hierarchies, but rather superimposed new patterns of behavior on a still race-conscious society. Cities like Selma, Alabama, where black activists battled white supremacists in the 1960s, today reflect two eras of race relations at once, giving no final sign of which will prevail.

Segregated neighborhoods persist in Selma, along with segregated social patterns. The Selma Country Club has no black members and until 1983 would not allow a black dance band inside. Elks Club members attend separate white and black chapters. Nearly a thousand white students attend two private academies founded with the express purpose of excluding blacks. Racial lines run through the city's economy: the overall jobless rate in Selma in 1985 was 16 percent but nearly twice as high for blacks as for whites. And in politics, residents tend to make racial choices for public office. The black community leader Frederick Reese won 40 percent of the mayoral vote in 1984 but only a handful of white supporters; Joseph Smitherman received 10 to 15 percent of the black vote but stayed in office with nearly 100 percent of the white vote.

Yet race relations in Selma have noticeably changed since the city's landmark civil rights demonstrations in 1965. The onetime "moderate segregationist" Smitherman began to tend an image as a facilitator of black mobility. In 1984 Smitherman observed proudly that 40 percent of the police force was black, including the assistant chief, several lieutenants, captains, and key department heads. The city's personnel board had three blacks and two whites, the eight-person library board was evenly composed of blacks and whites, and the school board had five blacks to four whites. Asphalt pavement, which had often stopped short of black neighborhoods, now stretched for miles throughout the town, covering over dirt roads and, with them, an era of flagrant neglect of black residents.

Perhaps most important to Selma's blacks and many whites, the movement reduced ignorance, fear, and hate. The black lawyer and civil rights activist J. L. Chestnut remarked in 1985, on the twentieth anniversary of his city's civil rights marches, that new attitudes were taking root: "My children don't think of white children as devils, and I don't think white children see my kids as watermelon-eating, tap-dancing idiots. If there is hope, it is in the fact that children in Selma today don't have to carry the baggage that Joe Smitherman and J. L. Chestnut carry. And that means they will never be scared the way we used to be scared." Teenagers at Selma's integrated public high school knew about the events of "Bloody Sunday" but viewed them as a mystery from another time. "Kids today, they're used to the way things are," explained Karyn Reddick, a black student. "Try as you can, you can't believe that white people once treated black people that way. It seems like something that happened long, long ago."

NO

Tom Wicker

Tragic Failure: Racial Integration in America

Introduction

Sharply conflicting white and black reactions to the O.J. Simpson verdict [not guilty of murder] dramatized the tragic fact that neither civil war in the nineteenth century nor the civil rights movement in the twentieth has brought racial equality, much less racial amity, to America.

I believe they can be reached only in the hearts of the people; wars will never achieve either, nor narrow legalities. Perhaps nothing can. Derrick Bell has written that African-Americans, despite surface changes in society, continue to be "the faces at the bottom of the well," the faces upon which whites, no matter how deprived themselves, can look down in the sure and comforting knowledge that at least *they* aren't black.

Having spent the first thirty-four years of my life in what was then the segregated South and the last thirty-five in what's only legally an integrated nation—and not always that—I believe the problem is not least that those black faces in the well are *reassuring* to most whites and *vital* to the self-esteem of the many disadvantaged among us, few of whom really want those faces to disappear.

The continuing separation of whites and blacks into hostile and unequal classes, however, is a fundamental cause of the political deadlock, economic inequity, and social rancor that mark American life. And if "a house divided against itself" could not stand in the era of chattel slavery, can it long endure in today's destructive atmosphere of black disadvantage, white anger, and racial animosity?

Long before O.J. Simpson went on trial, it was obvious that genuine racial equality—despite laws and legal decisions—had not been achieved in America. The high proportion of African-Americans[1] males in U.S. prisons and the low economic status of more than half the black population were evidence enough for anyone willing to see it, but few were. Even as the Simpson trial unfolded, white resentment erupted over affirmative action—an effort to overcome black disadvantages that's now widely seen, despite little evidence, as reverse racism.

When a Los Angeles jury brought in the Simpson verdict, the hard truth finally was too visible to be ignored. Whites denounced what they saw as black racial prejudice by a predominantly black jury in favor of a black hero despite the evidence. African-Americans, on the other hand, hailed black jurors for a courageous stand against white racial prejudice and constitutionally impermissible evidence provided by the racist Los Angeles police.

Throughout the long trial, "the white position [that Simpson was guilty] was treated as the rational, normal, acceptable one," David Shaw of the *Los Angeles Times* said on October 25, 1995, in a panel discussion of media coverage of the Freedom Forum. "The black perception [that Simpson was not guilty] was treated as irrational."

It's almost irrelevant [that] the black or white judgment might be more nearly correct. In my view, what mattered was the demonstration that whites and blacks, though living in the same America, see themselves in different worlds. Similarly conflicting views were evident in the responses of African-American journalists and their mostly white supervisors to a survey question of whether U.S. press organizations are "committed to retaining and promoting black journalists." Of the white supervisors, 94 percent believed newspapers and broadcasters were so committed; 67 percent of the black (mostly middle-class) journalists thought not. Both worked in the same newsrooms; neither saw the same world of work.

The Simpson trial and verdict were followed immediately by the so-called "Million-Man March," in which at least hundreds of thousands of orderly African-American males demonstrated peacefully on the Mall in Washington in October 1995. Despite a demagogic speech by Louis Farrakhan of the Nation of Islam, the marchers espoused what white Americans, watching on television, could readily recognize as middle-class values—thus confounding the recent white view of black men as lawless and shiftless, as well as conveying the message that African-Americans still are far from equal citizenship in a supposedly integrated nation.

The march emphasized the strong growth of the black middle class in the last three decades—to perhaps 40 percent of the African-American population. Even that growth has not banished the faces from the bottom of the well, any more than it has produced real racial equality. Middle-class African-Americans testify copiously to the indignities and embarrassments they still suffer from the white assumption of black inferiority, black income and wealth still are far below white levels, housing remains largely segregated by race, and *all* African-Americans tend to be judged by the unacceptable behavior of the worst off among them.

I consider it the saddest racial development of the last quarter century that as the black middle class expanded, the urban underclass grew even faster. The scary and undisciplined behavior of that largely black underclass—those African-Americans who for lack of jobs and hope and discipline turned in the seventies and eighties to crime and welfare and drugs and were sent to prison in droves—was seen (often graphically, on television) by frightened whites as the behavior of African-Americans generally.

In one panicked and self-destructive result, whites turned against social welfare programs designed to benefit the white as well as the black poor—hence society generally. Worse, African-Americans once seen as bravely facing the police dogs and cattle prods of Bull Connor in the name of freedom came to be regarded, instead, as irresponsible muggers, drug dealers, addicts, rapists, and welfare queens.

The same period exposed the failure of the African-American political empowerment that white and black civil rights leaders of the sixties had hoped would be the remedy for black disadvantages. One of them, Dr. Kenneth Clark, sadly conceded in 1993 that greater numbers of black elected officials had been "unable to increase justice and humanity for those who have been forgotten in the inner cities."

Thirty-five years of failing integration have convinced me that economic as well as political empowerment is needed if African-American disadvantages —particularly those of the underclass—are to be overcome. Only when the faces at the bottom of the well achieve generally higher economic status might they —as well as those talented and energetic blacks in the middle class—reach genuine equality in the hearts of whites, and only through economic gains for all might the threatening underclass become a more constructive element in a more amicable American life.

Such an economic transformation will not be easily or soon accomplished, and it probably never will be if the task is left to today's major political parties. Neither any longer even talks of such ambitious goals; both are less concerned with the truly disadvantaged than with the numerically dominant white middle class, with its plaints about an unfair tax burden and unfair preferences for blacks. The Republicans offer a new home to white defectors from a Democratic party the defectors regarded as too partial to blacks, and the supposedly "liberal" Democrats, alarmed by the loss of white votes, pay scant attention to the interests of African-Americans, whose allegiance causes the white defections.

In their own interest, therefore, but also in that of a racially torn nation, blacks should turn away from the Democrats to form a new party dedicated to economic equality through economic growth for whites and blacks alike. Such a new party could build upon predicted demographic change that in the next century will bring today's minority groups into rough numerical equality with non-Hispanic whites. It might even win the support of those millions of despairing Americans who now take no part in the politics of a prosperous nation they believe ruled by the affluent and for the affluent.

The new party might never win the presidency, but in the historical tradition of third parties, it could have [a] profound effect upon the other two and upon society generally. That's why I've suggested in this book that such a radically conceived party might also have the potential to do what our old, familiar politics-as-usual never can: "To achieve real democracy—to change American life by attacking its inequities—perhaps to save us from ourselves."

The End of Integration

Integration is like Prohibition. If the people don't want it, a whole army can't enforce it.

— Paul Johnson,
governor of Mississippi

The sweeping conservative victory in the elections of 1994 returned control of Congress to Republicans, repudiated what was left of liberal government, and dramatized the tragic failure of racial integration in America.

Race, as it always is in a modern American election, was the underlying issue. In the autumn of 1994 that issue was a prime determinant of the outcome, as white voters everywhere expressed unmistakable yearning for a lost time, before "they" forced themselves into the nation's consciousness.

White animosity toward and fear of African-Americans—seen largely as criminals and welfare cheats—gave emotional edge and added energy to the election's ostensible issues, and the campaign was fought out in code words and symbolism that disclosed rather than disguised its racial character.

- Fierce denunciations of crime and welfare, in white eyes the most prominent products of the black underclass
- Withering blasts at liberals and liberalism as the "social engineers" behind the "big government" that tried to force racial integration and brought higher taxes
- Diatribes against "spending" and "the redistribution of wealth" to the poor, a euphemism for social programs believed primarily to aid African-Americans
- Loud promises to extend the death penalty, from which African-Americans suffer proportionally far more than whites
- Overwrought demands for a return to "family values" (a term of many meanings, one of which is the sexual restraint that blacks are supposed by whites to disdain)

Anyone who might have misunderstood what had happened in the 1994 elections should have been set straight on January 23, 1995. That day, in the ornate hearing room of the House Rules Committee, the victorious Republicans removed a portrait of former Representative Claude Pepper of Florida, a renowned white liberal Democrat. That was understandable, but the new Republican committee chairman, Gerald Solomon of New York, had ordered the Pepper portrait replaced by that of *another Democrat,* the late Howard Smith of Virginia, a last-ditch segregationist and in his many years as Rules Committee chairman one of the most powerful opponents of the civil rights legislation of the sixties.

Blacks clearly believed race was the principal issue in the campaign; the reason, said Robert Smith, a professor of political science at San Francisco State University, was "absolute disgust" with the campaign among blacks of all walks.

"It took us black people so long to get the vote," T. J. Smith of Philadelphia told Richard Berke of *The New York Times* in 1994. "Now they're making us not want to vote" by neglecting black interests. Chris Williams, a Philadelphia ironworker, agreed: "Why do they talk about just building jails? Why don't they talk about building schools?"

The returns, if anything, left African-Americans feeling even more frustrated. Black turnout—perhaps fueled by fear—more than doubled nationally, over the 1990 midterm elections, with black voters going heavily Democratic; yet the Republicans won in a landslide and not a single Republican incumbent was defeated. Clearly, *white* voters had turned to the Republicans.

Fifty-one percent of the whites, moreover, who had responded to an election-year survey by the Times Mirror Center for the People and the Press said openly that they believed "equal rights" had been pushed too far—an increase of nine percentage points since 1992.

California, the nation's most populous state, voted by an overwhelming margin for Proposition 187, a ballot initiative designed to deprive illegal immigrants—mostly Latinos in California—of education, health, and welfare benefits. Governor Pete Wilson, whose reelection made him seem at the time a strong contender for the Republican presidential nomination, derived substantial political profit from his support for this initiative.

California's approval of Prop 187, which Democratic candidates for governor and senator opposed, may well have been symbolic of the 1994 elections as a whole. It was not an "anti-black" measure, nor was it an anti-black election *by definition.* The vote favoring Prop 187, however, clearly reflected the angry and vengeful or at least resentful racial attitudes many white Americans had developed since the high-water mark of the civil rights movement in the sixties. The entire selection reflected such white attitudes.

❧

If those attitudes reached a political peak in 1994, they had been a long time in the making. Racial integration in America had been failing for years, even though legal segregation in the southern states was ended in the sixties. The elections of 1994 only dramatized a fact that had long existed.

By that year integration had failed nationally because too few white Americans wanted it or were willing to sacrifice for it. Integration had failed too because whites' sterotypical view of blacks had been reshaped by the violence, idleness, and drug reliance of the urban black underclass. And the kind of political empowerment integration brought to blacks had proved unable to provide most African-Americans the economic and social gains needed for acceptance in white America.

The angry and fearful white reaction to undisciplined ghetto behavior also blinded whites to the concurrent growth of a substantial black middle class. Perhaps worse, that reaction had undermined white support for economic and social programs beneficial not only to the black poor but to millions of impoverished whites as well.

In actual practice, as a result of all this, integration had not been the policy of either Republican or Democratic administrations since the accession of Ronald Reagan to the presidency in 1981. In the decade before that, integration had been pursued only halfheartedly; zeal for enforcement of equal rights in education, housing, and employment had declined as antagonism to African-Americans rose.

Crime, though its victims as well as its perpetrators often were black, and welfare, widely considered a dole and an aid to shiftless blacks' supposed instinct to spawn, had long been favored targets of public and political anger.

Now the primary national approach to the ills of the urban underclass, endorsed in the polling booths of 1994, is to imprison poor blacks—an expensive, ineffective, misdirected, and self-destructive course sustained by white fear, politicians' posturing, and the sensationalism of the white press. More executions, mostly of blacks, an equally punitive and ill-considered response to crimes that already have been committed, are promised in response to the conservative landslide of 1994. Early in 1995 New York's new Republican governor, George Pataki, signed a death penalty law after nearly a quarter century of vetoes by the Democratic governors Hugh Carey and Mario Cuomo.

The inner city does teem with crime, idleness, and anger, spilling dangerously outward. Black family disintegration and welfare dependence are serious concerns. But for better or for worse, the American community necessarily *includes* the black community—African-Americans, some Latinos, many from the Caribbean. The Census Bureau predicts the black community will grow far larger. Its exclusion in anything like a democratic or humane manner would be impossible and would not solve the nation's most pressing problems; rather it would worsen some old problems and create many new ones.

Glaring economic inequities and class distinctions abound, among *both* blacks and whites. Technological or administrative competence, a prerequisite in today's economy, is seldom within the reach of poor and ill-educated Americans, of whom there are more and more of both races. Millions of whites and blacks are out of any kind of work, in the city and on the farm, and more will be in a newly competitive and technological era, with even profitable corporations laying off workers by the thousands. Manufacturing wages have declined for all. The real gap between rich and poor is widening. Unemployment, which strikes blacks first and worst, also hits whites hard—yet is fostered by a government too fearful of inflation to push economic growth strenuously and by a "lean and mean" business sector in which cost cutting has become the new panacea for all problems.

A seventh of the nation lives in poverty: more than forty million people, by no means all of them black, and including more than a fifth of all American children. Families of all races are disintegrating. The economy, measured against population growth and expected living standards, is not adequately expanding. Demographic changes predicted by the Census Bureau for the next fifty years will be of incalculable effect.

What the brash conservatives who triumphed in 1994 may be able to do about any of these troublesome truths remains, at this writing, largely to be seen. But the end of integration more or less subtly marked by their victory will not remove or diminish those ills, each of which, in large part or small, is linked to or affected by race, the continuing, the cancerous, the unconfronted American dilemma.

•❰◉❱•

In the fifties and the first half of the sixties, owing mostly to effective black demonstrations and demands, the shameful institutions of legally established racial segregation in the South at last were abolished. But this shining hour for the civil rights movement proved to be brief and limited.

In the late sixties and the seventies, efforts to broaden integration into a national, not just a southern, reality caused anxiety and anger in the nonsouthern white majority. Outside the old Confederacy, integration came to be seen as moving too fast and going too far—faster and farther than most whites in the rest of the nation had expected or wanted.

A "backlash" of white resistance to civil rights quickly gathered momentum, importantly furthered by the presidential campaigns of Governor George Wallace of Alabama. The long national retreat from integration was under way within a year or two after its greatest triumphs.

Such a turnabout had hardly seemed possible in the period when anti-segregation laws were being passed—slowly but, as it seemed, inevitably—by Congress under pressure from the Eisenhower, Kennedy, and Johnson administrations and over die-hard southern opposition. Even, however, in the Goldwater debacle of 1964—the most smashing Democratic and liberal presidential victory since Franklin Roosevelt's in 1936—the Republicans had carried four southern states.

The old Solid South had been shattered, a development that did not surprise the victorious President Lyndon Johnson, a southerner himself. The night Congress passed the massive Civil Rights Act of 1964, proposed by President Kennedy and pushed through by Johnson, a young White House aide named Bill Moyers called the president to congratulate him on the success of the legislation.

"Bill," Johnson replied, "I think we Democrats just lost the South for the rest of my life."

Inasmuch as LBJ died in 1972, it turned out to be for considerably longer than that. In 1994, thirty years later, the Democratic share of the vote in House races in the South dropped to 13.4 percent of eligible voters.

To most observers in 1964—including Tom Wicker, a *New York Times* political reporter—the southern defections had seemed relatively unimportant. After all, LBJ had defeated Goldwater by 486 to 52 in the electoral college. The Republicans had carried only one state (Goldwater's Arizona) outside the South, had lost 38 seats in the House and retained only 140, their lowest total since 1936. They also had lost 2 Senate seats and held only 32, no more than they had had in 1940. Republican defeats in state and local elections had been so severe as to cause frequent laments that the GOP was no longer an effective national party.

Only two years later, in a vigorous 1966 campaign led by Richard M. Nixon (out of office since 1961 but obviously on the road back), Republicans picked up forty-seven House seats, three in the Senate, and eight governorships, most significantly in California, where the political newcomer and old movie star Ronald Reagan first won political office. The Republican comeback was marked by a superb organizing and fundraising effort in the wake of Goldwater's defeat and by Nixon's leadership. But it benefited above all from *the Democratic party's and Johnson's racial liberalism.*

The president and his party had pushed through the Civil Rights Act of 1964, guaranteeing equal access to public facilities and banning racial discrimination in the workplace. They had achieved the Voting Rights Act of 1965, putting the federal government behind blacks' right to vote. Johnson himself had proclaimed to Congress the battle cry of Martin Luther King and his followers: "We shall overcome!" LBJ and John F. Kennedy rather reluctantly before him had identified their party more closely with African-Americans than any president since Lincoln.

Three decades later, in his 1995 inaugural speech as the new Republican Speaker of the House, Newt Gingrich—magnanimously praising the opposition, or so it appeared—noted that Democrats had been "the greatest leaders in fighting for an integrated America." He added pointedly: "It was the liberal wing of the Democratic party that ended segregation."

These honeyed words, intentionally or not, were political poison. Voters had shown in 1994 and earlier that they were well aware, and not favorably, of the Democrats' racial record. It had been apparent for years that this record was a political liability not just in the South but with the nation's white majority.

In early 1964, the year of Goldwater's defeat, a Gallup poll had found that 72 percent of nonsouthern whites believed the Johnson administration's pace toward civil rights was "about right" or even too slow. But as civil rights legislation began to touch life *outside* the South, although it had been expected generally that only the old Confederacy would be much affected, nonsouthern whites began to fear for property values, job security, local government, neighborhood cohesion—for the old, inherited, comfortable (for them) order of things.

By 1966 opinion surveys were showing a startling reversal: Three quarters of white voters thought blacks were moving ahead too fast, demanding and "being given" too much, at the expense of whites. As white backlash mounted, polls the next year suggested that "the number one concern" of most respondents was fear that black gains would damage the well-being of whites. And as the decade continued, blacks rioting in the cities—fearfully or angrily watched by a nation becoming addicted to television—and blacks raising clenched fists in the black power salute seemed not only threatening but ungrateful for white "concessions" (as whites tended to see changes in the old racial order).

The black separatist and "black is beautiful" movements, the anti-integrationist rhetoric of Malcolm X, the militant stance and demands of organizations like the Black Panthers and the Student Nonviolent Coordinating Committee (SNCC) all stirred white animosity and anxiety. So did aggressive African-Americans like H. Rap Brown, Stokely Carmichael, Huey Newton, and

Bobby Seale. The student and anti-Vietnam demonstrations were assumed by many whites to be a predictable consequence of black protests. Crime was increasing, much of it perpetrated by poor blacks, with television dramatizing it in the living room.

In 1967, as a result of the urban riots, President Johnson appointed a bipartisan commission, chaired by Governor Otto Kerner of Illinois, to look into the riots' causes. After extensive inquiry the Kerner Commission dismissed the notion that integration was proceeding too swiftly. Its report contended instead that despite the apparent success of the civil rights movement, black disadvantages still were so overwhelming that "our nation is moving toward two societies, one black, one white—separate but unequal."

Many prominent Americans, white and black, shared and approved this view, but many others resented it. Hadn't enough already been done for blacks? Even Lyndon Johnson, with a presidential election impending and the nation alarmed at what many believed to be insurrection in the cities, disliked the commission's conclusion and might have disavowed it if he could have. The backlash was not reversed; the riots undoubtedly heightened it.

Thus in 1968 fear and resentment of African-Americans underlay the "law and order" issue loudly demagogued by George Wallace and more subtly exploited by Richard Nixon in the "southern strategy" by which he narrowly won the presidency. The national loss of confidence in "Johnson's war" in Vietnam and destructive divisions within the party hurt the Democrats. But primarily, I believe, it was white racial anxieties that brought disaster to the party of Kennedy and Johnson only four years after its greatest victory. And the black community's impressive gains were becoming the cause of alarming losses of white support for Democrats.

Wallace campaigned widely and effectively, using code words and flamboyant oratory to stimulate white fears and to castigate the federal government. He finished a relatively distant third in the 1968 election, receiving votes from Democrats deserting the old civil rights advocate Hubert Humphrey and from Republicans who preferred Wallace's tough talk to Nixon's subtler appeal to white sentiment. In retrospect, however, Wallace's campaign was one of the most consequential of the postwar years. It effectively moved the country to the right, making racial fears seem more legitimate and paving the way for Ronald Reagan to win the presidency twelve years later.

Nixon's election and Wallace's campaign in 1968 sped along the national retreat from integration (though the courts forced President Nixon to push southern school desegregation in 1970). During the seventies affirmative action and "busing" were widely resented, even in Boston, once the seat of abolitionism. Low-income whites who could not afford private schools for their children and who felt their job security threatened by new competition from minority groups and women were especially alienated.

The Democrats and the integration they had pushed and supported were blamed for these perceived threats to the established order. Twenty-four years of Republican and conservative ascendancy, broken only briefly and feebly by Jimmy Carter's single presidential term (1977–81),[2] followed the election of 1968 with near inevitability.

During the seventies escalating fears of busing, affirmative action, and neighborhood breakdown caused many whites to see integration not as laudable national policy but as "racism in reverse." The deterioration of cities and the increase in crime and violence were largely blamed on blacks. This development of the newly visible underclass, moreover, sharpened white fear and anger.

Whites continued to look down at the black "faces at the bottom of society's well," those "magical faces" of which Derrick Bell has written that "[e]ven the poorest whites, those who must live their lives only a few levels above, gain their self-esteem by gazing down at us." Those black faces had always been there, viewed merely with contempt and complacency by some, with bitter relief by the poor, the disadvantaged, the despised, who had little of value but their white skins. Despite civil rights laws, surely those "faces at the bottom of the well" always would be there.

Their absence would announce to whites not just the end of segregation in the South but the arrival of an all but unimaginable new world, making life less comfortable for some whites, nearly unbearable for others. And those black faces imposed a double imperative on whites: Not only must they be kept at the bottom of the well, but those who would bring them to the top, or nearer to it, must be feared, castigated, opposed.

And then came Reagan.

•◦❂◦•

On August 3, 1980, looking virile and businesslike, he spoke in shirtsleeves to a cheering crowd of about ten thousand people, nearly all white, at the Neshoba County Fairgrounds near Philadelphia, Mississippi.

"I believe in states' rights," Reagan declared that day in the well-modulated voice that was to become so familiar to Americans. The Republican presidential nominee then promised a restoration to the states and to local governments of "the power that properly belongs to them."

Fresh from his Republican National Convention victory at Detroit, Ronald Reagan was making the first formal appearance of his presidential campaign, and his choice of a site for that opening appearance was powerfully symbolic: Philadelphia, Mississippi, was the place where three volunteer civil rights workers in the Mississippi Summer Project of 1964, two Jews and a black—Andrew Goodman, Michael Schwerner, and James Chaney—had been murdered. The sheriff and deputy sheriff of Neshoba County had been charged with these crimes. Most of the county's white population, by its silence, had been either complicit or oblivious.

No presidential candidate before Reagan had visited remote Neshoba County, in a state that had been the last stronghold of resistance to blacks' civil rights. Reagan was there because a Mississippi member of Congress, Trent Lott (now the [Senate majority leader]), had assured him that a personal visit to the state would carry it for him against President Carter.

The candidate might not fully have grasped the significance of Philadelphia, as later he would not understand the opposition to his visit to the Bitburg

Cemetery in Germany, where members of the Nazi SS were buried. But if Reagan didn't know about Philadelphia, Mississippi, he should have. It could not conceivably have been a routine campaign stop. One week after the bodies of Goodman, Schwerner, and Chaney had been discovered buried in a nearby earthen dam in 1964, Governor Paul Johnson—without a word of sympathy for the dead youths or their families—had told a crowd of six thousand at the Neshoba County fair that no Mississippian, including state officials, had any obligation to obey the Civil Rights Act of 1964.

"Integration," Johnson declaimed, "is like Prohibition. If the people don't want it, a whole army can't enforce it."

In 1964 that was the voice of last-ditch resistance, soon to be overwhelmed by events. But by 1980, as Ronald Reagan stood where the governor had stood, looking out upon much the same sea of white faces, it was possible to see Paul Johnson as a national prophet, no longer as a southern relic. Reagan's mere appearance at Philadelphia—unthinkable for a major-party presidential candidate even a few years earlier—was evidence that times had changed, radically. And when the candidate chose to open his campaign where Schwerner, Chaney, and Goodman had made the last sacrifice to rabid segregationist resistance, he sent the nation a message many Americans *wanted* to hear. That message was far more powerful and far more convincing than the deceptive plausibility with which Reagan was later to call for a "color-blind society" and insist that he was "heart and soul in favor of the things that have been done in the name of civil rights and desegregation. . . ."

Reagan's actual policies exposed those words as lip service, and anyway, much of the nation was watching what he did—visiting Philadelphia, Mississippi, for instance—rather than listening to what he said. Even before his speech at Philadelphia, Reagan had openly opposed the Civil Rights Act of 1964, the Voting Rights Act of 1965, the Opening Housing Act of 1968 and in numerous other ways had demonstrated his fundamental opposition to the *fact*, if not the concept, of integration. And by the time he sought the presidency—nearly winning the Republican nomination in 1976, taking it easily in 1980—neither his clear anti-integration record nor even his appearance in Mississippi was a political liability. It was, in fact, largely *because* of these that Ronald Reagan was elected to the White House.

Reagan did not single-handedly and from his own convictions turn the nation against integration. Rather a national reversal had begun not long after the civil rights triumphs of the sixties and his own entry into public life in California. In those years, as outlined above, national reluctance—neither confined to the South nor always most pronounced there—moved steadily toward opposition to integration. That movement owed more to crime, the underclass, busing, affirmative action, and *fear* (as much of the unknown as of any observable phenomena) than to the words or deeds of any one politician, even George Wallace. Reagan benefited politically from a greatly changed public mood even as he contributed to that mood.

Once he was in the Oval Office, moreover, the anti-civil rights record Reagan accumulated was so lengthy and substantial that he could not have compiled it without the acquiescence and support of white Americans. "From

Philadelphia to the Bitburg cemetery to the veto on sanctions against South Africa," Jesse Jackson observed toward the end of the Reagan years, "it's one unbroken ideological line."

That was true enough, but it was also true that Reagan had read accurately a public mood of disenchantment with racial integration. If even a beloved president thought blacks were being "given too much," as his actions (if not always his words) suggested, then surely ordinary Americans could think so too.

With tacit support from a popular president, it became respectable for whites to express loudly their misgivings about integration and to act on their fearful or hostile instincts about black neighbors or employees or schoolmates or job competitors. Those misgivings were many and fierce, those instincts had been frequently offended; so all too many white Americans were grateful that Reagan seemed to share their views. They took full advantage of what seemed to be approval from the top.

Notes

1. The author is aware that not all black Americans approve of the designation "African-American," or consider it accurate. The term is used interchangeably with "black" throughout this [selection] and no disrespect is intended in either case.

2. Carter's narrow victory over Gerald Ford derived mostly from reaction against the Watergate scandal of the Nixon years and Ford's pardon of Nixon himself. Without those counterbalancing factors, the Democrats might well have lost the close election of 1976 too, owing to the party's racial record and Carter's relatively liberal stance.

POSTSCRIPT

Did the Civil Rights Movement Improve Race Relations in the United States?

Regardless of how one assesses the civil rights movement, there can be little doubt that the struggle for equality produced an important legacy. First, the movement had a critical impact on the civil rights struggles of groups other than African Americans. Women demanding equality, the American Indian movement, and gay rights protesters have all employed activities and strategies inherited from the civil rights movement. Second, there is an obvious tie between the forms of civil disobedience advocated by African American leaders and those carried out in protests against U.S. involvement in Southeast Asia. In fact, antiwar activists have linked continuing racism at home with their perception of American racism abroad. Third, the civil rights movement inadvertently produced a serious white backlash, based on the notion that majority rights were being overwhelmed by the will of a minority of the nation's citizens, which stymied further advances toward full equality.

The literature on the civil rights movement is extensive. August Meier, Elliott Rudwick, and Francis L. Broderick, eds., *Black Protest Thought in the Twentieth Century*, 2d ed. (Bobbs-Merrill, 1971) presents a collection of documents that places the activities of the 1950s and 1960s in a larger framework. The reflections of many of the participants of the movement are included in Howell Raines, *My Soul Is Rested: The Story of the Civil Rights Movement in the Deep South* (G. P. Putnam, 1977). Students should also consult Aldon D. Morris, *The Origins of the Civil Rights Movement: Black Communities Organizing for Change* (Free Press, 1984).

August Meier's contemporary assessment "On the Role of Martin Luther King," *Crisis* (1965) in many ways remains the most insightful analysis of King's leadership. More detailed studies include David L. Lewis, *King: A Critical Biography* (Praeger, 1970); Stephen B. Oates, *Let the Trumpet Sound: The Life of Martin Luther King, Jr.* (Harper & Row, 1982); David J. Garrow's Pulitzer Prize–winning *Bearing the Cross: Martin Luther King, Jr., and the Southern Christian Leadership Conference* (William Morrow, 1986); and Adam Fairclough, *To Redeem the Soul of America: The Southern Christian Leadership Conference and Martin Luther King, Jr.* (University of Georgia Press, 1987). Taylor Branch's *Parting the Waters: America in the King Years, 1954–63* (Simon & Schuster, 1988) is interesting.

A critical assessment of the legacy of the civil rights movement is presented in two books by political scientist Robert C. Smith: *We Have No Leaders: African Americans in the Post–Civil Rights Era* (State University of New York Press, 1994) and *Racism in the Post–Civil Rights Era: Now You See It, Now You Don't* (State University of New York Press, 1996).

ISSUE 14

Was America's Escalation of the War in Vietnam Inevitable?

YES: Brian VanDeMark, from *Into the Quagmire: Lyndon Johnson and the Escalation of the Vietnam War* (Oxford University Press, 1991)

NO: H. R. McMaster, from *Dereliction of Duty: Lyndon Johnson, Robert McNamara, the Joint Chiefs of Staff, and the Lies That Led to Vietnam* (HarperCollins, 1997)

ISSUE SUMMARY

YES: Professor of history Brian VanDeMark argues that President Lyndon Johnson failed to question the viability of increasing U.S. involvement in the Vietnam War because he was a prisoner of America's global containment policy and because he did not want his opponents to accuse him of being soft on communism or endanger support for his Great Society reforms.

NO: H. R. McMaster, an active-duty army tanker, maintains that the Vietnam disaster was not inevitable but a uniquely human failure whose responsibility was shared by President Johnson and his principal military and civilian advisers.

At the end of World War II, imperialism was coming to a close in Asia. Japan's defeat spelled the end of its control over China, Korea, and the countries of Southeast Asia. Attempts by the European nations to reestablish their empires were doomed. Anti-imperialist movements emerged all over Asia and Africa, often producing chaos.

The United States faced a dilemma. America was a nation conceived in revolution and was sympathetic to the struggles of Third World nations. But the United States was afraid that many of the revolutionary leaders were Communists who would place their countries under the control of the expanding empire of the Soviet Union. By the late 1940s the Truman administration decided that it was necessary to stop the spread of communism. The policy that resulted was known as containment.

Vietnam provided a test of the containment doctrine in Asia. Vietnam had been a French protectorate from 1885 until Japan took control of it during World War II. Shortly before the war ended, the Japanese gave Vietnam its independence, but the French were determined to reestablish their influence in the area. Conflicts emerged between the French-led nationalist forces of South Vietnam and the Communist-dominated provisional government of the Democratic Republic of Vietnam (DRV), which was established in Hanoi in August 1945. Ho Chi Minh was the president of the DRV. An avowed Communist since the 1920s, Ho had also become the major nationalist figure in Vietnam. As the leader of the anti-imperialist movement against French and Japanese colonialism for over 30 years, Ho managed to tie together the communist and nationalist movements in Vietnam.

A full-scale war broke out in 1946 between the communist government of North Vietnam and the French-dominated country of South Vietnam. After the Communists defeated the French at the battle of Dien Bien Phu in May 1954, the latter decided to pull out. At the Geneva Conference that summer, Vietnam was divided at the 17th parallel, pending elections.

The United States became directly involved in Vietnam after the French withdrew. In 1955 the Republican president Dwight D. Eisenhower refused to recognize the Geneva Accord but supported the establishment of the South Vietnamese government. In 1956 South Vietnam's leader, Ngo Dinh Diem, with U.S. approval, refused to hold elections, which would have provided a unified government for Vietnam in accordance with the Geneva Agreement. The Communists in the north responded by again taking up the armed struggle. The war continued for another 19 years.

Both President Eisenhower and his successor, John F. Kennedy, were anxious to prevent South Vietnam from being taken over by the Communists, so economic assistance and military aid were provided. Kennedy's successor, Lyndon B. Johnson, changed the character of American policy in Vietnam by escalating the air war and increasing the number of ground forces from 21,000 in 1965 to a full fighting force of 550,000 at its peak in 1968.

The next president, Richard Nixon, adopted a new policy of "Vietnamization" of the war. Military aid to South Vietnam was increased to ensure the defeat of the Communists. At the same time, American troops were gradually withdrawn from Vietnam. South Vietnamese president Thieu recognized the weakness of his own position without the support of U.S. troops. He reluctantly signed the Paris Accords in January 1973 only after being told by Secretary of State Henry Kissinger that the United States would sign them alone. Once U.S. soldiers were withdrawn, Thieu's regime was doomed. In spring 1975 a full-scale war broke out, and the South Vietnamese government collapsed.

In the following selection, Brian VanDeMark argues that President Johnson failed to question the viability of increasing U.S. involvement in Vietnam because he was a prisoner of America's global containment policy and he did not want his opponents to accuse him of being soft on communism. In the second selection, H. R. McMaster argues that the Vietnam disaster was not inevitable but a uniquely human failure whose responsibility was shared by Johnson and his civilian and military advisers.

Brian VanDeMark

YES

Into the Quagmire

Vietnam divided America more deeply and painfully than any event since the Civil War. It split political leaders and ordinary people alike in profound and lasting ways. Whatever the conflicting judgments about this controversial war—and there are many—Vietnam undeniably stands as the greatest tragedy of twentieth-century U.S. foreign relations.

America's involvement in Vietnam has, as a result, attracted much critical scrutiny, frequently addressed to the question, "Who was guilty?"—"Who led the United States into this tragedy?" A more enlightening question, it seems, is "How and why did this tragedy occur?" The study of Vietnam should be a search for explanation and understanding, rather than for scapegoats.

Focusing on one important period in this long and complicated story—the brief but critical months from November 1964 to July 1965, when America crossed the threshold from limited to large-scale war in Vietnam—helps to answer that question. For the crucial decisions of this period resulted from the interplay of longstanding ideological attitudes, diplomatic assumptions and political pressures with decisive contemporaneous events in America and Vietnam.

Victory in World War II produced a sea change in America's perception of its role in world affairs. Political leaders of both parties embraced a sweepingly new vision of the United States as the defender against the perceived threat of monolithic communist expansion everywhere in the world. This vision of American power and purpose, shaped at the start of the Cold War, grew increasingly rigid over the years. By 1964–1965, it had become an ironbound and unshakable dogma, a received faith which policymakers unquestionably accepted—even though the circumstances which had fostered its creation had changed dramatically amid diffused authority and power among communist states and nationalist upheaval in the colonial world.

Policymakers' blind devotion to this static Cold War vision led America into misfortune in Vietnam. Lacking the critical perspective and sensibility to reappraise basic tenets of U.S. foreign policy in the light of changed events and local circumstances, policymakers failed to perceive Vietnamese realities accurately and thus to gauge American interests in the area prudently. Policymakers, as a consequence, misread an indigenous, communist-led nationalist movement as part of a larger, centrally directed challenge to world order and stability; tied American fortunes to a non-communist regime of slim popular legitimacy and effectiveness; and intervened militarily in the region far out of proportion to U.S. security requirements.

An arrogant and stubborn faith in America's power to shape the course of foreign events compounded the dangers sown by ideological rigidity. Policymakers in 1964–1965 shared a common postwar conviction that the United States not only should, but could, control political conditions in South Vietnam, as elsewhere throughout much of the world. This conviction had led Washington to intervene progressively deeper in South Vietnamese affairs over the years. And when—despite Washington's increasing exertions—Saigon's political situation declined precipitously during 1964–1965, this conviction prompted policymakers to escalate the war against Hanoi, in the belief that America could stimulate political order in South Vietnam through the application of military force against North Vietnam.

Domestic political pressures exerted an equally powerful, if less obvious, influence over the course of U.S. involvement in Vietnam. The fall of China in 1949 and the ugly McCarthyism it aroused embittered American foreign policy for a generation. By crippling President Truman's political fortunes, it taught his Democratic successors, John Kennedy and Lyndon Johnson [LBJ], a strong and sobering lesson: that another "loss" to communism in East Asia risked renewed and devastating attacks from the right. This fear of reawakened McCarthyism remained a paramount concern as policymakers pondered what course to follow as conditions in South Vietnam deteriorated rapidly in 1964–1965.

⋅◆⋅

Enduring traditions of ideological rigidity, diplomatic arrogance, and political vulnerability heavily influenced the way policymakers approached decisions in Vietnam in 1964–1965. Understanding the decisions of this period fully, however, also requires close attention to contemporary developments in America and South Vietnam. These years marked a tumultuous time in both countries, which affected the course of events in subtle but significant ways.

Policymakers in 1964–1965 lived in a period of extraordinary domestic political upheaval sparked by the civil rights movement. It is difficult to overstate the impact of this upheaval on American politics in the mid-1960s. During 1964–1965, the United States—particularly the American South—experienced profound and long overdue change in the economic, political, and social rights of blacks. This change, consciously embraced by the liberal administration of Lyndon Johnson, engendered sharp political hostility among conservative southern whites and their deputies in Congress—hostility which the politically astute Johnson sensed could spill over into the realm of foreign affairs, where angry civil rights opponents could exact their revenge should LBJ stumble and "lose" a crumbling South Vietnam. This danger, reinforced by the memory of McCarthyism, stirred deep political fears in Johnson, together with an abiding aversion to failure in Vietnam.

LBJ feared defeat in South Vietnam, but he craved success and glory at home. A forceful, driving President of boundless ambition, Johnson sought to harness the political momentum created by the civil rights movement to enact a far-reaching domestic reform agenda under the rubric of the Great Society. LBJ would achieve the greatness he sought by leading America toward justice and opportunity for all its citizens, through his historic legislative program.

Johnson's domestic aspirations fundamentally conflicted with his uneasy involvement in Vietnam. An experienced and perceptive politician, LBJ knew his domestic reforms required the sustained focus and cooperation of Congress. He also knew a larger war in Vietnam jeopardized these reforms by drawing away political attention and economic resources. America's increasing military intervention in 1964–1965 cast this tension between Vietnam and the Great Society into sharp relief.

Johnson saw his predicament clearly. But he failed to resolve it for fear that acknowledging the growing extent and cost of the war would thwart his domestic reforms, while pursuing a course of withdrawal risked political ruin. LBJ, instead, chose to obscure the magnitude of his dilemma by obscuring America's deepening involvement as South Vietnam began to fail. That grave compromise of candor opened the way to Johnson's eventual downfall.

Events in South Vietnam during 1964–1965 proved equally fateful. A historically weak and divided land, South Vietnam's deeply rooted ethnic, political, and religious turmoil intensified sharply in the winter of 1964–1965. This mounting turmoil, combined with increased communist military attacks, pushed Saigon to the brink of political collapse.

South Vietnam's accelerating crisis alarmed American policymakers, driving them to deepen U.S. involvement considerably in an effort to arrest Saigon's political failure. Abandoning the concept of stability in the South *before* escalation against the North, policymakers now embraced the concept of stability *through* escalation, in the desperate hope that military action against Hanoi would prompt a stubbornly elusive political order in Saigon.

This shift triggered swift and ominous consequences scarcely anticipated by its architects. Policymakers soon confronted intense military, political, and bureaucratic pressures to widen the war. Unsettled by these largely unforeseen pressures, policymakers reacted confusedly and defensively. Rational men, they struggled to control increasingly irrational forces. But their reaction only clouded their attention to basic assumptions and ultimate costs as the war rapidly spun out of control in the spring and summer of 1965. In their desperation to make Vietnam policy work amid this rising tide of war pressures, they thus failed ever to question whether it could work—or at what ultimate price. Their failure recalls the warning of a prescient political scientist, who years before had cautioned against those policymakers with "an infinite capacity for making ends of [their] means."

The decisions of 1964–1965 bespeak a larger and deeper failure as well. Throughout this period—as, indeed, throughout the course of America's Vietnam involvement—U.S. policymakers strove principally to create a viable noncommunist regime in South Vietnam. For many years and at great effort and cost, Washington had endeavored to achieve political stability and competence in Saigon. Despite these efforts, South Vietnam's political disarray persisted and deepened, until, in 1965, America intervened with massive military force to avert its total collapse.

Few policymakers in 1964–1965 paused to mull this telling fact, to ponder its implications about Saigon's viability as a political entity. The failure to re-examine this and other fundamental premises of U.S. policy—chief among them Vietnam's importance to American national interests and Washington's ability to forge political order through military power—proved a costly and tragic lapse of statesmanship. . . .

･❀･

The legacy of Vietnam, like the war itself, remains a difficult and painful sub-ject for Americans. As passions subside and time bestows greater perspective, Americans still struggle to understand Vietnam's meaning and lessons for the country. They still wonder how the United States found itself ensnared in an ambiguous, costly, and divisive war, and how it can avoid repeating such an ordeal in the future.

The experience of Lyndon Johnson and his advisers during the decisive years 1964–1965 offers much insight into those questions. For their decisions, which fundamentally transformed U.S. participation in the war, both reflected and defined much of the larger history of America's Vietnam involvement.

Their decisions may also, one hopes, yield kernels of wisdom for the fu-ture; the past, after all, can teach us lessons. But history's lessons, as Vietnam showed, are themselves dependent on each generation's knowledge and under-standing of the past. So it proved for 1960s policymakers, whose ignorance and misperception of Southeast Asian history, culture, and politics pulled America progressively deeper into the war. LBJ, [Secretary of State Dean] Rusk, [Robert] McNamara, [McGeorge] Bundy, [Ambassador Maxwell] Taylor—most of their generation, in fact—mistakenly viewed Vietnam through the simplistic ideolog-ical prism of the Cold War. They perceived a deeply complex and ambiguous regional struggle as a grave challenge to world order and stability, fomented by communist China acting through its local surrogate, North Vietnam.

This perception, given their mixture of memories—the West's capitula-tion to Hitler at Munich, Stalin's postwar truculence, Mao's belligerent rhetoric —appears altogether understandable in retrospect. But it also proved deeply flawed and oblivious to abiding historical realities. Constrained by their mem-ories and ideology, American policymakers neglected the subtle but enduring force of nationalism in Southeast Asia. Powerful and decisive currents—the deep and historic tension between Vietnam and China; regional friction among the Indochinese states of Vietnam, Laos, and Cambodia; and, above all, Hanoi's fa-natical will to unification—went unnoticed or unweighed because they failed to fit Washington's worldview. Although it is true, as Secretary of State Rusk once said, that "one cannot escape one's experience," Rusk and his fellow poli-cymakers seriously erred by falling uncritical prisoners of their experience.

Another shared experience plagued 1960s policymakers like a ghost: the ominous specter of McCarthyism. This frightful political memory haunted LBJ and his Democratic colleagues like a barely suppressed demon in the national psyche. Barely ten years removed from the traumatic "loss" of China and its devastating domestic repercussions, Johnson and his advisers remembered its consequences vividly and shuddered at a similar fate in Vietnam. They talked about this only privately, but then with genuine and palpable fear. Defense Secretary McNamara, in a guarded moment, confided to a newsman in the spring of 1965 that U.S. disengagement from South Vietnam threatened "a disastrous political fight that could... freeze American political debate and even affect political freedom."

Such fears resonated deeply in policymakers' minds. Nothing, it seemed, could be worse than the "loss" of Vietnam—not even an intensifying stalemate secured at increasing military and political risk. For a President determined to fulfill liberalism's postwar agenda, Truman's ordeal in China seemed a powerfully forbidding lesson. It hung over LBJ in Vietnam like a dark shadow he could not shake, an agony he would not repeat.

McCarthyism's long shadow into the mid-1960s underscores a persistent and troubling phenomenon of postwar American politics: the peculiar vulnerability besetting liberal Presidents thrust into the maelstrom of world politics. In America's postwar political climate—dominated by the culture of anti-communism—Democratic leaders from Truman to Kennedy to Johnson remained acutely sensitive to the domestic repercussions of foreign policy failure. This fear of right-wing reaction sharply inhibited liberals like LBJ, narrowing what they considered their range of politically acceptable options, while diminishing their willingness to disengage from untenable foreign commitments. Thus, when Johnson did confront the bitter choice between defeat in Vietnam and fighting a major, inconclusive war, he reluctantly chose the second because he could not tolerate the domestic consequences of the first. Committed to fulfilling the Great Society, fearful of resurgent McCarthyism, and afraid that disengagement meant sacrificing the former to the latter, LBJ perceived least political danger in holding on.

But if Johnson resigned never to "lose" South Vietnam, he also resigned never to sacrifice his cherished Great Society in the process. LBJ's determination, however understandable, nonetheless led him deliberately and seriously to obscure the nature and cost of America's deepening involvement in the war during 1964–1965. This decision bought Johnson the short-term political maneuverability he wanted, but at a costly long-term political price. As LBJ's credibility on the war subsequently eroded, public confidence in his leadership slowly but irretrievably evaporated. And this, more than any other factor, is what finally drove Johnson from the White House.

It also tarnished the presidency and damaged popular faith in American government for more than a decade. Trapped between deeply conflicting pressures, LBJ never shared his dilemma with the public. Johnson would not, or felt he dare not, trust his problems with the American people. LBJ's decision, however human, tragically undermined the reciprocal faith between President and public indispensable to effective governance in a democracy. Just as tragically, it fostered a pattern of presidential behavior which led his successor, Richard Nixon, to eventual ruin amid even greater popular political alienation.

Time slowly healed most of these wounds to the American political process, while reconfirming the fundamental importance of presidential credibility in a democracy. Johnson's Vietnam travail underscored the necessity of public trust and support to presidential success. Without them, as LBJ painfully discovered, Presidents are doomed to disaster.

Johnson, in retrospect, might have handled his domestic dilemma more forthrightly. An equally serious dilemma, however, remained always beyond his —or Washington's—power to mend: the root problem of political disarray in South Vietnam. The perennial absence of stable and responsive government in Saigon troubled Washington policymakers profoundly; they understood, only too well, its pivotal importance to the war effort and to the social and economic reforms essential to the country's survival. Over and over again, American officials stressed the necessity of political cooperation to their embattled South Vietnamese allies. But to no avail. As one top American in Saigon later lamented, "[Y]ou could tell them all 'you've got to get together [and stop] this haggling and fighting among yourselves,' but how do you make them do it?" he said. "How do you make them do it?"

Washington, alas, could not. As Ambassador Taylor conceded early in the war, "[You] cannot order good government. You can't get it by fiat." This stubborn but telling truth eventually came to haunt Taylor and others. South Vietnam never marshaled the political will necessary to create an effective and enduring government; it never produced leaders addressing the aspirations and thus attracting the allegiance of the South Vietnamese people. Increasing levels of U.S. troops and firepower, moreover, never offset this fundamental debility. America, as a consequence, built its massive military effort on a foundation of political quicksand.

The causes of this elemental flaw lay deeply imbedded in the social and political history of the region. Neither before nor after 1954 was South Vietnam ever really a nation in spirit. Divided by profound ethnic and religious cleavages dating back centuries and perpetuated under French colonial rule, the people of South Vietnam never developed a common political identity. Instead, political factionalism and rivalry always held sway. The result: a chronic and fatal political disorder.

Saigon's fundamental weakness bore anguished witness to the limits of U.S. power. South Vietnam's shortcomings taught a proud and mighty nation that it could not save a people in spite of themselves—that American power, in the last analysis, offered no viable substitute for indigenous political resolve. Without this basic ingredient, as Saigon's turbulent history demonstrated, Washington's most dedicated and strenuous efforts will prove extremely vulnerable, if not futile.

This is not a happy or popular lesson. But it is a wise and prudent one, attuned to the imperfect realities of an imperfect world. One of America's sagest diplomats, George Kennan, understood and articulated this lesson well when he observed: "When it comes to helping people to resist Communist pressures, . . . no assistance . . . can be effective unless the people themselves have a very high degree of determination and a willingness to help themselves. The moment they begin to place the bulk of the burden on us," Kennan warned, "the whole situation is lost." This, tragically, is precisely what befell America in South Vietnam during 1964–1965. Hereafter, as perhaps always before—*external* U.S. economic, military, and political support provided the vital elements of stability and strength in South Vietnam. Without that *external* support, as events following America's long-delayed withdrawal in 1973 showed, South Vietnam's government quickly failed.

Washington's effort to forge political order through military power spawned another tragedy as well. It ignited unexpected pressures which quickly overwhelmed U.S. policymakers, and pulled them ever deeper into the war. LBJ and his advisers began bombing North Vietnam in early 1965 in a desperate attempt to spur political resolve in South Vietnam. But their effort boomeranged wildly. Rather than stabilizing the situation, it instead unleashed forces that soon put Johnson at the mercy of circumstances, a hostage to the war's accelerating momentum. LBJ, as a result, began steering with an ever looser hand. By the summer of 1965, President Johnson found himself not the controller of events but largely controlled by them. He had lost the political leader's "continual struggle," in the words of Henry Kissinger, "to rescue an element of choice from the pressure of circumstance."

LBJ's experience speaks powerfully across the years. With each Vietnam decision, Johnson's vulnerability to military pressure and bureaucratic momentum intensified sharply. Each step generated demands for another, even bigger step—which LBJ found increasingly difficult to resist. His predicament confirmed George Ball's admonition that war is a fiercely unpredictable force, often generating its own inexorable momentum.

Johnson sensed this danger almost intuitively. He quickly grasped the dilemma and difficulties confronting him in Vietnam. But LBJ lacked the inner strength—the security and self-confidence—to overrule the counsel of his inherited advisers.

Most of those advisers, on the other hand—especially McGeorge Bundy and Robert McNamara—failed to anticipate such perils. Imbued with an overweening faith in their ability to "manage" crises and "control" escalation, Bundy and McNamara, along with Maxwell Taylor, first pushed military action against the North as a lever to force political improvement in the South. But bombing did not rectify Saigon's political problems; it only exacerbated them, while igniting turbulent military pressures that rapidly overwhelmed these advisers' confident calculations.

These advisers' preoccupation with technique, with the application of power, characterized much of America's approach to the Vietnam War. Bundy and McNamara epitomized a postwar generation confident in the exercise and efficacy of U.S. power. Despite the dark and troubled history of European intervention in Indochina, these men stubbornly refused to equate America's situation in the mid-1960s to France's earlier ordeal. To them, the United States possessed limitless ability, wisdom, and virtue; it would therefore prevail where other western powers had failed.

This arrogance born of power led policymakers to ignore manifest dangers, to persist in the face of ever darkening circumstances. Like figures in Greek tragedy, pride compelled these supremely confident men further into disaster.

They succumbed to the affliction common to great powers throughout the ages —the dangerous "self-esteem engendered by power," as the political philosopher Hans Morgenthau once wrote, "which equates power and virtue, [and] in the process loses all sense of moral and political proportion."

Tradition, as well as personality, nurtured such thinking. For in many ways, America's military intervention in Vietnam represented the logical fulfillment of a policy and outlook axiomatically accepted by U.S. policymakers for nearly two decades—the doctrine of global containment. Fashioned at the outset of the Cold War, global containment extended American interests and obligations across vast new areas of the world in defense against perceived monolithic communist expansion. It remained the lodestar of America foreign policy, moreover, even as the constellation of international forces shifted dramatically amid diffused authority and power among communist states and nationalist upheaval in the post-colonial world.

Vietnam exposed the limitations and contradictions of this static doctrine in a world of flux. It also revealed the dangers and flaws of an undiscriminating, universalist policy which perceptive critics of global containment, such as the eminent journalist Walter Lippmann, had anticipated from the beginning. As Lippmann warned about global containment in 1947:

> Satellite states and puppet governments are not good material out of which to construct unassailable barriers [for American defense]. A diplomatic war conducted as this policy demands, that is to say conducted indirectly, means that we must stake our own security and the peace of the world upon satellites, puppets, clients, agents about whom we can know very little. Frequently they will act for their own reasons, and on their own judgments, presenting us with accomplished facts that we did not intend, and with crises for which we are unready. The "unassailable barriers" will present us with an unending series of insoluble dilemmas. We shall have either to disown our puppets, which would be tantamount to appeasement and defeat and loss of face, or must support them at an incalculable cost. . . .

Here lay the heart of America's Vietnam troubles. Driven by unquestioning allegiance to an ossified and extravagant doctrine, Washington officials plunged deeply into a struggle which itself dramatized the changed realities and complexities of the postwar world. Their action teaches both the importance of re-examining premises as circumstances change and the costly consequences of failing to recognize and adapt to them.

Vietnam represented a failure not just of American foreign policy but also of American statesmanship. For once drawn into the war, LBJ and his advisers quickly sensed Vietnam's immense difficulties and dangers—Saigon's congenital political problems, the war's spiraling military costs, the remote likelihood of victory—and plunged in deeper nonetheless. In their determination to preserve America's international credibility and protect their domestic political standing, they continued down an ever costlier path.

That path proved a distressing, multifaceted paradox. Fearing injury to the perception of American power, diminished faith in U.S. resolve, and a conservative political firestorm, policymakers rigidly pursued a course which ultimately injured the substance of American power by consuming exorbitant lives and resources, shook allied confidence in U.S. strategic judgment, and shattered liberalism's political unity and vigor by polarizing and paralyzing American society.

Herein lies Vietnam's most painful but pressing lesson. Statesmanship requires judgment, sensibility, and, above all, wisdom in foreign affairs—the wisdom to calculate national interests prudently and to balance commitments with effective power. It requires that most difficult task of political leaders: "to distinguish between what is desireable and what is possible, . . . between what is desireable and what is essential."

This is important in peace; it is indispensable in war. As the great tutor of statesmen, Carl von Clausewitz, wrote, "Since war is not an act of senseless passion but is controlled by its political object, the value of this object must determine the sacrifices to be made for it in *magnitude* and also in *duration.* Once the expenditure of effort exceeds the value of the political object," Clausewitz admonished, "the object must be renounced. . . ." His maxim, in hindsight, seems painfully relevant to a war which, as even America's military commander in Vietnam, General William Westmoreland, concluded, "the vital security of the United States was not and possibly could not be clearly demonstrated and understood. . . ."

LBJ and his advisers failed to heed this fundamental principle of statesmanship. They failed to weigh American costs in Vietnam against Vietnam's relative importance to American national interests and its effect on overall American power. Compelled by events in Vietnam and, especially, coercive political pressures at home, they deepened an unsound, peripheral commitment and pursued manifestly unpromising and immensely costly objectives. Their failure of statesmanship, then, proved a failure of judgment and, above all, of proportion.

NO ✔

H. R. McMaster

Dereliction of Duty

The Americanization of the Vietnam War between 1963 and 1965 was the product of an unusual interaction of personalities and circumstances. The escalation of U.S. military intervention grew out of a complicated chain of events and a complex web of decisions that slowly transformed the conflict in Vietnam into an American war.

Much of the literature on Vietnam has argued that the "Cold War mentality" put such pressure on President Johnson that the Americanization of the war was inevitable. The imperative to contain Communism was an important factor in Vietnam policy, but neither American entry into the war nor the manner in which the war was conducted was inevitable. The United States went to war in Vietnam in a manner unique in American history. Vietnam was not forced on the United States by a tidal wave of Cold War ideology. It slunk in on cat's feet.

Between November 1963 and July 1965, LBJ made the critical decisions that took the United States into war almost without realizing it. The decisions, and the way in which he made them, profoundly affected the way the United States fought in Vietnam. Although impersonal forces, such as the ideological imperative of containing Communism, the bureaucratic structure, and institutional priorities, influenced the president's Vietnam decisions, those decisions depended primarily on his character, his motivations, and his relationships with his principal advisers.

⁂

Most investigations of how the United States entered the war have devoted little attention to the crucial developments which shaped LBJ's approach to Vietnam and set conditions for a gradual intervention. The first of several "turning points" in the American escalation comprised the near-contemporaneous assassinations of Ngo Dinh Diem and John F. Kennedy. The legacy of the Kennedy administration included an expanded commitment to South Vietnam as an "experiment" in countering Communist insurgencies and a deep distrust of the military that manifested itself in the appointment of officers who would prove supportive of the administration's policies. After November 1963 the United

From H. R. McMaster, *Dereliction of Duty: Lyndon Johnson, Robert McNamara, the Joint Chiefs of Staff, and the Lies That Led to Vietnam* (HarperCollins, 1997). Copyright © 1997 by H. R. McMaster. Reprinted by permission of HarperCollins Publishers, Inc. Notes omitted.

States confronted what in many ways was a new war in South Vietnam. Having deposed the government of Ngo Dinh Diem and his brother Nhu, and having supported actions that led to their deaths, Washington assumed responsibility for the new South Vietnamese leaders. Intensified Viet Cong activity added impetus to U.S. deliberations, leading Johnson and his advisers to conclude that the situation in South Vietnam demanded action beyond military advice and support. Next, in the spring of 1964, the Johnson administration adopted graduated pressure as its strategic concept for the Vietnam War. Rooted in Maxwell Taylor's national security strategy of flexible response, graduated pressure evolved over the next year, becoming the blueprint for the deepening American commitment to maintaining South Vietnam's independence. Then, in August 1964, in response to the Gulf of Tonkin incident, the United States crossed the threshold of direct American military action against North Vietnam.

The Gulf of Tonkin resolution gave the president carte blanche for escalating the war. During the ostensibly benign "holding period" from September 1964 to February 1965, LBJ was preoccupied with his domestic political agenda, and McNamara built consensus behind graduated pressure. In early 1965 the president raised U.S. intervention to a higher level again, deciding on February 9 to begin a systematic program of limited air strikes on targets in North Vietnam and, on February 26, to commit U.S. ground forces to the South. Last, in March 1965, he quietly gave U.S. ground forces the mission of "killing Viet Cong." That series of decisions, none in itself tantamount to a clearly discernable decision to go to war, nevertheless transformed America's commitment in Vietnam.

❧❦❧

Viewed together, those decisions might create the impression of a deliberate determination on the part of the Johnson administration to go to war. On the contrary, the president did not want to go to war in Vietnam and was not planning to do so. Indeed, as early as May 1964, LBJ seemed to realize that an American war in Vietnam would be a costly failure. He confided to McGeorge Bundy, "... looks like to me that we're getting into another Korea. It just worries the hell out of me. I don't see what we can ever hope to get out of this." It was, Johnson observed, "the biggest damn mess that I ever saw.... It's damn easy to get into a war, but... it's going to be harder to ever extricate yourself if you get in." Despite his recognition that the situation in Vietnam demanded that he consider alternative courses of action and make a difficult decision, LBJ sought to avoid or to postpone indefinitely an explicit choice between war and disengagement from South Vietnam. In the ensuing months, however, each decision he made moved the United States closer to war, although he seemed not to recognize that fact.

The president's fixation on short-term political goals, combined with his character and the personalities of his principal civilian and military advisers, rendered the administration incapable of dealing adequately with the complexities of the situation in Vietnam. LBJ's advisory system was structured to achieve consensus and to prevent potentially damaging leaks. Profoundly insecure and distrustful of anyone but his closest civilian advisers, the president viewed the JCS [Joint Chiefs of Staff] with suspicion. When the situation in Vietnam seemed to demand military action, Johnson did not turn to his military advisers to determine how to solve the problem. He turned instead to his civilian advisers to determine how to postpone a decision. The relationship between the president, the secretary of defense, and the Joint Chiefs led to the curious situation in which the nation went to war without the benefit of effective military advice from the organization having the statutory responsibility to be the nation's "principal military advisers."

⁂

What Johnson feared most in 1964 was losing his chance to win the presidency in his own right. He saw Vietnam principally as a danger to that goal. After the election, he feared that an American military response to the deteriorating situation in Vietnam would jeopardize chances that his Great Society would pass through Congress. The Great Society was to be Lyndon Johnson's great domestic political legacy, and he could not tolerate the risk of its failure. McNamara would help the president first protect his electoral chances and then pass the Great Society by offering a strategy for Vietnam that appeared cheap and could be conducted with minimal public and congressional attention. McNamara's strategy of graduated pressure permitted Johnson to pursue his objective of not losing the war in Vietnam while postponing the "day of reckoning" and keeping the whole question out of public debate all the while.

McNamara was confident in his ability to satisfy the president's needs. He believed fervently that nuclear weapons and the Cold War international political environment had made traditional military experience and thinking not only irrelevant, but often dangerous for contemporary policy. Accordingly, McNamara, along with systems analysts and other civilian members of his own department and the Department of State, developed his own strategy for Vietnam. Bolstered by what he regarded as a personal triumph during the Cuban missile crisis, McNamara drew heavily on that experience and applied it to Vietnam. Based on the assumption that carefully controlled and sharply limited military actions were reversible, and therefore could be carried out at minimal risk and cost, graduated pressure allowed McNamara and Johnson to avoid confronting many of the possible consequences of military action.

⁂

Johnson and McNamara succeeded in creating the illusion that the decisions to attack North Vietnam were alternatives to war rather than war itself. Graduated pressure defined military action as a form of communication, the object of which was to affect the enemy's calculation of interests and dissuade him from a particular activity. Because the favored means of communication (bombing fixed installations and economic targets) were not appropriate for the mobile forces of the Viet Cong, who lacked an infrastructure and whose strength in the

South was political as well as military, McNamara and his colleagues pointed to the infiltration of men and supplies into South Vietnam as proof that the source and center of the enemy's power in Vietnam lay north of the seventeenth parallel, and specifically in Hanoi. Their definition of the enemy's source of strength was derived from that strategy rather than from a critical examination of the full reality in South Vietnam—and turned out to be inaccurate.

Graduated pressure was fundamentally flawed in other ways. The strategy ignored the uncertainty of war and the unpredictable psychology of an activity that involves killing, death, and destruction. To the North Vietnamese, military action, involving as it did attacks on their forces and bombing of their territory, was not simply a means of communication. Human sacrifices in war evoke strong emotions, creating a dynamic that defies systems analysis quantification. Once the United States crossed the threshold of war against North Vietnam with covert raids and the Gulf of Tonkin "reprisals," the future course of events depended not only on decisions made in Washington but also on enemy responses and actions that were unpredictable. McNamara, however, viewed the war as another business management problem that, he assumed, would ultimately succumb to his reasoned judgment and others' rational calculations. He and his assistants thought that they could predict with great precision what amount of force applied in Vietnam would achieve the results they desired and they believed that they could control that force with great precision from halfway around the world. There were compelling contemporaneous arguments that graduated pressure would not affect Hanoi's will sufficiently to convince the North to desist from its support of the South, and that such a strategy would probably lead to an escalation of the war. Others expressed doubts about the utility of attacking North Vietnam by air to win a conflict in South Vietnam. Nevertheless, McNamara refused to consider the consequences of his recommendations and forged ahead oblivious of the human and psychological complexities of war.

◈

Despite their recognition that graduated pressure was fundamentally flawed, the JCS were unable to articulate effectively either their objections or alternatives. Interservice rivalry was a significant impediment. Although differing perspectives were understandable given the Chiefs' long experience in their own services and their need to protect the interests of their services, the president's principal military advisers were obligated by law to render their best advice. The Chiefs' failure to do so, and their willingness to present single-service remedies to a complex military problem, prevented them from developing a comprehensive estimate of the situation or from thinking effectively about strategy.

When it became clear to the Chiefs that they were to have little influence on the policy-making process, they failed to confront the president with their objections to McNamara's approach to the war. Instead they attempted to work within that strategy in order to remove over time the limitations to further action. Unable to develop a strategic alternative to graduated pressure, the Chiefs became fixated on means by which the war could be conducted and pressed for an escalation of the war by degrees. They hoped that graduated pressure would evolve over time into a fundamentally different strategy, more in keeping with their belief in the necessity of greater force and its more resolute application. In so doing, they gave tacit approval to graduated pressure during the critical period in which the president escalated the war. They did not recommend the total force they believed would ultimately be required in Vietnam and accepted a strategy they knew would lead to a large but inadequate commitment of troops, for an extended period of time, with little hope for success.

⋅⟨⊙⟩⋅

McNamara and Lyndon Johnson were far from disappointed with the joint Chiefs' failings. Because his priorities were domestic, Johnson had little use for military advice that recommended actions inconsistent with those priorities. McNamara and his assistants in the Department of Defense, on the other hand, were arrogant. They disparaged military advice because they thought that their intelligence and analytical methods could compensate for their lack of military experience and education. Indeed military experience seemed to them a liability because military officers took too narrow a view and based their advice on antiquated notions of war. Geopolitical and technological changes of the last fifteen years, they believed, had rendered advice based on military experience irrelevant and, in fact, dangerous. McNamara's disregard for military experience and for history left him to draw principally on his staff in the Department of Defense and led him to conclude that his only real experience with the planning and direction of military force, the Cuban missile crisis, was the most relevant analogy to Vietnam.

While they slowly deepened American military involvement in Vietnam, Johnson and McNamara pushed the Chiefs further away from the decision-making process. There was no meaningful structure through which the Chiefs could voice their views—even the chairman was not a reliable conduit. NSC meetings were strictly *pro forma* affairs in which the president endeavored to build consensus for decisions already made. Johnson continued Kennedy's practice of meeting with small groups of his most trusted advisers. Indeed he made his most important decisions at the Tuesday lunch meetings in which Rusk, McGeorge Bundy, and McNamara were the only regular participants. The president and McNamara shifted responsibility for real planning away from the JCS to ad hoc committees composed principally of civilian analysts and attorneys, whose main goal was to obtain a consensus consistent with the president's pursuit of the middle ground between disengagement and war. The products of those efforts carried the undeserved credibility of proposals that had been agreed on by all departments and were therefore hard to oppose. McNamara and Johnson endeavored to get the advice they wanted by placing conditions and qualifications on questions that they asked the Chiefs. When the Chiefs' advice was not consistent with his own recommendations, McNamara, with the aid of the chairman of the Joint Chiefs of Staff, lied in meetings of the National Security Council about the Chiefs' views.

Rather than advice McNamara and Johnson extracted from the JCS acquiescence and silent support for decisions already made. Even as they relegated the Chiefs to a peripheral position in the policy-making process, they were careful to preserve the facade of consultation to prevent the JCS from opposing the administration's policies either openly or behind the scenes. As American involvement in the war escalated, Johnson's vulnerability to disaffected senior military officers increased because he was purposely deceiving the Congress and the public about the nature of the American military effort in Vietnam. The president and the secretary of defense deliberately obscured the nature of decisions made and left undefined the limits that they envisioned on the use of force. They indicated to the Chiefs that they would take actions that they never intended to pursue. McNamara and his assistants, who considered communication the purpose of military action, kept the nature of their objective from the JCS, who viewed "winning" as the only viable goal in war. Finally, Johnson appealed directly to them, referring to himself as the "coach" and them as "his team." To dampen their calls for further action, Lyndon Johnson attempted to generate sympathy from the JCS for the great pressures that he was feeling from those who opposed escalation.

The ultimate test of the Chiefs' loyalty came in July 1965. The administration's lies to the American public had grown in magnitude as the American military effort in Vietnam escalated. The president's plan of deception depended on tacit approval or silence from the JCS. LBJ had misrepresented the mission of U.S. ground forces in Vietnam, distorted the views of the Chiefs to lend credibility to his decision against mobilization, grossly understated the numbers of troops General Westmoreland had requested, and lied to the Congress about the monetary cost of actions already approved and of those awaiting final decision. The Chiefs did not disappoint the president. In the days before the president made his duplicitous public announcement concerning Westmoreland's request, the Chiefs, with the exception of commandant of the Marine Corps Greene, withheld from congressmen their estimates of the amount of force that would be needed in Vietnam. As he had during the Gulf of Tonkin hearings, Wheeler lent his support to the president's deception of Congress. The "five silent men" on the Joint Chiefs made possible the way the United States went to war in Vietnam.

Several factors kept the Chiefs from challenging the president's subterfuges. The professional code of the military officer prohibits him or her from engaging in political activity. Actions that could have undermined the administration's credibility and derailed its Vietnam policy could not have been undertaken lightly. The Chiefs felt loyalty to their commander in chief. The Truman-MacArthur controversy during the Korean War had warned the Chiefs about the dangers of overstepping the bounds of civilian control. Loyalty to their services also weighed against opposing the president and the secretary of defense. Harold Johnson, for example, decided against resignation because he thought he had to remain in office to protect the Army's interests as best he could. Admiral McDonald and Marine Corps Commandant Greene compromised their views on Vietnam in exchange for concessions to their respective services. Greene achieved a dramatic expansion of the Marine Corps, and McDonald ensured that the Navy retained control of Pacific Command. None of the Chiefs had sworn an oath to his service, however. They had all sworn, rather, to "support and defend the Constitution of the United States."

General Greene recalled that direct requests by congressmen for his assessment put him in a difficult situation. The president was lying, and he expected the Chiefs to lie as well or, at least, to withhold the whole truth. Although the president should not have placed the Chiefs in that position, the flag officers should not have tolerated it when he had.

Because the Constitution locates civilian control of the military in Congress as well as in the executive branch, the Chiefs could not have been justified in deceiving the peoples' representatives about Vietnam. Wheeler in particular allowed his duty to the president to overwhelm his obligations under the Constitution. As cadets are taught at the United States Military Academy, the JCS relationship with the Congress is challenging and demands that military officers possess a strong character and keen intellect. While the Chiefs must present Congress with their best advice based on their professional experience and education, they must be careful not to undermine their credibility by crossing the line between advice and advocacy of service interests.

Maxwell Taylor had a profound influence on the nature of the civil-military relationship during the escalation of American involvement in Vietnam. In contrast to Army Chief of Staff George C. Marshall, who, at the start of World War II, recognized the need for the JCS to suppress service parochialism to provide advice consistent with national interests, Taylor exacerbated service differences to help McNamara and Johnson keep the Chiefs divided and, thus, marginal to the policy process. Taylor recommended men for appointment to the JCS who were less likely than their predecessors to challenge the direction of the administration's military policy, even when they knew that that policy was fundamentally flawed. Taylor's behavior is perhaps best explained by his close personal friendship with the Kennedy family; McNamara; and, later, Johnson. In contrast again to Marshall, who thought it important to keep a professional distance from President Franklin Roosevelt, Taylor abandoned an earlier view similar to Marshall's in favor of a belief that the JCS and the president should enjoy "an intimate, easy relationship, born of friendship and mutual regard."

⋘⊚⋙

The way in which the United States went to war in the period between November 1963 and July 1965 had, not surprisingly, a profound influence on the conduct of the war and on its outcome. Because Vietnam policy decisions were made based on domestic political expediency, and because the president was intent on forging a consensus position behind what he believed was a middle policy, the administration deliberately avoided clarifying its policy objectives and postponed discussing the level of force that the president was willing to commit to the effort. Indeed, because the president was seeking domestic political consensus, members of the administration believed that ambiguity in the objectives for fighting in Vietnam was a strength rather than a weakness. Determined to prevent dissent from the JCS, the administration concealed its development of "fall-back" objectives.

Over time the maintenance of U.S. credibility quietly supplanted the stated policy objective of a free and independent South Vietnam. The principal civilian planners had determined that to guarantee American credibility, it was not necessary to win in Vietnam. That conclusion, combined with the belief that the use of force was merely another form of diplomatic communication, directed the military effort in the South at achieving stalemate rather than victory. Those charged with planning the war believed that it would be possible to preserve American credibility even if the United States armed forces withdrew from the South, after a show of force against the North and in the South in which American forces were "bloodied." After the United States became committed to war, however, and more American soldiers, airmen, and Marines had died in the conflict, it would become impossible simply to disengage and declare America's credibility intact, a fact that should have been foreseen. The Chiefs sensed the shift in objectives, but did not challenge directly the views of civilian planners in that connection. McNamara and Johnson recognized that, once committed to war, the JCS would not agree to an objective other than imposing a solution on the enemy consistent with U.S. interests. The JCS deliberately avoided clarifying the objective as well. As a result, when the United States went to war, the JCS pursued objectives different from those of the president. When the Chiefs requested permission to apply force consistent with their conception of U.S. objectives, the president and McNamara, based on their goals and domestic political constraints, rejected JCS requests, or granted them only in part. The result was that the JCS and McNamara became fixated on the means rather than on the ends, and on the manner in which the war was conducted instead of a military strategy that could connect military actions to achievable policy goals.

Because forthright communication between top civilian and military officials in the Johnson administration was never developed, there was no reconciliation of McNamara's intention to limit the American military effort sharply and the Chiefs' assessment that the United States could not possibly win under such conditions. If they had attempted to reconcile those positions, they could not have helped but recognize the futility of the American war effort.

The Joint Chiefs of Staff became accomplices in the president's deception and focused on a tactical task, killing the enemy. General Westmoreland's "strategy" of attrition in South Vietnam, was, in essence, the absence of a strategy. The result was military activity (bombing North Vietnam and killing the enemy in South Vietnam) that did not aim to achieve a clearly defined objective. It was unclear how quantitative measures by which McNamara interpreted the success and failure of the use of military force were contributing to an end of the war. As American casualties mounted and the futility of the strategy became apparent, the American public lost faith in the effort. The Chiefs did not request the number of troops they believed necessary to impose a military solution in South Vietnam until after the Tet offensive in 1968. By that time, however, the president was besieged by opposition to the war and was unable even to consider the request. LBJ, who had gone to such great lengths to ensure a crushing defeat over Barry Goldwater in 1964, declared that he was withdrawing from the race for his party's presidential nomination.

Johnson thought that he would be able to control the U.S. involvement in Vietnam. That belief, based on the strategy of graduated pressure and McNamara's confident assurances, proved in dramatic fashion to be false. If the president was surprised by the consequences of his decisions between November 1963 and July 1965, he should not have been so. He had disregarded the advice he did not want to hear in favor of a policy based on the pursuit of his own political fortunes and his beloved domestic programs.

ᴇᴥᴼ⋗ᴠ

The war in Vietnam was not lost in the field, nor was it lost on the front pages of the *New York Times* or on the college campuses. It was lost in Washington, D.C., even before Americans assumed sole responsibility for the fighting in 1965 and before they realized the country was at war; indeed, even before the first American units were deployed. The disaster in Vietnam was not the result of impersonal forces but a uniquely human failure, the responsibility for which was shared by President Johnson and his principal military and civilian advisers. The failings were many and reinforcing: arrogance, weakness, lying in the pursuit of self-interest, and, above all, the abdication of responsibility to the American people.

POSTSCRIPT

Was America's Escalation of the War in Vietnam Inevitable?

The book from which VanDeMark's selection was excerpted is a detailed study of the circumstances surrounding the decisions that President Lyndon Johnson made to increase America's presence in Vietnam via the bombing raids of North Vietnam in February 1965 and the introduction of ground troops the following July. VanDeMark agrees with McMaster that Johnson did not consult the Joint Chiefs of Staff about the wisdom of the policy of escalating the war. In fact, Johnson's decisions of "graduated pressure" were made in increments by the civilian advisers surrounding Secretary of Defense Robert McNamara. The policy, if it can be called such, was to prevent the National Liberation Front and its Viet Cong army from taking over South Vietnam. Each service branch fought its own war without coordinating with one another or with the government of South Vietnam. In VanDeMark's view, U.S. intervention was doomed to failure because South Vietnam was an artificial and very corrupt nation-state created by the French and later supported by the Americans. It was unfortunate that the nationalist revolution was tied up with the Communists led by Ho Chi Minh, who had been fighting French colonialism and Japanese imperialism since the 1920s—unlike Korea and Malaysia, which had alternative, noncommunist, nationalist movements.

Why did Johnson plunge "into the quagmire"? For one thing, Johnson remembered how previous democratic presidents Franklin D. Roosevelt and Harry S. Truman had been charged with being soft on communism and accused of losing Eastern Europe to the Russians after the Second World War and China to the Communists in the Chinese Civil War in 1949. In addition, both presidents were charged by Senator Joseph McCarthy and others of harboring Communists in U.S. government agencies. If Johnson was tough in Vietnam, he could stop communist aggression. At the same time, he could ensure that his Great Society social programs of Medicare and job retraining, as well as the impending civil rights legislation, would be passed by Congress.

As an army officer who fought in the Persian Gulf War, McMaster offers a unique perspective on the decision-making processes used by government policymakers. McMaster spares no one in his critique of what he considers the flawed Vietnam policy of "graduated pressure." He says that McNamara, bolstered by the success of America during the Cuban Missile Crisis, believed that the traditional methods of fighting wars were obsolete. Johnson believed in McNamara's approach, and the president's own need for consensus in the decision-making process kept the Joint Chiefs of Staff out of the loop.

Unlike other military historians, who generally absolve the military from responsibility for the strategy employed during the war, McMaster argues that the Joint Chiefs of Staff were responsible for not standing up to Johnson and telling him that his military strategy was seriously flawed. McMaster's views are not as new as some reviewers of his book seem to think. Bruce Palmer, Jr., in *The Twenty-Five Year War: America's Military Role in Vietnam* (University Press of Kentucky, 1984), and Harry G. Summers, Jr., in *On Strategy: A Critical Analysis of the Vietnam War* (Presidio Press, 1982), also see a flawed strategy of war. Summers argues that Johnson should have asked Congress for a declaration of war and fought a conventional war against North Vietnam.

One scholar has claimed that over 7,000 books about the Vietnam War have been published. The starting point for the current issue is Lloyd Gardner and Ted Gittinger, eds., *Vietnam: The Early Decisions* (University of Texas Press, 1997). See also Larry Berman, *Planning a Tragedy: The Americanization of the War in Vietnam* (W. W. Norton, 1982) and *Lyndon Johnson's War* (W. W. Norton, 1989); David Halberstam, *The Best and the Brightest* (Random House, 1972); and Lloyd C. Gardner, *Pay Any Price: Lyndon Johnson and the Wars for Vietnam* (Ivan Dee, 1995). Primary sources can be found in the U.S. Department of State's two-volume *Foreign Relations of the United States, 1964–1968: Vietnam* (Government Printing Office, 1996) and in the relevant sections of one of the most useful collections of primary sources and essays, *Major Problems in the History of the Vietnam War,* 2d ed., by Robert J. McMahon (Houghton Mifflin, 2000).

The bureaucratic perspective can be found in a series of essays by George C. Herring entitled *LBJ and Vietnam: A Different Kind of War* (University of Texas Press, 1995). Herring is also the author of the widely used text *America's Longest War: the United States and Vietnam* (Alfred A. Knopf, 1986). A brilliant article often found in anthologies is by historian and former policymaker James Thompson, "How Could Vietnam Happen: An Autopsy," *The Atlantic Monthly* (April 1968). An interesting comparison of the 1954 Dien Bien Phu and 1965 U.S. escalation decisions is Fred I. Greenstein and John P. Burke, "The Dynamics of Presidential Reality Testing: Evidence From Two Vietnam Decisions," *Political Science Quarterly* (Winter 1989–1990). A nice review essay on Vietnam's impact on today's military thinking is Michael C. Desch's "Wounded Warriors and the Lessons of Vietnam," *Orbis* (Summer 1998).

ISSUE 15

Should America Remain a Nation of Immigrants?

YES: Reed Ueda, from "The Permanently Unfinished Country," *The World & I* (October 1992)

NO: Richard D. Lamm, from "Truth, Like Roses, Often Comes With Thorns," *Vital Speeches of the Day* (December 1, 1994)

ISSUE SUMMARY

YES: Professor of history Reed Ueda maintains that the sheer magnitude and diversity of immigrants continually reshapes the American character, making America a "permanently unfinished country."

NO: Former Colorado governor Richard D. Lamm argues that immigration should be severely curtailed. He contends that the most recent immigrants are members of the underclass who are culturally unassimilable and who take jobs away from the poorest citizens in an already overpopulated America.

Historians of immigration tend to divide the forces that encouraged voluntary migrations from one country to another into push and pull factors. Historically, the major reason why people left their native countries was the breakdown of feudalism and the subsequent rise of a commercially oriented economy. Peasants were pushed off the feudal estates of which they had been a part for generations. In addition, religious and political persecution for dissenting groups and the lack of economic opportunities for many middle-class émigrés also contributed to the migrations from Europe to the New World.

America was attractive to settlers long before the American Revolution took place. While the United States may not have been completely devoid of feudal traditions, immigrants perceived the United States as a country with a fluid social structure where opportunities abounded for everyone. By the mid-nineteenth century, the Industrial Revolution had provided opportunities for jobs in a nation that had always experienced chronic labor shortages.

There were four major periods of migration to the United States: 1607–1830, 1830–1890, 1890–1925, and 1968 to the present. In the seventeenth and eighteenth centuries, the white settlers came primarily, though not entirely, from the British Isles. They were joined by millions of African slaves. Both groups lived in proximity to several hundred thousand Native Americans. In those years the cultural values of Americans were a combination of what history professor Gary Nash has referred to as "red, white, and black." In the 30 years before the Civil War, a second phase began when immigrants came from other countries in northern and western Europe as well as China. Two European groups dominated. Large numbers of Irish Catholics emigrated in the 1850s because of the potato famine. Religious and political factors were as instrumental as economic factors in pushing the Germans to America. Chinese immigrants were also encouraged to come during the middle and later decades of the nineteenth century in order to help build the western portion of America's first transcontinental railroad and to work in low-paying service industries like laundries and restaurants.

By 1890 a third period of immigration had begun. Attracted by the unskilled jobs provided by the Industrial Revolution and the cheap transportation costs of fast-traveling, steam-powered ocean vessels, immigrants poured in at a rate of close to 1 million a year from Italy, Greece, Russia, and other countries of southern and eastern Europe. This flood continued until the early 1920s, when fears of a foreign takeover led Congress to pass legislation restricting the number of immigrants into the United States to 150,000 per year.

For the next 40 years America was ethnically frozen. The restriction laws of the 1920s favored northern and western European groups and were biased against southern and eastern Europeans. The depression of the 1930s, World War II in the 1940s, and minimal changes in the immigration laws of the 1950s kept migrations to the United States at a minimum level.

In the 1960s the immigration laws were drastically revised. The civil rights acts of 1964 and 1965, which ended legal discrimination against African Americans, were also the impetus for immigration reform. The 1965 Immigration Act represented a turning point in U.S. history. But it had unintended consequences. In conjunction with the 1990 Immigration Act, discrimination against non-European nations was abolished and preferences were given to family-based migrants over refugees and those with special skills. Immigrants from Latin American and Asian countries have dominated the fourth wave of migration and have used the loophole in the legislation to bring into the country "immediate relatives," such as spouses, children, and parents of American citizens who are exempt from the numerical ceilings of the immigration laws.

Should America remain a nation of immigrants? In the following selection, Reed Ueda maintains that America is a permanently unfinished country as a result of immigration. In the second selection, Richard D. Lamm makes a case for restricting current immigration to a total of 300,000 per year, a 75 percent reduction from the 1.2 million who have entered each year in the 1990s, because immigration has harmed America's participation in the global economy.

➡ **YES**

The Permanently Unfinished Country

The twentieth century has been called the "American century" because of the rise of the United States to world leadership. It has also been the era when the country became a world immigrant nation. The historical role of the United States as the quintessential magnetic society built from immigration has expanded to accommodate greater ethnic diversity. By the 1990s, the flow of newcomers included people from every region and culture of the globe.

However, this "new diversity" is merely a child of old historic patterns. Unless this is grasped, we are likely to mistake this new diversity as a new threat or new utopia, when it is in reality an outgrowth of roots imbedded in our national past. Thus the question "How new is diversity?" should actually be, "How old is diversity?"

The historical record shows that ethnic diversity is as old as the United States. The first U.S. census in 1790 revealed that the majority of Americans then were not of English origin. California had a higher proportion of Asians in 1880 than it did in 1980. In 1900, the majority of inhabitants in the largest cities were immigrants or the children of immigrants. In 1910, more than 50 languages were spoken by immigrants in the United States. Government and census records of the past amply prove the longstanding reality of American diversity.

This phenomenal ethnic diversity is largely due to certain unique characteristics of American immigration. The first key feature is the sheer magnitude of immigration: By 1990, 57 million people had migrated to the United States, the largest international movement of population in history. More immigrants came to the United States than to all other major immigrant-receiving countries combined. From 1820 to 1930, 38 million people moved to the United States, while 24 million migrated to Canada, Argentina, Brazil, Australia, New Zealand, and South Africa combined. The United States attracted three-fifths of the population flocking to major immigration countries. From the mid-nineteenth century to the Great Depression, the United States received more than 30 million newcomers, while Argentina received 6.4 million, Canada 5.2 million, Brazil 4.4 million, and Australia 2.9 million.

The second defining feature of American immigration is that it encompasses the greatest variety of nationalities among all the modern international

From Reed Ueda, "The Permanently Unfinished Country," *The World & I* (October 1992). Copyright © 1992 by *The World & I*. Reprinted by permission of *The World & I*, a publication of The Washington Times Corporation.

population movements. Fifteen percent of American immigrants came from Germany, 11 percent from Italy, 10 percent from Ireland, 9 percent from Austria-Hungary, 8 percent from Canada, and only 7 percent from England. More Latin American, Caribbean, and Asian immigrants have journeyed to America than to any other nation. By contrast, other English-speaking immigrant countries have drawn new settlers almost wholly from other English-speaking nations. Eighty percent of immigrants to Australia came from Great Britain, while in Canada 37 percent arrived from Great Britain and another 37 percent from the United States. Immigration into Latin America is limited chiefly to those of Iberian or Italian origin. In Argentina, 47 percent of the immigrants came from Italy and 32 percent from Spain; in Brazil, 34 percent came from Italy, 29 percent from Portugal, and 14 percent from Spain.

Every immigrant, from the Mexican farm laborer to the Polish steelworker, has been a bold adventurer on a voyage of discovery. Emma Lazarus was wrong in describing immigrants as "wretched refuse" in her poem "The New Colossus" that adorns the Statue of Liberty. In reality, the immigrants are brave, resourceful, and vigorous, with the immigrant resiliency to cope with tremendous social change and social loss.

The early immigrants made enormous sacrifices, and persevered to realize a new vision of man and society. They found that the novel American conditions of tolerance toward pluralism and variety made the forging of new identities and cultural ties inescapable. The immigrant American is a person who absorbs new ways from neighboring people who are different. The children of Japanese immigrants in Hawaii learn new games, new words, new values, new tastes in food, new dress and hairstyles, new friendships and relationships from their neighbors, who are Hawaiian, Filipino, German, Chinese, and Portuguese. Americans are not bound to tradition but are open to change and choices that come from outsiders. They learn from people unlike themselves about different foods, music, skills, arts and values. The American language is an immigrant language, a blending of many ethnic vocabularies.

A New Society

American immigrants have created a new society completely different from old societies like Sweden, Scotland, or Japan. These societies had taken strength from homogeneity. Solidarity came from all people being the same. American immigrants have built a society that substitutes a radical new self-definition for the nation. In the United States, the strength of the nation comes from the immense multiplicity of ethnic groups. Moreover, it hinges upon the existence of conditions that permit dissimilar groups to act and live together. The resultant mutual fusion and interdependency help integrate the nation. The large majority of nations in the world have little historical experience or political interest in operating as an immigrant-receiving nation. The German political leader Volker Ruhe expressed this viewpoint in 1991 by announcing "We [in Germany] are not an immigration country and we will not become one." But other societies—such as Japan, Norway, Scotland, Sweden, or Korea—also have no tradition of immigration and little interest in developing one.

By contrast, immigration has been the shaping force of the American nation and its role in world history. It has contributed an endless flux to American social history, making the nation, in the words of sociologist Nathan Glazer, "the permanently unfinished country." Immigration to America has adjusted the balance of human and material resources between nations, creating new international economic and cultural ties. Otto von Bismarck, the "Iron Chancellor" who unified Germany, called American immigration the "decisive fact" of the modern world.

Thus, at the heart of American history lies the cycle of national creation and recreation through immigration. The social foundation of the political nation has been a historical immigrant nation that has been ever-changing. Historically, three immigrant nations arose successively and fused into each other in the two centuries after the American Revolution, producing immense changes in social organization, cultural life, and nationality. The new republic built by Protestant colonials from the British Isles had to accommodate, by the Civil War, an immigrant nation of Irish Catholics and newcomers from Germany and Scandinavia. After the turn of the century, a new immigrant nation formed principally from migrations from southern and eastern Europe, with input also from east Asia, Mexico, and the Caribbean. In the late twentieth century, a multicultural immigrant nation coalesced out of the expansion of immigration onto a global stage. The United States, on the eve of the twenty-first century, is a cumulative fusion of these immigrant nations, a synthesis that has come to embody a "world" or international culture.

The contemporary multicultural focus on the differences and separate experiences of diverse groups often starts from a myopia toward the enormous magnitude of ethnic assimilation that is part of American history. When David Dinkins, the first black mayor of New York City, delivered his inaugural address, he paid homage to his city as a "beautiful mosaic." The discrete and static parts of the mosaic form an image employed to legitimize a model of ethnic relations that favors cultural preservationism. This image, however, only pictures one part of American social history, the unmelted elements found among all groups. The other part of the picture has been the chemistry of change in status, culture, and identity. This process has not been as far-reaching or uniform as the earlier image for ethnic relations, the melting pot, once described and predicted. But it would be unrealistic to ignore the dimensions of social mobility and acculturation experienced over the span of generations by every group since the arrival of immigrant ancestors.

It is a cliché to disparage the melting-pot model of ethnic relations as a path toward homogenization or even "Anglo-conformity." It is true that Anglo-Saxon nativists of the early twentieth century prescribed this method of dealing with ethnic pluralism. But, recently, this sterotypical view of the melting-pot culture has been resuscitated by journalists and advocates seeking to use it as a target for the movement to promote multicultural difference.

The melting pot as a social and cultural reality in history was never Anglo-conformist or homogeneous. It was the shared national culture, a fusion of elements taken from a multitude of group cultures. Assimilation has been a multidirectional process, undertaken with mutual concern among local groups.

Groups changed and merged like the images of a kaleidoscope, with astounding and unpredictable patterns of diversity that yet cohered into a unity. Moreover, many features of group life were left unmelted and unfused. Melting has been incomplete, not always linear, and it proceeded at a variety of paces for different groups. Northern European groups that were two or more generations removed from the Old World had the most attenuated sense of ethnic identity. Some examples of European groups that no longer stressed specific loyalties have been the Scotch-Irish, the Welsh, and the Dutch. Although they retained a stronger sense of special identity, the Norwegians, Danes, Swedes, and Germans have also grown distant from an ethnic identity based on the homeland. Americans descended from forebears who came from southern and eastern Europe, Asia, the Caribbean, and Latin America exhibited a stronger tendency to retain distinctive ethnic features.

One of the most sensitive signs of mutual assimilation or multidirectional fusion of American society has been intermarriage. The Japanese Americans and Jews who most stressed marriage within the ethnic group early in the twentieth century now marry out at the highest rates, about one out of two marrying spouses of other ethnic backgrounds. The dramatic story of the rise of intermarriage is recorded in the multiple ancestry table of the 1980 federal census.

Prejudice and discrimination based on ethnic identity have affected all groups at one time or other, but the immigrants found niches on the social pyramid that would provide a foothold for further ascent. The new immigrants —such as the Greeks, Jews, Italians, Slavs, Armenians, Chinese, Japanese, and Mexicans—faced severe exclusion from jobs, schools, and neighborhoods. Most workers advanced little and lived a life of transiency and grinding poverty. But equality of opportunity increased for their children and grandchildren, upon which they capitalized to chart a course of multigenerational advancement. The descendants of even the most impoverished and powerless immigrants have obtained better jobs, more education, and higher status than their immigrant forebears. In the media culture and political culture of mass parties they have achieved more representation and greater voice than their ancestors. Recent immigrants from Latin America, Asia, the Caribbean, and the Middle East appear to be starting their own multigenerational cycle of social mobility. Any verdict on America's identity as a land of opportunity must rest on the broader view of the promise of American life as directed to the children and grandchildren of immigrants.

The groups that were involuntarily incorporated into the nation through conquest and slavery, American Indians and African blacks, encountered greater difficulty in achieving social mobility. Treated as separate quasi-nations, Indians were quarantined in the reservation system; blacks had to struggle against slavery and its residual barriers. The elimination of poverty within the Indian and black populations remains a crucial challenge.

The immigrant's need to deal with outsiders who were different in order to survive made ethnic boundary crossing practical and opportunistic. An individual's opportunities increased according to the ability to diversify social contacts. To tap the full range of opportunity, it was necessary to overlook ethnic differences and loyalties. Ethnic group members were willing to ignore the religion or ancestry of the person with whom they developed instrumental and mutually beneficial social relations and economic ties. Immigrants could only gain political power and office by forming alliances with outsiders. No ethnic group constituted a secure majority except at the most localized level. In order to become a force, groups had to form coalitions that leapfrogged ethnic divisions. Ethnic groups in America lacked the size and power to isolate their members. Their members forged and dissolved linkages with people from other groups as made necessary by self-interest and permitted by the limits of discriminatory boundaries. The dynamic conditions of American society that detached people from families and groups of origin and reabsorbed them into new families and new communities created novel combinations of ethnic identity.

The kaleidoscopic complexity of American identity also reveals that the dynamics of social history have made ethnicity only a part of human identity. The nature of ethnic identity changed as it was outflanked and decentered by the forming of multiple identities and competing loyalties. Members of ethnic minorities forged overlapping bonds with other types of communities that increased as one generation succeeded the next. Even the youngest new Americans are shaped by the heterogeneous world of classmates and playmates.

In fact, many Americans have come not to identify with a particular ethnic group; their identity derives primarily from their occupation, consumer habits, generation, geographic location, and mass culture. In a special census survey in 1970, nearly half of the sample group of European origins chose not to identify with a specific ethnic heritage. If the sample had included Hawaiian persons of mixed ancestry, a similar pattern probably would have emerged. These populations represent a transnational group that has grown in size and importance, inclusive of the increasing numbers of people of mixed ethnic and racial parentage.

The conditions that promoted intergroup and intercultural fusion nevertheless retained the capacity to support the preservation of cultural heritages. American conditions have allowed the melted and the unmelted to coexist in equilibrium. The Jews, Koreans, Irish, and Armenians and others who were persecuted in their homelands saw melting-pot America as the land where they were at greatest liberty to maintain their way of life. This was the advantage of democracy that made the difficult journey worth it. Here, government left them alone to pursue their religion, build their neighborhood institutions, start their own schools. The tendency today is to see the historic United States as callously assimilationist. But let us not forget that immigrants throughout history voted with their feet that the United States was the most tolerant nation in the world. Today's sophisticates give in too readily to skepticism or cynicism about the historic nation as a haven of multicultural pluralism. The unsophisticated immigrants of 1910 found in America a place of refuge to protect their group life and culture. The Irish, Italians, Greeks, Japanese, Chinese, and Mexicans did not have activist government programs to protect their cultures, yet the historical record shows that their cultural identities were systematically and enduringly preserved. Irish parochial schools, Jewish religious schools, and German and Japanese language schools reached a flourishing pinnacle in the late nineteenth and early twentieth centuries, when public institutions did not give them support.

Americans have long seen their country as the land of opportunity and individual freedom. However, fears that the United States would disintegrate through the social disorders wrought by immigration have surfaced time and again. American authorities, such as the great economist Francis Walker and anthropologist Madison Grant, have sounded the alarm that immigration is a force corroding the nation.

Ultimately, their views gave way to the ascendant idea that immigration played a positive role in the nation's development. The intellectual turning points in this ideological change were marked by the work of historians Marcus Lee Hansen and Oscar Handlin. They viewed immigration as a source of the national ethos of liberty and individualism. Handlin's historical writings on immigration formed the intellectual and ethical capstone of the view of immigration as a liberating and nationalizing force. In his work, immigration was transfigured into a myth-history of the creation of modern identity. The immigrant American became the archetype of the individual freed from the shackles of prescribed roles by moving into an alien world to discover a new empowering identity. Immigration facilitated the fulfillment of the national and global destiny of the United States as the prototypical modern nation unified by the joint effort of dissimilar groups.

The vision of Hansen and Handlin can help refocus the public mind on the historic liberal conditions conducive to forging a national community. It is needed in our time to allay destructive anxiety over the new diversity. It also is needed to counteract the artificial division of society into separate ethnic classes under government social policies. The historically rooted forces that made American identity heterogeneous and transcendent of differences were ineluctable and are still vital. The mutual assimilation of immigrants, their need to establish interdependency with surrounding groups, and their vision of American democracy as the best haven for cultural pluralism probably ensure that voluntary and fluid identities will continue to make immigration a nationalizing experience.

Richard D. Lamm

 **NO**

Truth, Like Roses, Often Comes With Thorns

Delivered before the 1994 Harris Bank Family Conference, Chicago, Illinois, October, 15, 1994

I have never started a speech by citing Joseph Stalin, but I do so today. Joseph Stalin once said: "One man's death; that's a tragedy, a million men's death; that's a statistic." I have been intrigued with that quote in the health care context. In American health care, we have the rule of rescue where we will go to unfathomable expense to save an individual, but yet we have over 30 million people without basic health insurance. Hundreds of thousands of American women give birth without adequate prenatal care, and 40 percent of our city youths are not fully vaccinated ... yet, we spend hundreds of millions of dollars on "long shot" medicine at the end of life.

Individualism is fine, and it is one of the things that has made America great. But when you come to social policies, quite often the focus on the individual is at conflict with what should be the ends of your social policy.

"The divergence between what is good for the individual and what is good for society is one of the key elements in the health care debate," observes one scholar.

This is true not only of the health care debate, but it is central to the debates about many other important national issues. Does the right of a homeless person, for instance, to loiter in a public library because it is his only form of shelter, supersede the right of the rest of society to use the library in safety and in comfort?

Does the right of a welfare mother to have additional children take precedence over the taxpayers' interest in her not having more kids?

It is a dilemma that we find when we try to formulate our immigration policies as well. Should we give greater weight to the interest of the individual immigrant, who simply wants to improve his or her life by settling in the U.S., than we do the interest society has in limiting immigration?

To govern is to choose. Yet, choosing does not come easy to Americans. Our whole cultural heritage is that we can do everything for everybody, not only in the health care area, but in virtually every other area. Walt Whitman called America "the bulging store house and the endless freight train." The idea of any limit is abhorrent.

Yet, we are borrowing over a billion dollars a day from our children and our grandchildren, and recklessly running up nation-threatening deficits. By not having the maturity to ask hard questions about our limited resources, we are not only doing many people injustice, but we are doing the future injustice. We are stealing from our children's heritage.

It is this kind of lack of forethought or consideration of consequences that has been the hallmark of our immigration policy for decades. Factoring in legal immigration, admission of refugees, political asylum seekers and illegal immigrants who settle permanently, the United States now admits between 1.2 million and 1.4 million people a year.

These are abstract numbers, so let me put them into context for you. I live in Denver, a city of approximately half a million people. In other words, our immigration policies are responsible for the equivalent of a new Denver every five months! And we will go on adding a new Denver every five months indefinitely, with no end in sight.

What's even more astounding is that nobody really seems to know why. It is perhaps the only important public policy that has no definable objective. We cannot even articulate a national interest here. Ask the people who make the immigration laws why we have large-scale immigration and your response is likely to be a platitude. "We're a nation of immigrants," or someone will recite Emma Lazarus' poem.

Thus, as far as anyone can discern, we are adding a new Denver every five months out of habit, or because a schoolgirl wrote a nice poem in 1883. We have an immigration policy that is doomed to fail because nobody knows what we're aiming for, because we have never even defined what a successful immigration policy might be. And, like so many of our other failures, it will be our children and grandchildren who will live with the consequences of our unwillingness to even think about what we're doing.

We have all heard the expression about the road to hell being paved with good intentions. In America, the road to overpopulation, social tensions, cultural conflict and economic instability is being paved with a well-meaning, but thoughtless, immigration policy.

When you see an immigrant on television, our whole heritage says we must be doing the right thing. But, I increasingly question whether we are. Of the 160 countries that belong to the United Nations, only three take any appreciable number of legal immigrants. The United States takes about one million a year, Canada takes about 150,000 per year, and Australia takes about 125,000. So, perhaps, 1.25 million people in a total pool of 3 billion people are lucky enough to come to one of the immigrant receiving countries. Yet, that pool increases about 90 million people a year, almost all of the increase in underdeveloped countries.

The maximum amount of "good" that the immigrant receiving countries can do to alleviate the pressures on those countries where people want to migrate is infinitesimally small—less than .05 percent.

The maximum amount of "good" that we can do from the standpoint of alleviating those pressures is ridiculously small. We may be able to save a few highly identified individuals that appear on the evening news. But, in terms of alleviating the pressures of world population, economic disruption, revolts, and revolutions, it is small. Most people will have to solve their problems within their country of origin. In an increasingly crowded world, we have to take great care not to engender unrealistic expectations.

What should be our immigration policy? I believe we should do what is right for America.

The United States accepted more than 9 million immigrants during the 1980s. In contrast to its European and Asian trading partners, the United States is the only major nation accepting large numbers of newcomers. Does the United States stand alone as the major immigration country because it knows something about immigrants that Europe and Japan do not? Or, has the United States resisted a revision of its immigration policies in a changing world?

We backed into this role as the major destination of immigrants without planning for the current wave of newcomers that are crowding our metropolitan areas and are posing massive problems for our health and educational institutions. Yet, today, many voices are heard arguing for more and more immigration and they come from the right and left. One commentator said it well:

> "The conservatives love their cheap labor; the liberals love their cheap cause."

Unfortunately, advocates of more immigration often confuse "pro-immigrant" and "pro-immigration." They believe that more must be done by government for the Hispanic and Asian immigrants currently arriving on our shores, and that doing more for the immigrants who are already here also means supporting further immigration. I am strongly "pro-immigrant" and favor assisting those already here to join our mainstream as soon as possible. I also believe that it is necessary to reduce the number of future immigrants if we are to adequately assist those already here.

Why do I, along with significant majority of the American people (according to recent polls), favor a reduction in levels of immigration? First, the presence of newcomers in such large numbers makes it impossible to deal with America's poor (whether native-born or immigrants) in compassionate and effective ways. The United States has a large, and growing, number of people —especially in the inner cities—with weak ties to the labor market, but strong links to welfare programs, crime, and drugs. Many immigrants also live in these cities. These immigrants gain a foothold in the labor market and then preserve the status quo because they do not complain about inferior wages or working conditions.

As long as eager immigrants are available, private employers are not going to make the difficult and costly adjustments needed to employ the American underclass. Instead, they continue to operate their sweatshops and complain about the unwillingness of Americans with welfare and other options to be enthusiastic seamstresses or hotel maids alongside the immigrants. If we are going to end "welfare as we now know it" we are going to have to end immigration "as we now know it."

The availability of immigrants keep private business from experimenting with effective ways to integrate the underclass into the work force. Yet, a tight labor market could provide a unique opportunity for private businesses to help lift people out of poverty and into the mainstream of American society. At a time when American minorities, Hispanic as well as African-American, suffer from double-digit unemployment, I believe it is immoral to continue accepting so many newcomers to compete with Americans for the jobs that are available. I believe a tight labor market is a great friend to the poor.

Hannah Arendt once observed that there is nothing more dangerous to a society than to have large numbers of human beings who are not economically vital. With or without immigration, changing technology and global economy are marginalizing large segments of people in our society.

We see evidence of it every day. The once self-sufficient blue collar worker who is now struggling to hang on, doing menial labor for menial wages. The proliferation of homeless, who have ceased even to have marginal value to our economy. These people already pose a monumental challenge to our society. Armies of people who have no personal stake in the current order, and a society that has no real use for such people, is a formula for disaster, as Arendt warned.

Not only are we failing to come to grips with this dangerous social pathology, but we are exacerbating it through our immigration policies. By tens of millions, we are importing immigrants to compete with our own economically marginal citizens.

The jobs that used to give the less educated in our country a stake in our society—the ability to contribute, to own a home, a college education for their children—those jobs are being lost to global competition. At a time when we should be engaging in a national effort to retrain such workers, to make them economically vital, we are doing something far different. We are forcing them to compete with a constantly growing pool of immigrant labor that further drives down wages and working conditions for those jobs that remain.

In the future, probably the not too distant future, we will pay the price for the short-term benefits of these immigration policies. We undermine the working class of this country at our own peril.

The second reason for reducing immigration is that the availability of such workers steers some of the economy in a losing direction. American products have to compete in international markets. The United States' competitive edge can be technological sophistication, quality and reliability, or price. Although large numbers of unskilled immigrants may help American businesses hold down wages and thus prices in order to remain competitive, a low-wage and low-price strategy simply cannot succeed in the global economy. Developing countries are becoming more adept at producing goods, such as garments and agricultural products, that are currently made in the United States by immigrant workers. Consequently, even wages which are low by United States standards are not low enough to compete with Malaysian seamstresses or Mexican farm workers.

Industries which rely on immigrant workers are often slow to innovate, and when developing countries ship similar products produced at even lower wages to the United States, these American businesses often turn protectionist. The result is familiar. The American industry which "needed" immigrant workers to survive and ensure, for example, that grapes do not cost $2.00 per pound soon complains that cheaper foreign grapes threaten the survival of the American grape industry and asks for restrictions on imports. This, in turn, drives up consumer prices.

The third reason for limiting immigration is to ease the adaptation of newcomers into American society and facilitate their acceptance by the resident population. Earlier immigration waves contributed to positive changes in American culture. Many of us here today are second and third generation Americans and we are justly proud of our heritage and the contributions our ancestors made to American society. However, the immigration wave at the turn of the twentieth century ended after 25 years, partly due to war and depression and also because of the 1920s restrictive legislation. As a result, immigration dropped from over one million annually in 1908–09 to under 100,000 in the 1930s. No such abrupt end to current immigration is in sight. The immigration laws of the 1920s were racist and are an embarrassing blot on the American conscience. Yet, by limiting the admission of newcomers, the new immigrants were encouraged to adapt to American society. And within two generations, they adapted with a vengeance—and in the process, improved society. Tsongas is now as American as Clinton. Valdez is as common as Smith.

Today, with immigration increasing year after year, it is difficult for new Americans to adapt to the United States as did previous immigrants. Rather, the old norms and languages are reinforced in ever-growing ethnic enclaves and we see a situation such as Miami where, according to the 1990 census, over half of the population of that city either do not speak English or speak it poorly.

Because of these dramatic shifts in demographic behavior, current and future immigrants—as well as the resident population—must adapt to a brand new social situation. Pressure was exerted on earlier waves of immigrants to "Americanize" and to conform to Anglo-Saxon norms. Instead, a new "melting pot" emerged within the population of European ancestry. What kind of cultural adaptation will be needed to insure that today's different ethnic groups assimilate into 21st century America? With a continuation of current levels of immigration, cultural separatism, where each group maintains its own identity at the expense of the greater whole, could easily emerge. I would argue strongly against such an eventuality.

The fourth reason to reduce immigration is to slow down rapid population growth. We are the world's fastest growing industrial nation. We add about three million people annually. If current demographic trends continue, with fertility once again above 2.0 and immigration levels surpassing one million annually, thanks to the 1990 legislation, our population could approach half a billion by 2050, or 145 million more people than today. Demographers Dennis Ahlburg and J.W. Vaupel foresee a population of 811 million by 2080—that's bigger than India today!

Several weeks ago, National Public Radio was airing a piece about politics in India. During the course of the report they aired a comment by a professor at an Indian university that ought to serve as a warning to those of us in America. The professor began his comments by saying:

"We are the world's largest democracy. But because India is so overpopulated, Indians have very few personal freedoms."

Personal liberty, the ability to "do our own thing" is very much dependent on the size of our population. The more people we have, the more rules and regulations we will require to govern what we do, when we do it, how we do it and where it can be done. When everyone is living cheek to jowl, it becomes impossible for you to do your own thing without it impinging on me.

As we grow not just in numbers, but in terms of people of different cultures living side by side, the tensions of overpopulation become even greater. A difficult situation is made all the more difficult because we begin to lose a consensus about how a crowded society should co-exist.

While population growth must eventually come to an end, when and at what point should that occur? Our infrastructure is already deteriorating; rapid population growth exacerbates this deterioration by increasing the burden on roads and water systems and creating demands for schools and other types of public investment. Americans are concerned about environmental issues, about air and water quality, and while population growth is not necessarily the major cause of environmental problems, more people are certainly an accomplice. Quality of life can improve more with reduced population growth.

I believe we must place our emphasis on helping those in need—where they are. In 1990, 58 percent of the $400 million that the United States committed to assisting refugees was spent to resettle 125,000 refugees in this country. By contrast, what we spent to help the 99 percent of world refugees we did not resettle, amounted to a paltry four cents a day per capita. Resettling the few, while neglecting the many, is at best stupid and at worst immoral.

In addition to what we spent resettling a handful of refugees, the federal government spent (according to the Center for Immigration Studies) in excess of $2 billion in 1990 to take care of the needs of recent immigrants. By all indications, those costs are rising rapidly. California reports that it cost $700 million last year to provide health care just to illegal aliens. That's not the cost for all immigrants in the state—that's just the health care bill for people who were in the country illegally to begin with!

From the point of view of the recently resettled refugee or immigrant, these have been resources well spent. For the countless millions barely surviving in the shanty towns of most of the third world, it was a gross misallocation of resources.

The underclass, the economic trajectory, cultural adaptation, and population growth are four reasons why I think that the United States should reevaluate its immigration policy. I am convinced that a continuation of current trends will produce problems that can be avoided.

I sincerely believe that legal immigration should be limited to no more than 300,000 people a year—a level that the majority of Americans feel comfortable with.

The sense that Americans want immigration of all kinds brought down to more manageable levels is growing more evident every day. In California, the national's most important political state and the national bellwether when it comes to political trends, this year's elections are being dominated by the immigration issue. In many respects, immigration has overshadowed the races for governor and senator in that state. Given California's political importance—it is unlikely that anyone can win the White House without winning California—any issue that so dominates the political agenda there is bound to become an issue in the 1996 presidential campaign.

We have an opportunity now for comprehensive immigration reform—and that is what is needed, a top to bottom overhaul of our immigration policies. During the last session of Congress, we saw the first encouraging moves in that direction. For the first time in nearly 30 years, legislation was introduced to reform a policy that most Americans agree does not serve the interests of our nation. Even more encouraging, these first attempts at serious immigration reform had bi-partisan support.

Limiting legal immigration and halting illegal immigration are often perceived as controversial issues. Quite the contrary. There is practically no other public policy matter on which there is greater political consensus among the American people. With a new congress... [and] with a clear message from the voters of California, ... we have an opportunity to make some real reforms....

Which brings me to the Federation for American Immigration Reform, or FAIR, a remarkable not-for-profit organization that I've been associated with now for almost fifteen years. It's made up of people from all across America, in all fifty states, governed by an all-volunteer Board of Directors from across the political spectrum. FAIR works more aggressively—and responsibly—than any other national organization to fight for the kinds of sensible changes I'm talking about here. With an annual budget of only about three million dollars, FAIR has taken on some of the entrenched interests on this issue, and, despite the rough and tumble nature of this debate, has emerged in the forefront of the national immigration dialogue today.

FAIR's program includes research and public education as well as comprehensive legislative solutions to control the costs of illegal immigration, end illegal immigration, set a national policy for legal immigration, and find ways to streamline and reduce the immigration flow down the line. But we can't do it all alone. We need your interest and support to achieve these monumental objectives....

One way or the other, our immigration dilemma will be resolved. As George Kennan has suggested, it will be resolved either by rational decisions at this end—or by the achievement of some sort of a balance of misery between this country and the vast pools of poverty that confront it. The choice is ours to make, and the longer we put it off, the more difficult it will be to make those rational decisions and the more certain it will be that that balance of misery will be achieved.

POSTSCRIPT

Should America Remain a Nation of Immigrants?

There are a number of similarities among the four waves of migration. The "push" factors of political oppression, religious persecution, and lack of economic opportunities have continued to attract immigrants to the United States. Contrary to legend, many mainstream Americans have never welcomed "the huddled masses." Politicians like Patrick Buchanan may deplore the large numbers of nonwhite Hispanics and Asians entering the United States, yet over 200 years ago Benjamin Franklin echoed similar sentiments about the "Palatine boors" from Germany who swarmed into Pennsylvania with little respect or knowledge of the English language and its customs.

The major differences among the four waves of migration center around America's evolving economy. Eighteenth-century colonial America's economy was primarily subsistence agriculture; between 1850 and 1925 America shifted to a market-oriented agricultural- and industrial-producing economy; since the 1950s America has shifted to a postindustrial, technetronic, consumption-based economic system. Meanwhile illegal immigrants from Mexico, who work at seasonal back-breaking jobs for agribusinesses, stream into the United States at a rate of 250,000 per year.

What effect will the recent immigration have on America's core culture? Since the newest phase only started in 1968, it is probably too soon to tell whether or not the "ethnic enclaves" of the Cubans in Miami and the Asian neighborhoods of New York City and Los Angeles will disperse, as occurred in earlier generations.

There is an enormous bibliography on the newest immigrants. A good starting point, which clearly explains the immigration laws and their impact on the development of American society, is Kenneth K. Lee, *Huddled Masses, Muddled Laws: Why Contemporary Immigration Policy Fails to Reflect Public Opinion* (Praeger, 1998). Another book that concisely summarizes both sides of the debate and contains a useful glossary of terms is Gerald Leinwand, *American Immigration: Should the Open Door Be Closed?* (Franklin Watts, 1995).

Because historians take a long-range view of immigration, they tend to weigh in on the pro side of the debate. See L. Edward Purcell, *Immigration: Social Issues in American History Series* (Oryx Press, 1995); Ueda's *Postwar America: A Social History* (Bedford Books, 1995); and David M. Reimers, *Still the Golden Door: The Third World War Comes to America,* 2d. ed. (Columbia University Press, 1997) and *Unwelcome Strangers: American Identity and the Turn Against Immigration* (Columbia University Press, 1998).

ISSUE 16

Did President Reagan Win the Cold War?

YES: John Lewis Gaddis, from *The United States and the End of the Cold War: Implications, Reconsiderations, Provocations* (Oxford University Press, 1992)

NO: Daniel Deudney and G. John Ikenberry, from "Who Won the Cold War?" *Foreign Policy* (Summer 1992)

ISSUE SUMMARY

YES: Professor of history John Lewis Gaddis argues that President Reagan combined a policy of militancy and operational pragmatism to bring about the most significant improvement in Soviet-American relations since the end of World War II.

NO: Professors of political science Daniel Deudney and G. John Ikenberry contend that the cold war ended only when Soviet president Gorbachev accepted Western liberal values and the need for global cooperation.

The term *cold war* was first coined by the American financial whiz and presidential adviser Bernard Baruch in 1947. Cold war refers to the extended but restricted conflict that existed between the United States and the Soviet Union from the end of World War II in 1945 until 1990. Looking back, it appears that the conflicting values and goals of a democratic/capitalist United States and a communist Soviet Union reinforced this state of affairs between the two countries. Basically, the cold war ended when the Soviet Union gave up its control over the Eastern European nations and ceased to be a unified country itself.

The Nazi invasion of Russia in June 1941 and the Japanese attack on America's Pacific outposts in December united the United States and the Soviet Union against the Axis powers during World War II. Nevertheless, complications ensued during the top-level allied discussions to coordinate war strategy. The first meeting between the big three—U.S. president Franklin Roosevelt, British prime minister Winston Churchill, and Soviet premier Joseph Stalin—took place in Teheran in 1943 followed by another at Yalta in February 1945. These high-level negotiations were held under the assumption that wartime harmony among Britain, the United States, and the Soviet Union would continue; that Stalin, Churchill, and Roosevelt would lead the postwar world as they had conducted the war; and that the details of the general policies and agreements would be resolved at a less pressing time.

But none of these premises were fulfilled. By the time the Potsdam Conference (to discuss possible action against Japan) took place in July 1945, Churchill had been defeated in a parliamentary election, Roosevelt had died, and President Harry S. Truman had been thrust, unprepared, into his place. Of the big three, only Stalin remained as a symbol of continuity. Details about the promises at Teheran and Yalta faded into the background. Power politics, nuclear weapons, and mutual fears and distrust replaced the reasonably harmonious working relationships of the three big powers during World War II.

By 1947 the Truman administration had adopted a conscious policy of containment toward the Russians. This meant maintaining the status quo in Europe through various U.S. assistance programs. The NATO alliance of 1949 completed the shift of U.S. policy away from its pre–World War II isolationist policy and toward a commitment to the defense of Western Europe.

In the 1960s the largest problem facing the two superpowers was controlling the spread of nuclear weapons. The first attempt at arms control took place in the 1950s. After Stalin died in 1953, the Eisenhower administration made an "open-skies" proposal. This was rejected by the Russians, who felt (correctly) that they were behind the Americans in the arms race. In the summer of 1962 Soviet premier Nikita Khrushchev attempted to redress the balance of power by secretly installing missiles in Cuba that could be employed to launch nuclear attacks against U.S. cities. This sparked the Cuban Missile Crisis, the high point of the cold war, which brought both nations to the brink of nuclear war before the Russians agreed to withdraw the missiles.

During the Leonid Brezhnev–Richard Nixon years, the policy of *détente* (relaxation of tensions) resulted in a series of summit meetings. Most important was the SALT I agreement, which outlawed national antiballistic missile defenses and placed a five-year moratorium on the building of new strategic ballistic missiles.

Soviet-American relations took a turn for the worse when the Soviets invaded Afghanistan in December 1979. In response, President Jimmy Carter postponed presenting SALT II to the Senate and imposed an American boycott of the 1980 Olympic Games, which were held in Moscow.

Détente remained dead during President Ronald Reagan's first administration. Reagan not only promoted a military budget of $1.5 trillion over a five-year period, he also was the first president since Truman to refuse to meet the Soviet leader. Major changes, however, took place during Reagan's second administration. In the following selections, John Lewis Gaddis argues that President Reagan combined a policy of militancy and operational pragmatism to bring about significant improvements in Soviet-American relations, while Daniel Deudney and G. John Ikenberry credit Soviet president Mikhail Gorbachev with ending the cold war because he accepted Western liberal values and the need for global cooperation.

John Lewis Gaddis  **YES**

The Unexpected Ronald Reagan

T he task of the historian is, very largely, one of explaining how we got from where we were to where we are today. To say that the Reagan administration's policy toward the Soviet Union is going to pose special challenges to historians is to understate the matter: rarely has there been a greater gap between the expectations held for an administration at the beginning of its term and the results it actually produced. The last thing one would have anticipated at the time Ronald Reagan took office in 1981 was that he would use his eight years in the White House to bring about the most significant improvement in Soviet-American relations since the end of World War II. I am not at all sure that President Reagan himself foresaw this result. And yet, that is precisely what happened, with—admittedly—a good deal of help from Mikhail Gorbachev.

The question of how this happened and to what extent it was the product of accident or of conscious design is going to preoccupy scholars for years to come. The observations that follow are a rough first attempt to grapple with that question. Because we lack access to the archives or even very much memoir material as yet, what I will have to say is of necessity preliminary, incomplete, and almost certainly in several places dead wrong. Those are the hazards of working with contemporary history, though; if historians are not willing to run these risks, political scientists and journalists surely will. That prospect in itself provides ample justification for plunging ahead.

The Hard-Liner

... President Reagan in March, 1983, made his most memorable pronouncement on the Soviet Union: condemning the tendency of his critics to hold both sides responsible for the nuclear arms race, he denounced the U.S.S.R. as an "evil empire" and as "the focus of evil in the modern world." Two weeks later, the President surprised even his closest associates by calling for a long-term research and development program to create defense against attacks by strategic missiles, with a view, ultimately, to "rendering these nuclear weapons impotent and obsolete." The Strategic Defense Initiative was the most fundamental challenge to existing orthodoxies on arms control since negotiations on that subject had begun with the Russians almost three decades earlier. Once again it

From John Lewis Gaddis, *The United States and the End of the Cold War: Implications, Reconsiderations, Provocations* (Oxford University Press, 1992). Copyright © 1992 by John Lewis Gaddis. Reprinted by permission of Oxford University Press, Inc. Notes omitted.

called into question the President's seriousness in seeking an end to—or even a significant moderation of—the strategic arms race.

Anyone who listened to the "evil empire" speech or who considered the implications of "Star Wars" might well have concluded that Reagan saw the Soviet-American relationship as an elemental confrontation between virtue and wickedness that would allow neither negotiation nor conciliation in any form; his tone seemed more appropriate to a medieval crusade than to a revival of containment. Certainly there were those within his administration who held such views, and their influence, for a time, was considerable. But to see the President's policies solely in terms of his rhetoric, it is now clear, would have been quite wrong.

For President Reagan appears to have understood—or to have quickly learned—the dangers of basing foreign policy solely on ideology: he combined militancy with a surprising degree of operational pragmatism and a shrewd sense of timing. To the astonishment of his own hard-line supporters, what appeared to be an enthusiastic return to the Cold War in fact turned out to be a more solidly based approach to detente than anything the Nixon, Ford, or Carter administrations had been able to accomplish.

The Negotiator

There had always been a certain ambivalence in the Reagan administration's image of the Soviet Union. On the one hand, dire warnings about Moscow's growing military strength suggested an almost Spenglerian gloom [reflecting the theory of philosopher Oswald Spengler, which holds that all major cultures grow, mature, and decay in a natural cycle] about the future: time, it appeared, was on the Russians' side. But mixed with this pessimism was a strong sense of self-confidence, growing out of the ascendancy of conservatism within the United States and an increasing enthusiasm for capitalism overseas, that assumed the unworkability of Marxism as a form of political, social, and economic organization: "The West won't contain communism, it will transcend communism," the President predicted in May, 1981. "It won't bother to . . . denounce it, it will dismiss it as some bizarre chapter in human history whose last pages are even now being written." By this logic, the Soviet Union had already reached the apex of its strength as a world power, and time in fact was on the side of the West.

Events proved the optimism to have been more justified than the pessimism, for over the next four years the Soviet Union would undergo one of the most rapid erosions both of internal self-confidence and external influence in modern history; that this happened just as Moscow's long and costly military buildup should have begun to pay political dividends made the situation all the more frustrating for the Russians. It may have been luck for President Reagan to have come into office at a peak in the fortunes of the Soviet Union and at a trough in those of the United States: things would almost certainly have improved regardless of who entered the White House in 1981. But it took more than luck to recognize what was happening, and to capitalize on it to the extent that the Reagan administration did.

Indications of Soviet decline took several forms. The occupation of Afghanistan had produced only a bloody Vietnam-like stalemate, with Soviet troops unable to suppress the rebellion, or to protect themselves and their clients, or to withdraw. In Poland a long history of economic mismanagement had produced, in the form of the Solidarity trade union, a rare phenomenon within the Soviet bloc: a true workers' movement. Soviet ineffectiveness became apparent in the Middle East in 1982 when the Russians were unable to provide any significant help to the Palestinian Liberation Organization during the Israeli invasion of Lebanon; even more embarrassing, Israeli pilots using American-built fighters shot down over eighty Soviet-supplied Syrian jets without a single loss of their own. Meanwhile, the Soviet domestic economy which [former Soviet premier Nikita] Khrushchev had once predicted would overtake that of the United States, had in fact stagnated during the early 1980s, Japan by some indices actually overtook the U.S.S.R. as the world's second largest producer of goods and services, and even China, a nation with four times the population of the Soviet Union, now became an agricultural exporter at a time when Moscow still required food imports from the West to feed its own people.

What all of this meant was that the Soviet Union's appeal as a model for Third World political and economic development—once formidable—had virtually disappeared, indeed as Moscow's military presence in those regions grew during the late 1970s, the Russians increasingly came to be seen, not as liberators, but as latter-day imperialists themselves. The Reagan administration moved swiftly to take advantage of this situation by funneling military assistance—sometimes openly sometimes covertly—to rebel groups (or "freedom fighters," as the President insisted on calling them) seeking to overthrow Soviet-backed regimes in Afghanistan, Angola, Ethiopia, Cambodia, and Nicaragua; in October, 1983, to huge domestic acclaim but with dubious legality Reagan even ordered the direct use of American military forces to overthrow an unpopular Marxist government on the tiny Caribbean island of Grenada. The Reagan Doctrine, as this strategy became known, sought to exploit vulnerabilities the Russians had created for themselves in the Third World: this latter-day effort to "roll back" Soviet influence would, in time, produce impressive results at minimum cost and risk to the United States.

Compounding the Soviet Union's external difficulties was a long vacuum in internal leadership occasioned by [President Leonid] Brezhnev's slow enfeeblement and eventual death in November, 1982; by the installation as his successor of an already-ill Yuri Andropov, who himself died in February 1984; and by the installation of his equally geriatric successor, Konstantin Chernenko. At a time when a group of strong Western leaders had emerged—including not just President Reagan but also Prime Minister Margaret Thatcher in Great Britain, President François Mitterrand in France, and Chancellor Helmut Kohl in West Germany—this apparent inability to entrust leadership to anyone other than party stalwarts on their deathbeds was a severe commentary on what the sclerotic Soviet system had become. "We could go no further without hitting the end," one Russian later recalled of Chernenko's brief reign. "Here was the General Secretary of the party who is also the Chairman of the Presidium of the Supreme Soviet, the embodiment of our country, the personification of the party and he could barely stand up."

There was no disagreement within the Reagan administration about the desirability under these circumstances, of pressing the Russians hard. Unlike several of their predecessors, the President and his advisers did not see containment as requiring the application of sticks and carrots in equal proportion; wielders of sticks definitely predominated among them. But there were important differences over what the purpose of wielding the sticks was to be.

Some advisers, like [Secretary of Defense Casper] Weinberger, [Assistant Secretary of Defense for International Security Policy Richard] Perle, and [chief Soviet specialist on the National Security Council Richard] Pipes, saw the situation as a historic opportunity to exhaust the Soviet system. Noting that the Soviet economy was already stretched to the limit, they advocated taking advantage of American technological superiority to engage the Russians in an arms race of indefinite duration and indeterminate cost. Others, including Nitze, the Joint Chiefs of Staff, career Foreign Service officer Jack Matlock, who succeeded Pipes as chief Soviet expert at the NSC, and—most important—[Secretary of State Alexander M.] Haig's replacement after June, 1982, the unflamboyant but steady George Shultz, endorsed the principle of "negotiation from strength": the purpose of accumulating military hardware was not to debilitate the other side, but to convince it to negotiate.

The key question, of course, was what President Reagan's position would be. Despite his rhetoric, he had been careful not to rule out talks with the Russians once the proper conditions had been met: even while complaining, in his first press conference, about the Soviet propensity to lie, cheat, and steal, he had also noted that "when we can, ... we should start negotiations on the basis of trying to effect an actual reduction in the numbers of nuclear weapons. That would be real arms reduction." But most observers—and probably many of his own advisers—assumed that when the President endorsed negotiations leading toward the "reduction," as opposed to the "limitation," of strategic arms, or the "zero option" in the INF [intermediate-range nuclear forces] talks, or the Strategic Defense Initiative, he was really seeking to avoid negotiations by setting minimal demands above the maximum concessions the Russians could afford to make. He was looking for a way they believed, to gain credit for cooperativeness with both domestic and allied constituencies without actually having to give up anything.

That would turn out to be a gross misjudgment of President Reagan, who may have had cynical advisers but was not cynical himself. It would become apparent with the passage of time that when the Chief Executive talked about "reducing" strategic missiles he meant precisely that; the appeal of the "zero option" was that it really would get rid of intermediate-range nuclear forces; the Strategic Defense Initiative might in fact, just as the President had said, make nuclear weapons "impotent and obsolete." A simple and straightforward man, Reagan took the principle of "negotiation from strength" literally: once one had built strength, one negotiated.

The first indications that the President might be interested in something other than an indefinite arms race began to appear in the spring and summer of

1983. Widespread criticism of his "evil empire" speech apparently shook him: although his view of the Soviet system itself did not change, Reagan was careful, after that point, to use more restrained language in characterizing it. Clear evidence of the President's new moderation came with the Korean airliner incident of September, 1983. Despite his outrage, Reagan did not respond—as one might have expected him to—by reviving his "evil empire" rhetoric; instead he insisted that arms control negotiations would continue, and in a remarkably conciliatory television address early in 1984 he announced that the United States was "in its strongest position in years to establish a constructive and realistic working relationship with the Soviet Union." The President concluded this address by speculating on how a typical Soviet couple—Ivan and Anya—might find that they had much in common with a typical American couple—Jim and Sally: "They might even have decided that they were all going to get together for dinner some evening soon."

It was possible to construct self-serving motives for this startling shift in tone. With a presidential campaign under way the White House was sensitive to Democratic charges that Reagan was the only postwar president not to have met with a Soviet leader while in office. Certainly it was to the advantage of the United States in its relations with Western Europe to look as reasonable as possible in the face of Soviet intransigence. But events would show that the President's interest in an improved relationship was based on more than just electoral politics or the needs of the alliance: it was only the unfortunate tendency of Soviet leaders to die upon taking office that was depriving the American Chief Executive—himself a spry septuagenarian—of a partner with whom to negotiate.

By the end of September, 1984—and to the dismay of Democratic partisans who saw Republicans snatching the "peace" issue from them—a contrite Soviet Foreign Minister Andrei Gromyko had made the pilgrimage to Washington to re-establish contacts with the Reagan administration. Shortly after Reagan's landslide re-election over Walter Mondale in November, the United States and the Soviet Union announced that a new set of arms control negotiations would begin early the following year, linking together discussions on START [Strategic Arms Reduction Talks], INF, and weapons in space. And in December, a hitherto obscure member of the Soviet Politburo, Mikhail Gorbachev, announced while visiting Great Britain that the U.S.S.R. was prepared to seek "radical solutions" looking toward a ban on nuclear missiles altogether. Three months later, Konstantin Chernenko, the last in a series of feeble and unimaginative Soviet leaders, expired, and Gorbachev—a man who was in no way feeble and unimaginative—became the General Secretary of the Communist Party of the Soviet Union. Nothing would ever be quite the same again.

Reagan and Gorbachev

Several years after Gorbachev had come to power, George F. Kennan was asked in a television interview how so unconventional a Soviet leader could have risen to the top in a system that placed such a premium on conformity. Kennan's reply reflected the perplexity American experts on Soviet affairs have felt in seeking to account for the Gorbachev phenomenon: "I really cannot explain it." It seemed most improbable that a regime so lacking in the capacity for innovation, self-evaluation, or even minimally effective public relations should suddenly produce a leader who excelled in all of these qualities; even more remarkable was the fact that Gorbachev saw himself as a revolutionary—a breed not seen in Russia for decades—determined, as he put it, "to get out of the quagmire of conservatism, and to break the inertia of stagnation."

Whatever the circumstances that led to it, the accession of Gorbachev reversed almost overnight the pattern of the preceding four years: after March, 1985, it was the Soviet Union that seized the initiative in relations with the West. It did so in a way that was both reassuring and unnerving at the same time: by becoming so determinedly cooperative as to convince some supporters of containment in the United States and Western Europe—uneasy in the absence of the intransigence to which they had become accustomed—that the Russians were now seeking to defeat that strategy by depriving it, with sinister cleverness, of an object to be contained.

President Reagan, in contrast, welcomed the fresh breezes emanating from Moscow and moved quickly to establish a personal relationship with the new Soviet leader. Within four days of Gorbachev's taking power, the President was characterizing the Russians as "in a different frame of mind than they've been in the past. . . . [T]hey, I believe, are really going to try and, with us, negotiate a reduction in armaments." And within four months, the White House was announcing that Reagan would meet Gorbachev at Geneva in November for the first Soviet-American summit since 1979.

The Geneva summit, like so many before it, was long on symbolism and short on substance. The two leaders appeared to get along well with one another: they behaved, as one Reagan adviser later put it, "like a couple of fellows who had run into each other at the club and discovered that they had a lot in common." The President agreed to discuss deep cuts in strategic weapons and improved verification, but he made it clear that he was not prepared to forgo development of the Strategic Defense Initiative in order to get them. His reason —which Gorbachev may not have taken seriously until this point—had to do with his determination to retain SDI as a means ultimately of rendering nuclear weapons obsolete. The President's stubbornness on this point precluded progress, at least for the moment, on what was coming to be called the "grand compromise": Paul Nitze's idea of accepting limits on SDI in return for sweeping reductions in strategic missiles. But it did leave the way open for an alert Gorbachev, detecting the President's personal enthusiasm for nuclear abolition, to surprise the world in January, 1986, with his own plan for accomplishing that objective: a Soviet-American agreement to rid the world of nuclear weapons altogether by the year 2000.

It was easy to question Gorbachev's motives in making so radical a proposal in so public a manner with no advance warning. Certainly any discussion of even reducing—much less abolishing—nuclear arsenals would raise difficult questions for American allies, where an abhorrence of nuclear weapons continued to coexist uneasily alongside the conviction that only their presence could deter superior Soviet conventional forces. Nor was the Gorbachev proposal clear on how Russians and Americans could ever impose abolition, even if they themselves agreed to it, on other nuclear and non-nuclear powers. Still, the line between rhetoric and conviction is a thin one: the first Reagan-Gorbachev summit may not only have created a personal bond between the two leaders; it may also have sharpened a vague but growing sense in the minds of both men that, despite all the difficulties in constructing an alternative, an indefinite continuation of life under nuclear threat was not a tolerable condition for either of their countries, and that their own energies might very well be directed toward overcoming that situation.

That both Reagan and Gorbachev were thinking along these lines became clear at their second meeting, the most extraordinary Soviet-American summit of the postwar era, held on very short notice at Reykjavik, Iceland, in October, 1986. The months that preceded Reykjavik had seen little tangible progress toward arms control; there had also developed, in August, an unpleasant skirmish between intelligence agencies on both sides as the KGB, in apparent retaliation for the FBI's highly publicized arrest of a Soviet United Nations official in New York on espionage charges, set up, seized, and held *USNEWS* correspondent Nicholas Daniloff on trumped-up accusations for just under a month. It was a sobering reminder that the Soviet-American relationship existed at several different levels, and that cordiality in one did not rule out the possibility of confrontation in others. The Daniloff affair also brought opportunity though, for in the course of negotiations to settle it Gorbachev proposed a quick "preliminary" summit, to be held within two weeks, to try to break the stalemate in negotiations over intermediate-range nuclear forces in Europe, the aspect of arms control where progress at a more formal summit seemed likely. Reagan immediately agreed.

But when the President and his advisers arrived at Reykjavik, they found that Gorbachev had much more grandiose proposals in mind. These included not only an endorsement of 50 percent cuts in Soviet and American strategic weapons across the board, but also agreement not to demand the inclusion of British and French nuclear weapons in these calculations—a concession that removed a major stumbling block to START—and acceptance in principle of Reagan's 1981 "zero option" for intermediate-range nuclear forces, all in return for an American commitment not to undermine SALT I's ban on strategic defenses for the next ten years. Impressed by the scope of these concessions, the American side quickly put together a compromise that would have cut ballistic missiles to zero within a decade in return for the right, after that time, to deploy strategic defenses against the bomber and cruise missile forces that would be left. Gorbachev immediately countered by proposing the abolition of *all* nuclear weapons within ten years, thus moving his original deadline from the year 2000 to 1996. President Reagan is said to have replied: "*All* nuclear weapons? Well, Mikhail, that's exactly what I've been talking about all along.... That's always been my goal."

A series of events set in motion by a Soviet diplomat's arrest on a New York subway platform and by the reciprocal framing of an American journalist in Moscow had wound up with the two most powerful men in the world agreeing—for the moment, and to the astonishment of their aides—on the abolition of all nuclear weapons within ten years. But the moment did not last. Gorbachev went on to insist, as a condition for nuclear abolition, upon a ban on the laboratory testing of SDI, which Reagan immediately interpreted as an effort to kill strategic defense altogether. Because the ABM treaty does allow for some laboratory testing, the differences between the two positions were not all that great. But in the hothouse atmosphere of this cold-climate summit no one explored such details, and the meeting broke up in disarray, acrimony, and mutual disappointment.

It was probably just as well. The sweeping agreements contemplated at Reykjavik grew out of hasty improvisation and high-level posturing, not careful thought. They suffered from all the deficiencies of Gorbachev's unilateral proposal for nuclear abolition earlier in the year; they also revealed how susceptible the leaders of the United States and the Soviet Union had become to each other's amplitudinous rhetoric. It was as if Reagan and Gorbachev had been trying desperately to outbid the other in a gigantic but surrealistic auction, with the diaphanous prospect of a nuclear-free world somehow on the block....

Negotiations on arms control continued in the year that followed Reykjavik, however, with both sides edging toward the long-awaited "grand compromise" that would defer SDI in return for progress toward a START agreement. Reagan and Gorbachev did sign an intermediate-range nuclear forces treaty in Washington in December, 1987, which for the first time provided that Russians and Americans would actually dismantle and destroy—literally before each other's eyes—an entire category of nuclear missiles. There followed a triumphal Reagan visit to Moscow in May, 1988, featuring the unusual sight of a Soviet general secretary and an American president strolling amiably through Red Square, greeting tourists and bouncing babies in front of Lenin's tomb, while their respective military aides—each carrying the codes needed to launch nuclear missiles at each other's territory—stood discreetly in the background. Gorbachev made an equally triumphal visit to New York in December, 1988, to address the United Nations General Assembly: there he announced a *unilateral* Soviet cut of some 500,000 ground troops, a major step toward moving arms control into the realm of conventional forces.

When, on the same day Gorbachev spoke in New York, a disastrous earthquake killed some 25,000 Soviet Armenians, the outpouring of aid from the United States and other Western countries was unprecedented since the days of Lend Lease. One had the eerie feeling, watching anguished television reports from the rubble that had been the cities of Leninakan and Stipak—the breakdown of emergency services, the coffins stacked like logs in city parks, the mass burials—that one had glimpsed, on a small scale, something of what a nuclear war might actually be like. The images suggested just how vulnerable both super-powers remained after almost a half-century of trying to minimize vulnerabilities. They thereby reinforced what had become almost a ritual incantation pronounced by both Reagan and Gorbachev at each of their now-frequent summits: "A nuclear war cannot be won and must never be fought."

But as the Reagan administration prepared to leave office the following month, in an elegiac mood very different from the grim militancy with which it had assumed its responsibilities eight years earlier, the actual prospect of a nuclear holocaust seemed more remote than at any point since the Soviet-American nuclear rivalry had begun. Accidents, to be sure, could always happen. Irrationality though blessedly rare since 1945, could never be ruled out. There was reason for optimism, though, in the fact that as George Bush entered the White House early in 1989, the point at issue no longer seemed to be "how to fight the Cold War" at all, but rather "is the Cold War over?"

Ronald Reagan and the End of the Cold War

The record of the Reagan years suggests the need to avoid the common error of trying to predict outcomes from attributes. There is no question that the President and his advisers came into office with an ideological view of the world that appeared to allow for no compromise with the Russians; but ideology has a way of evolving to accommodate reality especially in the hands of skillful political leadership. Indeed a good working definition of leadership might be just this —the ability to accommodate ideology to practical reality—and by that standard, Reagan's achievements in relations with the Soviet Union will certainly compare favorably with, and perhaps even surpass, those of Richard Nixon and Henry Kissinger.

Did President Reagan intend for things to come out this way? That question is, of course, more difficult to determine, given our lack of access to the archives. But a careful reading of the public record would, I think, show that the President was expressing hopes for an improvement in Soviet-American relations from the moment he entered the White House, and that he began shifting American policy in that direction as early as the first months of 1983, almost two years before Mikhail Gorbachev came to power. Gorbachev's extraordinary receptiveness to such initiatives—as distinct from the literally moribund responses of his predecessors—greatly accelerated the improvement in relations, but it would be a mistake to credit him solely with the responsibility for what happened: Ronald Reagan deserves a great deal of the credit as well.

Critics have raised the question, though, of whether President Reagan was responsible for, or even aware of, the direction administration policy was taking. This argument is, I think, both incorrect and unfair. Reagan's opponents have been quick enough to hold him personally responsible for the failures of his administration; they should be equally prepared to acknowledge his successes. And there are points, even with the limited sources now available, where we can see that the President himself had a decisive impact upon the course of events. They include, among others: the Strategic Defense Initiative, which may have had its problems as a missile shield but which certainly worked in unsettling the Russians; endorsement of the "zero option" in the INF talks and real reductions in START, the rapidity with which the President entered into, and thereby legitimized, serious negotiations with Gorbachev once he came into office; and, most remarkably of all, his eagerness to contemplate alternatives to the nuclear arms race in a way no previous president had been willing to do.

Now, it may be objected that these were simple, unsophisticated, and, as people are given to saying these days, imperfectly "nuanced" ideas. I would not argue with that proposition. But it is important to remember that while complexity, sophistication, and nuance may be prerequisites for intellectual leadership, they are not necessarily so for political leadership, and can at times actually get in the way. President Reagan generally meant precisely what he said: when he came out in favor of negotiations from strength, or for strategic arms reductions as opposed to limitations, or even for making nuclear weapons ultimately irrelevant and obsolete, he did not do so in the "killer amendment" spirit favored by geopolitical sophisticates on the right; the President may have been conservative but he was never devious. The lesson here ought to be to beware of excessive convolution and subtlety in strategy, for sometimes simple-mindedness wins out, especially if it occurs in high places.

Finally President Reagan also understood something that many geopolitical sophisticates on the left have not understood: that although toughness may or may not be a prerequisite for successful negotiations with the Russians—there are arguments for both propositions—it is absolutely essential if the American people are to lend their support, over time, to what has been negotiated. Others may have seen in the doctrine of "negotiation from strength" a way of avoiding negotiations altogether, but it now seems clear that the President saw in that approach the means of constructing a domestic political base without which agreements with the Russians would almost certainly have foundered, as indeed many of them did in the 1970s. For unless one can sustain domestic support—and one does not do that by appearing weak—then it is hardly likely that whatever one has arranged with any adversary will actually come to anything.

There is one last irony to all of this: it is that it fell to Ronald Reagan to preside over the belated but decisive success of the strategy of containment George F. Kennan had first proposed more than four decades earlier. For what were Gorbachev's reforms if not the long-delayed "mellowing" of Soviet society that Kennan had said would take place with the passage of time? The Stalinist system that had required outside adversaries to justify its own existence now seemed at last to have passed from the scene; Gorbachev appeared to have concluded that the Soviet Union could continue to be a great power in world affairs only through the introduction of something approximating a market economy, democratic political institutions, official accountability, and respect for the rule of law at home. And that, in turn, suggested an even more remarkable conclusion: that the very survival of the ideology Lenin had imposed on Russia in 1917 now required infiltration—perhaps even subversion—by precisely the ideology the great revolutionary had sworn to overthrow

I have some reason to suspect that Professor Kennan is not entirely comfortable with the suggestion that Ronald Reagan successfully completed the execution of the strategy he originated. But as Kennan the historian would be the first to acknowledge, history is full of ironies, and this one, surely, will not rank among the least of them.

Daniel Deudney and
G. John Ikenberry

NO

Who Won the Cold War?

The end of the Cold War marks the most important historical divide in half a century. The magnitude of those developments has ushered in a wide-ranging debate over the reasons for its end—a debate that is likely to be as protracted, controversial, and politically significant as that over the Cold War's origins. The emerging debate over why the Cold War ended is of more than historical interest: At stake is the vindication and legitimation of an entire world view and foreign policy orientation.

In thinking about the Cold War's conclusion, it is vital to distinguish between the domestic origins of the crisis in Soviet communism and the external forces that influenced its timing and intensity, as well as the direction of the Soviet response. Undoubtedly, the ultimate cause of the Cold War's outcome lies in the failure of the Soviet system itself. At most, outside forces hastened and intensified the crisis. However, it was not inevitable that the Soviet Union would respond to this crisis as it did in the late 1980s—with domestic liberalization and foreign policy accommodation. After all, many Western experts expected that the USSR would respond to such a crisis with renewed repression at home and aggression abroad, as it had in the past.

At that fluid historic juncture, the complex matrix of pressures, opportunities, and attractions from the outside world influenced the direction of Soviet change, particularly in its foreign policy. The Soviets' field of vision was dominated by the West, the United States, and recent American foreign policy. Having spent more than 45 years attempting to influence the Soviet Union, Americans are now attempting to gauge the weight of their country's impact and, thus, the track record of U.S. policies.

In assessing the rest of the world's impact on Soviet change, a remarkably simplistic and self-serving conventional wisdom has emerged in the United States. This new conventional wisdom, the "Reagan victory school," holds that President Ronald Reagan's military and ideological assertiveness during the 1980s played the lead role in the collapse of Soviet communism and the "taming" of its foreign policy In that view the Reagan administration's ideological counter-offensive and military buildup delivered the knock-out punch to a system that was internally bankrupt and on the ropes. The Reagan Right's perspective is an ideologically pointed version of the more broadly held conventional

From Daniel Deudney and G. John Ikenberry, "Who Won the Cold War?" *Foreign Policy*, no. 87 (Summer 1992). Copyright © 1992 by The Carnegie Endowment for International Peace. Reprinted by permission.

wisdom on the end of the Cold War that emphasizes the success of the "peace-through-strength" strategy manifest in four decades of Western containment. After decades of waging a costly "twilight struggle," the West now celebrates the triumph of its military and ideological resolve.

The Reagan victory school and the broader peace-through-strength perspectives are, however, misleading and incomplete—both in their interpretation of events in the 1980s and in their understanding of deeper forces that led to the end of the Cold War. It is important to reconsider the emerging conventional wisdom before it truly becomes an article of faith on Cold War history and comes to distort the thinking of policymakers in America and elsewhere.

The collapse of the Cold War caught almost everyone, particularly hardliners, by surprise. Conservatives and most analysts in the U.S. national security establishment believed that the Soviet-U.S. struggle was a permanent feature of international relations. As former National Security Council adviser Zbigniew Brzezinski put it in 1986, "the American-Soviet contest is not some temporary aberration but a historical rivalry that will long endure." And to many hardliners, Soviet victory was far more likely than Soviet collapse. Many ringing predictions now echo as embarrassments.

The Cold War's end was a baby that arrived unexpectedly, but a long line of those claiming paternity has quickly formed. A parade of former Reagan administration officials and advocates has forthrightly asserted that Reagan's hardline policies were the decisive trigger for reorienting Soviet foreign policy and for the demise of communism. As former Pentagon officials like Caspar Weinberger and Richard Perle, columnist George Will, neoconservative thinker Irving Kristol, and other proponents of the Reagan victory school have argued, a combination of military and ideological pressures gave the Soviets little choice but to abandon expansionism abroad and repression at home. In that view, the Reagan military buildup foreclosed Soviet military options while pushing the Soviet economy to the breaking point. Reagan partisans stress that his dramatic "Star Wars" initiative put the Soviets on notice that the next phase of the arms race would be waged in areas where the West held a decisive technological edge.

Reagan and his administration's military initiatives, however, played a far different and more complicated role in inducing Soviet change than the Reagan victory school asserts. For every "hardening" there was a "softening": Reagan's rhetoric of the "Evil Empire" was matched by his vigorous anti-nuclearism; the military buildup in the West was matched by the resurgence of a large popular peace movement; and the Reagan Doctrine's toughening of containment was matched by major deviations from containment in East-West economic relations. Moreover, over the longer term, the strength marshaled in containment was matched by mutual weakness in the face of nuclear weapons, and efforts to engage the USSR were as important as efforts to contain it.

The Irony of Ronald Reagan

Perhaps the greatest anomaly of the Reagan victory school is the "Great Communicator" himself. The Reagan Right ignores that his anti-nuclearism was as strong as his anticommunism. Reagan's personal convictions on nuclear weapons were profoundly at odds with the beliefs of most in his administration. Staffed by officials who considered nuclear weapons a useful instrument of statecraft and who were openly disdainful of the moral critique of nuclear weapons articulated by the arms control community and the peace movement, the administration pursued the hardest line on nuclear policy and the Soviet Union in the postwar era. Then vice president George Bush's observation that nuclear weapons would be fired as a warning shot and Deputy Under Secretary of Defense T. K. Jones's widely quoted view that nuclear war was survivable captured the reigning ethos within the Reagan administration.

In contrast, there is abundant evidence that Reagan himself felt a deep antipathy for nuclear weapons and viewed their abolition to be a realistic and desirable goal. Reagan's call in his famous March 1983 "Star Wars" speech for a program to make nuclear weapons impotent and obsolete was viewed as cynical by many, but actually it expressed Reagan's heartfelt views, views that he came to act upon. As *Washington Post* reporter Lou Cannon's 1991 biography points out, Reagan was deeply disturbed by nuclear deterrence and attracted to abolitionist solutions. "I know I speak for people everywhere when I say our dream is to see the day when nuclear weapons will be banished from the face of the earth," Reagan said in November 1983. Whereas the Right saw anti-nuclearism as a threat to American military spending and the legitimacy of an important foreign policy tool, or as propaganda for domestic consumption, Reagan sincerely believed it. Reagan's anti-nuclearism was not just a personal sentiment. It surfaced at decisive junctures to affect Soviet perceptions of American policy. Sovietologist and strategic analyst Michael MccGwire has argued persuasively that Reagan's anti-nuclearism decisively influenced Soviet-U.S. relations during the early Gorbachev years.

Contrary to the conventional wisdom, the defense buildup did not produce Soviet capitulation. The initial Soviet response to the Reagan administration's buildup and belligerent rhetoric was to accelerate production of offensive weapons, both strategic and conventional. That impasse was broken not by Soviet capitulation but by an extraordinary convergence by Reagan and Mikhail Gorbachev on a vision of mutual nuclear vulnerability and disarmament. On the Soviet side, the dominance of the hardline response to the newly assertive America was thrown into question in early 1985 when Gorbachev became general secretary of the Communist party after the death of Konstantin Chernenko. Without a background in foreign affairs, Gorbachev was eager to assess American intentions directly and put his stamp on Soviet security policy. Reagan's strong antinuclear views expressed at the November 1985 Geneva summit were decisive in convincing Gorbachev that it was possible to work with the West in halting the nuclear arms race. The arms control diplomacy of the later Reagan years was successful because, as *Washington Post* journalist Don Oberdorfer has detailed in *The Turn: From the Cold War to a New Era* (1991), Secretary of State George Shultz picked up on Reagan's strong convictions and deftly side-stepped hard-line opposition to agreements. In fact, Shultz's success at linking presidential unease about nuclear weapons to Soviet overtures in the face of right-wing opposition provides a sharp contrast with John Foster Dulles's refusal to act on President Dwight Eisenhower's nuclear doubts and the opportunities presented by Nikita Khrushchev's détente overtures.

Reagan's commitment to anti-nuclearism and its potential for transforming the U.S-Soviet confrontation was more graphically demonstrated at the October 1986 Reykjavik summit when Reagan and Gorbachev came close to agreeing on a comprehensive program of global denuclearization that was far bolder than any seriously entertained by American strategists since the Baruch Plan of 1946. The sharp contrast between Reagan's and Gorbachev's shared skepticism toward nuclear weapons on the one hand, and the Washington security establishment's consensus on the other, was showcased in former secretary of defense James Schlesinger's scathing accusation that Reagan was engaged in "casual utopianism." But Reagan's anomalous anti-nuclearism provided the crucial signal to Gorbachev that bold initiatives would be reciprocated rather than exploited. Reagan's anti-nuclearism was more important than his administration's military buildup in catalyzing the end of the Cold War.

Neither anti-nuclearism nor its embrace by Reagan have received the credit they deserve for producing the Soviet-U.S. reconciliation. Reagan's accomplishment in this regard has been met with silence from all sides. Conservatives, not sharing Reagan's anti-nuclearism, have emphasized the role of traditional military strength. The popular peace movement, while holding deeply antinuclear views, was viscerally suspicious of Reagan. The establishment arms control community also found Reagan and his motives suspect, and his attack on deterrence conflicted with their desire to stabilize deterrence and establish their credentials as sober participants in security policy making. Reagan's radical anti-nuclearism should sustain his reputation as the ultimate Washington outsider.

The central role of Reagan's and Gorbachev's anti-nuclearism throws new light on the 1987 Treaty on Intermediate-range Nuclear Forces, the first genuine disarmament treaty of the nuclear era. The conventional wisdom emphasizes that this agreement was the fruit of a hard-line negotiating posture and the U.S. military buildup. Yet the superpowers' settlement on the "zero option" was not a vindication of the hard-line strategy. The zero option was originally fashioned by hardliners for propaganda purposes, and many backed off as its implementation became likely. The impasse the hard line created was transcended by the surprising Reagan-Gorbachev convergence against nuclear arms.

The Reagan victory school also overstates the overall impact of American and Western policy on the Soviet Union during the 1980s. The Reagan administration's posture was both evolving and inconsistent. Though loudly proclaiming its intention to go beyond the previous containment policies that were deemed too soft, the reality of Reagan's policies fell short. As Sovietologists Gail Lapidus and Alexander Dallin observed in a 1989 *Bulletin of the Atomic Scientists* article, the policies were "marked to the end by numerous zigzags and reversals, bureaucratic conflicts, and incoherence." Although rollback had long been a cherished goal of the Republican party's right wing, Reagan was unwilling and unable to implement it.

The hard-line tendencies of the Reagan administration were offset in two ways. First, and most important, Reagan's tough talk fueled a large peace movement in the United States and Western Europe in the 1980s, a movement that put significant political pressure upon Western governments to pursue far-reaching arms control proposals. That mobilization of Western opinion created a political climate in which the rhetoric and posture of the early Reagan administration was a significant political liability. By the 1984 U.S. presidential election, the administration had embraced arms control goals that it had previously ridiculed. Reagan's own anti-nuclearism matched that rising public concern, and Reagan emerged as the spokesman for comprehensive denuclearization. Paradoxically, Reagan administration policies substantially triggered the popular revolt against the nuclear hardline, and then Reagan came to pursue the popular agenda more successfully than any other postwar president.

Second, the Reagan administration's hard-line policies were also undercut by powerful Western interests that favored East-West economic ties. In the early months of Reagan's administration, the grain embargo imposed by President Jimmy Carter after the 1979 Soviet invasion of Afghanistan was lifted in order to keep the Republican party's promises to Midwestern farmers. Likewise, in 1981 the Reagan administration did little to challenge Soviet control of Eastern Europe after Moscow pressured Warsaw to suppress the independent Polish trade union Solidarity, in part because Poland might have defaulted on multibillion dollar loans made by Western banks. Also, despite strenuous opposition by the Reagan administration, the NATO allies pushed ahead with a natural gas pipeline linking the Soviet Union with Western Europe. That a project creating substantial economic interdependence could proceed during the worst period of Soviet-U.S. relations in the 1980s demonstrates the failure of the Reagan administration to present an unambiguous hard line toward the Soviet Union. More generally, NATO allies and the vocal European peace movement moderated and buffered hardline American tendencies.

In sum, the views of the Reagan victory school are flawed because they neglect powerful crosscurrents in the West during the 1980s. The conventional wisdom simplifies a complex story and ignores those aspects of Reagan administration policy inconsistent with the hardline rationale. Moreover, the Western "face" toward the Soviet Union did not consist exclusively of Reagan administration policies, but encompassed countervailing tendencies from the Western public, other governments, and economic interest groups.

Whether Reagan is seen as the consummate hardliner or the prophet of anti-nuclearism, one should not exaggerate the influence of his administration, or of other short-term forces. Within the Washington beltway, debates about postwar military and foreign policy would suggest that Western strategy fluctuated wildly, but in fact the basic thrust of Western policy toward the USSR remained remarkably consistent. Arguments from the New Right notwithstanding, Reagan's containment strategy was not that different from those of his predecessors. Indeed, the broader peace-through-strength perspective sees the Cold War's finale as the product of a long-term policy, applied over the decades.

In any case, although containment certainly played an important role in blocking Soviet expansionism, it cannot explain either the end of the Cold War or the direction of Soviet policy responses. The West's relationship with the Soviet Union was not limited to containment, but included important elements of mutual vulnerability and engagement. The Cold War's end was not simply a result of Western strength but of mutual weakness and intentional engagement as well.

Most dramatically, the mutual vulnerability created by nuclear weapons overshadowed containment. Nuclear weapons forced the United States and the Soviet Union to eschew war and the serious threat of war as tools of diplomacy and created imperatives for the cooperative regulation of nuclear capability. Both countries tried to fashion nuclear explosives into useful instruments of policy, but they came to the realization—as the joint Soviet-American statement issued from the 1985 Geneva summit put it—that "nuclear war cannot be won and must never be fought." Both countries slowly but surely came to view nuclear weapons as a common threat that must be regulated jointly. Not just containment, but also the overwhelming and common nuclear threat brought the Soviets to the negotiating table. In the shadow of nuclear destruction, common purpose defused traditional antagonisms.

A second error of the peace-through-strength perspective is the failure to recognize that the West offered an increasingly benign face to the communist world. Traditionally, the Soviets' Marxist-Leninist doctrine held that the capitalist West was inevitably hostile and aggressive, an expectation reinforced by the aggression of capitalist, fascist Germany. Since World War II, the Soviets' principal adversaries had been democratic capitalist states. Slowly but surely Soviet doctrine acknowledged that the West's behavior did not follow Leninist expectations, but was instead increasingly pacific and cooperative. The Soviet willingness to abandon the Brezhnev Doctrine in the late 1980s in favor of the "Sinatra Doctrine"—under which any East European country could sing, "I did it my way"—suggests a radical transformation in the prevailing Soviet perception of threat from the West. In 1990, the Soviet acceptance of the de facto absorption of communist East Germany into West Germany involved the same calculation with even higher stakes. In accepting the German reunification, despite that country's past aggression, Gorbachev acted on the assumption that the Western system was fundamentally pacific. As Russian foreign minister Andrei Kozyrev noted subsequently, that Western countries are pluralistic democracies "practically rules out the pursuance of an aggressive foreign policy." Thus the Cold War ended despite the assertiveness of Western hardliners, rather than because of it.

The War of Ideas

The second front of the Cold War, according to the Reagan victory school, was ideological. Reagan spearheaded a Western ideological offensive that dealt the USSR a death blow. For the Right, driving home the image of the Evil Empire was a decisive stroke rather than a rhetorical flourish. Ideological warfare was such a key front in the Cold War because the Soviet Union was, at its core, an ideological creation. According to the Reagan Right, the supreme vulnerability of the Soviet Union to ideological assault was greatly underappreciated by Western leaders and publics. In that view, the Cold War was won by the West's uncompromising assertion of the superiority of its values and its complete denial of the moral legitimacy of the Soviet system during the 1980s. Western military strength could prevent defeat, but only ideological breakthrough could bring victory.

Underlying that interpretation is a deeply ideological philosophy of politics and history. The Reagan Right tended to view politics as a war of ideas, an orientation that generated a particularly polemical type of politics. As writer Sidney Blumenthal has pointed out, many of the leading figures in the neoconservative movement since the 1960s came to conservatism after having begun their political careers as Marxists or socialists. That perspective sees the Soviet Union as primarily an ideological artifact, and therefore sees struggle with it in particularly ideological terms. The neoconservatives believe, like Lenin, that "ideas are more fatal than guns."

Convinced that Bolshevism was quintessentially an ideological phenomenon, activists of the New Right were contemptuous of Western efforts to accommodate Soviet needs, moderate Soviet aims, and integrate the USSR into the international system as a "normal" great power. In their view, the *realpolitik* strategy urged by George Kennan, Walter Lippmann, and Hans Morgenthau was based on a misunderstanding of the Soviet Union. It provided an incomplete roadmap for waging the Cold War, and guaranteed that it would never be won. A particular villain for the New Right was Secretary of State Henry Kissinger, whose program of détente implied, in their view, a "moral equivalence" between the West and the Soviet Union that amounted to unilateral ideological disarmament. Even more benighted were liberal attempts to engage and co-opt the Soviet Union in hopes that the two systems could ultimately reconcile. The New Right's view of politics was strikingly globalist in its assumption that the world had shrunk too much for two such different systems to survive, and that the contest was too tightly engaged for containment or Iron Curtains to work. As James Burnham, the ex-communist prophet of New Right anticommunism, insisted in the early postwar years, the smallness of our "one world" demanded a strategy of "rollback" for American survival.

The end of the Cold War indeed marked an ideological triumph for the West, but not of the sort fancied by the Reagan victory school. Ideology played a far different and more complicated role in inducing Soviet change than the Reagan school allows. As with the military sphere, the Reagan school presents an incomplete picture of Western ideological influence, ignoring the emergence of ideological common ground in stimulating Soviet change.

The ideological legitimacy of the Soviet system collapsed in the eyes of its own citizens not because of an assault by Western ex-leftists, but because of the appeal of Western affluence and permissiveness. The puritanical austerity of Bolshevism's "New Soviet Man" held far less appeal than the "bourgeois decadence" of the West. For the peoples of the USSR and Eastern Europe, it was not so much abstract liberal principles but rather the Western way of life—the material and cultural manifestations of the West's freedoms—that subverted the Soviet vision. Western popular culture—exemplified in rock and roll, television, film, and blue jeans—seduced the communist world far more effectively than ideological sermons by anticommunist activists. As journalist William Echikson noted in his 1990 book *Lighting the Night: Revolution in Eastern Europe,* "instead of listening to the liturgy of Marx and Lenin, generations of would-be socialists tuned into the Rolling Stones and the Beatles."

If Western popular culture and permissiveness helped subvert communist legitimacy, it is a development of profound irony. Domestically, the New Right battled precisely those cultural forms that had such global appeal. V. I. Lenin's most potent ideological foils were John Lennon and Paul McCartney, not Adam Smith and Thomas Jefferson. The Right fought a two-front war against communism abroad and hedonism and consumerism at home. Had it not lost the latter struggle, the West may not have won the former.

The Reagan victory school argues that ideological assertiveness precipitated the end of the Cold War. While it is true that right-wing American intellectuals were assertive toward the Soviet Union, other Western activists and intellectuals were building links with highly placed reformist intellectuals there. The Reagan victory school narrative ignores that Gorbachev's reform program was based upon "new thinking"—a body of ideas developed by globalist thinkers cooperating across the East-West divide. The key themes of new thinking—the common threat of nuclear destruction, the need for strong international institutions, and the importance of ecological sustainability—built upon the cosmopolitanism of the Marxist tradition and officially replaced the Communist party's class-conflict doctrine during the Gorbachev period.

It is widely recognized that a major source of Gorbachev's new thinking was his close aide and speechwriter, Georgi Shakhnazarov. A former president of the Soviet political science association, Shakhnazarov worked extensively with Western globalists, particularly the New York-based group known as the World Order Models Project. Goibachev's speeches and policy statements were replete with the language and ideas of globalism. The Cold War ended not with Soviet ideological capitulation to Reagan's anticommunism but rather with a Soviet embrace of globalist themes promoted by a network of liberal internationalists. Those intellectual influences were greatest with the state elite, who had greater access to the West and from whom the reforms originated.

Regardless of how one judges the impact of the ideological struggles during the Reagan years, it is implausible to focus solely on recent developments without accounting for longer-term shifts in underlying forces, particularly the widening gap between Western and Soviet economic performance. Over the long haul, the West's ideological appeal was based on the increasingly superior performance of the Western economic system. Although contrary to the expectation of Marx and Lenin, the robustness of capitalism in the West was increasingly acknowledged by Soviet analysts. Likewise, Soviet elites were increasingly troubled by their economy's comparative decline.

The Reagan victory school argues that the renewed emphasis on free-market principles championed by Reagan and then British prime minister Margaret Thatcher led to a global move toward market deregulation and privatization that the Soviets desired to follow. By rekindling the beacon of laissez-faire capitalism, Reagan illuminated the path of economic reform, thus vanquishing communism.

That view is misleading in two respects. First, it was West European social democracy rather than America's more free-wheeling capitalism that attracted Soviet reformers. Gorbachev wanted his reforms to emulate the Swedish model. His vision was not of laissez-faire capitalism but of a social democratic welfare state. Second, the Right's triumphalism in the economic sphere is ironic. The West's robust economies owe much of their relative stability and health to two generations of Keynesian intervention and government involvement that the Right opposed at every step. As with Western popular culture, the Right opposed tendencies in the West that proved vital in the West's victory.

There is almost universal agreement that the root cause of the Cold War's abrupt end was the grave domestic failure of Soviet communism. However, the Soviet response to this crisis—accommodation and liberalization rather than aggression and repression—was significantly influenced by outside pressures and opportunities, many from the West. As historians and analysts attempt to explain how recent U.S. foreign policy helped end the Cold War, a view giving most of the credit to Reagan-era assertiveness and Western strength has become the new conventional wisdom. Both the Reagan victory school and the peace-through-strength perspective on Western containment assign a central role in ending the Cold War to Western resolve and power. The lesson for American foreign policy being drawn from those events is that military strength and ideological warfare were the West's decisive assets in fighting the Cold War.

The new conventional wisdom, in both its variants, is seriously misleading. Operating over the last decade, Ronald Reagan's personal anti-nuclearism, rather than his administration's hardline, catalyzed the accommodations to end the Cold War. His administration's effort to go beyond containment and on the offensive was muddled, counter-balanced, and unsuccessful. Operating over the long term, containment helped thwart Soviet expansionism but cannot account for the Soviet domestic failure, the end of East-West struggle, or the direction of the USSR's reorientation. Contrary to the hard-line version, nuclear weapons were decisive in abandoning the conflict by creating common interests.

On the ideological front, the new conventional wisdom is also flawed. The conservatives' anticommunism was far less important in delegitimating the Soviet system than were that system's internal failures and the attraction of precisely the Western "permissive culture" abhorred by the Right. In addition, Gorbachev's attempts to reform communism in the late-1980s were less an ideological capitulation than a reflection of philosophical convergence on the globalist norms championed by liberal internationalists. And the West was more appealing not because of its laissez-faire purity, but because of the success of Keynesian and social welfare innovations whose use the Right resisted.

Behind the debate over who "won" the Cold War are competing images of the forces shaping recent history. Containment, strength, and confrontation—the trinity enshrined in conventional thinking on Western foreign policy's role in ending the Cold War—obscure the nature of these momentous changes. Engagement and interdependence, rather than containment, are the ruling trends of the age. Mutual vulnerability, not strength, drives security politics. Accommodation and integration, not confrontation, are the motors of change.

That such encouraging trends were established and deepened even as the Cold War raged demonstrates the considerable continuity underlying the West's support today for reform in the post-Soviet transition. Those trends also expose as one-sided and self-serving the New Right's attempt to take credit for the success of forces that, in truth, they opposed. In the end, Reagan partisans have been far more successful in claiming victory in the Cold War than they were in achieving it.

POSTSCRIPT

Did President Reagan Win the Cold War?

N ow that the cold war is over, historians must assess why it ended so suddenly and unexpectedly. Did President Reagan's military buildup in the 1980s force the Russians into economic bankruptcy? Gaddis gives Reagan high marks for ending the cold war. By combining a policy of militancy and operational pragmatism, says Gaddis, Reagan brought about the most significant improvement in Soviet-American relations since the end of World War II. Deudney and Ikenberry disagree. In their view the cold war ended only when the Russians saw the need for international cooperation in order to end the arms race, prevent a nuclear holocaust, and liberalize their economy. It was Western global ideas and not the hard-line containment policy of the early Reagan administration that caused Gorbachev to abandon traditional Russian communism, according to Deudney and Ikenberry.

Gaddis has established himself as the leading diplomatic historian of the cold war period. His assessment of Reagan's relations with the Soviet Union is balanced and probably more generous than that of most contemporary analysts. It is also very useful because it so succinctly describes the unexpected shift from a hard-line policy to one of détente. Gaddis admits that not even Reagan could have foreseen the total collapse of communism and the Soviet empire. While he allows that Reagan was not a profound thinker, Gaddis credits him with the leadership skills to overcome any prior ideological biases toward the Soviet Union and to take advantage of Gorbachev's offer to end the arms race. While many of the president's hard-liners could not believe that the collapse of the Soviet Union was for real, Reagan was consistent in his view that the American arms buildup in the early 1980s was for the purpose of ending the arms race. Reagan, says Gaddis, accomplished this goal.

Deudney and Ikenberry give less credit to Reagan than to global influences in ending the cold war. In their view, Gorbachev softened his hard-line foreign policy and abandoned orthodox Marxist economic programs because he was influenced by Western European cosmopolitans who were concerned about the "common threat of nuclear destruction, the need for strong international institutions, and the importance of ecological sustainability." Deudney and Ikenberry agree that Reagan became more accommodating toward the Russians in 1983, but they maintain that the cold war's end "was not simply a result of Western strength but of mutual weakness and intentional engagement as well."

There is a considerable bibliography assessing the Reagan administration. Three *Washington Post* reporters have provided an early liberal and critical assessment of Reagan. Lou Cannon's *President Reagan: The Role of a Lifetime* (Simon & Schuster, 1991) is a perceptive account of a reporter who has closely followed Reagan since he was governor of California. Haynes Johnson's *Sleep-walking Through History: America in the Reagan Years* (W. W. Norton, 1991) is more critical than Cannon's biography, but it is a readable account of Reagan's presidency. Don Oberdorfer, a former Moscow correspondent for the *Washington Post*, has written *The Turn: From the Cold War to a New Era: The United States and the Soviet Union, 1983–1990* (Poseidon Press, 1991). Oberdorfer credits Secretary of State George Schultz with Reagan's turnaround from a hard-line to a détente approach to foreign policy. Historian Michael R. Beschloss and *Time* magazine foreign correspondent Strobe Talbott interviewed Gorbachev for *At the Highest Levels: The Inside Story of the End of the Cold War* (Little, Brown, 1993), which carries the story from 1987 through the Bush administration.

Early evaluations of Reagan by historians and political scientists are useful, although any works written before 1991 are likely to be dated in their prognostications because of the collapse of the Soviet Union. Historian Michael Schaller, in *Reckoning With Reagan: America and Its President in the 1980s* (Oxford University Press, 1992), argues that Reagan created an illusion of national strength at the very time it was declining. Political scientist Coral Bell analyzes the disparity between Reagan's declaratory and operational policies in *The Reagan Paradox: U.S. Foreign Policy in the 1980s* (Rutgers University Press, 1989). A number of symposiums on the Reagan presidency have been published. Two of the best are David E. Kyvig, ed., *Reagan and the World* (Greenwood Press, 1990) and Dilys M. Hill, Raymond A. Moore, and Phil Williams, eds., *The Reagan Presidency: An Incomplete Revolution?* (St Martin's Press, 1990), which contains primarily discussions of domestic policy.

Not all scholars are critical of Reagan. Some of his academic and intellectual supporters include British professor David Mervin, in the admiring portrait *Ronald Reagan and the American Presidency* (Longman, 1990), and Patrick Glynn, in *Closing Pandora's Box: Arms Races, Arms Control, and the History of the Cold War* (Basic Books, 1992). A number of conservative magazines have published articles that argue that American foreign policy hard-liners won the cold war. Two of the most articulate essays written from this viewpoint are Arch Puddington, "The Anti–Cold War Brigade," *Commentary* (August 1990) and Owen Harries, "The Cold War and the Intellectuals," *Commentary* (October 1991).

Books on the end of the cold war will continue to proliferate. Michael J. Hogan has edited the earliest views of the major historians in *The End of the Cold War: Its Meaning and Implications* (Cambridge University Press, 1992). Michael Howard reviews five books on the end of the cold war in "Winning the Peace: How Both Kennan and Gorbachev Were Right," *Times Literary Supplement* (January 8, 1993).

ISSUE 17

Will History Consider William Jefferson Clinton a Reasonably Good Chief Executive?

YES: Lars-Erik Nelson, from "Clinton and His Enemies," *The New York Review of Books* (January 20, 2000)

NO: James MacGregor Burns and Georgia J. Sorenson et al., from *Dead Center: Clinton-Gore Leadership and the Perils of Moderation* (Scribner, 1999)

ISSUE SUMMARY

YES: Journalist Lars-Erik Nelson argues that President Bill Clinton is a sadly flawed human being but a reasonably good president whose administration was a time of peace and plenty for Americans.

NO: Political scientists James MacGregor Burns and Georgia J. Sorenson et al. argue that Clinton will not rank among the near-great presidents because he is a transactional broker who lacks the ideological commitment to tackle the big issues facing American society.

William Jefferson Clinton, born in Hope, Arkansas, on August 19, 1946, is the third-youngest president ever to hold the office. Similar to Abraham Lincoln, Clinton is considered a true embodiment of the "log cabin myth," which holds that anybody can become president. Both Lincoln and Clinton grew up in poor, dysfunctional southern families. Lincoln was born in Kentucky and was raised by a stepmother and a father whose unsuccessful ventures as a farmer caused the family to move four times before Lincoln was 21. Both had stepbrothers who were constantly in financial and legal trouble.

By the age of 16 Clinton knew he wanted to be a major professional politician. After graduating from Georgetown University in 1968 with an international affairs degree, Clinton won a Rhodes scholarship and studied for two years at Oxford University. Like a number of his liberal and conservative counterparts of the 1960s, Clinton avoided the draft and earned a law degree from Yale University in 1973. His first experience in politics was as the Texas coordinator of George McGovern's presidential campaign in 1972. Ironically,

Clinton served briefly as a staff attorney for the House Judiciary Committee, a year before the committee became preoccupied with investigating charges of impeachment against President Richard Nixon.

In the early 1970s, Clinton returned to his home state and briefly taught law at the University of Arkansas. But, like Lincoln, politics was his real ambition. In 1974 he made a strong showing against an entrenched Republican incumbent in the House of Representatives but fared better in 1976 when he ran Jimmy Carter's presidential campaign in his home state and was elected state attorney general. In 1978, at age 32, Clinton became one of the youngest governors ever elected to the office.

In his first term Clinton tried to govern as a New Deal Democrat. He upgraded the state's highways but was forced to raise taxes on gasoline and auto licensing fees to pay the costs. Meanwhile, riots by 18,000 Cuban refugees at Fort Chaffee, Arkansas, which he was forced to quell in conjunction with a perception that the governor and his staff exhibited a streak of arrogance and overambitiousness, hurt his bid for reelection in 1980. Carter's failed presidency and the taxpayer revolt, which started in California and spread to the rest of the nation, left Clinton unemployed.

Clinton was down but not out. He ostensibly practiced law, but his real goal was to get reelected as governor. He began his campaign on television with an apology to the voters for raising highway taxes, blamed his mistakes on "youthful ignorance," and toured the state in an effort to listen to the concerns of his citizens. This strategy paid off. Clinton defeated his Republican opponent by a wide margin in 1982 and was reelected on four more occasions with little opposition through 1992.

Clinton thought about running for president in 1988 but decided to wait until 1992. He was only 45 but it was a propitious time. President George Bush was extremely popular in the winter of 1991 because he had led UN forces to victory over the Iraqis in Kuwait. Prominent Democrats considered it futile to run against a popular incumbent president. The challengers were a group of lesser Democrats whom Clinton was able to defeat in the primaries. On November 3, 1992, Clinton received only 43 percent of the popular vote, Bush 38 percent, and H. Ross Perot 19 percent, which was the second-highest percentage in American history for a third-party candidate. The margin of victory was much wider in the electoral college—Clinton's 370 votes to Bush's 168. Clinton won the election running as a centrist Democrat from Arkansas. He got Reagan Democrats in the northeast and midwestern states to come back to the fold.

Will history rank Bill Clinton as a near-great, average, or below average president? In the following selection, Lars-Erik Nelson takes Clinton's detractors head-on and challenges a number of concepts that Americans believe about the presidency. In the second selection, James MacGregor Burns and Georgia J. Sorenson et al. argue that Clinton will not rank among the near-great presidents because he lacks the ideological commitment and overall vision to tackle the big issues facing American society.

⟶ **YES**

Clinton and His Enemies

Writing on the eve of the 1952 presidential election, the Cambridge political scientist D. W. Brogan described a peculiar trait in the American psyche, which he called "the illusion of American omnipotence." This, he elaborated, "is the illusion that any situation which distresses or endangers the United States can only exist because some Americans have been fools or knaves."[1]

Brogan was writing in the context of the debate over "Who lost China?," which was premised on the assumption that the convulsive Chinese Communist revolution, a forty-year struggle involving hundreds of millions of desperate people, could have been thwarted, or at least turned in a positive direction, by adroit diplomacy in Washington. The inanity of the China debate was instantly apparent (just as soon as Brogan put it into words), yet the illusion thrives. Even today, there are perfectly serious people who believe President Franklin D. Roosevelt was a knave for failing to stop the Nazi Holocaust or a fool for allowing the Red Army to occupy Eastern Europe at the end of World War II.

Brogan did not make the point, but the most obvious candidate for accusations of knavery is the president, especially now that whoever is in the White House is chief executive of the world's last superpower. In *Dead Center*, a survey of Bill Clinton's presidency, we see a modern extension of what Brogan described, the illusion of presidential omnipotence. In the current version, all that has gone wrong in America or the world at large—the slaughter in Kosovo, continuing inequality of wealth, the lack of national health insurance, even leaky roofs in our schools—can be blamed on Clinton. He is guilty, in the eyes of James MacGregor Burns and Georgia J. Sorenson, not because he is a knave or a fool, but, just as bad, because he is a centrist who shunned the radical changes and bold solutions that a more energetic and partisan leader could have achieved.

Burns and Sorenson, colleagues at the James MacGregor Burns Academy of Leadership at the University of Maryland, describe Clinton as a "transactional" president—one who makes deals—rather than a "transformational" one, who confronts political foes head-on and galvanizes the nation into taking fresh paths and shattering old habits. This is a fair assessment. Clinton has no large vision. As president, he has tried to reach across party lines. He has used opinion polls to assess and then act in accordance with the prevailing public sentiment, which will usually be more or less in the center. He has famously adopted a policy of "triangulation," trying to place himself at the apex of a triangle whose base angles are the preternaturally hostile congressional Republicans and Democrats. Though he is an eloquent speaker, he seldom directs his oratory against his enemies. Rather he lets them snarl themselves into incoherence.

.⚙.

The result is that Clinton has survived and prevailed over them. The Monica Lewinsky scandal guarantees that his presidency will be forever deemed a disappointment, not least to himself and his family. But by many measures his centrist strategy has worked. As Clinton enters his last year in the White House, the nation is not only at peace but it has no plausible foreign threats to its survival. Unemployment has remained low, and inflation has been held in check. Personal incomes are rising. Clinton's job approval rating hovers around 60 percent, even though his personal approval is about half that. Annual budget deficits, once projected to extend into infinity, have been eliminated. The national problem most debated at the moment appears to be nothing more immediate than shoring up the Social Security system so that it can pay its projected bills thirty years from now. Clinton has not only survived impeachment but outlasted his chief political opponents, former Senator Bob Dole of Kansas and former House Speaker Newt Gingrich of Georgia. Despite all the political shrieking against him that can be heard on radio and television, the country, under President Clinton, tootles along.

Burns and Sorenson, however, measure Clinton against a far stricter standard than mere peace and prosperity. They complain that he has failed to solve urgent national problems, and they attribute this failure to his centrism, which they regard as an inherently flawed ideology because it is incapable of effecting great, transformational change. Centrism would not have freed the slaves, or led America out of the Depression, or integrated the armed forces. Thus, in their eyes, Clinton is a failure. But the standard to which they hold him suffers from being based on the illusion of presidential omnipotence, and this illusion undermines their argument.

An example of the authors' complaint: Clinton prides himself on being the "Education President." And yet they write,

A *New York Times* article reported "leaky school roofs, buckling auditorium floors, antiquated coal furnaces, and dangerously rotted window frames." This was not a depression town in the 1930s but booming New York City in November 1998. Teachers and parents could report thousands and thousands of such situations across the country. Education was still in crisis.

In their eyes, the Education President had failed to transform local public education. Yes, we may agree; but what they do not say is that the federal government has only a small role in public education, and Clinton's Republican opponents have been trying to reduce even that, by abolishing the Education Department. To fault a sitting president, even indirectly, for the rotting window frames in a New York City school verges on the bizarre.

⋅✿⋅

As a second Clinton "failure," the authors cite "the grotesque income gap between the rich and the poor in America. Here again Clinton offered a host of proposals, some of which alleviated the direct symptoms of poverty." Yet income inequality remains. Why? "Clinton failed to exhibit the moral outrage that could have put inequality at the top of the nation's agenda." It is hard to believe that serious commentators would expect a moderate Democratic president, captive of the current campaign finance system, to agitate for class warfare against his own financial backers. But suppose he had: Would this or any other Congress have reenacted the steep progressive tax rates on income that were so triumphantly eliminated during the Reagan administration? Would the small business lobby have lessened its hostility to increases in the minimum wage? If Clinton had addressed income inequality in any meaningful way, he would have (a) failed to do much to change current income distribution and (b) been a one-term president.

On race, Clinton, in his open relations with African-Americans and his recruitment of them for his administration, has set an example that will be hard for successors to match. But even here he falls short of the Burns-Sorenson standard. "Historians of the future may see Clinton as a neoliberal, neo-civil-rights-radical, taking up Martin Luther King Jr.'s unfinished work toward an economic justice that transcends race," Burns and Sorenson concede.

> But while strong presidential leadership could potentially have created conditions and bridges across the racial divide, no such coalition—not even [Jesse] Jackson's Rainbow—had ever been sustained in the past. Such a coalition would take an act of transforming leadership on the order of the New Deal. It would take political capital, moral standing and the political will of Lincoln. Did Clinton have the will? The answer appeared to be no.

Clinton is not Lincoln.

Burns and Sorenson do not allow Clinton the excuse that he was presented with no opportunity to perform grand, Lincolnesque acts on race relations.

> Clinton had . . . misjudged Americans' relationship to their elected leaders. Again, as the sixties made plain, Americans would tolerate change—radical change—if leaders articulated values and visions consistently and succeeded in conveying a sense of urgency. Clinton did neither. His pursuit of racial justice was itself centrist.
>   In the end, Clinton was content to tinker, when he had a genuine opportunity to transform.

In the face of such ungenerous and unrealistic criticism, it is tempting to defend the Clinton presidency in spite of all its bungles, money-grubbing for contributions, foreign policy missteps, false starts, and changed directions. But we should not ignore some basic facts. Clinton, a moderate Democratic governor of Arkansas, was elected president in 1992 with 43 percent of the popular vote, hardly a mandate for sweeping personal leadership. As a governor of a small state, where politics were based more on personal relations than party divisions, he made appointments and dealt with the legislature without much concern for party affiliation. When he took office in Washington, he was supported by the smallest congressional majority of any president elected in this century (although some, most notably Richard Nixon, took office with one or both houses of Congress in the hands of the opposition). By nature and by circumstance, he was a centrist—a position that for him made political sense because, in his eyes, the Republican Party had moved so far to the right. There was a great political middle to be grabbed, and Clinton grabbed it.

To the Republicans, however, Clinton was no centrist. He was a pot-smoking, draft-dodging, anti–Vietnam War liberal with a socialist wife who wanted to strip away your right to see your family doctor. It was Clinton's great, and as yet unexplored, misfortune that he was the first Democratic president to take office since the astonishing rise of the demagogic radio talk-show hosts and their counterparts on cable television. A caricatured view of Clinton as a dangerous, even subversive liberal was broadcast for three hours a day, every day, from coast to coast by Rush Limbaugh and echoed by his imitators across the country. They questioned his patriotism and his right to be commander in chief. They complained when Hillary Rodham Clinton replaced the White House chef, as if she had no right to fire Barbara Bush's cook. They made a major scandal of an incident in which Clinton supposedly delayed air traffic at Los Angeles International Airport while he got a haircut aboard Air Force One. He did get the haircut, but no other aircraft was delayed. Nevertheless, the LAX incident survives in memory as a Clinton scandal.

Clinton's heavy-handed replacement of seven employees of the White House travel office, career government officials who enjoyed no civil service protection in that particular job, was also transformed into a scandal out of all proportion to its seriousness. He was dogged by questions about his Whitewater real estate investments, which proved to be more or less innocent, and hounded by investigations in the press, in the Congress, and by freelance inquisitors backed in large part by the reclusive Michigan multimillionaire Richard Mellon Scaife.

Clinton certainly made mistakes. One of his earliest actions was an attempt to order the military to accept homosexuals. The policy was well-intentioned, but homosexuals have protested that its application has led to more harassment, not less. Clinton failed to understand how deeply the military establishment and its supporters throughout the country would resent any change, and it added to the caricature image of him as a traditional liberal pandering to the most outspoken left-wing special interests. Some of his early appointments were badly bungled, particularly that of Lani Guinier, a longtime friend whom he nominated to head the Justice Department's civil rights division without anticipating the predictably harsh reaction against her support for race-based proportional representation.

⚫

To Burns and Sorenson, Clinton's biggest mistake was his health care plan, which tried to make use of existing insurance companies, doctors, hospitals, and health maintenance organizations rather than ignore these well-funded interest groups and start afresh. It was a relatively modest, well-intentioned initiative that was undermined by its complexity and the unnecessary secrecy with which it was drafted. The Health Insurance Association of America, which represents smaller insurance companies, ran TV commercials against it in which actors named "Harry" and "Louise" tried to frighten the public into believing that the government was about to take over and dictate their health care. Even *The New Republic*, which might have been expected to support a moderate Democratic president, ran a long, specious attack on the Clinton health plan's alleged failings.

Moderate though the plan was, it was too radical for the American political system. Clinton could be faulted for not trying, even after its defeat, to put forward a simpler and more modest plan so that at least some progress might have been made toward providing health care for the millions of people, mainly poor, who have no insurance whatever.

Yet Burns and Sorenson, who chide Clinton for the defeat and subsequent abandonment of his centrist proposal, argue that he should have pushed instead for a far more radical health reform, a Canadian-style "single-payer" system that would have taken all insurance companies out of the health care business and substituted for them a system of direct government payments to doctors. A single-payer plan has its virtues, but it would put an additional one seventh of the Gross National Product into the hands of government, and it would have gone down to defeat far faster and more decisively than the plan Clinton put forward. Nevertheless, Burns and Sorenson argue that only in this way can progress be made, by Hegelian clashes between extreme positions that might produce a new synthesis. It is an interesting theory, but it shows no awareness of political reality.

In his first two years in office, Clinton also pushed for a tax increase—promptly mischaracterized by his Republican opponents and a few Democrats as the biggest tax increase in history, even though it spared the middle class. One by one Republicans trooped to the House floor to warn the public that Clinton's 4.3-cent-a-gallon gasoline tax would cripple the economy and lead to widespread unemployment. They were wrong, but their charges that Clinton had raised everyone's taxes stuck in the public mind, nevertheless.

Clinton then antagonized congressional Democrats by pushing for approval of the North American Free Trade Agreement [NAFTA], promising that lowering the barriers to trade with Mexico would create hundreds of thousands of good new jobs. The labor unions and their congressional supporters were properly skeptical. NAFTA was approved, thousands of Americans lost their jobs as factories moved south across the border, and the hundreds of thousands of new jobs never materialized. NAFTA was not the disaster that labor feared—although it hit some workers so hard that their incomes have never recovered—but it was also not the panacea Clinton and his allies promised.

Third, he fought for approval of the Brady Bill, which put new restrictions on handgun sales and outlawed some types of semiautomatic rifles. This guaranteed him the hostility of one of the most powerful grass-roots lobbies in the country, the National Rifle Association, as well as enmity in even Democratic rural areas. Partly because of these three painful victories—the tax increase, NAFTA, and gun control—Clinton lost Democratic control of both House and Senate in the 1994 off-year congressional elections.

⋘◉⋙

From that point on, his presidency was under constant siege, a fact ignored by Burns and Sorenson, just as they ignore the relentless denunciations of Clinton and his wife by TV and radio commentators. This is an inexplicable omission. While trying to conduct the nation's business, the Clintons were investigated by two special prosecutors, Robert Fiske and Kenneth Starr, and a host of congressional committees. The Clintons were required to produce, under subpoena, documents going back decades. One inquisitor, Senator Alfonse D'Amato, subpoenaed the records of every telephone call from the White House to the 501 area code, i.e., Arkansas. Representative Dan Burton, an Indiana Republican, reenacted in his backyard the suicide of White House deputy counsel Vince Foster. A self-appointed gadfly, Larry Klayman of the group Judicial Watch, instituted a civil suit against the White House on behalf of Republicans whose FBI files had been stored there, and subjected White House officials to endless, rambling depositions. Utterly guiltless young men and women who had joined the Clinton administration in hopes of serving the country found themselves going into debt to pay lawyers' fees. So intense was the scrutiny that White House officials stopped taking notes in meetings or keeping records of their phone calls lest they be subpoenaed.

In addition to this, the Supreme Court ruled that a serving president could be subjected to a civil lawsuit while in office, which opened the way to the Paula Jones sexual harassment suit. This, in turn, led to the Lewinsky scandal. Four years after a special prosecutor was appointed to investigate him, Clinton finally committed a legal offense, falsely denying to Jones's lawyers that he had had sex with Lewinsky. By so doing he made himself fatally vulnerable to his enemies. The ensuing investigation and impeachment occupied the entire year of 1998 and the first month of 1999. So great was the congressional hostility to Clinton that at one point in 1997, when I asked then Speaker Gingrich seven times, in a semipublic forum, whether Clinton was the legitimately elected president of the United States, Gingrich, second in line to the presidency, seven times refused to say yes.

Dick Morris, Clinton's former pollster, records in *Vote.com* the burdens under which the Clinton White House labored:

> The sheer magnitude of the Clinton scandals is dizzying—Gennifer Flowers; the draft; pot smoking; the nanny tax; gays in the military; the $200 haircut; the travel-office firings; the Foster suicide; the Espy, Brown, Cisneros, and Babbitt investigations; Whitewater; the FBI files; the Rose Law Firm billing records; Chinese campaign contributions; advertising spending; Paula Jones; the China satellite waivers; the Web Hubbell job search; Chinese spies at Los Alamos.

It might be noted that in none of these controversies and scandals were the Clintons proved to have committed a crime, though at least one of them, the China-based fund-raising, stinks to high heaven.

⋅◈⋅

Under such unrelenting attack, it is remarkable that the Clinton White House was able to function at all. Robert Reich, who served as Clinton's first-term labor secretary, believes Clinton could and should have done more with his presidency. But in a critique written [in 1998] for *The Nation*, Reich noted that even Clinton's modest achievements have been overshadowed. "I fear," he writes, that "none will be remembered nearly as much as the viciousness of these years: the virulent spins and counterspins, the war rooms, the deadly battle over health care, the government shutdown and the stream of allegations over the White House travel office, Vince Foster's suicide, Whitewater, illegal fundraising and Gennifer, Paula, Kathy and Monica." Reich summed up Clinton's first-term plight this way: "A baby-boomer President who could charm snakes has tried to charm America and only infuriated the snakes." Clinton enraged the right with gun control, enraged organized labor with NAFTA, enraged liberals with welfare reform, and enraged Republicans by co-opting many of their issues.

And yet he wins consistently high job approval ratings. Morris explains part of this mystery in his book. Clinton, he says, was shrewdly—and with the help of Morris's polls—appealing to a younger generation, young families with children, whose concerns don't fit conventional political categories. Clinton's much-derided "small agenda" in fact meant a good deal to young parents. "He helped them get time off from work to bond with their newborn babies by passing the Family Leave Law," Morris writes.

> He made childhood immunization universal, inoculating children against disease and effectively inoculating their parents against Republican attacks on his administration.
>
> As their children came of preschool age, Clinton doubled the Head Start program so that it could accommodate all the children whose parents wanted it.... As their children grew older, X Generation parents worried more about issues like values, crime and violence. Clinton faced down the TV networks and made them implement a ratings system. Meanwhile, he got Congress to pass legislation requiring the installation of a V-chip in

each new television set. . . . To cut crime, Clinton got funds for 100,000 extra police and more money for drug counselors in schools.

When Clinton ensnared himself in a lurid scandal that had even grade schoolers asking about oral sex, many of the young parents blamed Republicans more for spreading their revelations into every household than they faulted Clinton for providing the ammunition. Clinton won their support, Morris says, by addressing, with careful political calculation, problems they actually faced at home. "He focused on topics like violence on television, teen smoking, national educational standards, school construction, and other areas that had never been part of the traditional congressional agenda."

Clinton's accomplishments may not seem like much in comparison to the Emancipation Proclamation or Dwight Eisenhower's support for the interstate highway system, the standards Burns and Sorenson use, but they improved the lives of a good many people in small but telling ways. Is that much of a legacy? We will not know for years to come.

In the eyes of Burns and Sorenson, Clinton fares no better on foreign policy. While Clinton vacillated on Bosnia, they write, 150,000 people were killed. They fault him for refusing to go it alone on Kosovo and for using air attacks rather than ground troops to repel Serbian forces. "The whole Kosovo episode once again illustrated the perils of moderation in foreign affairs, as in domestic," they write. Just how Clinton would have been able to use ground troops effectively in the face of vehement Pentagon and congressional opposition to taking losses Burns and Sorenson do not say.

William Hyland, a career national-security and intelligence expert who later served as editor of *Foreign Affairs,* is one of Clinton's more level-headed foreign-policy critics, and his survey of Clinton-era diplomacy, while stinging at times, is both more informed and more restrained than that of Burns and Sorenson. He faults the President chiefly for his inattention to foreign affairs until it is too late, creating a vacuum in which his subordinates "hijacked his foreign policy in the name of neo-Wilsonian internationalism, and for more than two years . . . engineered a series of failures and disasters."

In Hyland's view, Anthony Lake, Clinton's first National Security adviser, erred by putting too much stress on moral judgments as a driving force for American foreign policy, for example in Bosnia and China, while being unwilling, or unable, to devise policies to implement these judgments. He also accuses Secretary of State Madeleine Albright of being too willing to use force without an adequate sense of its dangers. Albright, who has seemed obsessed by the Munich agreement that sold out her native Czechoslovakia, has indeed been unusually bellicose. In a speech at Georgetown University in 1997, for example, she announced that America would never lift its economic sanctions against Iraq so long as Saddam Hussein was in power. It was a tough speech, but it gave Saddam no incentive to cooperate with United Nations arms inspections; Albright made it clear that even if he did, sanctions would continue. Similarly, Albright declared that Slobodan Milosevic understood no language other than force, which may have encouraged the Kosovo Liberation Army in the belief that America would support its stepped-up guerrilla war against Belgrade.

Hyland believes Clinton could have been more forceful in urging allies in 1993 to support the partition of Bosnia, according to the intricate plan worked out by former Secretary of State Cyrus Vance and former British Foreign Secretary David Owen. In addition, Clinton could have pressed harder for a policy of lifting the arms embargo on Bosnia's Muslims and carrying out air strikes against Bosnia's Serbs. The Bosnian Serbs, however, who controlled 70 percent of Bosnia, rejected the Vance-Owen plan, so it could only have been imposed—in all its complexity—at gunpoint. And the European allies, their peacekeeping troops on the ground outnumbered by the Serbs, wanted no US air strikes that might place their own troops at risk.

There is a whiff of the illusion of American omnipotence not only in Hyland's comments on the Balkans but also in the belief that more robust US diplomacy could have prevented the India-Pakistan nuclear arms race or averted the Asian economic collapse. But Hyland clearly recognizes the limits of US power when he dismisses the now current notion that more energetic American involvement could have created a free market and a functioning democracy in Russia.

The demoralization of Russia may be the most serious long-term development of the Clinton era, but here the administration's sins are more of style and tone than of substance. Certainly there was no need for US officials to act as cheerleaders and loan guarantors while so-called Russian reformers looted their country's wealth in the guise of privatization. Clinton's policymakers badly underestimated the depth of the corruption and criminality that pervades Russian society. But in dealing with Russia, Clinton had to work with the forces at hand. That meant backing Boris Yeltsin, with all his flaws, in preference to the resurgent Communist Party or the wacky fascism of Vladimir Zhirinovsky. As for another controversial part of Clinton's policy toward Russia, the expansion of the North Atlantic Treaty Organization to include Poland, Hungary, and the Czech Republic, Hyland seems dubious. While calling NATO expansion a significant achievement for the President, he also asserts that "building European security without, or against, Russia has not worked for four centuries."

❧❦❧

Clinton has to his credit genuine achievements in mediating the Northern Ireland dispute and pushing the Israelis and Palestinians farther along toward a permanent peace settlement. None of Clinton's supposed foreign policy fiascoes has been as bone-headed as, say, the Reagan administration's disastrous deployment of Marines in Lebanon in 1983 or its attempt to court supposed moderates in Iran by selling them antiaircraft missiles. In the 1996 election, Republicans chose not to make much of an issue of Clinton's foreign policy except for an effort to revive Reagan's Strategic Defense Initiative, an expensive and probably unworkable scheme that has many doubters among Republicans as well as Democrats. It is also the case that although the administration's policy has been marked by false steps, misjudgments, and shifts in direction, no one has put forward a clear, generally accepted alternative to it. Hyland freely admits that, on the major issues—whether in China, the Balkans, or Russia—he has none himself. Burns and Sorenson fault Clinton for lacking a grand strategy in foreign affairs, but they also note that no one else has one either.[2]

Hillary Clinton defended the administration's overall record to Burns and Sorenson by making the rather modest claim that Clinton has proven that government can be made to work for ordinary people and that it is not, as Ronald Reagan portrayed it, an enemy:

> So whether it's [the] Family and Medical Leave [Act] or the Brady Bill or taking assault weapons off the streets or even, as he has done, trumpeting small measures like curfews or school uniforms—that can give people a sense that all is not lost, that they're not living in this sort of libertarian wilderness where it's every person for himself.

Mrs. Clinton did not mention here the administration's major experiments such as welfare reform and the repeal of restrictions on banking. Senator Daniel Patrick Moynihan warned in the course of the welfare debate that in ten years' time we will be seeing children sleeping on grates. As Michael Massing recently observed in these pages, welfare reform has so far been a mixed success; but beginning in the year 2000, "the program's time limits will begin to take hold, and when they do, the levels of homelessness and hunger could sharply rise."[3] This program, moreover, has not yet been confronted with an economic downturn.

As Republicans compete to succeed Clinton, their chief stated goal is not to repeal the legislative accomplishments of his administration but to "restore dignity to the office" —dignity they themselves did much to besmirch. No one proposes rolling back the 4.3-cent gasoline tax or legalizing assault weapons. With a few minor exceptions, Governor George W. Bush's foreign policy speech at the Reagan Library in California in November could have come out of Clinton's speechwriting shop. Senator John McCain of Arizona, Bush's leading rival for the Republican presidential nomination, is concentrating on campaign finance reform, deriding Clinton's money-raising techniques even while he, McCain, freely acknowledges that under the current system he raises large sums from the corporations he oversees as chairman of the Senate Commerce Committee.

Clinton is not a candidate for Mount Rushmore. Blighted by its scandals, both real, and fabricated, his administration has been at best a tepid success. He repaired the damage of the crippling deficits produced by Reaganomics. He may have altered the image of the Democratic Party as a collection of tax-and-spend liberals who are soft on crime. He advanced the cause of racial justice largely through personal example. His vow to staff an administration that "looks like America" seemed hokey when announced, but he has made it stick.

He has also set an example, in this vituperative age, of showing no malice. It is hard to remember a single harsh word that Clinton has uttered against his many enemies. He will have, as Burns and Sorenson emphasize, no grand achievements like freeing the slaves, conquering the Depression, rolling back communism, or any of the other major transformations that they ascribe, somewhat simplistically, to previous presidents. Ordinary people, if not historians, are likely to remember him as they see him now, a sadly flawed human being but a reasonably good President whose administration was, for Americans, a time of peace and plenty.

Notes

1. "The Illusion of American Omnipotence," *Harper's,* December 1952, p. 21.
2. For anyone who thinks that in the post–cold war era a single grand strategy is possible, I recommend a book, *World Conflicts,* from Scarecrow Press. It lists, in encyclopedic form, virtually every one of the world's continuing ethnic, religious, tribal, and cross-border conflicts. It is an essential guide to the real world of the twenty-first century and, as it summons up the regional hatreds on all continents, a devastating antidote to any lingering illusion about American omnipotence. Its author, Patrick Brogan, is the son of D. W. Brogan.
3. "The End of Welfare?," *The New York Review,* October 7, 1999, pp. 22–26.

NO 👆

James MacGregor Burns and Georgia J. Sorenson et al.

What Kind of Leadership?

At some point a two-term president begins to think more about his place in history and less about his standing in the polls and at the polls. His hope for eternal fame rises most acutely after his reelection, of course, but not only then. Presidents are now held responsible for leading their party to win in congressional elections; thus Clinton, and Hillary Rodham Clinton too, were blamed for the Republican takeover of Congress in 1994, then credited for some Democratic gains in 1998. A president is also expected to help his vice president succeed him, but in 2000 that will be Al Gore's responsibility.

During much of his life—and perhaps as early as seizing JFK's hand—Clinton aspired to be not only president but a "great" president. One of his most crushing reactions to the Monica S. Lewinsky revelations was that his behavior had relegated him to the standing of a run-of-the-mill president. He might even be downgraded to failure—a rating inexplicably accorded Jimmy Carter in one polling of presidential scholars.

What is greatness in the White House? For years scholars have been rating presidents without a clear and agreed-on set of criteria. In our view, the bottom-line answer is conviction and commitment, plus the courage and competence to act on beliefs and promises. The scholarly rating game shows some volatility over the years in the standings of presidents—Harry Truman improved the more we got to know some of his successors—but the continuing "greats" over the years are the committed leaders Washington, Lincoln, and Franklin Roosevelt, with Thomas Jefferson just behind.

Monuments are another form of rating, especially in Washington. There is a pecking order in those memorials. For a century or more Washington and Lincoln have had their monuments, joined by Jefferson a half century ago and by FDR in the past decade. Washington's is the most imposing, Lincoln's the most evocative, Jefferson's the most philosophical, and Roosevelt's the most revealing about himself and his First Lady. Then there is Mount Rushmore, with Washington, Jefferson, and Lincoln carved in mighty stone, along with Theodore Roosevelt. Mean-spirited people complained that TR got there only because he and the sculptor were friends, but admirers of this "near great" are satisfied that he made it on his own.

Could Clinton aspire to a monument in Washington? Of course every president now gets his home library, no matter how great or nongreat. But Clinton might want more. Could he even hope for Mount Rushmore? There appears to be an open spot next to TR. But Franklin Roosevelt idolators see two spots that could be reserved for FDR and—yes—Eleanor. Still, what if someday the South Dakotans might balance the present three easterners and one midwesterner with a famous southerner?

Of course all this is terribly elitist. Dozens of other presidents, along with hundreds of governors, congressmen, local politicos, judges, and even professors are memorialized in thousands of courthouses, libraries, parks, and schools across the country. The warp and woof of American leadership, they are portrayed holding swords, canes, bibles, scrolls, constitutions, the reins of horses. Not one, so far as we know, brandishes a balanced budget law.

The Price of Centrism

A contradiction lay at the heart of Clinton's leadership: if he truly aspired to presidential greatness, the strategy he had chosen ensured that he would never achieve it. Rather, long before his presidency he had resolved on a centrist path that called for the kind of transactional leadership that he would exercise in abundance, especially in foreign policy. As a master broker he raised the art of the deal to world-class levels. But he rejected the kind of transformational leadership that might have placed him among the historic "greats."

What form did their transformational leadership take? Washington consolidated a whole new constitutional system that he had helped create. Jefferson recognized that political parties were necessary to unify and democratize that system, and he, with James Madison, fashioned the first opposition party. Lincoln moved on from demanding union at any price to demanding emancipation at any price and established a moral leadership that would vitalize his country for more than a century. FDR's remarkable foresight in broadening the antigovernment Bill of Rights into an "economic bill of rights" provided a "people's charter" that helped Americans cope with the ravages of the Depression and inequality.

The huge successes of these and other presidents displayed their transformational leadership: creativity in fashioning new policies; the courage to press for reforms and other changes despite popular apathy and opposition; the conviction to stick to grand principles no matter how long their realization might take; the commitment to the people to fight for their welfare at any personal cost. What was required for "greatness," in short, was a lifelong struggle to help achieve real, intended, principled, and lasting change.

Clinton could claim that he was just as committed to centrism as those great leaders had been committed to liberalism or progressivism. But just what was Clinton's centrism? The confusion over the term was vividly dramatized when his and Rodham Clinton's health bill of 1993–94 came to be categorized as a radical departure from his centrism. In fact in most respects the health plan epitomized moderate "mainstream" thinking. Rejecting the Canadian plan, it sought to attain a liberal goal, universal health care, without alienating conservatives, such as highly paid doctors and insurance companies. It had no particular ideology; it was neither socialist nor laissez-faire.

Confusion on this score was understandable because there seemed to be several brands of centrism. To some it was a kind of shopping list including moderate, liberal, and indeed conservative policies, from which the White House could pick items almost at will to meet immediate political and legislative exigencies. For others it was a nice balancing act, choosing conservative stands such as the death penalty and matching it with a liberal position on, say, gun control, without much in the middle.

The White House itself seemed unable to clarify this new form of government, or how it fit into the broader political system. In the summer of 1995, in a speech at Georgetown University, Clinton lamented that politics had become more and more fractured, and "just like the rest of us, pluralized. It's exciting in some ways, but as we divide into more and more and more sharply defined organized groups around more and more and more stratified issues, as we communicate more and more with people in extreme rhetoric through mass mailings or sometimes semihysterical messages right before election on the telephone, or thirty-second ads designed far more to inflame than to inform, as we see politicians actually getting language lessons on how to turn their adversaries into aliens, it is difficult to draw the conclusion that our political system is producing the sort of discussion that will give us the kind of results we need." Clinton seemed less than certain that mere goodwill among elected officials could paint over deep cracks in the polity.

Again and again the President invoked symbols of common ground, national unity, middle-class values, political partnership. Again and again he fell into pieties, such as civility, good citizenship, "strong families and faith," provoking in the minds of some listeners the only response to such shibboleths: "Of course, and who's against them?"

At that point, the President occupied the middle of the middle ground—so tenaciously that the liberal press searched for a Rasputin and found him in Dick Morris, who had come back to advise Clinton in 1995 after having worked for such conservatives as Jesse Helms and Paula Hawkins. But Clinton did not really need an advisor or a speechwriter for the Georgetown address. He was speaking from his heart and mind about his present political lodging place. Still, even this speech, lengthy though it was, omitted vital questions.

What about the Republicans? Were they supposed to suspend their partisanship to join the President on some peaceful ground? Clinton did not seem to recognize that he was confronted by one of the most disciplined and doctrinaire parties in this century, or if he did, he still assumed he could make deals with it. But the Republicans had won in 1994 with a most forthright platform, the Contract with America. Why should they break their promises to the people in order to trade with the President? These Republicans could hardly forget that Clinton had defeated a GOP governor in Arkansas and later driven their own president out of the White House. Who was he to talk conciliation?

And what about the Democrats? The President did not once mention the words *Democrat* or *Democratic party* in his Georgetown speech, though he was still using the old party catchwords—justice, equality, compassion, the Jeffersonian pursuit of happiness. Two hundred years earlier Jefferson and Madison were busy founding the Democratic-Republican party that would pursue the ancient values of liberty, equality, and fraternity. Was the modern Democratic party to stand by impotent while Clinton dickered with Republicans on his newly rediscovered common ground?

"Centrism is fine when it is the result of competing interests," William Safire wrote in late 1997. "Thesis; antithesis; synthesis. But centrism is vapid when it is the suffocator of interests, seeking to please rather than trying to move. Clinton's approach, in most cases, has been to follow the primrose path of polling down the middle: his motto has become a firm 'there must be no compromise without compromise.' "

Clinton's major failure was his inability, during his centrist phases, to frame a coordinated policy program that would make of his centrism not just an electoral strategy but a vital center of change. He was not against a political strategy in principle—he would tell aides that he wanted a "strategy" for some undertaking, as though strategies could be ordered up like tractors from John Deere. He loved strategy so much, someone quipped, that he had several of them, often at the same time. Clinton still clung to his overarching values of fairness and justice, but furthering such values to the degree he wished called for a strategy of change. Would centrist politics produce the kind of transformation that Clinton had so often championed and still seemed to support?

Perhaps it would if Clinton pursued his brokering kind of leadership persistently and skillfully. But in his heart he was not content to be only a dealer—at times his lofty values summoned him to a higher, transforming level of leadership. Such leadership, however, called for steady commitment to values such as equality and justice, priorities among those values, capacity to mobilize support both in his party and in movements that could be linked with the party, tenacity in pursuing his long-run visions and goals. It was not enough to know Niccolò Machiavelli's famous distinction between the courageous lion and the wily fox. He also needed to remember another Machiavelli dictum, which he quoted to a group of *Washington Post* reporters: "It must be considered that there is nothing more difficult to carry out or more doubtful of success, nor dangerous to handle, than to initiate a new order of things." For reformers have enemies, Machiavelli explained, and only "lukewarm defenders."

Clinton had lost many of his liberal defenders within three years of his somewhere-left-of-center 1992 campaign for the presidency. But he had not won over his centrist supporters, who feared another lurch to the left. Close observers had been tracking Clinton's ambivalence. Bob Woodward noted how Clinton sought to placate conservative foes of the energy (BTU) tax, stating, "I've been fighting the wrong folks." Elizabeth Drew reported that the President's ambivalence was raising again the "character issue," which could be overcome only if Clinton could move forcefully ahead on his program. It was not the first time someone pronounced, "Clinton was in a race against himself."

"On the one hand, the President badly wants to look like a problem-solver who will work with anyone to overcome the barriers of party and ideology," E. J. Dionne Jr. wrote in mid-1995. But Clinton also understood that "the Republicans have been dominating the political debate, and to change that, Democrats need to take on the large questions, challenging the Republican view of government fundamentally, and with conviction."

But Clinton could not resort to venomous politics. He could not hate those who hated him—not even the House Republicans who were targeting his favorite programs for extinction. "The Republicans were unanimous in their hatred for me—and I welcome their hatred," Franklin Roosevelt cried out to a roaring Democratic crowd at the height of the 1936 election campaign, as he scorched "economic royalists" who occupied positions similar to those of the Gingrich Republicans sixty years later. Clinton could not speak in such tones. Facing an ideological party, he could not be ideological because he was a transactional broker who was not always persistent and skillful enough to make his dealing stick, and was a would-be transforming leader without the deep conviction necessary to that strategy. No wonder some Americans considered him neither a fox nor a lion, but a chameleon.

◦◉◦

The clinching argument for centrism is simple: it works. While the ideologues are out there speechifying and pontificating, New Democrats are out there getting things done—not as fast as the "old" liberals would like, perhaps, but centrists get there step by step.

They have a point. The Clinton-Gore centrists can boast of hundreds of presidential and congressional acts leading to incremental progress. But the problem, as always, is not simply what the centrists have done. It is what they have done in comparison with the enormity of the problem and with the changes, some of them regressive, that others are fashioning. It is not only a battle of leaders but a battle of leaderships, economic and social and ideological as well as political.

"Government bureaucracies built a half or even a quarter century ago," Al From wrote in 1991, "are incapable of coping with the challenges of the 1990s—jobs lost to companies overseas, stagnant family incomes, a burgeoning underclass, homelessness, rampant drug abuse and crime and violence in our cities, crumbling roads and bridges, declining public schools, and a deterioration of moral and cultural values symbolized by the breakdown of the family. We need a new set of political innovations."

Eight years and trillions of dollars later, can we say that any of these fundamental problems have been solved? Some economic improvement, yes, but the problems still stare at us. Take education—a concern of Clinton and Rodham Clinton's from their earliest days in Arkansas and a key test of centrist strategy. "We have to be prepared to reform the systems we have made," Governor Bill Clinton told the Democratic Leadership Council in 1990. "As the governors' statement on national education goals says, we can't get there with the system we've got. That's why restructuring schools nationwide is so important."

Restructuring schools? Restructuring the educational *system*? In eight years we have seen a plethora of proposals and programs for federal loans, grants, testing (for teachers and students), school uniforms, aid to special education, recruiting volunteers to teach fourth-graders to read, the end of "social promotion" in schools, adding one hundred thousand new teachers in the primary grades—most of these worthy and helpful—but nothing that could be described as a transformation of our educational system. Centrism, with its incremental advances, cannot possibly achieve such a huge task. And education continues in crisis in the United States.

The centrists have an excuse—the intractability of the American political system. And one of the key arguments for centrism is that it is flexible enough to allow brokering within the interstices of the constitutional checks and balances. Still, it is the liberals, and the conservatives demanding systemic change, who have the main problem with all the veto traps and institutional blocks in the political system. But transformational leaders have learned that the system will respond if they work at it long enough and hard enough; and if this fails to work, they have ideas about rejuvenating the system. Centrists have hardly been forthcoming with ideas for "reconstruction": centrists don't do that sort of thing.

So, Clinton began his seventh year in office amid a political and institutional shambles. Indeed, as Alison Mitchell observed in the *New York Times*, when the 1997–98 Congress came to an end, "it stood identified less with any signature bill than with the paralysis of American politics near century's end." The lesson seemed clear; centrists can deal and bargain and transact from the center; they can gain incremental changes from the center; they cannot truly lead and transform from the center.

Thus, the cardinal question transcends Bill Clinton's or Al Gore's or Hillary Rodham Clinton's "greatness." It goes to core issues about the dynamics of progress, the role of conflict and consensus in democracy, the capacity of people to bring about far-reaching change, the requirements of leadership. It sharply poses the difference between the truly "vital center" that Arthur Schlesinger Jr. wrote about years ago and the mainstream, bipartisan, flaccid centrism of the 1990s.

The Myth of Presidential Virtue

While Clinton had been jibbing and yawing in his search for the political center, right, left, or middle, some close observers had been searching for a center in him, ethical, moral, or virtuous.

No words are more confused or abused than the language of good behavior. Dictionaries don't help; ours defines morality as ethics, ethics as morality, and virtue as both. But the distinctions are crucial. We define *virtue* as approved personal conduct, especially sexual; *ethical* as rectitude or right conduct, especially in nonprivate business or professional behavior; and moral as fidelity to the highest and broadest of national or community values, past and present, especially as proclaimed and continually reiterated in formal pronouncements such as presidential inaugural addresses over a long span of time.

The myth of the virtuous American president began early, with George Washington. The story of the cherry tree, although fabricated, symbolized the honesty and integrity that later ennobled the first president's leadership. Yet, he was succeeded, after the very proper John Adams, by his fellow Virginian Thomas Jefferson, who was shown many years later to have probably slept with his slave Sally Hemmings. This was not only unvirtuous but illegal as miscegenation under the laws of the day. But the myth survived and even flourished during the nineteenth century because the genteel press, though it might criticize a president's policies, would not conceive of investigating and exposing presidential peccadilloes, and even scholarly biographers rarely dug into sexual behavior.

Throughout the twentieth century, rumors drifted around about the extramarital sexual behavior—both before and during their presidencies—on the part of Harding, Franklin Roosevelt, Eisenhower, JFK, LBJ, and perhaps earlier of Woodrow Wilson. But the press was not yet so intrusive, or respectable biographers so bold, as to shatter the benign image of the virtuous president. Only years later did it become known, for example, that Harding had had sex with his young mistress in a White House "closet"; or that FDR had had a romance in his earlier Washington days with his wife's secretary or that the liaison was renewed in the White House during his final years; or that JFK had indulged in numerous trysts in the presidential mansion.

How long could the myth survive? Its destruction would require the combination of a reckless president, some bad luck, and rapacious journalists. This was the unintended feat of Bill Clinton. But when one strips away the exploitation of the "scandal" and considers the titillating specifics of the sexual behavior—the caressing, groping, undressing, and the rest—was there any difference between what literally went on in Harding's closet and in Bill and Monica's lovemaking? Only one differences so far as the myth was concerned—Harding's was never exposed in all its graphic detail by an independent prosecutor and sensationalized in the press.

Clinton was attacked not only for his sexual behavior, of course, but for lying about it. And few Americans would ever forget that indignant finger thrust out from the tube, as the President flatly denied the accusations against him. But the earlier transgressors had lied too—implicitly in the case of Jefferson, or with the covering-up by Harding and Kennedy, with the aid of a complicit press.

At issue is the president's right to privacy, including his right to protect it. Beginning with childhood, we all exercise that right, against intrusive parents, prying friends, interrogating employers. Whatever the law may say about the obstruction of justice, William Buckley Jr. wrote, "it is unrealistic to distinguish sharply between the offense of adultery and the offense of lying about it, inasmuch as the second offense goes hand in hand with the first. Anyone who commits adultery is expected to lie about it."

The right to privacy remains the issue. Perhaps presidents do not need it. Or perhaps they need it most of all.

·◍·

The tragedy of Monicagate was intensely personal—the horrendous invasions of the privacy of Monica S. Lewinsky herself at the hands of an alleged friend

[Linda Tripp], the privacy of Bill Clinton and countless others at the hands of a rampaging prosecutor, and the intense distress for Hillary Rodham Clinton and daughter Chelsea. Everything revolved around the definition of virtue as sex. The tragedy quickly became political, as a media frenzy turned the ethical lesson of Monicagate upside down, grotesquely overemphasizing sex in the Oval Office and ignoring the nonsexual ethical implications. As a result the whole era rivals the Age of McCarthy in its confused and perverted priorities. It ignored the great lesson of American history that ethical concerns must trump private virtue in the public realms.

To free a president from public accountability for behavior in the private realm does not free him from ethical responsibilities in the public realm. Rather, it is to pinion him all the more tightly to his public obligations. It is to confront him with the ethical standards that Americans learn from their parents, teachers, ministers, scoutmasters, coaches, indeed, from the lofty heritage of Christian and Judaic teachings. The standards are old-fashioned but eternally new—rectitude, integrity, compassion, loyalty, responsibility, trustworthiness, civility, respect for all regardless of status, race, gender, or age.

Both the political and economic demands of transactional leadership require a set of more specific but still significant qualities for brokers and mediators—honesty, accountability, reciprocity, credibility, and prudence. How well would the presidents of this century meet both the broader and narrower tests? The answer is difficult because qualities such as rectitude and credibility are not easily definable and certainly not quantifiable. But we do know that presidents lie, dissemble, cover up, break promises, but that they also show compassion, treat people with respect, work hard for their intended goals. As academics we would grade presidents of this century ethically at around a "gentleman's C," with Richard Nixon lowering the collective grade and Jimmy Carter raising it.

How would Bill Clinton fare in this ethical lineup? Measured by the presidential leadership we have studied, we would place him in the middle of the middle, on the basis of Clinton's promises not met, trust not given him, public integrity questioned, along with his incremental progress and his compassion and respect for Americans not sharing in the promise of America. His standing rises a bit when combined with the "straight arrow" of Hillary Rodham Clinton. These evaluations, anecdotal and impressionistic, may well be modified when the Clinton-Gore leadership is evaluated in longer perspective, and with more factual information.

A pressing question that allows a more easily measurable answer, based on extensive historical data, is whether presidential ethics have declined over two centuries, and if so, whether the deterioration will continue. From the lofty ethical standards of Washington and most of the other founders, those standards declined during the nineteenth century as our political system became more democratized and more subject to bossism and corruption. This tendency was balanced by relatively strong parties that could enforce a measure of discipline on individual miscreants in order to protect their national image and popular vote appeal. As parties have declined in the twentieth century, this kind of collective control has yielded to highly personalistic politics that encourages candidates and officeholders to set their own ethical standards, if any, free of external influence. Bill Clinton—far more a manipulator of the national Democratic party than a disciplined agent of it—well exemplifies this trend.

Will the apparent overall decline in presidential ethics continue in the twenty-first century? Probably yes, for two reasons, political and intellectual.

Increasingly our political institutions and practices are forcing office seekers and -holders to resort to manipulation and deception. Our constitutional checks and balances have long compelled our political executives and legislators to be extraordinarily skillful in threading their way through the devices that thwart collective action. In the absence of strong parties that can unify and empower the rank and file in Congress and the state legislatures, factional leaders within the parties pursue their narrower ends by mobilizing money, interest groups, and legions of lobbyists. Policy—or the blocking of policy—falls into the hands of "transactional opportunists."

Nothing suggests any improvement in this situation; on the contrary, the problem will only worsen, and with it the tendency of politicians, including presidents, to take ethical shortcuts, fueled by money. The Constitution cannot be reformed to make for more responsible and accountable collective action, and the power of corporate money is bound to increase. The sheer incapacity of Congress to pass any effective control of campaign finance is a symptom of the malaise. Nor can presidents solve this problem; increasingly they are part of it.

Behind these political forces lies a pervasive intellectual doctrine—pragmatism. It is ludicrous how often this pretentious term—which today means only expedient, narrow, and short-run self-interest—is used in the press to defend mediocre political actors. "Don't worry folks, Senator Smith, who might talk like a visionary, is really down-to-earth, a practical man. He coaches Little League and makes bookcases in his basement. He will not be carried away by his ideals or principles. He's okay—a pragmatist." This kind of pragmatism has come to mean, ethically, "anything goes, if you can get away with it." The test is "what immediately works?"—with no consideration of broader, long-term aspects.

Fashioned by Harvardmen William James and Charles Sanders Peirce and others a century ago, pragmatism was a philosophical theory about truth and a refreshing reaction against the heavy Anglo-Hegelian European dogmas that dominated philosophical teaching in America. Pragmatism called for fresh thinking, intellectual innovation, new truths, practical experience. James described his kind of pragmatist: he "turns away from abstraction and insufficiency, from verbal solutions, from bad *a priori* reasons, from fixed principles, closed systems, and pretended absolutes and origins. He turns toward concreteness and adequacy, toward facts, toward action and toward power." James did not flinch from mentioning pragmatism's "cash-value."

So analytically based was this kind of pragmatism, so clearheaded in clarifying different kinds of thought and action, so relevant to American politics and markets, that the new doctrine established a dominant role in American thought in the twentieth century. But during that century the doctrine has been both trivialized and barbarized. Trivialized in its application to almost any business or political act needing a positive spin. Barbarized in its use as "practicality" to defend ethically dubious persons or acts. Thus the FDR White

House joked about some of the disreputable city bosses who trafficked with it; the Kennedy White House admitted it made use of rascals, but these were "our rascals"; the Bush White House compromised with some of the most egregious Christian-right extremists.

So today's "pragmatism" is not an ethical test of political leadership—it is merely winning votes in the next election. Almost anything legal—and much that borders on the illegal—is justified as the "practical" thing to do. But the pragmatists ignore broader and more long-run aspects of elections. How is the contest being waged? What broader stakes than winning are involved? How will defeat or victory impact the future? Winning elections obviously calls for practicality—but what about the role of vision and idealism?

Above all today's pragmatism is anti-ideology. But the pragmatists have made an ideology of pragmatism.

Pragmatism encourages compartmentalization—the separation of self-serving acts from their ethical implications. Bill Clinton is said to deal with his varied problems by putting them into separate boxes—a personal relations box, a budget box, an election box, a Southern Baptist box, a civil rights box. Perhaps this is understandable since, in a broader sphere, our government itself is compartmentalized, as the constitutional separation of powers distributes authority and accountability among House, Senate, White House, and judiciary, and subdivisions thereof, even apart from the division of powers between the national and state governments.

As the most dynamic and innovative branch, can the presidency regain the moral leadership that certain administrations have displayed in the past?

The Real Test: Moral Leadership

"Are you having fun?" *Rolling Stone* reporters asked Bill Clinton. It was around the end of his first year in the White House.

"You bet," he answered. "I like it very much. Not every hour of the day is fun. The country is going through a period of change."

"But are you having fun in this job?"

"I genuinely enjoy it."

Later in the interview one of the reporters told Clinton of a young man who had been disappointed by the President's performance and had asked the reporter to pass on his question: What was Clinton "willing to stand up for and die for"?

The President furiously turned on the reporter, his face reddening as his voice rose.

"But that's the press's fault too, damn it. I have fought more damn battles here for more things than any President in the last twenty years." Clinton raged on: he had not "gotten one damn bit of credit for it from the knee-jerk liberal press, and I am sick and tired of it and you can put that in the damn article." He got up there "every day, and I work till late at night on everything from national service to the budget to the crime bill and all this stuff and you guys take it and you say, 'Fine, go on to something else, what else can I hit him about?' " Clinton ranted on and on. He was amazingly self-revealing, a bit paranoid, and wildly off the mark.

The "knee-jerk liberal press." All Democratic presidents—FDR, JFK, LBJ, Carter—were criticized by liberals farther to the left, sometimes unfairly. It came with the job.

"I have fought and fought and fought and fought." What had he fought about? He had pursued a number of policies tenaciously—as he would in the next five years—but he was hardly the image of the Andy Jackson fighting president.

"I . . ." "I . . ." "I . . ." Clinton was remarkably narcissistic, even for a president. In happier moments Clinton boasted of his "White House team." This was a time when the White House troika of Bill, Al, and Hillary was especially influential.

"So if you convince them I don't have any convictions, that's fine, but it's a damn lie. It's a lie." He pointed to a couple of his policies, such as tax reform. Already the most common criticism of the President was his "lack of principle." And again, this was a standard charge against presidents—it too came with the territory.

"Do I care if I don't get credit? No." Of course Clinton did care immensely—that's what the shouting was about. "And you get no credit around here for fighting and bleeding . . ." But Clinton had not fought and bled—he had brokered and negotiated and compromised on a wide range of policies.

And clearly he was not a happy president, at least at this point. Political psychologist Stanley Renshon noted his "bitter sense of futility," which suggested the active-negative character types. This was a reference to the distinction that presidential scholar James David Barber had drawn between active-positive presidents (FDR, Truman, JFK, Carter), who were the most psychologically healthy, and the active-negatives, who dutifully carried out their presidential chores (Wilson, Hoover, LBJ, Nixon) but gained little happiness on the job. Had the cheery, sunny Bill Clinton who had started office as an active-positive, but then, frustrated by Congress and criticism, turned active-negative?

Perhaps it signified something simpler, and even more significant—Clinton's dissatisfaction with himself. Over and beyond his centrist strategy, his endless brokerage, his incremental steps, perhaps he still visualized himself ideally as a principled and visionary leader. Would he ever be in a position to display that kind of political leadership?

In the next five years he became a more seasoned president, more resilient and self-assured. In part this resulted from the sheer experience of governing, and his winning in 1996 the most glorious prize of American politics, a second presidential term. His job satisfaction also rose, ironically, after the Republican sweep of Congress in 1994, forcing him to define and defend his own policies.

Then Monicagate. Anyone who had seen Clinton reveal his vulnerabilities in the *Rolling Stone* interview, or in other incidents where he had lost his cool, could understand Clinton's excruciating mortification later in the titillating revelations. And now he had no one to blame—no "knee-jerk liberals" or hostile press—for his troubles, only his own reckless behavior.

At the beginning of his presidency Bill Clinton had preached and promised change—big change. His presidential leadership would be measured by the success of his economic and social reform. While he was vague on some details, his and Hillary Rodham Clinton's plans became clearer when they proposed a comprehensive new health program. Facing a Democratic Congress, still in his presidential honeymoon, the President reasonably expected that, like FDR and others, he would be granted support and leeway.

The reaction to the rejection of the health bill still remains a mystery. The rejection itself was understandable—the First Lady's plan, developed with Ira Magaziner, had significant flaws, including overelaborate details that evidently tried to anticipate the flood of executive and administrative orders that usually follow the presidential signing of a major bill. In the long history of reform, first efforts often fail; the measure is revived and the fight goes on. Not so with the health bill. The rejection by a centrist Congress triggered a vituperative reaction against the proposers in the White House, not the destroyers on the Hill. The proposal was not only a failure; it was an outrage.

The most important of the overreactors was the President himself. Of all politicians he should have recognized the enormity of the high-powered and heavily financed attack the pharmaceutical and other lobbies had launched in Congress. But the conservatives won a double victory—the killing of the bill and Clinton's return to the centrist, incremental strategy that he and his Democratic Leadership Council [DLC] colleagues had embraced in the late 1980s.

So gradualism was back in favor. And over the next few years Clinton offered scores and scores of policy bytes, most of them welcomed by the public as promising to address specific problems and deficiencies. Supported by his Vice President and First Lady, he was imaginative and indefatigable in pressing for these small but benevolent changes. But he was most firm, most willing to spend his political capital, not on controversial liberal policies but on such centrist, DLC-backed programs at NAFTA [North American Free Trade Agreement] and budget balancing.

The tragedy of the Clinton administration was its failure to tackle the big changes needed to overcome the most glaring deficiencies and inequalities in American society.

Consider education. Clinton had prided himself on being the Education Governor of Arkansas, but even with the indispensable help of Rodham Clinton and a number of initiatives, Arkansas was still near the bottom of state standings on education when he left Little Rock. Then he would be, above all, the Education President, on the premise that the states could not do the job without ample funding from Washington. Soon he was initiating a host of education policy bytes, most of them worthy. But no teacher or parent could enjoy the illusion in 1999 that public education as a whole had been dramatically improved.

A *New York Times* article reported "leaky school roofs, buckling auditorium floors, antiquated coal furnaces, and dangerously rotted window frames." This was not a depression town in the 1930s but booming New York City in

November 1998. Teachers and parents could report thousands and thousands of such situations across the country. Education was still in crisis.

Or remember an even more deep-seated problem—the grotesque income gap between the rich and the poor in America. Here again Clinton offered a host of proposals, some of which alleviated the direct symptoms of poverty. But income data told the real story. "Overall, from the late sixties to the midnineties," according to Douglas A. Hicks of the University of Richmond, "income inequality, measured by the standard indicator called the Gini coefficient, increased by over twenty percent for families, and by almost twenty percent for households." Seen another way—in terms of quintiles of the U.S. population—the top 20 percent of our income distribution now receives almost half of the total national income. This is a greater share than the middle 60 percent earns and thirteen times the share of the poorest 20 percent. Clinton failed to exhibit the moral outrage that could have put inequality at the top of the nation's agenda.

Or take the "environmental challenge," Al Gore's special bailiwick. Early administration initiatives were either junked in Congress, as with the proposed BTU energy tax, or drastically cut, as with the proposed boost of the gasoline tax. After 1994, Clinton's and Gore's main efforts were devoted to thwarting Republican attempts to reverse recent gains in environmental policy. That policy —really a cluster of policies—was so complicated by global, national, regional, and special interest (oil industry) politics as to defy easy generalization, but it can be noted that Clinton and Gore's second term neared its end with their old environmental comrades disenchanted by the administration's centrist and weak leadership in this area.

The great excuse of Clinton and Gore—as of all American leaders trying to fashion major change—was the intractability of a constitutional system that utterly fragmented policy. Yet previous presidents had confronted the two-hundred-year-old Constitution and managed somehow to bring off huge changes—Roosevelt's New Deal programs, JFK's economic policies, LBJ's civil rights achievements. Of course, they enjoyed Democratic Congresses, but consider Ronald Reagan's conservative programs. He faced mainly Democratic Congresses but he put through his right-wing policies. He had two big things going for him: conviction and consistency.

The blockage of Clinton-Gore policies in Congress might have tempted Gore to propose major changes in the constitutional and political system. After all, he was in charge of REGO, the exciting project of Reinventing Government. With his strong philosophical interests, his legal and religious education, and his hands-on experience in politics and journalism, he might have at least proposed some constitutional changes for consideration—most notably the abolition of the midterm congressional elections, which had regularly wreaked havoc on presidents no matter how well or poorly they were leading. But the Vice President limited himself to downsizing the huge federal bureaucracy and experimenting with some managerial improvements. Government was hardly reinvented.

So if it was Government Lite under Clinton and Gore, as critics contended, how could they judge the President's efforts, for all his tenacity and compassion, as anything more than Leadership Lite?

POSTSCRIPT

Will History Consider William Jefferson Clinton a Reasonably Good Chief Executive?

Burns and Sorenson et al. distinguish between *transformational* leaders who confront foes head-on and push the nation in new directions and *transactional* leaders who make deals with their foes in Congress in order to win incremental changes. Clinton, they charge, lacked an overall vision; consequently, when he did bargain with the enemy on proposals for tax reform, gun control, and international trade agreements with the North American Free Trade Agreement (NAFTA) he ended up losing control of Congress to the Republicans in 1994. As Robert Reich, Clinton's first-term labor secretary put it, "A baby-boom president who could charm snakes has tried to charm America and only infuriated the snakes."

Burns and Sorenson et al. also criticize Clinton for governing like a centrist Democrat instead of acting like a true liberal, such as Franklin D. Roosevelt. They ask, Why didn't Clinton take on the "economic royalists" and enact real programs of redistributing wealth in the form of a single-pay, government-controlled health plan or a welfare-reform program of living wage income subsidies for the poor? Many would agree that had Clinton pushed for these programs he would never have been elected in 1992, much less reelected in 1996. Burns discusses FDR's leadership further in his classic biography *The Lion and a Fox* (Harcourt Brace Jovanovich, 1956). Many say that Roosevelt had no overall vision for curing the ills of the depression in 1933. Furthermore, his New Deal was a hodgepodge of relief, recovery, and reform programs, which were invented on an almost daily basis in a desperate search to bring back prosperity. In at least two cases—the Social Security Act and the National Labor Relations Act—Roosevelt was a transactional leader who jumped on the bandwagon when it was certain these acts would pass in Congress.

In Nelson's view, Clinton had to govern as a centrist because Congress and the extremely conservative press, along with their right-wing demagogues on the radio, curbed any radical changes Clinton could make in areas of health and welfare reforms and real income redistributions of wealth and power. Nelson argues that Clinton's centrist position allowed him to be reelected because he initiated programs, according to his centrist guru Richard Morris, "on topics like violence on television, teen smoking, national education standards, school construction, and other areas that had never been part of the traditional congressional agenda."

Nelson maintains that in the area of foreign policy Clinton made incremental changes in mediating the Northern Ireland dispute and pushed the

Israelis and Palestinians along toward a permanent peace settlement. The critics argue that these agreements could easily fall apart. They also contend that Clinton was very slow in getting involved in Bosnia and Kosovo, and he was unable to disentangle himself from Somalia, a situation he inherited from the Bush administration. Yet the critics have not been able to formulate an alternative foreign policy. This may be due to the fact that there may be no grand strategy that fits all situations in the post–cold war world.

Both Burns/Sorenson et al. and Nelson play down the importance of Clinton's aberrant private life, especially his affair with Monica Lewinsky. Burns contends that Clinton should never have been impeached because only a president's public morality should be questioned, not his private behavior. While this distinction should probably be followed, nevertheless the impeachment hearings dwarfed public policy and dominated the media for almost a year. Would the country have been better off if Clinton had resigned, as would have quickly occurred in a government run by a parliamentary system?

The Clinton presidency has been under constant assessment, which will certainly continue. The starting point for his prepresidential career is David Maraniss, *First in His Class: A Biography of Bill Clinton* (Simon & Schuster, 1995). An interesting account is Stanley A. Renshon, *High Hopes: The Clinton Presidency and the Politics of Ambition* (Routledge, 1998). Political scientists analyze the first term of Clinton's presidency and two election victories in Stanley A. Renshon, ed., *The Clinton Presidency: Campaigning, Governing and the Psychology of Leadership* (Westview Press, 1995) and in Colin Campbell and Bert A. Rockman, eds., *The Clinton Legacy* (Chatham House, 2000). The British weigh in with Paul S. Herrnson and Dilys M. Hill, eds., *The Clinton Presidency: The First Term 1992–1996* (St. Martin's Press, 1997).

The insiders have also started to weigh in. An easy read, which became a best-seller, is George Stephanopoulos, *All Too Human: A Political Education* (Little, Brown, 1999), which should be compared with Dick Morris, *Behind the Oval Office* (Random House, 1997). Morris was Clinton's chief strategist behind his "comeback from the grave" in 1995 and 1996. Reporters also weigh in with varying degrees of success. The earliest accounts are Elizabeth Drew, *On the Edge* (Simon & Schuster, 1994) and Bob Woodward, *The Agenda* (Simon & Schuster, 1994) and *Shadow* (Simon & Schuster, 1999).

Finally, three important works deserve mention. Jacob Weisberg, former *New Republic* editor, asserts that Clinton altered the office of the presidency in "The Governor-President, Bill Clinton," *New York Times Magazine* (January 17, 1999); the focus of *Washington Post* media critic Howard Kurtz's *Spin Cycle: Inside the Clinton Propaganda Machine* (Free Press, 1998) is self-evident; and senior Clinton pollster and adviser Stanley B. Greenberg's *Middle Class Dreams: The New American Majority,* rev. ed. (Yale University Press, 1996) is a book of wide-ranging historical analysis, which President Clinton read and apparently absorbed.

Contributors to This Volume

EDITORS

LARRY MADARAS is a professor of history and political science at Howard Community College in Columbia, Maryland. He received a B.A. from the College of the Holy Cross in 1959 and an M.A. and a Ph.D. from New York University in 1961 and 1964, respectively. He has also taught at Spring Hill College, the University of South Alabama, and the University of Maryland at College Park. He has been a Fulbright Fellow and has held two fellowships from the National Endowment for the Humanities. He is the author of dozens of journal articles and book reviews.

JAMES M. SoRELLE is a professor of history in and chair of the Department of History at Baylor University in Waco, Texas. He received a B.A. and an M.A. from the University of Houston in 1972 and 1974, respectively, and a Ph.D. from Kent State University in 1980. In addition to introductory courses in American history, he teaches upper-level sections in African American, urban, and late-nineteenth- and twentieth-century U.S. history. His scholarly articles have appeared in the *Houston Review, Southwestern Historical Quarterly,* and *Black Dixie: Essays in Afro-Texan History and Culture in Houston* edited by Howard Beeth and Cary D. Wintz (Texas A&M University Press, 1992). He has also contributed entries to *The Handbook of Texas, The Oxford Companion to Politics of the World,* and *Encyclopedia of the Confederacy.*

STAFF

Theodore Knight   List Manager
David Brackley   Senior Developmental Editor
Juliana Gribbins   Developmental Editor
Rose Gleich   Administrative Assistant
Brenda S. Filley   Director of Production/Design
Juliana Arbo   Typesetting Supervisor
Diane Barker   Proofreader
Richard Tietjen   Publishing Systems Manager
Larry Killian   Copier Coordinator

AUTHORS

RICHARD M. ABRAMS is a professor of history at the University of California, Berkeley, where he has been teaching since 1961. He is also associate dean of the International and Area Studies Teaching Program and director of the Political Economy of Industrial Societies Program. He has been a Fulbright professor in both London and Moscow and has taught and lectured in many countries throughout the world, including China, Austria, Norway, Italy, Japan, Germany, and Australia. He has published numerous articles in history, business, and law journals, and he is the author of *The Burdens of Progress* (Scott, Foresman, 1978).

GARY DEAN BEST is a professor of history at the University of Hawaii in Hilo, Hawaii. He is a former fellow of the American Historical Association and of the National Endowment for the Humanities, and he was a Fulbright Scholar in Japan from 1974 to 1975. His publications include *The Nickel and Dime Decade: American Popular Culture During the 1930s* (Praeger, 1993).

ROGER BILES is a professor in and chair of the history department at East Carolina University in Greenville, North Carolina. He is the author of *The South and the New Deal* (University Press of Kentucky, 1994) and *Richard J. Daly: Politics, Race, and the Governing of Chicago* (Northern Illinois Press, 1995).

JAMES MACGREGOR BURNS is the author of noted studies of presidents and other political leaders. As senior scholar, he teaches and researches leadership at the James MacGregor Burns Academy of Leadership at the University of Maryland in College Park, and he is an emeritus professor of political science at Williams College. He is the author of *State and Local Politics: Government by the People* (Prentice Hall, 2000) and editor of *Government by the People: National, State, and Local* (Simon & Schuster, 2000).

CARL N. DEGLER is the Margaret Byrne Professor Emeritus of American History at Stanford University in Stanford, California. He is a member of the editorial board for the Plantation Society, and he is a member and former president of the American History Society and the Organization of American Historians. His book *Neither Black nor White: Slavery and Race Relations in Brazil and the United States* (University of Wisconsin Press, 1972) won the 1972 Pulitzer Prize for history.

DANIEL DEUDNEY is an assistant professor in the Department of Political Science at the Johns Hopkins University in Baltimore, Maryland. He is the author of *Pax Atomica: Planetary Geopolitics and Republicanism* (Princeton University Press, 1993).

JOHN LEWIS GADDIS is the Robert A. Lovett Professor of History at Yale University in New Haven, Connecticut. He has also been the Distinguished Professor of History at Ohio University, where he founded the Contemporary History Institute, and he has held visiting appointments at the United States Naval War College, the University of Helsinki, Princeton University, and Oxford University. He is the author of many books, including *The Long Peace: Inquiries Into the History of the Cold War* (Oxford University

Press, 1987) and *The United States and the End of the Cold War: Implications, Reconsiderations, Provocations* (Oxford University Press, 1992).

ERNEST S. GRIFFITH (1896–1981), an editor and writer, was a professor of political science and political economy in the School of International Service at the American University in Washington, D.C. He also held academic appointments at Harvard University and Syracuse University, and he served as director of the legislative reference service at the Library of Congress. He is the author of *The American System of Government,* 6th edition (Routledge, 1984).

HERBERT G. GUTMAN (1928–1985) was internationally recognized as America's leading labor and social historian. He taught at many colleges and universities, including Stanford University, William and Mary College, and the Graduate Center of the City University of New York, where he founded the American Working Class History Project.

JACQUELYN DOWD HALL is the Julia Cherry Spruill Professor and director of the Southern Oral History Program at the University of North Carolina, Chapel Hill. Her research interests include U.S. women's history, southern history, working-class history, and biography. She has won a number of awards, including a Distinguished Teaching Award for graduate teaching. She is coauthor of *Like a Family: The Making of a Southern Cotton Mill World* (University of North Carolina Press, 1987).

MURIEL E. HIDY taught at the Harvard Business School for many years and was a pioneer in the field of business history. She is the author of *George Peabody, Merchant and Financier: 1829–1854* (Ayer, 1979) and coauthor, with Ralph W. Hidy and Roy V. Scott, of *The Great Northern Railway* (Harvard Business School Press, 1988).

RALPH W. HIDY taught at the Harvard Business School for many years and was a pioneer in the field of business history. He is the author of *House of Baring in American Trade and Finance: English Merchant Bankers at Work, 1763–1861* (Harvard University Press, 1949) and coauthor, with Muriel E. Hidy and Roy V. Scott, of *The Great Northern Railway* (Harvard Business School Press, 1988).

G. JOHN IKENBERRY, currently a Wilson Center Fellow, is a professor of political science at the University of Pennsylvania and a nonresident senior fellow at the Brookings Institution. He is the author of *After Victory: Institutions, Strategic Restraint and the Rebuilding of Order After Major Wars* (Princeton University Press, 2000) and *American Foreign Policy: Theoretical Essays,* 3rd ed. (Addison-Wesley Longman, 1998).

MATTHEW JOSEPHSON, who figured among the literary expatriots in France in the 1920s, is the author of numerous critical biographies and histories of the Gilded Age, including *Edison: A Biography* (McGraw-Hill, 1963) and *The President Makers: The Culture of Politics in an Age of Enlightenment* (Putnam, 1979).

ROBERT KORSTAD is an assistant professor in the Department of Public Policy Studies at Duke University, where he has been teaching since 1980. He has also taught at North Carolina Central University, and he has won a number of honors and awards. His work has appeared in such journals as *Journal of American History* and *Social Science History,* and he is coauthor of *Like a Family: The Making of a Southern Cotton Mill World* (University of North Carolina Press, 1987).

RICHARD D. LAMM is a former governor of Colorado. He has also served as executive director of the University of Denver's Center for Public Policy and Contemporary Issues, and he is the author or coauthor of several books, including *The Immigration Time Bomb: The Fragmenting of America* (Dutton/ Plume, 1985).

JAMES LELOUDIS is an associate professor, the associate dean for honors, and director of the James M. Johnston Center for Undergraduate Excellence at the University of North Carolina, Chapel Hill. His chief interest is in the history of the modern South, with emphases on women, labor, race, and reform. He is coauthor of *Like a Family: The Making of a Southern Cotton Mill World* (University of North Carolina Press, 1987) and the author of *Schooling the New South: Pedagogy, Self, and Society in North Carolina, 1880– 1920* (University of North Carolina Press, 1999).

ARTHUR S. LINK was a professor of history at Princeton University. He is coeditor of the Woodrow Wilson papers and the author of the definitive multivolume biography of President Wilson.

LEON F. LITWACK is the Alexander F. and May T. Morrison Professor of American History at the University of California, Berkeley. He is the author of *Been in the Storm So Long: The Aftermath of Slavery* (Alfred A. Knopf, 1980).

ELAINE TYLER MAY is a professor of American studies and history at the University of Minnesota in Minneapolis, Minnesota. She has also taught at Princeton University, and her research interests include family history and gender issues. She is the author of *Barren in the Promised Land: Childless Americans and the Pursuit of Happiness* (Basic Books, 1995).

RICHARD L. McCORMICK is president of the University of Washington in Seattle, Washington. Prior to that he served as provost and vice chancellor for academic affairs at the University of North Carolina at Chapel Hill. He received his Ph.D. in history from Yale University in 1976, and he is the author of *The Party Period and Public Policy: American Politics From the Age of Jackson to the Progressive Era* (Oxford University Press, 1986).

H. R. McMASTER graduated from the U.S. Military Academy at West Point in 1984. Since then he has held numerous command and staff positions in the military, and during the Persian Gulf War he commanded Eagle Troop, 2d Armored Cavalry Regiment in combat. He is the author of *A Distant Thunder* (HarperCollins, 1997).

DAVID NASAW is a professor of U.S. social history in the Graduate School and University Center of the City University of New York. He is the author of *Going Out: The Rise and Fall of Public Amusements* (Harvard University Press, 1999) and editor of *Course of U.S. History* (Wadsworth, 1987).

LARS-ERIK NELSON is a Washington columnist for the *New York Daily News* and a frequent contributor to *The New York Review of Books*.

WILLIAM L. O'NEILL is a professor in the Department of History at Rutgers University in New Brunswick, New Jersey, who specializes in twentieth-century American history. He is the author of many books, including *A Democracy at War: America's Fight at Home and Abroad in World War II* (Harvard University Press, 1995).

THOMAS G. PATERSON is a professor of history at the University of Connecticut in Storrs, Connecticut. His articles have appeared in the *Journal of American History* and *Diplomatic History*, the editorial boards of which he has served on, and the *American Historical Review*. A past president of the Society for Historians of American Foreign Relations, he has authored, coauthored, or edited many books, including *Contesting Castro* (Oxford University Press, 1994) and *On Every Front*, 2d ed. (W. W. Norton, 1993).

HOWARD N. RABINOWITZ (d. 1998) was a professor of history at the University of New Mexico and a historian of the urban South. Among his authored works are *Race Relations in the Urban South, 1865–1890* (University of Georgia Press, 1996) and *Race, Ethnicity, and Urbanization: Selected Essays* (University of Missouri Press, 1993).

GLENDA RILEY is a professor of history at Ball State University in Muncie, Indiana. She has written numerous articles and books on women in western history, including *Women and Nature: Saving the "Wild" West* (University of Nebraska Press, 1999) and *Diaries and Letters From the Western Trails, 1852: The California Trail* (University of Nebraska Press, 1997).

ANNE FIROR SCOTT is the William K. Boyd Professor of History Emeritus at Duke University in Durham, North Carolina. She has received numerous honors and professional citations, and she has served a term as president of the Organization of American Historians. She has contributed to many books on women's history, and she is the editor of *Unheard Voices: The First Historians of Southern Women* (University Press of Virginia, 1993).

GEORGIA J. SORENSON is a senior scholar and founding director of the James MacGregor Burns Academy of Leadership at the University of Maryland. Formerly a senior policy analyst with the Carter administration, she has served as a consultant to four presidential campaigns.

CHRISTINE STANSELL is a professor of history at Princeton University in Princeton, New Jersey. She is the author of *City of Women: Sex and Class in New York, 1790–1860* (Random House, 1986) and *American Bohemia: Art, Politics, and Modern Love* (Henry Holt, 1996).

W. A. SWANBERG was a freelance journalist and story writer who also had experience working on a railway. He studied English literature at the University of Minnesota, and during World War II he worked for a year and a half in the Office of War Information. He has written a number of biographies, including *Pulitzer* (Scribner, 1967).

JON C. TEAFORD is a professor of history at Purdue University in West Lafayette, Indiana. His publications include *Post-Suburbia: Government and*

Politics in the Edge Cities (Johns Hopkins University Press, 1996) and *Cities of the Heartland: The Rise and Fall of the Industrial Midwest* (Indiana University Press, 1994).

ROBERT A. THEOBALD was a retired rear admiral before his death. He was the commanding officer of Flotilla One, Destroyers, Pacific Fleet and was present at the Pearl Harbor attack. He testified on behalf of Admiral Husband E. Kimmel before the Roberts Commission, which had accused Kimmel of "dereliction of duty."

REED UEDA teaches history at Tufts University and has been a visiting professor at Harvard and Brandeis Universities. He is the author of *Postwar Immigrant America: A Social History* (St. Martin's Press, 1994).

BRIAN VANDEMARK teaches history at the United States Naval Academy at Annapolis. He served as research assistant on Clark Clifford's autobiography, *Counsel to the President: A Memoir* (Random House, 1991) and as collaborator on former secretary of defense Robert S. McNamara's Vietnam memoir, *In Retrospect: The Tragedy and Lessons of Vietnam* (Times Books, 1995).

ROBERT WEISBROT is a professor of history at Colby College in Waterville, Maine. He is also on the advisory committee for the African American studies program at Colby. He is the author of *From the Founding of the Southern Christian Leadership Conference to the Assassination of Malcolm X (1957-65)* (Chelsea House, 1994).

TOM WICKER, one-time chief of the Washington bureau of the *New York Times,* was a political columnist for the *New York Times* for 25 years, until he retired in 1991. His publications include *A Time to Die: The Attica Prison Revolt* (University of Nebraska Press, 1994) and *One of Us: Richard Nixon and the American Dream* (Random House, 1995).

ROBERTA WOHLSTETTER is a historian and a member of the Steering Committee of the Balkan Institute, which was formed to educate the public on the nature of the crisis in the Balkans and its humanitarian, political, and military consequences. She has earned the Presidential Medal of Freedom, and she is coauthor of *Nuclear Policies: Fuel Without the Bomb* (Harper Business, 1978).

Index